KU-324-176

FA Carling
PREMIERSHIP

POCKET ANNUAL 1997-98

Bruce Smith

5th Year of Publication

FA Carling Premiership Annual 1997-98

Copyright © Bruce Smith – Author 1997

ISBN: 07535 0122 8

The right of Bruce Smith to be identified as the Author of the Work has been asserted by him in accordance with the *Copyright, Designs and Patents Act 1988*.

First published August 1997 by
Virgin Publishing

Virgin Publishing Limited
332 Ladbroke Grove
London
W10 5AH

Typeset by Bruce Smith

All rights reserved. No part of this publication may be reproduced, stored in a retrieval system, or transmitted, in any form or by any means, without prior permission in writing of the publisher, nor be otherwise circulated in any form of binding or cover other than that in which it is published and without a similar condition including this condition being imposed on the subsequent purchaser.

Contact Bruce Smith at:

Bruce Smith,
PO Box 382, St. Albans,
Herts, AL2 3JD

email: Bruce-Smith@msn.com

Disclaimer

In a book of this type it is inevitable that some errors will creep in. While every effort has been made to ensure that the details given in this annual are correct at the time of going to press, neither the editor nor the publishers can accept any responsibility for errors within.

We welcome comments, corrections and additions to this annual. Please send them to Bruce Smith at the address opposite or email them direct to him at: Bruce-Smith@msn.com

Cover Repro by: Flame Limited
Printed by: Caledonian International Books, Glasgow, Scotland.

CONTENTS

FA Premier League Records 1996-97

FA Premier League All-Time Records

Championships, FA Cup, Coca-Cola Cup and Awards

European Club Competitions

England Internationals

FA Carling Premiership Club Directory 1997-98

Transfers Involving FA Premier League Clubs 1996-97

A-Z of FA Premier League Players 1996-97

A-Z of FA Premier League Managers

FA Premier League Ground Guide

Form 'n' Encounter Guide

Introduction...

To me season 1996-97 seemed to be one where the Premier League was catching its breath a little. There were some excellent games to be seen but equally there were some poor affairs which did little to promote the clubs involved or the league. That isn't to say the season wasn't exciting, and with so many clubs going into the final day in fear of relegation, the tension was maintained to the end.

This situation was rather typified by Leicester, who although they were safe after playing their penultimate game, found that a win at Blackburn Rovers catapulted them from around 17th position to a final ninth position. That win earned them close on a million pounds in prize money – more than their Coca-Cola Cup success.

Leicester's win over Middlesbrough sees them and any other club enter the UEFA Cup via this route for the very last time. UEFA have decreed that from now on clubs with top divisions of 18 clubs can only allocate UEFA Cup spots on league positions. This decision came about after the French FA applied to UEFA to allow their League Cup winners to enter. The implication here is clearly that UEFA are looking for all countries to come into line with an 18-club premier division. This is something I agree with and it would help relieve the fixture congestion that plagued the likes of Middlesbrough and Manchester United last season. Season extensions are not the question. The original concept behind the formation of the Premier League was a top flight of 18 clubs – of course, the clubs finally voted against when the crunch came.

The carrot of a UEFA Cup spot was the catalyst that made the League Cup attractive – its future as a competition where the Premier League clubs are involved in the long term must now be in doubt, and the rumours continue to circulate that Premier League clubs want changes to the competition. One-leg matches decided on the night would seem the most obvious. This might only be a short-term saviour though. Regular European matches for the majority of top clubs would seem to be only a matter of seasons away and this would surely be the final nail in the League Cup coffin. Already this season we see eight countries allowed two entries into the Champions' League and the format of both the UEFA Cup and the Cup Winners' Cup will surely take on a similar style to that of the senior partner.

The call is of course that the rich get richer, but there has in the last two seasons been talks between the Premier League and Football League clubs to work out a formulae as to how monies can be worked down to the smaller clubs to allow development of new talent. Football in England is characterised by its strength in depth and the demise of the smaller clubs would undermine the foundations of the English game. The fear of many Premier League club chairmen is that monies filtered down would simply be used to fund and inflate players' wages at this level and not go into youth and player development.

Club alliances may be another way ahead and in the spring of 1997 Liverpool and Crewe announced their desire to build an informal working relationship between the clubs, to both their benefits. This is something that already happens on the continent, especially in Spain.

The optimism generated by a successful England side continued into the summer and, after the World Cup defeat at Wembley at the hands of Italy, the performances in Le Tournoi in France have rekindled hopes. I reflect on how we and the rest of the world continue to marvel at the skills and commitment of Brazilian teams down the years. But isn't it significant that they were involved in a tournament and a world tour in preparation for France '98 while their domestic season continued on at home without many of their rising stars. The club versus country battle doesn't even exist in that part of South America. We aim to emulate but we remain blind as to how to start achieving it.

Back to the Premier League, and Barnsley become the 24th team to appear in the Premiership. They arrive with an excellent manager in Danny Wilson who rightly received the accolades of his contemporaries by being named Manager of the Season at the League Managers' Dinner in mid-May. He will win it again if they maintain their status.

Activity in the transfer market has been interesting during the early part of the close season and has almost been a battle between Chelsea and Arsenal – it will be fascinating to see if these clubs can do battle with Manchester United and Newcastle during 1997-98. If they do we will be in for possibly the most exciting FA Premier League season ever!

List of Acknowledgments
Many thanks to everyone who has contributed to this year's Annual – not least the following: David Tavener (Reviews), Mark Webb and Ben Dunn at Virgin.

Deadlines
After a relatively quiet close season on the transfer front things were starting to hot up just as we went to press. The cut-off date for this edition of the annual was July 1st 1997. Although many transfers were pending we have only included those that had actually physically taken place at this point.

Back Editions
Limited stocks of the previous editions of the FA Carling Premiership Pocket Annual are still available at £5.99 each including £1 p&p. Editions available are 1992-93, 1993-94, 1994-95 and 1995-96 and the complete set provides a full history of the FA Premier League. To obtain copies write with your requirements along with a cheque/PO payable to 'Words On Sport' to:
Words On Sport, PO Box, 382, St Albans, AL2 3DZ

Pre-Season

Southampton appoint Graeme Souness as manager following the dismissal of Dave Merrington. Blackburn Rovers turn down an offer from Manchester United for the top scorer in Euro 96 – Alan Shearer. Leeds United make Lee Bowyer the most expensive teenager in Britain by handing Charlton Athletic a cheque for £2.6m. West Ham United pay Spanish side Espanyol £2.4m for Romanian striker Florin Raducioiu but it's small fry compared to the £7m Middlesbrough splash out on 27-year-old Italian star Fabrizio Ravanelli and the £4m Bryan Robson also invests in his third Brazilian star, Emerson. They are joined in the Premiership by fellow international Roberto Di Matteo who joins Chelsea from Lazio for £4.9m. Manchester United, for once, are more modest and spend just £2.7m in bringing Norwegians Ronnie Johnsen and Ole Gunnar Solskjaer to Old Trafford. Alex Ferguson then further boosts the champions' squad with the £3.5m signing of Czech Republic midfielder Karel Poborsky. One overseas player not expected to see in the new season in England is Tomas Brolin who fails to turn up for pre-season training with Leeds United.

Keith Wiseman is named as successor to Bert Millichip as chairman of the Football Association.

Newly promoted Derby County add Dundee United midfielder Christian Dailly to their squad. Tit for tat – Blackburn, annoyed at speculation regarding Shearer's future, make a £4m bid for Eric Cantona. With the new season less than a month away, big money continues to change hands as Coventry City sign 31-year-old Scotland captain Gary McAllister from Leeds for £3m. The Yorkshire club then pay Crystal Palace £2.5m for goalkeeper Nigel Martyn. Tottenham Hotspur steer clear of the big names to sign Danish midfielder Allan Nielsen while Manchester United land Jordi Cruyff from Barcelona for around £1m.

Newcastle United set a new world record with the £15m capture of Alan Shearer as Kevin Keegan steps up his bid to bring the Premiership title to the north-east.

Bruce Rioch, after a blank summer in the transfer market, signs a contract after serving 14 months without one as Arsenal manager. Following the signing of Shearer, Newcastle sell all of their 300 executive season tickets at £1,500 a head. Middlesbrough supporters form a quarter of a mile queue to buy the club's new replica kit.

Ajax defeat Manchester United at Old Trafford in the Umbro Trophy and meet Chelsea in the final after Ruud Gullit's side beat Nottingham Forest on penalties. Chelsea lift the trophy with a 2-0 win at the City Ground.

A crowd of 20,000 greets Shearer as he makes his first public appearance in Newcastle; the Geordie is said to be on £1.2m a year. His first run out and goal comes during a 2-0 friendly win at Lincoln City. Sheffield Wednesday have a £5m bid for Georgiou Kinkladze rebuffed by Manchester City.

Manchester United announce to all and sundry that they have no intention of surrendering their double lightly and add the Charity Shield to their impressive collection with a remarkable 4-0 thrashing of Newcastle at Wembley.

Following defeats in Scotland by both Celtic and Rangers, Arsenal lose further friendlies to Fiorentina and Benfica. Just five days before the start of the Premiership season Arsenal sack Bruce Rioch; his 61-week reign is the shortest ever term in office for a Gunners boss. Stewart Houston is appointed caretaker manager. Not going to Highbury is Terry Venables. The former England coach is appointed director of football at Portsmouth. A hint that the new Gunners boss could be respected French coach Arsène Wenger, currently coach to Japanese side Nagoya Grampus Eight, is clearly given as the club sign the French duo of Patrick Vieira and Remi Garde for £3.5m and a free transfer respectively.

Liverpool complete the signing of Patrik Berger who scored for the Czech Republic in the final of Euro '96. Sunderland prepare for life in the top flight with the club record signing of Niall Quinn from Manchester City for £1.3m. As the new season dawns, only Blackburn, Leicester City and Southampton complete the close season without spending in excess of £1m on a single player.

Premiership sponsors Carling announce that the 1996-97 champions will receive more than £2m. Current champions Manchester United picked up less than half that figure for 1995-96.

August

Week 1 (Aug 17-23): Manchester United make an ominously good start, with a magnificent goal from the halfway line by David Beckham being the pick of the bunch in a 3-0 win over Wimbledon. New signing Gary Speed scores the second Everton goal in a 2-0 win over Newcastle while Liverpool get a point at Middlesbrough but play second fiddle to Ravanelli who scores a debut hat trick during a 3-3 draw at the Riverside. Six goals are also evenly shared at the Baseball Ground where Premiership new boys Derby County rescue a point against Leeds United. Dean Sturridge scores twice for Derby while Ian Rush is booked on his Leeds debut. Arsenal win the first London derby of the season, 2-0 over West Ham United, and Chris Armstrong scores twice as Tottenham Hotspur notch up a good victory over Blackburn Rovers at Ewood Park. Sheffield Wednesday make a promising start with a 2-1 win over fancied Aston Villa at Hillsborough. Joint biggest winners on the opening day are Nottingham Forest as a Kevin Campbell hat trick gives Forest an emphatic 3-0 win and ruins McAllister's Coventry City debut. The only games not to produce a goal are at Roker Park and the Dell where Sunderland and Southampton are held by Leicester City and Chelsea respectively, the latter match see Premiership debuts for Gianluca Vialli, Roberto Di Matteo and Frank Leboeuf.

The first Monday night match of the season sees Steve McManaman continue his Euro 96 form and score both Liverpool goals during a 2-0 victory over managerless Arsenal.

David Pleat's Sheffield Wednesday top the table after two games with Richie Humphreys and Andy Booth scoring the goals which clinch the points at Elland Road and add to the woes of Leeds boss Howard Wilkinson. Manchester United, in front of a massive crowd of 54,943, have to wipe out two Duncan Ferguson goals to deny Everton victory at Old Trafford and Christian Dailly scores a last-minute equaliser for Derby at Tottenham while Gareth Southgate's first goal since his infamous penalty miss at Wembley gives Aston Villa victory over Blackburn. Rovers' problems increase with the news that Kenny Dalglish will depart by mutual agreement. Sunderland crush Forest 4-1 at the City Ground to leave Wednesday as the only side with a 100% record after two games. Shearer, with a majestic free kick, scores his first goal for Newcastle as Wimbledon lose 2-0 at St James's Park to go to the foot of the Premiership. McAllister opens his account for Coventry in a 1-1 draw at West Ham. The exciting Emile Heskey does likewise with a brace for Leicester against Southampton and Di Matteo gives Chelsea victory over Middlesbrough at Stamford Bridge.

Week 2 (Aug 24-30): Eight Premiership matches produce just 14 goals but Sheffield Wednesday make it three wins out of three as goals from Peter Atherton and Guy Whittingham overturn a Shearer penalty and inflict on Newcastle an early defeat at fortress St James's Park. Chelsea stay two points behind Wednesday as Leboeuf and Vialli sink Coventry. Arsenal end Leicester's unbeaten record to move third. Liverpool are frustrated into a goalless draw with Sunderland at Anfield while on the Sunday, Manchester United drop two more home points as Blackburn get off the mark with a 2-2 draw.

The referee-bashing season gets into full swing at Stamford Bridge where Paul Danson is heavily criticised by Coventry who have Liam Daish sent off. Southampton have Frances Benali dismissed and Middlesbrough captain Nigel Pearson also sees red in a game of ten bookings at Nottingham Forest.

Lee Sharpe's first goal since his £4.5m move clinches Leeds' first win of the season on the 27th and leaves Wimbledon as the only Premier side without a point or a goal after three games.

September

Week 3 (Aug 31-Sep 6): Goals by Nick Barmby, Paul Gascoigne and Shearer earn England a 3-0 win in Moldova as August ends with no Premiership matches on the final weekend. The first match in September sees Richie Humphreys score his second spectacular goal of the season as Sheffield Wednesday – at the top of the table during the early weeks for the first time in 29 years – move five points clear with a 2-1 win over Leicester. Chelsea concede their first goals of the season during a 3-3 thriller at Highbury while Aston Villa move into second place when handing Everton their first defeat of the campaign. Newcastle, Liverpool and Leeds all notch up their first away wins at the second attempt and Wimbledon climb three places with a home win over Spurs but have Vinnie Jones dismissed for the 12th time in his career. Emerson and Ravanelli are amongst the scorers as West Ham are trounced 4-1 at the Riverside and for the third consecutive game Manchester United have to come from behind to pick up a point at Derby.

Week 4 (Sep 7-13): Sheffield Wednesday suffer their first setback on the first weekend of the month as Chelsea grab all three points at Hillsborough to reclaim second place. A last-minute Steve McManaman goal against Southampton lifts Liverpool to third. Champions Manchester United return to form with a 4-0 destruction of Leeds at Elland Road. Ravanelli scores two more, as does Juninho, as Boro crush bottom dogs Coventry 4-0. Wimbledon also run in four as Everton are hammered at Selhurst Park and Les Ferdinand bags a brace as Newcastle continue Spurs' poor run. A last-minute goal by Arsenal's Andy Linighan earns the Gunners a 2-2 and ends Villa's winning streak. The only midweek league match brings further misery for Blackburn Rovers who have just one point from five games as Derby clinch their first win of the season courtesy of a Sean Flynn goal.

Howard Wilkinson's eight-year stint as manager of Leeds United comes to an end on the 9th when he is dismissed as the club reels from Saturday's defeat and is faced with an upsurge of animosity from supporters towards their manager. A handshake believed to be worth a few quid softens the blow for Wilkinson. Just 24 hours later, Leeds install George Graham as their new manager; it is his first appointment since his 12-month ban from the game.

Newcastle defeat Halmstads 4-0 in the 1st Round 1st Leg of the UEFA Cup at St James's Park but fellow Swedes Helsingborgs hold Aston Villa to a 1-1 draw at Villa Park. Arsenal are beaten 3-2 at Highbury by Borussia Moenchengladbach. Off the pitch the Gunners confirm that their new manager will be Arsène Wenger although the date of his arrival in England is still uncertain.

Manchester United kick off their European Champions League campaign with a dismal display in Italy and are fortunate to go down to just a solitary goal defeat in the San Siro against Juventus. A week of European action closes with Liverpool defeating Finnish side MyPa-47 1-0 in Anjalankoski in the Cup Winners' Cup.

Friday 13th is a nightmare for Arsenal as caretaker manager Stewart Houston departs to take charge of Queens Park Rangers and their captain Tony Adams admits to being an alcoholic. Youth team coaches George Armstrong and Pat Rice stand in as Arsenal await Wenger's arrival.

Week 5 (Sep 14-20): Manchester United put their Euro misery behind them to destroy Forest 4-1 at Old Trafford with Cantona scoring twice in front of 54,984 fans while Wimbledon climb to eighth with a third successive victory – 2-0 at struggling West Ham. Somewhat predictably, Shearer scores from the penalty spo as Newcastle defeat Blackburn on Tyneside to send Ray Harford's side to the foot of the table. Middlesbrough further boost the north-east with goals from Barmby and Juninho being sufficient to maintain Everton's poor run. George Graham sees his side take a first-minute lead at Coventry before the Sky Blues bounce back for their first success of the campaign. Sunderland have defender Richard Ord sent off as Aljosa Asanovic converts a late penalty to give Derby their first win in the Premiership. Liverpool, playing on the Sunday, go top with two goals from Patrik Berger helping to account for Leicester 3-0 at Filbert Street. On the same day Andy Townsend scores a fine goal on his return to Stamford Bridge as Villa hold Chelsea to a draw.

For a club supposedly in turmoil, Arsenal find their touch against fading early pacesetters Sheffield Wednesday and, with Ian Wright scoring a hat trick on his way to 100 league and 150 career goals for the Gunners, they chalk up a 4-1 victory. Wednesday have former England defender Des Walker sent off for a 'professional foul' but Arsenal's mood is dampened by the news that defender Nigel Winterburn is to be charged with bringing the game into disrepute by the FA for alleged gestures made towards disabled Wednesday supporters.

Blackburn Rovers' first win of the season comes at Brentford, 2-1, in the Coca-Cola Cup but Derby are defeated 1-0 at Luton Town in 1st Leg ties of the 2nd Round. The following night sees more upsets as Coventry, Everton, Leeds and Sheffield Wednesday are held at home by Birmingham City, York City, Darlington and Oxford United respectively. West Ham can only draw at Barnet. On the plus side, Ravanelli scores four times as Middlesbrough crush Hereford United 7-0.

Week 6 (Sep 21-27): Returning to Premiership action, Chelsea head for Anfield looking for the win needed to lift them into pole position – the journey home is a solemn one following another Berger double in Liverpool's 5-1 victory. Villa and Manchester United are goalless at Villa Park but Arsenal, with Tony Adams back in the side, move to third with a 2-0 win at Middlesbrough. Shearer settles a bruising encounter at Elland Road and Carlton Palmer is dismissed. A tremendous volley by Steve Agnew clinches Sunderland's first home win of the season against Coventry and Greek George Donis scores his first for Blackburn in a 1-1 draw with Everton, who have Duncan Ferguson dismissed. Also sent off is West Ham's Marc Rieper during a 2-0 win at Forest. Leicester move out of the bottom three on the Sunday with a 2-1 victory at White Hart Lane.

Wimbledon continue their rise up the table with a 3-1 victory over bottom-but-one side Southampton. The midweek cup action kicks off with Newcastle United making progress in the UEFA Cup but Aston Villa go out on the away goals rule. York City and Oxford United remove Everton and Sheffield Wednesday from the Coca-Cola Cup while Forest pull through in extra time away to Wycombe Wanderers. Leeds win at Darlington.

Twenty-four hours later, Manchester United easily beat Rapid Vienna 2-0 at Old Trafford but Arsenal, with Wenger at last at the helm, are out of the UEFA Cup, defeated 6-4 on aggregate by Borussia Moenchengladbach. Chelsea lose 3-1 at home to Blackpool in the Coca-Cola Cup but squeeze through 5-4 on aggregate. Derby are out after only drawing at home with Luton. Liverpool complete a 4-1 aggregate win over MyPa-47 in the Cup Winners' Cup.

October

Week 7 (Sep 28-Oct 4): Arsenal join Liverpool at the summit with a 2-0 win over Sunderland at Highbury and Wimbledon boost the capital's title bid to move third with victory at the Baseball Ground. Arsenal's victory is soured by dismissals for the Sunderland duo Martin Scott and Paul Stewart, the latter for two deliberate handballs. Referee Paul Danson also sends Roker boss Peter Reid from the bench. Stewart's dismissal is later revoked as Danson reviews video evidence. Everton's poor run ends with victory over Sheffield Wednesday who slip out of the top six for the first time. Matt Le Tissier scores twice as Southampton thump Middlesbrough 4-0 at the Dell. On the final Sunday of September both Liverpool and Manchester United reaffirm their challenge with wins over West Ham and Spurs respectively, Solskjaer scoring twice for United.

Dwight Yorke ends a personal drought with a scintillating hat trick for Villa at Newcastle but he also deflects a Shearer shot into his own net as United go second with a fortuitous but exhilarating 4-3 victory.

Week 8 (Oct 5-11): A weekend of international football puts paid to the domestic action on the 5th and England have to wait until midweek before stuttering to a 2-1 victory over Poland at Wembley in a World Cup qualifier. Shearer scores both England goals in front of an excellent attendance of 74,663. Scotland's task is simplified by the non-appearance of hosts Estonia.

Week 9 (Oct 12-18): A crowd in excess of 55,000 look on as David Beckham's solitary goal ends Liverpool's unbeaten record and Manchester United move to within a point of Roy Evans' side. Newcastle seize the opportunity to return to the top thanks to Shearer's match-winning strike at Derby and equal their club record of six consecutive Premiership wins. Leeds notch their first victory under George Graham with a couple of Rod Wallace goals accounting for lowly Forest. A brace of Ian Wright goals keep Blackburn rooted to the foot of the table as the two sides immediately above them, Coventry and Southampton, share the points at Highfield Road with Dion Dublin grabbing City's last-minute equaliser. Wimbledon continue Sheffield Wednesday's downward spiral and clinch a club record – their sixth successive win in the Premiership. Dons keeper Neil Sullivan has put his early season embarrassments well behind him and saves a David Hirst penalty. The most controversial incident is at White Hart Lane where Aston Villa keeper Mark Bosnich is in trouble with the FA following a Nazi-style salute during Spurs' 1-0 win. Allan Nielsen's first goal for Tottenham clinches the Londoners' first home win since March and their first win over Villa in 15 meetings.

Sunderland have defender Richard Ord sent off for the second time this season but still manage to twice come from behind to draw with neighbours Middlesbrough at Roker Park. Boro's goals come from imports Ravanelli – his first not to be scored at the Riverside – and Emerson.

The FA hand out fines of £1,500 and £750 to managers Bryan Robson and Graeme Souness while Ian Wright is charged over personal remarks made about Sheffield Wednesday boss David Pleat, who delves into the transfer market to sign Benito Carbone from Inter Milan for £3m.

Shearer and Ferdinand score as Newcastle pull back a two-goal deficit away to legendary Hungarians Ferencvaros before succumbing 3-2 in the UEFA Cup. Manchester United's Champions League campaign is back on track as goals from Beckham and Cantona give the English champions maximum points from their trip to Istanbul to face Fenerbahce. Liverpool overturn a goal deficit through Robbie Fowler and John Barnes to gain a creditable 2-1 victory over Sion in Switzerland.

Back on the domestic front, Arsenal's disciplinary problems persist with Nigel Winterburn also charged for 'bringing the game into disrepute' and John Hartson is the first player this season to be suspended for reaching 21 penalty points. Retribution also hangs over the head of Paul Gascoigne, possibly in the form of being dropped by England, following revelations that he physically beat his new wife; just for good measure he is dismissed during Rangers' Champions League defeat by Ajax.

Week 10 (Oct 19-25): Wimbledon's surge up the table moves into top gear as the Crazy Gang hand Ruud Gullit's Chelsea their first home defeat of the season, 4-2, and it's the Dons who are praised for the quality of their football. Arsenal stay above Wimbledon in second place on goal difference despite being held at Highbury by Coventry who lose veteran goalkeeper Steve Ogrizovic with a broken nose following a clash with Ian Wright. West Ham slow their slide with victory over Leicester who have skipper Steve Walsh sent off. It is a bad day for the north-east as Middlesbrough and Sunderland both go down 3-0, Boro at home to Spurs and Sunderland at fellow strugglers Southampton. Newcastle, though, storm three points clear the following day with a staggering 5-0 destruction of Manchester United at St James's Park. The Magpies first league win over United for nine years is their seventh consecutive Premiership victory and is also the Reds' heaviest league defeat for 12 years – Ferguson's side had gone nine hours and nine minutes without conceding a goal.

Premiership sides are humbled in the Coca-Cola Cup on the 23rd as Stockport County win at Blackburn, Chelsea lose at Bolton and Luton hold Wimbledon at Selhurst Park. Coventry draw at Gillingham after leading by two goals. The football world is in shock the following day as news breaks that a helicopter crash has killed Chelsea vice chairman Matthew Harding and four others on their way back from Bolton.

Premiership sides have a better time in the Coca-Cola Cup on the 24th with Middlesbrough leading the way with a 5-1 thrashing of Huddersfield – overseas stars Juninho, Emerson, Mikkel Beck and Ravanelli (two) are the scorers. Iain Dowie scores twice in West Ham's 4-1 win over Notts Forest, Villa come back from one down to win at Elland Road and Sunderland lose to a last-minute Sol Campbell goal after leading at Tottenham. Liverpool and Arsenal draw away to Nationwide League opposition while the only surprise is Southampton being held at the Dell by Lincoln City.

November

Week 11 (Oct 26-Nov 1): A minute's silence is observed before every Premiership game on the 26th in memory of Matthew Harding. At a very emotional Stamford Bridge Ruud Gullit's side pay a suitable tribute with the manager scoring during a 3-1 victory over Spurs. Two goals inside the opening five minutes put Arsenal on course for a 3-0 victory over Leeds and a return to the summit of the table. After his first return to Highbury, George Graham admits it is going to be a long hard slog to get it right at his new club.

Newcastle surrender top place and their winning run with a shock 2-0 defeat at Filbert Street in which Foxes 'keeper Kasey Keller is outstanding. But the most amazing result of the day comes from the Dell where Manchester United are heavily beaten for a second time. Norwegian international Egil Ostendstadt grabs a hat trick as the Saints record an unlikely 6-3 victory during which Roy Keane headed for an early bath. Henning Berg fires Blackburn into an early lead at West Ham but his own goal five minutes from time condemns Ray Harford's side to another defeat as they slip a further point adrift of Coventry who draw at home with Sheffield Wednesday. Sunderland give a debut to French goalkeeper Lionel Perez during a home win over Aston Villa.

Everton climb to eighth with a Monday night win at Nottingham Forest, whose on-field problems are exacerbated by talks of a take-over. Joe Royle completes a good couple of days for the Toffeemen with the £5.75m signing of Nick Barmby from Middlesbrough. Faustino Asprilla scores twice and David Ginola conjures up

13

a magnificent goal as Newcastle make UEFA Cup progress with a 4-0 win over Ferencvaros at St James's. Manchester United put in a tame performance at Old Trafford and lose their 40-year unbeaten home record in Europe as Fenerbahce revive their Champions League ambitions with a deflected shot off David May, extending United's losing streak to three games. Liverpool suffer an evening of fluctuating fortunes at Anfield before finally seeing off Swiss side Sion 6-3 for an aggregate 8-4 victory in the Cup Winners' Cup.

Week 12 (Nov 2-8): Wimbledon stay in title race contention on the 2nd as a blood and thunder clash with Arsenal at Selhurst Park ends all square at 2-2. Goals from Michael Duberry and Gianluca Vialli put Chelsea on the path to handing Manchester United a fourth successive defeat, the Reds' first at home in the league this season. The surprises continue 24 hours later as Blackburn begin their recovery under caretaker manager Tony Parks with a 3-0 destruction of Liverpool; Chris Sutton scores twice as does Peter Beardsley as Newcastle reclaim pole position with a 3-1 home victory over neighbours Middlesbrough. Just two points separate 17th-placed Leeds from 10th-in-the-table Everton.

Alex Ferguson celebrates ten years at Old Trafford as his predecessor, Ron Atkinson, steps upstairs at Coventry to allow Gordon Strachan to move into the manager's seat. Both events, however, are eclipsed by the death of England legend Tommy Lawton at the age of 77. David Busst's career is over as he learns that the broken leg suffered against Manchester United will never again be strong enough to play football. Stan Collymore is fined two weeks' wages after refusing to play for Liverpool Reserves. Chelsea boost their total of overseas players by signing Italian international Gianfranco Zola from Parma for £4.5m.

Week 13 (Nov 9-15): Goals from Teddy Sheringham and Les Ferdinand move England closer to World Cup qualification with a 2-0 win over Georgia. The international fixture results in a blank weekend in the Premiership. Normality returns to the Coca-Cola Cup as Southampton and Wimbledon win replays at Lincoln and Luton respectively but the Dons come within a minute of going out. Arsenal and Liverpool also move through to the 4th Round the following evening but Coventry's problems deepen as Second Division Gillingham win 1-0 at Highfield Road.

Aston Villa goalkeeper Mark Bosnich is fined £1,000 by the FA for his 'Basil Fawlty – Hitler' impression at Tottenham.

Week 14 (Nov 16-22): A comical Nigel Winterburn own goal in front of 55,210 spectators at Old Trafford on the 16th brings the Reds' losing run to an end and allows Liverpool, 2-0 winners at Leeds, to climb into second place. Arsenal's misery is made complete by a rib injury sustained by England goalkeeper David Seaman. Newcastle stay top despite dropping two points at home to West Ham. Coventry ease their worries when battling back from two down to draw at Wimbledon and a draw for Blackburn at home to Chelsea lifts them above Notts Forest at the foot of the table. Gary Speed scores a hat trick and Andrei Kanchelskis a double as Everton blitz Southampton 7-1 at Goodison Park. Paul Stewart sees red as Sunderland go down 2-0 at Tottenham, for whom Andy Sinton scores his first goal.

Sheffield Wednesday, whose four straight wins at the start of the season took them to the top of the table, record a fifth Premiership victory after eight winless matches and climb back into the top ten with a 2-0 triumph over bottom side Notts Forest. Terry Venables makes a return to international football by accepting an invitation to be head coach to the Australian team.

A mistake by goalkeeper Pavel Srnicek restricts Newcastle to a 1-1 draw in their 3rd Round 1st Leg UEFA Cup tie with Metz in France but it is more than Manchester United can manage a day later as Juventus win 1-0 in Manchester in the Champions League. Juventus are supreme early on before a second half United onslaught almost rescues a point. In the Merseyside derby at Anfield – postponed earlier in the season due to flooding – Speed's late Everton equaliser floors Liverpool in their bid to topple Newcastle from the summit.

Regi Blinker of Sheffield Wednesday is handed a world-wide ban by FIFA over contractual problems the player had with one of his former clubs, Udinese.

Week 15 (Nov 23-29): Four of the top five sides face each other on the 23rd and each gains a point as Newcastle draw at Chelsea and Wimbledon do likewise at Liverpool, despite falling a goal behind inside the first-minute. Alan Shearer scores a superb goal for the league leaders in his first match after four weeks out following a groin operation. Craig Hignett's late penalty denies Manchester United victory at Middlesbrough while late strikes by Gary Kelly and Lee Sharpe hand Leeds their first away win under Graham and push Southampton deeper into trouble. Arsenal move to within a point of Newcastle on the Sunday with a deflected goal and a spectacular Dennis Bergkamp effort in the final three minutes clinches a 3-1 victory over Tottenham.

An injury-time equaliser by Forest's Colin Cooper salvages a point at the City Ground as Blackburn lose an opportunity to climb above 18th-placed Coventry. A crowd of just 7,573 witnesses Wimbledon's passage through to the quarter-finals of the Coca-Cola Cup with a fortuitous victory over holders Aston Villa at Selhurst Park. In the same competition, Southampton are held at Oxford United and 24 hours later West Ham, who get a full 90 minutes out of Florin Raducioiu for the first time since his £2.6m transfer in the summer, are forced into a replay by Stockport County. A weakened Manchester United side is defeated 2-0 at Leicester City while Middlesbrough see off Newcastle in a sizzling tie at the Riverside Stadium with what Bryan Robson describes as Boro's best performance of the season. North London will not be represented in the quarter-finals as Arsenal, having taken the lead at Anfield, are crushed 4-2 in an absorbing tie which sees Steve Bould dismissed for two bookable offences. Robbie Fowler continues his personal pilfering of the Arsenal defence with another double at their expense. But the Gunners' demise at Liverpool is more acceptable than that of their neighbours, Spurs, who are humiliated 6-1 by Nationwide League leaders Bolton Wanderers at Burnden Park; John McGinlay scores a hat trick.

December

Week 16 (Nov 30-Dec 6): Despite having Tony Adams harshly dismissed, Arsenal defeat Newcastle at St James's Park on the 30th to move to the top of the Premiership. Shearer scores for a personal record of seven consecutive games but is outshone by goals from Lee Dixon and Ian Wright. In addition to Adams' red card, referee Graham Barber hands out eight bookings. Manchester United, with their more recognised starting line-up, score three times in the final 15 minutes to gain a swift revenge over Leicester who reduce the deficit in the final minute. But United remain two points adrift of Wimbledon who stay fourth with a Robbie Earle goal seeing off Forest.

The surprise result of the day comes at Goodison where Everton, unbeaten in eight games, are overturned 3-1 by a Sunderland side which had lost its previous five away games. Eighteen-year-old Michael Bridges scores twice for Sunderland after coming on as substitute. Blackburn double their total of league victories with a 2-1 win over fellow strugglers Southampton who have Dutchman Ulrich van Gobbel controversially dismissed at Ewood Park. Coventry lose again, this time at Derby County whose victory carries the Rams into the top ten; manager Jim Smith wins the November Manager of the Month award. Leeds climb three places on the 1st with two early goals – including Ian Rush's first for the club at the 16th attempt – accounting for Chelsea at Elland Road.

The Monday match brings further gloom for Spurs as Liverpool join Arsenal as Premiership leaders with a 2-0 triumph at White Hart Lane. For the second time in less than a year Liverpool benefit from a bizarre ricochet off a divot as the ball bounces over Ian Walker's dive from a Steve McManaman shot for the second 'Pool goal.

Newcastle struggle to put their two defeats during the past week behind them before removing Metz from the UEFA Cup with two late goals from Faustino Asprilla for a 3-1 aggregate win. Less happy in the north-east are Middlesbrough, whose search for a league win is extended to ten games by Leicester who climb to 12th thanks to goals from Steve Claridge and Mustafa Izzet at the Riverside. Juninho and Emerson are absent from the Boro side.

Fears that England's representatives in the Champions' Cup will make one more early exit are banished as Manchester United cruise to a 2-0 win over Rapid in Vienna while Juventus's victory by the same score over Fenerbahce ensures United's passage to the quarter-finals. But United lose ground in the title race as Arsenal, boosted by Wright's 20th goal of the season, beat Southampton 3-1 at Highbury to move eight points clear of the sixth-placed champions. A third consecutive win for Aston Villa at Upton Park lifts them into fifth position.

Week 17 (Dec 7-13): With most of the top sides dropping points, Wimbledon seize the opportunity to climb into second place with a 3-1 win at Sunderland. Efan Ekoku scores twice as the Dons stretch their unbeaten run to a remarkable 18 games. Liverpool slip to third as Guy Whittingham's first-half goal clinches victory for Sheffield Wednesday at Anfield and Arsenal need a last-minute goal from Patrick Vieira to stop Derby from winning at Highbury; Dean Sturridge scores the first County goal with a glorious strike. Villa go fourth as an Andy Townsend goal condemns Southampton to a fifth successive defeat. Middlesbrough and Coventry have their respective winless runs extended to eleven games. Boro draw at home to Leeds while Coventry, facing a Spurs side which includes £2.5m new signing Steffen Iversen, go down 2-1. Everton bounce back to take a point off Chelsea in a 2-2 draw at Stamford Bridge and Blackburn move out of the bottom three with a point at Leicester. On the Sunday, Manchester United look likely to close the gap when taking a two-goal lead at Upton Park but two goals in three minutes for Raducioiu and Julian Dicks earn a share of the spoils. Spurs are back in the transfer market in a big way when adding John Scales of Liverpool to the midweek signing of Iversen for a further £2.6m.

Newcastle miss a chance to go second with an entertaining goalless draw at Forest in the Monday match; Forest's point dumps Coventry to the foot of the table.

Week 18 (Dec 14-20): Troubled Middlesbrough are on the receiving end as Robbie Fowler scores four times during a 5-1 drubbing at Anfield. Fowler's quartet includes his 100th goal for Liverpool in just 165 games, a feat achieved in one game less than Ian Rush. Wimbledon stay level on points with Roy Evans' side thanks to Dean Holdsworth's late winner against Blackburn. Leeds record their first home draw of the season and Spurs their first away draw in a goalless stalemate at Elland Road. After a slow start, Sunderland hammer three past Chelsea to move seven points clear of the relegation places.

December 15 kicks off with Vinnie Jones being fined £6,000 by Wimbledon for disparaging comments in a tabloid newspaper about his team mates. The day ends with Nick Barmby's 86th minute Everton winner denting Jim Smith's Manager of the Month celebrations. One day later and Fowler is back on the goal trail and Stan Collymore scores twice against his former club as Liverpool go top by virtue of a 4-2 victory over Forest. Forest not only set a new Premiership record of 16 games without a win but also drop to bottom place as Coventry notch an unlikely 2-1 win over Newcastle at Highfield Road. Goals for Darren Huckerby and Gary McAllister hand Gordon Strachan his first win as a manager.

Manchester United share the spoils with Sheffield Wednesday following an entertaining encounter at Hillsborough; United are now nine points adrift of Liverpool. Southampton edge out Oxford United in the Coca Cola Cup but West Ham are defeated at Stockport County whose 2-1 triumph features a memorable Iain Dowie own goal; Dowie's day is made complete as he suffers a broken ankle. The previous weekend Dowie was a hero when scoring twice for Northern Ireland against Albania in a World Cup qualifier.

Against a background of plummeting fortunes on the pitch and possible take-overs in the boardroom, Frank Clark resigns as manager of Nottingham Forest. Stuart Pearce is offered the position of caretaker manager. Fellow strugglers Middlesbrough could also be in trouble after calling off Saturday's match at Blackburn due to illness and injury.

Week 19 (Dec 21-27): Sunderland's revival is put on hold with Solskjaer and Cantona scoring twice each as United saunter home 5-0 at Old Trafford. Struggling Coventry, Southampton and Forest all win, the latter with a brace of Alf Inge Haarland goals accounting for Arsenal as Ian Wright is dismissed at the City Ground after an elaborate fall to the ground by Nikola Jerkan. Wimbledon miss out on a chance to go joint top when their 19-match unbeaten run is halted by a rampant Villa side for whom Yorke and Milosevic share four goals in a 5-0 thrashing at Villa Park. Shearer and Fowler are on target on the 23rd as Liverpool stay seven points clear of the Geordies and move three clear of the pack with a 1-1 draw at St James's Park. Middlesbrough head for Christmas amid more controversy following alleged derogatory comments about the club and English football by Ravanelli.

Better news for Boro on Boxing Day as Juninho caps an excellent performance with two goals in a 4-2 win over Everton, their first league success for 13 games. Another import, Zola, adds a pair as Chelsea consolidate their rise with a 2-0 win at

Villa and Spurs' Scandinavian signings Steffen Iversen and Allan Nielsen see off Southampton at White Hart Lane. Liverpool and Arsenal drop points with draws while the United goal machine adds four more as Forest are handed their first defeat under Pearce – 4-0 at the City Ground. Leeds' Premiership record of five consecutive clean sheets is undone by three Coventry goals in ten minutes including a Gary McAllister penalty against his former club. Blackburn stay in the bottom three despite a win over Newcastle, which further dents Keegan's title hopes.

Week 20 (Dec 28-Jan 3): England internationals Shearer, Ferdinand and Lee join in a goal spree as Newcastle annihilate Spurs 7-1, the third-highest winning margin in Premiership history. Manchester United settle for an Eric Cantona penalty to clinch victory over Leeds and move within two points of Liverpool. Wimbledon return to winning ways with a 3-1 success at fading Everton while Coventry complete a fourth consecutive victory, 3-0 over Middlesbrough, to climb to 14th thanks in no small part to the impressive Darren Huckerby. Liverpool re-establish a five-point advantage on the Sunday by adding to old boy Graeme Souness's worries with a bizarre opportunist John Barnes goal pinching victory at the Dell.

The new year kicks off with Chelsea keeping their championship ambitions alive with a Roberto Di Matteo goal handing Liverpool their third away defeat of the season. The Reds' defeat is seized on by Arsenal and Newcastle, who see off Middlesbrough and Leeds respectively. Boro's defeat is their sixth successive away failure as Ian Wright scores his 200th league goal. The Gunners have John Hartson dismissed in the final minute but the first red card of the year goes to Dion Dublin who started the game by scoring his fourth goal in as many games during Coventry's 2-2 draw with Sunderland. Manchester United are held by Villa at Old Trafford in front of another crowd in excess of 55,000 while Blackburn move out of the bottom three with victory at Everton and Forest suck West Ham back into trouble courtesy of Kevin Campbell's strike at Upton Park.

January

Week 21 (Jan 4-10): Premiership sides come through relatively unscathed in the 3rd Round of the Littlewoods-sponsored FA Cup on the 4th with only Southampton, beaten 3-1 at Reading, falling at the first attempt. Saints' boss Souness blasts referee Graham Poll for allowing the match to go ahead on a frozen surface. Top scorers are Sheffield Wednesday who notch up their biggest victory in the competition, 7-1, over Grimsby, for 65 years. Middlesbrough also win by six as Chester are thrashed and there are convincing three-goal wins for Chelsea and Nottingham Forest. French goalkeeper Lionel Perez is the toast of Sunderland after starring in a 1-1 draw at Highbury. West Ham come from behind to force a replay with Wrexham and 24 hours later Newcastle have their work cut out to hold Charlton at the Valley. Manchester United head for another domestic double as second half goals, including a majestic David Beckham free kick, account for injury-hit Spurs at Old Trafford and Everton ease their sorrows with a 3-0 win over Swindon who are livid after referee Neale Berry sends off defender Ian Culverhouse for handball after just 52 seconds.

Tottenham take their season's spending through the £10m barrier with the signing of Swiss international Ramon Vega from Cagliari on the 7th but one day later Kevin Keegan confirms that money does not guarantee success as he departs from Newcastle after rebuilding the club at a cost in excess of £60m. He recouped over £21m in sales. Keegan announced his resignation by stating that he had taken the club as far as he could and added that he had also offered his resignation at the end of the previous season.

On the pitch, Middlesbrough keep the spotlight on the north-east by virtue of an absorbing 2-1 quarter-final Coca-Cola Cup victory over Liverpool. Wimbledon make certain of their first appearance in the last four with a surprisingly comfortable 2-0 win at Bolton.

Week 22 (Jan 11-17): Liverpool fail to win for the sixth time in 12 home Premier Division matches as West Ham grab a vital point at Anfield. Arsenal and Chelsea, beaten at Sunderland and Forest, fail to close the gap while managerless Newcastle only draw at Villa after taking an early two-goal lead. Arsenal's case is not helped by Dennis Bergkamp picking up the Gunners' fifth red card in 10 games. Dion Dublin collects a seven-match suspension after departing early for the second consecutive match as Coventry are crushed 4-0 at Blackburn.

Manchester United are fast becoming title favourites and underline the point with one more Beckham special putting paid to a Spurs comeback in north London. Sheffield Wednesday's return to form continues with victory over Everton. The battle for survival hots up with a Jim Magilton penalty earning Southampton the points at the Riverside and Derby take a point at Wimbledon.

On the 14th, Middlesbrough have three points deducted and are fined £50,000 for their failure to show up for a Premiership match at Blackburn in December. A busy day for the club also sees Robson pay £2.5m for Italian Gianluca Festa.

Bad weather plays an increasing role in the story of the season and fans voice their frustration as FA Cup matches at Luton, Watford and Brentford are called off close to kick-off. A sudden mid-afternoon drop in the temperature caused the late postponements. In the matches that go ahead, Wimbledon, Leeds and Villa draw at Crewe, Crystal Palace and Notts County respectively. Derby's match at Gillingham is abandoned as the frost bites.

Newcastle United placate their supporters with the appointment of Kenny Dalglish as replacement for Keegan. Dalglish had only recently taken up a scouting position with Scottish champions Rangers. Although the team is picked by Terry McDermott and Arthur Cox, Dalglish's reign starts triumphantly with an Alan Shearer goal disposing of Charlton during extra time at St James's Park. Elsewhere, Bergkamp has a happier time at Roker Park as the last ever FA Cup tie at the ground ends in a 2-0 Arsenal victory; the Dutchman scores the opening goal. Goals either side of half time by Steve Claridge and Ian Marshall give Leicester victory over Southend. Coventry's home tie with Woking is added to the list of late postponements.

Chelsea's highly rated young defender Michael Duberry is out for the rest of the season after snapping an Achilles' tendon in training. West Ham part with Romanian Raducioiu and move for Celtic striker Pierre van Hooijdonk as Everton sell Anders Limpar to Birmingham.

Week 23 (Jan 18-24): Liverpool end their run of home draws with a goal from debutant Jamie Carragher setting the Reds on the path to a 3-0 win over Villa. United stay second with a 2-0 victory at Coventry. Southampton score twice in the final three minutes to salvage a point as Newcastle again let slip a two goal advantage. Welshman Mark Pembridge scores twice but is outgunned by overseas players Ravanelli, Festa – on his debut, Emerson and Juninho as Middlesbrough beat Wednesday 4-2. Ravanelli steps into more hot water as he is later dismissed. Derby's slide towards relegation continues as they go down 3-1 at Chelsea and have Christian Dailly sent off. Fellow midlanders Leicester defeat Wimbledon. Nottingham Forest overcome an early Andy Sinton goal to keep their good run going thanks to a pair of Bryan Roy goals as Spurs have Vega dismissed, and Arsenal maintain their title challenge at the expense of an increasingly desperate Everton.

Second-half goals for Gary Kelly and Lee Bowyer at Upton Park lift Leeds to 11th in the Monday match and deny West Ham the opportunity to climb out of the bottom three; Hammers fans criticise manager Harry Redknapp. Dalglish signs £2m rated Portuguese defender Raul on a free transfer courtesy of the Bosman ruling.

There are midweek FA Cup victories for Derby, Wimbledon and Aston Villa while Leicester move a step closer to Wembley with a quarter-final Coca-Cola Cup victory at Ipswich and Southampton, thanks to Egil Ostenstad's late equaliser, force a replay at Stockport.

Week 24 (Jan 25-31): The full magic of the FA Cup is experienced on the final weekend of the month. In the 3rd Round Coventry are embarrassed by a home draw with non-league cup specialists Woking and West Ham succumb to a last-minute winner from Wrexham's Kevin Russell. Everton's fall from grace accelerates with Chris Waddle scoring a stunning goal during Bradford City's 3-2 win at Goodison Park. Middlesbrough only squeeze through 3-2 at home to Vauxhall Conference side Hednesford Town but it is better than Manchester United can achieve as the holders are held by Robbie Earle's last-minute equaliser for Wimbledon at Old Trafford. Derby humble Aston Villa 3-1 at the Baseball Ground. The shocks continue on the Sunday with Chelsea overturning a two-goal deficit to defeat Liverpool 4-2 at the Bridge with Vialli scoring twice. Up at St James's Park the Geordies' season continues to disintegrate as Notts Forest battle back from one down to reach the 5th Round with a pair of Ian Woan goals.

A busy midweek programme sees Manchester United succeed where they failed at the weekend and beat Wimbledon to move to the top of the table. Arsenal also leapfrog Liverpool with a 2-1 win at West Ham, and Newcastle become Everton's latest beneficiaries, crushing Joe Royle's side 4-1. Coventry grab a lifeline with a 1-0 win at the City Ground. Southampton become the latest victims of a cup giant killing as Stockport win their Coca-Cola Cup replay 2-1 at the Dell.

February

Week 25 (Feb 1-7): A late Eric Cantona goal sees off Southampton at Old Trafford and keeps United a point clear at the summit from Liverpool who take maximum points at Derby, and Chelsea stay in the hunt with victory at Tottenham extending their unbeaten record at White Hart Lane to a decade. George Graham welcomes

20

Arsenal to Elland Road for a dreary goalless draw but goals prove no problem at St James's Park on the 2nd as Shearer scores a thrilling hat trick in the final 13 minutes to give the Magpies an unlikely 4-3 win over Leicester.

A magnificent save by Neil Sullivan from Gary Pallister paves the way for Wimbledon – playing their sixth match in 17 days – to dump Manchester United out of the FA Cup; Marcus Gayle heads the goal which ends United's domestic double dream. Coventry ride their luck at Kingfield before a Steve Foster own goal gives Strachan's side a formitous victory over Woking. Arsenal and Leeds meet again, this time at Highbury, and the Gunners are stunned as an early Rod Wallace goal puts the visitors through to the 5th Round.

Week 26 (Feb 8-14): No games are played in the Premiership on the second weekend of the month as national sides prepare for midweek World Cup qualifying ties. England coach Glenn Hoddle surprises many with his line-up and then looks on as Italy cast doubts on their 1998 qualification chances with a deflected shot by Zola securing the Italians a 1-0 victory at Wembley.

Week 27 (Feb 15-21): The FA Cup continues to surprise as Coventry overturn a first-minute deficit to win a 4th Round tie at Blackburn; veteran keeper Steve Ogrizovic saves a Chris Sutton penalty. In the 5th Round Nottingham Forest are beaten by a Tom Curtis penalty at Division Two side Chesterfield. But the result of the day is at Elland Road where Terry Venables' Division One Portsmouth puncture Leeds' normally solid defence three times for a shock 3-2 success. Middlesbrough make progress at Manchester City and Wimbledon end Queens Park Rangers' run. Outsiders Wrexham win at Birmingham. Two Sunday cup ties see Leicester battle back from two down to grab a replay with Chelsea, thanks to a last-minute own goal, while Sheffield Wednesday win at Blackburn, also with the aid of an own goal. Two Premiership matches produce just one goal but it is enough to boost Derby's survival hopes and leave West Ham in deep trouble.

Wimbledon, still contesting both domestic cup competitions and riding high in the league, draw 0-0 at Filbert Street with Leicester in the 1st Leg of the semi-final Coca-Cola Cup tie. Heavy rain causes the postponement of Stockport's home leg with Middlesbrough.

Manchester United tighten their grip on the championship with a 2-1 win at rainswept Highbury but the result is overshadowed by the running feud between Peter Schmeichel and Ian Wright which flares up again following an ugly two-footed lunge at the keeper by the England striker. The vendetta continues in the tunnel after the match. Liverpool at last have something to celebrate on home soil as Stan Collymore scores twice during a 4-0 destruction of Leeds.

David Hirst rescues a point for Sheffield Wednesday at Derby but a Dwight Yorke double leaves Coventry looking over their shoulders. Everton boss Joe Royle is warned by the FA following comments made to referee David Elleray back in September. David Busst, whose career ended a year earlier with a horrific broken leg at Old Trafford, faces a 15th operation on the damaged limb.

Week 28 (Feb 22-28): Zola and Beckham hit outstanding goals as Chelsea and United draw at the Bridge. Liverpool again slip up at home when held by Blackburn while Newcastle go third with a Ferdinand goal at luckless Middlesbrough. Ian Marshall strikes three times in Leicester's 4-2 over Derby and Sheffield Wednesday fight back from two down to win at Southampton as pressure mounts on Souness.

21

On the Sunday, Wimbledon's unbeaten record at Highbury is extended to ten years thanks to Vinnie Jones's volleyed winner.

West Ham add to the tension at the foot of the table and nudge Forest back into the bottom three with an absorbing 4-3 victory over Spurs; Julian Dicks scores twice and Hartson repays another chunk of his fee with a vital goal. Disappointment on the pitch for Forest is offset by events in the boardroom as a consortium including the former Tottenham chairman Irvine Scholar assumes control of the club and make in the region of £16m available for Stuart Pearce to acquire new players. Newcastle's hopes of European glory fade as it is announced that Alan Shearer is to undergo another groin operation.

Midweek cup ties throw up excitement and controversy galore. In a 5th Round FA Cup replay, Leicester City put in a tremendous display at Chelsea before succumbing to a penalty three minutes from the end of extra time. Referee Mike Reed is severely criticised for pointing to the spot after Chelsea substitute Frank Leboeuf appeared to jump into City defender Spencer Prior. Even the Prime Minister passes comment on the incident as the debate on the introduction of electrical wizardry gains momentum.

In a 5th Round tie Derby County stage a magnificent comeback as from two down at the Baseball Ground they storm through to the last eight thanks to Dean Sturridge's late winner. Middlesbrough move a step closer to their first Wembley appearance as Mikkel Beck and Ravanelli strike within six minutes of eachother to give the Premiership side a 2-0 Coca-Cola Cup semi-final 1st Leg advantage at Stockport. Southampton pick up just a point following a goalless home draw with Wimbledon and stay bottom but one. Changes continue at the City Ground as Dave Bassett is appointed general manager.

March

Week 29 (Mar 1-7): Coventry City's attempts to beat the drop look increasingly forlorn as two comical defensive errors inside the opening six minutes send them spinning to a 3-1 defeat at Manchester United move four points clear of second-placed Liverpool on the first day of the month. Ian Wright hits the headlines for the right reasons by scoring the opening goal in Arsenal's 2-0 win at Everton to lift the Gunners above Newcastle and into third place. Everton's plight looks serious as their run stretches to one win in ten and West Ham's fortunes dip as a Lee Sharpe goal sends them to defeat at Elland Road; it is Leeds' 15th clean sheet of the season as the Hammers have Michael Hughes sent off. Newcastle are felled at home by a Matt Le Tissier goal as Southampton move five points clear of bottom side Middlesbrough, who go down 3-1 at Hillsborough. Derby, twice trailing to Chelsea, win 3-2 for the second time in four days and Forest boost their survival hopes with a Dean Saunders goal clinching victory at Tottenham. Blackburn's unlikely relegation battle eases with a win over Sunderland while Leicester gain a psychological cup advantage over Wimbledon by virtue of a 3-1 win over the Dons at Selhurst Park; it is Wimbledon's first home defeat since the opening day of the season. Liverpool's title challenge falters on the Sunday with a late Ian Taylor goal earning Aston Villa the points at Villa Park.

The midweek matches kick off with Coventry dropping two points during a home draw with Wimbledon while Steffan Iversen hits a hat trick as Spurs trounce Sunderland 4-0 at Roker Park. Newcastle complete a miserable night in the north-east by losing the home leg of their UEFA Cup quarter-final with Monaco 1-0. The Magpies have Shearer, Ferdinand and Asprilla missing and concussion restricts Peter Beardsley to a seat on the bench.

England's standing in European club competitions gains a massive lift on the 5th as Manchester United rout Porto 4-0 at Old Trafford. David May, Eric Cantona, Ryan Giggs and Andy Cole score the goals which make the 2nd Leg of their quarter-final clash a formality. Also amongst the goals are Middlesbrough who hit six against Derby as their season moves into top gear. Ravanelli claims a hat trick as Boro win 6-1 but stay bottom of the Premier. Leicester continue their good run with victory over Aston Villa but Forest are well beaten 3-0 at home by in-form Sheffield Wednesday who rise to sixth. Southampton and Everton share the spoils at the Dell. A Robbie Fowler goal earns Liverpool a draw at Norwegian side Brann Bergen in the quarter-final of the Cup Winners' Cup.

Week 30 (Mar 8-14): The championship race is reopened as Manchester United crash to a shock 2-1 defeat at Roker Park. Arsenal close the gap to just one point with two Bergkamp goals seeing off Nottingham Forest at Highbury. Everton lose again, this time 1-0 at Leeds, and Coventry again fail to win at home when drawing with Leicester.

The 6th Round of the FA Cup brings little joy for the home sides. Of the two ties played on the Saturday, both Derby County and Sheffield Wednesday go down 2-0. Middlesbrough follow up their midweek thrashing of the Rams with goals from Juninho and Ravanelli edging them closer to their second possible final of the season. Wimbledon remain active on all three domestic fronts as goals from Robbie Earle and Dean Holdsworth end Yorkshire hopes at Hillsborough. Cup favourites Chelsea are in impressive form on the south coast and saunter to a 4-1 victory at Fratton Park with the buffeted Mark Hughes setting the Blues on the path to the semis. Chesterfield complete the semi-final quartet with a 1-0 win at Saltergate over fellow Division Two side Wrexham; Chris Beaumont scores the history-making goal.

In a complex deal, Celtic stand to receive £4.5m over a two-year period after selling Dutch striker Pierre van Hooijdonk to Nottingham Forest.

Eleven months on from Liverpool defeating Newcastle 4-3 at Anfield in a pulsating match, history virtually repeats itself as the Reds again triumph in a seven-goal thriller. Liverpool lead 3-0 through Steve McManaman, Patrik Berger and Fowler before Keith Gillespie, Asprilla and Warren Barton pull the Magpies level – the latter two goals coming in the 87th and 89th minutes. But it is to no avail as Fowler's 25th goal of the season completes a staggering finale at Anfield.

Leicester City defy the odds to salvage a 2nd Leg Coca-Cola Cup semi-final draw at Selhurst Park and knock Wimbledon out by virtue of the away goals rule to clinch their first Cup Final appearance since 1969. The Dons led through Marcus Gayle but were pegged back by Simon Grayson's powerful header. In the Premier, van Hooijdonk is booked on his debut as Forest grab a point at Blackburn Rovers. Middlesbrough join Leicester at Wembley but are made to sweat as Stockport win 1-0 at the Riverside and come so close to notching a second and taking the tie into extra time.

Leeds record another clean sheet with a goalless home draw with Southampton whose position is made all the more precarious by West Ham's 3-2 victory at Upton Park over Chelsea, Paul Kitson's last-minute strike lifting the Hammers above both the Saints and Forest. Sheffield Wednesday climb to fifth on the back of a 2-1 win over Sunderland.

Week 31 (Mar 15-21): Andy Cole and Karel Poborsky condemn Sheffield Wednesday to a 2-0 defeat at Old Trafford as United move three points clear of Liverpool who are held to a 1-1 draw at the City Ground. Arsenal stay in contention with a competent 2-0 win over Southampton. Kevin Gallacher scores his first hat trick for Blackburn as Wimbledon go down 3-1 and Coventry, who have Brian Borrows dismissed, are also on the receiving end as Newcastle win 4-0 at St James's Park. Middlesbrough add to the excitement at the foot of the table with a 3-1 win at Leicester but Robson's side remain one point adrift of Southampton. Sunderland are thrown back into the mire on the Sunday by a Chelsea side which scores three times in the final 12 minutes to clinch a 6-2 win.

West Ham, having drawn at Villa Park on Saturday, rescue another point with Stan Lazaridis's first goal for the club denying Wimbledon victory in the final minute at Selhurst Park on the 18th. Newcastle's European adventure comes to a crushing end with a 3-0 defeat by Monaco; Ginola requests a transfer. Arsenal are involved in talks with the local authority regarding increasing the Highbury capacity to over 50,000; the Gunners also sign 19-year-old Austrian goalkeeper Alexander Manninger.

Chris Waddle's career takes another twist with the 36-year-old former England player moving to the club he supported as a boy, Sunderland, from Bradford for £75,000.

Manchester United progress to the semi-finals of the Champions' Cup with a goalless draw in Portugal ousting Porto 4-0 on aggregate. Local police fire upon United fans with plastic bullets. Goals by Juninho and Ravanelli earn Middlesbrough a 2-1 win over Blackburn and push Southampton, who go down 1-0 at Chelsea, to the foot of the table. Liverpool close in on winning the European Cup Winners' Cup for the first time with a 3-0 (4-1 agg) win at Anfield over Brann Bergen; Fowler scores another brace.

Week 32 (Mar 22-28): Goals from Solskjaer and Cantona eradicate Manchester United fears of another European hangover as Everton are condemned to further misery with a 2-0 defeat at Goodison Park. In a possible FA Cup Final rehearsal Juninho scores a vital Premiership goal which gives Middlesbrough victory over Chelsea. Derby also pick up three points with a 4-2 win over Spurs, and Coventry are plunged deep into trouble as John Hartson scores twice in West Ham's 3-1 win at Highfield Road. Liverpool, on the 24th, seriously dent the capital's chances of lifting the championship with a controversial 2-1 win at Arsenal. Referee Gerald Ashby awards the visitors a penalty when Robbie Fowler tumbles convincingly in the penalty area after appearing to be caught by David Seaman. Remarkably, Fowler insists that it is not a foul and probably feels vindicated when Seaman saves his spot kick – only for Jason McAteer to sweep home the rebound.

Little is resolved at the foot of the table as Forest and Middlesbrough draw at the Riverside. Boro also receive no joy from an FA commission as their three-point deduction and £50,000 fine is upheld. Boro consider taking the matter further.

Everton's slump, and alleged differences with his chairman, force Joe Royle to end his 28-month reign as manager of the Toffeemen. Robbie Fowler is praised by Europe's top brass for his penalty honesty but is then fined £900 by UEFA for a slogan on a T-shirt exposed after scoring against Bergen.

April

Week 33 (Mar 29-Apr 4): The Easter weekend, traditionally make or break for many sides looking for honours or striving to avoid the drop, is eerily quiet in the Premiership due to World Cup qualifying matches. A weakened England side defeat Mexico 2-0 at Wembley in a friendly.

Long-serving defender Dave Watson becomes the second caretaker player/manager in the Premiership as Everton are prepared to wait patiently in their quest to appoint a top-class replacement for Joe Royle. On the same night that Poland hold Italy to a draw, Juninho plays for Brazil just five days before the Coca-Cola Cup Final.

Week 34 (Apr 5-11): Manchester United's vice-like grip on the title is loosened by Derby County whose shock 3-2 win at Old Trafford sees United concede three goals at home for the first time in over four years. Ashley Ward, debutant Paulo Wanchope and Dean Sturridge find the target as Arsenal rekindles their title aspirations with a conclusive 3-0 triumph over Chelsea at the Bridge. The closing of the gap does little to calm Alex Ferguson as the United boss becomes embroiled in a public row with Arsène Wenger as to whether the season should be extended or not. Newcastle are boosted as Shearer scores in his first match back since his latest operation but Michael Gray's goal is sufficient to earn Sunderland a vital point. Bottom dogs Southampton score two late goals through new signing Mickey Evans at the City Ground to edge Forest closer to almost inevitable relegation. Three goals in 14 minutes sustain Aston Villa's UEFA Cup ambitions and nudge Everton one step closer to trouble. Bolton clinch a return to the Premier League with victory over QPR.

In a remarkable match at Anfield on the Sunday, Coventry move out of the bottom three with Dion Dublin's injury-time winner after Liverpool had led. Victory would have taken the Reds to the summit. Extra-time goals at Wembley for Ravanelli and Emile Heskey – three minutes from time – force Middlesbrough and Leicester to do battle again in the final of the Coca-Cola Cup.

The midweek matches kick off with a dismal goalless encounter between Leeds and Blackburn during which Leeds give debuts to substitutes Derek Lilley and Pierre Laurent. Title favourites Manchester United fail to sparkle in Europe but return from Germany with just a 1-0 1st Leg Champions' Cup semi-final deficit to overcome courtesy of Tretschok's late goal for Borussia Dortmund. On the domestic front, strugglers Coventry, Southampton, West Ham and Middlesbrough all pick up points. The latter pair are goalless at Upton Park; a last-minute own goal rescues a point for the Saints at Derby but Coventry, having fallen behind at Highfield Road, move three points off third from bottom Middlesbrough with a 3-1 win over Chelsea. Liverpool's sudden loss of form continues into Europe where a shocking display, not aided by David James's erratic goalkeeping, results in a horrendous 3-0 defeat away to Paris St Germain.

Week 35 (Apr 12-18): The top ten sides end the 12th in the same positions in which they started the day. Manchester United remain three points clear of Arsenal with a 3-2 victory at Blackburn which leaves the 1995 champions just three points clear of the relegation places, while the Gunners see off Leicester 2-0 at Highbury. Southampton's belated surge towards safety gathers momentum as first-half goals for Evans and Berkovic account for West Ham at the Dell; the Saints even have to overcome the handicap of having defender Jason Dodd sent off. Everton and Derby move clear of danger with home wins over Villa and Spurs respectively. Villa keeper Mark Bosnich storms out after being dropped by manager Brian Little.

With just five games to go Liverpool stay within three points of United on the Sunday with a 2-1 win at Sunderland which includes Robbie Fowler's 30th goal of the season and confirms the Wearsiders' position in the bottom three. The FA Cup takes centre stage, though, as Chelsea, aided by a brace of goals from the irrepressible Mark Hughes, book their Wembley ticket with a 3-0 destruction of Wimbledon whose absorbing season is fast falling apart. Over at Old Trafford, Middlesbrough and Second Division Chesterfield conjure up one of the all-time classic cup semi-finals. Boro have defender Kinder sent off and trail to goals from Andy Morris and a Sean Dyche penalty with an hour gone. Ravanelli pulls one back before a highly contentious decision by referee David Elleray denies Chesterfield a third goal by ignoring a shot by Jonathan Howard which crosses the goal-line after hitting the underside of the bar. Craig Hignett takes the tie into extra time from the penalty spot and Boro go ahead for the first time with Gianluca Festa lashing the ball home. Amazingly, Chesterfield draw level a minute from time with Jamie Hewitt heading an opportunist goal when all seems lost.

There is further misery for Boro in midweek as an extra-time Steve Claridge goal decides a disappointing Coca-Cola Cup Final replay at Hillsborough in Leicester City's favour and grabs them a place in Europe for the first time in 35 years. There is no lack of passion back in the Premiership campaign as Fowler and David Unsworth are dismissed after exchanging blows during a 1-1 Merseyside draw at Goodison Park. Goals for Dean Holdsworth and Stewart Castledine earn Wimbledon their first home win for four months, 2-0 against Leeds. Shearer bags a pair as the Dons' cup conquerors, Chelsea, are defeated 3-1 at Newcastle.

Week 36 (Apr 19-25): Manchester United make light of a morning kick-off to effectively settle the title race with a convincing 3-1 victory at Anfield, a result which is cemented by two goals from Gary Pallister. Having lost a chance to move top in midweek, Liverpool now trail the champions by five points and have played a game more. United dominate throughout but are assisted by David James's continued poor form in the 'Pool goal; James is subsequently dropped from the England squad for the forthcoming match with Georgia. Gary Flitcroft scores a late equaliser for Blackburn during a game of nine bookings at Highbury; a point lifts Arsenal to second.

The battle for survival takes some dramatic twists, none more so than at the Riverside where Middlesbrough are beaten by a Darren Williams goal which takes Sunderland out of the bottom three. West Ham squander two points thanks to Duncan Ferguson grabbing a last-minute equaliser for Everton and Coventry also come back from two down to save a vital point at Southampton who stay clear of the drop on goal difference from the Hammers.

Coventry pick up their eighth point from four games during an entertaining home draw with Arsenal on the 21st and the value of that latest point is accentuated by Sunderland's demise at home to Southampton the following night. Egil Ostenstad's first-half goal allows the Saints to join the Sky Blues three points above the safety line although both sides have played two games more than most of the clubs fighting against the drop. Blackburn's worries ease with a 4-1 thrashing of Sheffield Wednesday while Chelsea inflict more misery on London rivals Wimbledon courtesy of a Dan Petrescu goal. Chesterfield's gallant FA Cup run is finally halted as the brilliant Juninho inspires Middlesbrough to a comprehensive 3-0 semi-final replay win at Hillsborough.

Manchester United's fifth Champions' League defeat of the season proves to be the end of the road for Alex Ferguson's side as Borussia Dortmund move through to the final with an aggregate 2-0 victory. Missed chances, particularly by Andy Cole, cost United dear.

West Ham keep Leicester on the edge of the relegation frame with a John Moncur goal at Filbert Street which spells greater problems for Sunderland who now look favourites to go down with Forest and Middlesbrough, a scenario which begins to look inevitable on the Thursday evening as the double cup finalists are defeated by Spurs at White Hart Lane. England's interest in Europe is over for another year despite Liverpool regaining a measure of pride with a determined 2-0 win over Paris St Germain at Anfield but the French side go through to the Cup Winners' Cup Final 3-2 on aggregate.

May

Week 37 (Apr 27-May 2): Although into the final throes, the race for the championship and lucrative Premier League survival is put on hold on the final Saturday in April as Hoddle gets his squad together for the midweek World Cup qualifying match at Wembley with Georgia. But it is business as usual in the Nationwide League where victory for Barnsley, 2-0 at home to Bradford City, ensures top-flight football at Oakwell for the 1997/98 season for the first time in the Yorkshire club's 110-year history.

Outstanding goals by Sheringham and Shearer enable England to complete the double over the Georgians and move level on points with group leaders Italy who are held to a goalless draw in Poland. The Italian contingent in England, however, are celebrating as Chelsea striker Gianfranco Zola is named as the football writers' Player of the Year.

Week 38 (May 3-9): Manchester United's latest title celebrations are kept on hold as Leicester storm into a two-goal lead inside 20 minutes at Filbert Street. A brace of goals for Solskjaer denies Leicester the maximum points required for Premiership safety but victories for Liverpool at home to Spurs and Newcastle away to Arsenal keep the destination of the trophy in some minor doubt. A day of astonishing results for several of the lowly clubs only confirms the fall from grace of Nottingham Forest who become the first club to twice be relegated from the Premier League.

Sunderland sign off from Roker Park in glorious style with a 3-0 thumping of Everton which brings renewed hope that the Rokermen's new ground will host top-flight football from its inception. Paul Stewart begins the spree with his first penalty for nine years and Chris Waddle opens his account for the team he supported as a boy as Sunderland dumps Coventry, beaten 2-1 at home by the now safe Derby, into a seemingly certain relegation position. Fabrizio Ravanelli breaks through the 30-goal barrier with two more for Middlesbrough as their slender survival hopes are boosted with a dramatic last-minute victory over Europe chasing Aston Villa. A stormy encounter at the Riverside sees Steve Staunton dismissed with others fortunate not to follow. Harry Redknapp's controversial big money splash out on Hartson and Kitson pays further valuable dividends as the duo share all five goals as Sheffield Wednesday are hammered again, this time 5-1, West Ham's biggest League win in 30 years. Kitson scores a hat-trick while David Hirst replies for Wednesday prior to being dismissed. Like West Ham, Southampton's remarkable transformation is almost complete with victory over Everton practically ensuring another successful battle against the drop.

Only one game is played on the Bank Holiday Monday but it is significant at both ends of the table as the league leaders are held at Old Trafford to a 3-3 draw by Middlesbrough. A crowd of 54,489 see Bryan Robson's side take the lead three times before another Solskjaer goal edges the champions to within one victory of retaining their crown - Boro remain on the brink of relegation.

Failure to win by both Liverpool, at Wimbledon, and Newcastle, at West Ham, on 6 May, saves Manchester United the trouble of winning the title under their own steam. Wimbledon's 2-1 win and West Ham's goalless draw hand United the title for the fourth time in five years, this time with two games to spare. But due to the latest tinkering with the European Cup, Liverpool, Newcastle and Arsenal could still qualify for that now greatly devalued tournament as runners-up to United.

Sheffield Wednesday's surprising dip in form continues as Leicester crown a memorable season for the Foxes with a late Matt Elliott goal securing Premiership safety for Martin O'Neill's side. West Ham and Blackburn are also smiling on the Thursday evening as a goalless draw at Ewood Park with the FA Cup finalists confirms their status for the following season but Middlesbrough's multi-million and multi-national side are facing a humbling return to the Nationwide League after just a two-year absence. Victory on the final day may not be sufficient to save Robson's boys and keep the foreign contingent on Teeside. Party mood prevails at Old Trafford where the two Uniteds, Manchester and Newcastle, draw a blank which puts Liverpool in the driving seat to claim second spot behind the Red Devils.

Stuart Pearce hands over control of team affairs to Dave Bassett at Nottingham Forest on the day that the FA reveal that they are reviewing their disciplinary procedures. The Football League dismiss a call to regionalise the bottom divisions to take in extra clubs from the Vauxhall Conference. Arsenal agree to pay Luton Town £1m for 18-year-old Matthew Upson who has yet to play a complete Nationwide league game for the Hatters.

Week 39 (May 10-16): The final round of league matches are delayed until Sunday 4 May and a sensational climax to the campaign is witnessed at many grounds. Another vast crowd pay homage to Manchester United as West Ham are seen off 2-0; United end the season with an average home attendance of just over 55,000. In the final-ever match at the Baseball Ground, Derby County take the lead and see visitors Arsenal reduced to ten men as Tony Adams picks up the Gunners' fifth red card of the season. Ian Wright scores twice as Arsenal storm back to win 3-1 but the Londoners have by far the worst disciplinary record in the Premiership. Arsenal's hopes of filling second place are shattered at St James's Park where Newcastle cut Forest to size with a 5-0 thrashing. Liverpool's poor run-in sees them drop to fourth on goal difference behind Arsenal and Newcastle as they can only salvage a point at Sheffield Wednesday with a late Jamie Redknapp equaliser.

At the bottom, Southampton look anxiously over their shoulders after losing at Aston Villa; their fears are heightened by Coventry City who start the day as favourites to go down but through an extraordinary set of circumstances extend their stay in the top division to 31 years with a 2-1 victory at Spurs. It is the ninth occasion in that time that they have pulled to safety on the final day. Newcastle aside, it is a tragic day for football in the north-east as Middlesbrough fail to get the win needed at Leeds to stay up. Boro are the first visiting side to score at Elland Road since mid December but Juninho's goal only cancels out Brian Deane's earlier strike and does not secure all three points. Sunderland, so long out of the bottom three, have their worst fears confirmed by Jason Euell's 85th-minute goal at Selhurst Park as they join Forest and Middlesbrough on the downward spiral.

Had Middlesbrough turned up for the game they walked away from at Blackburn in December and even lost 7-0 they would have survived but the three points docked by the Premier League sent them down. It therefore comes as little surprise that Boro plan to take their fight to get the points back to the High Court.

The league season may be over but the buying goes on and managerless Everton are quickest off the mark as they set a Premiership record for buying a defender when Slaven Bilic is signed from West Ham for £4.5m. Sol Campbell ends Manchester United and Liverpool's interest in him by signing a new contract with Tottenham.

Just which club will fill the final Division One promotion slot becomes a lot clearer as Sheffield United and Crystal Palace edge past Ipswich Town and Wolverhampton Wanderers respectively in the play-off semi finals. United beat Ipswich on the away goals rule while Palace are through to their second consecutive final by virtue of a 4-3 aggregate victory.

Week 40 (May 17-23): Middlesbrough's demise is expected to lead to the departure of many of their star names and Atletico Madrid are thought to be the first to bid for Juninho as they, allegedly, table an offer of £7.5m. Had Boro not been deducted those three points then a season which saw them reach both domestic cup finals would be regarded as a grand achievement for a club which has yet to win any silverware other than the Anglo-Scottish and Amateur Cups. As the day of the FA Cup Final dawns, Boro are looking to rescue their pride. Standing in their way is the Italian-inspired Chelsea side, so successfully moulded together by Ruud Gullit. The Londoners refuse to let sentiment stand in their way and, with a spectacular effort after just 43 seconds, Roberto di Matteo scores the quickest goal in Cup Final history. Eddie Newton makes sure the goes to SW6 for the first time in 27 years with a second Chelsea goal eight minutes from the end of a dreary encounter.

As Chelsea set about celebrating their success in the borough, the club have their thunder stolen by events at Old Trafford as Manchester United call a press conference to announce that Eric Cantona is to retire from football. A possible future in films is thought to be on the cards for the Frenchman. He leaves with five English Championship medals in his collection.

Derby add another overseas player to their squad with Stefano Eranio moving from AC Milan and Wimbledon look to bank around £4m from the sale of Oyvind Leonhardsen to Liverpool – the fee is to be set by a tribunal. Newly promoted Bolton Wanderers begin the dismantling of the Middlesbrough squad by paying £1.5m for defender Neil Cox and Sunderland part with £300,000 to capture goalkeeper Edwin Zoetebier from FC Volendam.

Week 41 (May 24-30): Southampton are rocked by the resignation of manager Graeme Souness after a disagreement with his chairman. Lawrie McMenemy follows close behind. The Saints' problems are compounded by the transfer of Eyal Berkovic to West Ham for £2.2m with all of the fee going to Berkovic's previous club rather than Southampton. With a quite superb goal by David Hopkin just ten seconds from full time in the play-off final with Sheffield United at Wembley, Crystal Palace, and manager Steve Coppell, return to the Premiership. ■

FINAL TABLES 1996-97

FA Carling Premiership

	P	W	D	L	F	A	W	D	L	F	A	Pts
		HOME					**AWAY**					
Manchester United	38	12	5	2	38	17	9	7	3	38	27	75
Newcastle United	38	13	3	3	54	20	6	8	5	19	20	68
Arsenal	38	10	5	4	36	18	9	6	4	26	14	68
Liverpool	38	10	6	3	38	19	9	5	5	24	18	68
Aston Villa	38	11	5	3	27	13	6	5	8	20	21	61
Chelsea	38	9	8	2	33	22	7	3	9	25	33	59
Sheffield Wednesday	38	8	10	1	25	16	6	5	8	25	35	57
Wimbledon	38	9	6	4	28	21	6	5	8	21	25	56
Leicester City	38	7	5	7	22	26	5	6	8	24	28	47
Tottenham Hotspur	38	8	4	7	19	17	5	3	11	25	34	46
Leeds United	38	7	7	5	15	13	4	6	9	13	25	46
Derby County	38	8	6	5	25	22	3	7	9	20	36	46
Blackburn Rovers	38	8	4	7	28	23	1	11	7	14	20	42
West Ham United	38	7	6	6	27	25	3	6	10	12	23	42
Everton	38	7	4	8	24	22	3	8	8	20	35	42
Southampton	38	6	7	6	32	24	4	4	11	18	32	41
Coventry City	38	4	8	7	19	23	5	6	8	19	31	41
Sunderland	38	7	6	6	20	18	3	4	12	15	35	40
Middlesbrough	38	8	5	6	34	25	2	7	10	17	35	39
Nottingham Forest	38	3	9	7	15	27	3	7	9	16	32	34

Middlesbrough deducted 3 points for failing to fulfil fixture.

Composite Table with Prize Money

Psn		P	W	D	L	F	A	Pts	Prize Money
1	Manchester United ...	38	21	12	5	76	44	75	£2,114,300
2	Newcastle United	38	19	11	8	73	40	68	£2,008,585
3	Arsenal	38	19	11	8	62	32	68	£1,902,870
4	Liverpool	38	19	11	8	62	37	68	£1,797,155
5	Aston Villa	38	17	10	11	47	34	61	£1,691,440
6	Chelsea	38	16	11	11	58	55	59	£1,585,725
7	Sheffield Wednesday ...	38	14	15	9	50	51	57	£1,480,010
8	Wimbledon	38	15	11	12	49	46	56	£1,374,295
9	Leicester City	38	12	11	15	46	54	47	£1,268,580
10	Tottenham Hotspur ...	38	13	7	18	44	51	46	£1,162,865
11	Leeds United	38	11	13	14	28	38	46	£1,057,150
12	Derby County	38	11	13	14	45	58	46	£951,435
13	Blackburn Rovers	38	9	15	14	42	43	42	£845,720
14	West Ham United	38	10	12	16	39	48	42	£740,005
15	Everton	38	10	12	16	44	57	42	£634,290
16	Southampton	38	10	11	17	50	56	41	£528,575
17	Coventry City	38	9	14	15	38	54	41	£422,860
18	Sunderland	38	10	10	18	35	53	40	£317,145
19	Middlesbrough	38	10	12	16	51	60	39	£211,430
20	Nottingham Forest... ...	38	6	16	16	31	59	34	£105,715

Middlesbrough deducted 3 points for failing to fulfil fixture.

Nationwide League Division 1

Psn		P	W	D	L	F	A	Pts	
1	Bolton Wanderers	46	28	14	4	100	53	98	P
2	Barnsley	46	22	14	10	76	55	80	P
3	Wolverhampton W.	46	22	10	14	68	51	76	
4	Ipswich Town	46	20	14	12	68	50	74	
5	Sheffield United	46	20	13	13	75	52	73	
6	Crystal Palace	46	19	14	13	78	48	71	P
7	Portsmouth	46	20	8	18	59	53	68	
8	Port Vale...	46	17	16	13	58	55	67	
9	QPR	46	18	12	16	64	60	66	
10	Birmingham City	46	17	15	14	52	48	66	
11	Tranmere Rovers	46	17	14	15	63	56	65	
12	Stoke City	46	18	10	18	51	57	64	
13	Norwich City	46	17	12	17	63	68	63	
14	Manchester City	46	17	10	19	59	60	61	
15	Charlton Athletic	46	16	11	19	52	66	59	
16	West Bromwich Albion	46	14	15	17	68	72	57	
17	Oxford United	46	16	9	21	64	68	57	

18	Reading	46	15	12	19	58	67	57	
19	Swindon Town	46	15	9	22	52	71	54	
20	Huddersfield Town	46	13	15	18	48	61	54	
21	Bradford City	46	12	12	22	47	72	48	
22	Grimsby Town	46	11	13	22	60	81	46	R
23	Oldham Athletic	46	10	13	23	51	66	43	R
24	Southend	46	8	15	23	42	86	39	R

Play-off final: Crystal Palace v Sheffield United: 1-0 at Wembley Stadium.

Nationwide League Division 2

Psn		P	W	D	L	F	A	Pts	
1	Bury	46	24	12	10	62	38	84	P
2	Stockport County	46	23	13	10	59	41	82	P
3	Luton Town	46	21	15	10	71	45	78	
4	Brentford	46	20	14	12	56	43	74	
5	Bristol City	46	21	10	15	69	51	73	
6	Crewe Alexandra	46	22	7	17	56	47	73	P
7	Blackpool	46	18	15	13	60	47	69	
8	Wrexham	46	17	18	11	54	50	69	
9	Burnley	46	19	11	16	71	55	68	
10	Chesterfield	46	18	14	14	42	39	68	
11	Gillingham	46	19	10	17	60	59	67	
12	Walsall	46	19	10	17	54	53	67	
13	Watford	46	16	19	11	45	38	67	
14	Millwall	46	16	13	17	50	55	61	
15	Preston North End	46	18	7	21	49	55	61	
16	Bournemouth	46	15	15	16	43	45	60	
17	Bristol Rovers	46	15	11	20	47	50	56	
18	Wycombe Wanderers	46	15	10	21	51	56	55	
19	Plymouth Argyle	46	12	18	16	47	58	54	
20	York City	46	13	13	20	47	68	52	
21	Peterborough United	46	11	14	21	55	73	47	R
22	Shrewsbury Town	46	11	13	22	49	74	46	R
23	Rotherham	46	7	14	25	39	70	35	R
24	Notts County	46	7	14	25	33	59	35	R

Psn		P	W	D	L	F	A	Pts	
1	Wigan Athletic	46	26	9	11	84	51	87	P
2	Fulham	46	25	12	9	72	38	87	P
3	Carlisle United	46	24	12	10	67	44	84	P
4	Northampton Town ...	46	20	12	14	67	44	72	P
5	Swansea City	46	21	8	17	62	58	71	
6	Chester City...	46	18	16	12	55	43	70	
7	Cardiff City	46	20	9	17	56	54	69	
8	Colchester United	46	17	17	12	62	51	68	
9	Lincoln City...	46	18	12	16	70	69	66	
10	Cambridge United	46	18	11	17	53	59	65	
11	Mansfield Town	46	16	16	14	47	45	64	
12	Scarborough	46	16	15	15	65	68	63	
13	Scunthorpe	46	18	9	19	59	62	63	
14	Rochdale...	46	14	16	16	58	58	58	
15	Barnet	46	14	16	16	46	51	58	
16	Leyton Orient	46	15	12	19	50	58	57	
17	Hull City...	46	13	18	15	44	50	57	
18	Darlington	46	14	10	22	64	78	52	
19	Doncaster United	46	14	10	22	52	66	52	
20	Hartlepool	46	14	9	23	53	66	51	
21	Torquay United	46	13	11	22	46	62	50	
22	Exeter City	46	12	12	22	48	73	48	
23	Brighton & Hove Alb...	46	13	10	23	53	70	47	
24	Hereford United	46	11	14	21	50	65	47	R

ALL-TIME TABLES
1992/93-96/97

Positions Based on Points

Psn		P	W	D	L	F	A	Pts	Yrs
1	Manchester United	202	123	52	27	373	176	421	5
2	Blackburn Rovers	202	99	50	53	314	211	347	5
3	Liverpool	202	93	53	56	318	218	332	5
4	Arsenal	202	82	63	57	256	179	309	5
5	Aston Villa	202	82	57	63	253	215	303	5
6	Newcastle United	160	86	37	37	288	165	295	4
7	Leeds United	202	73	64	65	249	234	283	5
8	Tottenham Hotspur ...	202	72	57	73	274	272	273	5
9	Wimbledon	202	72	56	74	264	289	272	5
10	Sheffield Wednesday ...	202	68	67	67	278	274	271	5
11	Chelsea	202	68	66	68	254	261	270	5
12	Everton	202	65	55	82	247	270	250	5
13	Coventry City	202	56	69	77	219	278	237	5
14	Southampton	202	56	58	88	248	298	226	5
15	QPR	164	59	39	66	224	232	216	4
16	Nottingham Forest	160	53	50	57	194	218	209	4
17	West Ham United	160	50	45	65	173	206	195	4
18	Manchester City	164	45	54	65	147	164	189	4
19	Norwich City	126	43	39	44	163	180	168	3
20	Middlesbrough	118	32	33	53	140	185	126 †	3
21	Ipswich Town	126	28	38	60	121	206	122	3
22	Crystal Palace	84	22	28	34	82	110	94	2
23	Sheffield United	84	22	28	34	96	113	94	2
24	Oldham Athletic	84	22	23	39	105	142	89	2
25	Leicester City	80	18	22	40	91	134	76	2
26	Derby County	38	11	13	14	45	58	46	1
27	Sunderland	38	10	10	18	35	53	40	1
28	Swindon Town	42	5	15	22	47	100	30	1
29	Bolton Wanderers	38	8	5	25	39	71	29	1

† *Middlesbrough three points deducted*

Psn		P	W	D	L	F	A	Pts	%
1	Manchester United	202	123	52	27	373	176	421	69.47
2	Newcastle United	160	86	37	37	288	165	295	61.46
3	Blackburn Rovers	202	99	50	53	314	211	347	57.26
4	Liverpool	202	93	53	56	318	218	332	54.79
5	Arsenal	202	82	63	57	256	179	309	50.99
6	Aston Villa	202	82	57	63	253	215	303	50.00
7	Leeds United	202	73	64	65	249	234	283	46.70
8	Tottenham Hotspur ...	202	72	57	73	274	272	273	45.05
9	Wimbledon	202	72	56	74	264	289	272	44.88
10	Sheffield Wednesday ...	202	68	67	67	278	274	271	44.72
11	Chelsea	202	68	66	68	254	261	270	44.55
12	Norwich City	126	43	39	44	163	180	168	44.44
13	QPR	164	59	39	66	224	232	216	43.90
14	Nottingham Forest ...	160	53	50	57	194	218	209	43.54
15	Everton	202	65	55	82	247	270	250	41.25
16	West Ham United	160	50	45	65	173	206	195	40.63
17	Derby County	38	11	13	14	45	58	46	40.35
18	Coventry City	202	56	69	77	219	278	237	39.11
19	Manchester City	164	45	54	65	147	164	189	38.41
20	Crystal Palace	84	22	28	34	82	110	94	37.30
21	Sheffield United	84	22	28	34	96	113	94	37.30
22	Southampton	202	56	58	88	248	298	226	37.29
23	Middlesbrough	118	32	33	53	140	185	126	35.59
24	Oldham Athletic	84	22	23	39	105	142	89	35.32
25	Sunderland	38	10	10	18	35	53	40	35.09
26	Ipswich Town	126	28	38	60	121	206	122	32.28
27	Leicester City	80	18	22	40	91	134	76	31.67
28	Bolton Wanderers	38	8	5	25	39	71	29	25.44
29	Swindon Town	42	5	15	22	47	100	30	23.81

Middlesbrough three points deducted

PROMOTIONS and RELEGATIONS

1996-97	Promoted	Bolton Wanderers	Champions
		Barnsley	Runners-up
		Crystal Palace	Play-off winners (6th)
	Relegated	Sunderland	20th
		Middlesbrough	21st
		Nottingham Forest	22nd
1995-96	Promoted	Sunderland	Champions
		Derby County	Runners-up
		Leicester City	Play-off winners (5th)
	Relegated	Manchester City	20th
		QPR	21st
		Bolton Wanderers	22nd
1994-95*	Promoted	Middlesbrough	Champions
		Bolton Wanderers	Play-off winners (3rd)
	Relegated	Crystal Palace	19th
		Norwich City	20th
		Leicester City	21st
		Ipswich Town	22nd
1993-94	Promoted	Crystal Palace	Champions
		Nottingham Forest	Runners-up
		Leicester City	Play-off winners (4th)
	Relegated	Sheffield United	20th
		Oldham Athletic	21st
		Swindon Town	22nd
1992-93	Promoted	Newcastle United	Champions
		West Ham United	Runners-up
		Swindon Town	Play-off winners (5th)
	Relegated	Crystal Palace	20th
		Middlesbrough	21st
		Nottingham Forest	22nd
1991-92†	Promoted	Ipswich Town	Champions
		Middlesbrough	Runners-up
		Blackburn Rovers	Play-off winners (6th)

FA Premier League reduced to 20 clubs
†*Promoted from Division 2 to newly formed FA Premier League*

	Arsenal	Aston Villa	Blackburn Rovers	Chelsea	Coventry City	Derby County	Everton	Leeds United	Leicester City	Liverpool
Arsenal	•	2-2	1-1	3-3	0-0	2-2	3-1	3-0	2-0	1-2
Aston Villa	2-2	•	1-0	0-2	2-1	2-0	3-1	2-0	1-3	1-0
Blackburn Rovers	0-2	0-2	•	1-1	4-0	1-2	1-1	0-1	2-4	3-0
Chelsea	0-3	1-1	1-1	•	2-0	3-1	2-2	0-0	2-1	1-0
Coventry City	1-1	1-2	0-0	3-1	•	1-2	0-0	2-1	0-0	0-1
Derby County	1-3	2-1	0-1	3-2	2-1	•	0-1	3-3	2-0	0-1
Everton	0-2	0-1	0-2	1-2	1-1	1-0	•	0-0	1-1	1-1
Leeds United	0-0	0-0	0-0	2-0	1-3	0-0	1-0	•	3-0	0-2
Leicester City	0-2	1-0	1-1	1-3	0-2	4-2	1-2	1-0	•	0-3
Liverpool	2-0	3-0	0-0	5-1	1-2	2-1	1-1	4-0	1-1	•
Manchester United	1-0	0-0	2-2	1-0	3-1	2-3	2-2	1-0	3-1	1-0
Middlesbrough	0-2	3-2	2-1	1-0	4-0	6-1	4-2	0-0	0-2	3-3
Newcastle United	1-2	4-3	2-1	3-1	4-0	3-1	4-1	3-0	4-3	1-1
N. Forest	2-1	0-0	2-2	2-0	0-1	1-1	0-1	1-1	0-0	1-1
Sheffield W.	0-0	2-1	1-1	0-2	0-0	0-0	2-1	2-2	2-1	0-1
Southampton	0-2	0-1	2-0	0-0	2-2	3-1	2-2	0-2	2-2	1-2
Sunderland	1-0	1-0	0-0	3-0	1-0	2-0	2-0	0-1	0-0	0-2
Tottenham H.	0-0	1-0	2-1	1-2	1-2	1-1	0-0	1-0	1-2	1-2
West Ham Utd	1-2	0-2	2-1	3-2	1-1	1-1	2-2	0-2	1-0	1-2
Wimbledon	2-2	0-2	1-0	0-1	2-2	1-1	4-0	2-0	1-3	2-1

	Manchester United	Middlesbrough	Newcastle United	Nottingham Forest	Sheffield Wednesday	Southampton	Sunderland	Tottenham Hotspur	West Ham United	Wimbledon
Arsenal	1-2	2-0	0-1	2-0	4-1	3-1	2-0	3-1	2-0	0-1
Aston Villa	0-0	1-0	2-2	2-0	0-1	1-0	0-0	1-1	0-0	5-0
Blackburn Rovers	2-3	0-0	1-0	1-1	4-1	2-1	1-0	0-2	2-1	3-1
Chelsea	1-1	1-0	1-1	1-1	2-2	1-0	6-2	3-1	3-1	2-4
Coventry City	0-2	3-0	2-1	0-3	0-0	1-1	2-2	1-2	1-3	1-1
Derby County	1-1	2-1	0-1	0-0	2-2	1-1	1-0	4-2	1-0	0-2
Everton	0-2	1-2	2-0	2-0	2-0	7-1	1-3	1-0	2-1	1-3
Leeds United	0-4	1-1	0-1	2-0	0-2	0-0	3-0	0-0	1-0	1-0
Leicester City	2-2	1-1	2-0	2-2	1-0	2-1	1-1	1-1	0-1	1-1
Liverpool	1-3	1-3	4-3	4-2	0-1	2-1	0-0	2-1	0-0	1-1
Manchester United	•	5-1	0-0	4-1	2-0	2-1	5-0	2-0	2-0	2-1
Middlesbrough	2-2	•	1-1	0-1	4-2	0-1	0-1	0-3	4-1	0-0
Newcastle United	5-0	3-1	•	5-0	1-2	1-3	1-1	7-1	1-1	2-0
N. Forest	0-4	1-1	0-0	•	0-3	1-1	1-4	2-1	0-2	1-1
Sheffield W.	1-1	3-1	2-0	2-0	•	1-1	2-1	2-1	0-2	3-1
Southampton	6-3	4-0	2-2	2-2	2-3	•	3-0	0-1	0-0	0-0
Sunderland	2-1	2-2	1-2	1-1	1-1	1-1	•	3-1	2-0	1-3
Tottenham H.	1-2	1-0	1-2	0-1	1-1	0-1	2-0	•	1-0	1-0
West Ham Utd	2-2	0-0	0-0	0-1	5-1	3-1	2-0	4-3	•	0-2
Wimbledon	0-3	1-1	1-1	1-3	4-2	3-1	1-0	1-0	1-1	•

FA PREMIER LEAGUE

	Arsenal	Aston Villa	Blackburn Rovers	Chelsea	Coventry City	Derby County	Everton	Leeds United	Leicester City	Liverpool
Arsenal	•	38,130	38,086	38,132	38,140	38,018	38,095	38,076	38,044	38,068
Aston Villa	37,944	•	32,257	39,339	30,409	34,646	39,339	39,051	36,193	39,399
Blackburn Rovers	24,303	24,274	•	27,229	24,055	19,214	27,091	23,226	25,881	29,598
Chelsea	28,182	27,729	25,784	•	25,024	22,839	28,418	28,277	27,723	28,239
Coventry City	19,998	21,340	17,032	19,917	•		19,497	17,297	19,220	23,021
Derby County	18,287	18,071	17,847	18,039	18,042	•	17,252	17,927	35,310	18,102
Everton	36,980	39,115	30,427	38,321	31,477	32,240	•	36,954	30,368	40,177
Leeds United	35,502	26,897	27,264	32,671		27,549	32,055	•	29,486	39,981
Leicester City	20,429	20,626	19,306		20,038	20,323	20,975	20,359	•	20,987
Liverpool	38,103	40,489	40,747	40,739	40,079	39,515	40,751	38,957	40,786	•
Manchester United	55,210	55,113	54,178	55,198	55,230	55,243	54,943	55,256	55,196	55,128
Middlesbrough	29,629	30,074	29,891	29,811	29,811	29,739	29,673	30,018	29,709	30,039
Newcastle United	36,565	36,400	36,424	36,320	36,571	36,553	36,143	36,489	36,396	36,570
N. Forest	27,384	25,239	17,525	28,358	22,619	27,771	19,892	25,565	24,105	29,181
Sheffield W.	23,245	26,861	22,191	30,983	21,793	23,934	24,175	30,373	17,657	38,943
Southampton	15,144	15,232	15,247	15,186	15,251	14,901	15,134	15,241	15,044	15,222
Sunderland	21,154	21,059	20,850	19,683	19,459	22,512	22,108	21,890	19,262	21,938
Tottenham H.	33,039	32,847	22,943	33,027	33,029	28,219	29,696	33,040	24,159	38,899
West Ham Utd	24,382	19,105	23,947	21,580	21,580	24,576	24,525		22,285	25,064
Wimbledon	25,521	9,015	13,246	14,601	10,307	11,467	13,684	7,979	11,487	20,016

ATTENDANCES 1996-97

	Manchester United	Middlesbrough	Newcastle United	Nottingham Forest	Sheffield Wednesda	Southampton	Sunderland	Tottenham Hotspur	West Ham United	Wimbledon
Arsenal	38,172	37,573	38,179	38,206	33,461	38,033	38,016	38,264	38,056	37,854
Aston Villa	39,339	39,053	39,339	35,310	26,726	39,339	32,491	39,339	35,995	28,875
Blackburn Rovers	30,476	27,411	30,398	20,485	20,345	23,018	24,208	26,960	21,994	23,333
Chelsea	28,336	28,272	28,401	27,673	27,467	28,079	24,072	28,373	28,315	28,020
Coventry City	23,085	20,617	21,538	19,468	17,267	15,485	17,700	19,675	22,291	15,273
Derby County	18,026	17,350	18,092	18,087	18,060	17,839	17,692	18,083	18,057	17,022
Everton	40,079	39,250	40,117	32,567	34,160	35,669	40,087	36,380	36,571	36,733
Leeds United	39,694	38,567	36,070	29,225	31,011	25,913	31,667	33,783	30,575	25,860
Leicester City	21,068	20,561	21,134	20,833	20,793	17,562	17,883	20,593	20,327	18,927
Liverpool	40,892	39,491	40,751	36,126	39,507	39,189	40,503	40,003	40,102	39,027
Manchester United	•	54,489	55,236	54,984	55,507	55,269	55,081	54,943	55,249	55,314
Middlesbrough	30,063	•	29,888	30,063	29,485	29,509	30,106	30,215	30,060	29,758
Newcastle United	36,579	36,577	•	36,554	36,452	36,446	36,582	36,308	36,552	36,385
N. Forest	29,032	24,705	25,762	•	21,485	25,134	22,874	27,303	23,352	19,865
Sheffield W.	37,671	28,206	33,798	16,390	•	20,106	20,294	27,667	22,231	26,957
Southampton	15,253	15,230	15,251	14,450	15,062	•	15,225	15,251	15,244	14,418
Sunderland	22,225	20,936	22,037	22,120	20,644	21,521	•	20,785	18,642	19,672
Tottenham H.	33,028	29,947	32,535	32,805	30,996	30,549	31,867	•	32,999	32,654
West Ham Utd	25,045	23,988	24,617	22,358	24,490	21,227	24,077	23,998	•	21,924
Wimbledon	25,786	15,046	23,175	12,608	10,512	8,572	21,338	17,506	15,771	•

FA PREMIER LEAGUE
RECORDS 1996-97
SCORERS

Top Scorers – All Competitions

Player	Club	L	F	C	E	Total
Robbie FOWLER	Liverpool	18	1	5	7	31
Fabrizio RAVANELLI	Middlesbrough	16	6	9	0	31
Ian WRIGHT	Arsenal	23	0	5	2	30
Alan SHEARER	Newcastle United	25	1	1	1	28
Les FERDINAND	Newcastle United	16	1	0	4	21
Dwight YORKE	Aston Villa	17	2	1	0	20
Ole Gunnar SOLSKJAER	Manchester United	18	0	0	1	19
Stan COLLYMORE	Liverpool	12	2	0	2	16
Matt LE TISSIER	Southampton	13	0	3	0	16
Steve CLARIDGE	Leicester City	12	1	2	0	15
JUNINHO	Middlesbrough	12	2	1	0	15

L=League, F=FA Cup, C=Coca-Cola Cup, E=Europe

FA Carling Premiership Top Scorers

Player	Club	Goals	All-time Total
Alan SHEARER	Newcastle United	25	137
Ian WRIGHT	Arsenal	23	94
Robbie FOWLER	Liverpool	18	83
Ole Gunnar SOLSKJAER	Manchester United	18	18
Dwight YORKE	Aston Villa	17	48
Les FERDINAND	Newcastle United	16	101
Fabrizio RAVANELLI	Middlesbrough	16	16
Dion DUBLIN	Coventry City	14	43
Matt LE TISSIER	Southampton	13	80
Dennis BERGKAMP	Arsenal	12	23
Stan COLLYMORE	Liverpool	12	49
Steve CLARIDGE	Leicester City	12	12
JUNINHO	Middlesbrough	12	12
Eric CANTONA	Manchester United	11	70
Efan EKOKU	Wimbledon	11	42

| Dean STURRIDGE | Derby County | 11 | 11 |
| Chris SUTTON | Blackburn Rovers | 11 | 59 |

FA Carling Premiership Club Top Scorers

Club	*Scorers*
Arsenal	Wright 23, Bergkamp 12, Merson 6
Aston Villa	Yorke 17, Milosevic 10, Johnson 4
Blackburn Rovers	Sutton 11, Gallagher 10, Sherwood 3
Chelsea	Vialli 9, M. Hughes 8, Zola 8
Coventry City	Dublin 14, Whelan 6, McAllister 6
Derby County	Sturridge 11, Ward 10, Asanovic 6
Everton	Ferguson 10, Speed 9, Stuart 5, Unsworth 5
Leeds United	Deane 5, Sharpe 5, Bowyer 4
Leicester City	Claridge 12, Heskey 10, Marshall 9
Liverpool	Fowler 18, Collymore 12, McManaman 7
Manchester United	Solskjaer 18, Cantona 11, Beckham 8
Middlesbrough	Ravanelli 16, Juninho 12, Beck 5
Newcastle United	Shearer 25, Ferdinand 16, R. Elliot 7
Nottingham Forest	Campbell 6, Haaland 6, Pearce 5
Sheffield Wednesday	Booth 10, Hirst 6, Pembridge 6
Southampton	Le Tissier 13, Ostenstad 10, Berkovic 4
Sunderland	Russell 4, Stewart 3, Quinn 3, Rae 3, Gray 3, Ball 3
Tottenham Hotspur	Sheringham 7, Iversen 6, Sinton 6
West Ham United	Kitson 8, Dicks 6, Hartson 5
Wimbledon	Ekoku 11, Gayle 8, Earle 7

FA Carling Premiership Hat-tricks

Player	*Goals*	*Match (result)*	*Date*
K. CAMPBELL	3	Coventry C. v N. FOREST (0-3)	17/08/96
F. RAVANELLI	3 (1p)	MIDDLESBROUGH v Liverpool (3-3)	17/08/96
I. WRIGHT	3 (1p)	ARSENAL v Sheffield W. (4-1)	16/09/96
E. OSTENSTADT	3	SOUTHAMPTON v Man. Utd (6-3)	26/10/96
D. YORKE	3	Newcastle Utd v ASTON VILLA (4-3)	30/09/96
G. SPEED	3	EVERTON v Southampton (7-1)	16/11/96
R. FOWLER	4	LIVERPOOL v Middlesbrough (5-1)	14/12/96
A. SHEARER	3	NEWCASTLE U. v Leicester C. (4-3)	02/02/97
I. MARSHALL	3	LEICESTER C. v Derby County (4-2)	22/02/97
S. IVERSEN	3	Sunderland v TOTTENHAM H. (0-4)	04/03/97
F. RAVANELLI	3	MIDDLESBROUGH v Derby Co. (6-1)	05/03/97
K. GALLACHER	3	BLACKBURN R. v Wimbledon (3-1)	15/03/97
P. KITSON	3	WEST HAM U. v Sheffield W. (5-1)	03/05/97

p = penalty

ATTENDANCES

Top Attendances by Club and Number

Club ... ... Posn	Total	Ave
Manchester United 1	1,046,527	55,080
Liverpool 4	755,757	39,777
Arsenal 3	718,603	37,821
Newcastle United 2	692,866	36,467
Everton 15	687,672	36,193
Aston Villa 5	684,383	36,020
Leeds United 11	610,235	32,118
Tottenham Hotspur 10	590,278	31,067
Middlesbrough 19	567,541	29,871
Chelsea 6	524,677	27,615
Sheffield Wednesday... 7	488,475	25,709
Blackburn Rovers 13	473,999	24,947
Nottingham Forest 20	467,151	24,587
West Ham United 14	441,131	23,217
Sunderland 18	398,497	20,974
Leicester City 9	383,490	20,184
Coventry City 17	372,560	19,608
Derby County 12	357,185	18,799
Wimbledon 8	287,637	15,139
Southampton 16	286,986	15,105
TOTAL	**10,835,650**	**28,515**

CLUBS BY TOTAL NUMBER OF PLAYERS USED

		Total	Start	Sub	Snu	Ps
1	Liverpool	462	418	44	146	44
2	Middlesbrough	465	418	47	142	47
3	Aston Villa	472	418	54	136	54
4	Newcastle United	472	418	54	135	54
5	Southampton	472	418	54	136	54
6	Leeds United	473	418	55	135	55
7	Everton	474	418	56	134	56
8	Blackburn Rovers	478	418	60	130	60

9	Coventry City 478	418	60	130	60
10	Tottenham Hotspur 481	418	63	127	63
11	Leicester City 482	418	64	126	64
12	Nottingham Forest... 482	418	64	126	64
13	Arsenal 484	418	66	124	66
14	Chelsea ..., ... 489	418	71	119	71
15	Wimbledon 491	418	73	117	73
16	Sunderland 492	418	74	116	74
17	Manchester United 493	418	75	115	75
18	West Ham United 500	418	82	108	82
19	Derby County 505	418	87	103	87
20	Sheffield Wednesday 510	418	92	98	92

BOOKINGS & DISMISSALS

Players Sent Off

	Player	Match	Date	Official
1	VENISON	Leicester v SOUTHAMPTON	21/08/96	M.Riley
2	DAISH	Chelsea v COVENTRY CITY	24/08/96	P.Danson
3	BENALI	West Ham v SOUTHAMPTON	24/08/96	D.Elleray
4	PEARSON	N. Forest v MIDDLESBROUGH	24/08/96	M.Riley
5	JONES	WIMBLEDON v Tottenham H.	03/09/96	S.Dunn
6	ORD	Derby Co. v SUNDERLAND	14/09/96	D.Elleray
7	WALKER	Arsenal v SHEFFIELD W.	16/09/96	M.Reed
8	FERGUSON	Blackburn R. v EVERTON	21/09/96	D.Elleray
9	PALMER	LEEDS UNITED v Newcastle U.	21/09/96	P.Alcock
10	RIEPER	N. Forest v WEST HAM	21/09/96	G.Willard
11	SCOTT	Arsenal v SUNDERLAND	28/09/96	P.Danson
12	STEWART	Arsenal v SUNDERLAND	28/09/96	P.Danson
13	DRAPER	Newcastle v ASTON VILLA	30/09/96	D.Elleray
14	ORD	SUNDERLAND v Middlesbrough	14/10/96	G.Poll
15	WALSH	West Ham v LEICESTER CITY	19/10/96	M.Riley
16	KEANE	Southampton v MAN. UTD	26/10/96	J.Winter
17	STEWART	Tottenham v SUNDERLAND	16/11/96	M.Reed
18	BATTY	Chelsea v NEWCASTLE U.	23/11/96	M.Reed
19	ADAMS	Newcastle v ARSENAL	30/11/96	G.Barber
20	VAN GOBBEL	Blackburn v SOUTHAMPTON	30/11/96	R.Dilkes
21	WRIGHT	N. Forest v ARSENAL	21/12/96	S.Lodge
22	DODD	SOUTHAMPTON v West Ham	12/04/97	S.Dunn
23	UNSWORTH	EVERTON v Liverpool	16/04/97	S.Lodge
24	FOWLER	Everton v LIVERPOOL	16/04/97	S.Lodge
25	STAUNTON	Middlesbrough v ASTON VILLA	03/05/97	P.Alcock

26	SHERWOOD	Southampton v BLACKBURN R.	03/05/97	G.Ashby
27	GILLESPIE	Arsenal v NEWCASTLE U.	03/05/97	M.Bodenham
28	HIRST	Southampton v SHEFFIELD W.	03/05/97	G.Ashby
29	ADAMS	Derby v ARSENAL	11/05/97	P.Durkin
30	GRODAS	Everton v CHELSEA	11/05/97	P.Jones
31	CLARKE	SHEFFIELD W. v Liverpool	11/05/97	D.Elleray

Referees by Number of Bookings Issued

More yellows less reds seemed to be the key to last season's card brigade – thus for the third season running the average bookings per game rose fractionally from 3.11 to 3.19. David Elleray saw red most of all, five times in fact, compared to the single *carte rouge* he produced in 1995-96. Referee Hegley certainly didn't hedge his bets with a massive nine cards in one game (Leicester City v West Ham United) – his one and only game of the Premiership season! Paul Danson maintained his normal high average, but Steve Lodge – last year's chart topper – fell with grace to 14th position. For the second season in succession 20 referees were used to cover the 380 Premiership games. The table below lists referees in order of the average booking rate per game – red cards are not included in the average.

*	Referee	Matches	Yellow	Red	Average
1	Hegley … … … … … … … … … 1		9	0	9.00
2	Danson … … … … … … … … 19		77	3	4.05
3	Reed … … … … … … … … … 24		97	3	4.04
4	Barber … … … … … … … … 21		83	1	3.95
5	Ashby … … … … … … … … … 14		54	2	3.86
6	Willard … … … … … … … … 18		67	1	3.72
7	Bodenham … … … … … … … 23		85	1	3.70
8	Riley … … … … … … … … … 20		73	3	3.65
9	Poll… … … … … … … … … … 22		79	1	3.59
10	Jones … … … … … … … … 20		69	1	3.45
11	Dunn … … … … … … … … … 23		75	2	3.26
12	Winter… … … … … … … … … 20		64	1	3.20
13	Elleray… … … … … … … … 21		64	5	3.05
14	Lodge … … … … … … … … 21		59	3	2.81
15	Burge … … … … … … … … 20		49	0	2.45
16	Alcock… … … … … … … … 21		51	2	2.43
17	Wilkie … … … … … … … … 23		54	0	2.35
18	Durkin… … … … … … … … 23		52	1	2.26
19	Gallagher … … … … … … … 9		20	0	2.22
20	Dilkes … … … … … … … … 20		30	1	1.50
	Averages … … … … … … … 380		*1211*	*31*	*3.19*

Dismissals by Club

Club	No	Player(s)
Arsenal	3	Adams (2), Wright
Aston Villa	2	Draper, Staunton
Blackburn Rovers	1	Sherwood
Chelsea	1	Grodas
Coventry City	1	Daish
Derby County	0	–
Everton	2	Ferguson, Unsworth
Leeds United	1	Palmer
Leicester City	1	Walsh
Liverpool	1	Fowler
Manchester United	1	Keane
Middlesbrough	1	Pearson
Newcastle United	2	Batty, Gillespie
Nottingham Forest	0	–
Sheffield Wednesday	3	Clarke, Hirst, Walker
Southampton	4	Benali, Dodd, Venison, van Gobbel
Sunderland	5	Ord (2), Scott, Stewart (2*)
Tottenham Hotspur	0	–
West Ham United	1	Rieper
Wimbledon	1	Jones

*Sent off twice but one v Arsenal struck out on appeal.

Referees – Who They Sent Off

Referee	No.	Players
ELLERAY	5	Benali, Ord, Ferguson, Draper, Clarke
REED	3	Walker, Stewart, Batty
DANSON	3	Daish, Scott, Stewart
LODGE	3	Wright, Unsworth, Fowler
RILEY	3	Pearson, Walsh, Venison
ALCOCK	2	Palmer, Staunton
ASHBY	2	Sherwood, Hirst
DUNN	2	Jones, Dodd
BARBER	1	Adams
BODENHAM	1	Gillespie
DILKES	1	van Gobbel
DURKIN	1	Adams
JONES	1	Grodas
POLL	1	Ord
WILLARD	1	Rieper
WINTER	1	Keane

Fair Play League

Talk about cleaning your act up! At the end of the 1995-96 season Wimbledon faced disciplinary action because of their seven sendings off and 56 bookings. This time round they top our Fair Play table, although it should be said that this table is calculated differently from those before. Nevertheless their 38 bookings was just one per game, well ahead of Liverpool who averaged out close on 1.50 per game.

Positions this year are calculated by counting a red card as two bookings and adding this to the yellow card total to give a Y-R rating which is divided by the number of games played.

Club	Games	Red	Yellow	Y-R	Ave
Wimbledon 38		38	1	39	1.03
Liverpool 38		45	1	46	1.21
Leicester City 38		50	1	51	1.34
Coventry City 38		52	1	53	1.39
Sheffield W. 38		50	3	53	1.39
Newcastle Utd 38		54	2	56	1.47
Aston Villa 38		55	2	57	1.50
Manchester Utd 38		57	1	58	1.53
Everton 38		57	2	59	1.55
Southampton 38		55	4	59	1.55
Sunderland 38		54	5	59	1.55
Derby County 38		62	0	62	1.63
N. Forest 38		63	0	63	1.66
Tottenham H. 38		64	0	64	1.68
Blackburn Rvrs 38		64	1	65	1.71
West Ham Utd 38		67	1	68	1.79
Chelsea 38		74	1	75	1.97
Middlesbrough 38		75	1	76	2.00
Leeds United 38		78	1	79	2.08
Arsenal 38		85	3	88	2.32

SCORES

Highest Aggregate Scorers

9	6-3	Southampton v Manchester United	26/10/96
8	7-1	Everton v Southampton	16/11/96
	7-1	Newcastle United v Tottenham Hotspur	28/12/96
	6-2	Chelsea v Sunderland	16/03/97

7	6-1	Middlesbrough v Derby County	05/03/97
	4-3	Liverpool v Newcastle United	10/03/97
	4-3	Newcastle United v Aston Villa	30/09/96
	4-3	Newcastle United v Leicester City	02/02/97
	4-3	West Ham United v Tottenham Hotspur	24/03/97

Biggest Home Wins

7-1	Everton v Southampton	28/12/96
7-1	Newcastle United v Tottenham Hotspur	05/03/97
6-1	Middlesbrough v Derby County	16/03/97
6-2	Chelsea v Sunderland	16/03/97
6-3	Southampton v Manchester United	26/10/96

Biggest Away Wins

0-4	Leeds v Manchester United	07/09/96
0-4	Nottingham Forest v Manchester United	26/12/96
0-4	Sunderland v Tottenham Hotspur	04/03/97
1-4	Nottingham Forest v Sunderland	21/08/96

Highest Score Draw

3-3	Derby County v Leeds United	17/08/96
3-3	Middlesbrough v Liverpool	17/08/96
3-3	Manchester United v Middlesbrough	05/03/97

Score Frequencies

Home Wins		6-1	1	2-3	3
Score	No.	6-2	1	2-4	2
1-0	38	6-3	1		
2-0	30	7-1	2	Draws	
3-0	9			Score	No.
4-0	6	Away Wins		0-0	41
5-0	4	Score	No.	1-1	49
2-1	30	0-1	26	2-2	25
3-1	19	0-2	24	3-3	4
3-2	3	0-3	6		
4-1	5	0-4	3		
4-2	6	1-2	22		
4-3	4	1-3	12		
5-1	3	1-4	1		

FA PREMIER LEAGUE ALL-TIME RECORDS

Premiership Titles by Number

4	Manchester United	1992-93, 1993-94, 1995-96, 1996-97
1	Blackburn Rovers	1994-95

Premiership Runners-up by Number

2	Newcastle United	1995-96, 1996-97
1	Aston Villa	1992-93
1	Blackburn Rovers	1993-94
1	Manchester United	1994-95

Championship Records

	Season	Champions	P	W	D	L	F	A	Pts	%
1	1992-93	Manchester United	42	24	12	6	67	31	84	66.67
2	1993-94	Manchester United	42	27	11	4	80	38	92	73.02
3	1994-95	Blackburn Rovers	42	27	8	7	80	39	89	70.63
4	1995-96	Manchester United	38	25	7	6	73	35	82	71.93
5	1996-97	Manchester United	38	21	12	5	76	44	75	65.79

All-Time Biggest Home Wins

9-0	Manchester United v Ipswich Town	04/03/95
7-0	Blackburn Rovers v Nottingham Forest	18/11/95
7-1	Aston Villa v Wimbledon	11/02/93
7-1	Blackburn Rovers v Norwich City	02/10/92
7-1	Newcastle United v Swindon Town	12/03/94
7-1	Everton v Southampton	28/12/96
7-1	Newcastle United v Tottenham Hotspur	05/03/97
6-0	Sheffield United v Tottenham Hotspur	02/03/93
6-0	Liverpool v Manchester City	28/10/95
6-1	Newcastle United v Wimbledon	21/10/95
6-1	Middlesbrough v Derby County	16/03/97
6-2	Sheffield Wednesday v Leeds United	16/12/95
6-2	Chelsea v Sunderland	16/03/97
6-3	Southampton v Manchester United	26/10/96

All-Time Biggest Away Wins

1-7	Sheffield Wednesday v Nottingham Forest	01/04/95
0-6	Bolton Wanderers v Manchester United	25/02/96
1-6	Crystal Palace v Liverpool	20/08/94
0-5	Swindon Town v Liverpool	22/08/93
0-5	Swindon Town v Leeds United	07/05/94
2-5	Sheffield Wednesday v Everton	27/04/96

All-Time Highest Aggregate Scores

9	9-0	Manchester United v Ipswich Town	04/03/95
	6-3	Southampton v Manchester United	26/10/96
8	7-1	Everton v Southampton	16/11/96
	7-1	Newcastle United v Tottenham Hotspur	28/12/96
	6-2	Sheffield Wednesday v Leeds United	16/12/95
	6-2	Chelsea v Sunderland	16/03/97
	7-1	Aston Villa v Wimbledon	11/02/93
	7-1	Blackburn Rovers v Norwich City	02/10/92
	7-1	Newcastle United v Swindon Town	12/03/94
	7-1	Everton v Southampton	28/12/96
	7-1	Newcastle United v Tottenham Hotspur	05/03/97
	4-4	Aston Villa v Leicester City	22/02/95

All-Time Highest Score Draws

4-4	Aston Villa v Leicester City	22/02/95
3-3	Crystal Palace v Blackburn Rovers	15/08/92
	Sheffield Wednesday v Manchester United	26/12/92
	West Ham United v Norwich City	24/01/93
	Swindon Town v Norwich City	19/02/93
	West Ham United v Southampton	07/05/93
	Coventry City v Leeds United	08/05/93
	Middlesbrough v Norwich City	08/05/93
	Oldham Athletic v Coventry City	24/08/93
	Sheffield Wednesday v Norwich City	01/09/93
	Southampton v Sheffield United	02/10/93
	Leeds United v Blackburn Rovers	23/10/93
	Sheffield Wednesday v Leeds United	30/10/93
	Tottenham Hotspur v Liverpool	18/12/93
	Sheffield Wednesday v Swindon Town	29/12/93
	Liverpool v Manchester United	04/01/94
	Everton v Chelsea	03/05/95
	Manchester City v Nottingham Forest	08/10/94

Manchester City v Southampton	05/11/94
Newcastle United v Tottenham Hotspur	03/05/95
Manchester City v Newcastle United	24/02/96
Wimbledon v Newcastle United	03/10/95
Coventry City v Wimbledon	25/11/95
Derby County v Leeds United	17/08/96
Middlesbrough v Liverpool	17/08/96
Manchester United v Middlesbrough	05/03/97

All-Time General Records – Home & Away

Most Goals Scored in a Season	Newcastle United	84	1993-94	42
	Manchester United	76	1996-97	38
Fewest Goals Scored in a Season	Crystal Palace	34	1994-95	42
	Manchester City	31	1996-97	38
Most Goals Conceded in a Season	Swindon Town	100	1993-94	42
	Bolton Wanderers	71	1995-96	38
Fewest Goals Conceded in a Season	Arsenal	28	1993-94	42
	Manchester United	28	1994-95	42
Most Points in a Season	Manchester United	92	1993-94	42
	Manchester United	82	1995-96	38
Fewest Points in a Season	Ipswich Town	27	1994-95	42
Most Wins in a Season	Manchester United	27	1993-94	42
	Blackburn Rovers	27	1994-95	42
Fewest Wins in a Season	Swindon Town	5	1993-94	42
Fewest Defeats in a Season	Manchester United	4	1993-94	42
Most Defeats in a Season	Ipswich Town	29	1994-95	42
	Bolton Wanderers	25	1995-96	38
Most Draws in a Season	Manchester City	18	1993-94	42
	Sheffield United	18	1993-94	42
	Southampton	18	1994-95	42
	Nottingham Forest	16	1996-97	38

NB: 38 or 42 refers to the number of games played in that season.

Record Attendances by Club

Club	Att	Opponents	Date
Arsenal	38,377	Tottenham Hotspur	29/04/95
Aston Villa	45,347	Liverpool	07/05/94
Blackburn Rovers	30,895	Liverpool	24/02/95
Bolton Wanderers	21,381	Manchester United	25/02/96
Chelsea	37,064	Manchester United	11/09/93
Coventry City	24,410	Manchester United	12/04/94
Crystal Palace	30,115	Manchester United	21/04/93

Derby County	18,287	Arsenal	11/05/97
Everton	40,177	Liverpool	16/04/97
Ipswich Town	22,559	Manchester United	01/05/94
Leeds United	41,125	Manchester United	27/04/94
Leicester City	21,393	Liverpool	26/12/94
Liverpool	44,619	Everton	20/03/93
Manchester City	37,136	Manchester United	20/03/93
Manchester United	55,314	Wimbledon	29/01/97
Middlesbrough	30,215	Tottenham Hotspur	19/10/96
Newcastle United	36,589	Tottenham Hotspur	05/05/96
Norwich City	21,843	Liverpool	29/04/95
Nottingham Forest	29,263	Manchester United	27/11/95
Queens Park Rangers	21,267	Manchester United	05/02/94
Sheffield United	30,044	Sheffield Wednesday	23/10/93
Sheffield Wednesday	38,943	Liverpool	11/05/97
Southampton	19,654	Tottenham Hotspur	15/08/92
Sunderland	22,512	Derby County	26/12/96
Swindon Town	18,108	Manchester United	19/03/94
Tottenham Hotspur	33,709	Arsenal	12/12/92
West Ham United	28,832	Manchester United	25/02/94
Wimbledon	30,115	Manchester United	08/05/93

Top 10 Attendances

Psn	Att	Match	Date
1	55,314	Manchester United v Wimbledon	29/01/97
2	55,269	Manchester United v Southampton	01/02/97
3	55,267	Manchester United v Sheffield Wednesday	15/03/97
4	55,256	Manchester United v Leeds United	28/12/96
5	55,249	Manchester United v West Ham United	12/05/97
6	55,243	Manchester United v Derby County	05/04/97
7	55,236	Manchester United v Newcastle United	08/05/97
8	55,230	Manchester United v Coventry City	01/03/97
9	55,210	Manchester United v Arsenal	16/11/96
10	55,198	Manchester United v Chelsea	02/11/96

Biggest attendance not at Old Trafford

| | 45,347 | Aston Villa v Liverpool | 07/05/94 |

Lowest Attendances by Club

Club	Att	Opponents	Date
Arsenal	18,253	Wimbledon	10/02/92
Aston Villa	16,180	Southampton	24/11/93

Blackburn Rovers	13,505	Sheffield United	18/10/93
Chelsea	8,923	Coventry City	04/05/94
Coventry City	9,526	Ipswich Town	10/10/94
Crystal Palace	10,422	Sheffield Wednesday	14/03/95
Derby County	17,022	Wimbledon	28/09/96
Everton	13,660	Southampton	04/12/93
Ipswich Town	10,747	Sheffield United	21/08/93
Leeds United	25,774	Wimbledon	15/08/92
Leicester City	15,489	Wimbledon	01/04/95
Liverpool	24,561	QPR	08/12/93
Manchester City	19,150	West Ham United	24/08/85
Manchester United	29,736	Crystal Palace	02/09/92
Middlesbrough	12,290	Oldham Athletic	22/03/93
Newcastle United	32,067	Southampton	22/01/94
Norwich City	12,452	Southampton	05/09/92
Nottingham Forest	17,525	Blackburn Rovers	25/11/96
Oldham Athletic	9,633	Wimbledon	28/08/93
Queens Park Rangers	9,875	Swindon Town	30/04/94
Sheffield United	13,646	West Ham United	28/03/94
Sheffield Wednesday	16,390	Nottingham Forest	18/11/96
Southampton	9,028	Ipswich Town	08/12/93
Sunderland	18,642	West Ham United	08/09/96
Swindon Town	11,970	Oldham Athletic	18/08/93
Tottenham Hotspur	17,452	Aston Villa	02/03/94
West Ham United	15,777	Swindon Town	11/09/93
Wimbledon	3,039	Everton	26/01/93

Lowest 10 Attendances

Psn	Att	Match	Date
1	3,039	Wimbledon v Everton	26/01/93
2	3,386	Wimbledon v Oldham Athletic	12/12/92
3	3,759	Wimbledon v Coventry City	22/08/92
4	3,979	Wimbledon v Sheffield United	20/02/93
5	4,534	Wimbledon v Southampton	06/03/93
6	4,714	Wimbledon v Manchester City	01/09/92
7	4,739	Wimbledon v Coventry City	26/12/93
8	4,954	Wimbledon v Ipswich Town	18/08/92
9	5,268	Wimbledon v Manchester City	21/03/95
10	5,536	Wimbledon v Sheffield Wednesday	15/01/94

THE GOALSCORERS

Top Goalscorers by Player

S/R=Strike rate – number of games per goal, ie Alan Shearer has a S/R of 1.23 – he scores a goal every 1.23 games on average. Club is the club where player made his last Premiership appearance as of the end of the 1996-97 season.

Player	Club	Goals	Tot	S/R	Sta	Sub
SHEARER, Alan	Newcastle United	137	169	1.23	163	6
FERDINAND, Les	Newcastle United	101	178	1.76	176	2
WRIGHT, Ian	Arsenal	94	167	1.78	160	7
FOWLER, Robbie	Liverpool	83	140	1.69	137	3
LE TISSIER, Matthew	Southampton	80	184	2.30	178	6
SHERINGHAM, Teddy	Tottenham Hotspur	76	169	2.22	166	3
COLE, Andy	Manchester United	72	130	1.81	117	13
CANTONA, Eric	Manchester United	70	156	2.23	154	2
SUTTON, Chris	Blackburn Rovers	59	157	2.66	146	11
BEARDSLEY, Peter	Newcastle United	58	168	2.90	165	3
HOLDSWORTH, Dean	Wimbledon	58	164	2.83	144	20
COTTEE, Tony	West Ham United	51	135	2.65	127	8
HUGHES, Mark	Chelsea	51	177	3.47	173	4
COLLYMORE, Stan	Aston Villa	49	99	2.02	91	8
BRIGHT, Mark	Sheffield Wednesday	48	138	2.88	117	21
RUSH, Ian	Leeds United	48	166	3.46	152	14
YORKE, Dwight	Aston Villa	48	148	3.08	129	19
DEANE, Brian	Leeds United	47	179	3.81	172	7
ARMSTRONG, Chris	Tottenham Hotspur	43	123	2.86	123	0
DUBLIN, Dion	Coventry City	43	111	2.58	102	9
KANCHELSKIS, Andrei	Everton	43	140	3.26	119	21
EKOKU, Efan	Wimbledon	42	122	2.90	106	16
SAUNDERS, Dean	Nottingham Forest	42	152	3.62	150	2
GIGGS, Ryan	Manchester United	37	167	4.51	156	11
SPENCER, John	QPR	36	103	2.86	75	28
NDLOVU, Peter	Coventry City	35	154	4.40	132	22
EARLE, Robbie	Wimbledon	34	162	4.76	162	0
HIRST, David	Sheffield Wednesday	34	99	2.91	90	9
DOWIE, Iain	West Ham United	33	163	4.94	156	7
QUINN, Niall	Sunderland	33	132	4.00	108	24
BARMBY, Nick	Everton	32	154	4.81	145	9
WALLACE, Rod	Leeds United	32	147	4.59	124	23
CAMPBELL, Kevin	Nottingham Forest	31	135	4.35	116	19

GALLACHER, Kevin	Blackburn Rovers	31	110	3.55	104	6
McALLISTER, Gary	Coventry City	31	189	6.10	189	0
NEVILLE, Gary	Manchester United	31	80	2.58	76	4
SPEED, Gary	Everton	31	180	5.81	179	1
FOX, Ruel	Tottenham Hotspur	29	143	4.93	139	4
LEE, Robert	Newcastle United	29	145	5.00	144	1
PEACOCK, Gavin	QPR	29	135	4.66	121	14
RIDEOUT, Paul	Everton	29	111	3.83	86	25
STUART, Graham	Everton	29	161	5.55	133	28
MERSON, Paul	Arsenal	28	160	5.71	150	10
MORRIS, Chris	Middlesbrough	27	52	1.93	47	5
McMANAMAN, Steve	Liverpool	26	176	6.77	171	5
PEARS, Stephen	Liverpool	26	26	1.00	26	0
ROBINS, Mark	Leicester City	26	92	3.54	78	14
WHITE, David	Leeds United	26	100	3.85	86	14
DICKS, Julian	West Ham United	25	125	5.00	125	0
OLNEY, Ian	Oldham Athletic	25	44	1.76	42	2
QUINN, Mick	Coventry City	25	64	2.56	57	7

All-Time Player: Most Goals in One Game

Gls	Player	Match	Date	Res
5	Andy COLE	MANCHESTER UTD v Ipswich Tn	04/03/95	9-0
4	Efan EKOKU	Everton v NORWICH CITY	25/09/93	1-5
4	Robbie FOWLER	LIVERPOOL v Middlesbrough	14/12/96	5-1

Player: Consecutive Games with Goals

7   **Mark Stein, Chelsea**   **1993-94**

	Dec 27	Southampton	Away	1-3	Stein
	Dec 28	Newcastle United	Home	1-0	Stein
	Jan 1	Swindon Town	Away	3-0	Stein
	Jan 3	Everton	Home	4-2	Stein x 2 (1 penalty)
	Jan 15	Norwich City	Away	1-1	Stein
	Jan 22	Aston Villa	Home	1-1	Stein
	Feb 5	Everton	Away	2-4	Stein x 2 (1 penalty)

(Stein actually scored 9 goals – inc. two penalties – in this sequence.
These goals were scored in consecutive Chelsea matches as well.)

7   **Alan Shearer, Newcastle United**   **1996-97**

	Sep 14	Blackburn Rovers	Home	2-1	Shearer (penalty)
	Sep 21	Leeds United	Away	1-0	Shearer
	Sep 30	Aston Villa	Home	4-3	Shearer
	Oct 12	Derby Co.	Away	1-0	Shearer

Oct 20	Manchester United	Home	5-0	Shearer
Nov 23	Chelsea	Away	1-1	Shearer
Nov 30	Arsenal	Home	1-2	Shearer

(Newcastle played Leicester City, Middlesbrough and West Ham after playing Man. United and before Chelsea, however Shearer was injured for these matches.)

Fastest Goals in a Game

| 13 seconds | Chris Sutton | BLACKBURN ROVERS v Everton | 01/04/94 |
| 17 seconds | John Spencer | CHELSEA v Leicester City | 08/10/94 |

Fastest Hat-trick in a Game

4 min 33 secs Robbie Fowler LIVERPOOL v Arsenal   28/08/94

Player: Most Hat-tricks in a Season

5   Alan Shearer, Blackburn Rovers   1995-96
        v Coventry City, Nottingham Forest, West Ham United, Bolton Wanderers
             and Tottenham Hotspur

Player: Hat-trick Hall of Fame

No.	Player	Team(s)
9	Alan Shearer	Blackburn Rovers and Newcastle United
5	Robbie Fowler	Liverpool
4	Matt Le Tissier	Southampton
	Ian Wright	Arsenal
3	Kevin Campbell	Arsenal and Nottingham Forest
	Andy Cole	Newcastle United
	Tony Cottee	Everton
	Les Ferdinand	QPR
2	Andrei Kanchelskis	Everton
	Fabrizio Ravanelli	Middlesbrough
	Teddy Sheringham	Tottenham Hotspur
	Chris Sutton	Norwich City
	Tony Yeboah	Leeds United

THE GOALKEEPERS

Goalkeepers by Total App-Goals Ratio

Surname	Club	App	Sub	GA	GkA	CS	GaR
SEAMAN	Arsenal	169	0	179	136	73	0.80
SCHMEICHEL	Manchester United	186	0	176	163	88	0.88
JAMES	Liverpool	160	1	218	158	55	0.98
FLOWERS	Blackburn Rovers	195	0	292	214	58	1.10
BOSNICH	Aston Villa	133	0	215	148	45	1.11
COTON	Sunderland	103	1	217	117	27	1.13
LUKIC	Arsenal	144	0	228	169	49	1.17
MARTYN	Leeds United	116	0	148	140	45	1.21
KHARINE	Chelsea	107	0	261	135	37	1.26
MIKLOSKO	West Ham United	156	0	206	199	47	1.28
SEGERS	Wimbledon	116	2	243	153	30	1.30
SOUTHALL	Everton	195	0	271	254	59	1.30
OGRIZOVIC	Coventry City	162	0	278	215	40	1.33
WALKER	Tottenham H.	143	1	272	194	38	1.35
CROSSLEY	Nottingham Forest	150	0	218	204	36	1.36
PRESSMAN	Sheffield W.	137	0	274	192	34	1.40
BEASANT	Southampton	103	2	291	148	24	1.41

Key: GA=Goals conceded by team overall; GkA=Goals conceded by goalkeeper; CS =number of Clean Sheets; GaR=GkA divided by total appearances (App+Sub) to give number of goals conceded per game on average. Only players with 100+ appearances are listed.

Goalkeepers by Total Most Clean Sheets

Surname	Club	CS	Apps	%
SCHMEICHEL	Manchester United	88	186	47.31
SEAMAN	Arsenal	73	169	43.20
SOUTHALL	Everton	59	195	30.26
FLOWERS	Blackburn Rovers	58	195	29.74
JAMES	Liverpool	55	161	34.16
LUKIC	Arsenal	49	144	34.03
MIKLOSKO	West Ham United	47	156	30.13
BOSNICH	Aston Villa	45	133	33.83
MARTYN	Leeds United	45	116	38.79
OGRIZOVIC	Coventry City	40	162	24.69
WALKER	Tottenham Hotspur	38	144	26.39
KHARINE	Chelsea	37	107	34.58

CROSSLEY	Nottingham Forest	36	150	24.00
PRESSMAN	Sheffield Wednesday	34	137	24.82
SRNICEK	Newcastle Utd	33	96	34.38
SEGERS	Wimbledon	30	118	25.42

Goalkeepers by Consecutive Shut-outs

Surname	Club	CSO	Rp	CS	Season
SOUTHALL	Everton	7	0	14	1994-95
SCHMEICHEL	Manchester United	5	0	18	1992-93
SEAMAN	Arsenal	5	2	20	1993-94
WALKER	Tottenham Hotspur	5	0	11	1994-95
WALKER	Tottenham Hotspur	5	0	11	1995-96
SEAMAN	Arsenal	5	0	10	1996-97
JAMES	Liverpool	5	0	12	1996-97
MIMMS	Blackburn Rovers	4	0	18	1992-93
THORSTVEDT	Tottenham Hotspur	4	0	8	1992-93
FORREST	Ipswich Town	4	0	9	1993-94
FLOWERS	Blackburn Rovers	4	0	16	1994-95
SCHMEICHEL	Manchester United	4	2	24	1994-95
MARSHALL	Norwich City	4	0	7	1994-95
OGRIZOVIC	Coventry City	4	0	8	1995-96
SCHMEICHEL	Manchester United	4	0	18	1995-96
WALSH	Middlesbrough	4	0	9	1995-96
MARTYN	Leeds United	4	0	20	1996-97
SCHMEICHEL	Manchester United	4	0	13	1996-97
SRNICEK	Newcastle United	4	0	7	1996-97

CSO=Consecutive shut-outs (number of full games without conceding a goal); Rp=No. of times repeated; CS=Clean Sheets.

Goalkeepers by Most Clean Sheets/Season

Surname	Club	CS	Aps	%	GkA	Season
SCHMEICHEL	Manchester United	24	32	75.00	22	1994-95
MARTYN	Leeds United	20	37	54.05	38	1996-97
SEAMAN	Arsenal	20	39	51.28	24	1993-94
SCHMEICHEL	Manchester United	18	36	50.00	30	1995-96
MIMMS	Blackburn Rovers	18	42	42.86	46	1992-93
SCHMEICHEL	Manchester United	18	42	42.86	31	1992-93
JAMES	Liverpool	17	42	40.48	37	1994-95
LUKIC	Leeds United	17	42	40.48	38	1994-95
JAMES	Liverpool	16	38	42.11	34	1995-96
SEAMAN	Arsenal	16	38	42.11	32	1995-96
SEAMAN	Arsenal	16	39	41.03	34	1992-93

FLOWERS	Blackburn Rovers	16	39	41.03	30	1994-95
SOUTHALL	Everton	15	38	39.47	44	1995-96
SCHMEICHEL	Manchester United	15	40	37.50	38	1993-94
MARTYN	Crystal Palace	14	37	37.84	41	1994-95
SOUTHALL	Everton	14	41	34.15	51	1994-95
MIKLOSKO	West Ham United	14	42	33.33	58	1993-94
FLOWERS	Blackburn Rovers	13	29	44.83	23	1993-94
KHARINE	Chelsea	13	31	41.94	46	1994-95
SCHMEICHEL	Manchester United	13	36	36.11	42	1996-97
WALKER	Tottenham Hotspur	13	37	35.14	49	1996-97
SRNICEK	Newcastle United	13	38	34.21	43	1994-95
BOSNICH	Aston Villa	13	38	34.21	34	1995-96
SEGERS	Wimbledon	13	41	31.71	53	1992-93
CROSSLEY	Nottingham Forest	13	42	30.95	43	1994-95
MIKLOSKO	West Ham United	13	42	30.95	48	1994-95
JAMES	Liverpool	12	38	31.58	37	1996-97
SEAMAN	Arsenal	11	31	35.48	31	1994-95
OGRIZOVIC	Coventry City	11	33	33.33	32	1993-94
OGRIZOVIC	Coventry City	11	33	33.33	50	1994-95
MIKLOSKO	West Ham United	11	36	30.56	47	1995-96
SULLIVAN	Wimbledon	11	36	30.56	43	1996-97
WALKER	Tottenham Hotspur	11	38	28.95	38	1995-96
LUKIC	Leeds United	11	39	28.21	53	1992-93
COTON	Manchester City	11	40	27.50	44	1992-93
SOUTHALL	Everton	11	40	27.50	45	1992-93
KHARINE	Chelsea	11	40	27.50	48	1993-94
SEGERS	Wimbledon	11	41	26.83	50	1993-94
WALKER	Tottenham Hotspur	11	41	26.83	57	1994-95
GUNN	Norwich City	11	42	26.19	65	1992-93
MARTYN	Crystal Palace	11	42	26.19	61	1992-93
SOUTHALL	Everton	11	42	26.19	63	1993-94
SEAMAN	Arsenal	10	22	45.45	15	1996-97
KHARINE	Chelsea	10	26	38.46	29	1995-96
COTON	Manchester City	10	31	32.26	37	1993-94
BEASANT	Southampton	10	36	27.78	49	1995-96
FLOWERS	Blackburn Rovers	10	36	27.78	42	1996-97
PRESSMAN	Sheffield Wednesday	10	38	26.32	50	1996-97
GUNN	Norwich City	10	41	24.39	60	1993-94
FLOWERS	Southampton	10	42	23.81	61	1992-93

THE PLAYERS

Maximum number of games possible is 202.
NB: Clubs listed are those that player played last Premiership match with.

Player	Club	Tot	Start	Sub	Gls
FLOWERS, Tim	Blackburn Rovers	195	195	0	0
SOUTHALL, Neville	Everton	195	195	0	0
ATHERTON, Peter	Sheffield Wednesday	192	191	1	3
McALLISTER, Gary	Coventry City	189	189	0	31
SCHMEICHEL, Peter	Manchester United	186	186	0	0
SHERWOOD, Tim	Blackburn Rovers	186	185	1	17
IRWIN, Dennis	Manchester United	184	182	2	11
LE TISSIER, Matthew	Southampton	184	178	6	80
PEACOCK, Darren	Newcastle United	181	177	4	7
SPEED, Gary	Everton	180	179	1	31
DEANE, Brian	Leeds United	179	172	7	47
FERDINAND, Les	Newcastle United	178	176	2	101
HUGHES, Mark	Chelsea	177	173	4	51
KENNA, Jeff	Blackburn Rovers	176	173	3	5
McMANAMAN, Steve	Liverpool	176	171	5	26
RICHARDSON, Kevin	Coventry City	176	172	4	8
WINTERBURN, Nigel	Arsenal	176	176	0	3
PALLISTER, Gary	Manchester United	173	173	0	8
PALMER, Carlton	Leeds United	173	170	3	11
WILSON, Clive	Tottenham Hotspur	173	170	3	7
DIXON, Lee	Arsenal	171	169	2	5
HENDRY, Colin	Blackburn Rovers	170	169	1	7
TOWNSEND, Andy	Aston Villa	170	169	1	12
SEAMAN, David	Arsenal	169	169	0	0
SHEARER, Alan	Newcastle United	169	163	6	137
SHERINGHAM, Teddy	Tottenham Hotspur	169	166	3	76
WATSON, Dave	Everton	169	168	1	6
BEARDSLEY, Peter	Newcastle United	168	165	3	58
BARRETT, Earl	Everton	167	166	1	1
GIGGS, Ryan	Manchester United	167	156	11	37
WRIGHT, Ian	Arsenal	167	160	7	94
McGRATH, Paul	Derby County	166	160	6	6
RUSH, Ian	Leeds United	166	152	14	48
HOLDSWORTH, Dean	Wimbledon	164	144	20	58
DOWIE, Iain	West Ham United	163	156	7	33

BARNES, John	Liverpool	162	158	4	22
EARLE, Robbie	Wimbledon	162	162	0	34
OGRIZOVIC, Steve	Coventry City	162	162	0	0
BABB, Phil	Liverpool	161	152	9	4
JAMES, David	Liverpool	161	160	1	0
STUART, Graham	Everton	161	133	28	29
JONES, Vinny	Wimbledon	160	156	4	13
KEOWN, Martin	Arsenal	160	142	18	2
MERSON, Paul	Arsenal	160	150	10	28
BERG, Henning	Blackburn Rovers	159	154	5	4
BART-WILLIAMS, Chris	Nottingham Forest	158	132	26	18
RIPLEY, Stuart	Blackburn Rovers	158	147	11	11
SUTTON, Chris	Blackburn Rovers	157	146	11	59
CANTONA, Eric	Manchester United	156	154	2	70
MIKLOSKO, Ludek	West Ham United	156	156	0	0
BARMBY, Nick	Everton	154	145	9	32
KELLY, Gary	Leeds United	154	152	2	2
NDLOVU, Peter	Coventry City	154	132	22	35
BENALI, Francis	Southampton	153	140	13	0
KEANE, Roy	Manchester United	152	147	5	21
SAUNDERS, Dean	Nottingham Forest	152	150	2	42
WALKER, Des	Sheffield Wednesday	152	152	0	0
RUDDOCK, Neil	Liverpool	151	147	4	14
BARTON, Warren	Newcastle United	150	143	7	7
CROSSLEY, Mark	Nottingham Forest	150	150	0	0
REDKNAPP, Jamie	Liverpool	150	129	21	15

Top Substitute Appearances by Player

NB: Clubs listed are those that player played last Premiership match with.

Player	Club	Sub	Tot	Start	Gls
CLARKE, Andy	Wimbledon	57	53	110	11
ROSENTHAL, Ronny	Tottenham Hotspur	47	71	118	10
McCLAIR, Brian	Manchester United	45	104	149	18
BARLOW, Stuart	Everton	41	21	62	10
WATSON, Gordon	Southampton	40	54	94	21
FENTON, Graham	Blackburn Rovers	34	25	59	10
CLARK, Lee	Sunderland	32	69	101	7
LEE, Jason	Nottingham Forest	32	31	63	12
GOODMAN, Jon	Wimbledon	31	28	59	11
PARLOUR, Ray	Arsenal	31	99	130	5
WARHURST, Paul	Blackburn Rovers	31	59	90	10
HYDE, Graham	Sheffield Wednesday	29	88	117	8

SCHOLES, Paul	Manchester United	29	38	67	18
CORK, Alan	Wimbledon	28	18	46	5
SPENCER, John	Chelsea	28	75	103	36
STUART, Graham	Everton	28	133	161	29
WALTERS, Mark	Southampton	28	44	72	11
LIMPAR, Anders	Everton	27	72	99	16
BANGER, Nicky	Southampton	26	8	34	8
BART-WILLIAMS, Chris	Nottingham Forest	26	132	158	18
HARFORD, Mick	Wimbledon	26	64	90	19
THOMAS, Michael	Liverpool	26	69	95	5
ADAMS, Neil	Norwich City	25	67	92	12
BURLEY, Craig	Chelsea	25	79	104	7
HEANEY, Neil	Manchester City	25	48	73	5
RIDEOUT, Paul	Everton	25	86	111	29
QUINN, Niall	Sunderland	24	108	132	33
RADOSAVIJEVIC, Pedray	Everton	24	22	46	4
JOACHIM, Julian	Aston Villa	23	18	41	7
NETHERCOTT, Stuart	Tottenham Hotspur	23	31	54	0
WALLACE, Rod	Leeds United	23	124	147	32
ATKINS, Mark	Blackburn Rovers	22	62	84	12
GUENTCHEV, Bontcho	Ipswich Town	22	39	61	6
HUGHES, David	Southampton	22	9	31	3
McGREGOR, Paul	Nottingham Forest	22	7	29	3
NDLOVU, Peter	Coventry City	22	132	154	35
BLISSETT, Gary	Wimbledon	21	10	31	3
BRIGHT, Mark	Sheffield Wednesday	21	117	138	48
KANCHELSKIS, Andrei	Everton	21	119	140	43
LAWRENCE, Jamie	Leicester City	21	11	32	1
MATHIE, Alex	Ipswich Town	21	16	37	6
MORROW, Steve	Arsenal	21	39	60	1
REDKNAPP, Jamie	Liverpool	21	129	150	15
SLATER, Robbie	Southampton	21	52	73	4
STRACHAN, Gordon	Coventry City	21	75	96	7
WHELAN, Noel	Coventry City	21	83	104	21
FURLONG, Paul	Chelsea	20	44	64	13
HOLDSWORTH, Dean	Wimbledon	20	144	164	58
MATTEO, Dominic	Liverpool	20	29	49	0
PENRICE, Gary	QPR	20	42	62	17
SUTCH, Daryl	Norwich City	20	35	55	3

THE MANAGERS

Length of Tenure – Current Tenants

	Club	Manager	Arrived
1	Manchester United	Alex Ferguson	November '86
2	Wimbledon	Joe Kinnear	January '91
3	Liverpool	Roy Evans	January '94
4	Barnsley	Danny Wilson	June '94
5	West Ham United	Harry Redknapp	August '94
6	Aston Villa	Brian Little	November '94
7	Tottenham Hotspur	Gerry Francis	November '94
8	Derby County	Jim Smith	June '95
9	Sheffield Wednesday	David Pleat	July '95
10	Leicester City	Martin O'Neill	December '95
11	Leeds United	George Graham	September '96
12	Bolton Wanderers	Colin Todd	January '96
13	Chelsea	Ruud Gullitt	May '96
14	Arsenal	Arsène Wenger	August '96
15	Coventry City	Gordon Strachan	November '96
16	Newcastle United	Kenny Dalglish	January '97
17	Crystal Palace	Steve Coppell	March '97 *
18	Blackburn Rovers	Roy Hodgson	June '97
19	Southampton	Dave Jones	June '97
20	Everton	Howard Kendall	June '97

* Caretaker Manager

See later in this Annual for full records of all Premiership managers

Managers: Most Games in Charge

Manager	P	W	D	L	F	A	PTS	PPG
FERGUSON, Alex	202	123	52	27	373	176	421	2.08
KINNEAR, Joe	202	72	56	74	264	289	272	1.35
ROYLE, Joe	181	58	54	69	241	258	228	1.26
WILKINSON, Howard	174	66	53	55	231	214	250	1.44
FRANCIS, Gerry	161	64	46	51	227	197	238	1.48
ATKINSON, Ron	160	55	44	61	174	195	209	1.31
GRAHAM, George	145	50	50	45	155	127	200	1.38
KEEGAN, Kevin	143	78	30	35	253	147	264	1.85
DALGLISH, Kenny	142	80	34	28	244	137	274	1.93
EVANS, Roy	134	65	35	34	212	131	230	1.72
FRANCIS, Trevor	126	44	42	40	180	162	174	1.38

HODDLE, Glenn	122	38	41	43	145	152	155	1.27
REDKNAPP, Harry	118	37	32	49	126	148	143	1.21
LITTLE, Brian	117	45	33	39	145	124	168	1.44
WILKINS, Ray	108	35	25	48	136	156	130	1.2
SOUNESS, Graeme	106	38	29	39	156	143	143	1.35
LYALL, John	101	24	34	43	101	146	106	1.05
BALL, Alan	98	28	33	37	120	151	117	1.19
REID, Peter	84	25	23	36	92	109	98	1.27
CLARK, Frank	97	38	31	28	136	126	145	1.49
WALKER, Mike	96	37	25	34	126	143	136	1.42

Managers by Total Points Won

Manager	P	W	D	L	F	A	Pts
FERGUSON, Alex	202	123	52	27	373	176	421
DALGLISH, Kenny	142	80	34	28	244	137	274
KINNEAR, Joe	202	72	56	74	264	289	272
KEEGAN, Kevin	143	78	30	35	253	147	264
WILKINSON, Howard	174	66	53	55	231	214	250
FRANCIS, Gerry	161	64	46	51	227	197	238
EVANS, Roy	134	65	35	34	212	131	230
ROYLE, Joe	181	58	54	69	241	258	228
ATKINSON, Ron	160	55	44	61	174	195	209
GRAHAM, George	145	50	50	45	155	127	200
FRANCIS, Trevor	126	44	42	40	180	162	174
LITTLE, Brian	117	45	33	39	145	124	168
HODDLE, Glenn	122	38	41	43	145	152	155
CLARK, Frank	97	38	31	28	136	126	145
REDKNAPP, Harry	118	37	32	49	126	148	143
SOUNESS, Graeme	106	38	29	39	156	143	143
WALKER, Mike	96	37	25	34	126	143	136
WILKINS, Ray	108	35	25	48	136	156	130
BALL, Alan	98	28	33	37	120	151	117
LYALL, John	101	24	34	43	101	146	106
REID, Peter	84	25	23	36	92	109	98
PLEAT, David	76	24	25	27	98	112	97
BASSETT, Dave	84	22	28	34	96	113	94
HORTON, Brian	80	21	30	29	90	108	93
ROBSON, Bryan	76	21	22	33	86	110	82
KENDALL, Howard	60	22	11	27	73	78	77
NEAL, Phil	58	18	18	22	54	69	72
HARFORD, Ray	58	18	19	21	79	89	69
BRANFOOT, Ian	66	18	14	34	77	97	68
GOULD, Bobby	54	16	19	19	66	73	67
RIOCH, Bruce	38	17	12	9	49	32	63

ARDILES, Ossie	54	16	14	24	75	83	62
DEEHAN, John	61	12	23	26	66	89	59
LIVERMORE/CLEMENCE, Doug/Ray	42	16	11	15	60	66	59
GULLITT, Ruud	38	16	11	11	58	55	59
BONDS, Billy	42	13	13	16	47	58	52
WENGER, Arsène	30	14	9	7	45	24	51
COPPELL, Steve	42	11	16	15	48	61	49
O'NEILL, Martin	38	12	11	15	46	54	47
SMITH, Jim	38	11	13	14	45	58	46
SMITH, Alan	42	11	12	19	34	49	45
LAWRENCE, Lennie	42	11	11	20	54	75	44
CLOUGH, Brian	42	10	10	22	41	62	40
MERRINGTON, Dave	38	9	11	18	34	52	38
PORTERFIELD, Ian	29	9	10	10	32	36	37
STRACHAN, Gordon	28	8	11	9	34	40	35
GORMAN, John	42	5	15	22	47	100	30
PEARCE, Stuart	21	5	9	7	17	30	24
TODD, Colin	16	6	1	9	18	27	19
WEBB, David	13	5	4	4	19	18	19
McGHEE, Mark	24	3	7	14	26	47	16
BURLEY, George	22	4	2	16	16	53	14
McFARLAND, Roy	22	2	4	16	21	44	10

Managers by Average Points/Game

Manager	P	W	D	L	F	A	Pts	PPG
FERGUSON, Alex	202	123	52	27	373	176	421	2.08
DALGLISH, Kenny	142	80	34	28	244	137	274	1.93
KEEGAN, Kevin	143	78	30	35	253	147	264	1.85
EVANS, Roy	134	65	35	34	212	131	230	1.72
WENGER, Arsène	30	14	9	7	45	24	51	1.70
RIOCH, Bruce	38	17	12	9	49	32	63	1.66
GULLITT, Ruud	38	16	11	11	58	55	59	1.55
CLARK, Frank	97	38	31	28	136	126	145	1.49
FRANCIS, Gerry	161	64	46	51	227	197	238	1.48
WEBB, David	13	5	4	4	19	18	19	1.46
WILKINSON, Howard	174	66	53	55	231	214	250	1.44
LITTLE, Brian	117	45	33	39	145	124	168	1.44
WALKER, Mike	96	37	25	34	126	143	136	1.42
LIVERMORE/CLEMENCE, Doug/Ray	42	16	11	15	60	66	59	1.40
GRAHAM, George	145	50	50	45	155	127	200	1.38
FRANCIS, Trevor	126	44	42	40	180	162	174	1.38
KINNEAR, Joe	202	72	56	74	264	289	272	1.35

SOUNESS, Graeme	106	38	29	39	156	143	143	1.35
ATKINSON, Ron	160	55	44	61	174	195	209	1.31
PLEAT, David	76	24	25	27	98	112	97	1.28
KENDALL, Howard	60	22	11	27	73	78	77	1.28
PORTERFIELD, Ian	29	9	10	10	32	36	37	1.28
HODDLE, Glenn	122	38	41	43	145	152	155	1.27
ROYLE, Joe	181	58	54	69	241	258	228	1.26
STRACHAN, Gordon	28	8	11	9	34	40	35	1.25
NEAL, Phil	58	18	18	22	54	69	72	1.24
GOULD, Bobby	54	16	19	19	66	73	67	1.24
BONDS, Billy	42	13	13	16	47	58	52	1.24
O'NEILL, Martin	38	12	11	15	46	54	47	1.24
REDKNAPP, Harry	118	37	32	49	126	148	143	1.21
SMITH, Jim	38	11	13	14	45	58	46	1.21
WILKINS, Ray	108	35	25	48	136	156	130	1.20
BALL, Alan	98	28	33	37	120	151	117	1.19
HARFORD, Ray	58	18	19	21	79	89	69	1.19
TODD, Colin	16	6	1	9	18	27	19	1.19
COPPELL, Steve	42	11	16	15	48	61	49	1.17
REID, Peter	84	25	23	36	92	109	98	1.17
HORTON, Brian	80	21	30	29	90	108	93	1.16
ARDILES, Ossie	54	16	14	24	75	83	62	1.15
PEARCE, Stuart	21	5	9	7	17	30	24	1.14
BASSETT, Dave	84	22	28	34	96	113	94	1.12
ROBSON, Bryan	76	21	22	33	86	110	82	1.08
SMITH, Alan	42	11	12	19	34	49	45	1.07
LYALL, John	101	24	34	43	101	146	106	1.05
LAWRENCE, Lennie	42	11	11	20	54	75	44	1.05
BRANFOOT, Ian	66	18	14	34	77	97	68	1.03
MERRINGTON, Dave	38	9	11	18	34	52	38	1.00
DEEHAN, John	61	12	23	26	66	89	59	0.97
CLOUGH, Brian	42	10	10	22	41	62	40	0.95
GORMAN, John	42	5	15	22	47	100	30	0.71
McGHEE, Mark	24	3	7	14	26	47	16	0.67
BURLEY, George	22	4	2	16	16	53	14	0.64
McFARLAND, Roy	22	2	4	16	21	44	10	0.45

SEASON BY SEASON

Crime Count – Year-by-Year

Season	Games	Red Cards	Ave	Yellow Cards	Ave
1992-93	462	34	0.077	760	1.65
1993-94	462	25	0.054	599	1.30
1994-95	462	65	0.140	1294	2.80
1995-96	380	57	0.150	1180	3.11
1996-97	380	31	0.082	1211	3.18
Total	*2146*	*212*	*0.098*	*5044*	*2.35*

Last Day Championships

The FA Premier League Championship has twice gone to the last day of the season to be decided.

1994-95

	P	W	D	L	F	A	Pts	GD
Blackburn Rovers	41	27	8	6	79	37	89	+42
Manchester United	41	26	9	6	76	27	87	+48

On the last day of the season Blackburn travelled to Liverpool needing a win to secure the title. Manchester United went to Upton Park needing three points from West Ham and hoping that Rovers would fail to win. A last minute goal gave Liverpool a 2-1 win over Blackburn, but despite a succession of missed chances Manchester United could only draw and the title went to Blackburn Rovers.

1995-96

	P	W	D	L	F	A	Pts	GD
Manchester United	41	24	7	6	70	35	79	+35
Newcastle United	41	24	5	8	65	36	77	+29

At one point Newcastle led the table by 12 points but a string of last-minute reversals and a relentless attack by the Red Devils allowed them to peg the Magpies back. On the final day of the season the United of Manchester travelled to the north-east to play Middlesbrough, needing a point to take the title. Newcastle entertained Spurs at home and needed to win and look a few miles south for a result. The United of Manchester prevailed, winning 3-0 at the Riverside as Newcastle drew 1-1 with Spurs.

		P	W	D	L	F	A	Pts	
1	Manchester United	42	24	12	6	67	31	84	
2	Aston Villa	42	21	11	10	57	40	74	
3	Norwich City	42	21	9	12	61	65	72	
4	Blackburn Rovers	42	20	11	11	68	46	71	
5	QPR	42	17	12	13	63	55	63	
6	Liverpool	42	16	11	15	62	55	59	
7	Sheffield Wednesday	42	15	14	13	55	51	59	
8	Tottenham Hotspur	42	16	11	15	60	66	59	
9	Manchester City	42	15	12	15	56	51	57	
10	Arsenal	42	15	11	16	40	38	56	
11	Chelsea	42	14	14	14	51	54	56	
12	Wimbledon	42	14	12	16	56	55	54	
13	Everton	42	15	8	19	53	55	53	
14	Sheffield United	42	14	10	18	54	53	52	
15	Coventry City	42	13	13	16	52	57	52	
16	Ipswich Town	42	12	14	16	50	55	52	
17	Leeds United	42	12	15	15	57	62	51	
18	Southampton	42	13	11	18	54	61	50	
19	Oldham Athletic	42	13	10	19	63	74	49	R
20	Crystal Palace	42	11	16	15	48	61	49	R
21	Middlesbrough	42	11	11	20	54	75	44	R
22	Nottingham Forest	42	10	10	22	41	62	40	R

Promoted:
Newcastle United – Champions
West Ham United – Runners-up
Swindon Town – Play-off Winners

		P	W	D	L	F	A	Pts	
1	Manchester United	42	27	11	4	80	38	92	
2	Blackburn Rovers	42	25	9	8	63	36	84	
3	Newcastle United	42	23	8	11	82	41	77	
4	Arsenal	42	18	17	7	53	28	71	
5	Leeds United	42	18	16	8	65	39	70	
6	Wimbledon	42	18	11	13	56	53	65	
7	Sheffield Wednesday	42	16	16	10	76	54	64	
8	Liverpool	42	17	9	16	59	55	60	
9	QPR	42	16	12	14	62	61	60	
10	Aston Villa	42	15	12	15	46	50	57	
11	Coventry City	42	14	14	14	43	45	56	
12	Norwich City	42	12	17	13	65	61	53	
13	West Ham United	42	13	13	16	47	58	52	
14	Chelsea	42	13	12	17	49	53	51	
15	Tottenham Hotspur	42	11	12	19	54	59	45	
16	Manchester City	42	9	18	15	38	49	45	
17	Everton	42	12	8	22	42	63	44	
18	Southampton	42	12	7	23	49	66	43	
19	Ipswich Town	42	9	16	17	35	58	43	
20	Sheffield United	42	8	18	16	42	60	42	R
21	Oldham Athletic	42	9	13	20	42	68	40	R
22	Swindon Town	42	5	15	22	47	100	30	R

Promoted:
Crystal Palace – Champions
Nottingham Forest – Runners-up
Leicester City – Play-off Winners

Final Table 1994-95 Season

		P	W	D	L	F	A	Pts	
1	Blackburn Rovers	42	27	8	7	80	39	89	
2	Manchester United	42	26	10	6	77	28	88	
3	Nottingham Forest	42	22	11	9	72	43	77	
4	Liverpool	42	21	11	10	65	37	74	
5	Leeds United	42	20	13	9	59	38	73	
6	Newcastle United	42	20	12	10	67	47	72	
7	Tottenham Hotspur	42	16	14	12	66	58	62	
8	Queens Park Rangers	42	17	9	16	61	59	60	
9	Wimbledon	42	15	11	16	48	65	56	
10	Southampton	42	12	18	12	61	63	54	
11	Chelsea	42	13	15	14	50	55	54	
12	Arsenal	42	13	12	17	52	49	51	
13	Sheffield Wednesday	42	13	12	17	49	57	51	
14	West Ham United	42	13	11	18	44	48	50	
15	Everton	42	11	17	14	44	51	50	
16	Coventry City	42	12	14	16	44	62	50	
17	Manchester City	42	12	13	17	53	64	49	
18	Aston Villa	42	11	15	16	51	56	48	
19	Crystal Palace	42	11	12	19	34	49	45	R
20	Norwich City	42	10	13	19	37	54	43	R
21	Leicester City	42	6	11	25	45	80	29	R
22	Ipswich Town	42	7	6	29	36	93	27	R

Promoted:
Middlesbrough – Champions
Bolton Wanderers – Play-off Winners

Final Table 1995-96 Season

		P	W	D	L	F	A	Pts	
1	Manchester United	38	25	7	6	73	35	82	
2	Newcastle United	38	24	6	8	66	37	78	
3	Liverpool	38	20	11	7	70	34	71	
4	Aston Villa	38	18	9	11	52	35	63	
5	Arsenal	38	17	12	9	49	32	63	
6	Everton	38	17	10	11	64	44	61	
7	Blackburn Rovers	38	18	7	13	61	47	61	
8	Tottenham Hotspur	38	16	13	9	50	38	61	
9	Nottingham Forest	38	15	13	10	50	54	58	
10	West Ham United	38	14	9	15	43	52	51	
11	Chelsea	38	12	14	12	46	44	50	
12	Middlesbrough	38	11	10	17	35	50	43	
13	Leeds United	38	12	7	19	40	57	43	
14	Wimbledon	38	10	11	17	55	70	41	
15	Sheffield Wednesday	38	10	10	18	48	61	40	
16	Coventry City	38	8	14	16	42	60	38	
17	Southampton	38	9	11	18	34	52	38	
18	Manchester City	38	9	11	18	33	58	38	
19	QPR	38	9	6	23	38	57	33	R
20	Bolton Wanderers	38	8	5	25	39	71	29	R

Promoted:
Sunderland – Champions
Derby County – Runners-up
Leicester City – Play-off Winners

LEAGUE CHAMPIONS' RECORDS

FOOTBALL LEAGUE

Season	Champions	P	W	D	L	F	A	Pts
1888-89	Preston North End	22	18	4	0	74	15	40
1889-90	Preston North End	22	15	3	4	71	30	33
1890-91	Everton	22	14	1	7	63	29	29
1891-92	Sunderland	26	21	0	5	93	36	42

FOOTBALL LEAGUE DIVISION 1

Season	Champions	P	W	D	L	F	A	Pts
1892-93	Sunderland	30	22	4	4	100	36	48
1893-94	Aston Villa	30	19	6	5	84	42	44
1894-95	Sunderland	30	21	5	4	80	37	47
1895-96	Aston Villa	30	20	5	5	78	45	45
1896-97	Aston Villa	30	21	5	4	73	38	47
1897-98	Sheffield United	30	17	8	5	56	31	42
1898-99	Aston Villa	34	19	7	8	76	40	45
1899-00	Aston Villa	34	22	6	6	77	35	50
1900-01	Liverpool	34	19	7	8	59	35	45
1901-02	Sunderland	34	19	6	9	50	35	44
1902-03	Sheffield Wednesday	34	19	4	11	54	36	42
1903-04	Sheffield Wednesday	34	20	7	7	48	28	47
1904-05	Newcastle United	34	23	2	9	72	33	48
1905-06	Liverpool	38	23	5	10	79	46	51
1906-07	Newcastle United	38	22	7	9	74	46	51
1907-08	Manchester United	38	23	6	9	81	48	52
1908-09	Newcastle United	38	24	5	9	65	41	53
1909-10	Aston Villa	38	23	7	8	84	42	53
1910-11	Manchester United	38	22	8	8	72	40	52
1911-12	Blackburn Rovers	38	20	9	9	60	43	49
1912-13	Sunderland	38	25	4	9	86	43	54
1913-14	Blackburn Rovers	38	20	11	7	78	42	51
1914-15	Everton	38	19	8	11	76	47	46
	World War I							
1919-20	West Bromwich Albion	42	28	4	10	104	47	60
1920-21	Burnley	42	23	13	6	79	36	59
1921-22	Liverpool	42	22	13	7	63	36	57
1922-23	Liverpool	42	26	8	8	70	31	60

Season	Champions	P	W	D	L	F	A	Pts
1923-24	Huddersfield Town *	42	23	11	8	60	33	57
1924-25	Huddersfield Town	42	21	16	5	69	28	58
1925-26	Huddersfield Town	42	23	11	8	92	60	57
1926-27	Newcastle United	42	25	6	11	96	58	56
1927-28	Everton	42	20	13	9	102	66	53
1928-29	Sheffield Wednesday	42	21	10	11	86	62	52
1929-30	Sheffield Wednesday	42	26	8	8	105	57	60
1930-31	Arsenal	42	28	10	4	127	59	66
1931-32	Everton	42	26	4	12	116	64	56
1932-33	Arsenal	42	25	8	9	118	61	58
1933-34	Arsenal	42	25	9	8	75	47	59
1934-35	Arsenal	42	23	12	7	115	46	58
1935-36	Sunderland	42	25	6	11	109	74	56
1936-37	Manchester City	42	22	13	7	107	61	57
1937-38	Arsenal	42	21	10	11	77	44	52
1938-39	Everton	42	27	5	10	88	52	59
	World War II							
1946-47	Liverpool	42	25	7	10	84	52	57
1947-48	Arsenal	42	23	13	6	81	32	59
1948-49	Portsmouth	42	25	8	9	84	42	58
1949-50	Portsmouth *	42	22	9	11	74	38	53
1950-51	Tottenham Hotspur	42	25	10	7	82	44	60
1951-52	Manchester United	42	23	11	8	95	52	57
1952-53	Arsenal *	42	21	12	9	97	64	54
1953-54	Wolverhampton W.	42	25	7	10	96	56	57
1954-55	Chelsea	42	20	12	10	81	57	52
1955-56	Manchester United	42	25	10	7	83	51	60
1956-57	Manchester United	42	28	8	6	103	54	64
1957-58	Wolverhampton W.	42	28	8	6	103	47	64
1958-59	Wolverhampton W.	42	28	5	9	110	49	61
1959-60	Burnley	42	24	7	11	85	61	55
1960-61	Tottenham Hotspur	42	31	4	7	115	55	66
1961-62	Ipswich Town	42	24	8	10	93	67	56
1962-63	Everton	42	25	11	6	84	42	61
1963-64	Liverpool	42	26	5	11	92	45	57
1964-65	Manchester United *	42	26	9	7	89	39	61
1965-66	Liverpool	42	26	9	7	79	34	61
1966-67	Manchester United	42	24	12	6	84	45	60
1967-68	Manchester City	42	26	6	10	86	43	58
1968-69	Leeds United	42	27	13	2	66	26	67
1969-70	Everton	42	29	8	5	72	34	66
1970-71	Arsenal	42	29	7	6	71	29	65
1971-72	Derby County	42	24	10	8	69	33	58

Season	Champions	P	W	D	L	F	A	Pts
1972-73	Liverpool	42	25	10	7	72	42	60
1973-74	Leeds United	42	24	14	4	66	31	62
1974-75	Derby County	42	21	11	10	67	49	53
1975-76	Liverpool	42	23	14	5	66	31	60
1976-77	Liverpool	42	23	11	8	62	33	57
1977-78	Nottingham Forest	42	25	14	3	69	24	64
1978-79	Liverpool	42	30	8	4	85	16	68
1979-80	Liverpool	42	25	10	7	81	30	60
1980-81	Aston Villa	42	26	8	8	72	40	60
1981-82	Liverpool	42	26	9	7	80	32	87
1982-83	Liverpool	42	24	10	8	87	37	82
1983-84	Liverpool	42	22	14	6	73	32	80
1984-85	Everton	42	28	6	8	88	43	90
1985-86	Liverpool	42	26	10	6	89	37	88
1986-87	Everton	42	26	8	8	76	31	86
1987-88	Liverpool	40	26	12	2	87	24	90
1988-89	Arsenal †	38	22	10	6	73	36	76
1989-90	Liverpool	38	23	10	5	78	37	79
1990-91	Arsenal +	38	24	13	1	74	18	83
1991-92	Leeds United	42	22	16	4	74	37	82

FA PREMIER LEAGUE

Season	Champions	P	W	D	L	F	A	Pts
1992-93	Manchester United	42	24	12	6	67	31	84
1993-94	Manchester United	42	27	11	4	80	38	92
1994-95	Blackburn Rovers	42	27	8	7	80	39	89
1995-96	Manchester United	38	25	7	6	73	35	82
1996-97	Manchester United	38	21	12	5	76	44	75

* won on goal average/goal difference
† won on goals scored
+ 2 points deducted

CHAMPIONSHIP WINS BY CLUB

FA Premier League and Football League Combined

Liverpool (18)	1901, 1906, 1922, 1923, 1947, 1964, 1966, 1973, 1976, 1977, 1979, 1980, 1982, 1983, 1984, 1986, 1988, 1990
Manchester United (11)	1908, 1911, 1952, 1956, 1957, 1965, 1967, 1993, 1994, 1996, 1997
Arsenal (10)	1931, 1933, 1934, 1935, 1938, 1948, 1953, 1971, 1989, 1991
Everton (9)	1891, 1915, 1927, 1932, 1934, 1963, 1970, 1985, 1987
Aston Villa (7)	1894, 1896, 1897, 1899, 1900, 1910, 1981
Sunderland (6)	1892, 1893, 1895, 1902, 1913, 1936
Newcastle United (4)	1905, 1907, 1909, 1927
Sheffield Wednesday (4)	1903, 1904, 1929, 1930
Huddersfield Town (3)	1924, 1925, 1926
Leeds United (3)	1966, 1974, 1992
Wolverhampton W. (3)	1954, 1958, 1959
Blackburn Rovers (3)	1912, 1914, 1995
Portsmouth (2)	1949, 1950
Preston NE (2)	1889, 1900
Burnley (2)	1921, 1960
Manchester City (2)	1937, 1968
Tottenham Hotspur (2)	1951, 1961
Derby County (2)	1972, 1975
Chelsea (1)	1955
Sheffield United (1)	1898
WBA (1)	1920
Ipswich Town (1)	1962
Nottingham Forest (1)	1978

FA CHALLENGE CUP
1996-97 Sponsored by Littlewoods

Note: Dates given are for official date of round – games may have taken place on different dates. † = after extra time.

Third Round – 4 January 1997

Arsenal	v	Sunderland	1-1	37,793
Barnsley	v	Oldham Athletic	2-0	9,936
Blackburn Rovers	v	Port Vale	1-0	19,891
Brentford	v	Manchester City	0-1	12,019
Carlisle	v	Tranmere Rovers	1-0	10,090
Charlton Athletic	v	Newcastle United	1-1	15,000
Chelsea	v	West Bromwich Albion	3-0	27,446
Chesterfield	v	Bristol City	2-0	5,193
Coventry City	v	Woking	1-1	16,040
Crewe Alexandra	v	Wimbledon	1-1	5,001
Crystal Palace	v	Leeds United	2-2	21,052
Everton	v	Swindon Town	3-0	20,411
Gillingham	v	Derby County	0-2	9,508
Hednesford Town	v	York City	1-0	3,169
Leicester City	v	Southend United	2-0	13,982
Liverpool	v	Burnley	1-0	33,252
Luton Town	v	Bolton Wanderers	1-1	7,414
Manchester United	v	Tottenham Hotspur	2-0	52,445
Middlesbrough	v	Chester City	6-0	18,684
Norwich City	v	Sheffield United	1-0	12,356
Nottingham Forest	v	Ipswich Town	3-0	14,681
Notts County	v	Aston Villa	0-0	13,315
Plymouth Argyle	v	Peterborough United	0-1	7,299
Queens Park Rangers	v	Huddersfield Town	1-1	11,776
Reading	v	Southampton	3-1	11,537
Sheffield Wednesday	v	Grimsby Town	7-1	20,590
Stevenage Borough	v	Birmingham City	0-2	15,365
		at Birmingham City FC		
Stoke City	v	Stockport County	0-2	9,961
Watford	v	Oxford United	2-0	9,502
Wolverhampton W.	v	Portsmouth	1-2	23,626
Wrexham	v	West Ham United	1-1	9,747

| Wycombe | v | Bradford City | 0-2 | 5,173 |

Third Round Replays

Aston Villa	v	Notts Co.	3-0	25,006
Bolton Wanderers	v	Luton Town	6-2	9,713
Huddersfield Town	v	Queens Park Rangers	1-2	18,813
Leeds United	v	Crystal Palace	1-0	21,903
Newcastle United	v	Charlton Athletic	2-1 †	36,639
Sunderland	v	Arsenal	0-2	15,518
West Ham United	v	Wrexham	0-1	16,763
Wimbledon	v	Crewe Alexandra	2-0	4,951
Woking	v	Coventry City	1-2	6,000

Fourth Round – 27 January 1997

Arsenal	v	Leeds United	0-1	38,115
Birmingham City	v	Stockport County	3-1	18,487
Blackburn Rovers	v	Coventry City	1-2	21,123
Bolton Wanderers	v	Chesterfield	2-3	10,854
Carlisle United	v	Sheffield Wednesday	0-2	16,104
Chelsea	v	Liverpool	4-2	27,950
Derby County	v	Aston Villa	3-1	17,977
Everton	v	Bradford City	2-3	30,007
Hednesford Town	v	Middlesbrough	2-3	27,511
		at Middlesbrough FC		
Leicester City	v	Norwich City	2-1	16,703
Manchester City	v	Watford	3-1	24,031
Manchester United	v	Wimbledon	1-1	53,342
Newcastle United	v	Nottingham Forest	1-2	36,434
Peterborough United	v	Wrexham	2-4	8,734
Portsmouth	v	Reading	3-0	15,003
Queens Park Rangers	v	Barnsley	3-2	14,317

Fourth Round Replays

| Wimbledon | v | Manchester United | 1-0 | 25,601 |

Fifth Round – 15 February 1997

Birmingham City	v	Wrexham	1-3	21,511
Bradford City	v	Sheffield Wednesday	0-1	17,830
Chesterfield	v	Nottingham Forest	1-0	8,890
Derby County	v	Coventry	3-2	18,003
Leeds United	v	Portsmouth	2-3	35,604
Leicester City	v	Chelsea	2-2	19,125

| Manchester City | v | Middlesbrough | 0-1 | 30,462 |
| Wimbledon | v | Queens Park Rangers | 2-1 | 22,395 |

Fifth Round Replays

| Chelsea | v | Leicester City | 1-0 | 26,053 |

Sixth Round – 8 March 1997

Chesterfield	v	Wrexham	1-0	8,735
Derby County	v	Middlesbrough	0-2	17,567
Portsmouth	v	Chelsea	1-4	15,701
Sheffield Wednesday	v	Wimbledon	0-2	25,032

Semi Finals – 13 April 1997

Middlesbrough	v	Chesterfield	3-3 †	49,640
		at Manchester United FC		
Wimbledon	v	Chelsea	0-3	32,674
		at Arsenal FC		

Semi Final Replay

| Chesterfield | v | Middlesbrough | 0-3 | 30,339 |
| | | *at Sheffield Wednesday FC* | | |

Final – 17 May 1996 at Wembley Stadium

| Chelsea | v | Middlesbrough | 2-0 | 79,160 |

Di Matteo (1), Newton (83)

Chelsea: Grodas, Clarke, Leboeuf, Sinclair, Minto, Petrescu, Newton, Di Matteo, Wise, Zola (Vialli 88), Hughes M. Subs not used: Myers, Hitchcock.
Booked: Newton, Di Matteo, Leboeuf.

Middlesbrough: Roberts, Fleming, Festa, Pearson, Blackmore, Hignett (Kinder 75), Stamp, Emerson, Mustoe (Vickers 28), Juninho, Ravanelli (Beck 23).
Booked: Festa.

Referee: Mr S. Lodge (Barnsley).

† after extra time

FA CHALLENGE CUP FINALS 1872-1997

Year	Winners	Runners-up	Score
1872	The Wanderers	Royal Engineers	1-0
1873	The Wanderers	Oxford University	2-0
1874	Oxford University	Royal Engineers	2-0
1875	Royal Engineers	Old Etonians	1-1
	Royal Engineers	Old Etonians	2-0
1876	The Wanderers	Old Etonians	1-1 †
	The Wanderers	Old Etonians	3-0
1877	The Wanderers	Oxford University	2-1 †
1878	The Wanderers*	Royal Engineers	3-1
1879	Old Etonians	Clapham Rovers	1-0
1880	Clapham Rovers	Oxford University	1-0
1881	Old Carthusians	Old Etonians	3-0
1882	Old Etonians	Blackburn Rovers	1-0
1883	Blackburn Olympic	Old Etonians	2-1 †
1884	Blackburn Rovers	Queen's Park, Glasgow	2-1
1885	Blackburn Rovers	Queen's Park, Glasgow	2-0
1886	Blackburn Rovers**	West Bromwich Albion	0-0
	Blackburn Rovers**	West Bromwich Albion	2-0
1887	Aston Villa	West Bromwich Albion	2-0
1888	West Bromwich Albion	Preston North End	2-1
1889	Preston North End	Wolverhampton Wanderers	3-0
1890	Blackburn Rovers	Sheffield Wednesday	6-1
1891	Blackburn Rovers	Notts County	3-1
1892	West Bromwich Albion	Aston Villa	3-0
1893	Wolverhampton Wanderers	Everton	1-0
1894	Notts County	Bolton Wanderers	4-1
1895	Aston Villa	West Bromwich Albion	1-0
1896	Sheffield Wednesday	Wolverhampton Wanderers	2-1
1897	Aston Villa	Everton	3-2
1898	Nottingham Forest	Derby County	3-1
1899	Sheffield United	Derby County	4-1
1900	Bury	Southampton	4-0
1901	Tottenham Hotspur	Sheffield United	2-2
	Tottenham Hotspur	Sheffield United	3-1
1902	Sheffield United	Southampton	1-1
	Sheffield United	Southampton	2-1
1903	Bury	Derby County	6-0

Year	Winners	Runners-up	Score
1904	Manchester City	Bolton Wanderers	1-0
1905	Aston Villa	Newcastle United	2-0
1906	Everton	Newcastle United	1-0
1907	Sheffield Wednesday	Everton	2-1
1908	Wolverhampton Wanderers	Newcastle United	3-1
1909	Manchester United	Bristol City	1-0
1910	Newcastle United	Barnsley	1-1
	Newcastle United	Barnsley	2-0
1911	Bradford City	Newcastle United	0-0
	Bradford City	Newcastle United	1-0
1912	Barnsley	West Bromwich Albion	0-0 †
	Barnsley	West Bromwich Albion	1-0
1913	Aston Villa	Sunderland	1-0
1914	Burnley	Liverpool	1- 0
1915	Sheffield United	Chelsea	3-0
1920	Aston Villa	Huddersfield Town	1-0 †
1921	Tottenham Hotspur	Wolverhampton Wanderers	1-0
1922	Huddersfield Town	Preston North End	1-0
1923	Bolton Wanderers	West Ham United	2-0
1924	Newcastle United	Aston Villa	2-0
1925	Sheffield United	Cardiff City	1-0
1926	Bolton Wanderers	Manchester City	1-0
1927	Cardiff City	Arsenal	1-0
1928	Blackburn Rovers	Huddersfield Town	3-1
1929	Bolton Wanderers	Portsmouth	2-0
1930	Arsenal	Huddersfield Town	2-0
1931	West Bromwich Albion	Birmingham	2-1
1932	Newcastle United	Arsenal	2-1
1933	Everton	Manchester City	3-0
1934	Manchester City	Portsmouth	2-1
1935	Sheffield Wednesday	West Bromwich Albion	4-2
1936	Arsenal	Sheffield United	1-0
1937	Sunderland	Preston North End	3-1
1938	Preston North End	Huddersfield Town	1-0 †
1939	Portsmouth	Wolverhampton Wanderers	4-1
1946	Derby County	Charlton Athletic	4-1 †
1947	Charlton Athletic	Burnley	1-0 †
1948	Manchester United	Blackpool	4-2
1949	Wolverhampton Wanderers	Leicester City	3-1
1950	Arsenal	Liverpool	2-0
1951	Newcastle United	Blackpool	2-0
1952	Newcastle United	Arsenal	1-0
1953	Blackpool	Bolton Wanderers	4-3

Year	Winners	Runners-up	Score
1954	West Bromwich Albion	Preston North End	3-2
1955	Newcastle United	Manchester City	3-1
1956	Manchester City	Birmingham City	3-1
1957	Aston Villa	Manchester United	2-1
1958	Bolton Wanderers	Manchester United	2-0
1959	Nottingham Forest	Luton Town	2-1
1960	Wolverhampton Wanderers	Blackburn Rovers	3-0
1961	Tottenham Hotspur	Leicester City	2-0
1962	Tottenham Hotspur	Burnley	3-1
1963	Manchester United	Leicester City	3-1
1964	West Ham United	Preston North End	3-2
1965	Liverpool	Leeds United	2-1 †
1966	Everton	Sheffield Wednesday	3-2
1967	Tottenham Hotspur	Chelsea	2-1
1968	West Bromwich Albion	Everton	1-0 †
1969	Manchester City	Leicester City	1-0
1970	Chelsea	Leeds United	2-2 †
	Chelsea	Leeds United	2-1 †
1971	Arsenal	Liverpool	2-1 †
1972	Leeds United	Arsenal	1-0
1973	Sunderland	Leeds United	1-0
1974	Liverpool	Newcastle United	3-0
1975	West Ham United	Fulham	2-0
1976	Southampton	Manchester United	1-0
1977	Manchester United	Liverpool	2-1
1978	Ipswich Town	Arsenal	1-0
1979	Arsenal	Manchester United	3-2
1980	West Ham United	Arsenal	1-0
1981	Tottenham Hotspur	Manchester City	1-1 †
	Tottenham Hotspur	Manchester City	3-2
1982	Tottenham Hotspur	Queens Park Rangers	1-1 †
	Tottenham Hotspur	Queens Park Rangers	1-0
1983	Manchester United	Brighton & Hove Albion	2-2
	Manchester United	Brighton & Hove Albion	4-0
1984	Everton	Watford	2-0
1985	Manchester United	Everton	1-0 †
1986	Liverpool	Everton	3- 1
1987	Coventry City	Tottenham Hotspur	3-2 †
1988	Wimbledon	Liverpool	1-0
1989	Liverpool	Everton	3-2 †
1990	Manchester United	Crystal Palace	3-3 †
	Manchester United	Crystal Palace	1-0
1991	Tottenham Hotspur	Nottingham Forest	2-1 †

Year	Winners	Runners-up	Score
1992	Liverpool	Sunderland	2-0
1993	Arsenal	Sheffield Wednesday	1-1 †
	Arsenal	Sheffield Wednesday	2-1 †
1994	Manchester United	Chelsea	4-0
1995	Everton	Manchester United	1-0
1996	Manchester United	Liverpool	1-0
1997	Chelsea	Middlesbrough	2-0

Final Venues

1872	Kennington Oval
1873	Lillie Bridge
1874-92	Kennington Oval
1893	Fallowfield, Manchester
1894	Everton
1895-1914	Crystal Palace
1915	Old Trafford
1920-22	Stamford Bridge
1923-1997	Wembley

Replay Venues

1886	Derby
1901	Bolton
1910	Everton
1911	Old Trafford
1912	Bramall Lane
1970	Old Trafford
1981	Wembley
1982	Wembley
1983	Wembley
1990	Wembley
1993	Wembley

* *Trophy won outright by The Wanderers, but restored to the FA.*
** *Special trophy awarded for a third consecutive win.*
† *after extra time.*

FA CHALLENGE CUP WINS BY CLUB

Manchester United (9)	1909, 1948, 1963, 1977, 1983, 1985, 1990, 1994, 1996
Tottenham Hotspur (8)	1901, 1921, 1961, 1962, 1967, 1981, 1982, 1991
Aston Villa (7)	1887, 1895, 1897, 1905, 1913, 1920, 1957
Arsenal (6)	1930, 1936, 1950, 1971, 1979, 1993
Blackburn Rovers (6)	1884, 1885, 1886, 1890, 1891, 1928
Newcastle United (6)	1910, 1924, 1932, 1951, 1952, 1955
Everton (5)	1894, 1906, 1933, 1966, 1995
Liverpool (5)	1965, 1974, 1986, 1989, 1992
The Wanderers (5)	1872, 1873, 1876, 1877, 1878
West Bromwich Albion (5)	1888, 1892, 1931, 1954, 1968
Bolton Wanderers (4)	1923, 1926, 1929, 1958
Manchester City (4)	1904, 1934, 1956, 1969
Sheffield United (4)	1899, 1902, 1915, 1925
Wolverhampton Wdrs (4)	1893, 1908, 1949, 1960
Sheffield Wednesday (3)	1896, 1907, 1935
West Ham United (3)	1964, 1975, 1980
Bury (2)	1900, 1903
Chelsea (2)	1970, 1997
Nottingham Forest (2)	1898, 1959
Old Etonians (2)	1879, 1882
Preston North End (2)	1889, 1938
Sunderland (2)	1937, 1973

Club	Year	Club	Year
Barnsley	1912	Notts County	1894
Blackburn Olympic	1883	Old Carthusians	1881
Blackpool	1953	Oxford University	1874
Bradford City	1911	Portsmouth	1939
Burnley	1914	Royal Engineers	1875
Cardiff City	1927	Southampton	1976
Charlton Athletic	1947	Wimbledon	1988
Clapham Rovers	1880		
Coventry City	1987		
Derby County	1946		
Huddersfield Town	1922		
Ipswich Town	1978		
Leeds United	1972		

FA CHARITY SHIELD WINNERS 1908-96

1908	Manchester United v Queens Park Rangers	4-0	
	after 1-1 draw		
1909	Newcastle United v Northampton Town	2-0	
1910	Brighton & Hove Albion v Aston Villa	1-0	
1911	Manchester United v Swindon Town	8-4	
1912	Blackburn Rovers v Queens Park Rangers	2-1	
1913	Professionals v Amateurs	7-2	
1919	West Bromwich Albion v Tottenham Hotspur	2-0	
1920	Tottenham Hotspur v Burnley	2-0	
1921	Huddersfield Town v Liverpool	1-0	
1922	*Not Played*		
1923	Professionals v Amateurs	2-0	
1924	Professionals v Amateurs	3-1	
1925	Amateurs v Professionals	6-1	
1926	Amateurs v Professionals	6-3	
1927	Cardiff City v Corinthians	2-1	
1928	Everton v Blackburn Rovers	2-1	
1929	Professionals v Amateurs	3-0	
1930	Arsenal v Sheffield Wednesday	2-1	
1931	Arsenal v West Bromwich Albion	1-0	
1932	Everton v Newcastle United	5-3	
1933	Arsenal v Everton	3-0	
1934	Arsenal v Manchester City	4-0	
1935	Sheffield Wednesday v Arsenal	1-0	
1936	Sunderland v Arsenal	2-1	
1937	Manchester City v Sunderland	2-0	
1938	Arsenal v Preston North End	2-1	
1948	Arsenal v Manchester United	4-3	
1949	Portsmouth v Wolverhampton Wanderers	1-1	*
1950	World Cup Team v Canadian Touring Team	4-2	
1951	Tottenham Hotspur v Newcastle United	2-1	
1952	Manchester United v Newcastle United	4-2	
1953	Arsenal v Blackpool	3-1	*
1954	Wolverhampton Wanderers v West Bromwich Albion	4-4	*
1955	Chelsea v Newcastle United	3-0	
1956	Manchester United v Manchester City	1-0	
1957	Manchester United v Aston Villa	4-0	

1958	Bolton Wanderers v Wolverhampton Wanderers	 4-1	
1959	Wolverhampton Wanderers v Nottingham Forest	 3-1	
1960	Burnley v Wolverhampton Wanderers 2-2		*
1961	Tottenham Hotspur v FA XI... 3-2		
1962	Tottenham Hotspur v Ipswich Town 5-1		
1963	Everton v Manchester United 4-0		
1964	Liverpool v West Ham United 2-2		*
1965	Manchester United v Liverpool 2-2		*
1966	Liverpool v Everton 1-0		
1967	Manchester United v Tottenham Hotspur... 3-3		*
1968	Manchester City v West Bromwich Albion 6-1		
1969	Leeds United v Manchester City 2-1		
1970	Everton v Chelsea 2-1		
1971	Leicester City v Liverpool 1-0		
1972	Manchester City v Aston Villa 1-0		
1973	Burnley v Manchester City 1-0		
1974	Liverpool v Leeds United 1-1		
	Liverpool won on penalties		
1975	Derby County v West Ham United... 2-0		
1976	Liverpool v Southampton 1-0		
1977	Liverpool v Manchester United 0-0		*
1978	Nottingham Forest v Ipswich Town 5-0		
1979	Liverpool v Arsenal 3-1		
1980	Liverpool v West Ham United 1-0		
1981	Aston Villa v Tottenham Hotspur 2-2		*
1982	Liverpool v Tottenham Hotspur... 1-0		
1983	Manchester United v Liverpool 2-0		
1984	Everton v Liverpool 1-0		
1985	Everton v Manchester United 2-0		
1986	Everton v Liverpool 1-1		*
1987	Everton v Coventry City 1-0		
1988	Liverpool v Wimbledon 2-1		
1989	Liverpool v Arsenal 1-0		
1990	Liverpool v Manchester United 1-1		*
1991	Arsenal v Tottenham Hotspur 0-0		*
1992	Leeds United v Liverpool 4-3		
1993	Manchester United v Arsenal 1-1		
	Manchester United won on penalties		
1994	Manchester United v Blackburn Rovers 2-0		
1995	Everton v Blackburn Rovers... 1-0		
1996	Manchester United v Newcastle United 4-0		
1997	Manchester United v Chelsea		

Each club retained Shield for six months

COCA-COLA FOOTBALL LEAGUE CUP 96-97

Second Round

			1st	2nd	Agg
Barnet	v	West Ham United	1-1	0-1	1-2
Barnsley	v	Gillingham	1-1	0-1	1-2
Blackpool	v	Chelsea	1-4	3-1	4-5
Brentford	v	Blackburn Rovers	1-2	0-2	1-4
Bristol City	v	Bolton Wanderers	0-0	1-3	1-3
Bury	v	Crystal Palace	1-3	0-4	1-7
Charlton Athletic	v	Burnley	4-1	2-1	6-2
Coventry City	v	Birmingham City	1-1	1-0	2-1
Everton	v	York City	1-1	2-3	3-4
Fulham	v	Ipswich Town	1-1	2-4	3-5
Huddersfield Town	v	Colchester United	1-1	2-0	3-1
Leeds United	v	Darlington	2-2	2-0	4-2
Lincoln City	v	Manchester City	4-1	1-0	5-1
Luton Town	v	Derby County	1-0	2-2	3-2
Middlesbrough	v	Hereford United	7-0	3-0	10-0
Nottingham Forest	v	Wycombe Wanderers	1-0	1-1	2-1
Oldham Athletic	v	Tranmere Rovers	2-2	1-0	3-2
Port Vale	v	Carlisle United	1-0	2-2	3-2
Preston NE	v	Tottenham Hotspur	1-1	0-3	1-4
Scarborough	v	Leicester City	0-2	1-2	1-4
Sheffield Wednesday	v	Oxford United	1-1	0-1	1-2
Southampton	v	Peterborough United	2-0	4-1	6-1
Stockport County	v	Sheffield United	2-1	5-2	7-3
Stoke City	v	Northampton Town	1-0	2-1	3-1
Swindon Town	v	QPR	1-2	3-1	4-3
Watford	v	Sunderland	0-2	0-1	0-3
Wimbledon	v	Portsmouth	1-0	1-1	2-1

Byes: Arsenal, Aston Villa, Liverpool, Manchester United, Newcastle United.

Third Round

Blackburn Rovers	v	Stockport County	0-1	14,622
Bolton Wanderers	v	Chelsea	2-1	16,867
Charlton Athletic	v	Liverpool	1-1	15,000
Gillingham	v	Coventry City	2-2	10,603
Ipswich Town	v	Crystal Palace	4-1	8,390
Leeds United	v	Aston Villa	1-2	15,803

Manchester United	v	Swindon Town	2-1	49,305
Middlesbrough	v	Huddersfield Town	5-1	26,615
Newcastle United	v	Oldham Athletic	1-0	36,314
Port Vale	v	Oxford United	0-0	4,942
Southampton	v	Lincoln City	2-2	14,516
Stoke City	v	Arsenal	1-1	20,804
Tottenham Hotspur	v	Sunderland	2-1	24,867
West Ham United	v	Nottingham Forest	4-1	19,402
Wimbledon	v	Luton Town	1-1	5,043
York City	v	Leicester City	0-2	8,406

Third Round Replays

Arsenal	v	Stoke City	5-2	33,962
Coventry City	v	Gillingham	0-1	12,639
Lincoln City	v	Southampton	1-3	10,523
Liverpool	v	Charlton Athletic	4-1	20,714
Luton Town	v	Wimbledon	1-2	8,076
Oxford United	v	Port Vale	2-0	5,279

Fourth Round

Bolton Wanderers	v	Tottenham Hotspur	6-1	18,621
Ipswich Town	v	Gillingham	1-0	13,537
Leicester City	v	Manchester United	2-0	20,428
Liverpool	v	Arsenal	4-2	32,814
Middlesbrough	v	Newcastle United	3-1	29,831
Oxford United	v	Southampton	1-1	9,473
West Ham United	v	Stockport County	1-1	20,061
Wimbledon	v	Aston Villa	1-0	7,573

Fourth Round Replays

| Southampton | v | Oxford United | 3-2 | 10,737 |
| Stockport County | v | West Ham United | 2-1 | 9,834 |

Fifth Round

Bolton Wanderers	v	Wimbledon	0-2	16,968
Middlesbrough	v	Liverpool	2-1	28,670
Ipswich Town	v	Leicester City	0-1	20,793
Stockport County	v	Southampton	2-2	9,840

Fifth Round Replays

| Southampton | v | Stockport County | 1-2 | 13,428 |

Semi-Finals First Leg

| Leicester City | v | Wimbledon | 0-0 | 16,021 |
| Stockport County | v | Middlesbrough | 0-2 | 11,778 |

Semi-Finals Second Leg

| Wimbledon | v | Leicester City | 1-1 | 17,810 |

(1-1 on aggregate. Leicester City win on away goals)

| Middlesbrough | v | Stockport County | 0-1 | 29,633 |

(Middlesbrough win 2-1 on aggregate)

Final – 6th April 1997 at Wembley Stadium

| Leicester City | v | Middlesbrough | 1-1 | 76,757 |
| Heskey (117) | | Ravanelli (95) | | aet |

Leicester City: Keller, Grayson, Whitlow (Robins 106), Walsh, Prior, Kaamark, Lennon, Parker, Izzet (Taylor 108), Heskey, Claridge. Sub not used: Poole.
Middlesbrough: Schwarzer, Fleming, Festa, Pearson, Cox, Emerson, Hignett, Mustoe, Ravanelli, Juninho, Beck. Subs not used: Vickers, Moore, Blackmore.
Ref: M. Bodenham.

Replay – 16th April 1997 at Hillsborough, Sheffield

| Leicester City | v | Middlesbrough | 1-0 | 39,428 |
| Claridge (100) | | | | aet |

Leicester City: Keller, Grayson, Whitlow (Lawrence 113),Walsh, Izzet, Lennon, Claridge (Robins 117), Kaamark, Parker, Prior, Heskey. Sub not used: Poole.
Middlesbrough: Roberts, Cox (Moore 106), Pearson, Emerson, Kinder, Mustoe, Juninho, Ravanelli, Blackmore, Festa (Vickers 76), Hignett (Beck 106).
Ref: M. Bodenham.

FOOTBALL LEAGUE CUP FINALS 1961-1997

Year	Winners	Runners-up	1st	2nd	Agg
1961	Aston Villa	Rotherham United	0-2	†3-0	3-2
1962	Norwich City	Rochdale	3-0	1-0	4-0
1963	Birmingham City	Aston Villa	3-1	0-0	3-1
1964	Leicester City	Stoke City	1-1	3-2	4-3
1965	Chelsea	Leicester City	3-2	0-0	3-2
1966	West Bromwich Albion	West Ham United	1-2	4-1	5-3
1967	Queens Park Rangers	West Bromwich Albion	3-2		
1968	Leeds United	Arsenal	1-0		
1969	Swindon Town	Arsenal	† 3-1		
1970	Manchester City	West Bromwich Albion	2-1		
1971	Tottenham Hotspur	Aston Villa	† 2-0		
1972	Stoke City	Chelsea	2-1		
1973	Tottenham Hotspur	Norwich City	1-0		
1974	Wolverhampton W.	Manchester City	2-1		
1975	Aston Villa	Norwich City	1-0		
1976	Manchester City	Newcastle United	2-1		
1977	Aston Villa	Everton	† 3-2		
	after 0-0 draw and 1-1 draw aet				
1978	Nottingham Forest	Liverpool	1-0		
	after 0-0 draw aet				
1979	Nottingham Forest	Southampton	3-2		
1980	Wolverhampton W.	Nottingham Forest	1-0		
1981	Liverpool	West Ham United	2-1		
	after 1-1 draw aet				

Milk Cup

1982	Liverpool	Tottenham Hotspur	† 3-1		
1983	Liverpool	Manchester United	† 2-1		
1984	Liverpool	Everton	1-0		
	after 0-0 draw aet				
1985	Norwich City	Sunderland	1-0		
1986	Oxford United	Queens Park Rangers	3-0		

Littlewoods Cup

1987	Arsenal	Liverpool	2-1		
1988	Luton Town	Arsenal	3-2		

| 1989 | Nottingham Forest | Luton Town | 3-1 |
| 1990 | Nottingham Forest | Oldham Athletic | 1-0 |

Rumbelows League Cup

| 1991 | Sheffield Wednesday | Manchester United | 1-0 |
| 1992 | Manchester United | Nottingham Forest | 1-0 |

Coca-Cola Cup

1993	Arsenal	Sheffield Wednesday	2-1
1994	Aston Villa	Manchester United	3-1
1995	Liverpool	Bolton Wanderers	2-1
1996	Aston Villa	Leeds United	3-0
1997	Leicester City	Middlesbrough	†1-0
	after 1-1 aet draw at Wembley		

† *after extra time*

FOOTBALL LEAGUE CUP WINS BY CLUB

Aston Villa (5) 1961, 1975, 1977, 1994, 1996
Liverpool (5) 1981, 1982, 1983, 1984, 1995
Nottingham Forest (4) 1978, 1979, 1989, 1990
Arsenal (2) 1987, 1993
Manchester City (2) 1970, 1976
Tottenham Hotspur (2) 1971, 1973
Norwich City (2) 1962, 1985
Wolverhampton Wders (2) 1974, 1980
Leicester City (2) 1964, 1997
Birmingham City 1963
Chelsea 1965
WBA 1966
QPR 1967
Leeds United 1968
Swindon Town 1969
Stoke City 1972
Oxford United 1986
Luton Town 1988
Sheffield Wednesday 1991
Manchester United 1992

FWA FOOTBALLER OF THE YEAR WINNERS

Season	Winner	Club
1947-48	Stanley Matthews	Blackpool & England
1948-49	Johnny Carey	Manchester United & Rep of Ireland
1949-50	Joe Mercer	Arsenal & England
1950-51	Harry Johnston	Blackpool & England
1951-52	Billy Wright	Wolverhampton Wanderers & England
1952-53	Nat Lofthouse	Bolton Wanderers & England
1953-54	Tom Finney	Preston North End & England
1954-55	Don Revie	Manchester City & England
1955-56	Bert Trautmann	Manchester City
1956-57	Tom Finney	Preston North End & England
1957-58	Danny Blanchflower	Tottenham Hotspur & Northern Ireland
1958-59	Syd Owen	Luton Town & England
1959-60	Bill Slater	Wolverhampton Wanderers & England
1960-61	Danny Blanchflower	Tottenham Hotspur & Northern Ireland
1961-62	Jimmy Adamson	Burnley
1962-63	Stanley Matthews	Stoke City & England
1963-64	Bobby Moore	West Ham United & England
1964-65	Bobby Collins	Leeds United & Scotland
1965-66	Bobby Charlton	Manchester United & England
1966-67	Jack Charlton	Leeds United & England
1967-68	George Best	Manchester United & Northern Ireland
1968-69	Dave Mackay	Derby County & Scotland
	Tony Book	Manchester City
1969-70	Billy Bremner	Leeds United & Scotland
1970-71	Frank McLintock	Arsenal & Scotland
1971-72	Gordon Banks	Stoke City & England
1972-73	Pat Jennings	Tottenham Hotspur & Northern Ireland
1973-74	Ian Callaghan	Liverpool & England
1974-75	Alan Mullery	Fulham & England
1975-76	Kevin Keegan	Liverpool & England
1976-77	Emlyn Hughes	Liverpool & England
1977-78	Kenny Burns	Nottingham Forest & Scotland
1978-79	Kenny Dalglish	Liverpool & Scotland
1979-80	Terry McDermott	Liverpool & England
1980-81	Frans Thijssen	Ipswich Town & Holland
1981-82	Steve Perryman	Tottenham Hotspur & England
1982-83	Kenny Dalglish	Liverpool & Scotland
1983-84	Ian Rush	Liverpool & Wales
1984-85	Neville Southall	Everton & Wales

1985-86	Gary Lineker	Everton & England
1986-87	Clive Allen	Tottenham Hotspur & England
1987-88	John Barnes	Liverpool & England
1988-89	Steve Nicol	Liverpool & England
1989-90	John Barnes	Liverpool & England
1990-91	Gordon Strachan	Leeds United & Scotland
1991-92	Gary Lineker	Tottenham Hotspur & England
1992-93	Chris Waddle	Sheffield Wednesday & England
1993-94	Alan Shearer	Blackburn Rovers & England
1994-95	Jurgen Klinsmann	Tottenham Hotspur & Germany
1995-96	Eric Cantona	Manchester United & France
1996-97	Gianfranco Zola	Chelsea & Italy

PFA AWARDS 1996-97

Player of the Year
1. Alan Shearer — Newcastle United
2. David Beckham — Manchester United
3. Ian Wright — Arsenal

Young Player of the Year
1. David Beckham — Manchester United
2. Emile Heskey — Leicester City
3. Robbie Fowler — Liverpool

Premiership Team
Goalkeeper	David Seaman	Arsenal
Defenders	Gary Neville	Manchester United
	Stig Inge Bjornebye	Liverpool
	Tony Adams	Arsenal
	Mark Wright	Liverpool
Midfield	David Beckham	Manchester United
	David Batty	Newcastle United
	Roy Keane	Manchester United
	Steve McManaman	Liverpool
Forwards	Ian Wright	Arsenal
	Alan Shearer	Newcastle United

Merit Award
Peter Beardsley — Newcastle United

CLUBS IN EUROPE 96-97

UEFA Champions' League – Manchester United

Group C Matches

Juventus Boksic (33)	**Manchester United**	**1-0**	50,000
Manchester United Solskjaer (20), Beckham (27)	**Rapid Vienna**	**2-0**	51,831
Fenerbahce	**Manchester United** Beckham (54), Cantona (60)	**0-2**	26,200
Manchester United	**Fenerbahce** Bolic (77)	**0-1**	53,297
Manchester United	**Juventus** del Piero (35)	**0-1**	53,529
Rapid Vienna	**Manchester United** Giggs (24), Cantona (72)	**0-2**	50,000

Final Group Table	P	W	D	L	F	A	Pts
Juventus	6	5	1	0	11	1	16
Manchester United	6	3	0	3	6	3	9
Fenerbahce	6	2	1	3	3	6	7
Rapid Vienna	6	0	2	4	2	12	2

Quarter Final

Manchester United May (22), Cantona (34), Giggs (60), Cole (80)	**FC Porto**	**4-0**	53,415
FC Porto	**Manchester United**	**0-0**	47,000

Manchester United win 4-0 on aggregate.

Semi Final

Borussia Dortmund Tretschok (33)	**Manchester United**	**1-0**	48,500
Manchester United	**Borussia Dortmund** Ricken (8)	**0-1**	53,606

Borussia Dortmund win 2-0 on aggregate.

Cup-Winners' Cup – Liverpool

1st Round

My Pa 47	**Liverpool**	**0-1** 5,500
	Bjornebye (61)	

Liverpool	My Pa 47	**3-1** 39,013
Berger (18), Collymore (60), Barnes (77)	Keskitalo (64)	

Liverpool win 4-1 on aggregate.

2nd Round

FC Sion	**Liverpool**	**1-2** 16,500
Bonvin (11)	Fowler (24), Barnes (60)	

Liverpool	FC Sion	**6-3** 38,514
McManaman (28), Bjornebye (54), Barnes (65), Fowler (70, 71), Berger (89)	Chassot (19, 64), Bonvin (23)	

Liverpool win 8-4 on aggregate.

Quarter Final

SK Brann	**Liverpool**	**1-1** 12,700
Hasund (47)	Fowler (9)	

Liverpool	SK Brann	**3-0** 40,326
Fowler (26 pen, 78), Collymore (62)		

Liverpool win 4-1 on aggregate.

Semi Final

Paris St Germain	**Liverpool**	**3-0** 35,142
Leonardo (11), Caudet (43), Leroy (83)		

Liverpool	Paris St Germain	**2-0** 38,984
Fowler (12), Wright (80)		

Paris St Germain win 3-2 on aggregate.

UEFA Cup – Arsenal, Aston Villa, Newcastle Utd

1st Round

Arsenal	**Borussia M'Gladbach**	**2-3** 36,894
Merson (54), Wright (89)	Juskowiak (37), Effenberg (46), Passlack (80)	

Borussia M'Gladbach	Arsenal	**3-2** 35,000
Juskowiak (23, 89), Effenberg (74)	Wright (43), Merson (49)	

Borussia M'Gladbach win 6-4 on aggregate.

Aston Villa	**Helsingborgs**	**1-1** 25,818
Johnson (14)	Wibran (80)	
Helsingborgs	**Aston Villa**	**0-0** 16,000

1-1 on aggregate. Helsingborgs win on away goals.

Newcastle United	**Halmstads**	**4-0** 28,124
Ferdinand (5), Asprilla (26), Albert (51),		
Beardsley (54)		
Halmstads	**Newcastle United**	**2-1** 7,847
Arvidson (74), Svensson H. (79)	Ferdinand (42)	

Newcastle United win 5-2 on aggregate.

2nd Round

Ferencvaros	**Newcastle United**	**3-2** 18,000
Horvath (6), Listzes (17, 56)	Ferdinand (24), Shearer (34)	
Newcastle United	**Ferencvaros**	**4-0** 35,740
Asprilla (42, 58), Ginola (65),		
Ferdinand (90)		

Newcastle United win 6-3 on aggregate.

3rd Round

Metz	**Newcastle United**	**1-1** 23,000
Traore (66)	Beardsley (31 pen)	
Newcastle United	**Metz**	**2-0** 35,641
Asprilla (80, 82)		

Newcastle United win 3-1 on aggregate.

Quarter Final

Newcastle United	**Monaco**	**0-1** 36,215
	Da Silva (59)	
Monaco	**Newcastle United**	**3-0** 14,400
Legwinski (41), Benarbia (50, 70)		

Monaco win 4-0 on aggregate.

UEFA CHAMPIONS' LEAGUE

GROUP A

	W	D	L	F	A	Pt
Auxerre	4	0	2	8	7	12
Ajax	4	0	2	8	4	12
Grasshopper	3	0	3	8	5	9
Rangers	1	0	5	5	13	3

GROUP B

	W	D	L	F	A	Pts
Atletico Madrid	4	1	1	12	4	13
B. Dortmund	4	1	1	14	8	13
Widzew Lodz	1	1	4	6	10	4
Steaua Buch.	1	1	4	4	5	4

GROUP C

	W	D	L	F	A	Pt
Juventus	5	1	0	11	1	16
Manchester Utd	3	0	3	6	3	9
Fenerbahce	2	1	3	3	6	7
Rapid Vienna	0	2	4	2	12	2

GROUP D

	W	D	L	F	A	Pt
FC Porto	5	1	0	12	4	16
Rosenborg	3	0	3	7	11	9
Milan	2	1	3	13	11	7
IFK Gotenburg	1	0	5	7	13	3

Quarter Finals

		1st	2nd	Agg
Ajax	Atletico Madrid	1-1	3-2	4-3
Borussia Dortmund	Auxerre	3-1	1-0	4-1
Manchester United	FC Porto	4-0	0-0	4-0
Rosenborg	Juventus	1-1	0-2	1-3

Semi Finals

		1st	2nd	Agg
Borussia Dortmund	Manchester United	1-0	1-0	2-0
Ajax	Juventus	1-2	1-4	2-6

Final   *Wednesday, May 28 at the Olympic Stadium in Munich.*

Juventus	B. Dortmund	1-3	55,500
Del Piero (64)	Riedle (29, 34), Ricken (71)		

CUP-WINNERS' CUP 1996-97

Quarter Finals

		1st	2nd	Agg
Barcelona	AIK Stockholm	3-1	1-1	4-2
Benfica	Fiorentina	0-2	1-0	1-2
Bran Bergen	Liverpool	1-1	0-3	1-4
Paris St Germain	AEK Athens	0-0	3-0	3-0

Semi Finals

		1st	2nd	Agg
Paris St Germain	Liverpool	3-0	0-2	3-2
Barcelona	Fiorentina	1-1	1-2	2-3

Final *Wednesday, May 14 in Rotterdam*

Barcelona	Fiorentina	1-0	52,000

Ronaldo (37 pen)

UEFA CUP 1996-97

Quarter Finals

		1st	2nd	Agg	
Anderlecht	Internazionale	1-1	1-2	2-3	
Newcastle United	Monaco	0-1	0-3	0-4	
Schalke 04	Valencia	2-0	1-1	3-1	
Tenerife	Brondby	1-1	1-0	2-1	†

Semi Finals

		1st	2nd	Agg	
Internazionale	Monaco	3-1	0-1	3-2	
Tenerife	Schalke 04	1-0	0-2	1-2	†

Final
1st Leg – Wednesday, May 7

Schalke 04	Internazionale	1-0	56,824

Wilmots (70)

2nd Leg – Wednesday, May 21

Internazionale	Schalke 04	1-0	81,675

Zamorano (84)

After extra time. 1-1 on aggregate. Schalke 04 win 4-1 on penalties.

ENGLAND

Kishinev, September 1st 1996 – World Cup Qualifying Group Two
MOLDOVA   **ENGLAND**   **0-3**   **8,000**
Barmby (24), Gascoigne (25), Shearer (61)
England: Seaman, Southgate, Pallister, Pearce, G. Neville, Beckham, Ince, Gascoigne (Batty 81), Hinchcliffe, Barmby (Le Tissier 81), Shearer. Subs not used: Walker (gk), Campbell, Stone, Draper, Ferdinand.

Wembley, October 9th 1996 – World Cup Qualifying Group Two
ENGLAND   **POLAND**   **2-1**   **74,663**
Shearer (24, 38)   Citko (7)
England: Seaman, G. Neville, Southgate (Pallister 51), Pearce, Ince, Beckham, McManaman, Gascoigne, Hinchcliffe, Shearer, Ferdinand. Subs not used: Walker (gk), Campbell, Platt, Le Tissier, Sheringham, Barmby.

Tiblisi, November 9th 1996 – World Cup Qualifying Group Two
GEORGIA   **ENGLAND**   **0-2**   **48,000**
Sheringham (15), Ferdinand (37)
England: Seaman, Campbell, Adams, Southgate, Beckham, Ince, Batty, Gascoigne, Hinchcliffe, Sheringham, Ferdinand (I. Wright 81). Subs not used: Walker (gk), G. Neville, Pearce, Platt, McManaman, Le Tissier.

Wembley, February 12th 1997 – World Cup Qualifying Group Two
ENGLAND   **ITALY**   **0-1**   **75,055**
Zola
England: Walker, G. Neville, Pearce, Campbell, Batty (I. Wright 89), McManaman (Merson 77), Beckham, Le Tissier (Ferdinand 61), Le Saux. Subs not used: James (gk), Southgate, Redknapp, Lee.

Wembley, March 29th 1997 – Friendly International
ENGLAND   **MEXICO**   **2-0**   **48,076**
Sheringham (20), Fowler (55)
England: James, Pearce, Keown, Southgate, Ince, Lee, Batty (Redknapp 52), Le Saux, Fowler, Sheringham (I. Wright 38), McManaman (Butt 68). Subs not used: Flowers (gk), P. Neville, May.

Wembley, April 30th 1997 – World Cup Qualifying Group Two
ENGLAND   **GEORGIA**   **2-0**   **71,208**
Sheringham (43), Shearer (90)
England: Seaman, G. Neville, Campbell, Batty, Adams (Southgate 88), Le Saux, Beckham, Ince (Redknapp 79), Shearer, Sheringham, Lee. Subs not used: Flowers (gk), Ferdinand, P. Neville.

Old Trafford, May 24th 1997 – Friendly International
ENGLAND   SOUTH AFRICA   2-1 52,676
Lee (21), Wright (75)
England: Martyn, P. Neville, Pearce, Keown, Le Saux (Beckham 68),
Redknapp (Batty 56), Gascoigne (Campbell 90), I. Wright, Sheringham
(Scholes 64), Lee (Butt 80). Subs not used: Flowers (gk), Cole.

Katowice, May 31st 1997 – World Cup Qualifying Group Two
POLAND   ENGLAND   0-2 35,000
                Shearer (5), Sheringham (90)
England: Seaman, G. Neville, Southgate, Campbell, Beckham (P. Neville
88), Ince, Gascoigne (Batty 16), Lee, Le Saux, Sheringham, Shearer.
Subs not used: Flowers (gk), Pearce, Keown, Scholes, Wright.

Nantes, June 4th 1997 – Le Tournoi
ENGLAND   ITALY   2-0 25,000
Wright (26), Scholes (43)
England: Flowers, Pearce, Keown, Southgate, P. Neville, Ince, Beckham,
Scholes, Le Saux (G. Neville 46), Sheringham (Gascoigne 79), I. Wright
(Cole 77). Subs not used: Seaman (gk), Shearer, Lee, Campbell, Scales,
Batty, Clark, Martyn (gk).

Montpellier, June 8th 1997 – Le Tournoi
FRANCE   ENGLAND   0-1 25,000
                Shearer (86)
England: Seaman, G. Neville, Southgate, Campbell, P. Neville, Beckham
(Lee 73), Batty (Ince 46), Gascoigne, Le Saux, Shearer, Wright (Sheringham
78). Subs not used: Flowers (gk), Pearce, Keown, Scales, Clark, Scholes,
Cole, Martyn (gk).

Paris, June 10th 1997 – Le Tournoi
BRAZIL   ENGLAND   1-0 50,000
Romario (6)
England: Seaman, Keown (G. Neville 20), Southgate, Campbell, P. Neville,
Ince, Gascoigne, Scholes (Lee 74), Le Saux, Sheringham (Wright 74),
Shearer. Subs not used: Flowers (gk), Pearce, Batty, Scales, Clark, Cole,
Martyn (gk).

Le Tournoi Final Table

	P	W	D	L	F	A	Pts
England … … … … …	3	2	0	1	3	1	6
Brazil … … … … …	3	1	2	0	5	4	5
France … … … … …	3	0	2	1	3	4	2
Italy … … … … …	3	0	2	1	5	7	2

Other Results

Brazil	3	Italy	3
France	2	Italy	2

England Record 1996-97

P	W	D	L	F	A	%
11	9	0	2	18	3	81.81

France '98 Qualification

Group 2

01/09/96	Moldova	England	0-1
05/10/96	Moldova	Italy	1-3
09/10/96	England	Poland	2-1
09/10/96	Italy	Georgia	1-0
09/11/96	Georgia	England	0-2
10/11/96	Poland	Moldova	2-1
12/02/97	England	Italy	0-1
29/03/97	Italy	Moldova	3-0
02/04/97	Poland	Italy	0-0
30/04/97	England	Georgia	2-0
30/04/97	Italy	Poland	3-0
31/05/97	Poland	England	0-2
07/06/97	Georgia	Moldova	2-0
14/06/97	Poland	Georgia	4-1
10/09/97	England	Moldova	
10/09/97	Georgia	Italy	
24/09/97	Moldova	Georgia	
07/10/97	Moldova	Poland	
11/10/97	Italy	England	
11/10/97	Georgia	Poland	

	P	W	D	L	F	A	Pts
Italy … … … … …	6	5	1	0	11	1	16
England … … … …	6	5	0	1	11	2	15
Poland … … … … …	6	2	1	3	7	9	7
Georgia … … … …	5	1	0	4	3	9	3
Moldova … … … …	5	0	0	5	2	13	0

Table as of 16 June 1997.

There are 15 qualifiers from Europe. France qualify as hosts. They are joined by the nine group winners and the best runner-up. The other eight runners-up are drawn against each other and play on a two leg, home and away basis.

These games are played on October 29th and November 19th. The four winners qualify for the finals.

1.	France – hosts	1
2.	Group winners	9
3.	Best runner-up	1
4.	Winners from other runners-up	4
	Total	15

The best runner-up in each group is determined by results against the first, third and fourth placed finishers – this ensures that any goal avelanche against the weakest group teams is not a factor. When teams finish level on points, positions are determined thus: 1, goal difference; 2, goals scored; 3, goal difference in two games between teams level on points. If teams cannot be separated, a play-off on a neutral ground will be used; this to be played on October 19th. The draw for the Finals will be made on December 4th.

Post-War England Manager Records

Manager	Tenure	P	W	D	L	F	A
Glenn Hoddle	7/96-	11	9	0	2	18	3
Terry Venables	01/94-6/96	23	11	11	1	35	13
Graham Taylor	08/90-11/93	38	18	12	8	62	32
Bobby Robson	08/82-07/90	95	47	30	18	158	60
Ron Greenwood	08/77-07/82	56	33	13	10	93	40
Don Revie	10/74-07/77	29	14	8	7	49	25
Joe Mercer	04/74-10/74	7	3	3	1	9	7
Sir Alf Ramsey	01/63-03/74	110	67	26	17	224	98
Sir Walter Winterbottom	08/46-12/62	139	78	33	28	383	196

Euro '96 games v Scotland, Holland, Spain and Germany officially listed as away matches by UEFA, but listed as home by FA. Does not include abandoned match in Dublin, although caps were awarded to players.

Goalscorer Summary 1996-97

	Player	Goals
Alan	SHEARER	8
Teddy	SHERINGHAM	4
Ian	WRIGHT	2
Nick	BARMBY	1
Les	FERDINAND	1
Robbie	FOWLER	1
Paul	GASCOIGNE	1
Robert	LEE	1
Paul	SCHOLES	1

Player Summary 1996-97

	Player	Club	Tot	St	Sub	SNU	PS
Tony	ADAMS	Arsenal	2	2	0	0	1
Nick	BARMBY	Middlesbrough	1	1	0	1	1
David	BATTY	Newcastle United	8	5	3	2	3
David	BECKHAM	Manchester United	9	8	1	0	2
Steve	BOULD	Arsenal	0	0	0	0	0
Nicky	BUTT	Manchester United	2	0	2	0	0
Sol	CAMPBELL	Tottenham Hotspur	7	6	1	3	0
Lee	CLARK	Sunderland	0	0	0	3	0
Andy	COLE	Manchester United	1	0	1	3	0
Stan	COLLYMORE	Liverpool	0	0	0	1	0
Mark	DRAPER	Aston Villa	0	0	0	1	0
Les	FERDINAND	Newcastle United	3	2	1	2	1
Tim	FLOWERS	Blackburn Rovers	1	1	0	5	0
Robbie	FOWLER	Liverpool	1	1	0	1	0
Paul	GASCOIGNE	Rangers	8	7	1	0	3
Andy	HINCHCLIFFE	Everton	3	3	0	0	0
Paul	INCE	Internazionale	10	9	1	0	1
David	JAMES	Liverpool	1	1	0	1	0
Martin	KEOWN	Arsenal	4	4	0	2	1
Graeme	LE SAUX	Blackburn Rovers	8	8	0	0	2
Matt	LE TISSIER	Southampton	2	1	1	2	1
Robert	LEE	Newcastle United	6	4	2	2	1
Nigel	MARTYN	Leeds United	1	1	0	3	0
David	MAY	Manchester United	0	0	0	1	0
Steve	McMANAMAN	Liverpool	3	3	0	1	2
Paul	MERSON	Arsenal	1	0	1	0	0
Gary	NEVILLE	Manchester United	8	6	2	1	0
Phil	NEVILLE	Manchester United	5	4	1	2	0
Gary	PALLISTER	Manchester United	2	1	1	0	0
Stuart	PEARCE	Nottingham Forest	6	6	0	4	0
David	PLATT	Arsenal	0	0	0	2	0
Jamie	REDKNAPP	Liverpool	3	1	2	1	1
John	SCALES	Tottenham Hotspur	0	0	0	3	0
Paul	SCHOLES	Manchester United	3	2	1	2	1
David	SEAMAN	Arsenal	7	7	0	1	0
Alan	SHEARER	Blackburn Rovers	7	7	0	1	0

	Player	*Club*	*Tot*	*St*	*Sub*	*SNU*	*PS*
Teddy	SHERINGHAM	Tottenham Hotspur	8	7	1	1	4
Gareth	SOUTHGATE	Aston Villa	10	9	1	1	1
Steve	STONE	Nottingham Forest	0	0	0	1	0
Ian	WALKER	Tottenham	1	1	0	3	0
Ian	WRIGHT	Arsenal	5	2	3	0	1
Mark	WRIGHT	Liverpool	2	1	1	1	1
	Totals		149	121	28	58	28

1996-97 APPEARANCE CHART

	Moldova	Poland	Georgia	Italy	Mexico	Georgia	S. Africa	Poland	Italy	France	Brazil
ADAMS	-	-	•	-	-	•(88)	-	-	-	-	-
BARMBY	•(81)	*	-	-	-	-	-	-	-	-	-
BATTY	*(81)	-	•	•(89)	•(52)	•	*(56)	*(16)	*	•(46)	*
BECKHAM	•	•	•	•	•	-	*(68)	•(88)	•	•(73)	-
BUTT	-	-	-	-	*(68)	-	*(80)	-	-	-	-
CAMPBELL	*	*	•	•	•	-	*(90)	•	*	•	•
CLARK	-	-	-	-	-	-	-	-	*	*	*
COLE	-	-	-	-	-	-	*	-	*(77)	*	*
COLLYMORE	-	-	-	-	*	-	-	-	-	-	-
DRAPER	*	-	-	-	-	-	-	-	-	-	-
FERDINAND	*	•	•(81)	*(61)	-	*	-	-	-	-	-
FLOWERS	-	-	-	-	*	*	*	*	•	-	*
FOWLER	-	-	-	-	•	-	-	-	-	*	-
GASCOIGNE	•(81)	•	•	•	-	-	•(90)	•(16)	*(79)	•	•
HINCHCLIFFE	•	•	-	-	-	-	-	-	-	-	-
INCE	•	•	•	•	-	•(79)	-	•	•	*(46)	•
JAMES	-	-	-	*	-	-	-	-	-	-	-
KEOWN	-	-	-	-	•	-	•	*	•	*	•(20)
LE SAUX	-	-	-	•	-	•	•(68)	-	•(46)	•	•
LE TISSIER	*(81)	*	*	•(61)	-	-	-	-	-	-	-
LEE	-	-	-	*	-	•	•(80)	-	*	*(73)	*(74)
MARTYN	-	-	-	-	-	-	•	-	*	*	*
MAY	-	-	-	-	*	-	-	-	-	-	-
McMANAMAN	-	•	*	•(77)	•(68)	-	-	-	-	-	-
MERSON	-	-	-	*(77)	-	-	-	-	-	-	-
NEVILLE G.	•	•	*	•	•	-	-	-	*(46)	•	*(20)
NEVILLE P.	-	-	-	-	*	*	•	*(88)	•	-	•
PALLISTER	•	*(51)	-	-	-	-	-	-	-	-	-
PEARCE	•	•	*	•	-	-	•	*	•	*	*
PLATT	-	*	*	-	-	-	-	-	-	-	-
REDKNAPP	-	-	-	*	*(52)	*(79)	•(56)	-	-	-	-
SCALES	-	-	-	-	-	-	-	-	*	*	*
SCHOLES	-	-	-	-	-	-	*(64)	*	•	*	•(74)
SEAMAN	•	•	•	-	-	-	-	-	•	*	•

• Started match. * Substitute - No appearance. A number next to an * indicates an

	Moldova	Poland	Georgia	Italy	Mexico	Georgia	S. Africa	Poland	Italy	France	Brazil
SHEARER	•	•	-	•	-	•	-	•	*	•	•
SHERINGHAM	-	*	•	-	•(38)	•	•(64)	•	•(79)	*(78)	•(74)
SOUTHGATE	•	•(51)	•	*	•	*(88)	•	•	•	-	-
STONE	*	-	-	-	-	-	-	-	-	-	-
WALKER	*	*	*	-	-	-	-	-	-	-	-
WRIGHT I.	-	-	-	*(89)	*(38)	-	•	*	•(77)	-	*(74)
WRIGHT M.	-	-	*(81)	-	-	-	-	-	-	•(78)	-

CLUB DIRECTORY
1997-98

Arsenal
Aston Villa
Barnsley
Blackburn Rovers
Bolton Wanderers
Chelsea
Coventry City
Crystal Palace
Derby County
Everton
Leeds United
Leicester City
Liverpool
Manchester United
Newcastle United
Sheffield Wednesday
Southampton
Tottenham Hotspur
West Ham United
Wimbledon

Arsenal

Formed as Dial Square, a workshop in Woolwich Arsenal with a sundial over the entrance, in October 1886, becoming Royal Arsenal, the 'Royal' possibly from a local public house, later the same year. Turned professional and became Woolwich Arsenal in 1891. Selected for an expanded Football League Division Two in 1893, the first southern team to join.

Moved from the Manor Ground, Plumstead, south-east London, to Highbury, north London, in 1913, changing name again at the same time. Elected from fifth in Division Two to the expanded First Division for the 1919-20 season and never relegated. Premier League founder members 1992.

Ground: Arsenal Stadium, Avenell Road, Highbury, London N5 1BU
Club No.: 0171-704-4000   **Information:** 0171-704-4242
Box Office: 0171-704-4040   **CC Bookings:** 0171-413-3366
News: 0891 20 20 21
Capacity: 39,497   **Pitch size:** 110 yds x 71 yds
Colours: Red/White sleeves, White, Red   **Nickname:** Gunners
Radio: 1548AM Capital Radio
Internet: http://www.arsenal.co.uk

Chairman: P.D. Hill-Wood   **Vice-Chairman:** David Dein
MD/Secretary: Ken Friar   **Manager:** Arsène Wenger
Assistant/Coach: Pat Rice   **Physio:** Gary Lewin MCSP SRP

League History: 1893 Elected to Division 2; 1904-13 Division 1; 1913-19 Division 2; 1919-92 Division 1; 1992- FA Premier League.

Honours: *Football League: Division 1 – Champions:* 1930-31, 1932-33, 1933-34, 1934-35, 1937-38, 1947-48, 1952-53, 1970-71, 1988-89, 1990-91; *Runners-up:* 1925-26, 1931-32, 1972-73; *Division 2 – Runners-up:* 1903-04. *FA Cup: Winners:* 1929-30, 1935-36, 1949-50, 1970-71, 1978-79, 1992-93; *Runners-up:* 1926-27, 1931-32, 1951-52, 1971-72, 1977-78, 1979-80. *Football League Cup: Winners:* 1986-87, 1992-93; *Runners-up:* 1967-68, 1968-69, 1987-88. *League-Cup Double Performed:* 1970-71. *Cup-Double Performed:* 1992-93; *Cup-Winners' Cup Winners:* 1993-94 (winners), *Runners-up:* 1979-80, 1994-95; *Fairs Cup Winners:* 1969-70. *European Super Cup Runners-up:* 1994-95.

European Record: Champions' Cup (2): 71-72 (QF), 91-92 (2); Cup-Winners' Cup (3): 79-80 (F), 93-94 (W), 94-95 (F); UEFA Cup (7): 63-64 (2), 69-70 (W), 71-70 (Q), 78-79 (3), 81-82 (2), 82-83 (1), 96-97 (1).

Managers: Sam Hollis 1894-97; Tom Mitchell 1897-98; George Elcoat 1898-99; Harry Bradshaw 1899-1904; Phil Kelso 1904-08; George Morrell 1908-15; Leslie Knighton 1919-25; Herbert Chapman 1925-34; George Allison 1934-47; Tom Whittaker 1947-56; Jack Crayston 1956-58; George Swindin 1958 62; Billy Wright 1962-66; Bertie Mee 1966-76; Terry Neill 1976-83; Don Howe 1984-86; *(FAPL)* George Graham May 1986-Feb 1995; Stewart Houston (caretaker) Feb 1995-May 1995; Bruce Rioch May 1995-Aug 1996; Stewart Houston (caretaker) Aug 1996; Pat Rice (caretaker) Sept 1996; Arsène Wenger Sept 1996-.

Season 1996-97

Biggest Home Win:	4-1 v Sheffield Wednesday
Biggest Home Defeat:	1-2 v Liverpool
Biggest Away Win:	3-0 v Chelsea
Biggest Away Defeat:	0-2 v Liverpool
Biggest Home Att:	38,264 v Tottenham Hotspur
Smallest Home Att:	33,461 v Sheffield Wednesday
Average Attendance:	37,821 (3rd)
Leading Scorers:	23 – Ian Wright, 12 – Dennis Bergkamp

All-Time Records

Record FAPL Win:	5-1 v Ipswich Town, 5/02/94 & Norwich City 1/4/95
Record FAPL Defeat:	0-3 v Leeds Utd, 21/11/92; Coventry City 14/8/93; Liverpool 28/8/94; Man. United 22/3/95
Record FL Win:	12-0 v Loughborough Town, Division 2, 12/3/1900
Record FL Defeat:	0-8 v Loughborough Town, Division 2, 12/12/1896
Record Cup Win:	11-1 v Darwen, FA Cup R3, 9/1/32
Record Fee Received:	£3.2m rising to £5m, John Hartson, West Ham United, 3/97
Record Fee Paid:	£7.5m Dennis Bergkamp, Internazionale, 6/95
Most FL Apps:	547 – David O'Leary, 1975-92
Most FAPL Apps:	176 – Nigel Winterburn, 1992-97
Most FAPL Goals:	94 – Ian Wright, 1992-97
Highest Scorer in FAPL Season:	Ian Wright, 30, 1992-93
Record Attendance (all-time):	73,295 v Sunderland, Division 1, 9/3/35
Record Attendance (FAPL):	38,377 v Tottenham Hotspur 29/4/95
Most FAPL Goals in Season:	62, 1996-97 – 38 games
Most FAPL Points in Season:	71, 1993-94 – 42 games

Player	Tot	St	Sb	Snu	PS	Gls	Y	R	Fa	La	Fg	Lg
ADAMS	28	27	1	0	2	3	5	2	3	3	0	0
ANELKA	4	0	4	1	0	0	0	0	0	0	0	0
BARTRAM	0	0	0	9	0	0	0	0	0	0	0	0
BERGKAMP ...	29	28	1	0	8	12	6	0	2	2	1	1
BOULD	33	33	0	1	2	0	6	0	3	3	0	0
DICKOV †	1	0	1	0	0	0	0	0	0	0	0	0
DIXON	32	31	1	0	3	2	8	0	1	3	0	0
GARDE	11	7	4	2	5	0	2	0	0	0	0	0
HARPER	1	1	0	9	0	0	0	0	0	0	0	0
HARTSON † ...	19	14	5	2	8	3	9	0	2	3	1	0
HELDER	2	0	2	3	0	0	0	0	0	0	0	0
HILLIER †	2	0	2	0	0	0	0	0	0	0	0	0
HUGHES	14	9	5	3	6	1	1	0	2	0	1	0
KEOWN	33	33	0	0	2	1	7	0	3	3	0	0
KIWOMYA	0	0	0	0	0	0	0	0	0	0	0	0
LINIGHAN † ...	11	10	1	11	1	1	2	0	0	0	0	0
LUKIC	15	15	0	20	0	0	0	0	1	1	0	0
MARSHALL † ...	8	6	2	10	1	0	1	0	0	0	0	0
McGOWAN	1	1	0	0	1	0	0	0	0	0	0	0
MERSON †	32	32	0	2	5	6	1	0	3	3	0	1
MORROW †... ...	14	5	9	12	3	0	1	0	2	2	0	0
PARLOUR	30	17	13	4	2	2	6	0	3	1	0	0
PLATT	28	27	1	0	5	4	4	0	1	3	0	1
RANKIN	0	0	0	3	0	0	0	0	0	0	0	0
ROSE †	1	1	0	12	1	0	0	0	0	0	0	0
SEAMAN	22	22	0	0	0	0	0	0	2	2	0	0
SELLEY	1	0	1	3	0	0	0	0	0	0	0	0
SHAW	8	1	7	17	1	2	0	0	1	0	0	0
VIEIRA	31	30	1	0	3	2	11	0	3	3	0	0
WINTERBURN ...	38	38	0	0	3	0	5	0	2	3	0	0
WRIGHT	35	30	5	0	4	23	10	1	1	3	0	5

UEFA Cup Appearances
(Start+Substitute/Goals)

Adams 1+0; Bergkamp 1+0; Bould 1+1; Dixon 1+0; Hartson 2+0; Helder 0+2; Keown 2+0; Linighan 2+0; Merson 2+0/2; Parlour 1+1; Platt 2+0; Seaman 2+0; Vieira 1+0; Winterburn 2+0; Wright 2+0/2.

NB: A key to the abbreviations used in this *Club Directory* section can be found at the end of this club section after the entry for Sunderland.

Wenger Gets Gunners Set

Despite lifting Arsenal's league standing during his first season in charge at Highbury, Bruce Rioch found himself out of Highbury just five days before the start of the season. Stuart Houston stepped in for a second spell as caretaker-manager and boosted his cv but then surprised the club with a move across London to Queens Park Rangers as respected French coach Arsène Wenger waited in the wings to take charge of the club after seeing out his contract abroad.

Wenger's pre-arrival influence was clear as French stars Patrick Vieira and Remi Garde crossed the water for £3.5m and a free transfer respectively. With their pre-season problems well behind them, the Gunners kicked off the Premiership campaign with a 2-0 win over West Ham and it was to be a further six months before a visiting side would take maximum points from Highbury. Providing much of the inspiration for an early assault on the title was the irrepressible Ian Wright who scored a hat trick during a 4-1 thrashing of Sheffield Wednesday in mid September which included his 100th league goal for the club. Wright was to later score the 200th league goal of his career and reclaim a place in the England side but it was not a season without its problems as he was hauled before the FA for another of the indiscretions which have frequently blighted his career.

Wenger finally joined the Gunners on 1 October and after a home draw with Coventry later that month the club topped the table. A 3-0 thumping of former manager George Graham's new side Leeds maintained pole position but a calamitous Nigel Winterburn own goal at Old Trafford saw them edged off top spot. Two late goals at home to Spurs and an excellent win at Newcastle – despite having Tony Adams dismissed – took Arsenal back to the summit but they were toppled for the final time just before Christmas with a shock defeat at Forest.

Arsenal continued to mount the only serious title challenge from the capital but, ironically, it was ultimately a loss of form at Highbury which ensured that the title would not be going to north London for the first time in six years. Having gone unbeaten at home in the league for 13 months, Arsenal lost four of their last seven games at Highbury, including crucial reversals against Manchester United and Liverpool. A 3-1 win at Derby on the final day of the season proved to be almost academic as a home defeat by Newcastle a week earlier condemned them to third place and a Champions' League place was missed by goal difference.

Arsenal may have enjoyed great cup success through the nineties but a 1st Round defeat was suffered in the UEFA Cup with Borussia Moenchengladbach winning both legs 3-2, while in the Coca-Cola Cup two games were required to see off Stoke City before Liverpool won a 4th Round tie 4-2 at Anfield. The FA Cup looked to be more to their liking as an impressive 3rd Round replay victory at Sunderland secured an enticing clash with Leeds. This time Graham took full revenge with a 1-0 triumph at Highbury.

Arsenal drew praise for the quality of their football as the less direct approach of earlier in the decade was replaced by a more welcome passing game. Less commendable was Arsenal's disciplinary record – 85 bookings and five dismissals in 38 league games.

Wenger was the most active of managers during the close season with a host of top signings bound for Highbury – Marc Overmars the most notable at £7 million – as the Gunners get set for a more sustained assault on the Premiership title. ∎

Results 1996-97

Date	Opponents	Ven	Res	Pos	Atten	Scorers
17-Aug	West Ham Utd	H	2-0	–	38,056	Hartson (22); Bergkamp (39 pen)
19-Aug	Liverpool	A	0-2	–	38,103	
24-Aug	Leicester C.	A	2-0	3	20,429	Bergkamp (26 pen); Wright (90)
04-Sep	Chelsea	H	3-3	5	38,132	Merson (44); Keown (66); Wright (77)
07-Sep	Aston Villa	A	2-2	8	37,944	Merson (70); Linighan (89)
16-Sep	Sheffield W.	H	4-1	6	33,461	Platt (58); Wright (62 pen, 78, 89)
21-Sep	Middlesbrough	A	2-0	3	29,629	Hartson (3); Wright (27)
28-Sep	Sunderland	H	2-0	3	38,016	Hartson (76); Parlour (88)
12-Oct	Blackburn R.	A	2-0	2	24,303	Wright (3, 51)
19-Oct	Coventry C.	H	0-0	1	38,140	
26-Oct	Leeds Utd	H	3-0	1	38,076	Dixon (1); Bergkamp (5); Wright (65)
02-Nov	Wimbledon	A	2-2	1	25,521	Wright (6); Merson (65)
16-Nov	Man. Utd	A	0-1	3	55,210	
24-Nov	Tottenham H.	H	3-1	2	38,264	Wright (27 pen); Adams (87); Bergkamp (89)
30-Nov	Newcastle Utd	A	2-1	1	36,565	Dixon (10); Wright (59)
04-Dec	Southampton	H	3-1	1	38,033	Merson (43); Wright (57 pen); Shaw (89)
07-Dec	Derby Co.	H	2-2	1	38,018	Adams (45); Vieira (90)
21-Dec	N. Forest	A	1-2	2	27,384	Wright (63)
26-Dec	Sheffield W.	A	0-0	2	23,245	
28-Dec	Aston Villa	H	2-2	3	38,130	Wright (12); Merson (73)
01-Jan	Middlesbrough	H	2-0	2	37,573	Bergkamp (14); Wright (44)
11-Jan	Sunderland	A	0-1	3	21,154	
19-Jan	Everton	H	3-1	2	38,095	Bergkamp (54); Vieira (56); Merson (68)
29-Jan	West Ham Utd	A	2-1	2	24,382	Parlour (7); Wright (66)
01-Feb	Leeds Utd	A	0-0	3	35,502	
15-Feb	Tottenham H.	A	0-0	3	33,093	
19-Feb	Man. Utd	H	1-2	3	38,172	Bergkamp (69)
23-Feb	Wimbledon	H	0-1	4	37,854	
01-Mar	Everton	A	2-0	3	36,980	Bergkamp (21); Wright (27)
08-Mar	N. Forest	H	2-0	2	38,206	Bergkamp (49, 78)
15-Mar	Southampton	A	2-0	3	15,441	Hughes (41); Shaw (72)
24-Mar	Liverpool	H	1-2	3	38,068	Wright (78)

05-Apr	Chelsea	A	3-0	3	28,182	Wright (22); Platt (53); Bergkamp (81)
12-Apr	Leicester C.	H	2-0	2	38,044	Adams (34); Platt (64)
19-Apr	Blackburn R.	H	1-1	2	38,086	Platt (19)
21-Apr	Coventry C.	A	1-1	2	19,998	Wright (19 pen)
03-May	Newcastle Utd	H	0-1	3	38,179	
11-May	Derby Co.	A	3-1	3	18,287	Wright (55, 90); Bergkamp (82)

FA Challenge Cup

Sponsored by Littlewoods Pools

Date	Opponents	Vn	Rnd	Res	Atten	Scorers
04-Jan	Sunderland	H	3R	1-1	37,793	Hartson (10)
15-Jan	Sunderland	A	3RR	2-0	15,277	Bergkamp (46); Hughes (64)
04-Feb	Leeds Utd	H	4R	0-1	38,115	

Coca-Cola League Cup

Date	Opponents	Vn	Rnd	Res	Atten	Scorers
23-Oct	Stoke City	A	3R	1-1	20,804	Wright (77)
13-Nov	Stoke City	H	3RR	5-2	33,962	Wright (41 pen, 63); Platt (46); Bergkamp (67); Merson (73)
27-Nov	Liverpool	A	4R	2-4	32,814	Wright (13 pen, 67 pen)

UEFA Cup

Date	Opponents	Vn	Rnd	Res	Atten	Scorers
10-Sep	B. M'Gladbach	H	1R1L	2-3	38,894	Merson (54); Wright (89)
25-Sep	B. M'Gladbach	A	1R2L	2-3	35,000	Wright (43); Merson (49)

Borussia Moenchengladbach win 6-4 on aggregate.

5-Year Record

	Div.	P	W	D	L	F	A	Pts	Pos	FAC	FLC
92-93	PL	42	15	11	16	40	38	56	10	W	W
93-94	PL	42	18	17	7	53	28	71	4	4	4
94-95	PL	42	13	12	17	52	49	51	12	3	5
95-96	PL	38	17	12	9	49	32	63	5	3	SF
96-97	PL	38	19	11	8	62	32	68	3	4	4

Aston Villa

Founded in 1874 by cricketers from the Aston Wesleyan Chapel, Lozells, who played on Aston Park, moving to a field in Wellington Road, Perry Barr in 1876. Prominent nationally, the club was a founder member of the Football League in 1888.

The landlord at Perry Barr made such demands that the club sought its own ground and eventually moved back to Aston occupying the Aston Lower Grounds, which had already been used for some big games. Not known as Villa Park until some time later, the ground first saw league football in 1897. Premier League founder members 1992.

Ground: Villa Park, Trinity Rd, Birmingham, B6 6HE
Club No.: 0121-327 2299
Box Office: 0121-327 5353   **CC Bookings:** 0121 607 8000
News: 0891 12 11 48   **Ticket:** 0891 12 18 48
Capacity: 40,530   **Pitch:** 115 yds x 75 yds
Colours: Claret/Blue, White, Blue/Claret   **Nickname:** The Villains
Radio: 1152AM Sport Extra
Internet: –

President: J.A. Alderson   **Chairman:** Doug Ellis
Secretary: Steven Stride
Manager: Brian Little   **Assistant:** Allan Evans
First Team Coach: Kevin MacDonald   **Physio:** Jim Walker

League History: 1888 Founder Member of the League; 1936-38 Division 2; 1938-59 Division 1; 1959-60 Division 2; 1960-67 Division 1; 1967-70 Division 2; 1970-72 Division 3; 1972-75 Division 2; 1975-87 Division 1; 1987-88 Division 2; 1988-92 Division 1; 1992- FA Premier League.

Honours: *FA Premier League – Runners-up* 1992-93; *Football League: Division 1 – Champions* 1893-94, 1895-96, 1896-97, 1898-99, 1899-1900, 1909-10, 1980-81; *Runners-up* 1888-89, 1902-03, 1907-08, 1910-11, 1912-13, 1913-14, 1930-31, 1932-33, 1989-90; *Division 2 – Champions* 1937-38, 1959-60; *Runners-up* 1974-75, 1987-88; *Division 3 – Champions* 1971-72. *FA Cup: Winners* 1887, 1895, 1897, 1905, 1913, 1920, 1957; *Runners-up* 1892, 1924. *League-Cup Double Performed:* 1896-97. *Football League Cup: Winners* 1961, 1975, 1977, 1994, 1996; *Runners-up* 1963, 1971. *Champions' Cup Winners –* 1981-82; *European Super Cup Winners*: 1982-83; *World Club Championship Runners-up:* 1982-83.

European Record: CC (2): 81-82 (W), 82-83 (QF); CWC (0); UEFA (7): 75-76 (1), 77-78 (Q), 83-84 (2), 90-91 (2), 93-94 (2), 94-95 (2), 96-97 (1).

Managers: George Ramsay 1884-1926; W.J. Smith 1926-34; Jimmy McMullan 1934-35; Jimmy Hogan 1936-44; Alex Massie 1945-50; George Martin 1950-53; Eric Houghton 1953-58; Joe Mercer 1958-64; Dick Taylor 1965-67; Tommy Cummings 1967-68; Tommy Docherty 1968-70; Vic Crowe 1970-74; Ron Saunders 1974-82; Tony Barton 1982-84; Graham Turner 1984-86; Billy McNeill 1986-87; Graham Taylor 1987-91; Dr Jozef Venglos 1990-91; *(FAPL)* Ron Atkinson June 1991-Nov 1994; Brian Little Nov 1994-

Season 1996-97

Biggest Home Win:	5-0 v Wimbledon
Biggest Home Defeat:	1-3 v Leicester City
Biggest Away Win:	2-0 v Blackburn Rvrs, West Ham Utd, Wimbledon
Biggest Away Defeat:	3-4 v Newcastle Utd; 0-3 v Liverpool
Biggest Home Att:	39,339 (7 occasions)
Smallest Home Att:	26,726 v Sheffield Wednesday
Average Attendance:	33,020 (6th)
Leading Scorers:	17 – Yorke, 10 – Milosevic

All-Time Records

Record FAPL Win:	7-1 v Wimbledon, 11/2/95
Record FAPL Defeat:	1-5 v Newcastle United, 27/4/94
Record FL Win:	12-2 v Accrington S, Division 1, 12/3/1892
Record FL Defeat:	1-8 v Blackburn R, FA Cup R3, 16/2/1889
Record Cup Win:	13-0 v Wednesbury Old Ath, FA Cup R1, 30/10/1886
Record Fee Received:	£5.5m from Bari for David Platt, 8/1991
Record Fee Paid:	£7m to Liverpool for Stan Collymore, 5/97
Most FL Apps:	Charlie Aitken, 561, 1961-76
Most FAPL Apps:	142 – Paul McGrath, 1992-97
Most FAPL Goals:	48 – Dwight Yorke, 1992-97
Highest Scorer in FAPL season:	Dean Saunders, 17, 1992-93; Dwight Yorke, 17, 1995-96 and 1996-97

Record Attendance (all-time): 76,588 v Derby Co., FA Cup R6, 2/2/1946
Record Attendance (FAPL): 45,347 v Liverpool, 7/5/94
Most FAPL Goals in Season: 57, 1992-93 – 42 games
Most FAPL Points in Season: 74, 1992-93 – 42 games

Summary 1996-97

Player	Tot	St	Sb	Snu	PS	Gls	Y	R	Fa	La	Fg	Lg
BOSNICH	20	20	0	3	2	0	2	0	3	1	0	0
BROCK	0	0	0	2	0	0	0	0	0	0	0	0
CURCIC	22	17	5	6	10	0	4	0	2	1	1	0
DAVIS	0	0	0	1	0	0	0	0	0	0	0	0
DRAPER	29	28	1	2	10	0	4	1	0	2	0	0
EHIOGU	38	38	0	0	0	3	4	0	3	2	1	0
FARRELLY †	3	1	2	15	0	0	0	0	0	0	0	0
HENDRIE	4	0	4	12	0	0	0	0	3	0	0	0
HUGHES	7	4	3	5	1	0	1	0	0	0	0	0
JOACHIM	15	3	12	21	2	3	0	0	1	1	0	0
JOHNSON	20	10	10	6	2	4	4	0	2	1	0	0
McGRATH †	0	0	0	7	0	0	0	0	0	0	0	0
MILOSEVIC	30	29	1	0	8	10	6	0	3	1	0	0
MURRAY	1	1	0	8	1	0	0	0	0	0	0	0
NELSON	34	33	1	1	4	0	6	0	1	2	0	0
OAKES	20	18	2	17	0	0	0	0	0	1	0	0
RACHEL	0	0	0	14	0	0	0	0	0	0	0	0
SCIMECA	17	11	6	9	0	0	1	0	3	2	0	0
SOUTHGATE	28	28	0	0	1	1	1	0	3	1	0	0
STAUNTON	30	30	0	0	5	2	5	1	2	1	0	0
TAYLOR	34	29	5	0	2	2	4	0	0	2	0	1
TILER †	11	9	2	7	1	1	1	0	2	1	0	0
TOWNSEND	34	34	0	0	2	2	8	0	3	2	0	0
WRIGHT	38	38	0	0	0	1	2	0	3	2	0	0
YORKE	37	37	0	0	3	17	2	0	2	2	2	1
OGs						1						

UEFA Cup Appearances

(Start+Substitute/Goals)

Draper 2+0; Ehiogu 2+0; Johnson 1+1/1; McGrath 0+1; Milosevic 2+0;
Nelson 2+0; Oakes 2+0; Southgate 2+0; Staunton 2+0; Taylor 1+0;
Townsend 2+0; Wright 2+0; Yorke 2+0.

5-Year Record

	Div.	P	W	D	L	F	A	Pts	Pos	FAC	FLC
92-93	PL	42	21	11	10	57	40	74	2	4	4
93-94	PL	42	15	12	15	46	50	57	10	5	W
94-95	PL	42	11	15	16	51	56	48	18	4	4
95-96	PL	38	18	9	11	52	35	63	4	SF	W
96-97	PL	38	17	10	11	47	34	61	5	4	4

Villa Fail to Build on Success

Winning the Coca-Cola Cup, reaching the semi-finals of the FA Cup and a rise of 14 places in the Premiership was always going to be a tough act for Brian Little's Aston Villa side to follow and, with early exits from all the cup competitions, it could be argued that, in many respects, the 1996-97 campaign was a disappointing time for the club.

Little released just one player and brought in Fernando Nelson from Sporting Lisbon for £1.75m and the exciting Sasa Curcic from Bolton Wanderers for a club record of £4m. Sadly Curcic failed to settle at Villa Park and could not hold down a first team place. Neither player was in the side for Villa's opening match, a 2-1 defeat at Sheffield Wednesday, and it was Gareth Southgate who kick-started the campaign with the winning goal against Blackburn Rovers three days later. That win began a six-match unbeaten run which included three straight wins and a brief flirtation with a season's high position of second behind early pacesetters Wednesday. But with just two victories from nine Premiership matches, Villa slipped down to ninth and were never seriously in contention.

Villa's best spell was a run of five straight wins, starting in late November, which were their most successful for five years. The first quartet came against struggling opposition but Little's side demonstrated its class with a 5-0 thrashing of Wimbledon, who were looking to extend a remarkable 19-match unbeaten run of their own. This was followed by a six-match winless run.

Villa's return to Europe after a year's absence was surprisingly short-lived as a 0-0 draw in Sweden with Helsingborgs, a fortnight after a late goal had denied Villa victory at home, condemned the Midlands side to an away goals defeat. First port of call in Villa's defence of the Coca-Cola Cup was at Elland Road, and Leeds –, the side which Villa comprehensively defeated in the previous season's final – threatened their grip on the trophy by taking the lead, only for late goals from Ian Taylor and Yorke, a penalty, to continue Villa's supremacy over the Yorkshire side. But hopes of another glorious march to Wembley evaporated in the 3rd Round at Selhurst Park in front of less than eight thousand supporters when Wimbledon clinched a 1-0 victory despite the visitors dominating proceedings.

The last of Villa's six FA Cup wins came way back in 1957 and hopes of celebrating the centenary of their league and cup double were boosted by a 3-0 3rd Round victory over Notts County. By the time of the 4th Round, though, Villa were struggling for form and went down 3-1 to Derby County at the Baseball Ground with Curcic scoring his first goal of a personally unsettled season.

Leading scorer, with 17 Premiership goals for the second consecutive season, was Dwight Yorke who struck a hat trick during a thrilling 4-3 defeat at Newcastle. Yorke had a dismal run of nine goalless games, followed by eleven goals in twelve games. Savo Milosevic also got into double figures for the second successive season but was frequently linked with a possible transfer. Defensively Villa were more than proficient with no side conceding fewer goals on home territory. Both Ugo Ehiogu and Alan Wright were ever present. Paul McGrath moved to Derby in October and Carl Tiler to Sheffield United in March for £650,000.

Little moved swiftly and boldly in the transfer market at the end of the season when bolstering his attacking options with the £7m club record signing of one-time Villa supporter Stan Collymore. ∎

Results 1996-97

Date	Opponents	Ven	Res	Pos	Atten	Scorers
17-Aug	Sheffield W.	A	1-2	–	26,861	Johnson (88)
20-Aug	Blackburn R.	H	1-0	–	32,257	Southgate (64)
24-Aug	Derby Co.	H	2-0	4	34,646	Joachim (18); Johnson (46 pen)
04-Sep	Everton	A	1-0		39,115	Ehiogu (62)
07-Sep	Arsenal	H	2-2		37,944	Milosevic (39, 63)
15-Sep	Chelsea	A	1-1		27,729	Townsend (18)
21-Sep	Man. Utd	H	0-0	6	39,339	
30-Sep	Newcastle Utd	A	3-4	8	36,400	Yorke (5, 59, 69)
12-Oct	Tottenham H.	A	0-1	8	32,847	
19-Oct	Leeds Utd	H	2-0	7	39,051	Yorke (58); Johnson (65)
26-Oct	Sunderland	A	0-1	7	21,059	
02-Nov	N. Forest	H	2-0	7	35,310	Tiler (20); Yorke (65)
16-Nov	Leicester C.	H	1-3	9	36,193	Yorke (16)
23-Nov	Coventry C.	A	2-1	8	21,340	Joachim (29); Staunton (85)
30-Nov	Middlesbrough	H	1-0	7	39,053	Yorke (39 pen)
04-Dec	West Ham Utd	A	2-0	5	19,105	Ehiogu (37); Yorke (73)
07-Dec	Southampton	H	1-0	4	15,232	Townsend (34)
22-Dec	Wimbledon	H	5-0	4	28,875	Yorke (38, 86); Milosevic (41, 75); Taylor (61)
26-Dec	Chelsea	H	0-2	5	39,339	
28-Dec	Arsenal	A	2-2	6	38,130	Milosevic (67); Yorke (74)
01-Jan	Man. Utd	A	0-0	6	55,133	
11-Jan	Newcastle Utd	H	2-2	6	39,339	Yorke (39); Milosevic (52)
18-Jan	Liverpool	A	0-3	7	40,489	
29-Jan	Sheffield W.	H	0-1	7	26,726	
01-Feb	Sunderland	H	1-0	7	32,491	Milosevic (37)
19-Feb	Coventry C.	H	2-1	5	30,409	Yorke (43, 75)
22-Feb	N. Forest	A	0-0	5	25,329	
02-Mar	Liverpool	H	1-0	5	39,399	Taylor (83)
05-Mar	Leicester C.	A	0-1	5	20,626	
15-Mar	West Ham Utd	H	0-0	6	35,995	
22-Mar	Blackburn R.	A	0-2	5	24,274	Johnson (64); Yorke (79)
05-Apr	Everton	H	3-1	5	39,339	Milosevic (41); Staunton (50); Yorke (54)
09-Apr	Wimbledon	A	2-0	4	9,015	Milosevic (26); Wright (78)
12-Apr	Derby Co.	A	1-2	4	18,071	Joachim (84)
19-Apr	Tottenham H.	H	1-1	5	39,339	Yorke (81)
22-Apr	Leeds Utd	A	0-0	5	26,897	

| 03-May | Middlesbrough | A | 2-3 | 5 | 30,074 | Ehiogu (58); Milosevic (76) |
| 11-May | Southampton | H | 1-0 | 5 | 39,339 | OG (12, Dryden) |

FA Challenge Cup

Date	Opponents	Vn	Rnd	Res	Atten	Scorers
14-Jan	Notts. County	A	3	0-0	13,315	
22-Jan	Notts. County	H	3R	3-0	25,006	Yorke (24, 53); Ehiogu (67)
25-Jan	Derby Co.	A	4	1-3	17,997	Curcic (76)

Coca-Cola League Cup

Date	Opponents	Vn	Rnd	Res	Atten	Scorers
23-Oct	Leeds Utd	A	3	2-1	15,803	Taylor (70); Yorke (77 pen)
26-Nov	Wimbledon	A	4	0-1	7,573	

UEFA Cup

Date	Opponents	Vn	Rnd	Res	Atten	Scorers
10-Sep	Helsingborgs	H	1R1L	1-1	25,818	Johnson (14)
24-Sep	Helsingborgs	A	1R2L	0-0	16,000	

1-1 on aggregate. Helsingborgs win on away goals rule.

Villa – Premiership Fact File

- Gareth Southgate's goal for Villa against Blackburn in the second game of the season was only his second Premiership goal for the club. His first was also scored against Rovers in the 1995-96 season.

- Dwight Yorke had to wait until game number eight for his first Premiership goals of the season. They came at Newcastle in the form of a hat-trick but he still finished on the losing side.

- Carl Tiler's first goal for Villa came against Nottingham Forest – his former club.

- Wimbledon's 5-0 pasting in December was their first defeat in 20 games – it was Villa's fifth successive win. Villa then failed to win in the Premiership for another six games!

Barnsley

Formed in 1887 by the Rev. Preedy as Barnsley St Peter, a reflection of the church connection. St Peter was dropped ten years later, a year before Barnsley were elected to the Second Division of the Football League. The early years were unremarkable save the fact that the FA Cup was won in 1912, two years after they had been beaten finalists.

The club remained in the lower reaches of the league, dropping down to the old Fourth Division for three seasons from 1965-68. Division One status was achieved in 1992 and the club completed a remarkable rise into the Premiership at the end of 1997 as one of the least fancied clubs for promotion.

Ground: Oakwell Ground, Barnsley, South Yorkshire, S71 1ET
Phone: 01226-211211   **Box Office:** 01226-211211
Info: 0891-12 11 52
Capacity: 19,101   **Pitch:** 110 yds x 75 yds
Colours: Red, White, Red   **Nickname:** The Tykes or Reds

President: A. Raynor   **Chairman:** J.A. Dennis
Secretary: Michael Spinks
Manager: Danny Wilson   **Coach:** Eric Winstanley
Physio: Michael Tarmley
Internet: http://www.yorkshire-web.co.uk/bfc/BFC.HTML

League History: 1898 Elected to Division 2; 1932-34 Division 3N; 1934-38 Division 2; 1938-39 Division 3N; 1946-53 Division 2; 1953-55 Division 3N; 1955-59 Division 2; 1959-65 Division 3; 1965-68 Division 4; 1968-72 Division 3; 1972-79 Division 4; 1979-81 Division 3; 1981-92 Division 2; 1992-1997 Division 1; 1997- FAPL.

Honours: *FA Cup Winners* 1911-12; *Runners-up* 1909-10; *Division 1 Runners-up* 1996-97; *Division 3N Champions* 1933-34, 1938-39, 1954-55; *Runners-up* 1953-54; *Division 3 Runners-up* 1980-81; *Division 4 Runners-up* 1967-68; *Promoted* 1978-79.

European Record: Never qualified.

Managers: Arthur Fairclough 1898-1901; John McCartney 1901-04; Arthur Fairclough 1904-12; John Hastie 1912-14; Percy Lewis 1914-19; Peter Sant 1919-33; John Commins 1926-29; Arthur Fairclough 1929-30; Brough Fletcher 1930-37; Angus Seed 1937-53; Tim Ward 1953-60; Johnny Steele

118

1960-71; John McSeveney 1971-72; Johnny Steele 1972-73; Jim Iley 1973-78; Allan Clarke 1978-80; Norman Hunter 1980-84; Bobby Collins 1984-85; Allan Clarke 1985-89; Mel Machin 1989-93; Viv Anderson 1993-94; Danny Wilson June 1994-.

Season 1996-97

Biggest Home Win:	4-0 v Charlton Athletic
Biggest Home Defeat:	1-3 v QPR, Wolverhampton Wanderers
Biggest Away Win:	3-2 v Grimsby Town
Biggest Away Defeat:	1-5 v Oxford United
Biggest Home Att:	18,605 v Bradford City
Smallest Home Att:	6,337 v Oxford United
Average Attendance:	11,407
Leading Scorer:	15 – Neil Readfearn

All-Time Records

Record FAPL Win:	–
Record FAPL Defeat:	–
Record FL Win:	9-0 v Loughborough Town, Division 2, 28/1/1889
	9-0 v Accrington St, Division 3N, 3/2/34
Record FL Defeat:	0-9 v Notts County, Division 2, 19/11/27
Record Cup Win:	6-0 v Blackpool, FA Cup 1RR, 20/1/10 and
	6-0 v Peterborough Utd, Lg Cup, 1R2L, 15/9/81
Record Fee Received:	£1.5m from N. Forest for Carl Tiler, 5/91
Record Fee Paid:	£1.5m to Partizan Belgrade for Gjorgi Hristov, 6/97
Most FL Apps:	514, Barry Murphy, 1962-78
Most FAPL Apps:	–
Most FAPL Goals:	–
Highest Scorer in FAPL Season:	–
Record Attendance (all-time):	40,255 v Stoke City, FA Cup 5R, 15/2/36
Record Attendance (FAPL):	–
Most FAPL Goals in Season:	–
Most FAPL Points in Season:	–

Summary 1996-97

Player	Tot	St	Sb	Gls	Fa	La	Fg	Lg
APPLEBY	35	35	0	0	1	4	0	0
BOSANCIC	25	17	8	1	2	4	0	0
BULLOCK	30	7	23	0	2	2	1	0
DAVIES	24	24	0	3	0	4	0	0
DE ZEEUW	43	43	0	2	2	4	0	0
EADEN	46	46	0	3	2	4	0	0
HENDRIE	36	36	0	15	2	0	1	0
HURST	1	0	1	0	1	2	0	0
JONES	17	12	5	0	2	0	0	0
LIDDELL	38	25	13	8	2	3	0	0
MARCELLE	39	26	13	8	2	4	1	0
MOSES	28	25	3	2	2	0	0	0
REDFEARN	43	43	0	17	2	4	1	1
REGIS	4	0	4	0	0	3	0	1
SHERIDAN	41	39	2	2	2	2	0	0
SHIRTLIFF	13	12	1	0	0	0	0	0
TEN HEUVEL	2	0	2	0	0	0	0	0
THOMPSON	24	24	0	5	1	3	0	0
VAN DER VELDEN	2	1	1	0	0	1	0	0
WATSON	46	46	0	0	2	4	0	0
WILKINSON	45	45	0	9	2	4	0	2
OGs				1				

Tykes Scale New Heights

The glorious cup runs enjoyed by Chesterfield and Stockport amongst others prove that the romance of the cup competitions is thriving but, while those two clubs still have ambitions of drawing the big fish again in 1997-98, Barnsley start the new campaign shoulder to shoulder with Manchester United et al.

With just one win from their last ten games of the previous season, Barnsley were few people's tip for promotion. Manager Danny Wilson released nine players and drafted in six although only one, Matt Appleby, cost the Yorkshire club a fee.

Wilson's starting line-up for the first Division One fixture of the season saw seven changes from the one which ended the 1995-96 season and the impact was immediate as West Bromwich Albion were beaten 2-1 at the Hawthorns. Huddersfield Town, Reading, Manchester City and Stoke City went the same way as Barnsley stormed to the top of the table with maximum points from five games and 13 goals scored. With their best start to a season for 18 years, Barnsley possessed the only 100% winning record in English professional football. The run ended at home to QPR but with it went pole position to Bolton who had played a game more. Having begun the season with three consecutive victories at Oakwell, Barnsley were now having serious problems in picking up points at home and in a run of five draws following the Grimsby match three of them were at Oakwell. On the plus side the unbeaten away record was maintained with good draws at Ipswich and Bradford and victory at Port Vale. Portsmouth dented Barnsley's proud away record on 23 November but it was the sole blip in a 15-match spell which saw Barnsley underline their quality with draws home and away with Bolton. The Tykes returned to the summit on 21 December with a 1-0 victory away to a Sheffield United side which began the day in second place. Scorer of the winning goal was John Hendrie who, at 33, more than paid back the £250,000 Barnsley paid Middlesbrough for him in October as he went on to score 15 times in 36 appearances. Top scorer, though, was Redfearn, who got into double figures for the fourth consecutive season.

Barnsley's stay at the top was short-lived with Stoke winning 1-0 in the Potteries on Boxing Day and, following the turn of the year, a 3-2 win at Grimsby was the start of another consistent run of one defeat in 12 games. With second wins of the season over West Brom and Reading, second place was made their own at the end of March. Barnsley received high praise for the manner of their football throughout the season and their reward came on 26 April when, in front of their highest gate of the season, goals from free signings Paul Wilkinson and Clint Marcelle plunged Bradford deeper into the relegation mire and hoisted Barnsley into exalted company for the first time in their 110-year history. Although completely inconsequential, the season ended on a low note with a 5-1 hammering at Oxford United and the bookies offered odds of 1,000/1 for Barnsley to take the Premiership title at the first attempt.

Against Oldham in the FA Cup, goals from Marcelle and Martin Bullock, only his second in well over 100 games for the club, set up a 4th Round at QPR and for the third time during the season Rangers got the better of the Oakwell club. As for the Coca-Cola Cup campaign, after a 2-1 defeat at Rochdale, 2nd Leg goals from Redfearn and Wilkinson turned the tie around, but the run was cut short by a 2-1 aggregate defeat by Gillingham in the 2nd Round. Barnsley's season was capped with Manager Danny Wilson being named Manager of the Year. ∎

Results 1996-97

Nationwide Division One

Date	Opponents	Ven	Res	Atten	Scorers
07-Aug	WBA	A	2-1	18,561	Marcelle; Liddell
25-Aug	Huddersfield Tn	H	3-1	9,787	Marcelle; Redfearn; Wilkinson
28-Aug	Reading	H	3-0	7,523	Liddell (2); Sheridan
07-Sep	Man. City	A	2-1	26,464	Marcelle (2)
10-Sep	Stoke City	H	3-0	11,696	Davis; Liddell; Thompson
14-Sep	QPR	H	1-3	13,003	Wilkinson
21-Sep	Oldham Ath	A	1-0	7,043	Redfearn (pen)
28-Sep	Grimsby Tn	H	1-3	8,833	Liddell
01-Oct	Ipswich Tn	A	1-1	9,041	Redfearn (pen)
12-Oct	Crystal Palace	H	0-0	9,183	
15-Oct	Oxford Utd	H	0-0	6,337	
19-Oct	Bradford City	A	2-2	11,477	Davis; Liddell
25-Oct	Bolton W.	H	2-2	9,413	Redfearn (2, 1pen)
29-Oct	Port Vale	A	3-1	5,231	De Zeeuw; Hendrie: Marcelle
02-Nov	W'hanpton W.	A	3-3	22,840	Eaden; De Zeeuw; Redfearn (pen)
09-Nov	Norwich City	H	3-1	9,697	Moses; Hendrie; Wilkinson
16-Nov	Swindon Tn	A	0-3	10,837	
23-Nov	Portsmouth	H	3-2	7,449	Davis; Hendrie; Wilkinson
30-Nov	Bolton W.	A	2-2	16,852	Redfearn (2, 1 pen)
03-Dec	Birmingham C.	A	0-0	24,004	
07-Dec	Southend Utd	H	3-0	7,489	Hendrie; Wilkinson (2)
14-Dec	Tranmere Rvr	H	3-0	8,513	Hendrie; Redfearn (pen); Wilkinson
21-Dec	Sheffield Utd	H	1-0	24,384	Hendrie
26-Dec	Stoke City	A	0-1	19,025	
28-Dec	Man. City	H	2-0	17,159	Moses; Bosancic (pen)
11-Jan	QPR	A	1-3	12,058	Redfearn
18-Jan	Ipswich Tn	H	1-2	9,872	Liddell
28-Jan	Grimsby Town	A	3-2	6,323	Hendrie (3)
01-Feb	Norwich City	A	1-1	17,001	Eaden
08-Feb	Port Vale	H	1-0	12,246	Hendrie
15-Feb	Charlton Ath	A	2-2	9,104	Hendrie (2)
22-Feb	W'hampton W	A	1-3	18,024	Sheridan
01-Mar	Southend Utd	A	2-1	4,855	Redfearn (2)
04-Mar	Swindon Tn	H	1-1	8,518	Redfearn
07-Mar	Sheffield Utd	A	2-0	14,668	Eaden; Hendrie
15-Mar	Tranmere Rvr	A	1-1	7,347	Wilkinson
22-Mar	Huddersfield T	A	0-0	14,754	
28-Mar	WBA	H	2-0	12,087	Redfearn; Thompson (pen)
31-Mar	Reading	A	2-1	10,244	Liddell; OG
05-Apr	Birmingham C.	H	0-1	13,092	

12-Apr	Charlton Ath	H	4-0	11,701	Thompson (2); Hendrie; Marcelle
15-Apr	Oldham Ath	H	2-0	17,476	Hendrie; Marcelle
19-Apr	C.Palace	A	1-1	20,006	Thompson (pen)
22-Apr	Portsmouth	A	2-4	8,328	Redfearn (2)
26-Apr	Bradford C.	H	2-0	18,605	Wilkinson; Marcelle
05-May	Oxford U.	A	1-5	8,693	Redfearn

FA Challenge Cup

Sponsored by Littlewoods Pools

Date	Opponents	Vn	Rnd	Res	Atten	Scorers
14-Jan	Oldham Ath	H	3R	2-0	9,936	Marcelle; Bullock
25-Jan	QPR	A	4R	2-3	14,317	Hendrie; Redfearn

Coca-Cola League Cup

Date	Opponents	Vn	Rnd	Res	Atten	Scorers
20-Aug	Rochdale	A	1R1L	1-2	2,426	Wilkinson
03-Sep	Rochdale	H	1R2L	2-0	5,613	Redfearn; Wilkinson
	Barnsley win 3-2 on aggregate.					
17-Sep	Gillingham	H	2R1L	1-1	4,491	Regis
24-Sep	Gillingham	A	2R2L	0-1	5,666	
	Gillingham win 2-1 on aggregate.					

5-Year Record

	Div.	P	W	D	L	F	A	Pts	Pos	FAC	FLC
92-93	1	46	17	9	20	56	60	60	13	5	1
93-94	1	46	16	7	23	55	67	55	18	5	2
94-95	1	46	20	12	14	63	52	72	6	3	2
95-96	1	46	14	18	14	60	66	60	10	3	3
96-97	1	46	22	14	10	76	55	80	2	4	2

Blackburn Rovers

Founded in 1875 by local school-leavers. Used several pitches, including Alexander Meadows, the East Lancashire Cricket Club ground, and became known nationally for their FA Cup exploits, eclipsing the record of Blackburn Olympic, the first club to take the trophy away from London. Three consecutive wins in the 1880s, when in the finals Queen's Park (twice) and West Bromwich Albion were beaten, brought recognition by way of a special shield awarded by the FA to commemorate the achievement.

Founder member of the Football League in 1888, the club settled at Ewood Park in 1890, purchasing the ground outright in 1893-94. Premier League founder member 1992 and champions in 1994-95.

Ground:	Ewood Park, Blackburn, BB2 4JF		
Phone:	01254-698888		
Box Office:	01254 671666	**CC Bookings:** 01254 671666	
News:	0891-12 10 14		
Capacity:	30,591	**Pitch:** 115 yds x 76 yds	
Colours:	Blue/White, White, Blue	**Nickname:** Blue and Whites	
Radio:	999AM Red Rose Gold		
Internet:	http://www.rovers.co.uk		

Club President: W.H. Bancroft   **Snr-Vice President:** J. Walker
Chairman: R.D. Coar BSC   **Vice-Chairman:** R.L. Matthewman
Secretary: Tom Finn
Manager: Roy Hodgson   **Coach:** Tony Parkes
Physio: M. Pettigrew

League History: 1888 Founder member of the League; 1936-39 Division 2; 1946-48 Division 1; 1948-58 Division 2; 1958-66 Division 1; 1966-71 Division 2; 1971-75 Division 3; 1975-79 Division 2; 1979-80 Division 3; 1980-92 Division 2; 1992- FA Premier League.

Honours: *FA Premier League: Champions* 1994-95; *Runners-up* 1993-94; *Football League: Division 1 – Champions* 1911-12, 1913-14; *Division 2 – Champions* 1938-39; *Runners-up* 1957-58; *Division 3 – Champions* 1974-75; *Runners-up* 1979-1980. *FA Cup: Winners* 1884, 1885, 1886, 1890, 1891, 1928; *Runners-up* 1882, 1960. *Full Members' Cup: Winners* 1986-87.

European Record: CC (1): 95-96; CWC (0): UEFA (1): 94-95 (1).

Managers: Thomas Mitchell 1884-96; J. Walmsley 1896-1903; R.B. Middleton 1903-25; Jack Carr 1922-26 (TM under Middleton to 1925); Bob Crompton 1926-31 (Hon. TM); Arthur Barritt 1931-36 (had been Secretary from 1927); Reg Taylor 1936-38; Bob Crompton 1938-41; Eddie Hapgood 1944-47; Will Scott 1947; Jack Burton 1947-49; Jackie Bestall 1949-53; Johnny Carey 1953-58; Dally Duncan 1958-60; Jack Marshall 1960-67; Eddie Quigley 1967-70; Johnny Carey 1970-71; Ken Furphy 1971-73; Gordon Lee 1974-75; Jim Smith 1975-78; Jim Iley 1978; John Pickering 1978-79; Howard Kendall 1979-81; Bobby Saxton 1981-86; Don Mackay 1987-91; (FAPL) Kenny Dalglish October 1991-May 1995; Ray Harford May 1995-Oct 1996; Tony Parkes (caretaker) Oct 1996-June 97; Roy Hodgson July 97-

Season 1996-97

Biggest Home Win:	4-0 v Coventry City
Biggest Home Defeat:	2-4 v Leicester City
Biggest Away Win:	2-0 v Everton
Biggest Away Defeat:	0-2 v Southampton
Biggest Home Att:	30,476 v Manchester United
Smallest Home Att:	20,485 v Nottingham Forest
Average Attendance:	24,947 (12th)
Leading Scorers:	11 – Sutton, 10 – Gallacher

All-Time Records

Record FAPL Win:	7-0 v Nottingham Forest, 18/11/95, 7-1 v Norwich City, 3/10/92
Record FAPL Defeat:	0-5 v Coventry City, 9/1/95
Record FL Win:	9-0 v Middlesbrough, Division 2, 6/11/54
Record FL Defeat:	0-8 v Arsenal, Division 1, 25/2/33
Record Cup Win:	11-0 v Rossendale, FA Cup R1, 13/10/1884
Record Fee Received:	£15m from Newcastle Utd for Alan Shearer, 7/96
Record Fee Paid:	£5m to Norwich City for Chris Sutton, 7/94
Most FL Apps:	Derek Fazackerley, 596, 1970-86
Most FAPL Apps:	176 – Tim Flowers, 1992-97
Most FAPL Goals:	112 – Alan Shearer, 1992-96

Highest Scorer in FAPL Season: Alan Shearer, 34, 1994-95
Record Attendance (all-time): 61,783 v Bolton W, FA Cup R6, 2/3/29
Record Attendance (FAPL): 30,895 v Liverpool, 24/2/96
Most FAPL Goals in Season: 80, 1994-95 – 42 games
Most FAPL Points in Season: 89, 1994-95 – 42 games

Player	Tot	St	Sb	Snu	PS	Gls	Y	R	Fa	La	Fg	Lg
BEATTIE	1	1	0	0	0	0	0	0	0	1	0	0
BERG	36	36	0	0	0	2	3	0	2	3	0	0
BOHINEN	23	17	6	7	0	2	6	0	1	3	1	0
BROOMES	0	0	0	3	0	0	0	0	0	0	0	0
COLEMAN	8	8	0	0	2	0	3	0	0	1	0	0
CROFT	5	4	1	10	0	0	0	0	0	2	0	0
DONIS	22	11	11	9	4	2	0	0	1	3	0	0
DUFF	1	1	0	4	0	0	0	0	0	0	0	0
FENTON	13	5	8	6	0	1	3	0	1	2	0	0
FLITCROFT	28	27	1	2	8	3	1	0	1	2	0	1
FLOWERS	36	36	0	2	0	0	2	0	2	3	0	0
GALLACHER	34	34	0	0	10	10	6	0	2	3	0	1
GIVEN	2	2	0	36	0	0	0	0	0	1	0	0
GUDMUNDSSON	2	0	2	5	0	0	0	0	0	0	0	0
HENDRY	35	35	0	0	3	1	4	0	2	2	0	0
KENNA	37	37	0	0	3	0	2	0	2	3	0	0
LE SAUX	26	26	0	0	1	1	6	0	2	0	0	0
MARKER	7	5	2	22	0	0	0	0	1	1	0	0
McKINLAY	25	23	2	4	3	1	12	0	2	0	0	0
PEARCE	12	7	5	3	1	0	1	0	0	2	0	0
PEDERSEN	11	6	5	1	8	1	0	0	0	0	0	0
RIPLEY	13	5	8	4	3	0	0	0	0	0	0	0
SHERWOOD	37	37	0	0	3	3	7	1	2	3	1	1
SUTTON	25	24	1	0	3	11	4	0	2	2	0	1
WARHURST	11	5	6	10	3	2	1	0	0	1	0	0
WILCOX	28	26	2	2	5	2	3	0	2	2	0	0

5-Year Record

	Div.	P	W	D	L	F	A	Pts	Pos	FAC	FLC
92-93	PL	42	20	11	11	68	46	71	4	6	SF
93-94	PL	42	25	9	8	63	36	84	2	4	4
94-95	PL	42	27	8	7	80	39	89	1	3	4
95-96	PL	38	18	7	13	61	47	61	7	3	4
96-97	PL	38	9	15	14	42	43	42	13	4	3

High Hopes as Hodgson Moves In

If the 1995-96 season was a time of great disappointment for the Ewood Park faithful, then the 96-97 campaign can be classed as little short of a catastrophe. In England striker Alan Shearer, Blackburn possessed the most potent goalscorer in the short life of the Premiership, but even Rovers found Newcastle's offer of £15m too good to resist. His departure seemed to be the catalyst for further unrest at Ewood Park. With no wins from their opening eleven league games, Blackburn then lost their manager, lined up a replacement who changed his mind, suffered a humbling Coca-Cola Cup giant killing at home to Stockport and saw league attendances drop by ten percent. Hardly a season to relish.

The campaign began badly for Blackburn with a 2-0 defeat at Ewood Park against Tottenham on the opening day of the season, in stark contrast to the impressive home record Rovers enjoyed since winning promotion to the Premier League. Just to compound their problems, Blackburn's away form – which was poor the previous season – was a nightmare with their only success coming at Everton on New Year's Day. A single goal success at Aston Villa on 20 August was followed by a bombshell as Kenny Dalglish announced his departure from the club. Rovers responded positively by collecting a point at Old Trafford but just two points from the next eight games had Blackburn entrenched at the foot of the table.

Ray Harford quit after only four points had been won from the opening ten games. Blackburn wanted a top coach to revive their fortunes and announced, after a lengthy wait, that Swede Sven-Goran Eriksson would be the new man in charge once clear of his current contract. In the meantime, long-time Blackburn servant Tony Parkes, 27 years at Ewood Park, was named as caretaker manager. Parkes began the revival as Liverpool were hammered 3-0 at the start of November. Draws with Chelsea, Forest and Leicester, and a home win over Southampton, lifted the side to a dizzy 17th. Defeat at Wimbledon was little more than a minor hiccup as just one of the next 12 games was lost, and goalkeeper Tim Flowers confirmed his return to form with six consecutive clean sheets.

But Rovers failed to build on their winter form and by the spring were once again looking anxiously over their shoulders following a run of just one win in eight games, this despite both Chris Sutton and Kevin Gallacher getting into double figures. Blackburn's second highest win of the season, 4-1 over Sheffield Wednesday on 22 April, eased their worries, with safety finally being secured courtesy of a goalless draw with Middlesbrough on 8 May.

Any hopes in the FA Cup quickly evaporated with a single-goal victory at Port Vale being followed by a shock 2-1 home defeat by Coventry. The Coca-Cola Cup was even less kind when a 4-1 aggregate 2nd Round success over Brentford was quickly forgotten as Stockport pulled off an outstanding 1-0 win at Ewood Park.

During the close season one free transfer was made and throughout the season only Per Pederson, £2.5m, was signed for a substantial fee.

Throughout the turmoil suffered during the season on and off the pitch, one man held everything together: Tony Parkes. When Eriksson decided that Lancashire was not for him, Parkes stood firm and guided Rovers to safety. Blackburn finally got the man they really wanted, the former Swiss manager and then Internazionale coach Roy Hodgson, who took the Italians to the UEFA Cup Final only to miss out in a penalty shoot-out. ∎

Results 1996-97

Date	Opponents	Ven	Res	Pos	Atten	Scorers
17-Aug	Tottenham H.	H	0-2	–	26,960	
20-Aug	Aston Villa	A	0-1	–	32,257	
25-Aug	Man. Utd	A	2-2	18	54,178	Warhurst (33); Bohinen (50)
04-Sep	Leeds Utd	H	0-1	19	23,226	
09-Sep	Derby Co.	H	1-2	19	19,214	Sutton (11)
14-Sep	Newcastle Utd	A	1-2	20	36,424	Sutton (85)
21-Sep	Everton	H	1-1	20	27,091	Donis (31)
28-Sep	Coventry C.	A	0-0	20	17,032	
12-Oct	Arsenal	H	0-2	20	24,303	
19-Oct	Sheffield W.	A	1-1	20	22,191	Bohinen (74)
26-Oct	West Ham Utd	A	1-2	20	23,947	Berg (8)
03-Nov	Liverpool	H	3-0	20	29,598	Sutton (3 pen, 55); Wilcox (24)
16-Nov	Chelsea	H	1-1	19	27,229	Gallacher (56)
25-Nov	N. Forest	A	2-2	19	17,525	Gallacher (53); Wilcox (57)
30-Nov	Southampton	H	2-1	18	23,018	Sherwood (27); Sutton (87)
07-Dec	Leicester C.	A	1-1	17	19,306	Sutton (33)
14-Dec	Wimbledon	H	0-1	17	13,246	
26-Dec	Newcastle Utd	H	1-0	18	30,398	Gallacher (75)
28-Dec	Derby Co.	A	0-0	18	17,847	
01-Jan	Everton	A	2-0	17	30,427	Sherwood (18); Sutton (32)
11-Jan	Coventry C.	H	4-0	14	24,055	Sutton (16, 34); Gallacher (30); Donis (76)
18-Jan	Sunderland	A	0-0	14	20,850	
29-Jan	Tottenham H.	A	1-2	16	22,943	Hendry (57)
01-Feb	West Ham Utd	H	2-1	13	21,994	Gallacher (36); Sutton (39)
22-Feb	Liverpool	A	0-0	15	40,747	
01-Mar	Sunderland	H	1-0	14	24,208	Gallacher (84)
05-Mar	Chelsea	A	1-1	13	25,784	Pedersen (62)
11-Mar	N. Forest	H	1-1	12	20,485	Gallacher (64)
15-Mar	Wimbledon	A	3-1	12	23,333	Gallacher (6, 26, 57)
19-Mar	Middlesbrough	A	1-2	12	29,891	Sutton (68)
22-Mar	Aston Villa	H	0-2	12	24,274	
07-Apr	Leeds Utd	A	0-0	13	27,264	
12-Apr	Man. Utd	H	2-3	14	30,476	McKinlay (35); Warhurst (88)
19-Apr	Arsenal	A	1-1	13	38,086	Flitcroft (89)
22-Apr	Sheffield W.	H	4-1	13	20,845	Berg (6); Sherwood (24); Le Saux (40); Flitcroft (59)
03-May	Southampton	A	0-2	13	15,247	
08-May	Middlesbrough	H	0-0	13	27,411	

11-May Leicester C. H 2-4 13 25,881 Flitcroft (25); Fenton (66)

FA Challenge Cup

Date	Opponents	Vn	Rnd	Res	Atten	Scorers
04-Jan	Port Vale	H	3R	1-0	19,891	Bohinen (68)
15-Feb	Coventry C.	A	4R	1-2	21,123	Sherwood (1)

Coca-Cola League Cup

Date	Opponents	Vn	Rnd	Res	Atten	Scorers
17-Sep	Brentford	A	2R1L	2-1	8,938	Flitcroft (17); Sutton (20)
24-Sep	Brentford	H	2R2L	2-0	9,599	Gallacher (44); Sherwood (74)

Blackburn Rovers win 4-1 on aggregate.

22-Oct	Stockport Co.	H	3R	0-1	14,622	

Rovers – Premiership Fact File

- Blackburn Rovers had to wait until their 12th game of the season to record their first win in the Premiership for 1996-97. But it was the point in their next game against Chelsea that took them off the bottom of the table.

- Rovers' tally of nine wins from 38 games was the second worst of the season. Only bottom club Nottingham Forest recorded less victories with six.

- Blackburn recorded only one win away from home during 1996-97. It came on New Year's Day at Everton. Leeds United recorded no wins away from home in the 1992-93 season. Rovers drew more away games than any other club during 1996-97 – 11 in total.

Bolton Wanderers

Formed in 1874 as a Sunday School side, Christ Church. This connection ended in 1877 when they adopted their present name. Turned professional in 1895 and were Football League founder members. Moved from Pikes Lane to present ground in 1895. Members of the reorganised Division One on formation of the Premier League, they were promoted to the Premier League for the 1995-96 season and, after being relegated straight back, bounced back into the top flight at the first attempt as Division One Champions.

Ground: The Reebok Stadium, Mansell Way, Horwich, Bolton
Phone: 01204-698800   **Box Office:** 01204-389200
Info: 0891-12 11 64
Capacity: 25,000   **Pitch:** tba
Colours: White, Navy Blue,Navy Blue   **Nickname:** The Trotters

President: Nat Lofthouse OBE   **Chairman:** G. Hargreaves
Secretary: Des McBain
Manager: Colin Todd   **Coach:** Ian Porterfield
Physio: E. Simpson
Internet: http://www.boltonwfc.co.uk

League History: 1892 Founder members of League; 1899-00 Division 2; 1900-03 Division 1; 1903-05 Division 2; 1905-08 Division 1; 1900-09 Division 2; 1909-10 Division 1; 1910-11 Division 2; 1911-33 Division 1; 1933-35 Division 2; 1935-64 Division 1; 1964-71 Division 2; 1971-73 Division 3; 1973-78 Division 2; 1978-80 Division 1; Division 2; 1983-87 Division 3; 1987-88 Division 4; 1988-92 Division 3; 1992-93 Division 2; 1993-94 Division 1; 1994-96 FAPL; 1996-1997 Division ; 1997- FAPL

Honours: *FA Cup Winners:* 1922-23, 1925-26, 1928-29, 1957-58; *Runners-up:* 1883-84, 1903-04, 1952-53; *Division One Champions:* 1996-97. *Division Two Champions:* 1908-09, 1977-78; *Division Three Champions:* 1972-73; *League Cup Runners-up:* 1994-95; *FA Charity Shield Winners:* 1958; *Sherpa Van Trophy Winners:* 1988-89; *Freight Rover Trophy Runners-up:* 1985-86.

European Record: Never qualified.

Managers: Tom Rawthorne 1874-85; JJ Bentley 1885-86; WG Struthers 1886-87; Fitzroy Norris 1887; JJ Bentley 1887-95; Harry Downs 1895-96; Frank Brettell 1896-98; John Somerville 1889-1910; Will Settle 1910-15; Tom Mather 1915-19; Charles Foweraker 1991-44; Walter Rowley 1944-50; Bill Ridding 1951-68; Nat Lofthouse 1968-70; Jimmy McIlroy 1971; Jimmy

Meadows 1971; Nat Lofthouse 1971; Jimmy Armfield 1971-74; Ian Greaves 1974-80; Stan Anderson 1980-81; George Mulhall 1981-82; John McGovern 1982-85; Charlie Wright 1985; Phil Neal 1985-92; Bruce Rioch 1992-1995; *(FAPL)* Roy McFarland/Colin Todd June 1995-Jan 1996; Colin Todd Jan 1996-

Season 1996-97

Biggest Home Win:	7-0 v Swindon Town
Biggest Home Defeat:	1-2 v Ipswich Town
Biggest Away Win:	4-2 v Bradford City
Biggest Away Defeat:	2-5 v Southend United
Biggest Home Att:	21,880 v Charlton Athletic
Smallest Home Att:	12,448 v Grimsby Town
Average Attendance:	22,017
Leading Scorer:	24 – John McGinlay

All-Time Records

Record FAPL Win:	4-1 v Middlesbrough (away), 17/2/96
Record FAPL Defeat:	0-6 v Manchester United (home), 25/2/96
Record FL Win:	8-0 v Barnsley, Division 2, 6/10/34
Record FL Defeat:	0-7 v Burnley 1/3/1890, Sheffield Wednesday, 1/3/15 and Manchester City, 21/3/36 all Division 1 away.
Record Cup Win:	13-0 v Sheffield Utd, FAC 2Rd, 1/2/1890
Record Fee Received:	£4.5m from Liverpool for Jason McAteer, 9/95
Record Fee Paid:	£1.5m to Barnsley for Gerry Taggart 8/95 and £1.5m to Partizan Belgrade for Sasa Curcic
Most FL Apps:	Eddie Hopkinson, 519, 1956-70
Most FAPL Apps:	37 – Jimmy Phillips, 1995-96
Most FAPL Goals:	6 – John McGinlay, 1995-96

Highest Scorer in FAPL Season: 6 – John McGinlay, 1995-96

Record Attendance (all-time): 69,912 v Man City, FAC 5Rd, 18/2/33
at Burnden Park

Record Attendance (FAPL): 21,381 v Manchester United, 25/2/96
at Burnden Park

Most FAPL Goals in Season: 29, 1995-96 – 38 games

Most FAPL Points in Season: 39, 1995-96 – 38 games

Summary 1996-97

Player	Tot	St	Sb	Gls	Fa	La	Fg	Lg
BERGSSON	33	30	3	3	2	3	0	0
BLAKE	34	34	0	19	3	5	2	3
BRANAGAN	36	36	0	0	0	4	0	0
BURNETT	1	0	1	0	0	0	0	0
COLEMAN	0	0	0	0	1	0	0	0
FAIRCLOUGH	46	46	0	8	3	5	0	0
FRANDSEN	41	40	1	5	4	5	0	0
GREEN	12	7	5	1	3	1	2	0
JOHANSEN	32	24	8	5	2	3	0	0
LEE	25	13	12	2	2	4	0	0
McANESPIE	13	11	2	0	0	1	0	0
McGINLAY	43	43	0	24	1	5	1	5
PAATELAINEN	10	3	7	2	0	0	0	0
PHILLIPS	36	36	0	0	0	4	0	0
POLLOCK	20	18	2	4	3	1	2	0
SELLARS	42	40	2	8	2	4	0	0
SHERIDAN	19	12	7	2	2	2	0	0
SMALL	11	10	1	0	3	1	0	0
TAGGART	43	43	0	3	2	5	0	1
TAYLOR	11	2	9	1	1	3	1	1
THOMPSON	34	34	0	11	2	4	1	1
TODD	15	6	9	0	0	4	0	0
WARD	11	10	1	0	3	1	0	0
OGs				2				

Tons of Success

Promotion, relegation, promotion. Bolton Wanderers go into the 1997-98 season looking to break that little sequence of fortune over the past three seasons. Whether their rapid exit from the Premiership last time merely confirms that there is a vast chasm between the Premier and the Nationwide or whether Bolton under-invested is a moot point, but Wanderers will be wary of the fact that for each of the past seven seasons one of the promoted sides has gone back down at the first attempt.

Colin Todd had money to spend going into the 1996-97 season following the sale of local hero Sasa Curcic to Aston Villa and Alan Stubbs to Celtic for a combined fee of £7.5m. Around £2.5m of that income was used to entice Michael Johansen and Per Frandsen to Burnden Park from Copenhagen. Bolton scored just once in each of their first two games but from then on the side scored freely and only twice failed to locate the target.

Alan Thompson, one of three players to get into double figures, scored Bolton's first goal of the season in a 1-1 draw with Port Vale. Frandsen quickly made his mark with the goal which gave Wanderers their first win, at home to Manchester City, and Johansen chipped in with his first in a 3-1 win over Norwich as Bolton ended the opening week with seven points out of nine and at the top of the Nationwide League. A third straight win at QPR bolstered their position only for bottom-of-the-table Southend United to hammer out a 5-2 warning. Scorers John McGinlay and Nathan Blake were the duo who went on to share 43 league goals, Scottish international McGinlay claiming 24. Bolton crushed struggling Grimsby 6-1 three days later. It was the start of an 11-match unbeaten run of which eight were won, including a crucial 2-1 victory at Molineux. Birmingham City ended the successful streak and two games later, their 19th league match, Bolton failed to score for the first time. Todd's side was on a run of eight games without a win and not surprisingly this led to pole position being surrendered just prior to Christmas.

Wins over lowly Grimsby and Southend, a 3-1 revenge, saw Bolton back at the top for the New Year and now there was no stopping the Lancashire side as they began to run away with the championship. Sixteen wins from 19 games secured promotion by 5 April with five games still to play. The final few weeks of the season were party time: the 2-1 win over QPR confirmed Bolton's promotion on the day Todd received the March Manager of the Month award. The championship, Bolton's first since winning the old Division Two in 1978, was taken in grand style at Maine Road four days later. All that remained was for Bolton to score a century of goals and amass a ton of points. Two goals at Tranmere on the last day of the season sorted out the first part of the equation but a last-minute equaliser by the home side left Bolton stranded on 98 points.

In the Coca-Cola Cup two Premiership sides bit the dust. After disposing of Bristol City over two legs in the 2nd Round, Bolton beat Ruud Gullit's Chelsea at Burnden Park. In the 4th Round Bolton thrashed Tottenham, with McGinlay netting Wanderers' only hat trick of the season. But in the quarter final Bolton met their match when going down 2-0 at home to in-form Wimbledon.

In the FA Cup Bolton put six goals past Luton Town at Burnden Park, after being pegged back by a late equaliser at Kenilworth Road. A favourable home tie with Chesterfield in Round Four seemed ideal but this year belonged very much to the underdog and the Division Two side duly pulled off a shock 3-2 victory.

Results 1996-97

Date	Opponents	Ven	Res	Atten	Scorers
17-Aug	Port Vale	A	1-1	10,057	Thompson
20-Aug	Man. City	H	1-0	18,257	Frandsen
24-Aug	Norwich City	H	3-1	13,057	Johansen; Blake (2)
01-Sep	QPR	A	2-1	11,225	McGinlay; Thompson
07-Sep	Southend Utd	A	2-5	4,475	Blake; McGinlay
010-Sep	Grimsby Tn	H	6-1	12,448	Fairclough; Johansen (2); Lee; Blake; Taylor
14-Sep	Portsmouth	H	2-0	14,248	Fairclough; Blake
21-Sep	Bradford City	A	4-2	12,034	Frandsen; Blake (2); Thompson
28-Sep	Stoke City	H	1-1	16,195	Blake
02-Oct	Wolves	A	2-1	26,540	McGinlay (2)
12-Oct	Oldham Ath	A	3-1	14,813	Johansen; McGinlay (2)
15-Oct	Tranmere Rvr	H	1-0	14,136	Sellars
19-Oct	Charlton Athl	A	3-3	11,091	Blake; McGinlay (2)
25-Oct	Barnsley	A	2-2	9,413	McGinlay; Thompson
29-Oct	Reading	H	2-1	12,677	Sellars; McGinlay
02-Nov	Huddersfield	H	2-0	15,865	McGinlay; Thompson
13-Nov	Birm, City	A	1-3	17,003	Sheridan
16-Nov	Crystal Palace	A	2-2	16,892	McGinlay; Sheridan
19-Nov	Oxford United	A	0-0	7,517	
22-Nov	Sheffield Utd	A	1-1	17,069	Blake
30-Nov	Barnsley	H	2-2	16,852	Thompson; Blake
08-Dec	WBA	A	2-2	13,084	Fairclough; Frandsen
14-Dec	Ipswich Tn	H	1-2	13,314	Bergsson
22-Dec	Swindon Tn	A	2-2	8,948	McGinlay; Green
26-Dec	Grimsby Tn	A	2-1	8,185	Taggart; Blake
28-Dec	Southend Utd	H	3-1	16,357	Sellars (2); McGinlay
01-Jan	Bradford City	H	2-1	16,192	Sellars; Lee
11-Jan	Portsmouth	A	3-0	10,467	Blake (2); Johansen
18-Jan	Wolves	H	3-0	18,980	Blake; Green; OG (Curle)
29-Jan	Stoke City	A	2-1	15,645	Pollock; McGinlay
01-Feb	Birm. City	H	2-1	16,737	Pollock; McGinlay
08-Feb	Reading	A	2-3	10,739	Thompson; McGinlay
15-Feb	Sheffield Utd	H	2-2	17,922	Fairclough; Paatelainen
22-Feb	Huddersfield	A	2-1	16,061	Taggart; Fairclough
02-Mar	WBA	H	1-0	13,258	Blake
04-Mar	Crystal Palace	A	1-1	16,038	Fairclough
08-Mar	Swindon Tn	H	7-0	13,981	Bergsson (2); Pollock; Frandsen; Blake; McGinlay; Thompson
15-Mar	Ipswich Town	A	1-0	16,187	McGinlay

18-Mar	Port Vale	H	4-2	14,150	Frandsen; OG (Glover); Fairclough; Blake
22-Mar	Norwich City	A	1-0	17,585	Sellars
05-Apr	QPR	H	2-1	19,198	Fairclough; McGinlay
09-Apr	Man. City	A	2-1	28,026	Paatelainen; Sellars
12-Apr	Oxford Utd	H	4-0	15,994	Thompson (2); Sellars; Blake
19-Apr	Oldham Ath.	A	0-0	10,702	
25-Apr	Charlton Ath	H	4-1	21,880	Thompson; Taggart; McGinlay (2)
04-May	Tranmere Rvrs	A	2-2	14,309	McGinlay, Pollock

FA Challenge Cup

Sponsored by Littlewoods Pools

Date	Opponents	Vn	Rnd	Res	Atten	Scorers
21-Jan	Luton Town	A	3R	1-1	7,414	Pollock
25-Jan	Luton Town	H	3RR	6-2	9,713	Pollock; Blake (2); McGinlay; Green; Thompson
4-Feb	Chesterfield	H	4R	2-3	10,852	Green; Taylor

Coca-Cola League Cup

Date	Opponents	Vn	Rnd	Res	Atten	Scorers
18-Sep	Bristol City	A	Rd	0-0	6,351	
24-Sep	Bristol City	H	2R1L	3-1	6,367	Blake; Thompson; McGinlay
	Bolton Wanderers win 3-1 on aggregate.					
22-Oct	Chelsea	H		2-1	16,867	McGinlay; Blake
27-Nov	Tottenham	H	3R	6-1	18,621	McGinlay (3); Taggart; Blake; Taylor
08-Jan	Wimbledon	H	4R	0-2	16,968	

5-Year Record

	Div.	P	W	D	L	F	A	Pts	Pos	FAC	FLC
92-93	2	46	27	9	10	80	41	90	2	5	2
93-94	1	46	16	7	23	63	64	59	14	6	2
94-95	1	42	20	12	14	67	45	77	3	3	F
95-96	PL	38	8	5	25	39	71	29	20	4	4
96-97	1	46	28	14	4	100	53	98	1	4	4

Chelsea

Founded in 1905. The Mears brothers developed Stamford Bridge Athletic Ground, which they owned, into a football stadium for prestigious matches and, prospectively, nearby Fulham FC. But Fulham did not take up the chance so the Mears brothers established their own club, rejecting possible names such as 'London' and 'Kensington' in favour, eventually, of Chelsea.

Judging that the club would not be accepted into the Southern League, it sought membership of the Football League. This was gained at the first attempt and it started the 1906-07 season in Division Two. Premier League founder members 1992.

Ground: Stamford Bridge, London SW6 1HS
Phone: 0171-385 5545
Box Office: 0171-386 7799   **CC Booking:** 0171-386 7799
News: 0891 12 11 59   **Tickets:** 0891 12 10 11
Capacity: 33,000 (>37,000 10/97) **Pitch:** 110 yds x 72 yds
Colours: Royal Blue, Royal Blue, White   **Nickname:** The Blues
Radio: 1548AM Capital Gold
Internet: http://www.chelseafc.co.uk

Patron: Ruth Harding   **Chairman:** Ken W. Bates
MD: Colin Hutchinson
Match Secretary: Keith Lacy   **Company Secretary:** Alan Shaw
Manager: Ruud Gullit   **Assistant:** Graham Rix
Physio: Bob Ward

League History: 1905 Elected to Division 2; 1907-10 Division 1; 1910-12 Division 2; 1912-24 Division 1; 1924-30 Division 2; 1930-62 Division 1; 1962-63 Division 2; 1963-75 Division 1; 1975-77 Division 2; 1977-79 Division 1; 1979-84 Division 2; 1984-88 Division 1; 1988-89 Division 2; 1989-92 Division 1; 1992- FA Premier League.

Honours: *Football League: Division 1 Champions:* 1954-55; *Division 2 Champions:* 1983-84, 1988-89; *Runners-up:* 1906-7, 1911-12, 1929-30,1962-63, 1976-77. *FA Cup: Winners:* 1970, 1997; *Runners-up:* 1914-15, 1966-67, 1993-94. *Football League Cup: Winners:* 1964-65; *Runners-up:* 1971-72; *Full Members' Cup Winners:* 1985-86. *Zenith Data Systems Cup Winners:* 1989-90.

European Record: CC (0) – ; CWC (3): 70-71 (W), 71-72 (2), 94-95 (SF); UEFA (2): 65-66 (SF), 68-69 (2).

Managers: John Tait Robertson 1905-07; David Calderhead 1907-33; A. Leslie Knighton 1933-39; Billy Birrell 1939-52; Ted Drake 1952-61; Tommy Docherty 1962-67; Dave Sexton 1967-74; Ron Stuart 1974-75; Eddie McCreadie 1975-77; Ken Shellito 1977-78; Danny Blanchflower 1978-79; Geoff Hurst 1979-81; John Neal 1981 85 (Director to 1986); John Hollins 1985-88; Bobby Campbell 1988-91; *(FAPL)* Ian Porterfield June 1991-1993; Dave Webb 1993; Glenn Hoddle July 1993-June 1996; Ruud Gullit June 1996-

Season 1996-97

Biggest Home Win:	6-2 v Sunderland
Biggest Home Defeat:	0-3 v Arsenal
Biggest Away Win:	3-1 v Manchester United
Biggest Away Defeat:	1-5 v Liverpool
Biggest Home Att:	28,418 v Everton
Smallest Home Att:	25,024 v Coventry City
Average Attendance:	27,615 (10th)
Leading Scorers:	9 – Gianluca Vialli, 8 – Mark Hughes and Gianfranco Zola

All-Time Records

Record FAPL Win: 6-2 v Sunderland, 16/3/97
Record FAPL Defeat: 1-4 v Leeds United, 6/11/93,
1-4 v Manchester United, 21/10/95
Record FL Win: 9-2 v Glossop NE, Division 2, 1/9/1906
Record FL Defeat: 1-8 v Wolverhampton W, Division 1, 26/9/1953
Record Cup Win: 13-0 v Jeunesse Hautcharage, CWC, 1R2L, 29/9/1971
Record Fee Received: £2.5m from QPR for John Spencer, 11/96
Record Fee Paid: £4.9m to Lazio for Roberto Di Matteo, 7/96
Most FL Apps: Ron Harris, 655, 1962-80
Most FAPL Apps: 147 – Dennis Wise, 1992-97
Most FAPL Goals: 36 – John Spencer, 1992-97
Highest Scorer in FAPL Season: 13: Mark Stein (93/4), John Spencer (95/6)
Record Attendance (all-time): 82,905 v Arsenal, Div 1, 12/10/1935
Record Attendance (FAPL): 37,064 v Manchester United, 11/9/93
Most FAPL Goals in Season: 58, 1996-97 – 38 games
Most FAPL Points in Season: 59, 1996-97 – 38 games

Player	Tot	St	Sb	Snu	PS	Gls	Y	R	Fa	La	Fg	Lg
BURLEY	31	26	5	1	8	2	3	0	3	3	1	0
CLARKE	31	31	0	1	1	0	7	0	7	3	0	0
CLEMENT	1	1	0	5	1	0	1	0	0	0	0	0
COLGAN	1	1	0	15	0	0	0	0	0	0	0	0
DI MATTEO	34	33	1	3	5	6	5	0	7	3	2	0
DUBERRY	15	13	2	4	0	1	4	0	1	2	0	0
FORREST *	3	2	1	1	0	0	0	0	0	0	0	0
GRANVILLE	5	3	2	2	0	0	0	0	0	0	0	0
GRODAS	21	20	1	9	1	0	1	1	5	1	0	0
GULLIT	12	6	6	2	2	1	1	0	1	1	0	0
HITCHCOCK	12	10	2	9	1	0	1	0	2	2	0	0
HUGHES M.	35	32	3	0	5	8	6	0	7	2	5	1
HUGHES P.	12	8	4	3	6	2	1	0	1	0	0	0
JOHNSEN	18	14	4	7	3	0	3	0	3	1	0	0
KHARINE	5	5	0	0	1	0	0	0	0	0	0	0
LEBOEUF	26	26	0	1	1	6	7	0	7	2	1	0
LEE	1	1	0	5	1	1	0	0	0	1	0	0
MINTO †	25	24	1	4	6	4	6	0	6	2	0	1
MORRIS	12	6	6	8	3	0	1	0	0	2	0	1
MYERS	18	15	3	6	6	1	2	0	0	0	0	0
NEWTON	15	13	2	2	2	0	2	0	6	0	1	0
NICHOLLS	8	3	5	8	2	0	0	0	0	2	0	0
PARKER †	4	1	3	2	1	0	0	0	0	0	0	0
PEACOCK	0	0	0	2	0	0	0	0	0	0	0	0
PETRESCU	34	34	0	0	4	3	4	0	6	2	0	1
PHELAN †	3	1	2	2	0	0	0	0	0	1	0	0
SHEERIN	1	0	1	0	0	0	0	0	0	0	0	0
SINCLAIR	20	17	3	6	0	1	5	0	6	0	0	0
SPENCER †	4	0	4	5	0	0	2	0	0	3	0	2
VIALLI	28	23	5	5	3	9	5	0	5	1	2	0
WISE	31	27	4	0	4	4	7	0	7	2	3	0
ZOLA	23	22	1	1	4	8	0	0	7	0	4	0
OGs						1						

* previously on loan from Ipswich Town.

Cup Win Just the Start?

A generation has passed since Chelsea last lifted significant silverware, but with their 2-0 FA Cup Final success over Middlesbrough, the Blues, under the inspired leadership of Ruud Gullit, appear to be on the verge of their greatest days since Dave Sexton's side of the early seventies.

As a player, a fully fit Gullit was without peers, and as a manager he displays remarkable calmness and an appreciation of situations on and off the pitch which is highly refreshing. With the full support of chairman Ken Bates, Gullit was able to invest freely in the transfer market, usually with great success, although free-signing Gianluca Vialli was none too pleased at being almost resident substitute.

Gullit raised around £2.5m from selling three players during the close season, a figure which covered the signing of Frank Leboeuf, while a further £4.9m was needed to prise Roberto Di Matteo from Lazio. The jigsaw was completed in November when Parma accepted £4.5m for Gianfranco Zola, who went on to win the Football Writers' Player of the Year award. Chelsea's multi-national side was quickly into its stride with clean sheets being achieved in all of the opening four league matches. The character of the side was tested at Arsenal when a two-goal lead was overturned, but Dennis Wise salvaged a point with the Blues' sixth league goal of the season, although it was the first scored by an Englishman. But if a reminder was needed that building a side to challenge the best does take time then it came at Anfield on 21 September as Liverpool dished out a 5-1 thrashing.

During the onset of winter Chelsea failed to find good consistent winning form in the league and were little more than on the fringe of a place in the UEFA Cup, despite some excellent results which included victory over Liverpool, a home draw with Manchester United and a 6-2 hammering of Sunderland.

A 4-1 win at Blackpool in the Coca-Cola Cup certainly bode well for the future. But it was their last win in that competition as Blackpool won the return at the Bridge 3-1 and Bolton Wanderers won 2-1 in the next round after Scott Minto had given Chelsea an early lead.

Chelsea had no such problems in the FA Cup and breezed past West Bromwich Albion. Liverpool soared into a two-goal lead in the 4th Round but with the introduction of Mark Hughes at half time the Blues' season was transformed. Hughes paved the way for a stunning 4-2 victory with Vialli grabbing the last two goals. In the 5th Round Chelsea were held to a draw by Leicester at Filbert Street thanks to Eddie Newton's embarrassing last-minute own goal. The outcome of the replay was controversial to say the least, as Leboeuf stroked home a penalty three minutes from the end of extra time after Erland Johnsen had taken a dramatic tumble in the box. Chelsea's form in the quarter final was awesome as Portsmouth were dispatched 4-1 at Fratton Park. Chelsea also cruised through the semi final with a 3-0 victory over neighbours Wimbledon when Hughes took his FA Cup goals total for the season to five with a brace and Zola chipped in a gem.

The final will forever be remembered for Di Matteo's stunning long-range goal after just 43 seconds, the quickest in Wembley history. Chelsea's first significant Wembley win was secured late in the day when Newton scored from close in. It is difficult to believe that Chelsea will not build on this success, which many dedicated to the memory of former vice chairman Matthew Harding who, along with four others, perished in a helicopter crash. ■

Results 1996-97

FA Carling Premiership

Date	Opponents	Ven	Res	Pos	Atten	Scorers
18-Aug	Southampton	A	0-0	–	15,186	
21-Aug	Middlesbrough	H	1-0	–	28,272	Di Matteo (85)
24-Aug	Coventry C.	H	2-0	2	25,024	Leboeuf (28); Vialli (74)
04-Sep	Arsenal	A	3-3	3	38,132	Leboeuf (6 pen); Vialli (30); Wise (90)
07-Sep	Sheffield W.	A	2-0	2	30,983	Burley (28); Myers (83)
15-Sep	Aston Villa	H	1-1	3	27,729	Leboeuf (45)
21-Sep	Liverpool	H	1-5	7	40,739	Leboeuf (89 pen)
28-Sep	N. Forest	H	1-1	6	27,673	Vialli (51)
12-Oct	Leicester C.	A	3-1	6	20,766	Vialli (48); Di Matteo (64); Hughes, M. (80)
19-Oct	Wimbledon	H	2-4	6	28,020	Minto (11); Vialli (84 pen)
26-Oct	Tottenham H.	H	3-1	6	28,373	Gullit (27); Lee (55 pen); Di Matteo (81)
02-Nov	Man. Utd	A	2-1	5	55,198	Duberry (30); Vialli (59)
16-Nov	Blackburn R.	A	1-1	5	27,229	Petrescu (82)
23-Nov	Newcastle Utd	H	1-1	5	28,401	Vialli (25)
01-Dec	Leeds Utd	A	0-2	7	32,671	
07-Dec	Everton	H	2-2	7	28,418	Zola (12); Vialli (55)
14-Dec	Sunderland	A	0-3	7	19,683	
21-Dec	West Ham Utd	H	3-1	8	28,315	Hughes, M. (5, 36); Zola (10)
26-Dec	Aston Villa	A	2-0	7	39,339	Zola (66, 70)
28-Dec	Sheffield W.	H	2-2	7	27,467	Zola (10); Hughes, M. (22)
01-Jan	Liverpool	A	1-0	7	28,239	Di Matteo (44)
11-Jan	N. Forest	A	0-2	7	28,358	
18-Jan	Derby Co.	H	3-1	6	28,293	Wise (38); Leboeuf (45 pen); Hughes, P. (85)
01-Feb	Tottenham H.	A	2-1	5	33,027	OG (1, Campbell); Di Matteo (52)
22-Feb	Man. Utd	H	1-1	6	28,336	Zola (3)
01-Mar	Derby Co.	A	2-3	7	18,039	Minto (16); Leboeuf (53)
5-Mar	Blackburn	H	1-1	8	25,784	Minto (63)
12-Mar	West Ham Utd	A	2-3	8	24,502	Vialli (26); Hughes, M. (87)
16-Mar	Sunderland	H	6-2	7	24,072	Zola (38); Sinclair (42); Petrescu (50); Hughes, M. (76, 89); Di Matteo (90)
19-Mar	Southampton	H	1-0	5	28,079	Zola (21)
22-Mar	Middlesbrough	A	0-1	6	29,811	
05-Apr	Arsenal	H	0-3	6	28,182	

09-Apr	Coventry C.	A	1-3	7	19,917	Hughes, P. (43)
16-Apr	Newcastle Utd	A	1-3	8	36,320	Burley (62)
19-Apr	Leicester C.	H	2-1	7	27,723	Minto (13); Hughes, M. (72)
22-Apr	Wimbledon	A	1-0	7	14,601	Petrescu (14)
03-May	Leeds Utd	H	0-0	7	28,277	
11-May	Everton	A	2-1	6	38,321	Wise (14); Di Matteo (36)

FA Challenge Cup

Date	Opponents	Vn	Rnd	Res	Atten	Scorers
04-Jan	WBA	H	3R	3-0	27,446	Wise (39); Burley (74); Zola (90)
26-Jan	Liverpool	H	4R	4-2	27,950	Hughes, M. (47); Zola (58); Vialli (63, 75)
16-Feb	Leicester C.	A	5R	2-2	19,125	Di Matteo (16); Hughes, M. (35)
26-Feb	Leicester C.	H	5RR	1-0	26,053	Leboeuf (117 pen)
09-Mar	Portsmouth	A	6R	4-1	15,701	Hughes, M. (23); Wise (44, 86); Zola (55)
13-Apr	Wimbledon	*	SF	3-0	32,674	Hughes, M. (42, 90); Zola (63)
17-May	Middlesbrough	W	F	2-0	79,160	Di Matteo (1); Newton (82)

* at Highbury.

Coca-Cola League Cup

Date	Opponents	Vn	Rnd	Res	Atten	Scorers
18-Sep	Blackpool	A	2R1L	4-1	9,666	Morris (16); Petrescu (46); Hughes, M. (64); Spencer (85)
25-Sep	Blackpool	H	2R2L	1-3	11,732	Spencer (63)
	Chelsea win 5-4 on aggregate.					
22-Oct	Bolton W.	A	3R	1-2	16,867	Minto (2)

5-Year Record

	Div.	P	W	D	L	F	A	Pts	Pos	FAC	FLC
92-93	PL	42	14	14	14	51	54	56	11	3	4
93-94	PL	42	13	12	17	49	53	51	14	F	3
94-95	PL	42	13	15	14	50	55	54	11	4	3
95-96	PL	38	12	14	12	46	44	50	11	SF	2
96-97	PL	38	16	11	11	58	55	59	6	W	3

Coventry City

Founded as Singer's FC, cycle manufacturers, in 1883. Joined the Birmingham and District League in 1894; in 1898 changed name to Coventry City; and in 1905 moved to the Athletic Ground, Highfield Road. Elected to Division One of the Southern League in 1908, but relegated to the Second in 1914.

Joined the Wartime Midland Section of the Football League in 1918 and elected to an expanded Second Division of the Football League for 1919-20. Founder members of the Fourth Division in 1958. Promoted to Division One for the first time in 1967 and never relegated. Premier League founder members 1992.

Ground: Highfield Road Stadium, King Richard St, Coventry, CV2 4FW
Phone: 01203-234000
Box Office: 01203-234020   **CC Booking:** 01203-578000
News: 0891 12 11 66
Capacity: 24,021   **Pitch:** 110 yds x 75 yds
Colours: All Sky Blue   **Nickname:** Sky Blues
Radio: 95.6FM BBC Radio West Midlands
Internet: http://www.ccfc.co.uk

President: Eric Grove   **Chairman:** Bryan Richardson
Deputy-Chairman: Mike McGinnity **Secretary:** Graham Hover
Manager: Gordon Strachan OBE   **Assistant:** Alec Miller
Director of Football: Ron Atkinson
Physio: George Dalton

League History: 1919 Elected to Division 2; 1925-26 Division 3 (N); 1926-36 Division 3 (S); 1936-52 Division 2; 1952-58 Division 3 (S); 1958-59 Division 4; 1959-64 Division 3; 1964-67 Division 2; 1967-92 Division 1; 1992- FA Premier League.

Honours: *Football League Division 2 Champions:* 1966-67; *Division 3 Champions:* 1963-64; *Division 3 (S) Champions:* 1935-36; *Runners-up:* 1933-34; *Division 4 Runners-up:* 1958-59; *FA Cup Winners:* 1986-87.

European Record: CC (0): – ; CWC (0) – ; UEFA (1): 70-71 (2)

Managers: H.R. Buckle 1909-10; Robert Wallace 1910-13; Frank Scott-Walford 1913-15; William Clayton 1917-19; H. Pollitt 1919-20; Albert Evans 1920-24; Jimmy Ker 1924-28; James McIntyre 1928-31; Harry Storer 1931-

45; Dick Bayliss 1945-47; Billy Frith 1947-48; Harry Storer 1948-53; Jack Fairbrother 1953-54; Charlie Elliott 1954-55; Jesse Carver 1955-56; Harry Warren 1956-57; Billy Firth 1957-61; Jimmy Hill 1961-67; Noel Cantwell 1967-72; Bob Dennison 1972; Joe Mercer 1972-75; Gordon Milne 1972-81; Dave Sexton 1981-83; Bobby Gould 1983-84; Don Mackay 1985-86; George Curtis 1986-87 (became MD); John Sillett 1987-90; Terry Butcher 1990-92; Don Howe 1992; *(FAPL)* Bobby Gould July 1992-93; Phil Neal Nov 1993-Feb 1995; Ron Atkinson Feb 1995-Nov 1996; Gordon Strachan Nov 1996-

Season 1996-97

Biggest Home Win: 3-0 v Middlesbrough
Biggest Home Defeat: 0-3 v Nottingham Forest
Biggest Away Win: 3-1 v Leeds United
Biggest Away Defeat: 0-4 v Blackburn Rovers, Middlesbrough, Newcastle Utd
Biggest Home Att: 23,085 v Manchester United
Smallest Home Att: 15,273 v Wimbledon
Average Attendance: 19,608 (17th)
Leading Scorers: 14 – Dion Dublin, 6 – Gary McAllister

All-Time Records

Record FAPL Win: 5-0 v Blackburn Rovers, 9/12/95
5-1 v Liverpool, 19/12/92
Record FAPL Defeat: 0-5 v Manchester United, 28/12/92
Record FL Win: 9-0 v Bristol C, Division 3 (S), 28/4/34
Record FL Defeat: 2-10 v Norwich C, Division 3 (S), 15/3/30
Record Cup Win: 7-0 v Scunthorpe U, FA Cup R1, 24/11/34
Record Fee Received: £3.6m from Liverpool for Phil Babb, 9/94
Record Fee Paid: £3m to Leeds United for Gary McAllister, 7/96
Most FL Apps: George Curtis, 486, 1956-70
Most FAPL Apps: 162 – Steve Ogrizovic, 1992-97
Most FAPL Goals: 41 – Dion Dublin, 1992-97
Highest Scorer in FAPL Season: Mick Quinn, 17, 1992-93
Record Attendance (all-time): 51,455 v Wolves, Division 2, 29/4/67
Record Attendance (FAPL): 24,410 v Manchester United 12/04/93
Most FAPL Goals in Season: 62, 1992-93 – 42 games
Most FAPL Points in Season: 56, 1993-94 – 42 games

Summary 1996-97

Player	Tot	St	Sb	Snu	PS	Gls	Y	R	Fa	La	Fg	Lg
BOLAND	1	0	1	13	0	0	0	0	0	0	0	0
BORROWS	23	16	7	8	4	0	3	0	3	4	0	0
BREEN	9	8	1	4	0	0	0	0	0	0	0	0
BURROWS	18	17	1	6	3	0	5	0	0	2	0	0
DAISH	20	20	0	0	2	1	4	1	0	3	0	1
DUBLIN	34	33	1	0	2	14	5	0	1	4	0	0
DUCROS	5	1	4	4	0	0	0	0	0	0	0	0
EUSTACE	0	0	0	1	0	0	0	0	0	0	0	0
EVTUSHOK	3	3	0	4	2	0	0	0	0	0	0	0
FILAN	1	0	1	37	0	0	0	0	0	0	0	0
GENAUX	4	3	1	6	1	0	2	0	0	0	0	0
GOODWIN	0	0	0	1	0	0	0	0	0	0	0	0
HALL	13	10	3	6	2	0	0	0	3	0	0	0
HUCKERBY	25	21	4	0	7	5	2	0	4	0	2	0
ISAIAS	1	0	1	1	0	0	0	0	0	0	0	0
JESS †	27	19	8	7	10	0	0	0	4	1	2	0
McALLISTER	38	38	0	0	6	1	0	4	4	0	1
McMENAMIN	0	0	0	1	0	0	0	0	0	0	0	0
NDLOVU †	20	10	10	1	4	1	1	0	3	0	0	0
O'NEILL	1	1	0	1	3	1	0	0	0	0	0	0
OGRIZOVIC	38	38	0	0	1	0	1	0	4	4	0	0
PRINDERVILLE	0	0	0	1	0	0	0	0	0	0	0	0
RICHARDSON	28	25	3	7	2	0	2	0	4	4	0	0
SALAKO	24	23	1	0	2	1	0	0	1	4	0	0
SHAW	35	35	0	2	2	0	3	0	4	3	0	0
SHILTON	0	0	0	2	0	0	0	0	0	0	0	0
STRACHAN	9	3	6	9	3	0	1	0	1	1	0	0
TELFER	34	31	3	1	2	0	6	0	4	4	0	2
WHELAN	35	34	1	0	9	6	9	0	4	4	2	0
WILLIAMS P.	32	29	3	2	1	2	7	0	4	2	0	0
WILLIS	0	0	0	2	0	0	0	0	0	0	0	0
OGs						2				1		

5-Year Record

	Div.	P	W	D	L	F	A	Pts	Pos	FAC	FLC
92-93	PL	42	13	13	16	52	57	52	15	3	2
93-94	PL	42	14	14	14	43	45	56	11	3	3
94-95	PL	42	12	14	16	44	62	50	16	4	3
95-96	PL	38	8	14	16	42	60	38	16	4	4
96-97	PL	38	9	14	15	38	54	41	17	5	3

The Great Escape – Again

Optimism pervaded Highfield Road in the run up to the Sky Blues' 30th year in the top division and manager Ron Atkinson kept the momentum going with the £3m signing of 31-year-old Leeds and Scotland captain Gary McAllister. Big Ron also brought in Regis Genaux from Standard Liege for £1m and Michael O'Neill, a £500,000 signing from Hibernian. Most of Genaux's fee was recouped when he moved to Udinese in January.

For the opening match of the season a crowd 4,000 above the previous season's average saw Coventry's expectancy levels greatly reduced as Nottingham Forest stormed to a 3-0 victory. Just one point was taken from the next four games, during which McAllister scored City's only goal, before a first-minute deficit at home to Leeds on 14 September was overturned by goals from John Salako and Noel Whelan. A run of six consecutive draws was followed by three successive defeats as Coventry stayed firmly entrenched in the bottom three.

Atkinson and his assistant, Gordon Strachan, were twice in trouble with the FA on disrepute charges. Atkinson's one day promote Strachan to manager came to fruition in early November as Big Ron moved 'upstairs'. During the same month Darren Huckerby was signed from Newcastle for a bargain £1m.

Only Forest now sat below the Sky Blues. But with Huckerby, Dublin and McAllister scoring freely, Strachan's side won their remaining four games before the turn of the year. Dublin was sent off twice and handed a seven-match ban. Strachan was busy in the transfer market in January as he signed Gary Breen from Birmingham and Aleksandr Evtushok for £2.5m and £800,000 respectively.

The Blackburn defeat sparked a run of just one win from 12 games and City entered the final month of the campaign hot favourites for the drop. Amazingly though, Coventry began their second great revival of the season by taking advantage of Liverpool's indifferent home form to clinch a 2-1 success at Anfield through Dublin's injury-time goal on 6 April. Three days later Chelsea's cup-chasing stars were brought down to earth and a vital point was grabbed at Southampton after trailing by two goals. Another point was squeezed from Arsenal but a 2-1 defeat at Derby in the final Saturday match of the season seemed to have sealed the Sky Blues' fate.

For an astonishing ninth time Coventry needed favourable results on the last day of the season to avoid the drop. They got the required result at Tottenham with first half goals from Dublin and Paul Williams and, thanks to Sunderland losing to an 85th minute goal at Wimbledon, survived by one point.

City's poor league form was carried into both major cup competitions. After being held at home by Birmingham in the Coca-Cola Cup, the Sky Blues won the return match at St Andrews but were then embarrassed by Gillingham who won at Highfield Road after being held in Kent, the latter being Strachan's first match in charge. In the FA Cup, non-league heroes Woking held Coventry to a remarkable draw at Highfield Road in the 3rd Round and in the replay the Sky Blues came close to defeat before an own goal carried them through. It was Coventry's turn to cause a shock in the following round as Blackburn Rovers were overcome at Ewood Park. Indeed, City looked to be fully into their stride by the 5th Round as they swept into a two-goal lead at Derby before suffering the second of three defeats to the Rams during the season. ∎

Results 1996-97

Date	Opponents	Ven	Res	Pos	Atten	Scorers
17-Aug	N. Forest	H	0-3	–	19,468	
21-Aug	West Ham Utd	A	1-1	–	21,580	McAllister (11)
24-Aug	Chelsea	A	0-2	19	25,024	
04-Sep	Liverpool	A	0-1	20	23,021	
07-Sep	Middlesbrough	A	0-4	20	29,811	
14-Sep	Leeds Utd	H	2-1	18	17,297	Salako (57); Whelan (65)
21-Sep	Sunderland	A	0-1	18	19,459	
28-Sep	Blackburn R.	H	0-0	19	17,032	
13-Oct	Southampton	H	1-1	19	15,485	Dublin (90)
19-Oct	Arsenal	A	0-0	19	38,140	
26-Oct	Sheffield W.	H	0-0	19	17,267	
04-Nov	Everton	A	1-1	18	31,477	McAllister (68)
16-Nov	Wimbledon	A	2-2	18	10,307	Whelan (54); Dublin (68)
23-Nov	Aston Villa	H	1-2	18	21,340	Dublin (75)
30-Nov	Derby Co.	A	1-2	19	18,042	Dublin (42)
07-Dec	Tottenham H.	H	1-2	20	19,675	Whelan (61)
17-Dec	Newcastle Utd	H	2-1	19	21,538	Huckerby (6); McAllister (31)
21-Dec	Leicester C.	A	2-0	17	20,038	Dublin (10, 71)
26-Dec	Leeds Utd	A	3-1	15	36,465	Huckerby (30); Dublin (38); McAllister (40)
28-Dec	Middlesbrough	H	3-0	14	20,617	Huckerby (29); McAllister (64 pen); OG (85, Liddle)
01-Jan	Sunderland	H	2-2	12	17,700	Dublin (10); Daish (28)
11-Jan	Blackburn R.	A	0-4	15	24,055	
18-Jan	Man. Utd	H	0-2	16	23,085	
29-Jan	N. Forest	A	1-0	14	22,619	Huckerby (50)
01-Feb	Sheffield W.	A	0-0	15	21,793	
19-Feb	Aston Villa	A	1-2	16	30,409	OG (78, Staunton)
22-Feb	Everton	H	0-0	16	19,497	
01-Mar	Man. Utd	A	1-3	16	55,230	Huckerby (85)
03-Mar	Wimbledon	H	1-1	16	15,273	Dublin (37)
08-Mar	Leicester C.	H	0-0	16	19,220	
15-Mar	Newcastle Utd	A	0-4	16	36,571	
22-Mar	West Ham Utd	H	1-3	18	22,291	Dublin (9)
06-Apr	Liverpool	A	2-1	17	40,079	Whelan (65); Dublin (90)
09-Apr	Chelsea	H	3-1	15	19,917	Dublin (49); Williams (51); Whelan (58)
19-Apr	Southampton	A	2-2	15	15,251	Ndlovu (62); Whelan (74)
21-Apr	Arsenal	H	1-1	15	19,998	Dublin (1)

| 3-May | Derby Co. | H | 1-2 | 18 | 22,839 | McAllister (59) |
| 11-May | Tottenham H. | A | 2-1 | 17 | 33,029 | Dublin (13); Williams (39) |

FA Challenge Cup

Date	Opponents	Vn	Rnd	Res	Atten	Scorers
25-Jan	Woking	H	3R	1-1	16,011	Jess (76)
04-Feb	Woking	A	3RR	2-1	6,000	Whelan 12; OG (79, Foster)
15-Feb	Blackburn R.	A	4R	2-1	21,123	Jess (28); Huckerby (44)
26-Feb	Derby Co.	A	5R	2-3	18,003	Huckerby (7); Whelan (12)

Coca-Cola League Cup

Date	Opponents	Vn	Rnd	Res	Atten	Scorers
18-Sep	Birmingham C.	H	2R1L	1-1	11,828	Daish (88)
24-Sep	Birmingham C.	A	2R2L	1-0	15,218	McAllister (62)
	Coventry City win 2-1 on aggregate.					
22-Oct	Gillingham	A	3R	2-2	10,603	Telfer (25, 28)
13-Nov	Gillingham	H	3RR	0-1	12,639	

Sky Blues – Premiership Fact File

- The 1996-97 season saw the Sky Blues escape relegation on the last day of the season for the 9th time in 30 years!

- Steve Ogrizovic set a new City record of 544 first team appearances when he played against Middlesbrough on 28 December.

- Darren Huckerby scored his first Sky Blue goal against the club who sold him a few weeks earlier – Newcastle United.

- Coventry's tally of nine wins from 38 games was the second worst of the season. Only bottom club Nottingham Forest recorded less victories with six.

- City scored 29 Premiership goals both at home and away.

Crystal Palace

Founded in 1905 to play at the Crystal Palace Ground where, earlier, a Crystal Palace staff team had successfully played. Joined the Southern League for 1905-06 when they were Champions of Division Two. Soon moved to Herne Hill, then to The Nest, Selhurst. Founder members and first champions of the Football League Third Division 1920-21. Moved to Selhurst Park in 1924.

Founder members of the old Fourth Division in 1958, they reached the First Division for the first time as Second Division runners-up in 1969. Premier League founder members 1992. Relegated after one season, but promoted back at the first attempt, only to be relegated in 1994-95, winning their place back through the play-offs at the end of the 1996-97 season.

Ground:	Selhurst Park, South Norwood, London SE25 6PU		
Phone:	0181-768 6000	**Box Office:**	0181-771 8841
News:	0891 400 333		
Capacity:	26,995	**Pitch:**	110 yds x 74 yds.
Colours:	Red/Blue, Red, Red	**Nickname:**	The Eagles
Radio:	1548AM Capital Gold		
Internet:	–		

Chairman:	Ron G. Noades	**Club Secretary:**	Mike Hurst
Manager:	Steve Coppell	**Coach:**	Ray Lewington
Physio:	Gary Sadler		

League History: 1920 Original Members of Division 3; 1921-25 Division 2; 1925-58 Division 3(S); 1958-61 Division 4; 1961-64 Division 3, 1964-69 Division 2; 1969-73 Division 1; 1973-74 Division 2; 1974-77 Division 3; 1977-79 Division 2; 1979-81 Division 1; 1981-89 Division 2; 1989-92 Division 1; 1992-93 FA Premier League; 1993-94 Division 1; 1994-95 FA Premier League; 1995-97 Division 1; 1997- FAPL.

Honours: *Football League Division 1 Champions:* 1993-94; *Division 2 Champions:* 1978-79; *Runners-up:* 1968-69; *Play-off Winners:* 1996-97; *Division 3 Runners-up:* 1963-64; *Division 3(S) Champions:* 1920-21; *Runners-up:* 1928-29, 1930-31, 1938-39; *Division 4 Runners-up:* 1960-61. *FA Cup Runners-up:* 1989-90. *Zenith Data System Cup Winners:* 1991.

European Record: Never qualified.

Managers: John T. Robson 1905-07; Edmund Goodman 1907-25 (had been secretary since 1905 and afterwards continued in this position to 1933); Alec Maley 1925-27; Fred Maven 1927-30, Jack Tresadern 1930-35, Tom Bromilow 1935-36; R.S. Moyes 1936; Tom Bromilow 1936-39; George Irwin 1939-47; Jack Butler 1947-49; Ronnie Rooke 1949-50; Charlie Slade and Fred Dawes (joint managers) 1950-51; Laurie Scott 1951-54; Cyril Spiers 1954-58; George Smith 1958-60; Authur Rowe 1960-62; Dick Graham 1962-66; Bert Head 1966-72; Malcolm Allison 1973-76; Terry Venables 1976-80; Ernie Walley 1980; Malcolm Allison 1980-81; Dario Gradi 1981; Steve Kember 1981-82; Alan Mullery 1982-84; Steve Coppell 1984-93; Alan Smith June 1993-95; Steve Coppell (TD) 1995-96; Dave Bassett Feb 1996-97; Steve Coppell (Caretaker-manager) 1997-.

Season 1996-97

Biggest Home Win:	6-1 v Southend United
Biggest Home Defeat:	2-3 v Wolverhampton Wanderers
Biggest Away Win:	6-1 v Reading
Biggest Away Defeat:	0-3 v Sheffield United
Biggest Home Att:	21,410 v Wolverhampton Wanderers
Smallest Home Att:	11,382 v Stoke City
Average Attendance:	15,791
Leading Scorer:	17 – Bruce Dyer

All-Time Records

Record FAPL Win:	4-1 v Middlesbrough 12/4/93 and v Coventry City 2/11/95
Record FAPL Defeat:	1-6 v Liverpool 20/8/95
Record FL Win:	9-0 v Barrow, Division 4, 10/10/1959
Record FL Defeat:	0-9 v Burnley, FA Cup R2 replay, 10/2/1909 and 0-9 v Liverpool, Division 1, 12/9/90
Record Cup Win:	8-0 v Southend U, Rumbelows League Cup, R2 L2 25/9/90
Record Fee Received:	£2.5m from Arsenal for Ian Wright, 9/91
Record Fee Paid:	£2.25m to Millwall for Andy Roberts, 6/95
Most FAPL Apps:	79 – Nigel Martyn, 1992-95
Most FAPL Goals:	23 – Chris Armstrong, 1992-95
Most FL Apps:	Jim Cannon, 571, 1973-88

Record Attendance (all-time): 41,482 v Burnley, Division 2, 11/5/79

Record Attendance (FAPL): 30,115 v Manchester United, 21/4/93

Highest Scorer in FAPL season: Chris Armstrong, 15, 1992-93

Most FAPL Goals in Season: 48, 1992-93 – 42 games

Most FAPL Points in Season: 49, 1992-93 – 42 games

Player	Tot	St	Sb	Gls	Fa	La	Fg	Lg
ANDERSON	14	7	7	1	1	3	0	0
BOWALL	6	4	2	0	0	1	0	0
CYRUS	1	1	0	0	0	0	0	0
DAVIES	6	5	1	0	0	0	0	0
DAY	24	24	0	0	2	2	0	0
DYER	43	39	4	17	2	3	1	0
EDWORTHY	46	43	3	0	2	3	0	1
FREEDMAN	44	33	11	11	1	3	0	1
GORDON	29	25	4	3	2	3	0	0
HARRIS	2	0	2	0	0	2	0	0
HOPKIN	41	38	3	13	2	2	0	2
HOUGHTON	21	18	3	1	0	2	0	0
LINIGHAN	21	19	2	0	0	0	0	0
McKENZIE	21	4	17	2	2	1	0	0
MIMMS	1	1	0	0	0	0	0	0
MUSCAT	44	42	2	2	2	3	0	1
NASH	21	21	0	0	0	1	0	0
NDAH	25	5	20	3	2	2	0	0
PITCHER	3	3	0	0	0	0	0	0
QUINN	22	17	5	1	0	3	0	1
ROBERTS	47	45	2	0	2	3	0	0
RODGER	11	9	2	0	0	0	0	0
SCULLY	1	0	1	0	0	0	0	0
SHIPPERLEY	32	29	3	12	2	0	1	0
TROLLOPE	9	0	9	0	0	0	0	0
TUTTLE	41	39	2	0	1	3	0	0
VEART	39	35	4	6	2	3	0	2

Eagles Soar Once Again

As a player Steve Coppell will always be synonymous with Manchester United whilst as a manager it would appear that his name will be forever associated with Crystal Palace. His place in the Palace history books is assured after returning for the final couple of months of the season, following an astonishing change of heart at Manchester City, to guide the Eagles into the Premiership for a second time.

Having missed out on promotion through the play-offs the previous season, manager Dave Bassett was very active in the transfer market during the close season. Long-serving keeper Nigel Martyn went to Leeds in exchange for £2.25m and five other players also departed. Martyn was replaced by Chris Day from Spurs for an initial £225,000. Other players to cost a fee were Kevin Muscat at £200,000 and Carlo Nash from non-league side Clitheroe for £35,000.

Palace made a poor start to the season with a 3-1 victory over lowly Oldham being their sole victory from the opening six games, though three of them finished all square. The Eagles' season switched gears on 14 September with a 3-1 victory over Manchester City. Five days later Bassett rejected Francis Lee's overtures to go to Maine Road as manager. Two weeks later Coppell accepted City's challenge while Bassett's preference for life in London certainly boosted his squad as, in successive games, both Reading and Southend United were blitzed 6-1 with no player scoring more than once in either game. The good run was extended to 11 games unbeaten. But just when it seemed as though the club was well on course for a title challenge the wheels came off and, with just one victory in 11 games, they slumped to seventh and out of the play-off places. Maximum points from the next three games, including the double over QPR and a revenge win at Wolves, lifted the Eagles back into the top five but after a home defeat by Tranmere the club was stunned as Bassett left to become general manager at Nottingham Forest.

Two days later Coppell, having resigned as Manchester City manager after just 33 days, returned to Palace as caretaker manager. A good start was made on his return with a 4-1 win at Oxford United but Palace were down in 10th place with five games to play. Palace got back into their stride and a second draw with Barnsley was followed by victory over lowly Reading to take Coppell's side above Port Vale into the top six and an out-of-form Swindon side was defeated at the County Ground.

The 1st Leg of the play-off semi final with Wolves exploded in the final three minutes as Freedman, sent off against Vale, added to Shipperley's early strike. Wolves immediately hit back before Freedman struck again to give Palace a useful 3-1 advantage. In an emotion-packed 2nd Leg, David Hopkin's fine second half goal carried Palace through on aggregate and Hopkin was again the hero as, with a glorious last-minute effort at Wembley, he clinched Palace's promotion at the expense of Sheffield United. Hopkin was one of four players to get into double figures in front of goal and his Wembley classic certainly made a wider impact as he signed for Leeds as soon as the season was over.

Palace may have coped well with the knock-out football of the play-offs but in the FA Cup they went out in Round Three in a replay at Leeds. their Coca-Cola Cup adventure lasted slightly longer with Bury being beaten 7-1 over two legs before Ipswich, in addition to taking four points off Palace in the league, trounced them 4-1 at Portman Road. ∎

Results 1996-97

Nationwide Division One

Date	Opponents	Ven	Res	Atten	Scorers
18-Aug	Birmingham C.	A	0-1	18,765	
24-Aug	Oldham Ath.	H	3-1	13,675	Hopkin (2); Dyer
27-Aug	WBA	H	0-0	14,328	
31-Aug	Huddersfield T.	A	1-1	11,116	Freedman
07-Sep	Stoke City	A	2-2	13,540	Hopkin; Freedman
10-Sep	Ipswich Tn	H	0-0	12,978	
14-Sep	Man. City	H	3-1	18,205	Hopkin (2); Anderson
21-Sep	Reading	A	6-1	9,675	Muscat; Tuttle; Freedman; Dyer; Veart; Ndah
28-Sep	Southend Utd	H	6-1	15,222	Muscat; Houghton; Freedman; Dyer; Veart; Hopkin
01-Oct	Portsmouth	A	2-2	7,212	Freedman; Veart
12-Oct	Barnsley	A	0-0	9,183	
16-Oct	Port Vale	A	2-0	4,522	Roberts; Dyer
19-Oct	Swindon Tn	H	1-2	15,544	Dyer
26-Oct	Grimsby Tn	H	3-0	13,941	Dyer; Freedman; Veart
29-Oct	Bradford City	A	4-0	10,091	Shipperley (2); Hopkin; Freedman
02-Nov	Tranmere R.	A	3-1	8,613	Hopkin; Freedman; Dyer
10-Nov	QPR	H	3-0	16,136	Hopkin; Shipperley; Dyer
16-Nov	Bolton W.	H	2-2	16,892	Hopkin; Freedman
23-Nov	W'hampton W.	H	2-3	21,410	Dyer; Veart
20-Nov	Grimsby Tn	A	1-2	5,115	Shipperley
07-Dec	Oxford Utd	H	2-2	18,592	Dyer (2)
14-Dec	Norwich City	A	1-1	16,395	Shipperley
17-Dec	Sheffield Utd	H	0-1	12,801	
21-Dec	Charlton Ath	A	1-0	16,279	Shipperley
26-Dec	Ipswich Tn	A	1-3	16,020	Gordon
11-Jan	Man. City	A	1-1	27,395	Ndah
18-Jan	Portsmouth	H	1-2	15,771	Quinn
28-Jan	Southend Utd	A	1-2	5,061	Freedman
01-Feb	QPR	A	1-0	16,467	Hopkin
08-Feb	Bradford City	H	3-1	15,459	Freedman; Shipperley; Ndah
15-Feb	W'hampton W.	A	3-0	25,919	Tuttle; Veart; Dyer
22-Feb	Tranmere Rvrs	H	0-1	16,169	
01-Mar	Oxford Utd	A	4-1	8,572	Dyer (2); Gordon; Hopkin
04-Mar	Bolton W.	H	1-1	16,572	Linighan
08-Mar	Charlton Ath	A	1-2	15,000	Dyer
15-Mar	Norwich City	H	2-0	18,706	McKenzie, Gordon
23-Mar	Oldham Ath	A	1-0	5,282	McKenzie
29-Mar	Birmingham C.	H	0-1	16,331	

05-Apr	Huddersfield T.	H	1-1	13,541	Shipperley
09-Apr	WBA	A	0-1	12,866	
12-Apr	Sheffield Utd	A	0-3	20,051	
15-Apr	Stoke City	H	2-0	11,382	Dyer (2)
19-Apr	Barnsley	H	1-1	20,006	Shipperley
23-Apr	Reading	H	3-2	13,747	Linighan; Hopkin; Shipperley
26-Apr	Swindon Tn	A	2-0	10,447	Shipperley (2)
04-May	Port Vale	H	1-1	16,401	Roberts

Division One Play-off

Date	Opponents	Vn	Rd	Res	Atten	Scorers
10-May	W'hampton W.	H	SF1L	3-1	21,053	Shipperley; Freedman (2)
14-May	W'hampton W.	A	SF2L	2-1	26,403	Hopkin
	Crystal Palace win 4-3 on aggregate.					
26-May	Sheffield U.	W	F	1-0	64,383	Hopkin

FA Challenge Cup

Sponsored by Littlewoods Pools

Date	Opponents	Vn	Rnd	Res	Atten	Scorers
14-Jan	Leeds United	H	3R	2-2	21,441	Dyer; Veart
25-Jan	Leeds United	A	3RR	0-1	21,903	

Coca-Cola League Cup

Date	Opponents	Vn	Rnd	Res	Atten	Scorers
17-Sep	Bury	A	2R1L	3-1	3,317	Hopkin (2); Edworthy
24-Sep	Bury	H	2R2L	4-0	5,417	Muscat; Quinn; Freedman; Veart
	Crystal Palace win 7-1 on aggregate.					
22-Oct	Ipswich Town	A	3R	1-4	8,390	Veart

5-Year Record

	Div.	P	W	D	L	F	A	Pts	Pos	FAC	FLC
92/93	PL	42	11	16	15	48	61	49	20	3	SF
93/94	1	46	27	9	10	73	46	90	1	3	3
94/95	PL	42	11	12	19	34	49	45	19	SF	SF
95/96	1	46	20	15	11	67	48	75	3	3	3
96/97	1	46	19	14	13	78	48	71	6	3	3

Derby County

In 1884 members of the Derbyshire County Cricket team formed the football club as a way of boosting finances in the cricket close season. They played their first season at the Racecourse Ground and entered the FA Cup. A year later the club moved to the Baseball Ground where they remained until a move to Pride Park Stadium for the 1997-98 season. In 1888 they became founder members of the Football League. Since their formation they have fluctuated through the top divisions, but enjoyed a sparkling spell during the 1970s.

Ground: Pride Park Stadium
Phone: 01332-340105
Box Office: 01332 340105   **CC Bookings:** 01332-203030
News: 0891 12 11 87   **Tickets:** 0891 33 22 12
Capacity: 35,000   **Pitch:** 110 yds x 71 yds
Colours: White & Black, Black, White & Black
Nickname: The Rams
Radio: BBC Radio Derby 1116AM/104.5FM
Internet: –

Chairman: Lionel Pickering   **Vice-Chairman:** Peter Gadsby
CEO: Keith Loring   **Secretary:** Keith Pearson
Manager: Jim Smith   **Coach:** Steve McClaren
Physio: Peter Melville

League History: 1888 Founder members of Football League; 107-12 Division 1; 1912-14 Division 2; 1914-15 Division 1; 1915-21 Division 1; 1921-26 Division 2; 1926-53 Division 1; 1953-55 Division 2; 1955-57 Division 3N; 1957-69 Division 2; 1969-80 Division 1; 1980-84 Division 2; 1984-86 Division 3; 1986-87 Division 2; 1987-91 Division 1; 1991-92 Division 2; 1992-96 Division 1; 1996- FA Premier League.

Honours: *Football League Division 1 Champions:* 1971-72, 1974-75; *Runners-up:* 1895-96, 1929-30, 1935-36, 1995-96; *Division 2 Champions:* 1911-12, 1914-15, 1968-69, 1986-87; *Runners-up:* 1925-26; *Division 3N Champions:* 1956-57; *Runners-up:* 1955-56; *FA Cup Winners:* 1945-46; *Runners-up:* 1897-98, 1888-89, 1902-03; *Anglo Italian Cup Runners-up:* 1992-93.

European Record: CC (2): 1972-73 (SF), 1975-76 (2); CWC (0) – ; UEFA (2): 1974-75 (3), 1976-77 (2)

Managers: Harry Bradshaw 1904-09; Jimmy Methven 1906-22; Cecil Potter 1922-25; George Jobey 1925-41; Ted Manger 1944-46; Stuart McMillan 1946-53; Jack Barker 1953-55; Harry Storer 1955-62; Tim Ward 1962-67; Brian Clough 1967-73; Dave Mackay 1973-76; Colin Murphy 1977; Tommy Docherty 1977-79; Colin Addison 1979-82; Johnny Newman 1982; Peter Taylor 1982-84; Roy McFarland 1984, Arthur Cox 1984-93; Roy McFarland 1993-95; *(FAPL)* Jim Smith June 1995 .

Season 1996-97

Biggest Home Win:	4-2 v Tottenham Hotspur
Biggest Home Defeat:	1-3 v Arsenal
Biggest Away Win:	3-2 v Manchester United
Biggest Away Defeat:	1-6 v Middlesbrough
Biggest Home Att:	18,287 v Arsenal (last game at Baseball Ground)
Smallest Home Att:	17,022 v Wimbledon
Average Attendance:	17,889 (18th)
Leading Scorers:	11 – Dean Sturridge, 10 – Ashley Ward

All-Time Records

Record FAPL Win: 4-2 v Tottenham Hotspur, 22/3/97
Record FAPL Defeat: 1-6 v Middlesbrough, 5/3/97
Record FL Win: 9-0 v Wolverhampton Wanderers, Div.1 10/1/1891
Record Cup Win: 12-0 v Finn Harps, UEFA Cup 1R1L, 15/9/76
Record Fee Received: £2.9m from Liverpool for Dean Saunders, 7/91
Record Fee Paid: £2.5m to Notts County for Craig Short, 9/92
Most FL Apps: Kevin Hector, 486, 1966-78, 1980-82
Most FAPL Apps: 36 – Christian Dailly and Jacob Laursen, 1996-97
Most FAPL Goals: 11 – Dean Sturridge, 1996-97
Highest Scorer in FAPL season: 11 – Dean Sturridge, 1996-97
Record Attendance (all-time): 41,826 v Tottenham H., Division 1, 20/9/69
Record Attendance (FAPL): 18,287 v Arsenal
Most FAPL Goals in Season: 45, 1996-97 – 38 games
Most FAPL Points in Season: 46, 1996-97 – 38 games

Summary 1996-97

Player	Tot	St	Sb	Snu	PS	Gls	Y	R	Fa	La	Fg	Lg
ASANOVIC	34	34	0	0	11	6	3	0	3	3	0	0
CARBON	10	6	4	8	4	0	1	0	1	1	0	0
CARSLEY	24	15	9	4	3	0	2	0	2	2	0	0
COOPER	0	0	0	3	0	0	0	0	0	0	0	0
DAILLY	36	31	5	0	6	3	6	0	6	6	0	0
FLYNN	17	10	7	8	3	1	3	0	3	3	0	0
GABBIADINI	14	5	9	1	4	0	1	0	1	1	0	0
HOULT	32	31	1	5	0	0	0	0	0	0	0	0
KAVANAGH	0	0	0	0	0	0	0	0	0	0	0	0
LAURSEN	36	35	1	0	7	1	2	0	2	2	0	0
McGRATH	24	23	1	1	4	0	2	0	2	2	0	0
PARKER †	4	4	0	2	1	0	1	0	1	1	0	0
POOM	4	4	0	0	1	0	0	0	0	0	0	0
POWELL Chris	35	35	0	0	4	0	4	0	4	4	0	0
POWELL Darryl	33	27	6	0	5	1	7	0	7	7	0	0
QUY †	0	0	0	3	0	0	0	0	0	0	0	0
RAHMBERG	1	0	1	3	0	0	0	0	0	0	0	0
ROWETT	35	35	0	0	2	2	6	0	6	6	0	0
SIMPSON	19	0	19	12	0	2	0	0	0	0	0	1
SOLIS	2	0	2	2	0	0	0	0	0	0	0	0
STIMAC	21	21	0	0	1	0	9	0	9	9	0	0
STURRIDGE	30	29	1	0	5	11	9	0	9	9	2	1
TAYLOR	3	3	0	28	0	0	0	0	0	0	0	0
TROLLOPE	14	13	1	2	1	1	3	0	3	3	0	0
VAN DER LAAN	16	15	1	7	7	2	1	0	1	1	3	0
WANCHOPE	5	2	3	0	2	1	0	0	0	0	0	0
WARD	30	25	5	1	7	10	2	0	2	2	1	0
WILLEMS	16	7	9	8	7	2	0	0	0	0	2	0
WRIGHT	0	0	0	2	0	0	0	0	0	0	0	0
YATES	10	8	2	3	2	0	0	0	0	0	0	0
OGs						1						

5-Year Record

	Div.	P	W	D	L	F	A	Pts	Pos	FAC	FLC
92-93	1	46	19	9	18	68	57	66	8	6	3
93-94	1	46	20	11	15	73	68	71	6	3	3
94-95	1	46	18	12	16	66	51	66	9	3	4
95-96	1	46	21	16	9	71	51	79	2	3	3
96-97	PL	38	11	13	14	45	58	46	12	6	2

Rams Have New Pride

One of the downsides of the vast financial benefits of the Premier League is that sides promoted from the Nationwide League are expected to be little more than cannon fodder for the big boys. Against this background Derby County took their place in the top flight and sought to make their final year at the Baseball Ground a memorable campaign.

Manager Jim Smith released six players during the summer, two on loan, and spent wisely on bringing in Christian Dailly (£1m), Croatian Aljosa Asanovic (£950,000), Dane Jacob Laursen (£500,000) and the experienced Paul Parker on a free transfer. By the end of the season Dailly's value had risen greatly and his consistency did not go unnoticed as Scotland handed him his first cap. One of Smith's shrewdest moves was to take veteran defender Paul McGrath from Aston Villa, and his experience proved vital although his services were not retained at the end of the season.

It was the home-grown talent of Dean Sturridge which got Derby's season going as he scored a brace as the Rams rescued a point after trailing by two goals at home to Leeds on the opening day of the season. Three days later Dailly's last-minute equaliser denied Spurs victory at White Hart Lane. It was not until the fifth game of the season that Derby clinched their first victory in the Premiership, a 2-1 success at Blackburn which lifted them from a season's low of 16th. A successful penalty by Asanovic accounted for Sunderland at the Baseball Ground in Derby's next game and lifted them to a season's high of ninth.

A high percentage of Derby's points were gathered from sides towards the foot of the Premiership although successive home wins over Chelsea and Tottenham in March were followed by a magnificent 3-2 victory over Manchester United at Old Trafford which included a glorious debut goal for Costa Rican new signing Paulo Wanchope. That run, however, was interspersed by a horrendous 6-1 annihilation at Middlesbrough and a defeat at the hands of an out of sorts Everton and 14 goals were conceded in just four games during February and March.

Derby's future was not made certain until the penultimate game of the season when goals by Gary Rowett and Sturridge added to Coventry's problem. Sturridge's goal was his 11th league strike of the season as he became the Rams' top scorer for the second consecutive year. The only disappointment for Derby at the end of the season was that their 102-year existence at the Baseball Ground ended with a 3-1 defeat by Arsenal. That reversal also ended their best Premiership run of seven consecutive unbeaten home games.

The Rams may have equipped themselves admirably in the Premiership but they became victims of a giant cup killing in the Coca-Cola Cup at the hands of Luton Town. Goals from Ron Willems and Robin van der Laan at Gillingham set up a 4th Round meeting with Aston Villa in the FA Cup. Van der Laan and Willems were joined by top scorer Sturridge as County put Villa out 3-1. Blocking Derby's path to the quarter final were Coventry and with two dire defensive errors inside the opening fifteen minutes at the Baseball Ground, Derby looked finished. But with a more than spirited comeback the Rams ended a pulsating tie as 3-2 victors. Sturridge grabbed the winning goal after Ashley Ward and van der Laan had erased the deficit. Just three days after their six-goal mauling at Middlesbrough, they bowed out of the cup on home soil as Boro chalked up a comfortable 2-0 victory. ∎

157

Results 1996-97

Date	Opponents	Ven	Res	Pos	Atten	Scorers
17-Aug	Leeds Utd	H	3-3	–	17,927	Sturridge (77, 78); Simpson (88)
21-Aug	Tottenham H.	A	1-1	–	28,219	Dailly (90)
24-Aug	Aston Villa	A	0-2	15	34,646	
04-Sep	Man. Utd	H	1-1	16	18,026	Laursen (25)
09-Sep	Blackburn R.	A	2-1	12	19,214	Willems (1); Flynn (85)
14-Sep	Sunderland	H	1-0	9	17,692	Asanovic (84 pen)
21-Sep	Sheffield W.	A	0-0	9	23,934	
28-Sep	Wimbledon	H	0-2	11	17,022	
12-Oct	Newcastle Utd	H	0-1	13	18,092	
19-Oct	N. Forest	A	1-1	12	27,771	Dailly (57)
27-Oct	Liverpool	A	1-2	16	39,515	Ward (88)
02-Nov	Leicester C.	H	2-0	11	18,010	Ward (55); OG (88, Whitlow)
17-Nov	Middlesbrough	H	2-1	10	17,350	Asanovic (15); Ward (47)
23-Nov	West Ham Utd	A	1-1	11	24,576	Sturridge (42)
30-Nov	Coventry C.	H	2-1	9	18,042	Asanovic (12 pen); Ward (79)
07-Dec	Arsenal	A	2-2	11	38,018	Sturridge (62); Powell D. (71)
16-Dec	Everton	H	0-1	11	17,252	
21-Dec	Southampton	A	1-3	11	14,901	Dailly (8)
26-Dec	Sunderland	A	0-2	13	22,512	
28-Dec	Blackburn R.	H	0-0	13	17,847	
11-Jan	Wimbledon	A	1-1	13	11,467	Willems (84)
18-Jan	Chelsea	A	1-3	15	28,293	Asanovic (25)
29-Jan	Leeds Utd	A	0-0	15	27,549	
01-Feb	Liverpool	H	0-1	16	18,102	
15-Feb	West Ham Utd	H	1-0	13	18,057	Asanovic (53 pen)
19-Feb	Sheffield W.	H	2-2	12	18,060	Sturridge (34); Stimac (71)
22-Feb	Leicester C.	A	2-4	13	20,323	Sturridge (2, 47)
01-Mar	Chelsea	H	3-2	12	18,039	Ward (50, 90); Asanovic (61 pen)
05-Mar	Middlesbrough	A	1-6	14	29,739	Simpson (90)
15-Mar	Everton	A	0-1	14	32,140	
22-Mar	Tottenham H.	H	4-2	14	18,083	Van Der Laan (10); Trollope (22); Sturridge (68); Ward (69)
05-Apr	Man. Utd	A	3-2	12	55,243	Ward (29); Wanchope (35); Sturridge (75)
09-Apr	Southampton	H	1-1	12	17,839	Ward (66)
12-Apr	Aston Villa	H	2-1	10	18,071	Rowett (21); Van Der Laan (35)

19-Apr	Newcastle Utd A	1-3	12	36,553	Sturridge (1)
23-Apr	N. Forest H	0-0	11	18,087	
03-May	Coventry C. A	2-1	10	22,839	Rowett (50); Sturridge (62)
11-May	Arsenal H	1-3	12	18,287	Ward (9)

FA Challenge Cup

Date	Opponents	Vn	Rnd	Res	Atten	Scorers
21 Jan	Gillingham	A	3R	2-0	9,508	Willems (53); Van Der Laan (89)
25-Jan	Aston Villa	H	4R	3-1	17,977	Van Der Laan (39); Sturridge (40); Willems (70)
26-Feb	Coventry C.	H	5R	3-2	18,033	Ward (17); Van Der Laan (41); Sturridge (88)
08-Mar	Middlesbrough	H	6R	0-2	17,567	

Coca-Cola League Cup

Date	Opponents	Vn	Rnd	Res	Atten	Scorers
17-Sep	Luton Town	A	2R1L	0-1	4,459	
25-Sep	Luton Town	H	2R2L	2-2	13,569	Sturridge (40); Simpson (44)

Luton Town win 3-2 on aggregate.

Rams – Premiership Fact File

- Derby County played their last game ever at the Baseball Ground on 11th May before moving to their new Pride Park Stadium. Fulham may have a cottage in one corner of their ground but Derby now have a pub!

- Derby's point in the 0-0 at Sheffield Wednesday meant that the Rams haven't won at Hillsborough in 60 years!

- Derby made a stirring start to their Premiership life, coming back from 0-2 down to draw 3-3 with Leeds United on the opening day of the season.

- Dean Sturridge made his 100th senior appearance at Leicester in February.

Everton

The cricket team of St Domingo's Church turned to football around 1878. Playing in Stanley Park, in late 1879 changed name to Everton FC, the name of the district to the west of the park.

Moved to a field at Priory Road in 1882 and then, in 1884, moved to a site in Anfield Road. As one of the country's leading teams, became founder members of the Football League in 1888. Moved to Goodison Park, a field on the north side of Stanley Park, in 1892 following a dispute with the ground's landlord. Premier League founder members 1992.

Ground: Goodison Park, Liverpool, L4 4EL
Phone: 0151 330 2200
Box Office: 0151 330 2300   **CC Bookings:** 0151 471 8000
Info: 0891 12 11 99
Colours: Royal Blue, White, Blue   **Nickname:** The Toffees
Capacity: 40,160   **Pitch:** 112 yds x 78 yds
Radio: Radio Everton 1602AM
Internet: http://evertonfc.merseyworld.com

Chairman: Peter Johnson   **Secretary:** Michael Dunford
Manager: Howard Kendall   **Assistant:** Adrian Heath
Coach: **Physio:** Les Helm

League History: 1888 Founder Member of the Football League; 1930-31 Division 2; 1931-51 Division 1; 1951-54 Division 2; 1954-92 Division 1; 1992- FA Premier League.

Honours: *Football League Division 1 Champions:* 1890-91, 1914-15, 1927-28, 1931-32, 1938-39, 1962-63, 1969-70, 1984-85, 1986-87; *Runners-up:* 1889-90, 1894-95, 1901-02, 1904-05, 1908-09, 1911-12, 1985-86; *Division 2 Champions:* 1930-31; *Runners-up:* 1953-54. *FA Cup Winners:* 1906, 1933, 1966, 1984, 1995; *Runners-up:* 1893, 1897, 1907, 1968, 1985, 1986, 1989. *Football League Cup Runners-up:* 1976-77, 1983-84. *League Super Cup Runners-up:* 1986. *Cup-Winners' Cup Winners:* 1984-85; *Simod Cup Runners-up:* 1989. *Zenith Data Systems Cup Runners-up:* 1991.

European Record: CC (2): 63-64 (1), 70-71 (QF); CWC (3): 66-67 (2), 84-85 (W), 95-96 (2). UEFA (6): 62-63 (1), 64-65 (3), 65-66 (2), 75-76 (1), 78-79 (2), 79-80 (1).

Managers: W.E. Barclay 1888-89; Dick Molyneux 1889-1901; William C. Cuff 1901-18; W.J. Sawyer 1918-19; Thomas H. McIntosh 1919-35; Theo Kelly 1936-48; Cliff Britton 1948-56; Ian Buchan 1956-58; Johnny Carey 1958-61; Harry Catterick 1961-73; Billy Bingham 1973-77; Gordon Lee 1977-81; Howard Kendall 1981-87; Colin Harvey 1987-90; *(FAPL)* Howard Kendall Nov 1990-93; Mike Walker Jan 1993-Nov 1994; Joe Royle Nov 1994-Mar 1997; Dave Watson (Caretaker) Apr 1997-July 1997; Howard Kendall July 1997-.

Season 1996-97

Biggest Home Win:	7-1 v Southampton
Biggest Home Defeat:	1-3 v Sunderland and Wimbledon
Biggest Away Win:	2-1 v Leicester City
Biggest Away Defeat:	0-4 v Wimbledon
Biggest Home Att:	40,177 v Liverpool
Smallest Home Att:	30,427 v Blackburn Rovers
Average Attendance:	36,193
Leading Scorers:	10 – Duncan Ferguson, 6 – Craig Short

All-Time Records

Record FAPL Win:	7 1 v Southampton, 16/11/96
Record FAPL Defeat:	1-5 v Norwich City 25/9/93; Sheffield Wnd 2/4/94
Record FL Win:	9-1 v Manchester City, Division 1, 3/9/06; Plymouth Argyle, Division 2, 27/12/30
Record FL Defeat:	4-10 v Tottenham H, Division 1, 11/10/58
Record Cup Win:	11-2 v Derby County, FA Cup R1, 18/1/90
Record Fee Received:	£8m from Fiorentina for Andrei Kanchelskis, 1/97
Record Fee Paid:	£5.75m to Middlesbrough for Nick Barmby, 10/96
Most FL Apps:	Ted Sagar, 465, 1929-53
Most FAPL Apps:	195 – Neville Southall, 1992-97
Most FAPL Goals:	29 – Paul Rideout, 1992-97
Highest Scorer in FAPL season:	16 – Tony Cottee, 93-94 and Andrei Kanchelskis 95-96

Record Attendance (all-time): 78,299 v Liverpool, Division 1, 18/9/48
Record Attendance (FAPL): 40,177 v Liverpool, 16/04/97
Most FAPL Goals in Season: 64, 1995-96 – 38 games
Most FAPL Points in Season: 61, 1995-96 – 38 games

Player	Tot	St	Sb	Snu	PS	Gls	Y	R	Fa	La	Fg	Lg
ALLEN	1	0	1	8	1	0	0	0	0	0	0	0
BALL	5	2	3	3	1	0	1	0	0	0	0	0
BARMBY	25	22	3	1	5	4	0	0	2	0	1	0
BARRETT	36	36	0	0	0	0	1	0	2	2	0	0
BRANCH	25	13	12	7	7	3	2	0	1	1	0	0
CADAMARTERI	1	0	1	0	0	0	0	0	0	0	0	0
DUNNE	7	6	1	4	1	0	2	0	1	0	0	0
EATON	0	0	0	1	0	0	0	0	0	0	0	0
EBBRELL	7	7	0	3	2	0	2	0	0	1	0	0
FERGUSON	33	31	2	1	0	10	5	1	2	1	1	0
GERRARD	5	4	1	30	0	0	0	0	0	0	0	0
GRANT	18	11	7	4	3	0	3	0	2	1	0	0
HILLS	3	1	2	4	0	0	0	0	0	0	0	0
HINCHCLIFFE	18	18	0	0	2	1	2	0	0	2	0	0
HOTTIGER	8	4	4	22	1	0	0	0	0	1	0	0
JACKSON	0	0	0	2	0	0	0	0	0	0	0	0
KANCHELSKIS †	20	20	0	0	5	4	0	0	2	2	1	1
LIMPAR †	2	1	1	10	1	0	0	0	0	1	0	0
McCANN	0	0	0	1	0	0	0	0	0	0	0	0
O'CONNOR	0	0	0	3	0	0	0	0	0	0	0	0
PARKINSON	28	28	0	0	4	0	4	0	1	2	0	0
PHELAN	15	15	0	0	3	0	1	0	1	0	0	0
RIDEOUT	9	4	5	15	2	0	2	0	1	2	0	1
SHORT	23	19	4	6	4	2	6	0	1	1	0	0
SOUTHALL	34	34	0	4	1	0	2	0	2	2	0	0
SPEARE	0	0	0	3	0	0	0	0	0	0	0	0
SPEED	37	37	0	0	9	9	8	0	2	2	1	1
STUART	35	29	6	2	3	5	4	0	2	1	0	0
THOMSEN	16	15	1	0	5	0	3	0	0	0	0	0
UNSWORTH	34	32	2	0	3	5	5	1	0	2	0	0
WATSON	29	29	0	0	2	1	4	0	2	0	0	0
OGs												1

Royle Departure

Cup winners in 1994-95, a significant rise up the Premier League a year later and a couple of large investments in the transfer market seemed to be the foundations upon which Everton favourite Joe Royle would build a side to bring the glory days back to Merseyside. During the close season Gary Ablett departed as did Daniel Amokachi after failing to reproduce the form which lit up the latter stages of the Toffeemen's FA Cup success. Paul Gerrard was signed from Oldham for £1m and Royle raided Leeds to snap up Gary Speed for £3.5m. The minor tinkering with the side paid instant dividends as Everton kicked off the season with a 2-0 win at Goodison Park over Newcastle. Speed marked his debut with a goal after David Unsworth had opened the scoring from the penalty spot. Duncan Ferguson scored twice four days later in a 2-2 draw at Old Trafford.

Another point was taken from Tottenham the following Saturday but suddenly Everton's world fell apart as a run of poor results in the Premiership coincided with a humiliating Coca-Cola Cup defeat. September began with two successive league defeats, including a 4-0 drubbing at Wimbledon, and just for good measure Ferguson was dismissed when the losing run ended with a 1-1 draw at Blackburn.

Having slumped to 15th in the table, Everton quickly sprung back up the league to sixth. Nick Barmby joined at the end of October for £5.75m.

By 23 November Everton had moved into a position, six points off the top, but the month ended with a shattering 3-1 home defeat by Sunderland. A win at Derby and draws with Chelsea and Leeds did little to halt the slide as the Blues then capitulated to six consecutive defeats. Andrei Kanchelskis, the Toffees' leading scorer the previous season but with just three league goals to his credit this time around, departed to Fiorentina for £8m on the eve of a 4-1 reversal at Newcastle.

Such was Everton's dramatic slump that there was always the possibility of the club slipping into the bottom three. A Dave Watson goal on 15 March eased such fears as Derby were seen off but Manchester United hastened the end of the Joe Royle era with a 2-0 win at Goodison. Five days later, on the 27 March, Royle left the club by mutual consent, although he is believed to have disagreed with his chairman regarding possible moves in the transfer market. Long-serving defender Watson accepted the dual responsibility of player/manager but Everton picked up just a further six points from their last seven games of the season.

Everton had already suffered three consecutive league defeats when they entertained York City in the 1st Leg of their 2nd Round Coca-Cola Cup tie in September. Kanchelskis's first goal of the season earned the Toffeemen no more than a draw and their demise was confirmed at Bootham Crescent as York went through 4-3 on aggregate just a year after removing Manchester United from the same competition. The next cup tie, on 5 January, also came on the back of three straight defeats but this time Everton took full advantage of Swindon defender Ian Culverhouse receiving the quickest red card in FA Cup history – 52 seconds – to cruise to a 3-0 victory. At half time in their 4th Round home tie with Bradford City, the sides were goalless, but within ten minutes of the restart Everton were two down and heading towards an inglorious 3-2 defeat.

The lack of a permanent manager did not stop the Blues from splashing out £4.5m on West Ham defender Slaven Bilic in May. Howard Kendall was appointed manager for the second time at the end of June. ■

163

Results 1996-97

FA Carling Premiership

Date	Opponents	Ven	Res	Pos	Atten	Scorers
17-Aug	Newcastle Utd	H	2-0	–	40,117	Unsworth (28 pen); Speed (40)
21-Aug	Man. Utd	A	2-2	–	54,943	Ferguson (34, 40)
24-Aug	Tottenham H.	A	0-0	7	29,696	
04-Sep	Aston Villa	H	0-1	11	39,115	
07-Sep	Wimbledon	A	0-4	15	13,684	
14-Sep	Middlesbrough	H	1-2	16	39,250	Short (8)
21-Sep	Blackburn R.	A	1-1	15	27,091	Unsworth (38)
28-Sep	Sheffield W.	H	2-0	13	34,160	Kanchelskis (17); Stuart (60)
12-Oct	West Ham Utd	H	2-1	8	36,571	Stuart (14); Speed (78)
28-Oct	N. Forest	A	1-0	7	19,892	Short (4)
04-Nov	Coventry C.	H	1-1	9	31,477	Stuart (45 pen)
16-Nov	Southampton	H	7-1	8	35,669	Stuart (13); Kanchelskis (22, 35); Speed (30, 32, 72); Barmby (58)
20-Nov	Liverpool	A	1-1	7	40,751	Speed (81)
23-Nov	Leicester C.	A	2-1	6	20,975	Hinchcliffe (12); Unsworth (52)
30-Nov	Sunderland	H	1-3	8	40,087	Ferguson (64)
07-Dec	Chelsea	A	2-2	8	28,418	Branch (17); Kanchelskis (28)
16-Dec	Derby Co.	A	1-0	7	17,252	Barmby (86)
21-Dec	Leeds Utd	H	0-0	7	36,954	
26-Dec	Middlesbrough	A	2-4	8	29,673	Unsworth (31); Ferguson (45)
28-Dec	Wimbledon	H	1-3	8	36,733	Stuart (23)
01-Jan	Blackburn R.	H	0-2	8	30,427	
11-Jan	Sheffield W.	A	1-2	9	24,175	Ferguson (63)
19-Jan	Arsenal	A	1-3	9	38,095	Ferguson (89)
29-Jan	Newcastle Utd	A	1-4	12	36,143	Speed (2)
01-Feb	N. Forest	H	2-0	9	32,567	Ferguson (47); Barmby (67)
22-Feb	Coventry C.	A	0-0	10	19,497	
01-Mar	Arsenal	H	0-2	11	36,980	
05-Mar	Southampton	A	2-2	12	15,134	Ferguson (10); Speed (27)
08-Mar	Leeds Utd	A	0-1	12	32,055	
15-Mar	Derby Co.	H	1-0	13	32,240	Watson (79)
22-Mar	Man. Utd	H	0-2	13	40,079	
05-Apr	Aston Villa	A	1-3	14	39,339	Unsworth (15)
09-Apr	Leicester C.	H	1-1	14	30,368	Branch (17)
12-Apr	Tottenham H.	H	1-0	12	36,380	Speed (11)
16-Apr	Liverpool	H	1-1	12	40,177	Ferguson (65)
19-Apr	West Ham Utd	A	2-2	11	24,525	Branch (78); Ferguson (89)

| 03-May | Southampton | A | 0-3 | 12 | 22,108 | |
| 11-May | Chelsea | H | 1-2 | 15 | 38,321 | Barmby (77) |

FA Challenge Cup

Date	Opponents	Vn	Rnd	Res	Atten	Scorers
05-Jan	Swindon T.	H	3R	3-0	20,411	Kanchelskis (2); Barmby (18); Ferguson (50)
25-Jan	Bradford C.	H	4R	2-3	30,007	OG (54, O'Brien); Speed (90)

Coca-Cola League Cup

Date	Opponents	Vn	Rnd	Res	Atten	Scorers
18-Sep	York City	H	2R1L	1-1	11,527	Kanchelskis (57)
24-Sep	York City	A	2R2L	2-3	7,854	Rideout (29); Speed (90)

York City win 4-3 on aggregate.

Everton – Premiership Fact File

- Neville Southall made his 700th appearance for Everton when he played in their opening fixture of the season.
- Duncan Ferguson's goals at Old Trafford in the second game of the season were the first Manchester United had conceded at home in the Premiership in 1996.
- Everton's 7-1 win over Southampton in November was their biggest ever in the Premiership.
- Gary Speed made the most Premiership appearances in an Everton shirt in 1996-97. He played in 37 of their 38 games.
- Everton have only finished in the top ten of the Premiership once in the five years it has been in existence.

5-Year Record

	Div.	P	W	D	L	F	A	Pts	Pos	FAC	FLC
92-93	PL	42	15	8	19	53	55	53	13	3	4
93-94	PL	42	12	8	22	42	63	44	17	3	4
94-95	PL	42	11	17	14	44	51	50	15	W	2
95-96	PL	38	17	10	11	64	44	61	6	4	2
96-97	PL	38	10	12	16	44	57	42	15	4	2

Leeds United

Leeds City, founded in 1904, took over the Elland Road ground of the defunct Holbeck Club and in 1905 gained a Football League Division Two place. The club was, however, expelled in 1919 for disciplinary reasons associated with payments to players during the War. The club closed down.

Leeds United FC, a new professional club, emerged the same year and competed in the Midland League. The club was elected to Football League Division Two for season 1920-21. The club has subsequently never been out of the top two divisions. Premier League founder member 1992.

Ground: Elland Road, Leeds, LS11 0ES
Phone: 0113-226 6000
Box Office: 0113-226 1000   **CC Bookings:** 0113-271 0710
Info: 0891 12 11 80
Colours: All White   **Nickname:** United
Capacity: 39,704   **Pitch:** 117 yds x 76 yds
Radio: Radio Leeds United 1323AM
Internet: http://www.lufc.co.uk

President: RtHn The Earl of Harewood
Chairman: Peter Ridsdale   **MD:** Jeremy Fenn
Secretary: Nigel Pleasants
Manager: George Graham   **Assistant:** David O'Leary
Coaches: Eddie Gray, David Williams, Robin Wray
Physios: David Swift and Alan Sutton

League History: 1920 Elected to Division 2; 1924-27 Division 1; 1927-28 Division 2; 1928-31 Division 1; 1931-32 Division 2; 1932-47 Division 1; 1947-56 Division 2; 1956-60 Division 1; 1960-64 Division 2; 1964-82 Division 1; 1982-90 Division 2; 1990-92 Division 1; 1992- FA Premier League.

Honours: *Football League Division 1 Champions:* 1968-69, 1973-74, 1991-92; *Runners-up:* 1964-65, 1965-66, 1969-70, 1970-71, 1971-72; *Division 2 Champions:* 1923-24, 1963-64, 1989-90; *Runners-up:* 1927-28, 1931-32, 1955-56. *FA Cup Winners:* 1971-72; *Runners-up:* 1964-65, 1969-70, 1972-73. *Football League Cup Winners:* 1967-68. *Runners-up:* 1995-96 *Champions' Cup Runners-up:* 1974-75; *Cup-Winners' Cup Runners-up:* 1972-73; *UEFA Cup Winners:* 1967-68, 1970-71; *Runners-up:* 1966-67.

European Record: CC (3): 69-70 (SF), 74-75 (F), 92-93 (2). CWC (1): 72-73 (F); UEFA (9): 65-66 (SF), 66-67 (F), 67-68 (W), 68-69 (QF), 70-71 (W), 71-72 (1), 73-74 (3), 79-80 (2), 95-96 (2).

Managers: Dick Ray 1919-20; Arthur Fairclough 1920-27; Dick Ray 1927-35; Bill Hampson 1935-47; Willis Edwards 1947-48; Major Frank Buckley 1948-53; Raich Carter 1953-58; Bill Lambton 1958-59; Jack Taylor 1959-61; Don Revie 1961-74; Brian Clough 1974; Jimmy Armfield 1974-78; Jock Stein 1978; Jimmy Adamson 1978-80; Allan Clarke 1980-82; Eddie Gray 1982-85; Billy Bremner 1985-88; *(FAPL)* Howard Wilkinson October 1988-Sept 1996; George Graham Sept 1996-.

Season 1996-97

Biggest Home Win:	3-0 v Sunderland and Leicester City
Biggest Home Defeat:	0-4 v Manchester United
Biggest Away Win:	2-0 v Southampton and West Ham United
Biggest Away Defeat:	0-4 v Liverpool
Biggest Home Att:	39,981 v Liverpool
Smallest Home Att:	25,860 v Wimbledon
Average Attendance:	32,118 (7th)
Leading Scorers:	5 – Brian Deane, Lee Sharpe

All-Time Records

Record FAPL Win:	5-0 v Tottenham H, 25/8/92; Swindon Tn, 7/5/94
Record FAPL Defeat:	2-6 v Sheffield Wednesday (A), 16/12/95
Record FL Win:	8-0 v Leicester City, Division 1, 7/4/1934
Record FL Defeat:	1-8 v Stoke City, Division 1, 27/8/1934
Record Cup Win:	10-0 v Lyn (Oslo), European Cup, 1R1L, 17/9/69
Record Fee Received:	£2.75 from Blackburn R. for David Batty, 10/93
Record Fee Paid:	£4.5m to Parma for Tomas Brolin, 11/95
Most FL Apps:	Jack Charlton, 629, 1953-73
Most FAPL Apps:	151 – Gary McAllister, 1992-96
Most FAPL Goals:	47 – Brian Deane, 1992-97

Highest Scorer in FAPL Season: Rod Wallace, 17, 1993-94

Record Attendance (all-time): 57,892 v Sunderland, FA Cup 5R replay, 15/3/67

Record Attendance (FAPL): 41,125 v Manchester United, 27/4/94

Most FAPL Goals in Season: 65, 1993-94 – 42 games

Most FAPL Points in Season: 73, 1994-95 – 42 games

Summary 1996-97

Player	Tot	St	Sb	Snu	PS	Gls	Y	R	Fa	La	Fg	Lg
BEENEY	1	1	0	37	0	0	0	0	0	1	0	0
BEESLEY †	12	11	1	4	1	0	5	0	1	1	0	0
BLUNT...	1	0	1	2	0	0	0	0	0	0	0	0
BOWYER	32	32	0	0	4	4	6	0	4	0	2	0
BOYLE...	1	0	1	1	0	0	0	0	0	0	0	0
COUZENS	10	7	3	4	7	1	2	0	0	3	0	0
DEANE	28	27	1	0	4	5	2	0	4	0	1	0
DORIGO	18	15	3	0	1	0	5	0	4	0	0	0
EVANS	0	0	0	1	0	0	0	0	0	0	0	0
FORD	16	15	1	13	6	1	4	0	0	3	0	0
GRAY	7	1	6	4	1	0	0	0	0	2	0	0
HALLE	20	20	0	0	0	0	2	0	3	0	0	0
HARTE	14	10	4	21	0	2	1	0	1	3	0	1
HATLEY †	6	5	1	1	1	0	0	0	0	0	0	0
JACKSON	17	11	6	11	1	0	1	0	4	0	0	0
JOBSON	10	10	0	0	0	0	2	0	0	3	0	0
KELLY	36	34	2	0	2	2	5	0	4	3	0	0
KEWELL	1	0	1	4	0	0	0	0	0	0	0	0
LAURENT	4	2	2	2	1	0	0	0	0	0	0	0
LILLEY	6	4	2	0	0	0	0	0	0	0	0	0
MARTYN	37	37	0	0	0	0	1	0	4	3	0	0
MOLENAAR	12	12	0	4	0	1	5	0	2	0	0	0
PALMER	28	26	2	1	1	0	10	1	3	2	0	0
RADEBE...	32	28	4	2	3	0	6	0	3	1	0	0
RUSH	36	34	2	0	4	3	6	0	4	2	0	0
SHARPE	26	26	0	3	4	5	1	0	1	3	0	1
SHEPHERD	1	1	0	0	0	0	0	0	0	0	0	0
TINKLER	3	1	2	1	1	0	0	0	0	0	0	0
WALLACE	22	17	5	8	7	3	5	0	4	3	2	3
WETHERALL	29	25	4	7	3	0	7	0	2	3	0	0
YEBOAH	7	6	1	4	3	0	2	0	0	0	0	0
OGs						1					1	

5-Year Record

	Div.	P	W	D	L	F	A	Pts	Pos	FAC	FLC
92-93	PL	42	12	15	15	57	62	51	17	4	3
93-94	PL	42	18	16	8	65	39	70	5	4	2
94-95	PL	42	20	13	9	59	38	73	5	5	2
95-96	PL	38	12	7	19	40	57	43	13	QF	F
96-97	PL	38	11	13	14	28	38	46	11	5	3

Graham Constructs Mean Machine

Manager Howard Wilkinson went into the 1996-97 season as the joint second favourite manager not to see out the season with his present employers. Wilkinson obviously paid little attention to such negative thoughts and made a number of changes to his side with Gary Speed (£3.5m), Gary McAllister (£3m), Phil Masinga (£500,000), John Lukic and Nigel Worthington amongst those leaving during the summer. Thomas Brolin was again absent come the start of the campaign. Six new signings were made which included a free transfer for Ian Rush from Liverpool whilst £9.5m was spent on taking Lee Sharpe, Lee Bowyer and Nigel Martyn from Manchester United, Charlton Athletic and Crystal Palace respectively.

The new campaign began dramatically with a 3-3 draw at Derby, from two down. There was no such revival the following Tuesday as Sheffield Wednesday won the Yorkshire derby 2-0 at Elland Road. Goals by Sharpe and Ian Harte, the latter three days after his 19th birthday, clinched wins over Wimbledon and Blackburn but Wilkinson's fate was sealed on 7 September when Sharpe's former club gave Leeds a 4-0 drubbing on home soil. Leeds moved swiftly and the manager was sacked 48 hours later after eight years with the club.

Little time was wasted in appointing former Arsenal boss George Graham as Wilkinson's replacement following the completion of the game. Graham's suspension from the game. Graham's tenure got off to a flying start as Andy Couzens' first goal for the club put Leeds into a first-minute lead at Coventry, but City fought back to hand United another defeat. The run of defeats stretched to four games before two Rod Wallace goals earned maximum points from the visit of relegation-bound Nottingham Forest. United slipped to 17th before 2-0 wins over Southampton and Chelsea – at the start of five consecutive games without conceding a goal – lifted the gloom. Indeed, goals for and against became a compelling feature of Graham's early reign. A run of three consecutive 1-0 victories followed a 4-0 defeat at Liverpool but United could only draw seven and lose two of their final nine games.

During the season only five league games saw Leeds and their opposition score in the same match while in one remarkable run 13 clean sheets were kept in 17 games. Leeds scored in just 10 of those 17 games. With just 28 goals in 38 games they were, by far, the lowest scorers in the Premiership. Sharpe and Brian Deane topped the strikers' pile with five league goals apiece. Rush was goalless for 15 games before opening his account for his new club.

Wallace and Harte ensured that no mistake was made in the 2nd Leg of the Coca-Cola Cup tie against Darlington as Leeds went through 4-2 on aggregate. But hopes of repeating the previous season's journey to Wembley were cast aside in the 3rd Round when Aston Villa won 2-1 at Elland Road.

Twenty-five years have passed since Leeds won the FA Cup for the only time and they progressed at home after a tricky 3rd Round draw at Crystal Palace. Graham savoured his finest moment since leaving Arsenal on 4 February when his new side, thanks to another Wallace goal, walked away from Highbury with a 4th Round victory under their belts. But if that result was a surprise it was nothing compared to the shock which lay in wait in the following round as Portsmouth pulled off a stunning 3-2 victory at Elland Road.

Leeds clearly have the defensive strength to achieve better things but one was left with the impression that a more adventurous approach will be required. ∎

Results 1996-97

FA Carling Premiership

Date	Opponents	Ven	Res	Pos	Atten	Scorers
17-Aug	Derby Co.	A	3-3	–	17,927	OG (19, Laursen); Harte (72); Bowyer (85)
20-Aug	Sheffield W.	H	0-2	–	31,011	
26-Aug	Wimbledon	H	1-0	11	25,860	Sharpe (58)
04-Sep	Blackburn R.	A	1-0	6	23,226	Harte (40)
07-Sep	Man. Utd	H	0-4	9	39,694	
14-Sep	Coventry C.	A	1-2	12	17,297	Couzens (1)
21-Sep	Newcastle Utd	H	0-1	14	36,070	
28-Sep	Leicester C.	A	0-1	17	20,359	
12-Oct	N. Forest	H	2-0	14	29,225	Wallace (46, 90)
19-Oct	Aston Villa	A	0-2	16	39,051	
26-Oct	Arsenal	A	0-3	17	38,076	
02-Nov	Sunderland	H	3-0	17	31,667	Ford (27); Sharpe (62); Deane (68)
16-Nov	Liverpool	H	0-2	17	39,981	
23-Nov	Southampton	A	2-0	14	15,241	Kelly (82); Sharpe (89)
01-Dec	Chelsea	H	2-0	12	32,671	Deane (8); Rush (10)
7-Dec	Middlesbrough	A	0-0	13	30,018	
14-Dec	Tottenham H.	H	0-0	13	33,783	
21-Dec	Everton	A	0-0	12	36,954	
26-Dec	Coventry C.	H	1-3	14	36,465	Deane (9)
28-Dec	Man. Utd	A	0-1	15	55,256	
01-Jan	Newcastle Utd	A	0-3	15	36,489	
11-Jan	Leicester C.	H	3-0	12	29,486	Bowyer (40); Rush (45, 69)
20-Jan	West Ham Utd	A	2-0	11	19,441	Kelly (52); Bowyer (69)
29-Jan	Derby Co.	H	0-0	10	27,549	
01-Feb	Arsenal	H	0-0	11	35,502	
19-Feb	Liverpool	A	0-4	11	38.957	
22-Feb	Sunderland	A	1-0	9	21,890	Bowyer (48)
01-Mar	West Ham Utd	H	1-0	9	30,575	Sharpe (47)
08-Mar	Everton	H	1-0	9	32,055	Molenaar (28)
12-Mar	Southampton	H	0-0	9	25,913	
15-Mar	Tottenham H.	A	0-1	9	33,040	
22-Mar	Sheffield W.	A	2-2	9	30,373	Sharpe (17); Wallace (21)
07-Apr	Blackburn R.	H	0-0	10	27,264	
16-Apr	Wimbledon	A	0-2	11	7,979	
19-Apr	N. Forest	A	1-1	10	25,565	Deane (66)
22-Apr	Aston Villa	H	0-0	9	26,897	
03-May	Chelsea	A	0-0	11	28,277	
11-May	Middlesbrough	H	1-1	11	38,567	Deane (77)

FA Challenge Cup

Date	Opponents	Vn	Rnd	Res	Atten	Scorers
14-Jan	C. Palace	A	3R	2-2	21,052	Deane (3); OG (7, Andersen)
25-Jan	C. Palace	H	3RR	1-0	21,903	Wallace (42)
04 Feb	Arsenal	A	4R	1-0	38,115	Wallace (12)
15-Feb	Portsmouth	H	5R	2-3	35,604	Bowyer (52, 90)

Coca-Cola League Cup

Date	Opponents	Vn	Rnd	Res	Atten	Scorers
18-Sep	Darlington	H	2R1L	2-2	15,711	Wallace (15, 50)
24-Sep	Darlington	A	2R2L	2-0	6,298	Wallace (18); Harte (30)
	Leeds United win 4-2 on aggregate.					
23-Oct	Aston Villa	H	3R	1-2	15,803	Sharpe (69)

Leeds United – Premiership Fact File

- Leeds United's 28 goals in the Premiership were not only the lowest tally achieved by a team during 1996-97, but also the lowest tally ever, in the Premiership's five-year history.

- Leeds fans' favourite song during the latter half of the season was sung to the tune of "We'll Meet Again" and went, "We'll score again, don't know where, don't know when..."

- United kept five successive clean sheets from 23 November.

- Goalkeeper Nigel Martyn was voted Leeds Player of the Year and the club's matchday programme was runner-up in the Premiership Programme of the Year Award.

Leicester City

Founded in 1884 as Leicester Fosse by former pupils of the Wyggeston School from the western part of the city near the old Roman Fosse Way. Moved to their present ground in 1891 and from the Midland League joined Division Two of the Football League in 1894. Promoted for the first time in 1908, they have been relegated seven times from the top flight.

FA Cup runners-up four times, they gained European Cup-Winners' Cup experience in 1961-62. Members of the new Division One in its first season, 1992-93, and promoted to the Premier League following play-off success in 1994. Relegated straight back but re-promoted, again via the play-offs at the end of the 1995-96 season. Won the League Cup in 1997.

Ground:	City Stadium, Filbert Street, Leicester LE2 7FL		
Phone:	0116 255 5000		
Box Office:	0116 291 5232	**CC Bookings:**	0116 291 5232
Info:	0891-12 11 85		
Colours:	All Blue	**Club Nickname:**	Filberts or Foxes
Capacity:	22,517	**Pitch:**	112 x 75 yds

President:	Ken Brigstock	**Chairman:**	Tom Smearton
CEO:	Barrie Pierpoint	**Secretary:**	Ian Silvester
Manager:	Martin O'Neill	**Assistant:**	John Robinson
Coaches:	Paul Franklin, Steve Walford		
Physios:	Alan Smith, Mick Yeoman		
Radio:	104.9FM BBC Radio Leicester		
Internet:	http://www.lcfc.co.uk		

League History: 1894 Elected to Division 2; 1908-09 Division 1; 1009-25 Division 2; 1925-35 Division 1; 1935-37 Division 2; 1937-39 Division 1; 1946-54 Division 2; 1954-55 Division 1; 1955-57 Division 2; 1957-69 Division 1; 1969-71 Division 2; 1971-78 Division 1; 1978-80 Division 2; 1980-81 Division 1; 1981-83 Division 2; 1983-87 Division 1; 1987-92 Division 2; 1992-94 Division 1; 1994-95 FA Premier League. 1995-96 Division 1. 1996- FA Premier League.

Honours: *Football League Division 1:* Runners-up 1928-29; *Division 2 Champions:* 1924-25, 1936-37, 1953-54, 1956-57, 1970-71, 1979-80; *Runners-up:* 1907-08. *FA Cup Runners-up:* 1949, 1961, 1963, 1969. *Football League Cup Winners:* 1964, 1997; *Runners-up:* 1965.

European Competitions: CC (0) – ; CWC (1): 61-62 (2); UEFA (0) –

Managers (and Secretary-managers): William Clarke 1896-97, George Johnson 1898-1907, James Blessington 1907-09, Andy Aitkin 1909-11, J.W. Bartlett 1912-14, Peter Hodge 1919-26, William Orr 1926-32, Peter Hodge 1932-34, Andy Lochead 1934-36, Frank Womack 1936-39, Tom Bromilow 1939-45, Tom Mather 1945-46, Johnny Duncan 1946-49, Norman Bullock 1949-55, David Halliday 1955-58, Matt Gillies 1959-68, Frank O'Farrell 1968-71, Jimmy Bloomfield 1971-77, Frank McLintock 1977-78, Jock Wallace 1978-82, Gordon Milne 1982-86, Bryan Hamilton 1986-87, David Pleat 1987-91, Brian Little May 1991-Nov 94; Mark McGhee Dec 94-Dec 95, *(FAPL)*: Martin O'Neill Dec 95 –.

Season 1996-97

Biggest Home Win: 4-2 v Derby County
Biggest Home Defeat: 0-3 v Liverpool
Biggest Away Win: 4-2 v Blackburn Rovers
Biggest Away Defeat: 3-4 v Newcastle United, 0-3 v Leeds United
Biggest Home Attendance: 21,068 v Manchester United
Smallest Home Attendance: 17,562 v Southampton
Average Attendance: 20,184 (16th)
Leading Scorer: 12 – Steve Claridge, 10 – Emile Heskey

All-Time Records

Record FAPL Win: 4-2 v Derby County 22/2/97,
                              4-2 v Blackburn Rovers 11/5/97
Record FAPL Defeat: 0-4 v Manchester United, 15/4/95
Record FL Win: 10-0 v Portsmouth, Division 1, 20/10/28
Record FL Defeat: 0-12 v Nottingham Forest, Division 1, 21/4/09
Record Cup Win: 8-1 v Coventry City (away), LC R5, 1/12/64
Record Fee Received: £3.5m from Aston Villa for Mark Draper, 7/95
Record Fee Paid: £1.25m to Notts County for Mark Draper, 8/94
Most FL Apps: Adam Black, 528, 1920-35
Most FAPL Apps: 70 – Simon Grayson, 1994-97
Most FAPL Goals: 12 – Steve Claridge, 1996-97
Highest Scorer in FAPL season: 12 – Steve Claridge, 1996-97
Record Attendance (all-time): 47,298 v Tottenham H, FAC Rd5, 18/2/28
Record Attendance (FAPL): 21,393 v Liverpool, 26/12/94
Most FAPL Goals in Season: 49, 1994-95 – 42 games
Most FAPL Points in Season: 47, 1996-97 – 38 games

Player	Tot	St	Sb	Snu	PS	Gls	Y	R	Fa	La	Fg	Lg
ANDREWS	0	0	0	3	0	0	0	0	0	0	0	0
CAMPBELL	10	4	6	10	2	0	0	0	2	2	0	0
CLARIDGE	32	29	3	1	7	12	2	0	4	8	1	2
ELLIOT	16	16	0	0	0	4	3	0	2	0	0	0
FOX	0	0	0	1	0	0	0	0	0	0	0	0
GRAYSON	36	36	0	0	1	0	4	0	3	7	0	2
GUPPY	13	12	1	0	1	0	2	0	0	0	0	0
HESKEY	35	35	0	0	4	10	8	0	3	9	0	2
HILL	7	6	1	9	4	0	2	0	0	2	0	0
HYDE	0	0	0	3	0	0	0	0	0	0	0	0
IZZET	35	34	1	0	6	3	6	0	3	8	0	1
KAAMARK	10	9	1	2	3	0	0	0	2	3	0	0
KELLER	31	31	0	0	0	0	0	0	4	8	0	0
LAWRENCE	15	2	13	16	0	0	0	0	2	7	0	2
LENHART	0	0	0	0	0	0	0	0	0	1	0	0
LENNON	35	35	0	0	0	1	8	0	2	7	0	1
LEWIS	6	4	2	2	4	0	0	0	0	2	0	0
MARSHALL	28	19	9	1	4	8	1	0	4	0	2	0
McMAHON	0	0	0	1	0	0	0	0	0	0	0	0
PARKER †	31	22	9	1	5	2	0	0	4	9	1	1
POOLE	7	7	0	31	0	0	0	0	0	1	0	0
PRIOR	34	33	1	1	4	0	4	0	4	7	0	0
ROBINS	8	5	3	18	4	1	0	0	2	6	0	1
ROLLING	1	1	0	6	1	0	0	0	0	2	0	0
SLATER	0	0	0	1	0	0	0	0	0	0	0	0
TAYLOR	25	20	5	4	9	0	2	0	2	7	0	0
ULLATHORNE	0	0	0	0	0	0	0	0	0	1	0	0
WALSH	22	22	0	0	0	2	3	1	2	8	1	0
WATTS	26	22	4	8	4	1	3	0	3	6	0	0
WHITLOW	17	14	3	5	1	0	2	0	4	0	0	0
WILSON	2	0	2	2	0	1	0	0	1	0	0	0
OGs						1					1	

5-Year Record

	Div.	P	W	D	L	F	A	Pts	Pos	FAC	FLC
92-93	1	46	22	10	14	71	64	76	6	3	3
93-94	1	46	19	16	11	72	59	73	4	3	3
94-95	PL	42	6	11	25	45	80	29	21	5	2
95-96	1	46	19	14	13	66	60	71	5	3	3
96-97	PL	38	12	11	15	46	54	47	9	5	W

Surprise Package Out-Fox Big Guns

Given the gulf between the Premiership and the Nationwide League, and Leicester City's habit of jumping between the two, the bookies were less than kind to the Foxes as they were deemed favourites for the drop and Martin O'Neill tipped the manager least likely to survive the whole season with the same club. O'Neill raised over £1m with the sale of top scorer Iwan Roberts and Brian Carey, but invested over £3m on Ian Marshall, Muzzy Isset, Spencer Prior and keeper Kasey Keller.

Leicester kicked off the season with a draw at Sunderland and a win at home to Southampton, courtesy of two goals from the emerging talent of Emile Heskey. But with just one victory from the opening six games, the Foxes were down in 16th position by mid September. Towards the end of the month the Foxes won Premiership matches back to back for the first time but failed to build on those successes with lengthy inconsistent spells.

The away match with Newcastle ended in an amazing 4-3 defeat after Leicester led 3-1 with 13 minutes remaining, but City then hit a purple patch. Marshall scored City's first Premiership hat trick during a 4-2 win over Derby and Matt Elliott, an outstanding £1.6m signing from Oxford United, scored twice in a 3-1 win at Wimbledon. O'Neill further spent a total of £1.45m on Steve Guppy and Robert Ullathorne, only for the latter to suffer a broken ankle in his first match.

A third consecutive victory was secured on 5 March when journeyman striker Steve Claridge scored the winner against Villa and a goalless draw at Coventry kept the Foxes in the top ten. But with just four draws from the next eight games, City slid towards the danger zone. Even so, safety was secured with a game to spare thanks to Elliott's late winner against Sheffield Wednesday. City celebrated with a 4-2 success at Blackburn as the club rose to a season's high of ninth.

Southend United and Norwich City were dispatched from the early rounds of the FA Cup at Filbert Street but O'Neill was forced to field a weakened side at home to Chelsea in Round Five and looked well beaten at two down by the interval. Such is the majesty of the cup however, and Leicester drew level in injury time through an own goal. That finish was dramatic enough but it was nothing compared to the furore which exploded when referee Mike Reed awarded Chelsea a farcical penalty three minutes from the end of the replay when Erland Johnsen dived in the visitors' penalty area. City complaints were rejected and out they went as Leboeuf scored from the spot.

Success for City was always more likely to come in the Coca-Cola Cup and progress was swiftly made as Scarborough and York City were beaten to set up a 4th Round tie with Manchester United. The champions fielded a weakened side of 'only' five internationals and paid the price as Claridge and Heskey took City through to a 5th Round meeting at Ipswich. Mark Robins, back in the side after four months on the sidelines, settled that tie to give Leicester a semi final showdown with Wimbledon. After being held to a 0-0 home draw in the 1st Leg, things looked bleak but Leicester came back from a goal down in the return match to book a place in the final on the away goals rule thanks to Simon Grayson's equaliser. Sadly the final with Middlesbrough was disappointing although it had a dramatic climax with Heskey equalising three minutes from the end of extra time. The two closely matched sides also took the replay at Hillsborough to extra time and this time Claridge struck ten minutes from time to clinch victory. ∎

175

Results 1996-97

Date	Opponents	Ven	Res	Pos	Atten	Scorers
17-Aug	Sunderland	A	0-0	–	19,262	
21-Aug	Southampton	H	2-1	–	17,562	Heskey (5, 42)
24-Aug	Arsenal	H	0-2	12	20,429	
02-Sep	Sheffield W.	A	1-2	13	17,657	Claridge (28)
07-Sep	N. Forest	A	0-0	14	24,105	
15-Sep	Liverpool	H	0-3	16	20,987	
22-Sep	Tottenham H.	A	2-1	14	24,159	Claridge (22); Marshall (86)
28-Sep	Leeds Utd	H	1-0	10	20,359	Heskey (60)
12-Oct	Chelsea	H	1-3	12	20,766	Watts (44)
19-Oct	West Ham Utd	A	0-1	14	22,285	
26-Oct	Newcastle Utd	H	2-0	11	21,134	Claridge (17); Heskey (79)
02-Nov	Derby Co.	A	0-2	13	35,310	
16-Nov	Aston Villa	A	3-1	10	36,193	Claridge (8); Parker (44 pen); Izzet (84)
23-Nov	Everton	H	1-2	12	20,975	Walsh (83)
30-Nov	Man. Utd	A	1-3	14	55,196	Lennon (90)
03-Dec	Middlesbrough	A	2-0	12	29,709	Claridge (45); Izzet (47)
07-Dec	Blackburn R.	H	1-1	12	19,306	Marshall (78)
21-Dec	Coventry C.	H	0-2	13	20,038	
26-Dec	Liverpool	A	1-1	13	40,786	Claridge (76)
28-Dec	N. Forest	H	2-2	12	20,833	Heskey (10); Izzet (63)
11-Jan	Leeds Utd	A	0-3	16	29,486	
18-Jan	Wimbledon	H	1-0	12	18,927	Heskey (72)
29-Jan	Sunderland	H	1-1	13	17,883	Parker (32 pen)
02-Feb	Newcastle Utd	A	3-4	14	36,396	Elliott (55); Claridge (60); Heskey (68)
22-Feb	Derby Co.	H	4-2	12	20,323	Marshall (6, 24, 27); Claridge (58)
01-Mar	Wimbledon	A	3-1	10	11,487	Elliott (17, 27); Robins (23)
05-Mar	Aston Villa	H	1-0	10	20,626	Claridge (66)
08-Mar	Coventry C.	A	0-0	10	19,220	
15-Mar	Middlesbrough	H	1-3	11	20,561	Marshall (47)
20-Mar	Tottenham H.	H	1-1	11	20,593	Claridge (74)
22-Mar	Southampton	A	2-2	11	15,044	Heskey (47); Claridge (71)
09-Apr	Everton	A	1-1	11	30,368	Marshall (70)
12-Apr	Arsenal	A	0-2	13	38,044	
19-Apr	Chelsea	A	1-2	13	27,723	OG (47, Sinclair)
23-Apr	West Ham Utd	A	0-1	14	20,327	
03-May	Man. Utd	H	2-2	12	21,068	Walsh (15); Marshall (20)
07-May	Sheffield W.	H	1-0	12	20,793	Elliott (86)

| 11-May | Blackburn R. | A | 4-2 | 9 | 25,881 | Heskey (13, 56); Claridge (55); Wilson (81) |

FA Challenge Cup

Date	Opponents	Vn	Rnd	Res	Atten	Scorers
15-Jan	Southend Utd	H	3R	2-0	13,982	Claridge (40); Marshall (48)
25-Jan	Norwich C.	H	4R	2-1	18,700	Marshall (90); Parker (67 pen)
16-Feb	Chelsea	H	5R	2-2	19,125	Walsh (52); OG (88, Newton)
26-Feb	Chelsea	A	5RR	0-1	26,053	

Coca-Cola League Cup

Date	Opponents	Vn	Rnd	Res	Atten	Scorers
17-Sep	Scarborough	A	2R1L	2-0	4,168	Izzet (9); Lawrence (81)
25-Sep	Scarborough	H	2R2L	2-1	10,793	Lawrence (40); Parker (90 pen)
	Leicester City win 4-1 on aggregate.					
22-Oct	York City	A	3R	2-0	8,406	Lennon (60); Grayson (87)
27-Nov	Man. Utd	H	4R	2-0	20,428	Claridge (38); Heskey (77)
21-Jan	Ipswich Town	A	5R	1-0	20,793	Robins (41)
18-Feb	Wimbledon	H	SF1L	0-0	16,021	
11-Mar	Wimbledon	A	SF2L	1-1	17,810	Grayson (52)
	1-1 on aggregate after extra time. Leicester City win on away goals rule.					
06-Apr	Middlesbrough	W	F	1-1	76,757	Heskey (117)
16-Apr	Middlesbrough	Hbr	FR	1-0	39,428	Claridge (100)

Foxes – Premiership Fact File

- Leicester City won the Premiership Programme of the Year Award. Each issue boosts over 100 pictures and represents the umpteenth award editor Paul Mace has amassed.

- Kevin Poole took part in all 38 of City's Premiership games last season. He made only seven appearances though – the other 31 matches he was an unused substitute. Who'd be a goalkeeper?

- Leicester were threatened with relegation on the last day of the season. They won 4-2 at Blackburn and ended up in 9th place. That position earned them over £1.2m in prize money – nearly three times as much as their Coca-Cola Cup success paid them.

Liverpool

Following a dispute between Everton and its Anfield landlord a new club, Liverpool AFC, was formed in 1892 by the landlord, former Everton committee-man John Houlding, with its headquarters at Anfield. An application for Football League membership was rejected without being put to the vote. Instead the team joined the Lancashire League and immediately won the championship.

After that one campaign, when the Liverpool Cup was won but there was early FA Cup elimination, Liverpool was selected to fill one of two vacancies in an expanded Football League Second Division in 1893. Premier League founder members 1992.

Ground: Anfield Road, Liverpool L4 0TH
Phone: 0151-263 2361   **Match Info:** 0151-260 9999 (24 hrs)
Box Office: 0151-260 8680   **CC Bookings:** 0151263 5727
News: 0891 12 11 84   **Ticket Info:** 0891 12 15 85
Capacity: 41,000   **Pitch:** 110 yds x 75 yds
Colours: All Red/White Trim   **Nickname:** Reds or Pool
Radio: 1485AM/95.8FM BBC Radio Merseyside
Internet: –

Chairman: D.R. Moores   **CEO:** Rick Parry
Secretary: Bryce Morrison
Manager: Roy Evans   **Coach:** Ronnie Moran

League History: 1893 Elected to Division 2; 1894-95 Division 1; 1895-96 Division 2; 1896-1904 Division 1; 1904-05 Division 2; 1905-54 Division 1; 1954-62 Division 2; 1962-92 Division 1; 1992- FA Premier League.

Honours: *Football League Division 1 Champions:* 1900-01, 1905-06, 1921-22, 1922-23, 1946-47, 1963-64, 1965-66, 1972-73, 1975-76, 1976-77, 1978-79, 1979-80, 1981-82, 1982-83, 1983-84, 1985-86, 1987-88, 1989-90; *Runners-up:* 1898-99, 1909-10, 1968-69, 1973-74, 1974-75, 1977-78, 1984-85, 1986-87, 1988-89, 1990-91; *Division 2 Champions:* 1893-94, 1895-96, 1904-05, 1961-62. *FA Cup Winners:* 1964-65, 1973-74, 1985-86, 1988-89, 1991-92; *Runners-up:* 1913-14, 1949-50, 1970-71, 1976-77, 1987-88, 1995-96; *Football League Cup Winners:* 1980-81, 1981-82, 1982-83, 1983-84, 1994-95; *Runners-up:* 1977-78, 1986-87, 1995-96; *League Super Cup Winners:* 1985-86; *Champions' Cup Winners:* 1976-77; 1977-78, 1980-81; 1983-84; *Runners-up:* 1984-85; *Cup-Winners' Cup Runners-up:* 1965-66;

UEFA Cup Winners: 1972-73, 1975-76; *European Super Cup Winners:* 1977; *Runners-up:* 1984; *World Club Championship Runners-up:* 1981, 1984.

European Record: CC (12): 64-65 (SF), 66-67 (2), 73-74 (2), 76-77 (W), 77-78 (W), 78-79 (1), 79-80 (1), 80-81 (W), 81-82 (QF), 82-83 (QF), 83-84 (W), 84-85 (F); CWC (5): 65-66 (F), 71-72 (2), 74-75 (2), 92-93 (2), 96-97 (SF); UEFA (8) 67-68 (3), 68-69 (1), 69-70 (2), 70-71 (SF), 72-73 (W), 75-76 (W), 91-92 (QF), 94-95 (2).

Managers: W.E. Barclay 1892-96; Tom Watson 1896-1915; David Ashworth 1920-22; Matt McQueen 1923-28; George Patterson 1928-36 (continued as secretary); George Kay 1936-51; Don Welsh 1951-56; Phil Taylor 1956-59; Bill Shankly 1959-74; Bob Paisley 1974-83; Joe Fagan 1983-85; Kenny Dalglish 1985-91; *(FAPL)* Graeme Souness 1991-94; Roy Evans January 1994-

Season 1996-97

Biggest Home Win:	5-1 v Chelsea and Middlesbrough
Biggest Home Defeat:	1-3 v Manchester United
Biggest Away Win:	3-0 v Leicester City
Biggest Away Defeat:	0-3 v Blackburn Rovers
Biggest Home Att:	40,892 v Manchester United
Smallest Home Att:	36,126 v Nottingham Forest
Average Attendance:	39,777 (2nd)
Leading Scorer:	18 – Robbie Fowler, 12 – Stan Collymore

All-Time Records

Record FAPL Win:	6-0 v Manchester City, 28/10/95
Record FAPL Defeat:	1-5 v Coventry City, 19/12/92
Record FL Win:	10-1 v Rotherham Town, Division 2, 18/2/1896 *and* 9-0 v Crystal Palace, Division 1, 12/9/89
Record FL Defeat:	1-9 v Birmingham City, Division 2, 11/12/54
Record Cup Win:	11-0 v Stromsgodset Drammen, CWC 1R1L, 17/9/74
Record Fee Received:	£7m from Aston Villa for Stan Collymore, 5/97
Record Fee Paid:	£8.5m to N. Forest for Stan Collymore, 6/95
Most FL Apps:	Ian Callaghan, 640, 1960-78
Most FAPL Apps:	176 – Steve McManaman, 1992-97
Most FAPL Goals:	83 – Robbie Fowler, 1993-97

Highest Scorer in FAPL Season: Robbie Fowler, 28 1995-96
Record Attendance (all-time): 61,905 v Wolves, FA Cup R4, 2/2/52
Record Attendance (FAPL): 44,619 v Everton, 20/3/93
Most FAPL Goals in Season: 65, 1994-95 – 42 games
Most FAPL Points in Season: 74, 1994-95 – 42 games

Player	Tot	St	Sb	Snu	PS	Gls	Y	R	Fa	La	Fg	Lg
BABB	22	21	1	2	4	1	5	0	1	3	0	0
BARNES	35	34	1	2	2	4	0	0	2	3	0	0
BERGER	23	13	10	9	5	6	0	0	2	3	0	1
BJORNEBYE	38	38	0	0	3	2	3	0	2	4	0	0
CARRAGHER	2	1	1	7	0	1	1	0	0	1	0	0
CASSIDY	0	0	0	1	0	0	0	0	0	0	0	0
COLLYMORE † ...	30	25	5	5	9	12	3	0	2	0	2	0
FOWLER...	32	32	0	0	4	18	4	1	1	4	1	5
HARKNESS	7	5	2	5	0	0	0	0	0	0	0	0
JAMES	38	38	0	0	0	0	0	0	2	4	0	0
JONES L.	2	0	2	15	0	0	0	0	0	0	0	0
JONES R.	2	2	0	4	1	0	1	0	0	1	0	0
KENNEDY	5	0	5	20	0	0	0	0	1	1	0	0
KVARME	15	15	0	0	2	0	1	0	1	0	0	0
MATTEO	26	22	4	7	1	0	2	0	2	3	0	0
McATEER	37	36	1	0	2	1	6	0	2	4	0	0
McMANAMAN ...	37	37	0	0	1	7	5	0	2	4	0	2
OWEN	2	1	1	2	0	1	0	0	0	0	0	0
REDKNAPP...	23	18	5	6	0	3	0	0	1	1	0	2
RUDDOCK	17	15	2	17	3	1	2	0	0	2	0	0
SCALES	3	3	0	1	2	0	0	0	0	1	0	0
THOMAS	30	28	2	3	2	3	4	0	1	4	0	0
THOMPSON	3	1	2	2	0	0	2	0	0	0	0	0
WARNER	0	0	0	38	0	0	0	0	0	0	0	0
WRIGHT...	33	33	0	0	3	0	6	0	2	3	0	1
OGs						2						

Cup Winners' Cup Appearances

Babb 4+1; Barnes 7+0/3; Berger 6+0/2; Bjornebye 8+0/2; Collymore 4+1/2;
Fowler 7+0/7; Harkness 3+0; James 8+0; Kennedy 0+1; Matteo 7+0;
McAteer 8+0; McManaman 8+0/1; Redknapp 4+3; Ruddock 2+1; Scales
2+1; Thomas 5+1; Wright 5+0/1.

5-Year Record

	Div.	P	W	D	L	F	A	Pts	Pos	FAC	FLC
92-93	PL	42	16	11	15	62	55	59	6	3	4
93-94	PL	42	17	9	16	59	55	60	8	3	4
94-95	PL	42	21	11	10	65	37	74	4	QF	W
95-96	PL	38	20	11	7	70	34	71	3	F	4
96-97	PL	38	19	11	8	62	37	68	4	4	QF

Fortress Anfield Falls

The Championship has not visited Anfield since 1990 but manager Roy Evans kept faith with most of the squad who finished the previous season in third place. The most notable changes saw Ian Rush depart on a free transfer to Leeds and Patrik Berger join from Borussia Dortmund for £3.25m.

Evans' judgement seemed well founded as Liverpool slipped into gear and, after sharing a 3-3 draw at Middlesbrough, the Reds chalked up six wins and a draw, conceding just four goals in the process. Their place at the summit of the Premiership was cemented by a 2-1 win over West Ham but, despite playing well in their next game, Liverpool suffered a painful defeat away to Manchester United. A 2-1 win over Derby maintained an unbeaten home record to the end of October but it was to be another six weeks before they would win two consecutive Premier League matches. Emphatic 5-1 and 4-2 victories over lowly Middlesbrough and Forest hoisted Liverpool back to the top with Fowler striking four times against Boro, as he notched his 100th 'Pool goal in a new club record of 165 games. Liverpool stayed top for the next six games but with just one win from the first five their position was under constant threat and between a 3-0 thumping of Aston Villa and a 1-0 victory at Derby, top place was surrendered to Manchester United.

One year on from a seven-goal thriller at Anfield with Newcastle, home fans' nerves were again tested as Newcastle wiped out a three-goal disadvantage before succumbing to Fowler's last-minute winner. Fowler and McManaman scored at Highbury but Fowler grabbed the headlines by telling referee Gerald Ashby he was wrong to award a penalty after Fowler himself appeared to be brought down by David Seaman; the penalty was saved. Liverpool faced a less than daunting run-in but their hopes were immediately hit by a shock injury-time defeat at home to Coventry. Four points from games at Sunderland and Everton ultimately counted for little as Manchester United practically wrapped up the title for another year with a surprisingly comfortable 3-1 success at Anfield.

Liverpool began positively in the Coca-Cola Cup with a 4-1 replay win over Charlton and a 4-2 victory over Arsenal, with Fowler adding another couple to his impressive tally against the Gunners. The run ended during a pulsating tie at Middlesbrough. FA Cup finalists the previous season, Liverpool sought to go one better in 1996-97 and set off on Wembley way with a single goal win over a defensively minded Burnley. First half goals from Fowler and Collymore put Liverpool in control at Chelsea in Round Four but the Reds capitulated in most unexpected fashion to crash out 4-2.

Thanks to Manchester United's double in 1995-96, Liverpool were admitted to the Cup Winners' Cup and made good early progress. The double was completed over Finns MyPa-47 and a 2-1 win at the home of FC Sion was followed by a 6-3 triumph over the French side. Hopes of success in Europe for the first time in 13 years continued with a 4-1 aggregate quarter final victory over Norwegians SK Brann, but after a dismal display in the 1st Leg of their semi final with Paris St Germain, the Reds were left with a mountain to climb at 3-0 down. Pride was restored at Anfield but goals from Fowler and Mark Wright could not stave off an aggregate defeat. With no silverware to hold up, Evans was criticised by some supporters but the indifferent form of some of his top players was beyond his control. Collymore was sold to Aston Villa for £7m after two years at Anfield. ∎

Results 1996-97

Date	Opponents	Ven	Res	Pos	Atten	Scorers
17-Aug	Middlesbrough	A	3-3	–	30,039	Bjornebye (4); Barnes (29); Fowler (65)
19-Aug	Arsenal	H	2-0	–	38,103	McManaman (68, 74)
24-Aug	Sunderland	H	0-0	7	40,503	
04-Sep	Coventry C.	A	1-0	4	23,021	Babb (68)
07-Sep	Southampton	H	2-1	3	39,189	Collymore (40); McManaman (89)
15-Sep	Leicester C.	A	3-0	1	20,987	Berger (58, 77); Thomas (62)
21-Sep	Chelsea	H	5-1	1	40,739	Fowler (14); Berger (42, 48); OG (45 Myers); Barnes (57)
29-Sep	West Ham Utd	A	2-1	1	25,064	Collymore (2); Thomas (55)
12-Oct	Man. Utd	A	0-1	3	55,128	
27-Oct	Derby Co.	H	2-1	3	39,515	Fowler (47, 51)
03-Nov	Blackburn R.	A	0-3	4	29,598	
16-Nov	Leeds Utd	A	2-0	2	39,981	Ruddock (13); McManaman (90)
20-Nov	Everton	H	1-1	2	40,751	Fowler (30)
23-Nov	Wimbledon	H	1-1	3	39,027	Collymore (1)
02-Dec	Tottenham H.	A	2-0	2	32,899	Thomas (45); McManaman (49)
07-Dec	Sheffield W.	H	0-1	3	39,507	
14-Dec	Middlesbrough	H	5-1	2	39,491	Fowler (1, 28, 77, 85); Bjornebye (45)
17-Dec	N. Forest	H	4-2	1	36,126	Collymore (6, 63); Fowler (27); OG (51, Lyttle)
23-Dec	Newcastle Utd	A	1-1	1	36,570	Fowler (45)
26-Dec	Leicester C.	H	1-1	1	40,786	Collymore (80)
29-Dec	Southampton	A	1-0	1	15,222	Barnes (77)
01-Jan	Chelsea	A	0-1	1	28,329	
11-Jan	West Ham Utd	H	0-0	1	40,102	
18-Jan	Aston Villa	H	3-0	1	40,489	Carragher (50); Collymore (58); Fowler (63)
01-Feb	Derby Co.	A	1-0	2	18,102	Collymore (75)
19-Feb	Leeds Utd	H	4-0	2	38,957	Fowler (22); Collymore (36, 38); Redknapp (87)
22-Feb	Blackburn R.	H	0-0	2	40,747	
02-Mar	Aston Villa	A	0-1	2	39,339	
10-Mar	Newcastle Utd	H	4-3	2	40,751	McManaman (29); Berger (30); Fowler (42, 90)
15-Mar	N. Forest	A	1-1	2	29,181	Fowler (3)

182

24-Mar	Arsenal	A	2-1	2	38,068	Collymore (50); McAteer (65)
06-Apr	Coventry C.	H	1-2	3	40,079	Fowler (53)
13-Apr	Sunderland	A	2-1	3	21,938	Fowler (33); McManaman (47)
16-Apr	Everton	A	1-1	2	40,177	Redknapp (27)
19-Apr	Man. Utd	H	1-3	3	40,892	Barnes (19)
03-May	Tottenham H.	H	2-1	2	40,003	Collymore (15), Berger (43)
06-May	Wimbledon	A	1-2	3	20,016	Owen (74)
11-May	Sheffield W.	A	1-1	4	38,943	Redknapp (83)

FA Challenge Cup

Date	Opponents	Vn	Rnd	Res	Atten	Scorers
04-Jan	Burnley	H	3R	1-0	33,252	Collymore (12)
26-Jan	Chelsea	A	4R	2-4	27,950	Fowler (10); Collymore (21)

Coca-Cola League Cup

23-Oct	Charlton Ath.	A	3	1-1	15,000	Fowler (21)
13-Nov	Charlton Ath.	H	3R	4-1	20,714	Wright (14); Redknapp (17); Fowler (48, 72)
27-Nov	Arsenal	H	4R	4-2	32,814	McManaman (26); Fowler (39 pen, 52), Berger (72)
8-Jan	Middlesbrough	A	QF	1-2	28,670	McManaman (64)

Cup-Winners' Cup

Date	Opponents	Vn	Rnd	Res	Atten	Scorers
12-Sep	MyPa-47	A	1R1L	1-0	5,500	Bjornebye (61)
26-Sep	MyPa-47	H	1R2L	3-1	39,013	Berger (18); Collymore (60); Barnes (77)

Liverpool win 4-1 on aggregate.

| 17-Oct | FC Sion | A | 2R1L | 2-1 | 16,500 | Fowler (24); Barnes (60) |
| 31-Oct | FC Sion | H | 2R2L | 6-3 | 38,514 | McManaman (28);
Bjornebye (54); Barnes (65);
Fowler (70, 71); Berger (89) |

Liverpool win 8-4 on aggregate.

| 6-Mar | SK Brann | A | QF1L | 1-1 | 12,700 | Fowler (9) |
| 20-Mar | SK Brann | H | QF2L | 3-0 | 40,326 | Fowler (26 pen, 78);
Collymore (62) |

Liverpool win 4-1 on aggregate.

| 10-Apr | PSG | A | SF1L | 0-3 | 35,142 | |
| 24-Apr | PSG | H | SF2L | 2-0 | 39,984 | Fowler (12); Wright (80) |

Paris St Germain win 3-2 on aggregate.

Manchester United

Came into being in 1902 upon the bankruptcy of Newton Heath. Predecessors appear to have been formed in 1878 as Newton Heath (LYR) when workers at the Carriage and Wagon Department at the Lancashire and Yorkshire Railway formed a club. This soon outgrew railway competition.

Turned professional in 1885 and founder member of Football Alliance in 1889. In 1892 Alliance runners-up Newton Heath was elected to an enlarged Division One of the Football League. In 1902 the club became Manchester United and, in February 1910, moved from Bank Street, Clayton, to Old Trafford. Premier League founder member 1992. Four times Premiership champions and the only side to have completed the Double twice.

Ground:	Old Trafford, Manchester, M16 0RA		
Phone:	0161-872 1661	**Box Office:**	0161-872 0199
Info:	0891 12 11 61		
Capacity:	44,622	**Pitch:**	116 yds x 76 yds
Colours:	Red, White, Black	**Nickname:**	Red Devils
Radio:	Manchester United Radio 1413AM		
Internet:	http://www.sky.co.uk/sports/manu/index.htm		

Chairman/Chief Executive: Martin Edwards
Secretary: Kenneth Merrett
Manager: Alex Ferguson   **Assistant:** Brian Kidd

League History: 1892 Newton Heath elected to Division 1; 1894-1906 Division 2; 1906-22 Division 1; 1922-25 Division 2; 1925-31 Division 1; 1931-36 Division 2; 1936-37 Division 1; 1937-38 Division 2; 1938-74 Division 1; 1974-75 Division 2; 1975-92 Division 1; 1992- FA Premier League.

Honours: *FA Premier League Champions:* 1992-93, 1993-94, 1995-96, 1996-97; *Runners-up:* 1994-95; *Football League: Division 1 Champions:* 1907-8, 1910-11, 1951-52, 1955-56, 1956-57, 1964-65, 1966-67; *Runners-up:* 1946-47, 1947-48, 1948-49, 1950-51, 1958-59, 1963-64, 1967-68, 1979-80, 1987-88, 1991-92. *Division 2 Champions:* 1935-36, 1974-75; *Runners-up:* 1896-97, 1905-06, 1924-25, 1937-38. *FA Cup Winners:* 1908-09, 1947-48, 1962-63, 1976-77, 1982-83, 1984-85, 1989-90, 1993-94, 1995-96; *Runners-up:* 1957, 1958, 1976, 1979, 1995; *Football League Cup Winners:* 1991-92; *Runners-up:* 1982-83, 1990-91, 1993-94. *Champions' Cup Winners:* 1967-68; *Cup-Winners' Cup Winners:* 1990-91. *League/Cup Double Performed:* 1993-94, 1995-96.

European Record: CC (8): 56-57 (SF), 57-58 (SF), 65-66 (SF), 67-68 (W), 68-69 (SF), 93-94 (SF), 94-95 (CL), 96-97 (SF): CWC (5): 63-64 (QF), 77-78 (2), 83-84 (SF), 90-91 (W), 91-92 (2). UEFA (7): 64-65 (SF), 76-77 (2), 80-81 (1), 82-83 (1), 84-85 (QF), 92-93 (1), 95-96 (1).

Managers: Ernest Magnall 1900-12; John Robson 1914-21; John Chapman 1921-26; Clarence Hildrith 1926-27; Herbert Bamlett 1927-31; Walter Crickmer 1931-32; Scott Duncan 1932-37; Jimmy Porter 1938-44; Walter Crickmer 1944-45; Matt Busby 1945-69 (continued as GM then Director); Wilf McGuinness 1969-70; Frank O'Farrell 1971-72; Tommy Docherty 1972-77; Dave Sexton 1977-81; Ron Atkinson 1981-86; *(FAPL)* Alex Ferguson Nov 1986-

Season 1996-97

Biggest Home Win:	5-0 v Sunderland
Biggest Home Defeat:	1-3 v Chelsea
Biggest Away Win:	4-0 v Leeds United and Nottingham Forest
Biggest Away Defeat:	3-6 v Southampton, 0-5 v Newcastle Utd
Biggest Home Att:	55,314 v Wimbledon
Smallest Home Att:	54,178 v Blackburn Rovers
Average Attendance:	55,080 (1st)
Leading Scorer:	18 – Ole Gunnar Solskjaer, 11 – Eric Cantona

All-Time Records

Record FAPL Win:	9-0 v Ipswich Town, 4/3/95
Record FAPL Defeat:	3-6 v Southampton, 26/10/96
Record FL Win:	10-1 v Wolverhampton W, Division 2, 15/10/1892
Record FL Defeat:	0-7 v Blackburn R, Div. 1, 10/4/26; Aston Villa, Div. 1, 27/12/30; Wolves, Div. 2, 26/12/31
Record Cup Win:	10-0 v RSC Anderlecht, Champions Cup, Pr2L, 26/9/56
Record Fee Received:	£7m from Internazionale (Italy) for Paul Ince 6/95
Record Fee Paid:	£7m to Newcastle United for Andy Cole 1/95 (inc. part exchange of Keith Gillespie – £1m).
Most FL Apps:	Bobby Charlton, 606, 1956-73
Most FAPL Apps:	186 – Peter Schmeichel, 1992-97
Most FAPL Goals:	70 – Eric Cantona, 1992-97

Highest Scorer in FAPL Season: 18 – Cantona, 93-94 and Solskjaer, 96-97
Record Attendance (all-time): 70,504 v Aston Villa, Division 1, 27/12/20
Record Attendance (FAPL): 55,314 v Wimbledon, 29/1/97
Most FAPL Goals in Season: 80, 1993-94 – 42 games
Most FAPL Points in Season: 92, 1993-94 – 42 games

Player	Tot	St	Sb	Snu	PS	Gls	Y	R	Fa	La	Fg	Lg
APPLETON	0	0	0	2	0	0	0	0	0	2	0	0
BECKHAM	36	33	3	1	3	8	6	0	2	0	1	0
BUTT	26	24	2	0	8	5	5	0	0	0	0	0
CANTONA †	36	36	0	0	1	11	5	0	3	0	0	0
CASPER	2	0	2	3	0	0	0	0	1	2	0	0
CLEGG	4	3	1	1	1	0	0	0	1	1	0	0
COLE	20	10	10	3	2	6	1	0	3	0	0	0
COOKE	0	0	0	0	0	0	0	0	0	1	0	0
CRUYFF	16	11	5	8	6	3	2	0	0	1	0	0
DAVIES	0	0	0	0	0	0	0	0	0	2	0	0
GIBSON	0	0	0	1	0	0	0	0	0	0	0	0
GIGGS	26	25	1	1	6	3	2	0	3	0	0	0
IRWIN	31	29	2	3	2	1	1	0	3	0	0	0
JOHNSEN	31	26	5	2	6	0	3	0	2	0	0	0
KEANE	21	21	0	0	1	2	6	1	3	2	0	0
MAY	29	28	1	1	2	3	5	0	1	2	0	0
McCLAIR	19	4	15	16	0	0	1	0	3	2	0	0
NEVILLE G.	31	30	1	3	2	1	4	0	3	1	0	0
NEVILLE P.	18	15	3	5	1	0	2	0	0	1	0	0
O'KANE	1	1	0	0	1	0	0	0	0	2	0	0
PALLISTER	27	27	0	1	4	3	4	0	1	0	0	0
PILKINGTON	0	0	0	1	0	0	0	0	0	0	0	0
POBORSKY	22	15	7	15	10	3	1	0	2	2	0	1
SCHMEICHEL	36	36	0	0	0	0	2	0	3	0	0	0
SCHOLES	24	16	8	7	7	3	6	0	2	2	2	1
SOLSKJAER	33	25	8	2	11	18	1	0	3	0	0	0
THORNLEY	2	1	1	5	1	0	0	0	0	2	0	0
VAN DER GOUW	2	2	0	34	0	0	0	0	0	2	0	0
OGs						6						

UEFA Champions' League *(Start+Substitute/Goals)*

Beckham 10+0/2; Butt 7+1; Cantona 10+0/3; Casper 0+1; Cole 3+3/1; Cruyff 3+1; Giggs 7+1/2; Irwin 8+0; Johnsen 9+0; Keane 5+0; May 7+1/1; McClair 0+3; Neville G. 10+0; Neville P. 2+2; Pallister 8+0; Poborsky 3+3; Schmeichel 9+0; Scholes 0+4; Solskjaer 8+2/1; Van der Gouw 1+0.

5-Year Record

	Div.	P	W	D	L	F	A	Pts	Pos	FAC	FLC
92-93	PL	42	24	12	6	67	31	84	1	5	3
93-94	PL	42	27	11	4	80	38	92	1	W	F
94-95	PL	42	26	10	6	77	28	88	2	F	3
95-96	PL	38	25	7	6	73	35	82	1	W	2
96-97	PL	38	21	12	5	76	44	75	1	4	4

Champions' Dream Comes Closer

Having completed the English league and cup double twice in three years, Manchester United's declared desire was to lift the Champions' Cup for the first time in almost 30 years. Manager Alex Ferguson, the longest serving one-club manager in the top flight, signed six players from overseas clubs with Czech Republic star Karel Poborsky, Dutch winger Jordi Cruyff and defender Ronny Johnsen topping the list at a cost of around £6m. A large chunk of that fee was recouped from the £4.5m sale of Lee Sharpe; veteran Steve Bruce also departed.

United started the season in spectacular fashion with a 4-0 destruction of Newcastle in the Charity Shield and followed it with a first day of the season 3-0 canter at Wimbledon which included David Beckham's classic goal. Beckham made a habit of scoring outstanding goals and by the end of the campaign he was a regular in the England set-up. He certainly took some of the pressure off Eric Cantona, whose influence was well down on recent seasons, and come the end of the season the Frenchman announced his retirement. Early on United failed to live up to expectations but a run of three consecutive league draws ended abruptly with a 4-0 thrashing of Leeds and a 4-1 drubbing of Nottingham Forest, which took United to the top of the Premiership for the first time. A lack of league games cost them pole position and the unbeaten record was shattered at the end of October as Peter Schmeichel appeared a mere mortal as United crashed 5-0 at Newcastle and 6-3 at Southampton, where Roy Keane was dismissed. Next to go was the unbeaten home record as Chelsea won 3-1 at Old Trafford.

Ferguson's side, which often did not include his summer signings, now put together a 16-match unbeaten Premiership run which included five straight victories. The double was achieved over Arsenal and top place was recaptured with victory over Wimbledon in front of their largest gate of 55,314. Surprising defeats were suffered at Sunderland and at home to Derby but when Liverpool were crushed 3-1 at Anfield, a fourth title in five years was virtually assured.

European commitments earned United exemption from the Coca-Cola Cup until the 3rd Round where a scratch side beat Swindon but then lost 2-0 at Leicester. United's bid to clinch an unprecedented third league and cup double made a convincing start with a 2-0 3rd Round FA Cup win over Spurs. But after taking, and then losing, a late lead at home to Wimbledon, the Red Devils lost in the replay.

In the Champions' League United were given a footballing lesson by holders Juventus, only to storm back with a superb first half performance at home to Rapid Vienna and a well controlled victory in Turkey against Fenerbahce. In the return, cautious approach contributed to a 1-0 end of their 41-year undefeated record at Old Trafford in European competitions. Juventus again gave United the run around in the return in England, at least for 45 minutes, but a stirring second half fightback should have saved a point, had United not been found wanting in front of goal. No such problems were experienced as Rapid were easily beaten in Vienna to clinch a place in the last eight. Portuguese champions FA Porto were ripped to shreds at Old Trafford as Ryan Giggs inspired United to a marvellous 4-0 triumph; the 0-0 draw in the 2nd Leg becoming rather academic. The semi-final proved a bitter experience for United as Borussia Dortmund gained a deserved 1st Leg lead in Germany. Having underperformed in Dortmund, the Reds excelled on home soil but ultimately went down 2-0 on aggregate, thanks to some shocking finishing. ∎

Results 1996-97

FA Carling Premiership

Date	Opponents	Ven	Res	Pos	Atten	Scorers
17-Aug	Wimbledon	A	3-0	–	25,786	Cantona (25); Irwin (58); Beckham (87)
21-Aug	Everton	H	2-2	–	54,943	Cruyff (70); OG (81, Unsworth)
25-Aug	Blackburn	H	2-2	7	54,178	Cruyff (38); Solskjaer (68)
04-Sep	Derby Co.	A	1-1	7	18,026	Beckham (38)
07-Sep	Leeds Utd	A	4-0	5	39,694	OG (2, Martyn); Butt (46); Poborsky (76); Cantona (90)
14-Sep	N. Forest	H	4-1	1	54,984	Solskjaer (21); Giggs (42); Cantona (82, 90 pen)
21-Sep	Aston Villa	A	0-0	4	39,339	
29-Sep	Tottenham H.	H	2-0	4	54,943	Solskjaer (38, 58)
12-Oct	Liverpool	H	1-0	4	55,128	Beckham (23)
20-Oct	Newcastle Utd	A	0-5	5	36,579	
26-Oct	Southampton	A	3-6	5	15,253	Beckham (41); May (56); Scholes (88)
02-Nov	Chelsea	H	1-3	6	55,198	Poborsky (80)
16-Nov	Arsenal	H	1-0	6	55,210	OG (61, Winterburn)
23-Nov	Middlesbrough	A	2-2	7	30,063	Keane (17); May (72)
30-Nov	Leicester C.	H	3-1	5	55,196	Butt (75, 86); Solskjaer (84)
08-Dec	West Ham Utd	H	2-2	6	25,045	Solskjaer (53); Beckham (74)
18-Dec	Sheffield W.	A	1-1	6	37,671	Scholes (62)
21-Dec	Sunderland	H	5-0	5	55,081	Solskjaer (35, 47); Cantona (43 pen, 79); Butt (58)
26-Dec	N. Forest	A	4-0	3	29,032	Beckham (25); Butt (44); Solskjaer (66); Cole (74)
28-Dec	Leeds Utd	H	1-0	2	55,256	Cantona (9 pen)
01-Jan	Aston Villa	H	0-0	3	55,113	
12-Jan	Tottenham H.	A	2-1	2	33,026	Solskjaer (22); Beckham (75)
18-Jan	Coventry C.	A	2-0	2	23,085	Giggs (60); Solskjaer (79)
29-Jan	Wimbledon	H	2-1	1	55,314	Giggs (75); Cole (82)
01-Feb	Southampton	H	2-1	1	55,269	Pallister (18); Cantona (79)
19-Feb	Arsenal	A	2-1	1	38,172	Cole (8); Solskjaer (32)
22-Feb	Chelsea	H	1-1	1	28,336	Beckham (68)
01-Mar	Coventry C.	H	3-1	1	55,230	OG (4, Breen); OG (5); Poborsky (47)
08-Mar	Sunderland	A	1-2	1	22,225	OG (77, Melville)
15-Mar	Sheffield W.	H	2-0	1	55,267	Cole (20); Poborsky (60)
22-Mar	Everton	A	2-0	1	40,079	Solskjaer (35); Cantona (79)
05-Apr	Derby Co.	H	2-3	1	55,243	Cantona (47); Solskjaer (76)

12-Apr	Blackburn R.	A	3-2	1	30,476	Cole (32); Scholes (42); Cantona (81)
19-Apr	Liverpool	A	3-1	1	40,892	Pallister (13, 42); Cole (63)
03-May	Leicester C.	A	2-2	1	21,068	Walsh (15); Marshall (20)
05-May	Middlesbrough	H	3-3	1	54,489	Keane (34); Neville, G. (42); Solskjaer (67)
08-May	Newcastle Utd	H	0-0	1	55,236	
12-May	West Ham Utd	H	2 0	1	55,249	Solskjaer (11); Cruyff (84)

FA Challenge Cup

Date	Opponents	Vn	Rnd	Res	Atten	Scorers
05-Jan	Tottenham H.	H	3R	2-0	52,445	Scholes (50); Beckham (86)
25-Jan	Wimbledon	H	4R	1-1	53,342	Scholes (88)
04-Feb	Wimbledon	A	4RR	0-1	25,601	

Coca-Cola League Cup

Date	Opponents	Vn	Rnd	Res	Atten	Scorers
23-Oct	Swindon T.	H	3R	2-1	49,305	Poborsky (19); Scholes (72)
27-Nov	Leicester C.	A	4R	0-2	20,428	

UEFA Champions' League

Date	Opponents	Vn	Rnd	Res	Atten	Scorers
11-Sep	Juventus	A	GpC	0-1	50,000	
25-Sep	Rapid Vienna	H	GpC	2-0	51,831	Solskjaer (20); Beckham (27)
16-Oct	Fenerbahce	A	GpC	2-0	26,200	Beckham (54); Cantona (60)
30-Oct	Fenerbahce	H	GpC	0-1	53,297	
20-Nov	Juventus	H	GpC	0-1	53,529	
04-Dec	Rapid Vienna	A	GpC	2-0	50,000	Giggs (24); Cantona (72)
05-Mar	FC Porto	H	QF1L	4-0	53,415	May (22); Cantona (34); Giggs (60); Cole (80)
19-Mar	FC Porto	A	QF2L	0-0	47,000	
	Manchester United win 4-0 on aggregate.					
09-Apr	B. Dortmund	A	SF1L	0-1	48,500	
23-Apr	B. Dortmund	H	SF2L	0-1	53,606	
	Borussia Dortmund win 2-0 on aggregate.					

FA Charity Shield

Date	Opponents	Venue	Rd	Res	Atten	Scorers
11-Aug	Newcastle United	W		4-0	73,241	Cantona (24); Butt (30); Beckham (85); Keane (87)

Newcastle United

Formed 1882 as Newcastle East End on the amalgamation of Stanley and Rosewood. Founder members, as a professional club, of the Northern League in 1889. Moved from Chillington Road, Heaton, in 1892 to take over the home of the defunct Newcastle West End, with several of those associated with the West End side joining the newcomers.

Applied for Football League Division One membership in 1892, failed and decided against a place in the new Second Division, staying in the Northern League. Later in 1892 changed name to Newcastle United. Elected to an expanded Football League Division Two in 1893.

Ground: St James' Park, Newcastle-upon-Tyne, NE1 4ST
Phone: 0191-201 8400   **Fax:** 0191-201 8600
Box Office: 0191-261 1571   **CC Bookings:** 0191-261 1571
Info: 0891 12 11 90   **Clubshop:** 0191-201-8426
Colours: Black/White, Black, Black   **Nickname:** Magpies
Capacity: 36,401   **Pitch:** 115 yds x 75 yds
Radio: 97.1FM Metro Radio
Internet: http://www.newcastle-utd.co.uk/nufc

President: Bob Young   **Chairman:** Sir John Hall
CEO: Freddie Fletcher   **GM/Secretary:** Russell Cushing
Manager: Kenny Dalglish
Assistants: Terry McDermott, Kenny Burns
Coaches: Chris McMenemy, Arthur Cox
Physio: Derek Wright

League History: 1893 Elected to Division 2; 1898-1934 Division 1; 1934-48 Division 2; 1948-61 Division 1; 1961-65 Division 2; 1965-78 Division 1; 1978-84 Division 2; 1984-89 Division 1; 1989-92 Division 2; 1992-1993 Division 1; 1993- FA Premier League.

Honours: *Football League: Division 1 Champions:* 1904-05, 1906-07, 1908-09, 1926-27, 1992-93; *FA Premier League Runners-up:* 1995-96, 1996-97; *Division 2 Champions:* 1964-65; *Runners-up:* 1897-98, 1947-48. *FA Cup Winners:* 1910, 1924, 1932, 1951, 1952, 1955; *Runners-up:* 1905, 1906, 1908, 1911, 1974; *Football League Cup Runners-up:* 1975-76; *Texaco Cup Winners:* 1973-74, 1974-75. *UEFA Cup Winners:* 1968-69.

European Record: CC (0): –; CWC (0): – ; UEFA (6): 68-69 (W), 69-70 (QF), 70-71 (2), 77-78 (2), 94-95 (2), 96-97 (QF).

Managers: Frank Watt 1895-1932 (secretary until 1932); Andy Cunningham 1930-35; Tom Mather 1935-39; Stan Seymour 1939-47 (hon manager); George Martin 1947-50; Stan Seymour 1950-54 (hon manager); Duggie Livingstone; 1954-56, Stan Seymour (hon manager) 1956-58; Charlie Mitten 1958-61; Norman Smith 1961-62; Joe Harvey 1962-75; Gordon Lee 1975-77; Richard Dinnis 1977; Bill McGarry 1977-80; Arthur Cox 1980-84; Jack Charlton 1984; Willie McFaul 1985-88; Jim Smith 1988 91; Ossie Ardiles 1991-92; *(FAPL)* Kevin Keegan Feb 1992-Jan 1997; Kenny Dalglish Jan 1997-.

Season 1996-97

Biggest Home Win:	7-1 v Tottenham Hotspur
Biggest Home Defeat:	1-2 v Sheffield Wednesday and Arsenal
Biggest Away Win:	2-1 v Sunderland and Tottenham Hotspur
Biggest Away Defeat:	3-4 v Liverpool
Biggest Home Att:	36,582 v Sunderland
Smallest Home Att:	36,143 v Everton
Average Attendance:	36,193 (5th)
Leading Scorer:	25 – Alan Shearer, 16 Les Ferdinand

All-Time Records

Record FAPL Win:	7-1 v Swindon Town, 12/3/94
	7-1 v Tottenham Hotspur, 28/12/96
Record FAPL Defeat:	0-3 v Queens Park Rangers, 4/2/95
Record FL Win:	13-0 v Newport County, Division 2, 5/10/46
Record FL Defeat:	0-9 v Burton Wanderers, Division 2, 15/4/1895
Record Cup Win:	9-0 v Southport (at Hillsborough),
	FA Cup R4, 1/2/32
Record Fee Received:	£7m from Manchester United for Andy Cole,
	1/95 (inc part exchange)
Record Fee Paid:	£6m to QPR for Les Ferdinand, 6/95
Most FL Apps:	Jim Lawrence, 432, 1904-22
Most FAPL Apps:	129 – Peter Beardsley, 1993-97
Most FAPL Goals:	55 – Andy Cole, 1993-95

Highest Scorer in FAPL Season: Andy Cole, 34, 1993-94
Record Attendance (all-time): 68,386 v Chelsea, Division 1, 3/9/30
Record Attendance (FAPL): 36,589 v Tottenham Hotspur, 5/5/96
Most FAPL Goals in Season: 82, 1993-94 – 42 games
Most FAPL Points in Season: 78, 1995-96 – 38 games

Player	Tot	St	Sb	Snu	PS	Gls	Y	R	Fa	La	Fg	Lg
ALBERT	27	27	0	5	1	2	6	0	2	2	0	0
ASPRILLA	24	17	7	4	12	4	1	0	0	2	0	0
BARTON	18	14	4	10	0	1	1	0	2	1	0	0
BATTY	32	32	0	0	1	1	10	1	3	2	0	0
BEARDSLEY	25	22	3	12	4	5	3	0	3	2	0	1
BERESFORD	19	18	1	5	0	0	4	0	3	0	0	0
BRAYSON	0	0	0	4	0	0	0	0	0	0	0	0
CLARK	25	9	16	12	2	2	1	0	3	1	1	0
CRAWFORD	2	0	2	6	0	0	0	0	0	0	0	0
ELLIOT R.	29	29	0	6	1	7	3	0	2	2	0	0
ELLIOT S.	0	0	0	1	0	0	0	0	0	0	0	0
FERDINAND	31	30	1	1	8	16	3	0	3	1	1	0
GILLESPIE	32	23	9	5	8	1	2	1	2	1	0	0
GINOLA	24	20	4	7	6	1	3	0	2	2	0	0
HAMILTON	0	0	0	3	0	0	0	0	0	0	0	0
HISLOP	16	16	0	22	0	0	0	0	3	1	0	0
HOWEY	8	8	0	1	0	1	0	0	0	0	0	0
HUGHES	0	0	0	1	0	0	0	0	0	0	0	0
KITSON	3	0	3	9	0	0	0	0	2	2	0	0
LEE	33	32	1	0	7	5	7	0	2	1	1	0
PEACOCK	35	35	0	3	0	1	2	0	3	2	0	0
SHEARER	31	31	0	0	1	25	5	0	3	1	1	1
SRNICEK	22	22	0	16	0	0	0	0	0	1	0	0
WATSON	36	33	3	2	3	1	3	0	3	1	0	0

UEFA Cup *(Start+Substitute/Goals)*
Albert 7+1/1; Asprilla 6+0/5; Barton 4+2; Batty 7+0; Beardsley 6+0/2;
Beresford 3+1; Clark 2+3; Elliot R. 4+1; Ferdinand 4+0/4; Gillespie 6+2;
Ginola 6+1/1; Hislop 2+0; Howey 1+0; Kitson 0+1; Lee 8+0; Peacock 8+0;
Shearer 4+0/1; Srnicek 6+0; Watson 4+1.

5-Year Record

	Div.	P	W	D	L	F	A	Pts	Pos	FAC	FLC
92-93	1	46	29	4	8	85	37	93	1	5	3
93-94	PL	42	23	8	11	82	41	77	3	4	3
94-95	PL	42	20	12	10	67	47	72	6	QF	4
95-96	PL	38	24	6	8	66	37	78	2	3	QF
96-97	PL	38	19	11	8	73	40	68	2	4	4

Champion Repayment

Newcastle stunned the football world in the build-up to the season when stealing Alan Shearer, apparently from under the noses of Manchester United, from Blackburn for a staggering world record £15m. Shearer, despite being hindered by injury, duly lived up to expectations although overall United did not quite deliver.

The season's curtain raiser saw Newcastle trundle home from Wembley well beaten 4-0 by Manchester United and by the time three league games had been completed another two defeats had been suffered. Shearer, though, had already opened his account, along with David Batty, during a 2-0 win over Wimbledon. The Magpies finally clicked at the start of September with a 2-1 victory at Sunderland which paved the way for a seven match-winning run and a rise from 14th position to top. Along the way Aston Villa were beaten 4-3 in an amazing match at St James's, then quite sensationally Manchester United were thrashed 5-0 with a series of top quality goals when the visitors had actually played reasonably well. Leicester put the charge on hold and their season went into a measure of decline at the end of November when Arsenal, despite having Tony Adams dismissed, won 2-1 at St James's Park. No wins from the next four games sent the side down to sixth before Tottenham were routed 7-1. But as the club celebrated a return to form on the pitch, it went into a state of shock off it as Keegan quit on 8 January to end almost five years as manager, during which time the club had changed beyond all recognition but still did not feature on any honours lists.

The man who succeeded Keegan at Liverpool as a player, Kenny Dalglish, now did likewise at St James's. Dalglish tasted victory for the first time on 29 January when four goals during the final 16 minutes put paid to Everton. Les Ferdinand's 13th Premiership goal of the season completed the double over Middlesbrough but their title hopes faltered with successive defeats by Southampton and Liverpool, their only league reversals after the turn of the year. The latter encounter saw Newcastle pull level in the 88th minute after trailing 3-0 but then fall to Fowler's last-minute winner. Along with Liverpool and Arsenal, though, they clung on to the hope of finishing second to grab the extra place in the Champions' League and with three straight wins, two draws and a 5-0 destruction of Nottingham Forest on the final day the Geordies pinched that money-spinning second place.

Under Keegan, Newcastle made little headway in the cup competitions and the trend was not altered during his final few months in charge. In the FA Cup the Geordies drew at Charlton Athletic before giving Dalglish a hero's welcome for the replay. Charlton almost stole the headlines before the Magpies clinched victory in extra time. The celebrations were somewhat premature as bottom-of-the-table Nottingham Forest pulled off a shock 2-1 win at St James's Park in Round Four. Their Coca-Cola Cup progress also failed to impress as, following a 1-0 win over Oldham Athletic, Keegan's side were well beaten 3-1 at Middlesbrough.

Domestic cup failure, though, would have been acceptable had the UEFA Cup come to rest in the north-east. Superb 4-0 home victories over Halmstads of Sweden and Ferencvaros made away defeats irrelevant and a 2-0 triumph over French side Metz took United through to the quarter final 3-1 on aggregate. The quarter final showdown with Monaco came at a time when United were a touch out of form and, after going down to a disappointing defeat on home soil, Newcastle were well beaten 3-0 in the 2nd Leg. ∎

Results 1996-97

Date	Opponents	Ven	Res	Pos	Atten	Scorers
17-Aug	Everton	A	0-0	–	40,117	
21-Aug	Wimbledon	H	2-0	–	36,385	Batty (4); Shearer (87)
24-Aug	Sheffield W.	H	1-2	14	36,452	Shearer (12 pen)
04-Sep	Sunderland	A	2-1	8	22,037	Beardsley (52); Ferdinand (62)
07-Sep	Tottenham H.	A	2-1	6	32,535	Ferdinand (36, 80)
14-Sep	Blackburn R.	H	2-1	4	36,424	Shearer (44 pen); Ferdinand (60)
21-Sep	Leeds Utd	A	1-0	2	36,070	Shearer (59)
30-Sep	Aston Villa	H	4-3	2	36,400	Ferdinand (5, 22); Shearer (38); Howey (67)
12-Oct	Derby Co.	A	1-0	1	18,092	Shearer (76)
20-Oct	Man. Utd	H	5-0	1	36,579	Peacock (12); Ginola (30); Ferdinand (62); Shearer (74); Albert (83)
26-Oct	Leicester C.	A	0-2	2	21,134	
03-Nov	Middlesbrough	H	3-1	1	36,577	Beardsley (40 pen, 69); Lee (74)
16-Nov	West Ham Utd	H	1-1	1	36,552	Beardsley (82)
23-Nov	Chelsea	A	1-1	1	28,401	Shearer (42)
30-Nov	Arsenal	H	1-2	3	36,565	Shearer (20)
09-Dec	N. Forest	A	0-0	4	25,762	
17-Dec	Coventry C.	A	1-2	4	21,538	Shearer (61)
23-Dec	Liverpool	H	1-1	6	36,570	Shearer (29)
26-Dec	Blackburn R.	A	0-1	6	30,398	
28-Dec	Tottenham H.	H	7-1	5	36,308	Shearer (19, 82); Ferdinand (22, 58); Lee (60, 87); Albert (78)
01-Jan	Leeds Utd	H	3-0	4	36,489	Shearer (4, 77); Ferdinand (87)
11-Jan	Aston Villa	A	2-2	4	39,339	Shearer (16); Clark (22)
18-Jan	Southampton	A	2-2	4	15,251	Ferdinand (13); Clark (82)
29-Jan	Everton	H	4-1	4	36,143	Ferdinand (74); Lee (79); Shearer (87 pen); Elliot, R.(90)
02-Feb	Leicester C.	H	4-3	4	36,396	Elliott, R. (3); Shearer (77, 83, 90)
22-Feb	Middlesbrough	A	1-0	3	30,063	Ferdinand (8)
01-Mar	Southampton	H	0-1	4	36,446	
10-Mar	Liverpool	A	3-4	4	40,751	Gillespie (71); Asprilla (87); Barton (88)

15-Mar	Coventry C.	H	4-0	4	36,571	Watson (11); Lee (44); Beardsley (75 pen); Elliott, R. (86)
23-Mar	Wimbledon	A	1-1	4	23,175	Asprilla (52)
05-Apr	Sunderland	H	1-1	4	36,582	Shearer (77)
13-Apr	Sheffield W.	A	1-1	5	33,798	Elliot, R. (38)
16-Apr	Chelsea	H	3-1	4	36,320	Shearer (11, 35); Asprilla (30)
19-Apr	Derby Co.	H	3-1	4	36,553	Elliot, R. (11); Ferdinand (51); Shearer (74)
03-May	Arsenal	A	1-0	4	38,179	Elliot, R. (44)
06-May	West Ham Utd	A	0-0	4	24,617	
08-May	Man. Utd	A	0-0	3	55,236	
11-May	N. Forest	H	5-0	2	36,554	Asprilla (20); Ferdinand (23, 26); Shearer (36); Elliot, R. (77)

FA Challenge Cup

Date	Opponents	Vn	Rnd	Res	Atten	Scorers
05-Jan	Charlton Ath.	A	3R	1-1	15,000	Lee (32)
15-Jan	Charlton Ath.	H	3RR	2-1	36,398	Clark (33); Shearer (100)
26-Jan	N. Forest	H	4R	1-2	36,434	Ferdinand (60)

Coca-Cola League Cup

Date	Opponents	Vn	Rnd	Res	Atten	Scorers
23-Oct	Oldham Ath.	H	3R	1-0	36,314	Beardsley (24 pen)
27-Nov	Middlesbrough	A	4R	1-3	29,831	Shearer (44)

UEFA Cup

Date	Opponents	Vn	Rnd	Res	Atten	Scorers
10-Sep	Halmstads	H	1R1L	4-0	28,124	Ferdinand (5); Asprilla (26); Albert (51); Beardsley (54)
24-Sep	Halmstads	A	1R2L	1-2	7,847	Ferdinand (42) *5-2 on agg*
16-Oct	Ferencvaros	A	2R1L	2-3	18,000	Ferdinand (24); Shearer (34)
28-Oct	Ferencvaros	H	2R2L	4-0	35,740	Asprilla (42, 58); Ginola (65); Ferdinand (90)
	Newcastle win 6-3 on aggregate.					
19-Nov	Metz	A	3R1L	1-1	23,000	Beardsley (31 pen)
03-Dec	Metz	H	3R2L	2-0	35,641	Asprilla (80, 82) *6-3 on agg*
04-Mar	Monaco	H	QF1L	0-1	36,215	
18-Mar	Monaco	A	QF2L	0-3	14,400	*Monaco win 4-0 on aggregate.*

FA Charity Shield

Date	Opponents	Vn	Rnd	Res	Atten	Scorers
11-Aug	Man. Utd	W		0-4	73,241	

Sheffield Wednesday

Founded in 1867 by members of the Wednesday Cricket Club and played at Highfield before moving to Myrtle Road. Were first holders of the Sheffield FA Cup. The club played at Sheaf House then Endcliff and became professionals in 1886. In 1887 moved to Olive Grove.

Refused admission to the Football League, the club was founder member, and first champions, of the Football Alliance in 1889. In 1892 most Alliance clubs became founder members of Football League Division Two, but Wednesday were elected to an enlarged top division. The club moved to Hillsborough in 1899. Founder member of the Premier League 1992.

Ground: Hillsborough, Sheffield, S6 1SW
Phone: 0114-221 2121   **News:** 0891 12 11 86
Box Office: 0114-221 2400
Capacity: 36,020   **Pitch:** 115 yds x 77 yds
Colours: Blue/White, Blue, Blue   **Nickname:** The Owls
Radio: BBC Radio Sheffield 88.6 and 104.1FM
Internet: http://www.cyberws.co.uk

Chairman: D.G. Richards   **Vice-Chairman:** K.T. Addy
Secretary: Graham Mackrell FCCA
Manager: David Pleat   **Assistant:** Danny Bergara
Physio: D. Galley

League History: 1892 Elected to Division 1; 1899-1900 Division 2; 1900-20 Division 1; 1920-26 Division 2; 1926-37 Division 1; 1937-50 Division 2; 1950-51 Division 1; 1951-52 Division 2; 1952-55 Division 1; 1955-56 Division 2; 1956-58 Division 1; 1958-59 Division 2; 1959-70 Division 1; 1970-75 Division 2; 1975-80 Division 3; 1980-84 Division 2; 1984-90 Division 1; 1990-91 Division 2; 1991-92 Division 1; 1992- FA Premier League.

Honours: *Football League: Division 1 Champions:* 1902-03, 1903-04, 1928-29, 1929-30; *Runners-up:* 1960-61; *Division 2 Champions:* 1899-1900, 1925-26, 1951-52, 1955-56, 1958-59; *Runners-up:* 1949-50, 1983-84. *FA Cup Winners:* 1895-96, 1906-07, 1934-35; *Runners-up:* 1889-90, 1965-66, 1992-93; *Football League Cup Winners:* 1990-91; *Runners-up:* 1992-93.

European Record: CC (0): –; CWC (0): – ; UEFA (3): 61-62 (QF), 63-64 (2), 92-93 (2).

Managers: Arthur Dickinson 1891-1920; Robert Brown 1920-33; Billy Walker 1933-37; Jimmy McMullan 1937-42; Eric Taylor 1942-58 (continued as GM to 1974); Harry Catterick 1958-61; Vic Buckingham 1961-64; Alan Brown 1964-68; Jack Marshall 1968-69; Danny Williams 1969-71; Derek Dooley 1971-73; Steve Burtenshaw 1974-75; Len Ashurst 1975-77; Jackie Charlton 1977-83; Howard Wilkinson 1983-88; Peter Eustace 1988-89; Ron Atkinson 1989-91; *(FAPL)* Trevor Francis June 1991-May 1995; David Pleat July 1995-

Season 1996-97

Biggest Home Win:	3-1 v Wimbledon
Biggest Home Defeat:	0-2 v Chelsea
Biggest Away Win:	3-0 v Nottingham Forest
Biggest Away Defeat:	1-5 v West Ham United
Biggest Home Att:	38,943 v Liverpool
Smallest Home Att:	16,390 v Nottingham Forest
Average Attendance:	25,709 (11th)
Leading Scorer:	10 – Andy Booth, 6 – Benito Carbone, David Hirst, Mark Pembridge

All-Time Records

Record FAPL Win:	6-2 v Leeds United, 16/12/95
Record FAPL Defeat:	1-7 v Nottingham Forest, 1/4/95
Record FL Win:	9-1 v Birmingham, Division 1, 13/12/30
Record FL Defeat:	0-10 v Aston Villa, Division 1, 5/10/12
Record Cup Win:	12-0 v Halliwell, FA Cup R1, 17/1/1891
Record Fee Received:	£2.7m from Blackburn R. for Paul Warhurst, 9/93
Record Fee Paid:	£3m to Internazionale for Benito Carbone, 10/96
Most FL Apps:	Andy Wilson, 502, 1900-20
Most FAPL Apps:	192 – Peter Atherton, 1992-97
Most FAPL Goals:	48 – Mark Bright, 1992-97
Highest Scorer in FAPL Season:	Bright, 19, 1993-94
Record Attendance (all-time):	72,841 v Man City, FA Cup R5, 17/2/34
Record Attendance (FAPL):	38,943 v Liverpool, 11/5/97
Most FAPL Goals in Season:	76, 1993-94 – 42 games
Most FAPL Points in Season:	64, 1993-94 – 42 games

Player	Tot	St	Sb	Snu	PS	Gls	Y	R	Fa	La	Fg	Lg
ATHERTON	37	37	0	0	1	2	7	0	4	2	0	0
BLINKER	33	15	18	2	5	1	6	0	1	2	0	0
BOOTH	35	32	3	0	7	10	3	0	4	2	3	0
BRIGHT †	1	0	1	0	0	0	0	0	0	0	0	0
BRISCOE	6	5	1	5	1	0	0	0	0	0	0	0
CARBONE	25	24	1	0	11	6	3	0	2	0	0	0
CLARKE	1	0	1	37	0	0	0	1	0	0	0	0
COLLINS	12	8	4	7	3	1	1	0	1	0	0	0
DONALDSON	5	2	3	4	0	2	0	0	0	0	0	0
HIRST	25	20	5	0	11	6	3	1	2	1	0	0
HUMPHREYS	29	14	15	8	11	3	2	0	4	1	2	0
HYDE	19	15	4	0	3	2	4	0	4	1	1	0
LINIGHAN	0	0	0	1	0	0	0	0	0	0	0	0
NEWSOME	10	10	0	1	0	1	1	0	3	1	0	0
NICOL	23	19	4	9	8	0	0	0	3	0	0	0
NOLAN	38	38	0	0	1	1	1	0	4	2	0	0
OAKES	19	7	12	9	5	1	1	0	0	0	0	0
PEMBRIDGE	34	33	1	0	2	6	7	0	4	1	1	0
PRESSMAN	38	38	0	0	1	0	0	0	4	2	0	0
SHERIDAN †	2	0	2	2	0	0	0	0	0	0	0	0
STEFANOVIC	29	27	2	5	3	2	6	0	1	1	0	0
TRUSTFULL	19	9	10	7	8	3	3	0	1	2	0	0
WALKER	36	36	0	0	1	0	1	1	4	1	0	0
WHITTINGHAM	33	29	4	1	10	3	1	0	3	2	1	1
WILLIAMS	1	0	1	0	0	0	0	0	0	1	0	0
OGs						2						

	Div.	P	W	D	L	F	A	Pts	Pos	FAC	FLC
92-93	PL	42	15	14	13	55	51	59	7	F	F
93-94	PL	42	16	16	10	76	54	64	7	4	SF
94-95	PL	42	13	12	17	49	57	51	13	4	4
95-96	PL	38	10	10	18	48	61	40	15	3	4
96-97	PL	38	14	15	9	50	51	57	7	6	2

Early Promise Goes Unfulfilled

With his side having ended the previous campaign with little more than a whimper, Sheffield Wednesday boss David Pleat made several changes to his squad during the summer with Andy Booth, Scott Oakes, Matt Clarke and Wayne Collins moving to Hillsborough. At £2.75m Booth, from Huddersfield, became Wednesday's joint highest purchase. As the season progressed Pleat delved into the transfer market twice more to sign Italian Benito Carbone for £3m and Peterborough's David Billington for £500,000. Pleat's first attempt to sign an Italian during the summer ended in failure when Attilo Lombardo stalled over a £3.5m deal. The Owls recouped £4.5m in a clearout which included free transfers for former England players Chris Waddle and Chris Woods.

The start enjoyed by Wednesday was nothing short of sensational as local teenager Richie Humphreys scored a marvellous goal during a 2-1 win over Aston Villa. By the end of the first week another six points had been taken from county rivals Leeds and, most impressively, at St James's Park from Newcastle. Pleat, joint second manager for the chop according to the bookies at the start of the season, was the proud boss of the Premier League leaders. Wednesday were clearly enjoying topping the table for the first time in 29 years and, with the help of another wonderful goal from Humphreys, defeated Leicester 2-1 to open up a five-point lead from second-placed Chelsea. Humphreys's early season form was a great boost for the club as they awaited the return from an Achilles' injury of England striker David Hirst. Pleat's relatively inexperienced side had a genuine opportunity to cement their position when Chelsea visited Hillsborough for their fifth game of the season but the bubble burst as the Owls went down 2-0 for their only home defeat of the season. Booth put the Yorkshire side ahead in their next league match at Arsenal but they crumbled 4-1 and slipped to fifth.

Indeed, another three-point haul was not forthcoming until mid-November when bottom dogs Notts Forest were beaten – their sole victory in 11 games. After a run of draws, the Owls went on their second four-match-winning run, scoring 11 goals in the process. All of those victories came against sides towards the foot of the table and took Wednesday back into the top five. A disappointing end saw Wednesday swept away to successive 4-1 and 5-1 defeats by sides, Blackburn and West Ham, desperate for the points. Defeat at Leicester and a home draw with Liverpool finally put paid to their UEFA Cup ambitions.

Since reaching the final of both domestic cup competitions in 1993, and the Coca-Cola Cup semi final one year later, Sheffield Wednesday have fared poorly in the knock-out competitions. They were held 1-1 at home by Oxford United in the Coca-Cola Cup and duly went down 1-0 in the 2nd Leg at the Manor Ground. In the FA Cup the Owls were presented with draws which could be perceived either as potential humiliations or as generous paths to the latter stages. Certainly no problem was experienced in thrashing Grimsby Town 7-1 at Hillsborough in the 3rd Round with both Humphreys and Booth scoring twice. Bradford City battled hard to hold the Owls in the 5th Round, only for an 84th-minute own goal to hand Wednesday a quarter final meeting with in-form Wimbledon, and it was the Dons who proved more adept in taking chances as Wednesday bowed out at Hillsborough.

Wednesday's disciplinary record, despite three players being dismissed, was generally good as they had the second lowest number of cautions. ∎

Results 1996-97

FA Carling Premiership

Date	Opponents	Ven	Res	Pos	Atten	Scorers
17-Aug	Aston Villa	H	2-1	–	26,861	Humphreys (56); Whittingham (84)
20-Aug	Leeds Utd	A	2-0	–	31,011	Humphreys (14); Booth (90)
24-Aug	Newcastle Utd	A	2-1	1	36,452	Atherton (14); Whittingham (79)
02-Sep	Leicester C.	H	2-1	1	17,657	Humphreys (25); Booth (51)
07-Sep	Chelsea	H	0-2	1	30,983	
16-Sep	Arsenal	A	1-4	5	33,461	Booth (25)
21-Sep	Derby Co.	H	0-0	5	23,934	
28-Sep	Everton	A	0-2	7	34,160	
12-Oct	Wimbledon	A	2-4	7	10,512	Booth (4); Hyde (72)
19-Oct	Blackburn R.	H	1-1	9	22,191	Booth (3)
26-Oct	Coventry C.	A	0-0	8	17,267	
02-Nov	Southampton	H	1-1	9	20,106	Newsome (14)
18-Nov	N. Forest	H	2-0	9	16,390	Trustfull (63); Carbone (85)
23-Nov	Sunderland	A	1-1	10	20,644	Oakes (64)
30-Nov	West Ham Utd	H	0-0	10	22,231	
07-Dec	Liverpool	A	1-0	9	39,507	Whittingham (21)
18-Dec	Man. Utd	H	1-1	9	37,671	Carbone (57)
21-Dec	Tottenham H.	A	1-1	9	30,996	Nolan (16)
26-Dec	Arsenal	H	0-0	10	23,245	
28-Dec	Chelsea	A	2-2	9	27,467	Pembridge (23); Stefanovic (90)
11-Jan	Everton	H	2-1	8	24,175	Pembridge (22); Hirst (50)
18-Jan	Middlesbrough	A	2-4	8	29,485	Pembridge (29, 80)
29-Jan	Aston Villa	A	1-0	8	26,726	Booth (69)
01-Feb	Coventry C.	H	0-0	8	21,793	
19-Feb	Derby Co.	A	2-2	8	18,060	Collins (9); Hirst (76)
22-Feb	Southampton	A	3-2	8	15,062	Hirst (49, 55); Booth (78)
01-Mar	Middlesbrough	H	3-1	8	28,206	Booth (21); Hyde (42); Pembridge (90 pen)
05-Mar	N. Forest	A	3-0	6	21,485	Carbone (52, 86); Blinker (57)
12-Mar	Sunderland	H	2-1	5	20,294	Hirst (42); Stefanovic (63)
15-Mar	Man. Utd	A	0-2	5	55,267	
22-Mar	Leeds Utd	H	2-2	7	30,373	Hirst (20); Booth (51)
09-Apr	Tottenham H.	H	2-1	6	22,667	Atherton (18); Booth (70)
13-Apr	Newcastle Utd	H	1-1	6	33,798	Pembridge (57)
19-Apr	Wimbledon	H	3-1	6	26,957	Donaldson (42); Trustfull (78, 83)

22-Apr	Blackburn R.	A	1-4	6	20,845	Carbone (84 pen)
03-May	West Ham Utd	A	1-5	7	24,960	Carbone (82)
07-May	Leicester C.	A	0-1	7	20,793	
11-May	Liverpool	H	1-1	7	38,943	Donaldson (25)

FA Challenge Cup

Date	Opponents	Vn	Rnd	Res	Atten	Scorers
04-Jan	Grimsby Tn	H	3R	7-1	20,590	Humphreys (15, 48); Booth (34, 69); OG (45, Fickling); Hyde (54); Pembridge (83)
25-Jan	Carlisle Utd	A	4R	2-0	16,104	Whittingham (12); Booth (46)
16-Feb	Bradford C.	A	5R	1-0	17,830	OG (84, Mohan)
9-Mar	Wimbledon	H	6R	0-2	25,032	

Coca-Cola League Cup

Date	Opponents	Vn	Rnd	Res	Atten	Scorers
18-Sep	Oxford Utd	H	2R1L	1-1	7,499	Whittingham (13)
24-Sep	Oxford Utd	A	2R2L	0-1	6,863	

Oxford Utd win 2-1 on aggregate.

Wednesday – Premiership Fact File

- Wednesday used more substitutes than any other team last season – 92 in all. Liverpool used just 44!

- Kevin Pressman and Ian Nolan played in all 38 Premiership games – both were substituted once during the season though.

- Matt Clarke made his debut in goal for Wednesday when he replaced the injured Kevin Pressman after 73 minutes. His debut lasted just nine minutes though when he was sent off by David Elleray for handling outside his area. Clarke had been on the bench for the previous 37 matches!

- Wednesday had their best start to a season ever when they won their first four games to go five points clear at the top. Their 0-2 defeat by Chelsea was the start of eight games without a win.

Southampton

Formed 1885 by members of the St Mary's Young Men's Association, St Mary's FC. The church link was dropped, though the name retained, in 1893. In 1895 applied for a Southern League place, but was refused only to be invited to fill a subsequent vacancy. 'St Mary's' was dropped after two seasons. Moved from the County Cricket Ground to the Dell in 1898.

Six times Southern League champions, Southampton were founder members of Football League Division Three in 1920 (this becoming Division Three (South) the following season), of Division Three at the end of regionalisation in 1958, and of the Premier League, 1992.

Ground: The Dell, Milton Road, Southampton, SO9 4XX
Phone: 01703-220505   **News:** 0891 12 15 93
Box Office: 01703-228575
Capacity: 15,288   **Pitch:** 110 yds x 72 yds
Colours: Red/White, Black, Black   **Nickname:** The Saints
Radio: Radio Solent 96.1FM
Internet: http://www.soton.ac.uk

President: J. Corbett   **Chairman:** F.G. Askham FCA
Vice-Chairman: K. St. J. Wiseman   **Secretary:** Brian Truscott
Manager: David Jones   **Assistant:** John Sainty
Physio: Don Taylor

League History: 1920 Original Member of Division 3; 1921 Division 3 (S); 1922-53 Division 2; 1953-58 Division 3 (S); 1958-60 Division 3; 1960-66 Division 2; 1966-74 Division 1; 1974-78 Division 2; 1978-92 Division 1; 1992- FA Premier League.

Honours: *Football League: Division 1 Runners-up:* 1983-84; *Division 2 Runners-up:* 1965-66, 1977-78; *Division 3 (S) Champions:* 1921-22; *Runners-up:* 1920-21; *Division 3 Champions:* 1959-60. *FA Cup Winners:* 1975-76; *Runners-up:* 1900, 1902. *Football League Cup Runners-up:* 1978-79. *Zenith Data Systems Cup Runners-up:* 1991-92.

European Record: CWC (1): 76-77 (QF). UEFA (5): 69-70 (3), 71-72 (1), 81-82 (2), 82-83 (1), 84-85 (1).

Managers: Cecil Knight 1894-95; Charles Robson 1895-97; E. Arnfield 1897-1911 (continued as secretary); George Swift 1911-12; E. Arnfield 1912-19; Jimmy McIntyre 1919-24; Arthur Chadwick 1925-31; George Kay 1931-

36; George Cross 1936-37; Tom Parker 1937-43; (J.R. Sarjantson stepped down from the board to act as secretary-manager 1943-47 with the next two listed being team managers during this period); Arthur Dominy 1943-46; Bill Dodgin Snr 1946-49; Sid Cann 1949-51; George Roughton 1952-55; Ted Bates 1955-73; Lawrie McMenemy 1973-85; Chris Nicholl 1985-91; *(FAPL)* Ian Branfoot 1991-94; Alan Ball Jan 1994-July 1995; Dave Merrington July 1995-June 1996; Graeme Souness July 1996-May 1997; David Jones July 1997–.

Season 1996-97

Biggest Home Win:	6-3 v Manchester United
Biggest Home Defeat:	0-2 v Arsenal and Leeds United
Biggest Away Win:	3-1 v Nottingham Forest
Biggest Away Defeat:	1-7 v Everton
Biggest Home Att:	15,253 v Manchester United
Smallest Home Att:	14,418 v Wimbledon
Average Attendance:	15,105 (20th)
Leading Scorer:	13 – Le Tissier, 10 – Egil Ostenstad

All-Time Records

Record FAPL Win:	6-3 v Manchester United, 20/10/96
Record FAPL Defeat:	1-7 v Everton, 16/11/96
Record FL Win:	9-3 v Wolverhampton Wds, Division 2, 18/9/65
Record FL Defeat:	0-8 v Tottenham Hotspur, Division 2, 28/3/36; Everton, Division 1, 20/11/71
Record Cup Win:	7-1 v Ipswich Town, FA Cup R3, 7/1/61
Record Fee Received:	£3.3m from Blackburn R. for Alan Shearer, 7/92
Record Fee Paid:	£1.3m to Galatasary for Ulrich van Gobbel, 10/96
Most FL Apps:	Terry Payne, 713, 1956-74
Most FAPL Apps:	184 – Matt Le Tissier, 1992-97
Most FAPL Goals:	80 – Matt Le Tissier, 1992-97

Highest Scorer in FAPL Season: 25, Matthew Le Tissier, 1993-94
Record Attendance (all-time): 31,044 v Man United, Division 1, 8/10/69
Record Attendance (FAPL): 19,654 v Tottenham Hotspur, 15/8/92
Most FAPL Goals in Season: 61, 1994-95 – 42 games
Most FAPL Points in Season: 54, 1994-95 – 42 games

Player	Tot	St	Sb	Snu	PS	Gls	Y	R	Fa	La	Fg	Lg
BASHAM	6	1	5	14	0	0	0	0	0	0	0	0
BEASANT	14	13	1	20	0	0	0	0	1	4	0	0
BENALI	18	14	4	4	2	0	3	1	1	0	0	0
BERKOVIC †	28	26	2	2	11	4	4	0	1	6	0	2
CHARLTON	26	24	2	1	8	0	1	0	1	6	0	1
DIA	1	0	1	0	1	0	0	0	0	0	0	0
DODD	23	23	0	0	3	1	2	1	0	3	0	0
DRYDEN	29	28	1	4	3	1	5	0	0	6	0	3
EVANS	12	8	4	0	0	4	1	0	0	0	0	0
FLAHAVAN	0	0	0	2	0	0	0	0	0	0	0	0
HEANEY	8	4	4	0	5	1	1	0	0	0	0	0
HUGHES	6	1	5	1	0	0	1	0	0	2	0	0
Le TISSIER	31	25	6	0	8	13	5	0	1	6	0	3
LUNDEKVAM	29	28	1	1	3	0	6	0	1	8	0	0
MADDISON	17	14	3	16	5	1	4	0	1	4	0	0
MAGILTON	37	31	6	1	7	4	4	0	1	8	0	2
MONKOU	13	8	5	1	0	0	6	0	0	6	0	0
MOSS	3	3	0	14	0	0	0	0	0	2	0	0
NEILSON	29	24	5	3	2	0	4	0	0	5	0	0
OAKLEY	28	23	5	0	11	3	0	0	1	7	0	0
OSTENSTADT	30	29	1	0	5	10	3	0	1	6	1	3
POTTER	8	2	6	6	1	0	0	0	0	2	0	0
ROBINSON	7	3	4	1	1	0	0	0	1	0	0	0
SHIPPERLEY	10	9	1	0	3	1	0	0	0	2	0	0
SLATER	30	22	8	1	3	2	5	0	1	7	0	0
TAYLOR	18	18	0	0	0	0	1	0	0	0	0	0
VAN GOBBEL	25	24	1	1	3	1	10	1	1	6	0	1
VENISON	2	2	0	0	0	0	1	1	0	0	0	0
WARREN	1	0	1	1	0	0	0	0	0	0	0	0
WATKINSON	2	0	2	1	0	0	0	0	1	1	0	0
WATSON	15	7	8	3	6	2	0	0	0	6	0	3
WOODS	4	4	0	0	1	0	0	0	0	1	0	0
OGs						2						

Salvation Assured Again

Since the inception of the Premier League, Southampton have only once finished inside the top ten and, despite the arrival of Graeme Souness as manager, few predicted that the trend was about to change. Souness brought in several low-key signings during the summer but within a month of the season starting he'd invested £1.3m in Galatasary defender Ulrich van Gobbel, £1m in Eyal Berkovic from Haifa Maccabi, a further £2m on Norwegians Egil Ostenstad and Claus Lundekvam. On the credit side, around £3m was collected from the sale of Richard Hall and Tommy Widdrington, while veterans Bruce Grobbelaar and Mark Walters also left the Dell.

A disappointing goalless draw against Chelsea opened the season but there was little other calmness on the south coast through to the end of September as the Saints failed to win any of their first seven league games. Following a 3-1 defeat at Wimbledon on the 23rd, they sat level on points with Blackburn at the foot of the table. Souness commented that he was not too concerned about the Saints' form, so perhaps he was not overly surprised when Middlesbrough were whipped 4-0. Matt Le Tissier, back at his best, scored twice against Middlesbrough and then proceeded to score in each of the next four Premier League games. The Saints moved out of the bottom three with their first away point, a 1-1 draw at Coventry, and the momentum gathered pace with a 3-0 victory over Sunderland and a staggering 6-3 drubbing of Manchester United in front of their largest gate of the season. Three of the goals came late in the day with Le Tissier playing second fiddle to Ostenstad who scored a hat trick, and man of the match Berkovic who notched a brace. A Southampton side showing six changes from the one which started the season continued the good run with a point at Sheffield Wednesday as the Saints wallowed in a relatively healthy 14th position.

A 7-1 caning at Everton had serious repercussions as the Saints went on to lose five successive league games and were back deep in relegation trouble. In the first three months of 1997 just two games out of 11, against north-east sides Middlesbrough and Newcastle, ended in victory. April kicked off with a vital win at the now bottom side Forest. It was the perfect platform for a series of games against lowly opposition and the Saints took full advantage to pick up another 11 points from five games and to retain their Premier League status.

Southampton have never managed to build on their FA Cup triumph of 1976 and years on they made an inglorious exit at Reading on a frozen pitch which was not well received by Souness. Eight games were played in the Coca-Cola Cup despite progressing through just three rounds. Peterborough United were defeated home and away in the 2nd Round but three late goals were needed in a 3rd Round replay at Lincoln City to avoid a premature departure. Life was little easier in the 4th Round against Oxford United who held out for a draw at the Manor Ground and only went down 3-2 at the Dell. Southampton drew more lower level opposition in the quarter final with an away tie at Stockport County. Ostenstad's second goal of the game five minutes from time clinched a replay but the Saints became another statistic at the Dell as the Second Division side overturned an early deficit.

A turbulent season for the club had another twist in the tail with Souness and Lawrie McMenemy quitting the club, The successful Stockport manager, Dave Jones, was appointed manager at the end of June. His first move was to get Le Tissier to sign a new four-year contract. ■

Results 1996-97

Date	Opponents	Ven	Res	Pos	Atten	Scorers
18-Aug	Chelsea	H	0-0	–	15,186	
21-Aug	Leicester C.	A	1-2	–	17,562	Le Tissier (68)
24-Aug	West Ham Utd	A	1-2	17	21,227	Heaney (17)
04-Sep	N. Forest	H	2-2		14,450	Dryden (53); Le Tissier (89)
07-Sep	Liverpool	A	1-2	18	39,189	Magilton (57)
14-Sep	Tottenham H.	H	0-1	19	15,251	
23-Sep	Wimbledon	A	1-3	19	8,572	Oakley (76)
28-Sep	Middlesbrough	H	4-0	18	15,230	Oakley (10); Le Tissier (28, 47); Watson (82)
13-Oct	Coventry C.	A	1-1	17	15,485	Le Tissier (17)
19-Oct	Sunderland	H	3-0	17	15,225	Dodd (38); Le Tissier (53pen); Shipperley (89)
26-Oct	Man. Utd	H	6-3	14	15,253	Berkovic (6, 83); Le Tissier (34); Ostenstad (44, 85, 89)
02-Nov	Sheffield W.	A	1-1	14	20,106	Le Tissier (55 pen)
16-Nov	Everton	A	1-7	14	35,669	Ostenstad (39)
23-Nov	Leeds Utd	H	0-2	17	15,241	
30-Nov	Blackburn R.	A	1-2	17	23,018	Ostenstad (62)
04-Dec	Arsenal	A	1-3	17	38,033	Berkovic (81)
07-Dec	Aston Villa	H	0-1	18	15,232	
21-Dec	Derby Co.	H	3-1	16	14,901	Watson (9); Oakley (12); Magilton (89 pen)
26-Dec	Tottenham H.	A	1-3	19	30,549	Le Tissier (39)
29-Dec	Liverpool	H	0-1	19	15,222	
11-Jan	Middlesbrough	A	1-0	19	29,509	Magilton (58)
18-Jan	Newcastle U.	H	2-2	19	15,251	Maddison (88); Le Tissier (90)
01-Feb	Man. Utd	A	1-2	19	55,269	Ostenstad (10)
22-Feb	Sheffield W.	H	2-3	19	15,062	Ostenstad (28); Le Tissier (32 pen)
26-Feb	Wimbledon	H	0-0	19	14,418	
01-Mar	Newcastle Utd	A	1-0	19	36,446	Le Tissier (55)
05-Mar	Everton	H	2-2	19	15,134	Slater (59); OG (62, Short)
12-Mar	Leeds Utd	A	0-0	19	25,913	
15-Mar	Arsenal	H	0-2	19	15,144	
19-Mar	Chelsea	A	0-1	20	28,079	
22-Mar	Leicester C.	H	2-2	20	15,044	Ostenstad (31); van Gobbel (50)

05-Apr	N. Forest	A	3-1	20	25,134	Magilton (7); Evans (85, 89)
09-Apr	Derby Co.	A	1-1	19	17,839	OG (90, Powell, D.)
12-Apr	West Ham Utd	H	2-0	16	15,244	Evans (12); Berkovic (36)
19-Apr	Coventry C.	H	2-2	17	15,251	Evans (27); Ostenstad (47)
22-Apr	Sunderland	A	1-0	15	21,521	Ostenstad (22)
03-May	Blackburn R.	H	2-0	15	15,247	Slater (22); Le Tissier (73)
11 May	Aston Villa	A	0-1	16	39,339	

FA Challenge Cup

| Date | Opponents | Vn | Rnd | Res | Atten | Scorers |
| 04-Jan | Reading | A | 3R | 1-3 | 11,537 | Ostenstad (49) |

Coca-Cola League Cup

Date	Opponents	Vn	Rnd	Res	Atten	Scorers
18-Sep	Peterboro' Utd	H	2R1L	2-0	12,467	Le Tissier (19); Watson (81)
25-Sep	Peterboro' Utd	A	2R2L	4-1	8,220	Watson (33); Charlton (35); Magilton (55); Dryden (78)
	Southampton win 6-1 on aggregate.					
23-Oct	Lincoln City	H	3R	2-2	14,516	Le Tissier (46); van Gobbel (54)
12-Nov	Lincoln City	A	3RR	3-1	10,523	Magilton (75 pen); Watson (85); Berkovic (90)
26-Nov	Oxford United	A	4R	1-1	9,473	Dryden (26)
18-Dec	Oxford United	H	4RR	3-2	10,737	Berkovic (21); Dryden (52); Ostenstad (58)
22-Jan	Stockport Co.	A	QF	2-2	9,840	Ostenstad (16, 85)
29-Jan	Stockport Co.	H	QFR	1-2	13,428	Le Tissier (8)

5-Year Record

	Div.	P	W	D	L	F	A	Pts	Pos	FAC	FLC
92-93	PL	42	13	11	18	54	61	50	18	3	3
93-94	PL	42	12	7	23	49	66	43	18	3	2
94-95	PL	42	12	18	12	61	63	54	10	5	3
95-96	PL	38	9	11	18	34	52	38	17	QF	4
96-97	PL	38	10	11	17	50	56	41	16	3	QF

Tottenham Hotspur

Formed in 1882 by members of the schoolboys' Hotspur CC as Hotspur FC and had early church connections. Added 'Tottenham' in 1884 to distinguish club from London Hotspur FC. Turned professional in 1895 and elected to the Southern League in 1896 having been rebuffed by the Football League.

Played at two grounds (Tottenham Marshes and Northumberland Park) before moving to the site which became known as White Hart Lane in 1899. Joined the Football League Second Division 1908. Having failed to gain a place in the re-election voting, it secured a vacancy caused by a late resignation. Premier League founder members 1992.

Ground:	748 High Road, Tottenham, London, N17 0AP	
Phone:	0181-365 5000	**News:** 0891 33 55 55
Box Office:	0181-365 5050	**Tickets:** 0891 33 55 66
Capacity:	30,246	**Pitch:** 110 yds x 73 yds
Colours:	White, Navy Blue, White	**Nickname:** Spurs
Radio:	1548AM Capital Gold	
Internet:	http://www.spurs.co.uk	

Chairman:	Alan Sugar	**President:** W.E. Nicholson OBE
CEO:	Claude Littner	**Secretary:** Peter Barnes
Manager:	Gerry Francis	**Physio:** Tony Lenaghan

League History: 1908 Elected to Division 2; 1909-15 Division 1; 1919-20 Division 2; 1920-28 Division 1; 1928-33 Division 2; 1933-35 Division 1; 1935-50 Division 2; 1950-77 Division 1; 1977-78 Division 2; 1978-92 Division 1; 1992- FA Premier League.

Honours: *Football League: Division 1 Champions: 1950-51, 1960-61; Runners-up: 1921-22, 1951-52, 1956-57, 1962-63; Division 2 Champions: 1919-20, 1949-50; Runners-up: 1908-09, 1932-33; FA Cup Winners: 1900-01, 1920-21, 1960-61, 1961-62, 1966-67, 1980-81, 1981-82, 1990-91; Runners-up: 1986-87; Football League Cup Winners: 1970-71, 1972-73; Runners-up: 1981-82; Cup-Winners' Cup Winners: 1962-63; Runners-up: 1981-82; UEFA Cup Winners: 1971-72, 1983-84; Runners-up: 1973-74.*

European Record: CC (1): 61-62 (SF); CWC (6): 62-63 (W), 63-64 (2), 67-68 (2), 81-82 (SF), 82-83 (2), 91-92 (QF). UEFA (5): 71-72 (W), 72-73 (SF), 73-74 (F), 83-84 (W), 84-85 (QF).

Managers: Frank Brettell 1898-99; John Cameron 1899-1907; Fred Kirkham 1907-08; Peter McWilliam 1912-27; Billy Minter 1927-29; Percy Smith 1930-35; Jack Tresadern 1935-38; Peter McWilliam 1938-42; Arthur Turner 1942-46; Joe Hulme 1946-49; Arthur Rowe 1949-55; Jimmy Anderson 1955-58; Bill Nicholson 1958-74; Terry Neill 1974-76; Keith Burkinshaw 1976-84; Peter Shreeves 1984-86; David Pleat 1986-87; Terry Venables 1987-91; Peter Shreeves 1991-92; *(FAPL)* Doug Livermore 1992-June 1993; Ossie Ardiles June 1993-Nov 1994; Gerry Francis Nov 1994-.

Season 1996-97

Biggest Home Win:	3-1 v Southampton
Biggest Home Defeat:	0-2 v Liverpool
Biggest Away Win:	4-0 v Sunderland
Biggest Away Defeat:	1-7 v Newcastle United
Biggest Home Att:	33,040 v Leeds United
Smallest Home Att:	22,943 v Blackburn Rovers
Average Attendance:	31,067 (8th)
Leading Scorer:	7 – Teddy Sheringham

All-Time Records

Record FAPL Win:	5-0 v Oldham Athletic, 18/9/93
Record FAPL Defeat:	1-7 v Newcastle United, 28/12/96
Record FL Win:	9-0 v Bristol Rovers, Division 2, 22/10/77
Record FL Defeat:	0-7 v Liverpool, Division 1, 2/9/1978
Record Cup Win:	13-2 v Crewe Alex, FA Cup, R4 replay, 3/2/60
Record Fee Received:	£5.5m from Lazio for Paul Gascoigne, 5/92
Record Fee Paid:	£4.5m to Crystal Palace for Chris Armstrong, 6/95
Most FL Apps:	Steve Perryman, 655, 1969-86
Most FAPL Apps:	166 – Teddy Sheringham, 1992-97
Most FAPL Goals:	76 – Teddy Sheringham, 1992-97

Highest Scorer in FAPL Season: Jurgen Klinsmann, 24, 1994-95
Record Attendance (all-time): 75,038 v Sunderland, FA Cup R6, 5/3/38
Record Attendance (FAPL): 33,709 v Arsenal, 12/12/92
Most FAPL Goals in Season: 66, 1994-95 – 42 games
Most FAPL Points in Season: 62, 1994-95 – 42 games

Player	Tot	St	Sb	Snu	PS	Gls	Y	R	Fa	La	Fg	Lg
ALLEN	12	9	3	12	3	2	4	0	1	3	0	2
ANDERTON	16	14	2	0	7	3	4	0	0	3	0	2
ARBER	0	0	0	1	0	0	0	0	0	0	0	0
ARMSTRONG	12	12	0	0	2	5	2	0	0	3	0	1
AUSTIN	15	13	2	8	2	0	3	0	1	0	0	0
BAARDSEN	2	1	1	36	0	0	0	0	0	0	0	0
BRADY	0	0	0	3	0	0	0	0	0	0	0	0
BROWN	0	0	0	1	0	0	0	0	0	0	0	0
CALDERWOOD	34	33	1	1	0	0	6	0	1	4	0	0
CAMPBELL	38	38	0	0	2	0	1	0	1	4	0	1
CARR	26	24	2	7	3	0	1	0	1	3	0	0
CLAPHAM	1	0	1	1	0	0	0	0	0	0	0	0
DOZZELL	17	10	7	7	2	2	2	0	0	1	0	0
EDINBURGH	24	21	3	6	2	0	11	0	1	2	0	0
FENN	4	0	4	3	0	0	0	0	1	0	0	0
FOX	25	19	6	3	6	1	1	0	0	4	0	0
HILL	0	0	0	3	0	0	0	0	0	0	0	0
HOWELLS	32	32	0	0	6	2	7	0	1	4	0	0
IVERSEN	16	16	0	0	1	6	1	0	0	0	0	0
KERSLAKE	0	0	0	3	0	0	0	0	0	0	0	0
MABBUTT	1	1	0	0	1	0	0	0	0	0	0	0
McMAHON	0	0	0	1	0	0	0	0	0	0	0	0
McVEIGH	3	2	1	2	2	1	0	0	0	0	0	0
NETHERCOTT	9	2	7	19	2	0	2	0	0	0	0	0
NIELSEN	29	28	1	1	8	6	6	0	1	3	0	0
ROSENTHAL	20	4	16	6	0	1	0	0	0	0	0	0
SCALES	12	10	2	0	1	0	0	0	0	0	0	0
SHERINGHAM †	29	29	0	0	0	7	6	0	0	3	0	1
SINTON	33	32	1	0	9	6	5	0	1	2	0	0
VEGA	8	8	0	0	2	1	2	0	0	0	0	0
WALKER	37	37	0	0	1	0	0	0	1	4	0	0
WILSON	26	23	3	3	1	1	0	0	0	4	0	0

A Season of Anonymity

With Arsenal once again leading the south's challenge for the championship and Chelsea taking the FA Cup, this was a season in which Tottenham supporters suffered as Gerry Francis's side spent much of the season in the middle of the Premiership table and made little impression in the cup competitions. After a low-key season the previous year, Francis was subdued in the transfer market during the summer as he released several fringe players and brought in just Allan Nielsen from Brondby for £1.65m. Francis himself had operated without a contract since joining the club in November 1994 but finally agreed to sign a two-year deal.

Despite the impression that Tottenham would once again not be threatening Manchester United's supremacy, the club made a decent start with the formidable partnership of Teddy Sheringham and Chris Armstrong quickly amongst the goals. Armstrong scored both in an opening-day win at Blackburn and only a late Derby equaliser denied Sheringham giving Spurs a winning start at White Hart Lane. The win at Blackburn was achieved at some cost, with Gary Mabbutt adding a broken leg to the numerous injuries to have blighted his career. With Mabbutt out of the side, a lot of responsibility fell on the shoulders of Sol Campbell, who rose to the challenge to become a prominent member of the England squad.

Tottenham's next home match, with Everton, merely confirmed though that their renowned problems with winning at home were back to haunt them. Newcastle and Leicester both took maximum points from their visits to the Lane. As with the previous season this was a campaign in which many of Francis's plans were ruined by injury, with Sheringham, Armstrong and long-term absentee Darren Anderton spending much of their time on the sidelines. Sheringham, who put in a transfer request at the end of the season, was still Tottenham's top scorer but just seven league goals tells its own story. Spurs' best spell came during the early part of winter when wins over Aston Villa, Middlesbrough, West Ham and Sunderland came either side of a defeat at Chelsea. But two late goals at Arsenal sent them spinning to a 3-1 reversal and a fall from a season's high of seventh place. Rock bottom was reached on 28 December at St James's Park as the Toon Army celebrated a staggering 7-1 slaughter. Spurs' next outing was equally daunting with the visit of Manchester United to London and although Spurs went down 2-1, the performance of young Rory Allen brightened the locals' outlook.

Francis answered supporters' criticism of a lack of ambition by gradually drafting in new signings. In fact, he spent almost £10m in two months on bringing Steffen Iversen, John Scales and Ramon Vega to White Hart Lane. Scales was troubled by injury and Vega was sent off in only his second game. Iversen, at Sunderland in March, scored Spurs' first league hat trick for over two years but the season ended on a low note with one victory from six games.

Tottenham Hotspur's reputation as a cup-fighting unit has taken a slight knock over the five seasons since the FA Cup was last won and when a weakened side took to Old Trafford in the 3rd Round of this season's competition, it was of little surprise when Spurs lost 2-0. In the 3rd Round of the Coca-Cola Cup, Spurs reversed Sunderland's early strike to make the 4th Round at Bolton thanks to Campbell's last-minute winner – his only goal of the season. On their way to relegation the previous season, Bolton's first away point came at Tottenham. This time Spurs suffered a complete humiliation as Wanderers ran riot 6-1. ∎

211

Results 1996-97

FA Carling Premiership

Date	Opponents	Ven	Res	Pos	Atten	Scorers
17-Aug	Blackburn R.	A	2-0	–	26,960	Armstrong (33, 68)
21-Aug	Derby Co.	H	1-1	–	28,219	Sheringham (33)
24-Aug	Everton	H	0-0	8	29,696	
04-Sep	Wimbledon	A	0-1	12	17,506	
07-Sep	Newcastle Utd	H	1-2	13	32,535	Allen (28)
14-Sep	Southampton	A	1-0	11	15,251	Armstrong (65 pen)
22-Sep	Leicester C.	H	1-2	12	24,159	Wilson (64 pen)
29-Sep	Man. Utd	A	0-2	14	54,943	
12-Oct	Aston Villa	H	1-0	11	32,847	Nielsen (60)
19-Oct	Middlesbrough	A	3-0	8	30,215	Sheringham (21, 89); Fox (23)
26-Oct	Chelsea	A	1-3	9	28,373	Armstrong (41)
02-Nov	West Ham Utd	H	1-0	8	32,999	Armstrong (67)
16-Nov	Sunderland	H	2-0	7	31,867	Sinton (13); Sheringham (82)
24-Nov	Arsenal	A	1-3	9	38,264	Sinton (67)
02-Dec	Liverpool	H	0-2	11	32,899	
07-Dec	Coventry C.	A	2-1	10	19,675	Sheringham (26); Sinton (75)
14-Dec	Leeds Utd	A	0-0	9	33,783	
21-Dec	Sheffield W.	H	1-1	10	30,996	Nielsen (29)
26-Dec	Southampton	H	3-1	8	30,549	Iversen (1, 30); Nielsen (63)
28-Dec	Newcastle Utd	A	1-7	10	36,308	Nielsen (88)
12-Jan	Man. Utd	H	1-2	10	33,028	Allen (43)
19-Jan	N. Forest	A	1-2	10	27,303	Sinton (1)
29-Jan	Blackburn R.	H	2-1	9	22,943	Iversen (41); Sinton (83)
01-Feb	Chelsea	H	1-2	10	33,027	Howells (82)
15-Feb	Arsenal	H	0-0	9	33,039	
24-Feb	West Ham Utd	A	3-4	11	23,998	Sheringham (6); Anderton (28); Howells (53)
01-Mar	N. Forest	H	0-1	13	32,805	
04-Mar	Sunderland	A	4-0	10	20,785	Iversen (2, 9, 64); Nielsen (26)
15-Mar	Leeds Utd	H	1-0	10	33,040	Anderton (26)
19-Mar	Leicester C.	A	1-1	10	20,593	Sheringham (90)
22-Mar	Derby Co.	A	2-4	10	18,083	Rosenthal (29); Dozzell (50)
05-Apr	Wimbledon	H	1-0	9	32,654	Dozzell (81)
09-Apr	Sheffield W.	A	1-2	9	22,667	Nielsen (43)
12-Apr	Everton	A	0-1	9	36,380	
19-Apr	Aston Villa	H	1-1	9	39,339	Vega (54)
24-Apr	Middlesbrough	H	1-0	9	29,947	Sinton (71)
03-May	Liverpool	A	1-2	9	40,003	Anderton (5)
11-May	Coventry C.	H	1-2	10	33,029	McVeigh (44)

FA Challenge Cup

Date	Opponents	Vn	Rnd	Res	Atten	Scorers
05-Jan	Man. Utd	A	3R	0-2	52,495	

Coca-Cola League Cup

Date	Opponents	Vn	Rnd	Res	Atten	Scorers
17-Sep	Preston NE	A	2R1L	1-1	16,258	Anderton (2)
25-Sep	Preston NE	H	2R2L	3-0	20,080	Anderton (30); Allen (62, 76)
	Tottenham Hotspur win 4-1 on aggregate.					
23-Oct	Sunderland	H	3R	2-1	24,867	Armstrong (71); Campbell (89)
27-Nov	Bolton Wdrs	A	4R	1-6	18,621	Sheringham (20)

Spurs – Premiership Fact File

- Spurs' 1-0 win over Aston Villa on 12th October was their first home win for six months.

- Sol Campbell was the only Spurs player to feature in all 38 of their Premiership games.

- Spurs' seven drawn games was the lowest tally by a Premiership side. Their 18 defeats equalled the number suffered by relegated Sunderland.

5-Year Record

	Div.	P	W	D	L	F	A	Pts	Pos	FAC	FLC
92-93	PL	42	16	11	15	60	66	59	8	SF	4
93-94	PL	42	11	12	19	54	59	45	15	4	5
94-95	PL	42	16	14	12	66	58	62	7	SF	3
95-96	PL	38	16	13	9	50	38	61	8	5	3
96-97	PL	38	13	7	18	44	51	46	10	3	4

West Ham United

Thames Ironworks founded 1895, to give recreation for the shipyard workers. Several different grounds were used as the club entered the London League (1896) and won the championship (1898). In 1899, having become professional, won the Southern League Second Division (London) and moved into Division One.

On becoming a limited liability company the name was changed to West Ham United. Moved from the Memorial Ground to a pitch in the Upton Park area, known originally as 'The Castle', in 1904. Elected to an expanded Football League Division Two for the 1919-20 season and never subsequently out of the top two divisions.

Ground: Boleyn Ground, Green Street, Upton Park, London E13 9AZ
Phone: 0181-548 2748   **News:** 0891 12 11 65
Box Office: 0181-548 2700
Capacity: 24,500   **Pitch:** 112 yds x 72 yds
Colours: Claret, White, White   **Nickname:** The Hammers
Radio: 1548AM Capital Gold
Internet: http://westhamunited.co.uk

Chairman: Terence Brown   **Vice-Chairman:** Martin Cearns
MD: Peter Storrie
Manager: Harry Redknapp   **Assistant:** Frank Lampard
First Team Coaches: Paul Hilton, Tony Carr
Physio: John Green

League History: 1919 Elected to Division 2; 1923-32 Division 1; 1932-58 Division 2; 1958-78 Division 1; 1978-81 Division 2; 1981-89 Division 1; 1989-91 Division 2; 1991-1993 Division 1; 1993- FA Premier League.

Honours: *Football League: Division 1 Runners-up:* 1992-93; *Division 2 Champions:* 1957-58, 1980-81; *Runners-up:* 1922-23, 1990-91. *FA Cup Winners:* 1964, 1975, 1980; *Runners-up:* 1922-23. *Football League Cup Runners-up:* 1966, 1981. *Cup-Winners' Cup Winners:* 1964-65; *Runners-up:* 1975-76.

European Record: CC (0): –; CWC (4): 64-65 (W), 65-66 (SF), 75-76 (F), 80-81 (QF); UEFA (0): –.

Managers: Syd King 1902-32; Charlie Paynter 1932-50; Ted Fenton 1950-61; Ron Greenwood 1961-74 (continued as GM to 1977); John Lyall 1974-

89; Lou Macari 1989-90; *(FAPL)* Billy Bonds Feb 1990-Aug 1994; Harry Redknapp Aug 1994-

Season 1996-97

Biggest Home Win:	5-1 v Sheffield Wednesday
Biggest Home Defeat:	0-2 v Aston Villa, Wimbledon and Leeds United
Biggest Away Win:	3-1 v Coventry City
Biggest Away Defeat:	1-4 v Middlesbrough
Biggest Home Att:	25,064 v Liverpool
Smallest Home Att:	19,105 v Aston Villa
Average Attendance:	23,217 (14th)
Leading Scorer:	8 – Paul Kitson, 6 – Julian Dicks

All-Time Records

Record FAPL Win: 5-1 v Sheffield Wednesday, 3/5/97

Record FAPL Defeat: 0-5 v Sheffield Wednesday, 18/12/93

Record FL Win: 8-0 v Rotherham United, Division 2, 8/3/58 and Sunderland, Division 1, 19/10/68

Record FL Defeat: 2-8 v Blackburn Rovers, Division 1, 26/12/63

Record Cup Win: 10-0 v Bury, League Cup, R2 2nd leg, 25/10/83

Record Fee Received: £4.5m from Everton for Slaven Bilic, 5/97

Record Fee Paid: £3.2m>£5m to Arsenal for John Hartson, 3/97

Most FL Apps: Billy Bonds, 663, 1967-88

Most FAPL Apps: 156 – Ludek Miklosko, 1992-97

Most FAPL Goals: 51 – Tony Cottee, 1992-97

Highest Scorer in FAPL Season: 13 – Trevor Morley, 1993-94 and Tony Cottee 1994-95

Record Attendance (all-time): 42,322 v Tottenham H., Div 1, 17/10/70

Record Attendance (FAPL): 28,832 v Manchester United, 26/2/94

Most FAPL Goals in Season: 47, 1993-94 – 42 games

Most FAPL Points in Season: 52, 1993-94 – 42 games

Summary 1996-97

Player	Tot	St	Sb	Snu	PS	Gls	Y	R	Fa	La	Fg	Lg
BILIC †	35	35	0	0	3	2	10	0	1	5	0	1
BISHOP	29	26	3	2	9	1	2	0	2	5	0	0
BOWEN †	17	15	2	5	5	1	2	0	0	3	0	0
BOYLIN	1	0	1	0	0	0	0	0	0	0	0	0
BREACKER	26	22	4	1	5	0	2	0	2	3	0	0
COTTEE †	3	2	1	0	2	0	1	0	0	2	0	1
DICKS	31	31	0	0	0	6	6	0	2	5	0	2
DOWIE	23	18	5	6	0	0	1	0	0	5	0	2
DUMITRESCU †	7	3	4	5	2	0	0	0	0	3	0	0
FERDINAND	15	11	4	2	3	2	2	0	1	1	0	0
FUTRE †	9	4	5	0	2	0	0	0	0	0	0	0
HALL	7	7	0	0	0	0	1	0	0	0	0	0
HARTSON	11	11	0	0	0	5	3	0	0	0	0	0
HODGES	0	0	0	1	0	0	0	0	0	0	0	0
HUGHES	33	31	2	0	1	3	5	0	2	4	0	0
JONES †	8	5	3	3	3	0	0	0	2	1	0	0
KITSON	14	14	0	0	2	8	2	0	0	0	0	0
LAMPARD	13	3	10	15	2	0	1	0	1	2	0	0
LAZARIDIS	22	13	9	3	6	1	2	0	1	4	0	0
LOMAS	7	7	0	0	1	0	0	0	0	0	0	0
MAUTONE	1	1	0	7	0	0	0	0	0	2	0	0
MEAN	0	0	0	2	0	0	0	0	0	0	0	0
MIKLOSKO	36	36	0	0	1	0	0	0	2	3	0	0
MONCUR	27	26	1	1	7	2	8	0	1	4	0	0
NEWELL*	7	6	1	0	2	0	2	0	0	0	0	0
OMOYINMI	1	0	1	0	0	0	0	0	0	0	0	0
PORFIRIO *	23	15	8	2	5	2	6	0	2	2	1	1
POTTS	20	17	3	5	3	0	2	0	1	1	0	0
RADUCIOIU †	11	6	5	2	4	2	0	0	0	1	0	1
RIEPER	28	26	2	3	3	1	3	1	1	4	0	0
ROWLAND	15	11	4	11	8	1	5	0	0	0	0	0
SEALEY	2	1	1	22	0	0	0	0	0	0	0	0
SHILTON †	0	0	0	8	0	0	0	0	0	0	0	0
SLATER †	3	2	1	0	1	0	1	0	0	0	0	0
WILLIAMSON	15	13	2	0	2	0	0	0	2	2	0	0
OGs						2						

216

Hartson and Kitson Hammer Home

Manager Harry Redknapp broke the West Ham United transfer record when signing the Espanyol player Florin Raducioiu for £2.2m to boost an attack which scored at a little over a goal a game the previous season. Richard Hall for £1.4m, Mark Bowen, Michael Hughes and Paolo Futre all moved to Upton Park. In October, the previous season's top scorer, Tony Cottee, was sold to Selengor. In keeping with their other two seasons in the Premiership, West Ham made another poor start.

A first day 2-0 defeat at Arsenal was followed by an early tumble down to 17th. West Ham's main problems were in scoring goals and stringing together two consecutive wins, something which was achieved just twice during the season. Prior to Christmas the Hammers had won just four league games but had picked up a creditable draw at Newcastle and rescued a point at home to Manchester United after trailing by two goals late in the game. The year ended with the brilliant Slaven Bilic opening the scoring and the outstandingly unimpressive Raducioiu adding a second in a 2-0 win at Upton Park against Sunderland. It was to be almost two months before West Ham were to win another game as a home defeat by Forest and a draw at Liverpool were followed by two more home and two away defeats. The run left Redknapp's side in the relegation zone and, having scored just two times in six Premiership matches, the manager was criticised by the fans.

Redknapp's response was sensational as West Ham began to move away from signing overseas players and turned to the domestic scene. In a bold double swoop Paul Kitson was prised away from Newcastle for £2.3m while Arsenal agreed a fee of £3.2m for the raw power of John Hartson, a fee which could eventually rise to £5m. Both were kept quiet on their debut at Derby but on a blustery evening at Upton Park on 24 February they opened their account and the irrepressible Julian Dicks scored twice in a thrilling 4-3 win over Spurs. That temporary move out of the bottom three was halted five days later by a 1-0 defeat at Leeds but West Ham now had renewed belief and, after seeing Chelsea equalise three minutes from time in their next game, the Hammers, through Kitson, still found time to grab a vital 3-2 win. It was the start of a five-match undefeated run which contained another important victory, this time 3-1 at Coventry with Hartson scoring twice. But another three-match winless run plunged them back into serious danger before a John Moncur goal laid the perfect foundation for safety, which was virtually secured when Kitson scored a hat trick and Hartson a brace in a 5-1 thrashing of Sheffield Wednesday. Another point was taken from a goalless draw at Upton Park with Newcastle on 6 May but their Premier League future was secured two days later when Blackburn and Middlesbrough drew.

In the FA Cup a superbly executed long-range goal by on-loan Portuguese star Hugo Porfirio secured a draw at snow-swept Wrexham. Any thoughts that the job was virtually done were destroyed in the final minute of the Upton Park replay as the Welsh club claimed a headline-grabbing winner. The Coca-Cola Cup was more to the Hammers' liking, although a 2-1 aggregate 2nd Round success over tiny Barnet hardly had the locals dreaming of Wembley. In the 3rd Round Nottingham Forest were conclusively beaten 4-1 with Iain Dowie scoring his only club goals of the season. After being held at home by the all-conquering Stockport County, the Hammers bowed out with a 2-1 defeat in the replay at Edgeley Park after taking the lead through Dicks.■

Results 1996-97

Date	Opponents	Ven	Res	Pos	Atten	Scorers
17-Aug	Arsenal	A	0-2	–	38,056	
21-Aug	Coventry C.	H	1-1	–	21,580	Rieper (78)
24-Aug	Southampton	H	2-1	11	21,227	Hughes (72); Dicks (81 pen)
04-Sep	Middlesbrough	A	1-4	15	30,060	Hughes (57)
08-Sep	Sunderland	A	0-0	16	18,642	
14-Sep	Wimbledon	H	0-2	17	21,924	
21-Sep	N. Forest	A	2-0	13	23,352	Bowen (44); Hughes (53)
29-Sep	Liverpool	H	1-2	15	25,064	Bilic (15)
12-Oct	Everton	A	1-2	16	36,571	Dicks (85 pen)
19-Oct	Leicester C.	H	1-0	13	22,285	Moncur (77)
26-Oct	Blackburn R.	H	2-1	10	23,947	Porfirio (76); OG (83, Berg)
02-Nov	Tottenham H.	A	0-1	12	32,999	
16-Nov	Newcastle Utd	A	1-1	12	36,552	Rowland (22)
23-Nov	Derby Co.	H	1-1	13	24,576	Bishop (16)
30-Nov	Sheffield W.	A	0-0	13	22,231	
04-Dec	Aston Villa	H	0-2	15	19,105	
08-Dec	Man. Utd	H	2-2	14	25,045	Raducioiu (77); Dicks (79 pen)
21-Dec	Chelsea	A	1-3	15	28,315	Porfirio (11)
28-Dec	Sunderland	H	2-0	16	24,077	Bilic (35); Raducioiu (89)
01-Jan	N. Forest	H	0-1	16	22,358	
11-Jan	Liverpool	A	0-0	17	40,102	
20-Jan	Leeds Utd	H	0-2	18	19,441	
29-Jan	Arsenal	H	1-2	18	24,382	OG (64, Rose)
01-Feb	Blackburn R.	A	1-2	18	21,994	Ferdinand (64)
15-Feb	Derby Co.	A	0-1	18	18,057	
24-Feb	Tottenham H.	H	4-3	17	23,998	Dicks (19, 71); Kitson (21); Hartson (36)
01-Mar	Leeds Utd	A	0-1	18	30,575	
12-Mar	Chelsea	H	3-2	17	24,502	Dicks (54 pen); Kitson (68, 90)
15-Mar	Aston Villa	A	0-0	17	35,992	
17-Mar	Wimbledon	A	1-1	16	15,771	Lazaridis (89)
22-Mar	Coventry C.	A	3-1	15	22,291	Hartson (27, 49); Ferdinand (33)
09-Apr	Middlesbrough	H	0-0	16	23,988	
12-Apr	Southampton	A	0-2	17	15,244	
19-Apr	Everton	H	2-2	18	24,525	Kitson (10, 32)
23-Apr	Leicester C.	A	1-0	16	20,327	Moncur (75)
03-May	Sheffield W.	H	5-1	15	24,490	Kitson (4, 12, 88); Hartson (29, 65)

| 06-May | Newcastle Utd | H | 0-0 | 12 | 24,617 | |
| 11-May | Man. Utd | A | 0-2 | 14 | 55,249 | |

FA Challenge Cup

Date	Opponents	Vn	Rnd	Res	Atten	Scorers
04 Jan	Wrexham	A	3R	1-1	9,747	Porfirio (44)
25-Jan	Wrexham	H	3RR	0-1	16,763	

Coca-Cola League Cup

Date	Opponents	Vn	Rnd	Res	Atten	Scorers
18-Sep	Barnet	A	2R1L	1-1	3,849	Cottee (78)
25-Sep	Barnet	H	2R2L	1-0	15,264	Bilic (46)
	West Ham win 2-1 on aggregate.					
23-Oct	N. Forest	H	3R	4-1	19,402	Dowie (14, 55); Porfirio (65); Dicks (72 pen)
27-Nov	Stockport Co.	H	4R	1-1	20,061	Raducioiu (11)
18-Dec	Stockport Co.	A	4RR	1-2	9,834	Dicks (22)

Hammers – Premiership Fact File

- United's 5-1 win over Sheffield Wednesday was their biggest ever in the Premiership. Interestingly West Ham's biggest defeat in the Premiership was by Sheffield Wednesday, 0-5.

- According to manager Harry Redknapp, West Ham will only end up paying £5m for John Hartson if the Hammers win the Champions' League. Watch out Borussia Dortmund!

- Full-back Julian Dicks was the Hammers' second top scorer.

5-Year Record

	Div.	P	W	D	L	F	A	Pts	Pos	FAC	FLC
92-93	1	46	26	10	10	81	41	88	2	4	2
93-94	PL	42	13	13	16	47	58	52	13	6	3
94-95	PL	42	13	11	18	44	48	50	14	4	4
95-96	PL	38	14	9	15	43	52	51	10	4	3
96-97	PL	38	10	12	16	39	48	42	14	3	4

Wimbledon

Founded 1889 as Wimbledon Old Centrals, an old boys' side of the Central School playing on Wimbledon Common. Member of the Southern Suburban League, the name was changed to Wimbledon in 1905. Moved to Plough Lane in 1912. Athenian League member for two seasons before joining the Isthmian League in 1921.

FA Amateur Cup winners 1963 and seven times Isthmian League champions. Turned professional in 1965, joining the Southern League, of which they were champions three times before being elected to Football League Division Four in 1977. Started ground sharing at Selhurst Park in 1991 and founder member of the Premier League 1992.

Ground: Selhurst Park, South Norwood, London SE25 6PY
Phone: 0181-771 2233   **News:** 0891 12 11 75
Box Office: 0181-771 8841
Colours: All Blue with Yellow trim   **Nickname:** The Dons
Capacity: 26,995   **Pitch:** 110 yds x 74 yds
Radio: 1548AM Capital Gold
Internet: –

Chairman: S.G. Reed   **Vice-Chairman:** J. Lelliott
Owner: Sam Hamman   **Chief Executive:** David Barnard
Secretary: Steve Rooke   **Manager:** Joe Kinnear
Assistant: Terry Burton   **Physio:** Steve Allen

League History: 1977 Elected to Division 4; 1979-80 Division 3; 1980-81 Division 4; 1981-82 Division 3; 1982-83 Division 4; 1983-84 Division 3; 1984-86 Division 2; 1986-92 Division 1; 1992- FA Premier League.

Honours: *Football League Division 3 Runners-up:* 1983-84; *Division 4 Champions:* 1982-83. *FA Cup Winners:* 1987-88. *FA Amateur Cup Winners:* 1963.

European Record: Never qualified. InterToto Cup (1995).

Managers: Les Henley 1955-71; Mike Everitt 1971-73; Dick Graham 1973-74; Allen Batsford 1974-78; Dario Gradi 1978-81; Dave Bassett 1981-87; Bobby Gould 1987-90; Ray Harford 1990-91; Peter Withe 1991; *(FAPL)* Joe Kinnear January 1992-

Season 1996-97

Biggest Home Win:	4-0 v Everton
Biggest Home Defeat:	0-3 v Manchester United
Biggest Away Win:	4-2 v Chelsea
Biggest Away Defeat:	0-5 v Aston Villa
Biggest Home Att:	25,786 v Manchester United
Smallest Home Att:	8,572 v Southampton
Average Attendance:	15,139 (19th)
Leading Scorer:	11 – Efan Ekoku, 7 – Robbie Earle

All-Time Records

Record FAPL Win:	4-0 v Crystal Palace, 9/4/93
	4-0 v Everton, 7/9/96
Record FAPL Defeat:	1-7 v Aston Villa, 11/2/95
Record FL Win:	6-0 v Newport County, Division 3, 3/9/83
Record FL Defeat:	0-8 v Everton, League Cup R2, 29/8/78
Record Cup Win:	7-2 v Windsor & Eton, FA Cup R1, 22/11/80
Record Fee Received:	£4.5m from Newcastle for Warren Barton, 6/95
Record Fee Paid:	£2m to Millwall for Ben Thatcher, 7/96
Most FL Apps:	Alan Cork, 430, 1977-92
Most FAPL Apps:	164 – Dean Holdsworth, 1992-97
Most FAPL Goals:	58 – Dean Holdsworth, 1992-97

Record Scorer in FAPL Season: Holdsworth, 19, 1992-93
Record Attendance (all-time): 30,115 v Manchester United, 8/5/93
Record Attendance (FAPL): 30,115 v Manchester United, 8/5/93
Most FAPL Goals in Season: 56, 1992-93 *and* 56, 1993-94 – 42 games
Most FAPL Points in Season: 65, 1993-94 – 42 games

Summary 1996-97

Player	Tot	St	Sb	Snu	PS	Gls	Y	R	Fa	La	Fg	Lg
ARDLEY	34	33	1	1	4	2	1	0	5	5	0	0
BLACKWELL	27	22	5	2	0	0	4	0	6	8	0	0
CASTLEDINE	6	4	2	0	0	1	0	0	0	1	0	1
CLARKE	11	4	7	9	2	1	1	0	1	6	0	0
CORT	1	0	1	0	0	0	0	0	0	0	0	0
CUNNINGHAM	36	36	0	0	2	0	5	0	7	7	0	0
EARLE	32	32	0	0	4	7	3	0	7	6	4	0
EKOKU	30	28	2	0	17	11	4	0	6	5	0	1
EUELL	7	4	3	2	0	2	0	0	0	1	0	0
FEAR	18	9	9	11	0	0	3	0	0	4	0	1
GAYLE	36	34	2	0	12	8	2	0	6	7	2	3
GOODMAN	13	6	7	6	6	1	0	0	3	1	0	0
HARFORD	13	3	10	15	1	1	2	0	2	5	0	0
HEALD	2	2	0	23	0	0	0	0	0	1	0	0
HOLDSWORTH	25	10	15	1	3	5	0	0	6	5	2	2
JONES	29	29	0	0	7	3	5	1	7	7	0	0
JUPP	6	6	0	9	2	0	1	0	2	1	0	0
KIMBLE	31	28	3	4	0	0	2	0	6	8	0	0
LEONHARDSEN †	27	27	0	1	8	5	0	0	7	7	0	1
McALLISTER	23	19	4	8	2	0	2	0	5	1	0	0
MURPHY	0	0	0	13	0	0	0	0	0	0	0	0
PERRY	37	37	0	0	2	1	0	0	7	7	1	0
REEVES	2	0	2	11	0	0	0	0	0	1	0	0
SULLIVAN	36	36	0	1	0	0	1	0	7	7	0	0
THATCHER	9	9	0	0	1	0	2	0	0	0	0	0
OGs						1						

5-Year Record

	Div.	P	W	D	L	F	A	Pts	Pos	FAC	FLC
92-93	PL	42	14	12	16	56	55	54	12	5	3
93-94	PL	42	18	11	13	56	53	65	6	5	5
94-95	PL	42	15	11	16	48	65	56	9	5	3
95-96	PL	38	10	11	17	55	70	41	14	QF	2
96-97	PL	38	15	11	12	49	46	56	8	SF	F

Dons Double Heartbreak

Wimbledon's FA Cup triumph of 1988 may be the finest achievement to date in the club's history but the 1996-97 season came so close to being the greatest in the still relatively young Football League life of a club which thrives on defeating the odds. The 'experts' were rubbing their hands with glee as the Dons failed to either score or pick up a single point from their first three Premiership games. Manager Joe Kinnear made few changes to his squad during the summer and, while there were no big-money sales, he bought modestly in spending £1.84m on taking Ben Thatcher from Millwall and an initial £125,000 on Fulham's Darren Jupp.

The Dons broke their duck on 3 September when Robbie Earle, the previous season's top scorer, notched the winning goal against Tottenham and four days later he was on target again as Wimbledon moved into top gear with a 4-0 drubbing of Everton. On the back of those results Wimbledon had risen from bottom to 11th and the run was maintained as West Ham, Southampton, Derby, Sheffield Wednesday and most notably of all, Chelsea, were swept aside during a glorious seven-match winning streak. Both Wednesday and neighbours Chelsea were beaten 4-2 before three successive draws saw the Dons slip from second to fourth. Their credentials were fully tested in draws with Arsenal and Liverpool while a 3-1 win at Sunderland early in December lifted the club back into second position. A late Dean Holdsworth goal against Blackburn extended Wimbledon's unbeaten league run to 14 games but their world caved in three days before Christmas at Villa Park as Villa meted out a 5-0 tonking. Having appeared almost impregnable prior to that match, Wimbledon were never to fully recover although the double was completed over Everton in their next match.

From then on league results declined sharply, possibly due to thrilling runs in the two knock-out competitions. Having scored a very commendable 33 goals in their opening 19 league games, the back of the net was found just a further 16 times from the final 19 games. Such was their slide down the table that even three wins in their last six games could not secure a place in Europe.

Ever since their historic FA Cup runs as a non-league side in the 1970s Wimbledon have been the club everyone wants to avoid. The Dons scraped through 2-1 on aggregate against Pompey but were within a minute of a replay defeat at Luton before Stewart Castledine took the tie into extra time and Peter Fear scored the winner. A Marcus Gayle goal clinched a fortuitous victory over Villa before early strikes by Efan Ekoku and Oyvind Leonhardsen earned an impressive victory at Bolton. A semi final showdown with Leicester looked to be going the Dons' way when Gayle put them ahead in the 2nd Leg following a goalless draw, but Grayson's second half equaliser put Wimbledon out on the away goals rule.

The Wembley dream looked to have been shattered by a late Manchester United goal in FA Cup Round Four at Old Trafford but Earle conjured up a last gasp equaliser. Gayle's powerful point blank header ended United's third double dream in the replay. Wimbledon marched on with a home win over QPR and a fine 2-0 victory at Sheffield Wednesday. But for the second time in a month Wimbledon fell at the final hurdle as Chelsea breezed to a comfortable 3-0 semi final victory.

This will also be seen as the season in which the Crazy Gang lost its bad boy image as they had far fewer bookings than any other side in the Premiership and just one player, predictably Jones, dismissed. ∎

Results 1996-97

Date	Opponents	Ven	Res	Pos	Atten	Scorers
17-Aug	Man. Utd	H	0-3	–	25,786	
21-Aug	Newcastle Utd	A	0-2	–	36,385	
26-Aug	Leeds Utd	A	0-1	20	25,860	
04-Sep	Tottenham H.	H	1-0		17,506	Earle (3)
07-Sep	Everton	H	4-0	11	13,684	Ardley (33); Gayle (46); Earle (58); Ekoku (73)
14-Sep	West Ham Utd	A	2-0	8	21,924	Clarke (54); Ekoku (84)
23-Sep	Southampton	H	3-1	6	8,572	Gayle (13); Ekoku (38, 74)
28-Sep	Derby Co.	A	2-0	3	17,022	Earle (49); Gayle (70)
12-Oct	Sheffield W.	H	4-2	5	10,512	Ekoku (3); Earle (32); Leonhardsen (66); Jones (86)
19-Oct	Chelsea	A	4-2	2	28,020	Earle (4); Ardley (18); Gayle (64); Ekoku (78)
26-Oct	Middlesbrough	A	0-0	3	29,758	
02-Nov	Arsenal	H	2-2	4	25,521	Jones (44); Gayle (69)
16-Nov	Coventry C.	H	2-2	4	10,307	Earle (45); Gayle (54)
23-Nov	Liverpool	A	1-1	4	39,027	Leonhardsen (67)
30-Nov	N. Forest	H	1-0	4	12,608	Earle (37)
07-Dec	Sunderland	A	3-1	2	19,672	Ekoku (8, 29); Holdsworth (89)
14-Dec	Blackburn R.	H	1-0	3	13,246	Holdsworth (85)
22-Dec	Aston Villa	A	0-5	3	28,875	
28-Dec	Everton	A	3-1	4	36,733	Ekoku (59); Leonhardsen (70); Gayle (76)
11-Jan	Derby Co.	H	1-1	5	11,467	Gayle (60)
18-Jan	Leicester C.	A	0-1	5	18,927	
29-Jan	Man. Utd	A	1-2	5	55,314	Perry (61)
01-Feb	Middlesbrough	H	1-1	6	15,046	OG (22, Cox)
23-Feb	Arsenal	A	1-0	6	37,854	Jones (21)
26-Feb	Southampton	A	0-0	5	14,418	
01-Mar	Leicester C.	H	1-3	6	11,487	Holdsworth (67)
03-Mar	Coventry C.	A	1-1	6	15,273	Ekoku (32)
15-Mar	Blackburn R.	A	1-3	8	23,333	Ekoku (39)
17-Mar	West Ham Utd	H	1-1	8	15,771	Harford (19)
23-Mar	Newcastle Utd	H	1-1	8	23,175	Leonhardsen (27)
05-Apr	Tottenham H.	A	0-1	8	32,654	
09-Apr	Aston Villa	H	0-2	8	9,015	
16-Apr	Leeds Utd	H	2-0	8	7,979	Holdsworth (18); Castledine (74)
19-Apr	Sheffield W.	A	1-3	8	26,957	Goodman (85)

Date		Vn	Res	Atten	Scorers
22-Apr	Chelsea	H	0-1	8	14,601	
03-May	N. Forest	A	1-1	8	19,865	Leonhardsen (15)
06-May	Liverpool	H	2-1	8	20,016	Euell (41); Holdsworth (55)
11-May	Sunderland	H	1-0	8	21,338	Euell (85)

FA Challenge Cup

Date	Opponents	Vn	Rnd	Res	Atten	Scorers
14-Jan	Crewe Alex.	A	3R	1-1	5,011	Perry (25)
21-Jan	Crewe Alex.	H	3RR	2-0	4,951	Earle (11); Holdsworth (46)
25-Jan	Man. Utd	A	4R	1-1	53,342	Earle (90)
04-Feb	Man. Utd	H	4RR	1-0	25,601	Gayle (63)
15-Feb	QPR	H	5R	2-1	22,395	Gayle (43); Earle (54)
09-Mar	Sheffield W.	A	6R	2-0	25,032	Earle (75); Holdsworth (90)
13-Apr	Chelsea	Hby	SF	0-3	32,674	

Coca-Cola League Cup

Date	Opponents	Vn	Rnd	Res	Atten	Scorers
18-Sep	Portsmouth	H	2R1L	1-0	3,811	Holdsworth (56)
25-Sep	Portsmouth	A	2R2L	1-1	4,006	Gayle (47)
	Wimbledon win 2-1 on aggregate.					
22-Oct	Luton Town	H	3R	1-1	5,188	Holdsworth (25)
12-Nov	Luton Town	A	3RR	2 1	8,076	Castledine (90); Fear (98)
26-Nov	Aston Villa	H	4R	1-0	7,573	Gayle (42)
08-Jan	Bolton W.	H	5R	2-0	16,968	Ekoku (3); Leonhardsen (22)
18-Feb	Leicester C.	A	SF1L	0-0	16,021	
11-Mar	Leicester C.	H	SF2L	1-1	17,771	Gayle (23)
	After extra time. Leicester City win on away goals rule.					

Dons – Premiership Fact File

- Wimbledon goalkeeper Neil Sullivan may be remembered for being the guy David Beckham beat from the halfway line, but the season finished in perfect style for the Dons keeper, who made his international debut for Scotland v Wales.

- Wimbledon reached second spot in the Premiership during the course of the season – their highest ever position.

- Wimbledon went 272 minutes into the season before scoring their first goal. They then had seven straight wins in the Premiership and went on to record 15 Premiership games without defeat; 19 in all competitions!

D1: Middlesbrough

Formed in 1876 and played first game in 1877. Turned professional in 1889, but reverted to amateur status shortly afterwards, being early winners of the FA Amateur Cup. League football was first played in Middlesbrough by the Ironpolis side for one season, 1893-94. Middlesbrough turned professional again, were elected to Division Two in 1899, and moved to Ayresome Park in 1903. They were founder members of the Premier League in 1993 but were relegated in their first season. Moved to purpose-built stadium in 1995 coinciding with return to Premiership. Reached and lost both Cup Finals in 1997 in addition to being relegated to Division 1.

Ground: The Cellnet Riverside Stadium, Middlesbrough, TS3 6RS
Phone: 01642 877700
Box Office: 01642 877745
Info: 0891 42 42 00 **Club Shop:** 01642 877720
Colours: Red with Black, White with Black, Red with Black
Capacity: 31,000 **Nickname:** The Boro
Radio: 100.7FM Century Radio
Internet: –

Chairman: Steve Gibson **CEO:** Keith Lamb
Secretary: Karen Nelson
Manager: Bryan Robson **Assistant:** Viv Anderson
First Team Coach: John Pickering **Physios:** Bob Ward, Tommy Johnson

League History: 1899 Elected to Division 2; 1902-24 Division 1; 1924-27 Division 2; 1927-28 Division 1; 1928-29 Division 2; 1929-54 Division 1; 1954-66 Division 2; 1966-67 Division 3; 1967-74 Division 2; 1974-82 Division 2; 1982-86 Division 2; 1986-87 Division 3; 1988-89 Division 1; 1989-92 Division 2; 1992-93 FAPL; 1993-95 Division 1; 1995-97 FAPL; 1997- Division 1

Honours: *Division 1 (new) Champions:* 1994-95; *Division 2 Champions* 1926-27, 1928-29, 1973-74; *Runners-up:* 1901-02, 1991-92; *Division 3 Runners up:* 1966-67, 1986-87; *FA Cup Runners-up:* 1996-97; *League Cup Runners-up:* 1996-97. *FA Amateur Cup Winners:* 1895, 1898; *Anglo-Scottish Cup Winners:* 1975-76.

European Record: Never qualified

Managers: John Robson 1899-05; Alex Massie 1905-06; Andy Atkin 1906-09; J. Gunter 1908-10; Andy Walker 1910-11; Tom McIntosh 1911-19; James Howie 1920-23; Herbert Bamlett 1923-26; Peter McWilliam 1927-34; Wilf Gillow 1933-44; David Jack 1944-52; Walter Rowley 1952-54; Bob Dennison 1954-63; Raich Carter 1963-66; Stan Anderson 1966-73; Jack Charlton 1973-77; John Neal 1977-81; Bobby Murdoch 1981-82; Malcolm Allison 1982-84; Willie Maddren 1984-86; Bruce Rioch 1986-90; Colin Todd 1990-91; Lennie Lawrence 1991-94; *(FAPL)* Bryan Robson May 1994-

Season 1996-97

Biggest Home Win:	6-1 v Derby County
Biggest Home Defeat:	0-3 v Tottenham Hotspur
Biggest Away Win:	3-1 v Leicester City
Biggest Away Defeat:	1-5 v Liverpool
Biggest Home Att:	30,215 v Tottenham Hotspur
Smallest Home Att:	29,485 v Sheffield Wednesday
Average Attendance:	29,871 (9th)
Leading Scorer:	16 – Fabrizio Ravanelli, 12 – Juninho

All-Time Records

Record FAPL Win:	4-1 v Leeds United, 22/8/92 and
	4-1 v Manchester City, 9/12/95
Record FAPL Defeat:	0-5 v Chelsea, 04/2/96 and
	1-5 v Aston Villa, 17/1/93
Record FL Win:	9-0 v Brighton & HA, D2 23/8/58
Record FL Defeat:	0-9 v Blackburn Rovers, D2 6/11/54
Record Cup Win:	9-3 v Goole Town, FAC1, 9/1/15
Record Fee Received:	£5.75m, from Everton for Nicky Barmby, 10/96
Record Fee Paid:	£7m to Juventus for Fabrizio Ravanelli, 7/96
Record Attendance (all-time):	53,596 v Newcastle Utd, D1 27/12/49
	at Ayresome Park
Record Attendance (FAPL):	30,215 v Tottenham Hotspur, 19/10/96
	at Cellnet Stadium – also record
Most FL Apps:	Tim Williamson, 563, 1902-23
Most FAPL Apps:	81 – Derek Whyte, 1992-97
Most FAPL Goals:	27 – Chris Morris, 1992-97
Highest Scorer in FAPL Season:	16 – Fabrizio Ravanelli, 1996-97
Most FAPL Goals in Season:	54, 1992-93 – 42 games
Most FAPL Points in Season:	44, 1992-93 – 42 games

Summary 1996-97

Player	Tot	St	Sb	Snu	PS	Gls	Y	R	Fa	La	Fg	Lg
BARMBY†	10	10	0	1	1	1	0	0	0	0	0	0
BECK	25	22	3	3	2	5	0	0	6	7	2	4
BLACKMORE	16	14	2	3	1	2	2	0	5	3	0	0
BRANCO †	2	1	1	5	0	0	0	0	0	2	0	2
CAMPBELL	3	0	3	2	0	0	0	0	0	0	0	0
COX †	31	29	2	4	0	0	7	0	3	7	1	0
EMERSON	32	32	0	0	6	4	8	0	5	8	1	2
FESTA	13	13	0	0	0	1	5	0	5	4	1	0
FJORTOFT †	5	2	3	7	0	1	0	0	2	1	1	0
FLEMING	30	30	0	1	0	0	4	0	5	7	0	1
FREESTONE	2	0	2	8	0	0	0	0	1	0	0	0
HENDRIE †	0	0	0	8	0	0	0	0	0	2	0	0
HIGNETT	22	19	3	6	6	4	3	0	6	6	2	1
JUNINHO †	35	34	1	0	4	12	5	0	6	7	2	1
KINDER	6	4	2	5	1	1	0	0	3	1	0	0
LIDDLE	5	5	0	5	0	0	1	0	1	0	0	0
MILLER †	10	10	0	2	0	0	1	0	0	2	0	0
MOORE	17	10	7	9	7	0	4	0	2	4	0	0
MORRIS	4	3	1	4	2	0	0	0	0	2	0	0
MUSTOE	31	31	0	0	1	2	9	0	7	8	0	0
ORMEROD	0	0	0	2	0	0	0	0	0	0	0	0
PEARSON	18	17	1	1	2	0	3	1	3	5	0	0
RAVANELLI	33	33	0	0	4	16	6	0	7	8	6	9
ROBERTS	10	9	1	25	0	0	1	0	6	2	0	0
ROBSON	2	1	1	1	0	0	0	0	0	0	0	0
SCHWARZER	7	7	0	1	1	0	0	0	0	3	0	0
STAMP	23	15	8	3	2	1	1	0	5	7	1	1
SUMMERBELL	2	0	2	4	0	0	1	0	0	0	0	0
VICKERS	29	26	3	4	3	0	4	0	6	6	0	1
WALSH	12	12	0	5	0	0	1	0	1	3	0	0
WHELAN	9	9	0	11	1	0	3	0	0	2	0	0
WHYTE	21	20	1	11	3	0	6	0	4	4	0	1
OGs						1						1

5-Year Record

	Div.	P	W	D	L	F	A	Pts	Pos	FAC	FLC
92-93	PL	42	11	11	20	54	75	44	21	4	2
93-94	1	46	18	13	15	66	54	67	9	3	3
94-95	1	46	23	13	10	67	40	82	1	3	3
95-96	PL	38	11	10	17	35	50	43	12	4	4
96-97	PL	38	10	12	16	51	60	39	19	F	F

Foreign Delights End in Disaster

Encouraged by the success of Juninho and not put off by the failure of Branco the previous season, Middlesbrough manager Bryan Robson continued to look abroad and invested a total of £11m on Italian Fabrizio Ravanelli and Brazilian Emerson. Mikkel Beck of Cologne also moved to the Riverside. Sadly, Emerson frequently went awol and struggled to make an impact while Beck was erratic, but Ravanelli was a sensation who marked his debut in English football with a hat trick in a 3-3 draw with Liverpool.

Juninho was in good form throughout the campaign and his determination to keep Boro in the Premiership won him many new admirers. After a defeat at Chelsea in their next match, Juninho scored his first goal of the season in a draw at Nottingham Forest. Goals then flowed at the expense of West Ham and Coventry. Boro rose to fourth with a 2-1 win at Everton but lost their form and went 12 matches without victory, starting with a 2-0 home defeat by Arsenal. Boro also caused a stir by failing to appear for a match at Blackburn on 21 December, citing injury and illness as causing player shortages. The Premier League dished out a £50,000 fine and a three point deduction. The squad was strengthened in January with the £2.75m signing of Internazionale defender Gianluca Festa.

During the bad run Nick Barmby departed to Everton for £5.75m. Three more defeats completed the fall to the foot of the table. March kicked off with another reversal, at Sheffield Wednesday, but Boro burst into life with Ravanelli scoring a hat trick in a 6-1 annihilation of Derby. Juninho scored in the next three games as maximum points were taken from Leicester, Blackburn and Chelsea. With eight games remaining, Boro were out of the bottom three but another four-match winless run took them into the final nine days – and four games – in a perilous position. A last-minute Ravanelli penalty secured a 3-2 win over West Ham but midweek draws at Manchester United, after leading three times, and Blackburn, left them needing to win at Leeds on the final day. Juninho was brilliant but only a draw was achieved as Boro became the most expensively assembled side to fall from the Premiership.

In the Coca-Cola Cup, Hereford were on the receiving end of four Ravanelli goals during a 7-0 defeat at the Riverside and Huddersfield were similarly thrashed. Boro then produced two of their most passionate displays to defeat Newcastle and Liverpool at the Riverside. Giant killers Stockport County were seen off 2-0 at Edgeley Park in the 1st leg of the semi final but Boro had a scare in the return as County only just failed to claw back the second goal. The final with Leicester was disappointing but when Ravanelli put Boro ahead in extra time it looked as though the club had won its first significant piece of silverware. Leicester, though, grabbed a late equaliser and took the trophy in a Hillsborough replay.

In the FA Cup, Boro ditched Chester 6-0 but only narrowly beat non-leaguers Hednesford Town. A Juninho goal accounted for Manchester City and Derby was removed. In the semi final Boro went down to ten Chesterfield men. Two swift strikes took the tie into extra time, in which Festa put Boro ahead, only for Chesterfield to grab a sensational equaliser seconds from time. Robson's multi-million pound side made no mistake in the Hillsborough replay, running out 3-0 victors. Just a week after being relegated, Boro faced Chelsea in the Wembley final but they never recovered from conceding a goal inside 43 seconds – a fitting finale

Results 1996-97

Date	Opponents	Ven	Res	Pos	Atten	Scorers
17-Aug	Liverpool	H	3-3	–	30,039	Ravanelli (26 pen, 35, 81)
21-Aug	Chelsea	A	0-1	–	28,272	
24-Aug	N. Forest	A	1-1	14	24,705	Juninho (48)
04-Sep	West Ham Utd	H	4-1	9	30,060	Emerson (12); Mustoe (28); Ravanelli (53); Stamp (83)
07-Sep	Coventry C.	H	4-0	7	29,811	Ravanelli (3, 73); Juninho (28, 80)
14-Sep	Everton	A	2-1	4	39,250	Barmby (61); Juninho (81)
21-Sep	Arsenal	H	0-2	8	29,629	
28-Sep	Southampton	A	0-4	9	15,230	
14-Oct	Sunderland	A	2-2	8	20,936	Emerson (17); Ravanelli (52)
19-Oct	Tottenham H.	H	0-3	11	30,215	
26-Oct	Wimbledon	H	0-0	13	29,758	
03-Nov	Newcastle Utd	A	1-3	15	36,577	Beck (88)
17-Nov	Derby Co.	A	1-2	15	17,350	Ravanelli (73)
23-Nov	Man. Utd	H	2-2	15	30,063	Ravanelli (27); Hignett (82 pen)
30-Nov	Aston Villa	A	0-1	16	39,053	
03-Dec	Leicester C.	H	0-2	16	29,709	
07-Dec	Leeds Utd	H	0-0	16	30,018	
14-Dec	Liverpool	A	1-5	16	39,491	Fjortoft (75)
26-Dec	Everton	H	4-2	17	29,673	Hignett (22); Blackmore (37); Juninho (58, 74)
28-Dec	Coventry C.	A	0-3	17	20,617	
01-Jan	Arsenal	A	0-2	18	37,573	
11-Jan	Southampton	H	0-1	20	29,509	
18-Jan	Sheffield W.	H	4-2	20	29,485	Ravanelli (14 pen); Festa (23); Emerson (72 pen); Juninho (90)
01-Feb	Wimbledon	A	1-1	20	15,046	Mustoe (75)
22-Feb	Newcastle Utd	H	0-1	20	30,063	
01-Mar	Sheffield W.	A	1-3	20	28,206	OG (71, Nicol)
05-Mar	Derby Co.	H	6-1	20	29,739	Kinder (24); Ravanelli (54, 83, 85); Hignett (70); Beck (84)
15-Mar	Leicester C.	A	3-1	20	20,561	Blackmore (8); Juninho (26); Beck (36)
19-Mar	Blackburn R.	H	2-1	19	29,891	Juninho (43); Ravanelli (60)
22-Mar	Chelsea	H	1-0	17	29,811	Juninho (53)
24-Mar	N. Forest	H	1-1	17	29,888	Beck (56)

09-Apr	West Ham Utd	A	0-0	18	23,988	
19-Apr	Sunderland	H	0-1	19	30,106	
24-Apr	Tottenham H.	A	0-1	19	29,947	
03-May	Aston Villa	H	3-2	19	30,074	Ravanelli (20, 90 pen); Beck 34)
05-May	Man. Utd	A	3-3	19	54,489	Juninho (15); Emerson (37); Hignett (40)
08-May	Blackburn R.	A	0-0	19	27,411	
11-May	Leeds Utd	A	1-1	19	38,567	Juninho (79)

FA Challenge Cup

Date	Opponents	Vn	Rnd	Res	Atten	Scorers
04-Jan	Chester C.	H	3R	6-0	18,684	Ravanelli (20, 50); Hignett (25); Cox (44); Beck (55); Stamp (79)
25-Jan	Hednesford T.	A	4R	3-2	27,511	OG (26, Lambert); Fjortoft (86); Ravanelli (88)
15-Feb	Manchester C.	A	5R	1-0	30,462	Juninho (77)
08-Mar	Derby Co.	A	6R	2-0	17,567	Juninho (39); Ravanelli (90)
13-Apr	Chesterfield	OT	SF	3-3	49,640	Ravanelli (62); Hignett (68 pen); Festa (100)
	after extra time					
22-Apr	Chesterfield	Hbr	SFR	3-0	30,339	Beck (12); Ravanelli (57); Emerson (89)
17-May	Chelsea	W	F	0-2	79,160	

Coca-Cola League Cup

Date	Opponents	Vn	Rnd	Res	Atten	Scorers
18-Sep	Hereford Utd	H	2R1L	7-0	17,136	Ravanelli (20, 37, 55, 72 pen); Emerson (32); Branco (57); Fleming (69)
24-Sep	Hereford Utd	A	2R2L	3-0	4,522	Beck (23); Stamp (49); Branco (51)
	Middlesbrough win 10-0 on aggregate.					
23-Oct	Huddersfield T.	H	3R	5-1	26,615	Juninho (17); Emerson (42); Ravanelli (72, 76); Beck (85)
27-Nov	Newcastle Utd	H	4R	3-1	29,831	Whyte (27); Beck (61); Ravanelli (89)
08-Jan	Liverpool	H	5R	2-1	28,670	Hignett (13); Vickers (27)
26-Feb	Stockport Co.	A	SF	2-0	11,778	Beck (73); Ravanelli (79)
12-Mar	Stockport Co.	H	SF	0-1	29,633	
06-Apr	Leicester C.	W	F	1-1	76,757	Ravanelli (95)
	after extra time					
16-Apr	Leicester C.	Hbr	FR	0 1	39,428	

D1: Nottingham Forest

Founded in 1865 by players of a hockey-like game, shinney, who played at the Forest Recreation Ground. They played their first game in 1866. Had several early homes, including a former Notts County ground, The Meadows, and Trent Bridge Cricket Ground.

Founder members of the Football Alliance in 1889 and champions in 1892 when elected to an extended Football League top division. In 1898 moved from the Town Ground to the City Ground at West Bridgford. Run by a committee until 1982, the last League club to become a limited company. Premier League founder members 1992. Relegated after one season, but promoted back at the first attempt, only to be relegated once again in 1997.

Ground: City Ground, Nottingham NG2 5FJ
Phone: 0115-952 6000   **Fax:** 0115-952 600
Box Office: 0115-952 6002   **CC Bookings:** 0115-971 8181
Info: 0115-952 6016 (24 hrs)
News: 0891 12 11 74   **Clubshop:** 0115-952-6026
Capacity: 30,539   **Pitch:** 115 yds x 78 yds
Colours: Red, White, Red   **Nickname:** Reds
Radio: 945AM/999AM GEM AM
Internet: –

Chairman: Irving Korn   **Deputy-Chairman:** Phillip Soar
Secretary: Paul White
Manager: Dave Bassett   **Team Manager:** Stuart Pearce
First Team Coach: Liam O'Kane   **Physio:** John Haselden

League History: 1892 elected to Division 1; 1906-07 Division 2; 1907-11 Division 1; 1911-22 Division 2; 1922-25 Division 1; 1925-49 Division 2; 1949-51 Division 3 (S); 1951-57 Division 2; 1957-72 Division 1; 1972-77 Division 2; 1977-92 Division 1; 1992-93 FA Premier League; 1993-94 Division 1; 1994- FA Premier League.

Honours: *Football League Division 1 Champions:* 1977-78; *Runners-up:* 1966-67, 1978-79; *Division 2 Champions:* 1906-07, 1921-22; *Runners-up:* 1956-57; *Division 3 (S) Champions:* 1950-51. *FA Cup Winners:* 1898, 1959; *Runners-up:* 1991. *Anglo-Scottish Cup Winners:* 1976-77. *Football League*

Cup Winners: 1977-78, 1978-79, 1988-89, 1989-90; *Runners-up:* 1979-80, 1991-92; *Simod Cup Winners:* 1989; *Zenith Data Systems Cup Winners:* 1991-92; *Champions' Cup Winners:* 1978-79, 1979-80; *European Super Cup Winners:* 1979-80; *Runners-up:* 1980-81. *World Club Championship Runners-up:* 1980-81.

European Record: CC (3): 78-79 (W), 79-80 (W), 80-81 (1); CWC (0): –; UEFA (5): 61-62 (1), 67-68 (2), 83-84 (3), 84-85 (1), 95-96 (QF).

Managers: Harry Radford 1889-97; Harry Haslam 1897-09; Fred Earp 1909-12; Bob Masters 1912-25; Jack Baynes 1925-29; Stan Hardy 1930-31; Noel Watson 1931-36; Harold Wightman 1936-39; Billy Walker 1939-60; Andy Beattie 1960-63; John Carey 1963-68; Matt Gillies 1969-72; Dave Mackay 1972-73; Allan Brown 1973-75; *(FAPL)* Brian Clough 1975-93; Frank Clark June 1993-Dec 1996; Stuart Pearce Dec 1996-

Season 1996-97

Biggest Home Win:	2-0 v Chelsea
Biggest Home Defeat:	0-4 v Manchester United
Biggest Away Win:	3-0 v Coventry City
Biggest Away Defeat:	5-0 v Newcastle United
Biggest Home Att:	29,181 v Liverpool
Smallest Home Att:	17,525 v Blackburn Rovers
Average Attendance:	24,587 (13th)
Leading Scorer:	6 – Kevin Campbell and Alf Inge Haaland

All-Time Records

Record FAPL Win:	7-1 v Sheffield Wednesday, 1/4/95
Record FAPL Defeat:	0-7 v Blackburn Rovers (away), 18/11/95
Record FL Win:	12-0 v Leicester Fosse, Division 1, 12/4/09
Record FL Defeat:	1-9 v Blackburn R, Division 2, 10/4/37
Record Cup Win:	14-0 v Clapton (away), FA Cup R1, 17/1/1891
Record Fee Received:	£8.5m from Liverpool for Stan Collymore, 6/95
Record Fee Paid:	£3.5m>4.5m to Celtic, Pierre van Hooijdonk, 3/97
Most FL Apps:	Bob McKinlay, 614, 1951-70
Most FAPL Apps:	150 – Mark Crossley, 1992-97
Most FAPL Goals:	24 – Bryan Roy, 1994-9
Record Attendance (all-time):	49,945 v Manchester Utd, Div 1 28/10/67
Record Attendance (FAPL):	29,263 v Manchester United, 27/11/95

Highest Scorer in FAPL Season: Stan Collymore, 23, 1994-95
Most FAPL Goals in Season: 72, 1994-95 – 42 games
Most FAPL Points in Season: 77, 1994-95 – 42 games

Summary 1996-97

Player	Tot	St	Sb	Snu	PS	Gls	Y	R	Fa	La	Fg	Lg
ALLEN	24	16	8	10	4	0	1	0	1	0	1	0
ARMSTRONG	0	0	0	1	0	0	0	0	0	0	0	0
BART-WILLIAMS	16	16	0	1	3	1	1	0	2	3	0	0
BLATHERWICK	7	7	0	4	2	0	2	0	1	2	0	0
BURNS	0	0	0	1	0	0	0	0	0	0	0	0
CAMPBELL	17	16	1	0	2	6	3	0	3	0	0	0
CHETTLE	32	31	1	3	0	0	3	0	3	1	0	0
CLOUGH	13	10	3	1	3	1	1	0	0	0	0	0
COOPER	36	36	0	0	1	2	6	0	3	3	0	1
CROSSLEY	33	33	0	0	0	0	1	0	3	3	0	0
FETTIS	4	4	0	32	0	0	0	0	1	0	0	0
GEMMILL	24	18	6	10	4	0	6	0	2	3	0	0
GUINAN	2	0	2	3	0	0	0	0	0	0	0	0
HAALAND	34	33	1	2	3	6	3	0	3	3	0	0
HENRY	0	0	0	4	0	0	0	0	0	0	0	0
HOWE	1	0	1	6	0	0	0	0	0	0	0	0
JERKAN	14	14	0	8	4	0	6	0	0	0	0	0
LEE	13	5	8	4	0	1	1	0	1	3	0	1
LYTTLE	32	30	2	4	4	1	5	0	3	2	0	0
McGREGOR	5	0	5	4	0	0	0	0	1	0	0	0
MOORE	5	1	4	2	0	0	0	0	0	0	0	0
O'NEIL	5	4	1	2	1	0	2	0	0	0	0	0
PEARCE	33	33	0	0	2	5	8	0	2	2	0	0
PHILLIPS	27	24	3	5	3	0	1	0	2	2	0	0
ROY	20	8	12	12	7	3	1	0	3	3	0	1
SAUNDERS	34	33	1	0	11	3	0	0	2	3	2	0
SILENZI	2	1	1	0	1	0	0	0	0	0	0	0
SMITH	0	0	0	2	0	0	0	0	0	0	0	0
STONE	5	5	0	0	2	0	2	0	0	0	0	0
VAN HOOIJDONK	8	8	0	0	0	1	3	0	0	0	0	0
WALKER	0	0	0	3	0	0	0	0	0	0	0	0
WARNER	3	2	1	0	0	0	0	0	0	0	0	0
WOAN	32	29	3	1	7	1	7	0	3	3	1	0
WRIGHT	1	1	0	1	0	0	0	0	0	0	0	0

Bassett Aims to Replant Forest

During the previous two seasons Nottingham Forest set a Premiership record of 25 games without defeat, but having conceded five goals in two of their final five games of the 1995-96 season, they did offer signs that all was not well at the City Ground. None-the-less, manager Frank Clark stayed loyal to his squad and made just three signings, Dean Saunders, Nikola Jerkan and Chris Allen, at a cost of almost £2m. Saunders and Jerkan made their debuts at Coventry on the opening day of the season but had to play second fiddle to Kevin Campbell who equalled his league tally for the previous campaign with all the goals in a 3-0 victory. But the optimism was dashed four days later as Sunderland romped to a 4-1 win in the Midlands. Three consecutive draws left Forest in 11th place but already it was evident that there were problems and supporters had to wait until the week before Christmas for another league victory. Despite their poor form Forest did not slump to the foot of the table until mid-November when Blackburn went above them on goal difference. A four-month spell without victory was all the more remarkable in that no game was lost by more than two goals. Their problems were at the opposite end as they failed to score in half those matches and Saunders managed a miserly three Premiership goals all season.

Forest's problems on the field of play were exacerbated by a protracted boardroom takeover and the frustration caused rumour to spread about Clark's future. The former Forest defender finally called it a day on 19 December, and England stalwart Stuart Pearce was offered the position of player manager. Pearce rang the changes for his first match at home to Arsenal. Out went three players and the response was startling as two goals from Alf Inge Haaland overturned a goal from the later dismissed Ian Wright. Manchester United reminded Forest that they remained at the bottom of the pile with a 4-0 rout at the City Ground on Boxing Day but Pearce's side stopped a run of five successive away defeats with a point at Leicester two days later. Campbell's sixth, and final, league goal of the season secured victory at West Ham and Pearce led from the front with the opening goal in a 2-0 win over Chelsea. Injuries forced Pearce to recall the out-of-favour Bryan Roy against Spurs and the Dutchman struck twice as Forest won 2-1 to climb out of the bottom three for the first time in over three months.

With peace breaking out in the boardroom, and a possible £14m to spend on players, Forest had 15 games in which to build on their three straight wins and secure a place in the Premiership. The club strengthened its team, supporting Pearce with Dave Bassett taking on the role of general manager. Forest then failed to score in five of their next six matches. March was most notable for a run of four successive 1-1 draws, the first of which saw record signing Pierre van Hooijdonk, a £3.5m signing from Celtic, make his debut and pick up a booking. Forest's fate was as good as sealed when Southampton gained a rare away win early in April. Following a 5-0 thrashing at Newcastle on the last day, Bassett was confirmed as manager for the following season.

In the Coca-Cola Cup a 3rd Round meeting at West Ham ended in a miserable 4-1 demolition. In a season of many lows, a high point was found in the FA Cup when a 3-0 3rd Round victory over Ipswich Town was followed by an outstanding 2-1 win away to Newcastle. But such was Forest's season that they went down to Chesterfield in the next round. ∎

Results 1996-97

Date	Opponents	Ven	Res	Pos	Atten	Scorers
17-Aug	Coventry C.	A	3-0	–	19,468	Campbell (13, 36, 47)
21-Aug	Sunderland	H	1-4	–	22,874	Haaland (26)
24-Aug	Middlesbrough	H	1-1	10	24,705	Pearce (67)
04-Sep	Southampton	A	2-2		14,450	Campbell (4); Saunders (23)
07-Sep	Leicester C.	H	0-0	11	24,105	
14-Sep	Man. Utd	A	1-4	14	54,984	Haaland (3)
21-Sep	West Ham Utd	H	0-2	16	23,352	
28-Sep	Chelsea	A	1-1	16	27,673	Lee (90)
12-Oct	Leeds Utd	A	0-2	17	29,225	
19-Oct	Derby Co.	H	1-1	18	27,771	Saunders (1)
28-Oct	Everton	H	0-1	18	19,892	
02-Nov	Aston Villa	A	0-2	18	35,310	
18-Nov	Sheffield W.	A	0-2	20	16,390	
25-Nov	Blackburn R.	H	2-2	20	17,525	Pearce (44 pen); Cooper (90)
30-Nov	Wimbledon	A	0-1	20	12,608	
09-Dec	Newcastle Utd	H	0-0	19	25,762	
17-Dec	Liverpool	A	2-4	20	36,126	Campbell (34); Pearce (60)
21-Dec	Arsenal	H	2-1	20	27,384	Haaland (64, 88)
26-Dec	Man. Utd	H	0-4	20	29,032	
28-Dec	Leicester C.	A	2-2	20	20,833	Clough (37); Cooper (87)
01-Jan	West Ham Utd	A	1-0	19	22,358	Campbell (37)
11-Jan	Chelsea	H	2-0	18	28,358	Pearce (39); Bart-Williams (57)
19-Jan	Tottenham H.	H	2-1	17	27,303	Roy (47, 61)
29-Jan	Coventry C.	H	0-1	17	22,619	
01-Feb	Everton	A	0-2	17	32,567	
22-Feb	Aston Villa	H	0-0	17	25,239	
01-Mar	Tottenham H.	A	1-0	17	32,805	Saunders (17)
05-Mar	Sheffield W.	H	0-3	17	21,485	
08-Mar	Arsenal	A	0-2	17	38,208	
11-Mar	Blackburn R.	A	1-1	17	20,485	Haaland (19)
15-Mar	Liverpool	H	1-1	18	29,181	Woan (29)
22-Mar	Sunderland	A	1-1	19	22,120	Lyttle (86)
24-Mar	Middlesbrough	A	1-1	18	29,888	Haaland (4)
05-Apr	Southampton	H	1-3	19	25,134	Pearce (88 pen)
19-Apr	Leeds Utd	H	1-1	20	25,565	van Hooijdonk (6)
23-Apr	Derby Co.	A	0-0	20	18,087	
03-May	Wimbledon	H	1-1	20	19,865	Roy (60)
11-May	Newcastle Utd	A	0-5	20	36,554	

FA Challenge Cup

Date	Opponents	Vn	Rnd	Res	Atten	Scorers
04-Jan	Ipswich T.	H	3R	3-0	14,681	Saunders (16, 74); Allen (26)
26-Jan	Newcastle Utd	A	4R	2-1	36,434	Woan (75, 80)
15-Feb	Chesterfield	A	5R	0-1	8,890	

Coca-Cola League Cup

Date	Opponents	Vn	Rnd	Res	Atten	Scorers
18-Sep	Wycombe W.	H	2R1L	1-0	6,482	Roy (47)
24-Sep	Wycombe W.	A	2R2L	1-1	6,310	Lee (102)
	After extra time. Nottingham Forest win 2-1 on aggregate.					
23-Oct	West Ham Utd	A	3R	1-4	19,402	Cooper (26)

Forest – Premiership Fact File

- Kevin Campbell marked his Forest debut with his first ever hat-trick. The former Arsenal striker only scored a further three Premiership goals.

- Forest managed only six Premier League wins throughout the season – this did include a double over Tottenham.

5-Year Record

	Div.	P	W	D	L	F	A	Pts	Pos	FAC	FLC
92-93	PL	42	10	10	22	41	62	40	22	5	5
93/94	1	46	23	14	9	74	49	83	2	3	5
94-95	PL	42	22	11	9	72	43	77	3	4	4
95-96	PL	38	15	13	10	50	54	58	9	QF	2
96-97	PL	38	6	16	16	31	59	34	20	5	3

D1: Sunderland

Formed in 1879 as The Sunderland and District Teachers' Association FC by James Allan, a Scottish school teacher. Originally membership was restricted to teachers only, but this requirement was soon removed. Became Sunderland AFC in 1880 and had their first ground at the Blue House pub. Played at a number of grounds until they moved to the Roker Park site in 1898. Elected to Division 2 of the Football League in 1890 and best remembered for their famous FA Cup win over Leeds United in 1973. Started the 1997-98 season in a new stadium.

Ground: Roker Park, Sunderland, SR6 9SW
Phone: 0191-514-0332   **News:** 0891 12 11 40
Box Office: 0191 514 0332
Capacity: 22,657   **Pitch:** tba
Colours: Red & White stripes, Black, Red with White trim
Nickname: The Rokermen
Radio: Radio Roker 103.4FM
Internet: http://www.sunderland-afc.com

Chairman: R.S. Murray   **CEO:** J.M. Ficking
Deputy Chairman: G.S. Wood   **Secretary:** Mark Blackbourne
Manager: Peter Reid   **Assistant:** Paul Bracewell
Head Coach: Bobby Saxton   **Physio:** Gordon Ellis

League History: 1890 Elected to Division 1; 1958-64 Division 2; 1964-70 Division 1; 1970-76 Division 2; 1976-77 Division 1; 1977-80 Division 2; 1980-85 Division 1; 1985-87 Division 2; 1987-88 Division 3; 1988-90 Division 2; 1990-91 Division 1; 1991-92 Division 2; 1992-96 Division 1; 1996-97 FAPL; 1997- Division 1

Honours: *Football League Division 1 Champions:* 1891-92, 1892-93, 1894-95, 1901-02, 1912-13, 1935-36, 1995-96; *Runners-up:* 1893-94, 1897-88; 1900-01, 1922-23, 1934-35; *Division 2 Champions:* 1975-76; *Runners-up:* 1963-64, 1979-80; *Division 3 Champions:* 1987-88; *FA Cup Winners:* 1936-37, 1972-73; *Runners-up:* 1912-13, 1991-92. *Football League Cup Runners-up:* 1984-85.

European Record: CC (0): – ; CWC (1) 1973-74 (2) ; UEFA (0): –

Managers: Tom Watson 1888-96, Bob Campbell 1896-99, Alex Mackie 1899-1905, Bob Kyle 1905-28, Johnny Cochrane 1928-39, Bill Murray 1939-

57, Alan Brown 1957-64, George Hardwick 1964-65, Ian McColl 1965-68, Alan Brown 1968-72, Bob Stokoe 1972-76, Jimmy Adamson 1976-78, Ken Knighton 1979-81, Alan Durban 1981-84, Len Ashurst 1984-85, Lawrie McMenemy 1985-87, Denis Smith 1987-91, Malcolm Crosby 1992-93, Terry Butcher 1993, Mick Buxton 1993-95, Peter Reid 1995-.

Season 1996-97

Biggest Home Win:	3-0 v Chelsea and Everton
Biggest Home Defeat:	0-4 v Tottenham Hotspur
Biggest Away Win:	3-1 v Everton
Biggest Away Defeat:	2-6 v Chelsea
Biggest Home Att:	22,512 v Derby County
Smallest Home Att:	18,642 v West Ham United
Average Attendance:	20,974 (15th)
Leading Scorer:	4 – Kevin Ball, Michael Gray, Craig Russell

All-Time Records

Record FAPL Win:	3-0 v Chelsea, 15/12/96
Record FAPL Defeat:	2-6 v Chelsea, 16/3/97
Record FL Win:	9-1 v Newcastle United (away), Div.1, 5/12/08
Record FL Defeat:	0-8 v West Ham United, Div. 1, 19/10/68 *and*
	0-8 v Watford Div. 1, 25/9/82
Record Cup Win:	11-1 v Fairfield, FA Cup 1st Rd, 2/2/1895
Record Fee Received:	£1.5m from C. Palace for Marco Gabbiadini, 9/91
Record Fee Paid:	£1.3m to Manchester City for Niall Quinn, 8/96
Most FL Apps:	Jim Montgomery, 537, 1966-77
Most FAPL Apps:	38 – Paul Bracewell, 1996-97
Most FAPL Goals:	4 Kevin Ball and Craig Russell, 1996-97

Highest Scorer in FAPL Season: 4 – Kevin Ball, Michael Gray
and Craig Russell, all 1996-97

Record Attendance (all-time): 75,118 v Derby County, FA Cup 6RR, 8/3/33

Record Attendance (FAPL): 22,512 v Derby County, 26/12/96

Most FAPL Goals in Season: 35, 1996-97 – 38 games

Most FAPL Points in Season: 40, 1996-97 – 38 games

Player	Tot	St	Sb	Snu	PS	Gls	Y	R	Fa	La	Fg	Lg
AGNEW	15	11	4	4	4	2	2	0	1	2	0	0
AISTON	2	0	2	9	0	0	0	0	2	0	0	0
BALL	32	32	0	0	2	3	5	0	0	3	0	1
BRACEWELL	38	38	0	0	6	0	3	0	1	2	0	0
BRIDGES	24	10	14	5	9	3	3	0	2	2	0	0
COTON	10	10	0	0	1	0	0	0	0	2	0	0
ERIKSSON	1	1	0	9	0	0	1	0	0	0	0	0
GRAY	35	32	3	3	9	3	4	0	2	2	1	0
HALL	32	32	0	6	5	0	1	0	2	3	0	0
HECKINGBOTTOM	0	0	0	4	0	0	0	0	0	0	0	0
HOLLOWAY	0	0	0	1	0	0	0	0	0	0	0	0
HOWEY	12	9	3	8	1	0	1	0	0	0	0	0
JOHNSTON	6	4	2	0	3	1	0	0	0	0	0	0
KELLY	24	23	1	3	3	0	4	0	2	2	0	0
KUBICKI	29	28	1	2	3	0	3	0	2	1	0	0
MELVILLE	30	30	0	0	0	1	2	0	2	3	0	0
MULLIN	10	9	1	1	4	1	2	0	2	0	0	0
NAISBETT	0	0	0	1	0	0	0	0	0	0	0	0
ORD	33	33	0	0	0	2	3	2	2	3	0	0
PEREZ	29	28	1	8	0	0	2	0	2	1	0	0
PICKERING	0	0	0	1	0	0	0	0	0	0	0	0
PREECE	0	0	0	22	0	0	0	0	0	0	0	0
QUINN	12	8	4	1	4	3	2	0	0	1	0	1
RAE	22	12	10	6	5	3	6	0	0	2	0	1
RUSSELL	29	10	19	3	3	4	1	0	2	3	0	0
SCOTT	15	15	0	0	0	1	4	1	0	2	0	1
SMITH	10	6	4	8	3	0	0	0	1	1	0	0
STEWART *	24	20	4	2	6	3	4	2	0	3	0	0
WADDLE	7	7	0	0	2	1	0	0	0	0	0	0
WILLIAMS	11	10	1	3	1	2	1	0	2	0	0	0
WOODS	0	0	0	6	0	0	0	0	0	0	0	0
OGs						2						

*Red card at Arsenal later withdrawn.

Grand Prix Record

Contested:	443	
Victories:	104	
Pole Positions:	79	
Fastest Laps:	69	
Constructors' World Titles:	7	(74, 84, 85, 88, 89, 90, 91)
Drivers' World Championships:	9	(74, 76, 84, 85, 86, 88, 89, 90, 91)
Most Points in a Season:	199	(1988)
Total World Championship Points: 1984.5		

Review

The 1996 season was another winless season for the Woking team who had promised much more in the lead-up to the season. Australia 1993 was the last McLaren win but there is no doubting that they have the talent and the car to get back onto the podium's top spot. Luck may be all that is lacking now – if they had had some at Monaco and also at Spa when a double top looked likely until the pace car spoiled things, they may have already turned that particular corner.

The Mercedes engine, now proven during 1996, should be one of the best in F1, rivalling the Renault and Peugeot for top-end power. Certainly improvements during last season left it looking as though it was the most potent powerplant on the track. The key now is the chassis and improvements have been made here, especially on the front wing mounting points which, it was discovered, had been flexing, which was causing downforce to fluctuate.

What McLaren do have is a talented drive duo of Mika Hakkinen and David Coulthard. Few can have anything but admiration for the way Mika Hakkinen recovered from the huge practice accident he had at Adelaide at the end of 1995. Many observers had written off his chances of racing competitively again. He proved them wrong and only failed to finish in four of his 16 races, and in 10 of those 12 races he finished in the points, amassing 31 in all – his best season ever!

After a season at the front with Williams, David Coulthard moved to McLaren with great hopes for 1996. In general when the car ran well so did Coulthard and his blinding starts, especially at Imola where he grabbed the lead from fourth on the grid, were an eye-catcher.

The MP4-12 is the designation of the 1997 car which incorporates numerous design innovations. In line with the updated FIA technical regulations the MP4-12 features a rear impact zone, collapsible steering column, reduced winglets areas and suspension designed within the limited aspect ratios designated by the technical regulations. The design is similar to that introduced at the Belgian Grand Prix in 1996.

There have also been a range of aerodynamic changes and further use of composites within the rear suspension. A newly packaged version of the longitudinal transmission introduced in 1996 will be in place for a second season and the cooling system philosophy has also been changed to capitalise on internal air flow.

For 1997 McLaren are without their almost symbolic red and white livery and Marlboro sponsor (whose name can now be found on the Ferrari). A bright (very bright) orange (shades of the early 1996 Jordan?) will distinguish the West McLaren Mercedes on the circuit. West are a tobacco brand of the Reemstma company. With a change of sponsor may come the change in fortunes that McLaren seeks.

Drivers and Results 1996

Driver	Races	Com	Ret	Dnq	HP	Pts	Psn	Comp%
David Coulthard	16	9	7	0	2	18	7/16	56.25
Mika Hakkinen	16	12	4	0	3	31	5/16	75.00

Grand Prix	David Coulthard	Mika Hakkinen
Australian	Retired	5th
Brazilian	Retired	4th
Argentinian	7th	Retired
European	3rd	8th
San Marino	Retired	8th
Monaco	2nd	Retired
Spanish	Retired	5th
Canadian	4th	5th
French	6th	5th
British	5th	3rd
German	5th	Retired
Hungarian	Retired	4th
Belgian	Retired	3rd
Italian	Retired	3rd
Portuguese	13th	Retired
Japanese	8th	3rd

McLaren MP4-12 Specifications

Engine:	Mercedes-Benz
Type:	V10 (75 degree)
Cylinders:	10 – 4 valves per cylinder
Injection:	TAG 2000 electronic system
Oil:	Mobil 1
Dimensions:	590mm (length), 546.4mm (width), 483mm (height)

Sad Finale for Roker Park

Manager Peter Reid was determined to see that Sunderland did not repeat their previous visit to the top division, which expired after just one season. Ten signings were completed pre-season with Niall Quinn the most expensive at £1.3m and goalkeeper Lionel Perez, at £200,000, possibly the most successful. One of four players to leave was Gordon Armstrong after 349 league games for the Rokermen. On their way to promotion the previous season, Sunderland conceded just 33 goals and the omens were good early on in their Premiership life, with just four goals conceded and two games lost from the first seven. But they were having problems finding the net. Two draws and a win had Sunderland inside the top five after a week but a win over Coventry on 21 September was needed to stay in the top ten.

It was to be the last time Sunderland were so highly placed but they did not fill one of the relegation spots until, crucially, the final three weeks of the season. Reid's side was probably the most inconsistent in the Premier League in that they never once won two consecutive games. Excellent away wins at Everton and Middlesbrough, in November and April, were immediately devalued by home reversals against Wimbledon and Southampton, the latter result giving the Saints a lifeline and making Sunderland's plight distinctly gloomy.

This was Sunderland's final season at Roker Park and it was good form on home soil around the turn of the year which offered the best hope for survival as the club went five games undefeated, which included a 1-0 victory over Arsenal. It was only from February that Sunderland began to slide into genuine difficulty. Four successive matches were lost, the first three 1-0 before Spurs handed out a 4-0 thrashing at Roker Park. Draws with Forest and neighbours Newcastle kept Sunderland just above the safety line but, with four games remaining, a 2-1 defeat at Liverpool plunged them into the bottom three for the first time. A lifeline appeared to have been grabbed with victory at Middlesbrough but a home defeat by Southampton piled on the agony. Sunderland's association with Roker Park closed on 3 May with a resounding 3-0 win over Everton to complete their sole double of the season. Chris Waddle, a late season £75,000 buy from Bradford, scored his only goal for the club he supported as a boy. But it was not enough to stave off relegation as an 85th-minute goal at Wimbledon on the last day of the season, coupled with Coventry's win at Tottenham, sent Sunderland down.

Some of Sunderland's early-season problems were self-inflicted with Richard Ord being dismissed at Derby and both Martin Scott and Paul Stewart, the latter harshly, departing during a 2-0 defeat at Arsenal. Stewart was also dismissed on his return to one of his former clubs, Spurs. Reid was called before the FA to explain certain comments directed at the referee in the Arsenal game. Injury ruled out Quinn for much of the season and Tony Coton was also sidelined with a double fracture. This at least allowed Frenchman Perez to enjoy a personally impressive season. Local youngster Michael Bridges was another to suggest that Sunderland's absence from the top flight could be short-lived.

In a gritty display at Highbury in the 3rd Round of the FA Cup the Rokermen dragged Arsenal back to the north-east. Arsenal, however, made no mistake in the replay. Watford were beaten in both legs of Sunderland's 2nd Round Coca-Cola Cup tie but the path to Wembley was blocked at Tottenham in Round Three – the first of three defeats against Spurs during the season. ■

Results 1996-97

FA Carling Premiership

Date	Opponents	Ven	Res	Pos	Atten	Scorers
17-Aug	Leicester C.	H	0-0	–	19,262	
21-Aug	N. Forest	A	4-1	–	22,874	Gray (7); Quinn (16, 31); Ord (42)
24-Aug	Liverpool	A	0-0	5	40,503	
04-Sep	Newcastle Utd	H	1-2	10	22,037	Scott (20 pen)
08-Sep	West Ham Utd	H	0-0	10	18,642	
14-Sep	Derby Co.	A	0-1	13	17,692	
21-Sep	Coventry C.	H	1-0	10	19,459	Agnew (51)
28-Sep	Arsenal	A	0-2	12	38,016	
14-Oct	Middlesbrough	H	2-2	15	20,936	Rae (21 pen); Russell (61)
19-Oct	Southampton	A	0-3	15	15,225	
26-Oct	Aston Villa	H	1-0	13	21,059	Stewart (25)
02-Nov	Leeds Utd	A	0-3	16	31,667	
16-Nov	Tottenham H.	A	0-2	16	31,867	
23-Nov	Sheffield W.	H	1-1	16	20,644	Melville (68)
30-Nov	Everton	A	3-1	12	40,087	Russell (54); Bridges (74, 87)
07-Dec	Wimbledon	H	1-3	14	19,672	Rae (53)
14-Dec	Chelsea	H	3-0	14	19,683	OG (30, Duberry); Ball (48); Russell (67)
21-Dec	Man. Utd	A	0-5	14	55,081	
26-Dec	Derby Co.	H	2-0	11	22,512	Ord (73); Russell (87)
28-Dec	West Ham Utd	A	0-2	13	24,077	
01-Jan	Coventry C.	A	2-2	11	17,700	Bridges (6); Agnew (18 pen)
11-Jan	Arsenal	H	1-0	11	21,154	OG (66, Adams)
18-Jan	Blackburn R.	H	0-0	12	20,850	
29-Jan	Leicester C.	A	1-1	11	17,883	Williams (18)
01-Feb	Aston Villa	A	0-1	12	32,491	
22-Feb	Leeds Utd	H	0-1	14	21,890	
01-Mar	Blackburn R.	A	0-1	15	24,208	
04-Mar	Tottenham H.	H	0-4	15	20,785	
08-Mar	Man. Utd	H	2-1	15	22,225	Gray (52); Mullin (76)
12-Mar	Sheffield W.	A	1-2	15	20,294	Ball (28)
16-Mar	Chelsea	A	2-6	15	24,027	Stewart (57); Rae (59)
22-Mar	N. Forest	H	1-1	16	22,120	Ball (61)
05-Apr	Newcastle Utd	A	1-1	15	36,582	Gray (31)
13-Apr	Liverpool	H	1-2	15	21,938	Stewart (52)
19-Apr	Middlesbrough	A	1-0	16	30,106	Williams (45)
22-Apr	Southampton	H	0-1	17	21,521	
03-May	Everton	H	3-0	17	22,108	Stewart (35); Waddle (57); Johnston (68)
11-May	Wimbledon	A	0-1	18	21,338	

FA Challenge Cup

Date	Opponents	Vn	Rnd	Res	Atten	Scorers
04-Jan	Arsenal	A	3R	1-1	37,793	Gray (20)
15-Jan	Arsenal	H	3RR	0-2	15,277	

Coca-Cola League Cup

Date	Opponents	Vn	Rnd	Res	Atten	Scorers
18-Sep	Watford	A	2R1L	2-0	9,136	Quinn (10); Rae (34)
24-Sep	Watford	H	2R2R	1-0	10,659	Scott (6)
	Sunderland win 3-0 on aggregate.					
23-Oct	Tottenham H.	A	3R	1-2	24,867	Ball (30)

Sunderland – Premiership Fact File

- Sunderland had three sent off at Highbury. Manager Peter Reid was shown the red card following the dismissals of Scott and Stewart. Stewart later had his red card rescinded.
- Sunderland lost more away games than any other team during the season – 12 in all. Their total of 18 defeats was only matched by Tottenham who finished in 10th position.
- Paul Bracewell featured in all 38 of Sunderland's Premiership games.

5-Year Record

	Div.	P	W	D	L	F	A	Pts	Pos	FAC	FLC
92-93	1	46	13	11	22	50	64	50	21	4	1
93-94	1	46	19	8	19	54	57	65	12	4	3
94-95	1	46	12	18	16	41	45	54	20	4	2
95-96	1	46	22	17	7	59	33	83	1	3	2
96-97	PL	38	10	10	18	35	53	40	18	3	3

Appearance Totals

Team	Tot	St	Sb	Snu	PS	Gls	Y	R	Fa	La	Fg	Lg
Arsenal	484	418	66	124	66	62	85	3	35	38	3	8
Aston Villa	472	418	54	136	54	47	55	2	36	25	4	2
Blackburn Rvrs ...	478	418	60	130	60	42	64	1	25	40	2	4
Chelsea	489	418	71	119	71	58	74	1	87	36	19	6
Coventry City	478	418	60	130	60	38	52	1	48	46	6	4
Derby County	505	418	87	103	87	45	62	0	62	62	8	2
Everton	474	418	56	134	56	44	57	2	24	24	5	3
Leeds United	473	418	55	135	55	28	78	1	48	36	6	5
Leicester City	482	418	64	126	64	46	50	1	49	115	6	12
Liverpool	462	418	44	146	44	62	45	1	24	46	3	10
Manchester Utd ...	493	418	75	115	75	76	57	1	39	27	3	2
Middlesbrough ...	465	418	47	142	47	51	75	1	89	111	18	23
Newcastle Utd ...	472	418	54	135	54	73	54	2	41	25	4	2
N. Forest	482	418	64	126	64	31	63	0	39	36	4	3
Sheffield W.	510	418	92	98	92	50	50	3	49	22	10	1
Southampton	472	418	54	136	54	47	55	4	36	25	4	2
Sunderland	492	418	74	116	74	35	54	5	27	38	1	4
Tottenham H.	481	418	63	127	63	44	64	0	11	47	0	7
West Ham Utd ...	500	418	82	108	82	39	67	1	23	62	1	8
Wimbledon	491	418	73	117	73	49	38	1	90	101	9	9

KEY TO CLUB DIRECTORY ABBREVIATIONS
Stats relating to FA Carling Premiership Season

Tot	Total appearances in season – this is St + Sb.
St	Total number of times player was in starting line-up.
Sb	Total number of times player came on as sub.
Snu	Total number of times player was sub but not used (Sub not used).
PS	Total number of times player was substituted (Player Subbed).
Gls	Total number of goals scored.
Y	Total number of Yellow cards received.
R	Total number of Red cards received. (Note: A red card issued due to a second yellow card is recorded as 1Y and 1R.)
Fa/La	Total number of appearances in FA Cup and League Cup.
Fg/Lg	Total number of goals scored in FA Cup and League Cup.
†	Player no longer with club at time of going to press.

FA PREMIER LEAGUE CLUB TRANSFERS 1996-97

August 1996

Player	From	To	Fee
Fabrizio Ravanelli	Juventus	Middlesbrough	£7,000,000
Lee Sharpe	Manchester United	Leeds United	£4,500,000
Sasa Curcic	Bolton Wanderers	Aston Villa	£4,000,000
Emerson	FC Porto	Middlesbrough	£4,000,000
Karel Poborsky	Slavia Prague	Manchester United	£3,500,000
Patrick Vieira	Milan	Arsenal	£3,500,000
Patrik Berger	B. Dortmund	Liverpool	£3,250,000
Florin Raducioiu	Espanyol	West Ham United	£2,400,000
Ole Gunnar Solskjaer	Molde	Manchester United	£1,500,000
Jordi Cruyff	Barcelona	Manchester United	£1,400,000
Niall Quinn	Manchester City	Sunderland	£1,300,000
Regis Genaux	Standard Liege	Coventry City	£1,000,000
Paul Gerrard	Oldham Athletic	Everton	£1,000,000
			Rising to £1,500,000
Christian Dailly	Dundee United	Derby County	£1,000,000
Paul Dickov	Arsenal	Manchester City	£1,000,000
Kasey Keller	Millwall	Leicester City	£900,000
Ian Marshall	Ipswich Town	Leicester City	£800,000
Orlando Trustfull	Feyenoord	Sheffield Wednesday	£750,000
Spencer Prior	Norwich City	Leicester City	£600,000
Scott Oakes	Luton Town	Sheffield Wednesday	£425,000
			Rising to £750,000
Ally Pickering	Coventry City	Stoke City	£280,000
Graham Potter	Stoke City	Southampton	£250,000
			Rising to £500,000
Robbie Slater	West Ham Utd	Southampton	£250,000
Chris Day	Tottenham Hotspur	Crystal Palace	£225,000
		Rising to £425,000 plus £100,000 on an England appearance	
Lionel Perez	Bordeaux	Sunderland	£200,000
Anthony Barness	Chelsea	Charlton Athletic	£165,000
Richard Dryden	Bristol City	Southampton	£150,000
Jaime Moreno	Middlesbrough	Washington	£100,000
Richard Baker	Sheffield Wednesday	Linfield	£40,000
Scott Canham	West Ham Utd	Brentford	£25,000
			Rising to £60,000

Brian Atkinson	Sunderland	Darlington	Free
Mikkel Beck	Fortuna Cologne	Middlesbrough	Free
Mark Blake	Leicester City	Walsall	Free
Iain Brunskill	Liverpool	Bury	Free
Lee Bryden	Liverpool	Darlington	Free
Chris Coffey	Arsenal	Crewe Alexandra	Free
David Faulkner	Sheffield Wednesday	Darlington	Free
Remi Garde	Strasbourg	Arsenal	Free
Dale Gordon	West Ham United	Bournemouth	Free
Jonathan Gould	Coventry City	Bradford	Free
Bruce Grobbelaar	Southampton	Plymouth Argyle	Free
Michael Holt	Blackburn Rovers	Preston NE	Free
Jorvan Kirovski	Manchester United	Borussia Dortmund	Free
David Lamour	Liverpool	Doncaster	Free
Alvin Martin	West Ham United	Leyton Orient	Free
Darren Mowbray	Middlesbrough	Scarborough	Free
Steve Pears	Liverpool	Hartlepool	Free
David Preece	Derby County	Cambridge United	Free
Zeke Rowe	Chelsea	Peterborough United	Free
Nigel Spackman	Chelsea	Sheffield United	Free
Steve Sutton	Derby County	Birmingham City	Free
Matthew Woods	Everton	Chester City	Free
Russell Kelly	Chelsea	Darlington	Non-Contract
Bobby Mimms	Blackburn Rovers	Crystal Palace	Non-Contract
Hans Segers	Wimbledon	Wolverhampton W.	Non-Contract
Neil Webb	Nottingham Forest	Grimsby Town	Non-Contract

September 1996

Player	From	To	Fee
Eyal Berkovitch	Maccabi Tel Aviv	Southampton	£1,000,000
Egil Ostenstad	Viking Stavanger	Southampton	£800,000
Gerard McMahon	Tottenham Hotspur	Stoke City	£450,000
Claus Lundekvam	SK Brann	Southampton	£400,000
Graham Kavanagh	Middlesbrough	Stoke City	£250,000
		Plus £250,000 after 50 appearances	
Andy Turner	Tottenham Hotspur	Portsmouth	£250,000
Gary Elkins	Wimbledon	Swindon Town	£100,000
Dave Hercock	Cambridge City	Sheffield Wednesday	Free
		Five-figure fee after 10 appearances	
Chris Knight	Everton	Erith & Bel.	Free
Sascha Lennart	Royal Antwerp	Leicester City	Free
Jamie Pollock	Middlesbrough	Osasuna	Free
Chris Waddle	Sheffield Wednesday	Falkirk	Free
Russell Watkinson	Woking	Southampton	Free
Andrew Mitchell	Aston Villa	Chesterfield	Non-Contract

246

October 1996

Player	From	To	Fee
Nick Barmby	Middlesbrough	Everton	£5,750,000
Benito Carbone	Internazionale	Sheffield Wednesday	£3,000,000
Ulrich van Gobbel	Galatasaray	Southampton	£1,300,000
Neil Shipperley	Southampton	Crystal Palace	£1,000,000
Tony Cottee	West Ham United	Selangor	£750,000
Chris Holland	Newcastle United	Birmingham City	£600,000
Eddie McGoldrick	Arsenal	Manchester City	£300,000
John Hendrie	Middlesbrough	Barnsley	£250,000
Adrian Whitbread	West Ham Utd	Portsmouth	£250,000
Paul McGrath	Aston Villa	Derby County	£100,000
			Rising to £200,000
Darren Williams	York City	Sunderland	£50,000
Franz Carr	Aston Villa	Reggiana	Free
Paul Sykes	Sheffield Wednesday	Bradford PA	Free
Branco	Middlesbrough	Released	
Paul Parker	Derby County	Released	
Jason Kearton	Everton	Crewe Alex.	Non-Contract
Stuart Slater	Ipswich Town	Leicester City	Non-Contract
Lee Farrell	Lincoln City	Leicester City	Monthly Contract
Mark Flatts	Arsenal	Watford	Monthly Contract

November 1996

Player	From	To	Fee
Gianfranco Zola	Parma	Chelsea	£4,500,000
John Spencer	Chelsea	QPR	£2,500,000
Steffen Iversen	Rosenborg	Tottenham Hotspur	£2,700,000
Jamie Pollock	Middlesbrough	Bolton Wanderers	£1,500,000
	Rejoined Middlesbrough from Osasuna on technicality before joining Bolton		
Darren Huckerby	Newcastle United	Coventry City	£1,000,000
Neil Heaney	Southampton	Manchester City	£500,000
Matt Jackson	Everton	Birmingham City	£500,000
David Hillier	Arsenal	Portsmouth	£250,000
Jason Cundy	Tottenham Hotspur	Ipswich Town	£200,000
Brett Angell	Sunderland	Stockport County	£120,000
Scott Mean	Bournemouth	West Ham United	£100,000
Jason Kavanagh	Derby County	Wycombe Wanderers	£20,000
Frankie Bennett	Southampton	Bristol Rovers	£15,000
Frode Grodas	Lillestroem	Chelsea	Free
Jason Kearton	Everton	Crewe Alex.	Free
Tommy Knarvik	IL Skjerjard	Leeds United	Free
Peter Holcroft	Everton	Swindon Town	Free

Les Sealey	Leyton Orient	West Ham United	Free
Aly Dia	(no club)	Southampton	Monthly Contract
Paul Parker	Derby County	Sheffield United	Monthly Contract
Peter Shilton	West Ham Utd	Leyton Orient	Monthly Contract

December 1996

Player	From	To	Fee
John Scales	Liverpool	Tottenham Hotspur	£2,600,000
Terry Phelan	Chelsea	Everton	£850,000
Ilie Dumitrescu	West Ham United	Club America	£800,000
Gavin Peacock	Chelsea	QPR	£800,000
			Rising to £1,000,000
Vinny Samways	Everton	Las Palmas	£600,000
Maik Taylor	Barnet	Southampton	£500,000
Gunnar Halle	Oldham Athletic	Leeds United	£400,000
John Sheridan	Sheffield Wednesday	Bolton Wanderers	£180,000
Phil Charnock	Liverpool	Crewe Alexandra	Unknown
Ian Ashbee	Derby County	Cambridge United	Free
Ashley Neal	Liverpool	Huddersfield Town	Free
Noel Imber	Arsenal	Woking	Free
Sam Stockley-Phillips	Southampton	Barnet	Free

January 1997

Player	From	To	Fee
Andrei Kanchelskis	Everton	Fiorentina	£8,000,000
Ramon Vega	Cagliari	Tottenham Hotspur	£3,750,000
Gianluca Festa	Internazionale	Middlesbrough	£2,700,000
Gary Breen	Birmingham City	Coventry City	£2,500,000
Matt Elliot	Oxford United	Leicester City	£1,600,000
Florin Raducioiu	West Ham United	Espanyol	£1,600,000
Vladimir Kinder	Slovan Bratislava	Middlesbrough	£1,000,000
Robert Molenaar	FC Volendam	Leeds United	£1,000,000
Claus Thomsen	Ipswich Town	Everton	£900,000
Reggie Genaux	Coventry City	Udinese	£800,000
Alex Evtushok	Dnepr	Coventry City	£800,000
Jan Aage Fjortoft	Middlesbrough	Sheffield United	£700,000
Gordon Watson	Southampton	Bradford City	£550,000
Jan Eriksson	Helsingborg	Sunderland	£250,000
Andy Linighan	Arsenal	Crystal Palace	£110,000
Anders Limpar	Everton	Birmingham City	£100,000
Kenny Brown	West Ham United	Birmingham City	£75,000
Mark Bright	Sheffield Wednesday	Sion	£70,000
Paul Read	Arsenal	Wycombe Wanderers	£35,000

Danny Shipp	West Ham United	Coleraine	£30,000
Nicolas Anelka	Paris St Germain	Arsenal	Undisclosed
Will Davies	Derby County	Cobh Rangers	Free
Phil Gee	Leicester City	Hednesford Town	Free
Bjorn Tore Kvarme	Rosenborg	Liverpool	Free
Neil Moore	Everton	Norwich City	Free

February 1997

Player	From	To	Fee
John Hartson	Arsenal	West Ham United	£3,200,000
			Could rise to £5,000,000
Per Pederson	OB	Blackburn Rovers	£2,500,000
Paul Kitson	Newcastle United	West Ham United	£2,300,000
Mark Schwarzer	Bradford City	Middlesbrough	£1,500,000
John Ebbrell	Everton	Sheffield United	£1,000,000
Steve Guppy	Port Vale	Leicester City	£850,000
			Could rise to £1,000,000
Robert Ullathorne	Osasuna	Leicester City	£600,000
Paul Beesley	Leeds United	Manchester City	£500,000
Steve Jones	West Ham United	Charlton Athletic	£400,000
Kevin Scott	Tottenham Hotspur	Norwich City	£250,000
Graham Potter	Southampton	WBA	£150,000
			Could rise to £300,000
Nathan Blamey	Southampton	Shrewsbury Town	Free
Robert Bowman	Leeds United	Rotherham United	Free
Stephen Brodie	Sunderland	Scarborough	Free
Richard Hope	Blackburn Rovers	Darlington	Free
Fabio Moreira	No club	Middlesbrough	Free
Paul Hyde	Leicester City	Leyton Orient	Non-Contract
			Returned to Leicester City

March 1997

Player	From	To	Fee
Pierre van Hooijdonk	Celtic	Nottingham Forest	£3,500,000
			Rising to £4,500,000
Celestine Babayaro	Anderlecht	Chelsea	£2,250,000
			Signed in April but joining in July
Steve Lomas	Manchester City	West Ham United	£1,600,000
			May rise to £2,000,000
Des Hamilton	Bradford City	Newcastle United	£1,500,000
			Plus £8,000 per game to a maximum of £800,000
Ian Moore	Tranmere Rovers	Nottingham Forest	£750,000
Carl Tiler	Aston Villa	Sheffield United	£650,000

Paulo Wanchope	CS Heridiano	Derby County	£600,000
Mauricio Solis	CS Heridiano	Derby County	£600,000
Allan Johnston	Rennes	Sunderland	£550,000
David Billington	Peterborough United	Sheffield Wednesday	£500,000
		May rise to £1,000,000	
Bjarni Gudjonsson	IA Akranes	Newcastle United	£500,000
Mart Poom	FC Flora Tallinn	Derby County	£500,000
Mike Evans	Plymouth Argyle	Southampton	£500,000
Pierre Laurent	Bastia	Leeds United	£500,000
Derek Lilley	Greenock Morton	Leeds United	£500,000
		May rise to £700,000	
Alex Manninger	Casino Salzburg	Arsenal	£500,000
		Signed in March, but joined club in July	
Alan Miller	Middlesbrough	WBA	£500,000
Steve Morrow	Arsenal	QPR	£500,000
Tommy Wright	Nottingham Forest	Manchester City	£450,000
Jorgen Nielsen	Hvidovre	Liverpool	£400,000
Danny Granville	Cambridge United	Chelsea	£300,000
Steve Mauntone	West Ham United	Reading	£250,000
Kim Hieselberg	Esbjerg FB	Sunderland	£125,000
Keith O'Halloran	Middlesbrough	St Johnstone	£50,000
Chris Waddle	Bradford City	Sunderland	£75,000
Mark Tinkler	Leeds United	York City	Undisclosed
Mark Bowen	West Ham United	Shimizu S-Pulse	Free
Paul Hyde	Leicester City	Leyton Orient	Free
Phil King	Aston Villa	Swindon Town	Free
Paul Parker	Fulham	Chelsea	Free
Sam Sharman	Sheffield Wednesday	Hull City	Free
Chris Woods	USSF	Sunderland	Free

May 1997

Player	From	To	Fee
Stan Collymore	Liverpool	Aston Villa	£7,000,000
Slaven Bilic	West Ham United	Everton	£4,500,000
Anton Drobnjak	Bastia	Leeds United	£4,000,000
Neil Cox	Middlesbrough	Bolton Wanderers	£1,500,000
Mathew Upson	Luton Town	Arsenal	£1,000,000
David Robertson	Rangers	Leeds United	£500,000
Mathew Rose	Arsenal	QPR	£500,000
Jonathan Hunt	Birmingham City	Derby County	£500,000
Darren Wassall	Derby County	Birmingham City	£100,000
Gustavo Poyet	Real Zaragoza	Chelsea	Free
Tore Andre Flo	SK Brann	Chelsea	tbc
Shay Given	Blackburn Rovers	Newcastle United	Contested
Stefano Eranio	Milan	Derby County	Free

Summer 1997

Marc Overmars	Ajax	Arsenal	£7,000,000
Paul Merson	Arsenal	Middlesbrough	£5,000,000
Teddy Sheringham	Tottenham Hotspur	Manchester United	£3,500,000
Oyvind Leonhardsen	Wimbledon	Liverpool	£3,500,000
Emmanuel Petit	Monaco	Arsenal	£3,000,000
Lee Clark	Newcastle United	Sunderland	£2,500,000
Ed De Gouy	Feyenoord	Chelsea	£2,250,000
Gilles Grimandi	Monaco	Arsenal	£2,000,000
Jimmy Floyd Hasselbaink			
	Boavista	Leeds United	£2,000,000
Eyal Berkovic	Southampton	West Ham United	£1,750,000
Luis Boamorte	Sporting Lisbon	Arsenal	£1,750,000
Bernard Lambourde	Bordeaux	Chelsea	£1,500,000
Gjorgi Hristov	Partizan Belgrade	Barnsley	£1,500,000
Kevin Miller	Watford	Crystal Palace	£1,550,000
Andrew Impey	QPR	West Ham United	£1,200,000
Mark Tinker	Cagliari	Barnsley	£650,000
Bruno Riberio	Vitoria Sctubal	Leeds United	£500,000
Ales Krizan	Maribor Branik	Barnsley	£450,000
Ceri Hughes	Luton Town	Wimbledon	£400,000
Lars Lees	Bayer Leverkusen	Barnsley	£250,000
Alf Inge Haarland	Nottingham Forest	Leeds United	Tribunal
Simon Grayson	Leicester City	Aston Villa	Tribunal
Gareth Farrelly	Aston Villa	Everton	Tribunal
Scott Minto	Chelsea	Benfica	Free
Alberto Mendez Rodriguez			
	FC Feucht (Germany)	Arsenal	Free
Lee Harper	Arsenal	QPR	tba

PLAYER LOANS 1996-97

August 1996

Player	From	To
Player	*From*	*To*
Tomas Brolin	Leeds United	FZ Zurich
Mark Hateley	QPR	Leeds United
Ben Roberts	Middlesbrough	Lincoln City

September 1996

Michael Barron	Middlesbrough	Hartlepool
Kenny Brown	West Ham United	Reading
David Burt	Newcastle United	Scunthorpe United
Phil Charnock	Liverpool	Crewe Alex.
James Crawford	Newcastle United	Rotherham United
Stuart Elliot	Newcastle United	Scunthorpe United
Chris Freestone	Middlesbrough	Preston NE
Frode Grodas	Lillestroem	Chelsea
Lee Hodges	West Ham United	Exeter City
Chris Holland	Newcastle United	Birmingham City
Darren Huckerby	Newcastle United	Millwall
Patrick McGibbon	Manchester United	Swansea City
Eddie McGoldrick	Arsenal	Manchester City
Steve Mauntone	West Ham United	Crewe Alex.
Ashley Neal	Liverpool	Brighton & HA
Emmanuel Omoyimni	West Ham United	Bournemouth
Hugo Porfirio	Sporting Lisbon	West Ham United
Malcolm Rigby	Nottingham Forest	Ilkeston Town
Wayne Sutton	Derby County	Hereford United
Martin Taylor	Derby County	Manchester City

October 1996

Craig Armstrong	Nottingham Forest	Notts County
Frankie Bennett	Southampton	Shrewsbury
Jason Cundy	Tottenham Hotspur	Ipswich Town
Simon Davis	Manchester United	Huddersfield Town
Neil Davis	Aston Villa	Wycombe Wanderers
Scott Fitzgerald	Wimbledon	Millwall
Marco Gabbiadini	Derby County	Birmingham City
Noel Imber	Chelsea	Stevenage Borough
Matt Jackson	Everton	Birmingham City
Craig Ludlam	Sheffield United	Notts County
John O'Kane	Manchester United	Bury
Grant Payne	Wimbledon	Woking

Player	From	To
Mark Robins	Leicester City	FC Copenhagen
Andrea Silenzi	Nottingham Forest	Vicenza
Mark Summerbell	Middlesbrough	Cork
Paul Trollope	Derby County	Crystal Palace
Robin Van der Laan	Derby County	Wolverhampton W.
Michael Williams	Sheffield Wednesday	Huddersfield Town
Chris Woods	Colorado Rapids	Southampton
Tommy Wright	Nottingham Forest	Reading

November 1996

Clayton Blackmore	Middlesbrough	Bristol City
Iyseden Christie	Coventry City	Bournemouth
Terry Cooke	Manchester United	Birmingham City
Rio Ferdinand	West Ham United	Bournemouth
Steven Harper	Newcastle United	Gateshead
Glenn Helder	Arsenal	Benfica
David Kerslake	Tottenham Hotspur	Swindon Town
Keith O'Halloran	Middlesbrough	Cardiff City
Shane O'Neill	Coventry City	Hereford United
Gavin Peacock	Chelsea	QPR
John Sheridan	Sheffield Wednesday	Bolton Wanderers
Mark Stein	Chelsea	Stoke City
Paul Tisdale	Southampton	Huddersfield Town

December 1996

Mark Bright	Sheffield Wednesday	Millwall
Stephen Brodie	Sunderland	Scarborough United
Kenny Brown	West Ham United	Birmingham City
Adrian Clarke	Arsenal	Rotherham United
Nigel Clough	Manchester City	Nottingham Forest
Scott Fitzgerald	Wimbledon	Millwall
Steve Harper	Newcastle United	Gateshead
Chris Kiwomya	Arsenal	Le Havre
Mike Newell	Birmingham City	West Ham United
Kevin Scott	Tottenham Hotspur	Charlton Athletic
Ian Selley	Arsenal	Southend
Paul Simpson	Derby County	Sheffield United

January 1997

Craig Armstrong	Nottingham Forest	Watford
Paul Brayson	Newcastle United	Swansea City
Tomas Brolin	Leeds United	Parma
		Parma paying £300,000 fee for loan
Marlon Broomes	Blackburn Rovers	Swindon Town

253

Player	From	To
Jamie Clapton	Tottenham Hotspur	Leyton Orient
John Hills	Everton	Swansea City
Marco Gabbiadini	Derby County	Oxford United
Richard Hope	Blackburn Rovers	Darlington
Stephen Howe	Nottingham Forest	Ipswich Town
Lee Jones	Liverpool	Wrexham
Sam McMahon	Leicester City	Kettering Town
Alan Miller	Middlesbrough	Huddersfield Town
John O'Kane	Manchester United	Bury
Kevin Pilkington	Manchester United	Rotherham United
Marino Rhamberg	Degerfors	Derby County
David Rocastle	Chelsea	Norwich City
Kevin Scott	Tottenham Hotspur	Norwich City
Paul Tisdale	Southampton	Ipswich Town
Tommy Wright	Nottingham Forest	Manchester City

February 1997

Sam Aiston	Sunderland	Chester City
Vince Bartram	Arsenal	Wolverhampton W.
Iyseden Christie	Coventry City	Mansfield Town
Carl Cort	Wimbledon	Lincoln City
Stuart Elliot	Newcastle United	Hull City
Les Hodges	West Ham United	Leyton Orient
Jason Lee	Nottingham Forest	Charlton Athletic
Steve Mautone	West Ham United	Reading
Alan Miller	Middlesbrough	WBA
Adem Poric	Sheffield Wednesday	Southend United
Chris Price	Everton	Oxford United
Adam Reed	Blackburn Rovers	Darlington
Simon Weaver	Sheffield Wednesday	Doncaster

March 1997

Sam Aiston	Sunderland	Chester City
Ian Andrews	Bournemouth	Leicester City
Craig Armstrong	Nottingham Forest	Watford
Steve Baitherwick	Nottingham Forest	Reading
Jamie Clapham	Tottenham Hotspur	Bristol Rovers
Adrian Clarke	Arsenal	Southampton
Kevin Cooper	Derby County	Stockport
Graham Coughlan	Blackburn Rovers	Swindon
Paul Evans	Leeds United	Bradford City
Tom Evans	Crystal Palace	Coventry City
Sean Flynn	Derby County	Stoke City
Craig Forrest	Ipswich Town	Chelsea
Chris Freestone	Middlesbrough	Carlisle United

Player	From	To
Niklas Gudmundsson	Blackburn Rovers	Ipswich Town
Steve Guinan	Nottingham Forest	Burnley
Steve Harper	Newcastle United	Stockport County
Lee Jones	Liverpool	Tranmere Rovers
Jason Lee	Nottingham Forest	Grimsby Town
Gavin McGowan	Arsenal	Luton Town
Paul Mahorn	Tottenham Hotspur	Brentford
Pat McGibbon	Manchester United	Bradford City
John O'Kane	Manchester United	Wrexham
Brian O'Neill	Celtic	Nottingham Forest
Martin Taylor	Derby County	Wycombe Wanderers
Christer Warren	Southampton	Fulham
Darren Wassall	Derby County	Birmingham City
Luke Weaver	Leyton Orient	West Ham United
Michael Williams	Sheffield Wednesday	Peterborough United

PLAYER TRIALS 1996-97

August 1996

Player	On Trial From	On Trial To
Gary Blissett	Wimbledon	Portsmouth
Kevin Dennis	Arsenal	Brentford
Richard Goddard-Crawley	Arsenal	Brentford
Kirk Jackson	Sheffield Wednesday	Scunthorpe

September 1996

Giorgio Bresciani	Bologna	Southampton
Franz Carr	Aston Villa	Reggiana
Thor-Andre Flo	SK Brann	Southampton
Roger Joseph	Wimbledon	Brighton
Luca Luzardi	Brescia	Tottenham Hotspur
Adie Smith	Bromsgrove Rovers	Coventry City

October 1996

Jerome Gnako	Sochaux	Sunderland
Rodney Jack	Torquay United	Newcastle United
Roger Joseph	Wimbledon	Swindon Town
Mirko Taccolo	Napoli	Coventry City
Robert Tomaschek	Slovan Bratislava	Everton

November 1996

Player	On Trial From	On Trial To
Ketil Clorius	B93	Derby County
Ronan Harazi	Beiter	Sunderland
Jan Hoffman	B93	Derby County
Bjorn Tore Kvarme	Rosenborg	Liverpool
Victor Leonenko	Dynamo Kiev	Sunderland
Eric Nevland	Viking Stavanger	Manchester United
Vinny Samways	Everton	Las Palmas
Stale Solbakken	Lillestroem	Southampton
Gary Sundgren	AIK	Sunderland

December 1996

Braatni Gudjonsson	Akranes	Newcastle United
Alexander Jewtuschok	Dnepr	Coventry City
Vladimir Kinder	Slovan Bratislava	Middlesbrough
Yuri Maximov	Dynamo Kiev	Southampton
Avi Nimni	Maccabi Tel Aviv	Chelsea
Mamado Viallo	Zeytinburnu	Sunderland
Kjetil Waehler	SF Lynn	Arsenal

January 1997

Joe Baker	Leyton Orient	Derby County
Marc Dittinger	Germany	Southampton
Ian Hendon	Leyton Orient	Sunderland
Uri Maximov	Dynamo Kiev	Southampton
Olof Mellberg	Degerfors	Newcastle United
Mirkola Taccola	Napoli	Middlesbrough
Artur Petrossian	Shimrak Gyumri	Arsenal
Richard Watson	Canberra Cos	Middlesbrough

February 1997

Bjarni Gudjonsson	IA Akranes	Newcastle Utd
Rodney Jack	Torquay United	Sunderland
Peter Lipcsei	FC Porto	Sheffield Wed
Jorgen Nielsen	Hvidovre	Liverpool
Alphonse Tchami	Boca Juniors	Sunderland
Mark Turner	Telford United	Leeds United
Gareth Whalley	Crewe Alexandra	Liverpool
Romeo Wouden	SC Heerenveen	Southampton

March 1997

Sam Bowen	Merthyr Tydfil	West Ham U
Gadi Bromer	Maccabi Tel Aviv	Manchester U
Keith Welch	Bristol City	Sunderland
Laurent Viaud	Monaco	Everton

A-Z
FA Premier League Players
1997-98

Notes: The players are listed in alphabetical order and are those who are likely to feature in the Premiership action during the 1997-98 season. As a rule, fringe players who played at least one game in 1996-97 are included. There are exceptions though – for instance, players making a large number of appearances on the bench without actually getting on the pitch. This is true for reserve goalkeepers. *Previous Clubs Details* includes all Premiership games played to date. Specific appearance details for 1996-97 can be found in the *Club Directory* section. A club with * next to it in the *Previous Clubs Details* list indicates that the figures do not include those for the 1996-97 season. NL=Non-League. When figures are given for a non-English club they refer to the relevant country's league and cup competitions.

ADAMS Tony   Arsenal
Full Name: Anthony Alexander Adams   DOB: 10-10-66 Romford, Essex
Debut: ARSENAL v Norwich City 15/8/92
Debut Goal: ARSENAL v Newcastle United 18/9/94

Previous Clubs Details

Club	Signed	Fee	Tot	Start	Sub	FA	FL	Lge	FA	FL
Arsenal	Jan-84	Amateur	395	391	4	35	57	27	5	5

FAPL Summary by Club

Club			Tot	Start	Sub	FA	FL	Lge	FA	FL
Arsenal	92-93 to 96-97		146	143	3	17	23	7	4	3
Total			*146*	*143*	*3*	*17*	*23*	*7*	*4*	*3*

ALBERT Philippe   Newcastle United
Full Name: Philippe Albert   DOB: 10-08-67 Bouillon, Belgium
Debut: Leicester City v NEWCASTLE UNITED 21/8/94
Debut Goal: NEWCASTLE UNITED v Leicester City 10/12/94

Previous Clubs Details

Club	Signed	Fee	Tot	Start	Sub	FA	FL	Lge	FA	FL
Anderlecht										
Newcastle U.	Aug-94	£2.65m	67	63	4	4	9	8	1	2

FAPL Summary by Club

Club			Tot	Start	Sub	FA	FL	Lge	FA	FL
Newcastle U.	94-95 to 96-97		67	63	4	4	9	8	1	2
Total			*67*	*63*	*4*	*4*	*9*	*8*	*1*	*2*

ALLEN Graham   Everton

Full Name: Graham Allen   DOB: 08-04-77 Franworth
Debut: Middlesbrough v EVERTON 26/12/96 as sub
Debut Goal:

Previous Clubs Details				Apps				Goals	
Club	Signed	Fee	Tot	Start	Sub	FA	FL	Lge	FA	FL
Everton			1	0	1	0	0	0	0	0
FAPL Summary by Club										
Everton	1996-97		1	0	1	0	0	0	0	0
Total			*1*	*0*	*1*	*0*	*0*	*0*	*0*	*0*

ALLEN Rory   Tottenham Hotspur

Full Name: Rory Allen   DOB: 17-10-77 Beckenham
Debut: Wimbledon v TOTTENHAM HOTSPUR 3/9/96 as sub
Debut Goal: TOTTENHAM HOTSPUR v Newcastle United 7/9/96

Previous Clubs Details				Apps				Goals	
Club	Signed	Fee	Tot	Start	Sub	FA	FL	Lge	FA	FL
Tottenham H.			12	9	3	1	3	2	0	2
FAPL Summary by Club										
Tottenham H.	1996-97		12	9	3	1	3	2	0	2
Total			*12*	*9*	*3*	*1*	*3*	*2*	*0*	*2*

ANDERSEN Leif   Crystal Palace

Full Name: Leif Erik Andersen   DOB: 19-04-71 Fredrickstad, Norway
Debut: Debut Goal:

Previous Clubs Details				Apps				Goals	
Club	Signed	Fee	Tot	Start	Sub	FA	FL	Lge	FA	FL
Moss FK										
Crystal Palace	Jan-96	£120,000	30	19	11	1	3	1	0	0

ANDERTON Darren   Tottenham Hotspur

Full Name: Darren Robert Anderton   DOB: 03-03-72 Southampton
Debut: Southampton v TOTTENHAM HOTSPUR 15/8/92
Debut Goal: TOTTENHAM HOTSPUR v Southampton 7/2/93

Previous Clubs Details				Apps				Goals	
Club	Signed	Fee	Tot	Start	Sub	FA	FL	Lge	FA	FL
Portsmouth	Feb-90		62	53	9	8	5	7	5	1
Tottenham H.	Jun-92	£1.75m	132	124	8	14	12	22	2	4
FAPL Summary by Club										
Tottenham H.	92-93 to 96-97		132	124	8	14	12	22	2	4
Total			*132*	*124*	*8*	*14*	*12*	*22*	*2*	*4*

ANELKA Nicolas   Arsenal

Full Name: Nicolas Anelka   DOB: 14-03-70 Versailles
Debut: Chelsea V ARSENAL 5/4/97 as sub
Debut Goal:

Previous Clubs Details			Apps				Goals		
Club	Signed	Fee	Tot	Start	Sub	FA	FL	Lge	FA	FL
Paris St G. *			2	0	2	0	0	0	0	0
Arsenal	Jan-97	£500,000	4	0	4	0	0	0	0	0
FAPL Summary by Club										
Arsenal		1996-97	4	0	4	0	0	0	0	0
Total			4	0	4	0	0	0	0	0

APPLEBY Matty   Barnsley

Full Name: Matthew Wilfred Appleby   DOB: 16-04-72 Middlesbrough
Debut: NEWCASTLE UNITED v Coventry City
Debut Goal:

Previous Clubs Details			Apps				Goals		
Club	Signed	Fee	Tot	Start	Sub	FA	FL	Lge	FA	FL
Newcastle U.	May-90	Trainee	20	18	2	2	3	0	0	0
Darlington	Nov-93	Loan	10	10	0	0	0	1	0	0
Darlington	Sep-94	Free	79	77	2	4	2	7	0	0
Barnsley			35	35	0	4	0	1	0	0
FAPL Summary by Club										
Newcastle U.	93-94 to 95-96		1	1	0	0	0	0	0	0
Total			1	1	0	0	0	0	0	0

ARDLEY Neal   Wimbledon

Full Name: Neal Christopher Ardley   DOB: 01-09-72 Epsom
Debut: WIMBLEDON v Arsenal 5/9/92 as sub
Debut Goal: WIMBLEDON v Blackburn Rovers 19/9/92

Previous Clubs Details			Apps				Goals		
Club	Signed	Fee	Tot	Start	Sub	FA	FL	Lge	FA	FL
Wimbledon	Jul-91		105	92	13	15	16	8	0	2
FAPL Summary by Club										
Wimbledon	92-93 to 96-97		96	84	12	15	16	8	0	2
Total			96	84	12	15	16	8	0	2

ARMSTRONG Chris   Tottenham Hotspur

Full Name: Christopher Peter Armstrong   DOB: 19-06-71 Newcastle
Debut: Manchester United v CRYSTAL PALACE 2/9/92
Debut Goal: CRYSTAL PALACE v Oldham Athletic 12/9/92

Previous Clubs Details			Apps				Goals		
Club	Signed	Fee	Tot	Start	Sub	FA	FL	Lge	FA	FL
Wrexham	Mar-89		60	40	20	1	3	13	0	0
Millwall	Aug-91	£50,000	28	11	17	1	4	5	0	2
C. Palace	Sep-92	£1m	123	123	0	12	11	43	9	9
Tottenham H.	Jul-94	£4.5m	48	48	0	6	6	20	4	4
FAPL Summary by Club										
C. Palace	92-93 to 94-95		123	123	0	12	11	43	9	9

| Tottenham H. | 95-96 to 96-97 | 48 | 48 | 0 | 6 | 6 | 20 | 4 | 4 |
| *Total* | | *171* | *171* | *0* | *18* | *17* | *63* | *13* | *13* |

ASANOVIC Aijosa   Derby County

Full Name: Aijosa Asanovic   DOB: 14-12-65 Split
Debut: DERBY COUNTY v Leeds United 17/8/96
Debut Goal:

| *Previous Clubs Details* | | | | *Apps* | | | | *Goals* | |
Club	Signed	Fee	Tot	Start	Sub	FA	FL	Lge	FA	FL
Hadjuk Split	Jul-96	£1m								
Derby County			34	34	0	3	3	6	0	0
FAPL Summary by Club										
Derby County	1996-97		34	34	0	3	3	6	0	0
Total			*34*	*34*	*0*	*3*	*3*	*6*	*0*	*0*

ASPRILLA Tino   Newcastle United

Full Name: Faustino Hernon Asprilla   DOB: 10-11-69 Colombia
Debut: Middlesbrough v NEWCASTLE UNITED 10/2/96 as sub
Debut Goal: Manchester City v NEWCASTLE UNITED 24/2/96

| *Previous Clubs Details* | | | | *Apps* | | | | *Goals* | |
Club	Signed	Fee	Tot	Start	Sub	FA	FL	Lge	FA	FL
Parma										
Newcastle U.	Feb-96	£6.7m	38	28	10	0	2	7	0	0
FAPL Summary by Club										
Newcastle U.	95-96 to 96-97		38	28	10	0	2	7	0	0
Total			*38*	*28*	*10*	*0*	*2*	*7*	*0*	*0*

ATHERTON Peter   Sheffield Wednesday

Full Name: Peter Atherton   DOB: 06-04-70 Orrell
Debut: COVENTRY CITY v Middlesbrough 15/8/92
Debut Goal: Aston Villa v SHEFFIELD WEDNESDAY 27/11/94

| *Previous Clubs Details* | | | | *Apps* | | | | *Goals* | |
Club	Signed	Fee	Tot	Start	Sub	FA	FL	Lge	FA	FL
Wigan Athletic	Feb-88		149	145	4	7	8	1	0	0
Coventry City	Aug-91	£300,000	114	113	1	2	4	0	0	0
Sheffield W.	Jun-94	£800,000	113	113	0	5	9	3	0	0
FAPL Summary by Club										
Coventry City	92-93 to 93-94		79	78	1	2	4	0	0	0
Sheffield W.	94-95 to 96-97		113	113	0	8	10	3	0	0
Total			*192*	*191*	*1*	*10*	*14*	*3*	*0*	*0*

AUSTIN Dean   Tottenham Hotspur

Full Name: Dean Barry Austin   DOB: 26-04-70 Hemel Hempstead
Debut: TOTTENHAM HOTSPUR v Crystal Palace 22/8/92
Debut Goal:

				Apps				Goals		
Previous Clubs Details										
Club	Signed	Fee	Tot	Start	Sub	FA	FL	Lge	FA	FL
Southend U.	Mar-90	£12,000	96	96	0	2	4	2	0	0
Tottenham H.	Jun-92	£375,000	124	117	7	17	9	0	0	0
FAPL Summary by Club										
Tottenham H.		92-93 to 96-97	124	117	7	17	9	0	0	0
Total			*124*	*117*	*7*	*17*	*9*	*0*	*0*	*0*

BAARDSEN Espen　　　　　　　　Tottenham Hotspur

Full Name: Espen Baardsen　　　　　　DOB: San Rafael, Ca.
Debut: 　Liverpool v TOTTENHAM HOTSPUR 3/5/97 as sub
Debut Goal:

				Apps				Goals		
Previous Clubs Details										
Club	Signed	Fee	Tot	Start	Sub	FA	FL	Lge	FA	FL
Tottenham H.			2	1	1	0	0	0	0	0
FAPL Summary by Club										
Tottenham H.		1996-97	2	1	1	0	0	0	0	0
Total			*2*	*1*	*1*	*0*	*0*	*0*	*0*	*0*

BABAYARO Celestine　　　　　　　　　　　Chelsea

Full Name: Celestine Babayaro　　　　　　DOB: 29-08-78 Nigeria

				Apps				Goals		
Previous Clubs Details										
Club	Signed	Fee	Tot	Start	Sub	FA	FL	Lge	FA	FL
Anderlecht										
Chelsea	Apr-97	£2.25m								

BABB Phil　　　　　　　　　　　　　　Liverpool

Full Name: Phillip Andrew Babb　　　　　　DOB: 30-11-70 London
Debut: 　COVENTRY CITY v Middlesbrough 15/8/92
Debut Goal: Arsenal v COVENTRY CITY 14/8/93

				Apps				Goals		
Previous Clubs Details										
Club	Signed	Fee	Tot	Start	Sub	FA	FL	Lge	FA	FL
Bradford City	Aug-90		80	73	7	3	6	14	0	0
Coventry City	Jul-92	£500,000	77	70	7	2	5	3	0	1
Liverpool	Sep-94	£3.6m	84	82	2	11	14	1	0	0
FAPL Summary by Club										
Coventry City		92-93 to 94-95	77	70	7	2	5	3	0	1
Liverpool		94-95 to 96-97	84	82	2	11	14	1	0	0
Total			*161*	*152*	*9*	*13*	*19*	*4*	*0*	*1*

BALL Michael　　　　　　　　　　　　　Everton

Full Name: Michael BALL　　　　　　DOB: 02-10-77 Liverpool
Debut: 　EVERTON v Tottenham Hotspur 12/4/97
Debut Goal:

Previous Clubs Details			Apps				Goals		
Club	Signed	Fee	Tot	Start	Sub	FA	FL	Lge	FA	FL
Everton			5	2	3	0	0	0	0	0
FAPL Summary by Club										
Everton		1996-97	5	2	3	0	0	0	0	0
Total			*5*	*2*	*3*	*0*	*0*	*0*	*0*	*0*

BARMBY Nicky — Everton

Full Name: Nicholas Jonathan Barmby　　　DOB: 11-02-74 Hull
Debut:　　Sheffield W. v TOTTENHAM H 7/9/92
Debut Goal: TOTTENHAM HOTSPUR v Middlesbrough 17/10/92

Previous Clubs Details			Apps					Goals		
Club	Signed	Fee	Tot	Start	Sub	FA	FL	Lge	FA	FL
Tottenham H.	Apr-91	Trainee	87	81	6	13	8	20	5	1
Middlesbrough	Aug-95	£5.25m	50	43	7	3	4	8	1	1
Everton	Oct-96	£5.75m	25	22	3	2	0	4	1	0
FAPL Summary by Club										
Tottenham H.	92-93 to 94-95		87	81	6	13	8	20	5	1
Middlesbrough	95-96 to 96-97		50	43	7	3	4	8	1	1
Everton	1996-97		25	22	3	2	0	4	1	0
Total			*162*	*146*	*16*	*18*	*12*	*32*	*7*	*2*

BARNES John — Liverpool

Full Name: John Charles Bryan Barnes　　　DOB: 07-11-63 Jamaica
Debut:　　QPR v LIVERPOOL 23/11/92 as sub
Debut Goal: LIVERPOOL v Aston Villa 9/1/92

Previous Clubs Details			Apps					Goals		
Club	Signed	Fee	Tot	Start	Sub	FA	FL	Lge	FA	FL
Watford	Jul-81		233	232	1	31	21	65	11	7
Liverpool	Jun-87	£900,000	314	310	4	51	26	84	16	3
FAPL Summary by Club										
Liverpool	92-93 to 96-97		162	158	4	19	16	22	0	0
Total			*162*	*158*	*4*	*19*	*16*	*22*	*0*	*0*

BARRETT Earl — Everton

Full Name: Earl Delisser Barrett　　　DOB: 28-04-67 Rochdale
Debut:　　Ipswich Town v ASTON VILLA 15/8/92
Debut Goal: ASTON VILLA v Everton 20/2/93

Previous Clubs Details			Apps					Goals		
Club	Signed	Fee	Tot	Start	Sub	FA	FL	Lge	FA	FL
Man. City	Apr-85		3	2	1	0	1	0	0	0
Chester City	Mar-86	Loan	12	12	0	0	0	0	0	0
Oldham Ath.	Nov-87	£35,000	183	181	2	14	20	7	1	1
Aston Villa	Feb-92	£1.7m	119	118	1	9	15	1	0	1
Everton	Jan-95	£1.7m	61	61	0	2	4	0	0	0

Aston Villa	92-93 to 94-95	106	105	1	9	15	1	0	0
Everton	94-95 to 96-97	61	61	0	2	4	0	0	0
Total		*167*	*166*	*1*	*11*	*19*	*1*	*0*	*0*

BARTON Warren   Newcastle United
Full Name: Warren Dean Barton   DOB: 19-03-69 Stoke Newington
Debut: Leeds United v WIMBLEDON 15/8/92
Debut Goal: Leeds Utd v WIMBLEDON 15/8/92

Previous Clubs Details			*Apps*				*Goals*		
Club	Signed	Fee	Tot	Start	Sub	FA	FL	Lge	FA	FL
Maidstone U.	Jul-87	£10,000	42	41	1	3	2	0	1	0
Wimbledon	Jun-90	£300,000	180	178	2	11	16	10	0	1
Newcastle U.	Jun-95	£4m+	49	44	5	4	6	1	0	0

FAPL Summary by Club

Wimbledon	92-93 to 94-95	101	99	2	6	12	6	0	1
Newcastle U.	95-96 to 96-97	49	44	5	4	6	1	0	1
Total		*150*	*143*	*7*	*10*	*18*	*7*	*0*	*2*

BARTRAM Vince   Arsenal
Full Name: Vincent Lee Bartram   DOB: 07-08-68 Birmingham
Debut: Nottingham Forest v ARSENAL 3/12/94
Debut Goal: (Goalkeeper)

Previous Clubs Details			*Apps*				*Goals*		
Club	Signed	Fee	Tot	Start	Sub	FA	FL	Lge	FA	FL
W'hampton W.	Aug-85		5	5	0	3	2	0	0	0
Blackpool	Oct-89	Loan	9	9	0	0	0	0	0	0
Bournemouth	Jul-91	£65,000	132	132	0	14	10	0	0	0
Arsenal	Aug-94	£400,000	11	11	0	0	1	0	0	0
W'hampton W.	Feb-97	Loan								

FAPL Summary by Club

| Arsenal | 94-95 to 95-96 | 11 | 11 | 0 | 0 | 1 | 0 | 0 | 0 |
| *Total* | | *11* | *11* | *0* | *0* | *1* | *0* | *0* | *0* |

BASHAM Steve   Southampton
Full Name: Steve Basham   DOB: 02-12-77 Southampton
Debut: SOUTHAMPTON v Chelsea 18/8/96 as sub
Debut Goal:

Previous Clubs Details			*Apps*				*Goals*		
Club	Signed	Fee	Tot	Start	Sub	FA	FL	Lge	FA	FL
Southampton			6	1	5	0	0	0	0	0

FAPL Summary by Club

| Southampton | 1996-97 | 6 | 1 | 5 | 0 | 0 | 0 | 0 | 0 |
| *Total* | | *6* | *1* | *5* | *0* | *0* | *0* | *0* | *0* |

BATTY David   Newcastle United

Full Name: David Batty   DOB: 02-12-68 Leeds
Debut: LEEDS UNITED v Wimbledon 15/8/92
Debut Goal: LEEDS UNITED v Middlesbrough 31/1/93

Previous Clubs Details

Club	Signed	Fee	Tot	Start	Sub	FA	FL	Lge	FA	FL
Leeds U.	Jul-87	Trainee	211	201	10	12	17	4	0	0
Blackburn R.	Oct-93	£2.75m	54	53	1	5	6	1	0	0
Newcastle U.	Feb-96	£3.75m	43	43	0	3	2	2	0	0

FAPL Summary by Club

Leeds U.	92-93 to 93-94		39	38	1	3	2	1	0	0
Blackburn R.	93-94 to 95-96		54	53	1	5	6	1	0	0
Newcastle U.	95-96 to 96-97		43	43	0	3	2	2	0	0
Total			*136*	*134*	*2*	*11*	*10*	*4*	*0*	*0*

BEARDSLEY Peter   Newcastle United

Full Name: Peter Andrew Beardsley   DOB: 18-01-61 Newcastle
Debut: EVERTON v Sheffield Wednesday 15/8/92
Debut Goal: Manchester United v EVERTON 19/8/92

Previous Clubs Details

Club	Signed	Fee	Tot	Start	Sub	FA	FL	Lge	FA	FL
Carlisle U.	Aug-79		104	93	11	15	7	22	7	0
Vancouver	Apr-81	£275,000	0	0	0	0	0	0	0	0
Manchester U.	Sep-82	£300,000	0	0	0	0	1	0	0	0
Vancouver	Sep-83		0	0	0	0	0	0	0	0
Newcastle U.	Sep-83	£150,000	147	146	1	6	10	61	0	0
Liverpool	Jul-87	£1.9m	131	120	11	25	14	46	11	1
Everton	Aug-91	£1m	81	81	0	4	8	25	1	5
Newcastle U.	Jul-93	£1.4m	129	126	3	11	11	48	3	4

FAPL Summary by Club

Everton	92-93 to 93-94		39	39	0	2	4	10	2	0
Newcastle U.	93-94 to 96-97		129	126	3	11	12	48	3	4
Total			*168*	*165*	*3*	*13*	*16*	*58*	*5*	*4*

BEASANT Dave   Southampton

Full Name: David John Beasant   DOB: 20-03-59 Willesden
Debut: CHELSEA v Oldham Athletic 15/8/92
Debut Goal: Goalkeeper

Previous Clubs Details

Club	Signed	Fee	Tot	Start	Sub	FA	FL	Lge	FA	FL
Wimbledon	Aug-79	£1,000	340	340	0	27	21	0	0	0
Newcastle U.	Jun-88	£800,000	20	20	0	2	2	0	0	0
Chelsea	Jan-89	£725,000	133	133	0	5	11	0	0	0
Grimsby Town	Oct-92	Loan	6	6	0	0	0	0	0	0

| Wolves | Jan-93 | Loan | 4 | 4 | 0 | 0 | 1 | 0 | 0 | 0 |
| Southampton | Nov-93 | £300,000 | 88 | 86 | 2 | 9 | 8 | 0 | 0 | 0 |

FAPL Summary by Club

Chelsea	92-93 to 93-94	17	17	0	0	0	0	0	0
Southampton	93-94 to 96-97	88	86	2	9	8	0	0	0
Total		*105*	*103*	*2*	*9*	*8*	*0*	*0*	*0*

BECKHAM David   Manchester United

Full Name: David Beckham   DOB: 02-05-75 Leytonstone
Debut: MANCHESTER UNITED v Leeds Utd 2/4/95
Debut Goal: Aston Villa v MANCHESTER UNITED 19/8/95

Previous Clubs Details				*Apps*				*Goals*		
Club	Signed	Fee	Tot	Start	Sub	FA	FL	Lge	FA	FL
Manchester U.	Jan-93	Trainee	73	61	12	7	5	15	2	0
Preston NE	Feb-95	Loan	5	4	1			2		

FAPL Summary by Club

| Manchester U. | 94-95 to 96-97 | 73 | 61 | 12 | 7 | 5 | 15 | 2 | 0 |
| *Total* | | *73* | *61* | *12* | *7* | *5* | *15* | *2* | *0* |

BEENEY Mark   Leeds United

Full Name: Mark Raymond Beeney   DOB: 30-12-67 Tunbridge Wells
Debut: Coventry City v LEEDS UNITED 8/5/93
Debut Goal:

Previous Clubs Details				*Apps*				*Goals*		
Club	Signed	Fee	Tot	Start	Sub	FA	FL	Lge	FA	FL
Gillingham	Aug-85		2	2	0	0	1	0	0	0
Maidstone U.	Feb-87		50	50	0	11	3	0	0	0
Aldershot	Mar-90	Loan	7	7	0	0	0	0	0	0
Brighton HA	Mar-91	£30,000	69	68	1	7	6	0	0	0
Leeds U.	Apr-93	£350,000	45	44	1	5	4	0	0	0

FAPL Summary by Club

| Leeds U. | 92-93 to 96-97 | 34 | 34 | 0 | 4 | 4 | 0 | 0 | 0 |
| *Total* | | *34* | *34* | *0* | *4* | *4* | *0* | *0* | *0* |

BENALI Francis   Southampton

Full Name: Francis Vincent Benali   DOB: 30-12-68 Southampton
Debut: SOUTHAMPTON v Tottenham Hotspur 15/8/92
Debut Goal:

Previous Clubs Details				*Apps*				*Goals*		
Club	Signed	Fee	Tot	Start	Sub	FA	FL	Lge	FA	FL
Southampton	Jan-87		220	193	27	19	23	0	0	0

FAPL Summary by Club

| Southampton | 1992-93 to 1995-96 | 153 | 140 | 13 | 8 | 12 | 0 | 0 | 0 |
| *Total* | | *153* | *140* | *13* | *8* | *12* | *0* | *0* | *0* |

BENNETT Frank

Bristol Rovers

Full Name: Frank Bennett
DOB: 03-01-69 Birmingham
Debut: SOUTHAMPTON v Everton 14/8/93
Debut Goal: SOUTHAMPTON v Chelsea 27/12/93

Previous Clubs Details

Club	Signed	Fee	Tot	Start	Sub	FA	FL	Lge	FA	FL
								Goals		
Southampton	Feb-93	£7,500	19	5	14	1	3	1	0	0
Shrewsbury T.	Sep-96	Loan								
Bristol R.	Nov-96	£15,000								

FAPL Summary by Club

Southampton	93-94 to 95-96	19	5	14	1	2	1	0	0
Total		*19*	*5*	*14*	*1*	*2*	*1*	*0*	*0*

BERESFORD John

Newcastle United

Full Name: John Beresford
DOB: 04-09-66 Sheffield
Debut: NEWCASTLE UNITED v Tottenham Hotspur 14/8/93
Debut Goal:

Previous Clubs Details

Club	Signed	Fee	Tot	Start	Sub	FA	FL	Lge	FA	FL
								Goals		
Man. City	Sep-83		0	0	0	0	0	0	0	0
Barnsley	Aug-86	Free	88	79	9	5	7	5	1	2
Portsmouth	Mar-89	£300,000	107	102	5	11	12	8	0	2
Newcastle U.	Jul-92	£650,000	161	159	2	15	14	1	1	0

FAPL Summary by Club

Newcastle U.	93-94 to 96-97	119	117	2	11	9	0	1	0
Total		*119*	*117*	*2*	*11*	*9*	*0*	*1*	*0*

BERG Henning

Blackburn Rovers

Full Name: Henning Berg
DOB: 01-09-69 Eidsvell
Debut: BLACKBURN ROVERS v Crystal Palace 2/2/93
Debut Goal: BLACKBURN ROVERS v Chelsea 14/8/93

Previous Clubs Details

Club	Signed	Fee	Tot	Start	Sub	FA	FL	Lge	FA	FL
								Goals		
Lillestrom			0	0	0	0	0	0	0	0
Blackburn R.	Jan-93	£400,000	159	154	5	10	16	4	0	0

FAPL Summary by Club

Blackburn R.	92-93 to 96-97	159	154	5	10	16	4	0	0
Total		*159*	*154*	*5*	*10*	*16*	*4*	*0*	*0*

BERGER Patrik

Liverpool

Full Name: Patrik Berger
DOB: 10-11-73 Prague
Debut: LIVERPOOL v Southampton 7/9/96 as sub
Debut Goal: Leicester City v LIVERPOOL 15/9/96

Previous Clubs Details				Apps				Goals		
Club	Signed	Fee	Tot	Start	Sub	FA	FL	Lge	FA	FL
Slavia Prague	1991		89	83	6			24		
B. Dortmund	1995		25	13	12			4		
Liverpool	Aug-96	£3.25m	23	13	10	2	3	6	0	0
FAPL Summary by Club										
Liverpool		1996-97	23	13	10	2	3	6	0	1
Total			*23*	*13*	*10*	*2*	*3*	*6*	*0*	*1*

BERGKAMP Dennis   Arsenal
Full Name: Dennis Nicolaas Bergkamp   DOB: 18-05-69 Amsterdam
Debut: ARSENAL v Middlesbrough 20/8/95
Debut Goal: ARSENAL v Southampton 23/9/96

Previous Clubs Details				Apps				Goals		
Club	Signed	Fee	Tot	Start	Sub	FA	FL	Lge	FA	FL
Ajax	Jul-86		185	185	0	0	0	103	0	0
Internazionale	Jul-93	£12m	52	50	2			11		
Arsenal	Jul-95	£7.5m	62	61	1	3	9	23	1	6
FAPL Summary by Club										
Arsenal		95-96 to 96-97	62	61	1	3	9	23	1	6
Total			*62*	*61*	*1*	*3*	*9*	*23*	*1*	*6*

BERGSSON Gudni   Bolton Wanderers
Full Name: Gudni Bergsson   DOB: 21-07-65 Iceland
Debut: TOTTENHAM HOTSPUR v Nottm Forest 28/12/92
Debut Goal:

Previous Clubs Details				Apps				Goals		
Club	Signed	Fee	Tot	Start	Sub	FA	FL	Lge	FA	FL
Tottenham H.	Dec-88	£100,000	71	51	20	4	6	3	0	0
Bolton W.	Mar-95	£65,000	75	72	3	2	10	7	0	0
FAPL Summary by Club										
Tottenham H.		92-93 to 94-95	5	0	5	1	0	0	0	0
Bolton W.		1995-96	34	34	0	0	6	4	0	0
Total			*39*	*34*	*5*	*1*	*6*	*4*	*0*	*0*

BERKOVIC Eyal   West Ham United
Full Name: Eyal Berkovic   DOB: 02-04-72 Haifa
Debut: Coventry City v SOUTHAMPTON 13/10/96 as sub
Debut Goal: SOUTHAMPTON v Manchester United 26/10/96

Previous Clubs Details				Apps				Goals		
Club	Signed	Fee	Tot	Start	Sub	FA	FL	Lge	FA	FL
Maccabi Haifa	1992		128	126	2	0	0	25	0	0
Southampton	Sep-96	£1m	28	26	2	1	6	4	0	2
West Ham U.	Jun-97	£1.75m								

| Southampton | 1996-97 | 28 | 26 | 2 | 1 | 6 | 4 | 0 | 2 |
| *Total* | | *28* | *26* | *2* | *1* | *6* | *4* | *0* | *2* |

BILIC Slaven   Everton
Full Name: Slaven Bilic   DOB: 11-09-68 Croatia
Debut: Tottenham Hotspur v WEST HAM UTD 12/2/96
Debut Goal: WEST HAM UTD v Liverpool 29/9/96

| *Previous Clubs Details* | | | *Apps* | | | | *Goals* | | |
Club	Signed	Fee	Tot	Start	Sub	FA	FL	Lge	FA	FL
Karlsruhe										
West Ham U.	Dec-95	£1.3m	48	48	0	1	5	2	0	1
Everton	May-97	£4.5m								

FAPL Summary by Club

| West Ham U. | 95-96 to 96-97 | 48 | 48 | 0 | 1 | 5 | 2 | 0 | 1 |
| *Total* | | *48* | *48* | *0* | *1* | *5* | *2* | *0* | *1* |

BISHOP Ian   West Ham United
Full Name: Ian William Bishop   DOB: 29-05-65 Liverpool
Debut: WEST HAM UNITED v Swindon Town 11/9/93
Debut Goal: Sheffield Utd v WEST HAM UNITED 28/3/94

| *Previous Clubs Details* | | | *Apps* | | | | | *Goals* | | |
Club	Signed	Fee	Tot	Start	Sub	FA	FL	Lge	FA	FL
Everton	May-83		1	0	1	0	0	0	0	0
Crewe Alex.	Mar-84	Loan	4	4	0	0	0	0	0	0
Carlisle U.	Oct-84	£15,000	132	131	1	5	8	14	1	1
Bournemouth	Jul-88	£35,000	44	44	0	5	4	2	0	0
Man. City	Aug-89	£465,000	19	18	1	0	4	2	0	1
West Ham U.	Dec-89	Exchange	251	237	14	23	51	11	3	1

FAPL Summary by Club

| West Ham U. | 93-94 to 96-97 | 131 | 128 | 3 | 13 | 14 | 4 | 1 | 1 |
| *Total* | | *131* | *128* | *3* | *13* | *14* | *4* | *1* | *1* |

BJORNEBYE Stig Inge   Liverpool
Full Name: Stig Inge Bjornebye   DOB: 11-12-69 Norway
Debut: Coventry City v LIVERPOOL 19/12/92
Debut Goal: Middlesbrough v LIVERPOOL 17/8/96

| *Previous Clubs Details* | | | *Apps* | | | | | *Goals* | | |
Club	Signed	Fee	Tot	Start	Sub	FA	FL	Lge	FA	FL
Rosenborg										
Liverpool	Dec-92	£600,000	91	88	3	11	11	2	11	0

FAPL Summary by Club

| Liverpool | 92-93 to 96-97 | 91 | 88 | 3 | 11 | 11 | 2 | 11 | 0 |
| *Total* | | *91* | *88* | *3* | *10* | *12* | *2* | *0* | *0* |

BLACKWELL Dean   Wimbledon

Full Name: Dean Robert Blackwell   DOB: 05-12-69 Camden
Debut: Leeds Utd v WIMBLEDON 15/8/92
Debut Goal:

Previous Clubs Details				*Apps*				*Goals*		
Club	Signed	Fee	Tot	Start	Sub	FA	FL	Lge	FA	FL
Wimbledon	Jul-88		119	97	22	14	11	1	0	0
Plymouth A.	Mar-90	Loan	7	5	2	0	0	0	0	0
FAPL Summary by Club										
Wimbledon	92-93 to 96-97		77	65	12	13	9	0	0	0
Total			*77*	*65*	*12*	*13*	*9*	*0*	*0*	*0*

BLAKE Nathan   Bolton Wanderers

Full Name: Nathan Alexander Blake   DOB: 27-01-72 Cardiff
Debut: Tottenham H. v BOLTON W. 23/12/95
Debut Goal: Middlesbrough v BOLTON W. 17/2/96

Previous Clubs Details				*Apps*				*Goals*		
Club	Signed	Fee	Tot	Start	Sub	FA	FL	Lge	FA	FL
Cardiff City	Aug-90		131	113	18	10	8	35	4	0
Sheffield U.	Feb 94	£300,000	69	55	14	1	4	34	0	1
Bolton W.	Dec-95	£1.5m	52	48	4	5	5	20	2	3
FAPL Summary by Club										
Bolton W.	1995-96		18	14	4	2	0	1	0	0
Total			*18*	*14*	*4*	*2*	*0*	*1*	*0*	*0*

BLINKER Regi   Sheffield Wednesday

Full Name: Regi Blinker   DOB: 06-04-69 Surinam
Debut: Aston Villa v SHEFFIELD W. 6/3/96
Debut Goal: Aston Villa v SHEFFIELD W. 6/3/96

Previous Clubs Details				*Apps*				*Goals*		
Club	Signed	Fee	Tot	Start	Sub	FA	FL	Lge	FA	FL
Feyenoord										
Sheffield W.	Mar-96	£275,000	42	24	18	1	2	3	0	0
FAPL Summary by Club										
Sheffield W.	95-96 to 96-97		42	24	18	1	2	3	0	0
Total			*42*	*24*	*18*	*1*	*2*	*3*	*0*	*0*

BLUNT Jason   Leeds United

Full Name: Jason Blunt   DOB: 16-08-77 Penzance
Debut: LEEDS UTD v Middlesbrough, 30/3/96 as sub
Debut Goal:

Previous Clubs Details				*Apps*				*Goals*		
Club	Signed	Fee	Tot	Start	Sub	FA	FL	Lge	FA	FL
Leeds U.	Jan-95	Trainee	4	2	2	0	0	0	0	0

| | | Leeds U. | 95-96 to 96-97 | 4 | 2 | 2 | 0 | 0 | 0 | 0 | 0 |
| *Total* | | | | *4* | *2* | *2* | *0* | *0* | | *0* | *0* | *0* |

BOHINEN Lars   Blackburn Rovers

Full Name: Lars Bohinen   DOB: 08-09-69 Vadso, Norway
Debut: Ipswich Town v NOTTM FOREST 20/8/94 as sub
Debut Goal: NOTTM FOREST v Sheffield Wednesday 10/9/94

				Apps					*Goals*		
Club	Signed	Fee	Tot	Start	Sub	FA	FL		Lge	FA	FL
Young Boys Berne											
N. Forest	Nov-93	£450,000	64	59	5	2	8		6	1	2
Blackburn R.	Oct-95	£700,000	43	35	8	2	3		6	1	0

FAPL Summary by Club

				Apps					*Goals*		
N. Forest	94-95 to 95-96		41	37	4	1	5		6	0	2
Blackburn R.	95-96 to 96-97		43	35	8	2	3		6	1	0
Total			*84*	*72*	*12*	*3*	*8*		*12*	*1*	*2*

BOLAND Willie   Coventry City

Full Name: Willie Boland   DOB: 06-08-75 Republic of Ireland
Debut: Chelsea v COVENTRY CITY 1/5/93 as sub
Debut Goal:

				Apps					*Goals*		
Club	Signed	Fee	Tot	Start	Sub	FA	FL		Lge	FA	FL
Coventry City	Nov-92	Juniors	44	35	9	0	4		0	0	0

FAPL Summary by Club

				Apps					*Goals*		
Coventry City	92-93 to 96-97		44	35	9	0	4		0	0	0
Total			*44*	*35*	*9*	*0*	*4*		*0*	*0*	*0*

BOOTH Andy   Sheffield Wednesday

Full Name: Andrew David Booth   DOB: 06-12-73 Huddersfield
Debut: SHEFFIELD WEDNESDAY v Aston Villa, 17/8/96
Debut Goal: Leeds Utd v SHEFFIELD WEDNESDAY 20/8/96

				Apps					*Goals*		
Club	Signed	Fee	Tot	Start	Sub	FA	FL		Lge	FA	FL
Huddersfield T.	Jul-92	Trainee	123	109	14	6	7		54	3	3
Sheffield W.	Jul-96	£2.7m	35	32	3	4	2		10	3	0

FAPL Summary by Club

				Apps					*Goals*		
Sheffield W.	1996-97		35	32	3	4	2		10	3	0
Total			*35*	*32*	*3*	*4*	*2*		*10*	*3*	*0*

BORROWS Brian   Coventry City

Full Name: Brian Borrows   DOB: 20-12-60 Liverpool
Debut: Sheffield Wednesday v COVENTRY CITY 2/9/92
Debut Goal: COVENTRY CITY v Liverpool 19/12/92

BOSANCIC Jovo   Barnsley

Full Name: Jovo Bosancic   DOB:
Debut: Debut Goal:

Previous Clubs Details				Apps				Goals		
Club	Signed	Fee	Tot	Start	Sub	FA	FL	Lge	FA	FL
Barnsley			25	17	8	2	4	0	0	0

BOSNICH Mark   Aston Villa

Full Name: Mark John Bosnich   DOB: 13-01-72 Sydney
Debut: Sheffield Wednesday v ASTON VILLA 5/12/92
Debut Goal: (Goalkeeper)

Previous Clubs Details				Apps				Goals		
Club	Signed	Fee	Tot	Start	Sub	FA	FL	Lge	FA	FL
Manchester U.	Jun-89		3	3	0	0	0	0	0	0
Croatia Sydney	Aug-91									
Aston Villa	Feb-92	Free	133	133	0	13	20	0	0	0
FAPL Summary by Club										
Aston Villa	92-93 to 96-97		133	133	0	13	20	0	0	0
Total			*133*	*133*	*0*	*13*	*20*	*0*	*0*	*0*

BOULD Steve   Arsenal

Full Name: Stephen Andrew Bould   DOB: 16-11-62 Stoke
Debut: ARSENAL v Norwich City 15/8/92
Debut Goal: ARSENAL v Norwich City 15/8/92

Previous Clubs Details				Apps				Goals		
Club	Signed	Fee	Tot	Start	Sub	FA	FL	Lge	FA	FL
Stoke City	Nov-80		183	179	4	10	13	6	0	1
Torquay U.	Oct-82	Loan	9	9	0	2	0	0	0	0
Arsenal	Jun-89	£390,000	244	236	8	20	31	5	0	1
FAPL Summary by Club										
Arsenal	1992-93 to 1996-97		132	129	3	8	21	1	0	1
Total			*132*	*129*	*3*	*8*	*21*	*1*	*0*	*1*

BOWYER Lee   Leeds United

Full Name: Lee David Bowyer   DOB: 03-01-77 London
Debut: Derby Co. v LEEDS UTD 17/8/96
Debut Goal: Derby Co. v LEEDS UTD 17/8/96

Previous Clubs Details

Club	Signed	Fee	Tot	Start	Sub	FA	FL	Lge	FA	FL
Charlton Ath	Apr-94	Trainee	46	46	0	3	7	8	1	5
Leeds U.	Jul-96	£3m	32	32	0	4	0	4	2	0

FAPL Summary by Club

| Leeds U. | | 1996-97 | 32 | 32 | 0 | 4 | 0 | 4 | 2 | 0 |
| *Total* | | | *32* | *32* | *0* | *4* | *0* | *4* | *2* | *0* |

BOXALL Danny   Crystal Palace

Full Name: Daniel James Boxall   DOB: 24-08-77 Croydon
Debut: Debut Goal:

Previous Clubs Details

Club	Signed	Fee	Tot	Start	Sub	FA	FL	Lge	FA	FL
C. Palace	Apr-94	Trainee	7	5	2	0	1	0	0	0

BRANAGAN Keith   Bolton Wanderers

Full Name: Keith Branagan   DOB: 10-07-66 Fulham
Debut: Wimbledon v BOLTON WANDERERS 19/8/95
Debut Goal:

Previous Clubs Details

Club	Signed	Fee	Tot	Start	Sub	FA	FL	Lge	FA	FL
Cambridge U.	Aug-83	Junior	110	110	0	6	12	0	0	0
Millwall	Mar-88	£100,000	46	46	0	5	1	0	0	0
Brentford	Nov-89	Loan	2	2	0	0	0	0	0	0
Gillingham	Oct-91	Loan	1	1	0	0	0	0	0	0
Bolton W.	Jul-92	Free	166	166	0	10	26	0	0	0

FAPL Summary by Club

| Bolton W. | | 1995-96 | 31 | 31 | 0 | 2 | 6 | 0 | 0 | 0 |
| *Total* | | | *31* | *31* | *0* | *2* | *6* | *0* | *0* | *0* |

BRANCH Michael   Everton

Full Name: Michael Paul Branch   DOB: 18-10-72 Liverpool
Debut: Manchester United v EVERTON 21/2/96 as sub
Debut Goal: Chelsea v EVERTON 7/12/96

Previous Clubs Details

Club	Signed	Fee	Tot	Start	Sub	FA	FL	Lge	FA	FL
Everton	Oct-95	Trainee	28	14	14	1	1	3	0	0

FAPL Summary by Club

| Everton | | 95-96 to 96-97 | 28 | 14 | 14 | 1 | 1 | 3 | 0 | 0 |
| *Total* | | | *28* | *14* | *14* | *1* | *1* | *3* | *0* | *0* |

272

BREACKER Tim West Ham United

Full Name: Timothy Sean Breacker DOB: 02-07-65 Bicester
Debut: WEST HAM UNITED v Wimbledon 14/8/93
Debut Goal: WEST HAM UNITED v Coventry City 11/12/93

Previous Clubs Details				*Apps*				*Goals*	
Club	Signed	Fee	Tot	Start	Sub	FA	FL	Lge	FA FL
Luton Town	May-83		210	204	6	21	24	3	0 0
West Ham U.	Oct-90	£600,000	218	209	9	24	16	8	0 0
FAPL Summary by Club									
West Ham U.	93-94 to 96-97		121	114	7	10	10	3	0 0
Total			*121*	*114*	*7*	*10*	*10*	*3*	*0 0*

BREEN Gary Coventry City

Full Name: Gary Patrick Breen DOB: 12-12-73 Hendon
Debut: Aston Villa v COVENTRY CITY 19/2/97
Debut Goal:

Previous Clubs Details				*Apps*				*Goals*	
Club	Signed	Fee	Tot	Start	Sub	FA	FL	Lge	FA FL
Maidstone U.	Mar-91	Free	19	19	0	0	0	0	0 0
Gillingham	Jul-92	Free	51	45	6	5	4	0	0 0
Peterboro' U.	Aug-94	£70,000	69	68	1	6	6	1	0 0
Bir'ham C. *	Feb-96	£400,000	18	17	1	0	0	1	0 0
Coventry City	Jan-97	£2.5m	9	8	1	0	0	0	0 0
FAPL Summary by Club									
Coventry City	1996-97		9	8	1	0	0	0	0 0
Total			*9*	*8*	*1*	*0*	*0*	*0*	*0 0*

BRISCOE Lee Sheffield Wednesday

Full Name: Lee Stephen Briscoe DOB: 30-09-75 Pontefract
Debut: Tottenham Hotspur v SHEFFIELD WED 5/2/94 as sub
Debut Goal:

Previous Clubs Details				*Apps*				*Goals*	
Club	Signed	Fee	Tot	Start	Sub	FA	FL	Lge	FA FL
Sheffield W.	May-94		38	33	5	0	1	0	0 0
FAPL Summary by Club									
Sheffield W.	93-94 to 96-97		38	33	5	0	1	0	0 0
Total			*38*	*33*	*5*	*0*	*1*	*0*	*0 0*

BROLIN Tomas Leeds United

Full Name: Tomas Brolin DOB: 29-11-69 Hudiksvall, Sweden
Debut: Newcastle United v LEEDS UNITED 25/11/95 as sub
Debut Goal: Sheffield Wed. v LEEDS UNITED 16/12/95

Previous Clubs Details				*Apps*				*Goals*	
Club	Signed	Fee	Tot	Start	Sub	FA	FL	Lge	FA FL
GIF Sundsvall	1987		51					13	

Norrkoping	1990		11					7		
Parma	1990		133	118	15			20		
Leeds U.	Nov-95	£4.5m	19	17	2	2	4	4	0	0
FC Zurich	Aug-96	Loan								
Parma	Jan-97	Loan + £300,000								

FAPL Summary by Club

| Leeds U. | 95-96 to 96-97 | 19 | 17 | 2 | 2 | 4 | 4 | 0 | 0 |
| *Total* | | *19* | *17* | *2* | *2* | *4* | *4* | *0* | *0* |

BULLOCK Martin   Barnsley

Full Name: Martin John Bullock   DOB: 05-03-75 Derby
Debut: Debut Goal:

Previous Clubs Details				*Apps*				*Goals*		
Club	Signed	Fee	Tot	Start	Sub	FA	FL	Lge	FA	FL
Barnsley	Sep-93	£15,000	NL100	49	51	5	4	1	1	1

BURLEY Craig   Chelsea

Full Name: Craig William Burley   DOB: 24-09-71 Irvine
Debut: Tottenham Hotspur v CHELSEA 5/12/92
Debut Goal: CHELSEA v Everton 3/1/94

Previous Clubs Details				*Apps*				*Goals*		
Club	Signed	Fee	Tot	Start	Sub	FA	FL	Lge	FA	FL
Chelsea	Sep-89	Trainee	113	85	28	16	8	7	4	0

FAPL Summary by Club

| Chelsea | 92-93 to 96-97 | 104 | 79 | 25 | 16 | 5 | 7 | 4 | 0 |
| *Total* | | *104* | *79* | *25* | *16* | *5* | *7* | *4* | *0* |

BURNETT Wayne   Bolton Wanderers

Full Name: Wayne Burnett   DOB: 04-09-71 Lambeth
Debut: BOLTON WDRS v Leeds Utd 27/12/95 as sub
Debut Goal:

Previous Clubs Details				*Apps*				*Goals*		
Club	Signed	Fee	Tot	Start	Sub	FA	FL	Lge	FA	FL
Leyton Orient	Nov-89	Trainee	40	34	6	4	4	0	0	1
Blackburn R.	Aug-92	£90,000	0	0	0	0	0	0	0	0
Plymouth A.	Aug-93		70	61	9	3	3	3	0	0
Bolton W.	Oct-95	£100,000	2	0	2	0	0	0	0	0

FAPL Summary by Club

| Bolton W. | 1995-96 | 1 | 0 | 1 | 0 | 0 | 0 | 0 | 0 |
| *Total* | | *1* | *0* | *1* | *0* | *0* | *0* | *0* | *0* |

BURROWS David   Coventry City

Full Name: David Burrows   DOB: 25-10-68 Dudley
Debut: Nottingham Forest v WEST HAM UNITED 16/8/92
Debut Goal: WEST HAM UNITED v Coventry City 11/12/93

Previous Clubs Details				*Apps*				*Goals*		
Club	Signed	Fee	Tot	Start	Sub	FA	FL	Lge	FA	FL
WBA	Oct-86		46	37	9	2	4	1	0	0
Liverpool	Oct-88	£550,000	146	135	11	17	16	3	0	0
West Ham U.	Sep-93	Swap	29	29	0	3	3	1	0	1
Everton	Sep-94	Swap +	19	19	0	2	2	0	0	0
Coventry City	Mar-95	£1.1m	42	41	1	1	2	0	0	0
FAPL Summary by Club										
Liverpool		1992-93	30	29	1	0	5	2	0	0
West Ham U.		93-94 to 94-95	29	29	0	3	3	1	0	1
Everton		1994-95	19	19	0	2	2	0	0	0
Coventry City		94-95 to 96-97	42	41	1	1	2	0	0	0
Total			*120*	*118*	*2*	*6*	*12*	*3*	*0*	*1*

BUTT Nicky   Manchester United
Full Name: Nicholas Butt   DOB: 21-01-75 Manchester
Debut: MANCHESTER UNITED v Oldham Athletic 21/11/92
Debut Goal: Southampton v MANCHESTER UNITED 31/12/94

Previous Clubs Details				*Apps*				*Goals*		
Club	Signed	Fee	Tot	Start	Sub	FA	FL	Lge	FA	FL
Manchester U.	Jan-93	Trainee	82	66	16	12	3	8	1	0
FAPL Summary by Club										
Manchester U.		92-93 to 96-97	82	66	16	12	3	8	1	0
Total			*82*	*66*	*16*	*12*	*3*	*8*	*1*	*0*

CADAMARTERI Danny   Everton
Full Name: Daniel Cadamarteri   DOB: 12-10-79 Bradford
Debut: EVERTON v Chelsea 11/5/97 as sub
Debut Goal:

Previous Clubs Details				*Apps*				*Goals*		
Club	Signed	Fee	Tot	Start	Sub	FA	FL	Lge	FA	FL
Everton			1	0	1	0	0	0	0	0
FAPL Summary by Club										
Everton		1996-97	1	0	1	0	0	0	0	0
Total			*1*	*0*	*1*	*0*	*0*	*0*	*0*	*0*

CALDERWOOD Colin   Tottenham Hotspur
Full Name: Colin Calderwood   DOB: 20-01-65 Stranraer
Debut: Newcastle United v TOTTENHAM HOTSPUR 14/8/93
Debut Goal: TOTTENHAM HOTSPUR v Sheffield Wed 10/12/94

Previous Clubs Details				*Apps*				*Goals*		
Club	Signed	Fee	Tot	Start	Sub	FA	FL	Lge	FA	FL
Mansfield T.	Mar-82		100	97	3	6	4	1	1	0
Swindon T.	Jul-85	£30,000	330	328	2	17	35	20	1	0
Tottenham H.	Jul-93	£1.25m	125	120	5	14	13	3	0	0

CAMPBELL Sol   Tottenham Hotspur

Full Name: Sulzeer Jeremiah Campbell   DOB: 18-09-74 Newham
Debut: TOTTENHAM HOTSPUR v Chelsea 5/12/92 as sub
Debut Goal: TOTTENHAM HOTSPUR v Chelsea 5/12/92

Previous Clubs Details			*Apps*				*Goals*		
Club	Signed	Fee	Tot	Start	Sub	FA	FL	Lge	FA FL
Tottenham H.	Sep-92	Trainee	134	125	9	13	13	2	0 0

FAPL Summary by Club
Tottenham H.	92-93 to 96-97	134	125	9	13	13	2	0	2
Total		*134*	*125*	*9*	*13*	*13*	*2*	*0*	*2*

CAMPBELL Stuart   Leicester City

Full Name: Stuart Campbell   DOB:
Debut: Manchester United v LEICESTER CITY 30/11/96
Debut Goal:

Previous Clubs Details			*Apps*				*Goals*		
Club	Signed	Fee	Tot	Start	Sub	FA	FL	Lge	FA FL
Leicester City			10	4	6	2	2	0	0 0

FAPL Summary by Club
Leicester City	1996-97	10	4	6	2	2	0	0	0
Total		*10*	*4*	*6*	*2*	*2*	*0*	*0*	*0*

CARBON Matt   Derby County

Full Name: Matthew Carbon   DOB: 08-06-75 Nottingham
Debut: DERBY CO. v Manchester Utd 3/9/96
Debut Goal:

Previous Clubs Details			*Apps*				*Goals*		
Club	Signed	Fee	Tot	Start	Sub	FA	FL	Lge	FA FL
Lincoln City	Apr-93	Trainee	69	66	3	3	4	10	0 1
Derby County	Mar-96	£385,000	16	8	8	1	1	0	0 0

FAPL Summary by Club
Derby County	1996-97	10	6	4	1	1	0	0	0
Total		*10*	*6*	*4*	*1*	*1*	*0*	*0*	*0*

CARBONE Benito   Sheffield Wednesday

Full Name: Benito Carbone   DOB: 14-08-71 Bagnara Calabra (Ita)
Debut: SHEFFIELD WEDNESDAY v Blackburn Rvrs 19/10/96
Debut Goal: SHEFFIELD WEDNESDAY v Nottingham Forest 18/11/96

Previous Clubs Details			*Apps*				*Goals*		
Club	Signed	Fee	Tot	Start	Sub	FA	FL	Lge	FA FL
Torino	1988		8					0	

Reggina (B)	1990		31					5			
Casertana (B)	1991		31					4			
Ascoli (B)	1992		28					6			
Torino	1993		28	25	3			6			
Napoli	1994		29	27	2			4			
Internazionale	1995		31	25	6			2			
Sheffield W.	Oct 96	£3m	25	24	1	2	0	6	0	0	

FAPL Summary by Club

Sheffield W.	1996-97	25	24	1	2	0	6	0	0
Total		*25*	*24*	*1*	*2*	*0*	*6*	*0*	*0*

CARR Stephen   Tottenham Hotspur

Full Name: Stephen Carr   DOB: 29-08-76 Dublin
Debut: Ipswich Town v TOTTENHAM HOTSPUR 26/9/93
Debut Goal:

Previous Clubs Details			Apps					Goals		
Club	Signed	Fee	Tot	Start	Sub	FA	FL	Lge	FA	FL
Tottenham H.	Aug-93		27	25	2	1	4	0	0	0

FAPL Summary by Club

Tottenham H.	93-94 to 96-97	27	25	2	1	4	0	0	0
Total		*27*	*25*	*2*	*1*	*4*	*0*	*0*	*0*

CARRAGHER Jamie   Liverpool

Full Name: James Carragher   DOB: 28-01-78 Bootle
Debut: LIVERPOOL v West Ham Utd 11/1/97 as sub
Debut Goal: LIVERPOOL v Aston Villa 18/1/97

Previous Clubs Details			Apps					Goals		
Club	Signed	Fee	Tot	Start	Sub	FA	FL	Lge	FA	FL
Liverpool		Trainee	2	1	1	0	1	1	0	0

FAPL Summary by Club

Liverpool	1996-97	2	1	1	0	1	1	0	0
Total		*2*	*1*	*1*	*0*	*1*	*1*	*0*	*0*

CARSLEY Lee   Derby County

Full Name: Lee Kevin Carsley   DOB: 28-04-74 Birmingham
Debut: Sheffield Wednesday v DERBY CO. 21/9/96
Debut Goal:

Previous Clubs Details			Apps					Goals		
Club	Signed	Fee	Tot	Start	Sub	FA	FL	Lge	FA	FL
Derby County	Jul-92	Trainee	82	68	14	3	8	3	0	0

FAPL Summary by Club

Derby County	1996-97	24	15	9	2	2	0	0	0
Total		*24*	*15*	*9*	*2*	*2*	*0*	*0*	*0*

CASPER Chris   **Manchester United**
Full Name: Christopher Martin Casper   DOB: 28-04-75 Burnley
Debut: Tottenham Hotspur v MANCHESTER UTD 12/1/97 as sub
Debut Goal:

Previous Clubs Details				*Apps*				*Goals*	
Club	Signed	Fee	Tot	Start	Sub	FA	FL	Lge	FA	FL
Manchester U.	Mar-93	Trainee	2	0	2	1	3	0	0	0
Bournemouth	Jan-96	Loan	16	16	0	0	0	1	0	0
FAPL Summary by Club									
Manchester U.	1996-97		2	0	2	1	2	0	0	0
Total			*2*	*0*	*2*	*1*	*2*	*0*	*0*	*0*

CASTLEDINE Stewart   **Wimbledon**
Full Name: Stewart Mark Castledine   DOB: 22-01-73 Wandsworth
Debut: Coventry City v WIMBLEDON 2/4/94
Debut Goal: Coventry City v WIMBLEDON 2/4/94

Previous Clubs Details				*Apps*				*Goals*	
Club	Signed	Fee	Tot	Start	Sub	FA	FL	Lge	FA	FL
Wimbledon	Jul-91		21	14	7	2	1	4	0	1
Wycombe W.	Aug-95	Loan	7	7	0	0	0	3	0	0
FAPL Summary by Club									
Wimbledon	93-94 to 96-97		19	14	5	2	1	4	0	1
Total			*19*	*14*	*5*	*2*	*1*	*4*	*0*	*1*

CHARLES Gary   **Aston Villa**
Full Name: Gary Andrew Charles   DOB: 13-04-70 Newham
Debut: Manchester United v ASTON VILLA 4/2/95
Debut Goal: ASTON VILLA v Southampton 8/4/96

Previous Clubs Details				*Apps*				*Goals*	
Club	Signed	Fee	Tot	Start	Sub	FA	FL	Lge	FA	FL
N. Forest	Nov-87		56	54	2	10	9	1	1	0
Leicester City	Mar-89	Loan	8	5	3	0	0	0	0	0
Derby County	Jul-93	£750,000	61	61	0	1	3	3	0	0
Aston Villa	Jan-95	£2.9m +	50	48	2	5	8	1	0	0
FAPL Summary by Club									
N. Forest	92-93 to 94-95		14	14	0	0	0	0	0	0
Aston Villa	94-95 to 95-96		50	48	2	5	8	1	0	0
Total			*64*	*62*	*2*	*5*	*8*	*1*	*0*	*0*

CHARLTON Simon   **Southampton**
Full Name: Simon Thomas Charlton   DOB: 25-10-71 Huddersfield
Debut: SOUTHAMPTON v Everton 14/8/93
Debut Goal: SOUTHAMPTON v Chelsea 27/12/93

Previous Clubs Details				*Apps*					*Goals*		
Club	Signed	Fee	Tot	Start	Sub	FA	FL		Lge	FA	FL
Huddersfield T.	Jul-89	Trainee	124	121	3	10	9		1	0	1
Southampton	Jun-93	£250,000	110	102	8	9	11		2	0	1
FAPL Summary by Club											
Southampton		93-94 to 96-97	110	102	8	9	11		2	0	1
Total			*110*	*102*	*8*	*9*	*11*		*2*	*0*	*1*

CLAPHAM Jamie   Tottenham Hotspur

Full Name: James Clapham   DOB: 07-12-75 Lincoln
Debut: TOTTENHAM v Coventry City 11/5/97 as sub
Debut Goal:

Previous Clubs Details				*Apps*					*Goals*		
Club	Signed	Fee	Tot	Start	Sub	FA	FL		Lge	FA	FL
Tottenham H.			1	0	1	0	0		0	0	0
FAPL Summary by Club											
Tottenham H.		1996-97	1	0	1	0	0		0	0	0
Total			*1*	*0*	*1*	*0*	*0*		*0*	*0*	*0*

CLARIDGE Steve   Leicester City

Full Name: Stephen Edward Claridge   DOB: 10-04-66 Portsmouth
Debut: LEICESTER CITY v Southampton 21/8/96
Debut Goal: Sheffield Wednesday v LEICESTER CITY 2/9/96

Previous Clubs Details				*Apps*					*Goals*		
Club	Signed	Fee	Tot	Start	Sub	FA	FL		Lge	FA	FL
Bournemouth	Nov-84	From NL	7	3	4	0	0		1	0	0
C. Palace	Oct-88										
Aldershot	Oct-88	£14,000	62	58	4	6	3		19	1	0
Cambridge U.	Feb-90	£75,000	79	56	23	1	6		28	0	2
Luton Town	Jul-92	£160,000	16	15	1	0	2		2	0	3
Cambridge U.	Nov-92	£195,000	53	53	0	4	4		18	0	3
Birmingham C.	Jan-94	£350,000	88	86	2	7	15		35	0	2
Leicester City	Mar-96	£1m	46	43	3	4	8		17	1	2
FAPL Summary by Club											
Leicester City		1996-97	32	29	3	4	8		12	1	2
Total			*32*	*29*	*3*	*4*	*8*		*12*	*1*	*2*

CLARKE Matt   Sheffield Wednesday

Full Name: Matthew John Clarke   DOB: 03-11-73 Sheffield
Debut: SHEFFIELD WEDNESDAY v Liverpool 11/5/97 as sub
Debut Goal: (Goalkeeper)

Previous Clubs Details				*Apps*					*Goals*		
Club	Signed	Fee	Tot	Start	Sub	FA	FL		Lge	FA	FL
Rotherham	Jul-92	Trainee	124	123	1	3	4		0	0	0
Sheffield W.			1	0	1	0	0		0	0	0

CLARKE Andy   Wimbledon

Full Name: Andrew Weston Clarke   DOB: 22-07-67 Islington
Debut: Leeds Utd v WIMBLEDON 15/8/92
Debut Goal: WIMBLEDON v Aston Villa 3/10/92

Previous Clubs Details				*Apps*					*Goals*	
Club	Signed	Fee	Tot	Start	Sub	FA	FL	Lge	FA	FL
Barnet	NL									
Wimbledon	Feb-91	£250,000	156	73	83	13	22	17	2	3
FAPL Summary by Club										
Wimbledon	1992-93 to 1996-97	110	53	57	8	11	11	2	1	
Total		*110*	*53*	*57*	*8*	*11*	*11*	*2*	*1*	

CLARKE Adrian   Arsenal

Full Name: Adrian James Clarke   DOB: 28-09-74 Cambridge
Debut: ARSENAL v QPR 31/12/94 as sub
Debut Goal:

Previous Clubs Details				*Apps*					*Goals*	
Club	Signed	Fee	Tot	Start	Sub	FA	FL	Lge	FA	FL
Arsenal	Jul-93	Trainee	7	4	3	2	0	0	0	0
Rotherham U.*	Dec-96	Loan								
Southampton *	Mar-97	Loan								
FAPL Summary by Club										
Arsenal	94-95 to 95-96	7	4	3	2	0	0	0	0	
Total		*7*	*4*	*3*	*2*	*0*	*0*	*0*	*0*	

CLARKE Steve   Chelsea

Full Name: Stephen Clarke   DOB: 29-08-63 Saltcoats
Debut: CHELSEA v Oldham Athletic 15/8/92
Debut Goal:

Previous Clubs Details				*Apps*					*Goals*	
Club	Signed	Fee	Tot	Start	Sub	FA	FL	Lge	FA	FL
St Mirren			0	0	0	0	0	0	0	0
Chelsea	Jan-87	£422,000	304	299	5	35	20	6	1	1
FAPL Summary by Club										
Chelsea	92-93 to 96-97	141	138	3	27	10	0	0	0	
Total		*141*	*138*	*3*	*27*	*10*	*0*	*0*	*0*	

CLEGG Michael   Manchester United

Full Name: Michael Clegg   DOB: 03-07-77 Tameside
Debut: Middlesbrough v MANCHESTER UTD 23/11/96
Debut Goal:

Previous Clubs Details				*Apps*				*Goals*		
Club	Signed	Fee	Tot	Start	Sub	FA	FL	Lge	FA	FL
Manchester U.			4	3	1	1	1	0	0	0
FAPL Summary by Club										
Manchester U.	1996-97		4	3	1	1	1	0	0	0
Total			*4*	*3*	*1*	*1*	*1*	*0*	*0*	*0*

COLE Andy   Manchester United

Full Name: Andrew Alexander Cole   DOB: 15-10-71 Nottingham
Debut: NEWCASTLE UNITED v Tottenham Hotspur 14/8/93
Debut Goal: Manchester United v NEWCASTLE UNITED 21/8/93

Previous Clubs Details				*Apps*				*Goals*		
Club	Signed	Fee	Tot	Start	Sub	FA	FL	Lge	FA	FL
Arsenal	Oct-89	Trainee	1	0	1	0	0	0	0	0
Fulham	Sep-91	Loan	13	13	0	0	0	3	0	0
Bristol City	Mar-92	£500,000	41	41	0	1	3	20	4	0
Newcastle U.	Mar-93	£1.75m	70	69	1	4	7	55	1	8
Manchester U.	Jan-95	£7m +	72	59	13	10	1	29	2	0
FAPL Summary by Club										
Newcastle U.	93-94 to 94-95		58	58	0	4	7	43	1	8
Manchester U.	94-95 to 96-97		72	59	13	10	1	29	2	0
Total			*130*	*117*	*13*	*14*	*8*	*72*	*3*	*8*

COLEMAN Chris   Blackburn Rovers

Full Name: Christopher Coleman   DOB: 10-06-70 Swansea
Debut: CRYSTAL PALACE v Blackburn R. 15/8/92
Debut Goal: Coventry City v CRYSTAL PALACE 3/12/92

Previous Clubs Details				*Apps*				*Goals*		
Club	Signed	Fee	Tot	Start	Sub	FA	FL	Lge	FA	FL
Swansea City	Sep-87		160	159	1	13	8	2	1	0
C.Palace	Jul-91	£275,000	154	143	11	8	26	13	1	2
Blackburn R.	Dec-95	£2.8m	28	27	1	2	1	0	0	0
FAPL Summary by Club										
C.Palace	92-93 to 94-95		73	66	7	7	14	6	1	2
Blackburn R.	95-96 to 96-97		28	27	1	2	1	0	0	0
Total			*101*	*93*	*8*	*9*	*15*	*6*	*1*	*2*

COLLINS Wayne   Sheffield Wednesday

Full Name: Wayne Collins   DOB: 04-03-69 Manchester
Debut: SHEFFIELD WEDNESDAY v Aston Villa 17/8/96
Debut Goal: Derby County v SHEFFIELD WEDNESDAY 19/2/97

Previous Clubs Details				*Apps*				*Goals*		
Club	Signed	Fee	Tot	Start	Sub	FA	FL	Lge	FA	FL
Crewe Alex.	Jul-93	£10k NL	117	102	15	9	5	14	0	1
Sheffield W.	Jul-96	£600,000	12	8	4	1	0	1	0	0

Sheffield W.	1996-97	12	8	4	1	0	1	0	0
Total		*12*	*8*	*4*	*1*	*0*	*1*	*0*	*0*

COLLYMORE Stan   Aston Villa

Full Name: Stanley Victor Collymore   DOB: 22-01-71 Stone
Debut: CRYSTAL PALACE v Southampton 26/9/92 as sub
Debut Goal: NOTTINGHAM FOREST v Manchester United 22/8/94

Previous Clubs Details				*Apps*				*Goals*	
Club	Signed	Fee	Tot	Start	Sub	FA	FL	Lge	FA FL
C. Palace	Jan-91	£100,000	20	4	16	0	5	1	0 1
Southend U.	Nov-92	£100,000	30	30	0	3	0	15	3 0
N. Forest	Jul-93	£2.0m	65	64	1	2	9	41	1 2
Liverpool	Jul-95	£8.5m	60	54	6	9	4	26	7 0
Aston Villa	May-97	£7m							

FAPL Summary by Club									
C. Palace		92-93	2	0	2	0	2	0	0 0
N. Forest		1994-95	37	37	0	2	4	23	1 2
Liverpool		95-96 to 96-97	60	54	6	9	4	26	7 0
Total			*99*	*91*	*8*	*11*	*10*	*49*	*8 2*

COOKE Terry   Manchester United

Full Name: Terence John Cooke   DOB: 05-08-76 Marston Green
Debut: MANCHESTER UTD v Bolton W. 16/9/95
Debut Goal:

Previous Clubs Details				*Apps*				*Goals*	
Club	Signed	Fee	Tot	Start	Sub	FA	FL	Lge	FA FL
Manchester U.	Jul-94	Trainee	4	1	3	0	3	0	0 0
Sunderland	Jan-96	Loan	6	6	0	0	0	0	0 0
Birmingham C.	Nov-96	Loan							

FAPL Summary by Club									
Manchester U.	95-96 to 96-97	4	1	3	0	3	0	0	0
Total		*4*	*1*	*3*	*0*	*3*	*0*	*0*	*0*

COUZENS Andy   Leeds United

Full Name: Andrew Couzens   DOB: 04-06-75 Shipley
Debut: LEEDS UNITED v Coventry City 18/3/95 as sub
Debut Goal: Coventry City v LEEDS UTD 14/9/96

Previous Clubs Details				*Apps*				*Goals*	
Club	Signed	Fee	Tot	Start	Sub	FA	FL	Lge	FA FL
Leeds U.	Mar-93	Trainee	28	17	11	0	5	1	0 1

FAPL Summary by Club									
Leeds U.	94-95 to 96-97	28	17	11	0	5	1	0	1
Total		*28*	*17*	*11*	*0*	*5*	*1*	*0*	*1*

COX Neil   Bolton Wanderers

Full Name: Neil James Cox   DOB: 08-10-71 Scunthorpe
Debut: Sheffield Wednesday v ASTON VILLA 5/12/92
Debut Goal: ASTON VILLA v Everton 20/2/93

Previous Clubs Details				*Apps*				*Goals*	
Club	Signed	Fee	Tot	Start	Sub	FA	FL	Lge	FA FL
Scunthorpe U.	Mar-90		17	17	0	4	0	1	0 0
Aston Villa	Feb-91	£400,000	42	26	16	6	7	3	1 0
Middlesbrough	Jul-94	£1m	75	74	1	2	8	3	0 0
Bolton W.	May-97	£1.5m							
FAPL Summary by Club									
Aston Villa	92-93 to 93-94		35	22	13	6	7	3	0 0
Middlesbrough	1995-96		35	35	0	2	5	2	0 0
Total			*70*	*57*	*13*	*8*	*12*	*5*	*0 0*

CRAWFORD Jimmy   Newcastle United

Full Name: James Crawford   DOB: Chicago, USA
Debut: Liverpool v NEWCASTLE UNITED 10/3/97 as sub
Debut Goal:

Previous Clubs Details				*Apps*				*Goals*	
Club	Signed	Fee	Tot	Start	Sub	FA	FL	Lge	FA FL
Bohemians (Ire)									
Newcastle U.	Mar-95	£75,000	2	0	2	0	0	0	0 0
Rotherham U.	Sep-96	Loan							
FAPL Summary by Club									
Newcastle U.	1996-97		2	0	2	0	0	0	0 0
Total			*2*	*0*	*2*	*0*	*0*	*0*	*0 0*

CROFT Gary   Blackburn Rovers

Full Name: Gary Croft   DOB: 17-02-74 Burton on Trent
Debut: Coventry City v BLACKBURN R. 28/9/96
Debut Goal:

Previous Clubs Details				*Apps*				*Goals*	
Club	Signed	Fee	Tot	Start	Sub	FA	FL	Lge	FA FL
Grimsby Town	Jul-92	Trainee	149	139	10	10	7	3	1 0
Blackburn R.	Mar-96	£1.7m	5	4	1	0	2	0	0 0
FAPL Summary by Club									
Blackburn R.	1996-97		5	4	1	0	2	0	0 0
Total			*5*	*4*	*1*	*0*	*2*	*0*	*0 0*

CRUYFF Jordi   Manchester United

Full Name: Johan Jordi Cruyff   DOB: 09-02-74 Amsterdam
Debut: Wimbledon v MANCHESTER UTD 17/8/96
Debut Goal: MANCHESTER UTD v Everton 21/8/96

Previous Clubs Details				*Apps*				*Goals*		
Club	Signed	Fee	Tot	Start	Sub	FA	FL	Lge	FA	FL
Barcelona	1994		41	32	9			11		
Manchester U.	Aug-96	£1.4m	16	11	5	0	1	3	0	0
FAPL Summary by Club										
Manchester U.		1996-97	16	11	5	0	1	3	0	0
Total			*16*	*11*	*5*	*0*	*1*	*3*	*0*	*0*

CUNNINGHAM Kenny — Wimbledon

Full Name: Kenneth Edward Cunningham DOB: 28-06-71 Dublin
Debut: WIMBLEDON v Newcastle United 19/11/94
Debut Goal:

Previous Clubs Details				*Apps*				*Goals*		
Club	Signed	Fee	Tot	Start	Sub	FA	FL	Lge	FA	FL
Millwall	Sep-89		136	132	4	1	10	1	0	0
Wimbledon	Nov-94	£1.3m +	97	96	1	19	9	0	0	0
FAPL Summary by Club										
Wimbledon	94-95 to 96-97		97	96	1	19	9	0	0	0
Total			*97*	*96*	*1*	*19*	*9*	*0*	*0*	*0*

CURCIC Sasa — Aston Villa

Full Name: Sasa Curcic DOB: 14-02-72 Belgrade
Debut: BOLTON WANDERERS v Arsenal, 30/10/95
Debut Goal: Chelsea v BOLTON WANDERERS 22/11/95

Previous Clubs Details				*Apps*				*Goals*		
Club	Signed	Fee	Tot	Start	Sub	FA	FL	Lge	FA	FL
OFK Belgrade	1990		52					5		
Part. Belgrade	1993		64					14		
Bolton W.	Oct-95	£1.5m	28	28	0	2	3	4	2	1
Aston Villa	Aug-96	£4m	22	17	5	2	1	0	1	0
FAPL Summary by Club										
Bolton W.		1995-96	28	28	0	2	3	4	2	1
Aston Villa		1996-97	22	17	5	2	1	0	1	0
Total			*50*	*45*	*5*	*4*	*4*	*4*	*3*	*1*

CYPRUS Andrew — Crystal Palace

Full Name: Andrew Cyprus DOB: 30-09-76 Lambeth
Debut: Debut Goal:

Previous Clubs Details				*Apps*				*Goals*		
Club	Signed	Fee	Tot	Start	Sub	FA	FL	Lge	FA	FL
C.Palace	Sep-95	Trainee	1	1	0	0	0	0	0	0

DAILLY Christian — Derby County

Full Name: Christian Dailly DOB: 23-10-73 Dundee
Debut: DERBY COUNTY v Leeds Utd 17/8/96
Debut Goal: Tottenham Hotspur v DERBY COUNTY 21/8/96

Previous Clubs Details				*Apps*				*Goals*		
Club	Signed	Fee	Tot	Start	Sub	FA	FL	Lge	FA	FL
Dundee U.	1990	S Form	140	108	32			16		
Derby County	Aug-96	£1m	36	31	5	6	6	3	0	0
FAPL Summary by Club										
Derby County		1996-97	36	31	5	6	6	3	0	0
Total			*36*	*31*	*5*	*6*	*6*	*3*	*0*	*0*

DAISH Liam   Coventry City

Full Name: Liam Sean Daish   DOB: 23-09-68 Portsmouth
Debut: COVENTRY CITY v Middlesbrough 24/2/96
Debut Goal: Everton v COVENTRY CITY 9/3/96

Previous Clubs Details				*Apps*				*Goals*		
Club	Signed	Fee	Tot	Start	Sub	FA	FL	Lge	FA	FL
Portsmouth	Aug-86	Apprentice	1	1	0	0	0	0	0	0
Cambridge U.	Jul-88	Free	139	138	1	17	11	5	0	0
Birmingham C.	Jan-94	£50,000	73	72	1	7	10	3	0	1
Coventry City	Feb-96	£1.5m	31	31	0	0	3	2	0	1
FAPL Summary by Club										
Coventry City	95-96 to 96-97		31	31	0	0	3	2	0	1
Total			*31*	*31*	*0*	*0*	*3*	*2*	*0*	*1*

DAVIES Simon   Manchester United

Full Name: Simon Ithel Davies   DOB: 23-04-74 Winsford
Debut: MANCHESTER UNITED v Crystal Palace 19/11/94
Debut Goal:

Previous Clubs Details				*Apps*				*Goals*		
Club	Signed	Fee	Tot	Start	Sub	FA	FL	Lge	FA	FL
Manchester U.	Jul-92	Trainee	11	4	7	0	6	0	0	0
Exeter City	Dec-93	Loan	6	5	1	1	0	1	0	0
FAPL Summary by Club										
Manchester U.	94-95 to 96-97		11	4	7	0	6	0	0	0
Total			*11*	*4*	*7*	*0*	*6*	*0*	*0*	*0*

DAVIES Gareth   Crystal Palace

Full Name: Gareth Melville Davies   DOB: 11-12-73 Hereford
Debut: Debut Goal:

Previous Clubs Details				*Apps*				*Goals*		
Club	Signed	Fee	Tot	Start	Sub	FA	FL	Lge	FA	FL
Hereford U.	Apr-92	Trainee	95	91	4	4	7	1	0	0
C. Palace	Jul-95	£120,000	26	22	4	2	0	2	0	0

DAY Chris   Crystal Palace

Full Name: Christopher Day   DOB: 28-07-75 Whipps Cross
Debut: Debut Goal: (Goalkeeper)

Club	Signed	Fee	Tot	Start	Sub	FA	FL	Lge	FA	FL
Tottenham H.	1992	Trainee	0	0	0	0	0	0	0	0
C. Palace	Aug-96	£225,000	24	24	0	2	2	0	0	0

DE GOUY Ed   Chelsea
Full Name: Edward De Gouy   DOB:
Debut: Debut Goal: (Goalkeeper)

Previous Clubs Details   *Apps*   *Goals*

Club	Signed	Fee	Tot	Start	Sub	FA	FL	Lge	FA	FL
Sparta Rotterdam										
Feyenoord *	1990		201	201	0					
Chelsea	Jun-97	£2.25m								

DE ZEEUW Arjan   Barnsley
Full Name: Adrianus Johannes De Zeeuw   DOB: 16-04-70 Holland
Debut: Debut Goal:

Previous Clubs Details   *Apps*   *Goals*

Club	Signed	Fee	Tot	Start	Sub	FA	FL	Lge	FA	FL
Telstar										
Barnsley	Nov-95	£250,000	31	31	0	2	0	2	0	0

DEANE Brian   Leeds United
Full Name: Brian Christopher Deane   DOB: 07-02-68 Leeds
Debut: LEEDS UNITED v Manchester United 15/8/93
Debut Goal: LEEDS UNITED v Manchester United 15/8/93

Previous Clubs Details   *Apps*   *Goals*

Club	Signed	Fee	Tot	Start	Sub	FA	FL	Lge	FA	FL
Doncaster R.	Dec-85	Juniors	66	59	7	3	3	12	1	0
Sheffield U.	Jul-88	£30,000	197	197	0	24	16	82	11	11
Leeds U.	Jul-93	£2.9m	138	131	7	16	11	32	4	2

FAPL Summary by Club

Club	Signed	Fee	Tot	Start	Sub	FA	FL	Lge	FA	FL
Sheffield U.		92-93	41	41	0	6	4	15	3	2
Leeds U.		93-94 to 96-97	138	131	7	16	10	32	4	2
Total			*179*	*172*	*7*	*22*	*14*	*47*	*7*	*4*

DI MATTEO Roberto   Chelsea
Full Name: Roberto Di Matteo   DOB: 29-05-70 Sciaffusa (Switz)
Debut: Southampton v CHELSEA 18/8/96
Debut Goal: CHELSEA v Middlesbrough 21/8/96

Previous Clubs Details   *Apps*   *Goals*

Club	Signed	Fee	Tot	Start	Sub	FA	FL	Lge	FA	FL
Schaffhausen	1988		50					2		
FC Zurich	1991		34					6		
Aarau	1992		31					1		

Lazio	1993		88					7		
Chelsea	Jul-96	£4.9m	34	33	1	7	3	6	2	0
FAPL Summary by Club										
Chelsea		1996-97	34	33	1	7	3	6	2	0
Total			*34*	*33*	*1*	*7*	*3*	*6*	*2*	*0*

DICKS Julian   West Ham United

Full Name: Julian Andrew Dicks   DOB: 08-08-68 Bristol
Debut: WEST HAM UNITED v Wimbledon 14/8/93
Debut Goal: Everton v LIVERPOOL 14/8/93

Previous Clubs Details				Apps					Goals	
Club	Signed	Fee	Tot	Start	Sub	FA	FL	Lge	FA	FL
Birmingham C.	Apr-86	Apprentice	89	83	6	5	6	1	0	0
West Ham U.	Mar-88	£300,000	159	159	0	14	19	29	2	5
Liverpool	Sep-93	£1.5m	24	24	0	1	3	3	0	0
West Ham U.	Oct-94	£500,000 +	94	94	0	7	10	21	0	3
FAPL Summary by Club										
West Ham U.		1993-94	7	7	0	0	0	1	0	0
Liverpool		1993-94	24	24	0	1	3	3	0	0
West Ham U.		94-95 to 96-97	94	94	0	7	10	21	0	3
Total			*125*	*125*	*0*	*8*	*13*	*25*	*0*	*3*

DIXON Lee   Arsenal

Full Name: Lee Michael Dixon   DOB: 17-03-64 Manchester
Debut: ARSENAL v Norwich City 15/8/92
Debut Goal: ARSENAL v Norwich City 1/4/95

Previous Clubs Details				Apps					Goals	
Club	Signed	Fee	Tot	Start	Sub	FA	FL	Lge	FA	FL
Burnley	Jul-82	Juniors	4	4	0	0	1	0	0	0
Chester City	Feb-84	Free	57	56	1	1	2	1	0	0
Bury	Jul-85	Free	45	45	0	8	4	5	1	0
Stoke City	Jul-86	£40,000	71	71	0	7	6	5	0	0
Arsenal	Jan-88	£400,000	324	320	4	29	42	20	1	0
FAPL Summary by Club										
Arsenal		92-93 to 96-97	171	169	2	16	26	5	0	0
Total			*171*	*169*	*2*	*16*	*26*	*5*	*0*	*0*

DODD Jason   Southampton

Full Name: Jason Robert Dodd   DOB: 02-11-70 Bath
Debut: SOUTHAMPTON v Tottenham Hotspur 15/8/92
Debut Goal: Sheffield Wednesday v SOUTHAMPTON 13/4/93

Previous Clubs Details				Apps					Goals	
Club	Signed	Fee	Tot	Start	Sub	FA	FL	Lge	FA	FL
Southampton	Mar-89	£50,000	194	178	16	21	26	6	1	0

287

Southampton	92-93 to 95-96	125	115	10	11	11	6	1	0
Total		*125*	*115*	*10*	*11*	*11*	*6*	*1*	*0*

DONALDSON O'Neill   Sheffield Wednesday
Full Name: O'Neill McKay Donaldson   DOB: 24-11-69, Birmingham
Debut: Manchester City v SHEFFIELD WEDNESDAY 18/3/95 as sub
Debut Goal: QPR v SHEFFIELD WEDNESDAY 9/9/95

Previous Clubs Details				*Apps*				*Goals*	
Club	Signed	Fee	Tot	Start	Sub	FA	FL	Lge	FA FL
Shrewsbury T.	Nov-91	Free NL	28	15	13	0	0	4	0 0
Doncaster R.	Aug-94	Free	9	7	2	0	2	2	0 0
Mansfield T.	Dec-94	Loan	4	4	0	1	0	6	1 0
Sheffield W.	Jan-95	£50,000	10	4	6	0	0	3	0 0
FAPL Summary by Club									
Sheffield W.	94-95 to 96-97	10	4	6	0	0	3	0	0
Total		*10*	*4*	*6*	*0*	*0*	*3*	*0*	*0*

DONIS George   Blackburn Rovers
Full Name: Georgio Donis   DOB: 29-10-69 Frankfurt
Debut: BLACKBURN ROVERS v Tottenham Hotspur 17/8/96
Debut Goal: BLACKBURN ROVERS v Everton 21/9/96

Previous Clubs Details				*Apps*				*Goals*	
Club	Signed	Fee	Tot	Start	Sub	FA	FL	Lge	FA FL
Panathinaikos (Greece)									
Blackburn R.	Jul-96	Free	22	11	11	1	3	2	0 0
FAPL Summary by Club									
Blackburn R.	1996-97	22	11	11	1	3	2	0	0
Total		*22*	*11*	*11*	*1*	*3*	*2*	*0*	*0*

DORIGO Tony   Leeds United
Full Name: Anthony Robert Dorigo   DOB: 31-12-65 Melbourne
Debut: LEEDS UNITED v Wimbledon 15/8/92
Debut Goal: LEEDS UNITED v Ipswich Town 27/2/93

Previous Clubs Details				*Apps*				*Goals*	
Club	Signed	Fee	Tot	Start	Sub	FA	FL	Lge	FA FL
Aston Villa	Jul-83	Apprentice	111	106	5	7	15	1	0 0
Chelsea	Jul-87	£475,000	146	146	0	4	14	11	0 0
Leeds U.	Jun-91	£1.3m	171	168	3	16	13	5	0 0
FAPL Summary by Club									
Leeds U.	92-93 to 96-97	133	130	3	15	8	2	0	0
Total		*133*	*130*	*3*	*15*	*8*	*2*	*0*	*0*

DOWIE Iain   West Ham United
Full Name: Iain Dowie   DOB: 09-01-65 Hatfield
Debut: QPR v SOUTHAMPTON 19/8/92
Debut Goal: Crystal Palace v SOUTHAMPTON 26/9/92

Previous Clubs Details | | | | *Apps* | | | | *Goals* | |
| --- | --- | --- | --- | --- | --- | --- | --- | --- | --- | --- |
| Club | Signed | Fee | Tot | Start | Sub | FA | FL | Lge | FA | FL |
| Luton Town | Dec-88 | £30,000 NL | 66 | 53 | 13 | 3 | 4 | 16 | 0 | 0 |
| Fulham | Sep-89 | Loan | 5 | 5 | 0 | 0 | 0 | 1 | 0 | 0 |
| West Ham U. | Mar-91 | £480,000 | 12 | 12 | 0 | 0 | 0 | 4 | 0 | 0 |
| Southampton | Sep-91 | £500,000 | 122 | 115 | 7 | 6 | 11 | 30 | 1 | 1 |
| C. Palace | Jan-95 | £400,000 | 19 | 19 | 0 | 6 | 0 | 4 | 4 | 0 |
| West Ham U. | Sep-95 | £125,000 + | 56 | 51 | 5 | 3 | 8 | 8 | 1 | 2 |

FAPL Summary by Club
Southampton	92-93 to 94-95		92	90	2	2	7	21	1	1
C. Palace	1994-95		15	15	0	6	0	4	4	0
West Ham U.	95-96 to 96-97		56	51	5	3	8	8	1	2
Total			*163*	*156*	*7*	*11*	*15*	*33*	*6*	*3*

DOZZELL Jason   Tottenham Hotspur
Full Name: Jason Alvin Winans Dozzell   DOB: 09-12-67 Ipswich
Debut: IPSWICH TOWN v Aston Villa 15/8/92
Debut Goal: IPSWICH TOWN v Liverpool 25/8/92

Previous Clubs Details | | | | *Apps* | | | | *Goals* | |
| --- | --- | --- | --- | --- | --- | --- | --- | --- | --- | --- |
| Club | Signed | Fee | Tot | Start | Sub | FA | FL | Lge | FA | FL |
| Ipswich Town | Dec-84 | | 332 | 312 | 20 | 18 | 23 | 52 | 10 | 3 |
| Tottenham H. | Aug-93 | £1.9m | 84 | 68 | 16 | 5 | 9 | 13 | 1 | 0 |

FAPL Summary by Club
Ipswich Town	92-93 to 94-95		41	41	0	4	7	7	2	0
Tottenham H.	93-94 to 96-97		84	68	16	5	9	13	1	0
Total			*125*	*109*	*16*	*9*	*16*	*20*	*3*	*0*

DRAPER Mark   Aston Villa
Full Name: Mark Draper   DOB: 11-11-70 Long Eaton
Debut: LEICESTER CITY v Newcastle United 21/8/94
Debut Goal: Everton v LEICESTER CITY 24/9/94

Previous Clubs Details | | | | *Apps* | | | | *Goals* | |
| --- | --- | --- | --- | --- | --- | --- | --- | --- | --- | --- |
| Club | Signed | Fee | Tot | Start | Sub | FA | FL | Lge | FA | FL |
| Notts County | Dec-88 | Trainee | 222 | 206 | 16 | 10 | 15 | 40 | 2 | 2 |
| Leicester City | Jul-94 | £1.25m | 39 | 39 | 0 | 2 | 2 | 5 | 0 | 0 |
| Aston Villa | Jul-95 | £3.25m | 65 | 64 | 1 | 5 | 10 | 2 | 2 | 1 |

FAPL Summary by Club
Leicester City	1994-95		39	39	0	2	2	5	0	0
Aston Villa	95-96 to 96-97		65	64	1	5	10	2	2	1
Total			*104*	*103*	*1*	*7*	*12*	*7*	*2*	*1*

DRYDEN Richard   Southampton

Full Name: Richard Andrew Dryden   DOB: 14-06-69 Stroud
Debut: SOUTHAMPTON v Chelsea 18/08/96
Debut Goal: SOUTHAMPTON v Nottingham Forest 03/09/96

Previous Clubs Details			*Apps*					*Goals*		
Club	Signed	Fee	Tot	Start	Sub	FA	FL	Lge	FA	FL
Bristol R.	Jul-87	Trainee	13	12	1	2	3	0	0	0
Exeter City	Sep-88	Loan	6	6	0	0	0	0	0	0
Exeter City	Mar-89		86	86	0	2	7	13	0	2
Notts County	Aug-91	£250,000	31	30	1	3	2	1	0	0
Plymouth A.	Nov-92	Loan	5	5	0	0	0	0	0	0
Birmingham C.	Mar-93	£165,000	48	48	0	1	5	0	0	0
Bristol City	Dec-94	£140,000	37	32	5	2	4	2	0	0
Southampton	Aug-96	£150,000	29	28	1	0	6	1	0	3
FAPL Summary by Club										
Southampton	1996-97		29	28	1	0	6	1	0	3
Total			*29*	*28*	*1*	*0*	*6*	*1*	*0*	*3*

DUBERRY Michael   Chelsea

Full Name: Michael Wayne Duberry   DOB: 14-10-75 London
Debut: CHELSEA v Coventry City 4/5/94
Debut Goal: Manchester United v CHELSEA 2/11/96

Previous Clubs Details			*Apps*					*Goals*		
Club	Signed	Fee	Tot	Start	Sub	FA	FL	Lge	FA	FL
Chelsea	Jun-93	Trainee	38	36	2	9	2	1	2	0
Bournemouth	Sep-95	Loan	7	7	0	0	0	0	0	0
FAPL Summary by Club										
Chelsea	93-94 to 96-97		38	36	2	9	2	1	2	0
Total			*38*	*36*	*2*	*9*	*2*	*1*	*2*	*0*

DUBLIN Dion   Coventry City

Full Name: Dion Dublin   DOB: 22-04-69 Leicester
Debut: Sheffield Utd v MANCHESTER UNITED 15/8/92 as sub
Debut Goal: Southampton v MANCHESTER UNITED 24/8/92

Previous Clubs Details			*Apps*					*Goals*		
Club	Signed	Fee	Tot	Start	Sub	FA	FL	Lge	FA	FL
Norwich City	Mar-88	Trainee	0	0	0	0	0	0	0	0
Cambridge U.	Aug-88		156	133	23	21	10	52	11	5
Manchester U.	Aug-92	£1m	12	4	8	2	2	2	0	1
Coventry City	Sep-94	£2m	99	98	1	8	9	41	3	2
FAPL Summary by Club										
Manchester U.	92-93 to 93-94		12	4	8	2	2	2	0	1
Coventry City	94-95 to 96-97		99	98	1	8	9	41	3	2
Total			*111*	*102*	*9*	*10*	*11*	*43*	*3*	*3*

DUCROS Andrew   Coventry City

Full Name: Andrew Ducros   DOB: 16-09-77 Evesham
Debut: COVENTRY CITY v Nottingham Forest 17/8/96 as sub
Debut Goal:

Previous Clubs Details				*Apps*				*Goals*		
Club	Signed	Fee	Tot	Start	Sub	FA	FL	Lge	FA	FL
Coventry City			5	1	4	0	0	0	0	0
FAPL Summary by Club										
Coventry City	1996-97		5	1	4	0	0	0	0	0
Total			*5*	*1*	*4*	*0*	*0*	*0*	*0*	*0*

DUNNE Richard   Everton

Full Name: Richard Dunne   DOB: 21-09-79 Dublin
Debut: Sheffield Wednesday v EVERTON 11/1/97
Debut Goal:

Previous Clubs Details				*Apps*				*Goals*		
Club	Signed	Fee	Tot	Start	Sub	FA	FL	Lge	FA	FL
Everton			7	6	1	1	0	0	0	0
FAPL Summary by Club										
Everton	1996-97		7	6	1	1	0	0	0	0
Total			*7*	*6*	*1*	*1*	*0*	*0*	*0*	*0*

DYER Bruce   Crystal Palace

Full Name: Bruce Antonio Dyer   DOB: 13-04-75 Ilford
Debut: CRYSTAL PALACE v Liverpool 20/8/94 as sub
Debut Goal: Manchester City v CRYSTAL PALACE 10/9/94

Previous Clubs Details				*Apps*				*Goals*		
Club	Signed	Fee	Tot	Start	Sub	FA	FL	Lge	FA	FL
Watford	Apr-93	Trainee	31	29	2	1	4	6	0	2
C. Palace	Mar-94	£1.1m	105	69	36	6	10	31	2	1
FAPL Summary by Club										
C. Palace	1994-95		16	7	9	3	3	1	0	1
Total			*16*	*7*	*9*	*3*	*3*	*1*	*0*	*1*

EADEN Nicky   Barnsley

Full Name: Nicholas Jeremy Eaden   DOB: 12-12-72 Sheffield
Debut: Debut Goal:

Previous Clubs Details				*Apps*				*Goals*		
Club	Signed	Fee	Tot	Start	Sub	FA	FL	Lge	FA	FL
Barnsley	Jun-91	Juniors	176	173	3	9	11	8	0	0

EARLE Robbie   Wimbledon

Full Name: Robert Gerald Earle   DOB: 27-01-65 Newcastle-under-Lyme
Debut: Leeds Utd v WIMBLEDON 15/8/92
Debut Goal: WIMBLEDON v Arsenal 5/9/92

Club	Signed	Fee	Tot	Start	Sub	FA	FL	Lge	FA	FL
				Apps					*Goals*	
Port Vale	Jul-82	Juniors	294	284	10	21	23	77	4	4
Wimbledon	Jul-91	£775,000	202	202	0	28	20	48	7	5

FAPL Summary by Club

Wimbledon	92-93 to 96-97	162	162	0	26	18	34	7	5
Total		*162*	*162*	*0*	*26*	*18*	*34*	*7*	*5*

EDINBURGH Justin   Tottenham Hotspur

Full Name: Justin Charles Edinburgh   DOB: 18-12-69 Brentwood
Debut: Southampton v TOTTENHAM HOTSPUR 15/8/92
Debut Goal:

Previous Clubs Details

Club	Signed	Fee	Tot	Start	Sub	FA	FL	Lge	FA	FL
				Apps					*Goals*	
Southend U.	Jul-88	Trainee	37	36	1	2	3	0	0	0
Tottenham H.	Jul-90	£150,000	173	156	17	22	21	1	0	0

FAPL Summary by Club

Tottenham H.	92-93 to 96-97	134	120	14	17	13	0	0	0
Total		*134*	*120*	*14*	*17*	*13*	*0*	*0*	*0*

EDWORTHY Marc   Crystal Palace

Full Name: Marc Edworthy   DOB: 24-12-74 Barnstaple
Debut: Debut Goal:

Previous Clubs Details

Club	Signed	Fee	Tot	Start	Sub	FA	FL	Lge	FA	FL
				Apps					*Goals*	
Plymouth A.	Mar-91	Trainee	69	52	17	7	7	1	0	0
C. Palace	Jun-95	£350,000	89	86	3	6	3	2	0	1

EHIOGU Ugo   Aston Villa

Full Name: Ugochuku Ehiogu   DOB: 03-11-72 Hackney
Debut: ASTON VILLA v Southampton 22/8/92
Debut Goal: Tottenham Hotspur v ASTON VILLA 23/8/95

Previous Clubs Details

Club	Signed	Fee	Tot	Start	Sub	FA	FL	Lge	FA	FL
				Apps					*Goals*	
WBA	Jul-89		2	0	2	0	0	0	0	0
Aston Villa	Jul-91	£40,000	142	131	11	12	15	7	1	1

FAPL Summary by Club

Aston Villa	92-93 to 96-97	134	127	7	11	15	4	1	1
Total		*134*	*127*	*7*	*11*	*15*	*4*	*1*	*1*

EKOKU Efan   Wimbledon

Full Name: Efangwu Goziem Ekoku   DOB: 08-06-67 Manchester
Debut: NORWICH CITY v Manchester United 5/4/93 as sub
Debut Goal: Tottenham Hotspur v NORWICH CITY 9/4/93

Previous Clubs Details				Apps					Goals		
Club	Signed	Fee	Tot	Start	Sub	FA	FL		Lge	FA	FL
Bournemouth	May-90	£100,000	62	43	19	7	2		21	2	0
Norwich City	Mar-93	£500,000	37	26	11	1	3		15	0	0
Wimbledon	Oct-94	£900,000	85	80	5	16	6		27	3	1
FAPL Summary by Club											
Norwich City	92-93 to 94-95		37	26	11	1	3		15	0	2
Wimbledon	94-95 to 96-97		85	80	5	16	6		27	3	1
Total			*122*	*106*	*16*	*17*	*9*		*42*	*3*	*3*

ELLIOT Matt   Leicester City
Full Name: Matthew Stephen Elliot   DOB: 01-11-68 Wandsworth
Debut: LEICESTER CITY v Wimbledon 18/1/97
Debut Goal: Newcastle United v LEICESTER CITY 2/2/97

Previous Clubs Details				Apps					Goals		
Club	Signed	Fee	Tot	Start	Sub	FA	FL		Lge	FA	FL
Charlton Ath	Sep-88	£5,000 NL	0	0	0	0	1		0	0	0
Torquay U.	Mar-89	£10,000	124	123	1	9	9		15	2	2
Scunthorpe U.	Mar-92	£50,000	61	61	0	2	6		8	0	0
Oxford Utd *	Nov-93	£150,000	139	122	17	11	8		0	2	0
Leicester City	Jan-97	£1.6m	16	16	0	2	0		4	0	0
FAPL Summary by Club											
Leicester City	1996-97		16	16	0	2	0		4	0	0
Total			*16*	*16*	*0*	*2*	*0*		*4*	*0*	*0*

ELLIOTT Robert   Newcastle United
Full Name: Robert James Elliott   DOB: 25-12-73 Newcastle
Debut: Oldham Athletic v NEWCASTLE UNITED 23/2/94
Debut Goal: Leicester City v NEWCASTLE UNITED 21/8/94 as sub

Previous Clubs Details				Apps					Goals		
Club	Signed	Fee	Tot	Start	Sub	FA	FL		Lge	FA	FL
Newcastle U.	Apr-91		79	71	8	9	5		9	0	0
FAPL Summary by Club											
Newcastle U.	93-94 to 96-97		64	57	7	9	4		9	0	0
Total			*64*	*57*	*7*	*9*	*4*		*9*	*0*	*0*

ERANIO Stefano   Derby County
Full Name: Stefano Eranio   DOB: 29-12-66 Genova
Debut: Debut Goal:

Previous Clubs Details				Apps					Goals		
Club	Signed	Fee	Tot	Start	Sub	FA	FL		Lge	FA	FL
Genoa	1985		213						13		
Milan *	1990		77						4		
Derby County	May-97	Free									

EUELL Jason — Wimbledon

Full Name: Jason Euell DOB: 06-02-77 South London
Debut: WIMBLEDON v Southampton 28/10/95
Debut Goal: WIMBLEDON v Southampton 28/10/95

Previous Clubs Details			Apps					Goals		
Club	Signed	Fee	Tot	Start	Sub	FA	FL	Lge	FA	FL
Wimbledon			16	8	8	6	1	4	0	0
FAPL Summary by Club										
Wimbledon	95-96 to 96-97		16	8	8	6	1	4	0	0
Total			*16*	*8*	*8*	*6*	*1*	*4*	*0*	*0*

EVANS Micky — Southampton

Full Name: Michael James Evans DOB: 01-01-73 Plymouth
Debut: SOUTHAMPTON v West Ham Utd 12/4/97 as sub
Debut Goal:

Previous Clubs Details			Apps					Goals		
Club	Signed	Fee	Tot	Start	Sub	FA	FL	Lge	FA	FL
Plymouth A. *	Mar-91	Trainee	130	97	33	7	5	26	2	0
Southampton	Mar-97	£500,000	12	8	4	0	0	4	0	0
FAPL Summary by Club										
Southampton	1996-97		12	8	4	0	0	4	0	0
Total			*12*	*8*	*4*	*0*	*0*	*4*	*0*	*0*

EVTUSHOK Alex — Coventry City

Full Name: Alex Evtushok DOB:
Debut: Manchester United v COVENTRY CITY 1/3/97
Debut Goal:

Previous Clubs Details			Apps					Goals		
Club	Signed	Fee	Tot	Start	Sub	FA	FL	Lge	FA	FL
Dnepr										
Coventry City	Jan-97	£800,000	3	3	0	0	0	0	0	0
FAPL Summary by Club										
Coventry City	1996-97		3	3	0	0	0	0	0	0
Total			*3*	*3*	*0*	*0*	*0*	*0*	*0*	*0*

FAIRCLOUGH Chris — Bolton Wanderers

Full Name: Courtney Huw Fairclough DOB: 12-04-64 Nottingham
Debut: LEEDS UNITED v Wimbledon 15/8/92
Debut Goal: LEEDS UNITED v Coventry City 31/10/92

Previous Clubs Details			Apps					Goals		
Club	Signed	Fee	Tot	Start	Sub	FA	FL	Lge	FA	FL
N. Forest	Oct-81		107	102	5	6	10	1	0	1
Tottenham H.	Jun-87	£387,000	60	60	0	3	7	5	0	0
Leeds U.	Mar-89	£500,000	193	187	6	15	19	23	0	2

Bolton W.	Jul-95	£500,000	79	79	0	5	11	8	0	0
FAPL Summary by Club										
Leeds U.	92-93 to 94-95		75	70	5	7	6	8	0	0
Bolton W.	1995-96		33	33	0	2	6	0	0	0
Total			*108*	*103*	*5*	*9*	*12*	*8*	*0*	*0*

FARRELLY Gareth   Everton

Full Name: Gareth Farrelly   DOB: 28-08-75 Dublin
Debut: ASTON VILLA v Leeds Utd 3/2/96 as sub
Debut Goal:

Previous Clubs Details				Apps					Goals	
Club	Signed	Fee	Tot	Start	Sub	FA	FL	Lge	FA	FL
Aston Villa	Jan-92	Trainee	7	2	5	0	1	0	0	0
Rotherham U.	Mar-95	Loan	10	9	1	0	0	2	0	0
Everton	Jul-97	tba								
FAPL Summary by Club										
Aston Villa	95-96 to 96-97		7	2	5	0	1	0	0	0
Total			*7*	*2*	*5*	*0*	*1*	*0*	*0*	*0*

FEAR Peter   Wimbledon

Full Name: Peter Stanley Fear   DOB: 10-09-73 Sutton
Debut: Arsenal v WIMBLEDON 10/2/93
Debut Goal: WIMBLEDON v Leeds Utd 26/3/94

Previous Clubs Details				Apps					Goals	
Club	Signed	Fee	Tot	Start	Sub	FA	FL	Lge	FA	FL
Wimbledon	Jul-92		63	46	17	3	9	2	0	1
FAPL Summary by Club										
Wimbledon	92-93 to 96-97		63	46	17	3	9	2	0	1
Total			*63*	*46*	*17*	*3*	*9*	*2*	*0*	*1*

FENN Neale   Tottenham Hotspur

Full Name: Neale Fenn   DOB: 18-01-77 Tottenham
Debut: TOTTENHAM HOTSPUR v Sheffield Wed 9/4/97 as sub
Debut Goal:

Previous Clubs Details				Apps					Goals	
Club	Signed	Fee	Tot	Start	Sub	FA	FL	Lge	FA	FL
Tottenham H.			4	0	4	1	0	0	0	0
FAPL Summary by Club										
Tottenham H.	1996-97		4	0	4	1	0	0	0	0
Total			*4*	*0*	*4*	*1*	*0*	*0*	*0*	*0*

FENTON Graham   Blackburn Rovers

Full Name: Graham Anthony Fenton   DOB: 22-05-74 Wallsend
Debut: ASTON VILLA v Manchester City 22/2/94
Debut Goal: Sheffield Utd v ASTON VILLA 16/4/94

Previous Clubs Details				*Apps*					*Goals*		
Club	Signed	Fee	Tot	Start	Sub	FA	FL		Lge	FA	FL
Aston Villa	Feb-92		32	16	16	0	7		3	0	0
WBA	Jan-94	Loan	7	7	0	0	0		3	0	0
Blackburn R.	Dec-95	£1.5m	27	9	18	1	2		7	0	0
FAPL Summary by Club											
Aston Villa	93-94 to 95-96		32	16	16	0	7		3	0	0
Blackburn R.	95-96 to 96-97		27	9	18	1	2		7	0	0
Total			*59*	*25*	*34*	*1*	*9*		*10*	*0*	*0*

FERDINAND Les   Newcastle United

Full Name: Leslie Ferdinand   DOB: 18-12-66 Acton
Debut: Manchester City v QPR 17/8/92
Debut Goal: QPR v Southampton 19/8/92

Previous Clubs Details				*Apps*					*Goals*		
Club	Signed	Fee	Tot	Start	Sub	FA	FL		Lge	FA	FL
QPR	Apr-87	£15,000	163	152	11	8	13		80	3	7
Brentford	Mar-88	Loan	3	3	0	0	0		0	0	0
Besiktas (Turkey)	Jun-88	Loan									
Newcastle U.	Jun-95	£6m	68	67	1	5	6		41	2	3
FAPL Summary by Club											
QPR	92-93 to 94-95		110	109	1	7	8		60	3	5
Newcastle U.	95-96 to 96-97		68	67	1	5	6		41	2	3
Total			*178*	*176*	*2*	*12*	*14*		*101*	*5*	*8*

FERDINAND Rio   West Ham United

Full Name: Rio Gavin Ferdinand   DOB: 07-11-78 London
Debut: WEST HAM UTD v Sheffield Wednesday 5/5/96 as sub
Debut Goal: Blackburn R. v WEST HAM UTD 1/2/97

Previous Clubs Details				*Apps*					*Goals*		
Club	Signed	Fee	Tot	Start	Sub	FA	FL		Lge	FA	FL
West Ham U.	Nov-95	Trainee	16	11	5	1	1		2	0	0
Bournemouth *	Nov-96	Loan									
FAPL Summary by Club											
West Ham U.	95-96 to 96-97		16	11	5	1	1		2	0	0
Total			*16*	*11*	*5*	*1*	*1*		*2*	*0*	*0*

FERGUSON Duncan   Everton

Full Name: Duncan Ferguson   DOB: 27-12-71 Stirling
Debut: EVERTON v Coventry City 15/10/94
Debut Goal: EVERTON v Liverpool 21/11/94

Previous Clubs Details				*Apps*					*Goals*		
Club	Signed	Fee	Tot	Start	Sub	FA	FL		Lge	FA	FL
Dundee United	Feb-90	NL	77	75	2	6	3		27	4	2

Rangers	Jul-93	£4m	14	8	6	3	4	2	0	3
Everton	Oct-94	£4m	74	69	5	8	2	22	4	0
FAPL Summary by Club										
Everton	94-95 to 96-97		74	69	5	8	2	22	4	0
Total			*74*	*69*	*5*	*8*	*2*	*22*	*4*	*0*

FILAN John   Coventry City

Full Name: John Richard Filan   DOB: 08-02-70 Sydney
Debut: Tottenham Hotspur v COVENTRY CITY 9/5/95
Debut Goal: (Goalkeeper)

Previous Clubs Details				*Apps*					*Goals*	
Club	Signed	Fee	Tot	Start	Sub	FA	FL	Lge	FA	FL
Sydney										
Cambridge U.	Mar-93	£40,000	68	68	0	3	6	0	0	0
N. Forest	Dec-94	Loan								
Coventry City	Mar-95	£300,000	16	15	1	0	2	0	0	0
FAPL Summary by Club										
Coventry City	94-95 to 96-97		16	15	1	0	2	0	0	0
Total			*16*	*15*	*1*	*0*	*2*	*0*	*0*	*0*

FLITCROFT Gary   Blackburn Rovers

Full Name: Gary William Flitcroft   DOB: 06-11-72 Bolton
Debut: MANCHESTER CITY v Oldham Athletic 29/8/92
Debut Goal: Ipswich Town v MANCHESTER CITY 12/12/92

Previous Clubs Details				*Apps*					*Goals*	
Club	Signed	Fee	Tot	Start	Sub	FA	FL	Lge	FA	FL
Man. City	Jul-91		115	109	6	14	12	13	2	0
Bury	Mar-92	Loan	12	12	0	0	0	0	0	0
Blackburn R.	Mar-96	£3.2m	31	30	1	1	2	3	0	1
FAPL Summary by Club										
Man. City	92-93 to 95-96		115	109	6	14	12	13	2	0
Blackburn R.	95-96 to 96-97		31	30	1	1	2	3	0	1
Total			*146*	*139*	*7*	*15*	*14*	*16*	*2*	*1*

FLO Tore Andre   Chelsea

Full Name: Tore Andre Flo   DOB: 15-06-73 Norway
Debut: Debut Goal:

Previous Clubs Details				*Apps*					*Goals*	
Club	Signed	Fee	Tot	Start	Sub	FA	FL	Lge	FA	FL
Tromso	1995		26					18		
SK Brann	1996		24					19		
Chelsea	May-97	tba								

FLOWERS Tim   Blackburn Rovers

Full Name: Timothy David Flowers   DOB: 03-02-67 Kenilworth
Debut: SOUTHAMPTON v Tottenham Hotspur 15/8/92
Debut Goal: (Goalkeeper)

Previous Clubs Details

Club	Signed	Fee	Tot	Start	Sub	FA	FL	Lge	FA	FL
Wolves	Aug-84		63	63	0	2	5	0	0	0
Southampton	Jun-86	£70,000	192	192	0	16	26	0	0	0
Swindon Town	Mar-87	Loan	2	2	0	0	0	0	0	0
Swindon Town	Nov-87	Loan	5	5	0	0	0	0	0	0
Blackburn R.	Nov-93	£2.4m	141	141	0	6	14	0	0	0

Premiership Record
FAPL Summary by Club

Southampton	92-93 to 93-94		54	54	0	1	5	0	0	0
Blackburn R.	93-94 to 96-97		141	141	0	6	14	0	0	0
Total			*195*	*195*	*0*	*7*	*19*	*0*	*0*	*0*

FLYNN Sean   Derby County

Full Name: Sean Michael Flynn   DOB: 13-03-68 Birmingham
Debut: COVENTRY CITY v Middlesbrough 15/8/92
Debut Goal: Arsenal v COVENTRY CITY 14/8/93

Previous Clubs Details

Club	Signed	Fee	Tot	Start	Sub	FA	FL	Lge	FA	FL
Coventry City	Dec-91	£20,000 NL	97	90	7	3	5	9	0	1
Derby County	Aug-95	£250,000	59	39	20	4	6	3	0	0
Stoke City	Mar-97	Loan								

FAPL Summary by Club

Coventry City	92-93 to 94-95		75	69	6	3	5	7	0	1
Derby County	96-97		17	10	7	3	3	1	0	0
Total			*92*	*79*	*13*	*6*	*8*	*8*	*0*	*1*

FORD Mark   Leeds United

Full Name: Mark Ford   DOB: 10-10-75 Pontefract
Debut: Swindon Town v LEEDS UNITED 7/5/94 as sub
Debut Goal: LEEDS UTD v Sunderland 2/11/96

Previous Clubs Details

Club	Signed	Fee	Tot	Start	Sub	FA	FL	Lge	FA	FL
Leeds U.			28	26	2	5	7	1	0	0

FAPL Summary by Club

Leeds U.	93-94 to 96-97		28	26	2	5	7	1	0	0
Total			*28*	*26*	*2*	*5*	*7*	*1*	*0*	*0*

FOWLER Robbie   Liverpool

Full Name: Robert Bernard Fowler   DOB: 09-04-75 Liverpool

Debut: Chelsea v LIVERPOOL 25/9/93
Debut Goal: LIVERPOOL v Oldham Athletic 16/10/93

Previous Clubs Details

Club	Signed	Fee	Tot	Start	Sub	FA	FL	Lge	FA	FL
					Apps				*Goals*	
Liverpool	Apr-92	Trainee	140	137	3	16	21	83	9	17

Premiership Record
FAPL Summary by Club

Liverpool	93-94 to 96-97	140	137	3	16	21	83	7	16
Total		*140*	*137*	*3*	*16*	*21*	*83*	*7*	*16*

FOX Ruel   Tottenham Hotspur

Full Name: Ruel Adrian Fox   DOB: 14-01-68 Ipswich
Debut: Arsenal v NORWICH CITY 15/8/92
Debut Goal: Arsenal v NORWICH CITY 15/8/92

Previous Clubs Details

Club	Signed	Fee	Tot	Start	Sub	FA	FL	Lge	FA	FL
					Apps				*Goals*	
Norwich City	Jan-86	Apprentice	172	148	24	15	16	22	0	3
Newcastle U.	Feb-94	£2.25m	58	56	2	5	3	12	0	1
Tottenham H.	Oct-95	£4.2m	51	45	6	6	4	7	0	0

FAPL Summary by Club

Norwich City	92-93 to 93-94	59	57	2	4	5	11	0	2
Newcastle U.	93-94 to 95-96	58	56	2	5	3	12	0	1
Tottenham H.	95-96 to 96-97	51	45	6	6	4	7	0	0
Total		*168*	*158*	*10*	*15*	*12*	*30*	*0*	*3*

FRANDSEN Per   Bolton Wanderers

Full Name: Per Frandsen   DOB:
Debut: Debut Goal:

Previous Clubs Details

Club	Signed	Fee	Tot	Start	Sub	FA	FL	Lge	FA	FL
					Apps				*Goals*	
Bolton W.			41	40	1	4	5	5	0	0

FREEDMAN Dougie   Crystal Palace

Full Name: Douglas Alan Freedman   DOB: 21-01-74 Glasgow
Debut: Debut Goal:

Previous Clubs Details

Club	Signed	Fee	Tot	Start	Sub	FA	FL	Lge	FA	FL
					Apps				*Goals*	
QPR	May-92	Trainee	0	0	0	0	0	0	0	0
Barnet	Jul-94	Free	47	47	0	2	6	27	0	5
C. Palace	Sep-95	£800,000	83	70	13	3	3	31	0	1

GALLACHER Kevin   Blackburn Rovers

Full Name: Kevin William Gallacher   DOB: 23-11-66 Clydebank
Debut: COVENTRY CITY v Blackburn R 29/8/92
Debut Goal: Oldham Athletic v COVENTRY CITY 5/9/92

Previous Clubs Details				Apps				Goals		
Club	Signed	Fee	Tot	Start	Sub	FA	FL	Lge	FA	FL
Coventry City	Jan-90	£900,000	100	99	1	4	11	28	0	7
Blackburn R.	Mar-93	£1.5m	90	85	5	8	7	25	1	1
FAPL Summary by Club										
Coventry City	1992-93		20	19	1	1	2	6	0	0
Blackburn R.	92-93 to 96-97		90	85	5	8	7	25	1	1
Total			*110*	*104*	*6*	*9*	*9*	*31*	*1*	*1*

GARDE Remi   Arsenal

Full Name: Remi Garde   DOB: 03-04-66 L'Arbesle
Debut: ARSENAL v Leeds Utd 26/10/96 as sub
Debut Goal:

Previous Clubs Details				Apps				Goals		
Club	Signed	Fee	Tot	Start	Sub	FA	FL	Lge	FA	FL
O. Lyonnais	1990		81	81	0			13		
RC Strasbourg	1995		68	64	4			3		
Arsenal	Aug-96	Free	11	7	4	0	0	0	0	0
FAPL Summary by Club										
Arsenal	1996-97		11	7	4	0	0	0	0	0
Total			*11*	*7*	*4*	*0*	*0*	*0*	*0*	*0*

GAYLE Marcus   Wimbledon

Full Name: Marcus Anthony Gayle   DOB: 27-09-70 Hammersmith
Debut: WIMBLEDON v Leeds Utd 26/3/94
Debut Goal: Nottingham Forest v WIMBLEDON 17/10/94

Previous Clubs Details				Apps				Goals		
Club	Signed	Fee	Tot	Start	Sub	FA	FL	Lge	FA	FL
Brentford	Jul-89		156	118	38	8	9	22	2	0
Wimbledon	Mar-94	£250,000	103	87	16	14	11	15	2	4
FAPL Summary by Club										
Wimbledon	93-94 to 96-97		103	87	16	14	11	15	2	4
Total			*103*	*87*	*16*	*14*	*11*	*15*	*2*	*4*

GERRARD Paul   Everton

Full Name: Paul William Gerrard   DOB: 22-01-73 Heywood
Debut: QPR v OLDHAM ATHLETIC 5/12/92
Debut Goal: (Goalkeeper)

Previous Clubs Details				Apps				Goals		
Club	Signed	Fee	Tot	Start	Sub	FA	FL	Lge	FA	FL
Oldham Ath.	Nov-91	Trainee	119	118	1	7	7	0	0	0
Everton	Aug-96	1.5m	5	4	1	0	0	0	0	0

Oldham Ath.	92-93 to 93-94	41	40	1	2	2	0	0	0
Everton	1996-97	5	4	1	0	0	0	0	0
Total		*46*	*44*	*2*	*2*	*2*	*0*	*0*	*0*

GIGGS Ryan
Manchester United

Full Name: Ryan Joseph Giggs DOB: 29-11-73 Cardiff
Debut: Sheffield Utd v MANCHESTER UNITED 15/8/92
Debut Goal: Nottingham Forest v MANCHESTER UNITED 29/8/92

Previous Clubs Details				*Apps*				*Goals*	
Club	Signed	Fee	Tot	Start	Sub	FA	FL	Lge	FA	FL
Manchester U.	Dec-90		207	189	18	29	20	42	5	6

FAPL Summary by Club

Manchester U.	92-93 to 96-97	167	156	11	26	12	37	5	3
Total		*167*	*156*	*11*	*26*	*12*	*37*	*5*	*3*

GILLESPIE Keith
Newcastle United

Full Name: Keith Robert Gillespie DOB: 18-02-75 Bangor
Debut: Sheffield Wednesday v MANCHESTER UTD 8/10/94
Debut Goal: MANCHESTER UTD v Newcastle United 29/10/94 as sub

Previous Clubs Details				*Apps*				*Goals*	
Club	Signed	Fee	Tot	Start	Sub	FA	FL	Lge	FA	FL
Manchester U.	Feb-93	Trainee	9	3	6	2	3	1	1	0
Wigan Athletic	Sep-93	Loan	8	8	0	0	0	4	0	0
Newcastle U.	Jan-95	£1m +	77	64	13	5	5	7	2	1

FAPL Summary by Club

Manchester U.	93-94 to 94-95	9	3	6	2	3	1	1	0
Newcastle U.	94-95 to 96-97	77	64	13	5	5	7	2	1
Total		*86*	*67*	*19*	*7*	*8*	*8*	*3*	*1*

GINOLA David
Newcastle United

Full Name: David Ginola DOB: 25-01-67 Gassin, nr St Tropez
Debut: NEWCASTLE UNITED v Coventry City 19/8/95
Debut Goal: Sheffield Wednesday v NEWCASTLE UNITED 27/8/95

Previous Clubs Details				*Apps*				*Goals*	
Club	Signed	Fee	Tot	Start	Sub	FA	FL	Lge	FA	FL
PSG (France)										
Newcastle U.	Jul-95	£2.5m	58	54	4	4	6	6	0	0

FAPL Summary by Club

Newcastle U.	95-96 to 96-97	58	54	4	4	6	6	0	0
Total		*58*	*54*	*4*	*4*	*6*	*6*	*0*	*0*

GIVEN Shay　　　　　　　　　　　　　Newcastle United

Full Name: Seamus John Given　　　DOB: 20-04-76 Lifford, Co. Donegal
Debut: Wimbledon v BLACKBURN ROVERS 14/12/96
Debut Goal: (Goalkeeper)

Previous Clubs Details

Club	Signed	Fee	Tot	Start	Sub	FA	FL	Lge	FA	FL
Celtic										
Blackburn R.	Aug-94	Free	2	2	0	0	1	0	0	0
Swindon Town	Jan-95	Loan	5	5	0	0	0	0	0	0
Sunderland	Jan-96	Loan	17	17	0	0	0	0	0	0
Newcastle U.	May-97	tba	2	2	0	0	0	0	0	0

FAPL Summary by Club

Blackburn R.		1996-97	2	2	0	0	1	0	0	0
Total			*2*	*2*	*0*	*0*	*1*	*0*	*0*	*0*

GOODMAN Jon　　　　　　　　　　　　　Wimbledon

Full Name: Jonathan Goodman　　　DOB: 02-06-71 Walthamstow
Debut: WIMBLEDON v Newcastle United 19/11/94
Debut Goal: Ipswich Town v WIMBLEDON 16/12/94

Previous Clubs Details

Club	Signed	Fee	Tot	Start	Sub	FA	FL	Lge	FA	FL
Bromley										
Millwall	Aug-90	£50,000	109	97	12	6	9	35	0	2
Wimbledon	Nov-94	£1.3m +	59	28	31	7	2	11	3	0

FAPL Summary by Club

Wimbledon		94-95 to 96-97	59	28	31	7	2	11	3	0
Total			*59*	*28*	*31*	*7*	*2*	*11*	*3*	*0*

GORDON Dean　　　　　　　　　　　　Crystal Palace

Full Name: Dean Dwight Gordon　　　DOB: 10-02-73 Croydon
Debut: Oldham Athletic v CRYSTAL PALACE 19/8/92
Debut Goal: Leeds Utd v CRYSTAL PALACE 30/8/94

Previous Clubs Details

Club	Signed	Fee	Tot	Start	Sub	FA	FL	Lge	FA	FL
C. Palace	Jul-91	Trainee	164	145	19	11	17	18	1	2

FAPL Summary by Club

C. Palace		92-93 to 94-95	51	44	7	6	9	2	1	1
Total			*51*	*44*	*7*	*6*	*9*	*2*	*1*	*1*

GRANT Tony　　　　　　　　　　　　　　Everton

Full Name: Anthony James Grant　　　DOB: 14-11-74 Liverpool
Debut: Newcastle United v EVERTON 1/2/95 as sub
Debut Goal: Middlesbrough v EVERTON 2/3/96

Previous Clubs Details			Apps					Goals		
Club	Signed	Fee	Tot	Start	Sub	FA	FL	Lge	FA	FL
Everton	Jul-93	Trainee	36	23	13	3	3	1	0	0
Swindon Town	Jan-96	Loan	3	3	0	0	0	1	0	0
FAPL Summary by Club										
Everton		94-95 to 96-97	36	23	13	3	3	1	0	0
Total			*36*	*23*	*13*	*3*	*3*	*1*	*0*	*0*

GRANVILLE Danny   Chelsea

Full Name: Daniel Patrick Granville   DOB. 19-01-75 Islington
Debut: CHELSEA v Arsenal 5/4/97
Debut Goal:

Previous Clubs Details			Apps					Goals		
Club	Signed	Fee	Tot	Start	Sub	FA	FL	Lge	FA	FL
Cambridge U.*	May-93	Trainee	62	52	10	2	3	7	0	0
Chelsea	Mar-97	£300,000	5	3	2	0	0	0	0	0
FAPL Summary by Club										
Chelsea		1996-97	5	3	2	0	0	0	0	0
Total			*5*	*3*	*2*	*0*	*0*	*0*	*0*	*0*

GRAY Andy   Leeds United

Full Name: Andrew David Gray   DOB: 15-11-77 Harrogate
Debut: LEEDS UTD v West Ham Utd 13/1/96 as sub
Debut Goal:

Previous Clubs Details			Apps					Goals		
Club	Signed	Fee	Tot	Start	Sub	FA	FL	Lge	FA	FL
Leeds U.	Jul-95	Trainee	22	13	9	2	4	0	0	0
FAPL Summary by Club										
Leeds U.		95-96 to 96-97	22	13	9	2	4	0	0	0
Total			*22*	*13*	*9*	*2*	*4*	*0*	*0*	*0*

GRAYSON Simon   Aston Villa

Full Name: Simon Nicholas Grayson   DOB: 16-12-69 Ripon
Debut: LEICESTER CITY v Newcastle United 21/8/94
Debut Goal:

Previous Clubs Details			Apps					Goals		
Club	Signed	Fee	Tot	Start	Sub	FA	FL	Lge	FA	FL
Leeds U.	Jun-88	Trainee	2	2	0	0	0	0	0	0
Leicester City	Mar-92	£50,000	188	175	13	9	18	4	0	2
Aston Villa	Jun-97	Free								
FAPL Summary by Club										
Leicester City		94-95 to 96-97	70	70	0	6	9	0	0	2
Total			*70*	*70*	*0*	*6*	*9*	*0*	*0*	*2*

GRIMANDI Gilles — Arsenal

Full Name: Gilles Grimandi
DOB: 11-11-70
Debut:
Debut Goal:

Previous Clubs Details

Club	Signed	Fee	Tot	Start	Sub	FA	FL	Lge	FA	FL
Monaco *	1990		66	39	27			2		
Arsenal	Jun-97	£2m								

GRODAS Frode — Chelsea

Full Name: Frode Grodas
DOB: 24-10-69 Norway
Debut: Blackburn Rovers v CHELSEA 16/11/96
Debut Goal: (Goalkeeper)

Previous Clubs Details

Club	Signed	Fee	Tot	Start	Sub	FA	FL	Lge	FA	FL
Lillestrom	1990		117	117	0			1		
Chelsea	Nov-96	Free	21	20	1	5	1	0	0	0

FAPL Summary by Club

Chelsea	1996-97		21	20	1	5	1	0	0	0
Total			21	20	1	5	1	0	0	0

GUDMUNDSSON Niklas — Blackburn Rovers

Full Name: Niklas Gudmundsson
DOB: 29-02-72 Halmstad
Debut: BLACKBURN RVRS v Sheffield Wednesday 20/1/96 as sub
Debut Goal:

Previous Clubs Details

Club	Signed	Fee	Tot	Start	Sub	FA	FL	Lge	FA	FL
Halmstads										
Blackburn R.	Dec-95	£750,000	6	1	5	0	0	0	0	0
Ipswich Town	Mar-97	Loan								

FAPL Summary by Club

Blackburn R.	95-96 to 96-97		6	1	5	0	0	0	0	0
Total			6	1	5	0	0	0	0	0

GULLIT Ruud — Chelsea

Full Name: Dil Ruud Gullit
DOB: 01-09-62 Amsterdam
Debut: CHELSEA v Everton 19/8/95
Debut Goal: CHELSEA v Southampton 16/9/95

Previous Clubs Details

Club	Signed	Fee	Tot	Start	Sub	FA	FL	Lge	FA	FL
Haarlem	Jul-79		91	91	0	0	0	32	0	0
Feyenoord	Jul-82		85	85	0	0	0	30	0	0
PSV	Jul-85		68	68	0	0	0	46	0	0
Milan	Jul-87		117	117	0	0	0	35	0	0
Sampdoria	Jul-93		22	21	1			8		
Chelsea	Jul-95	Free	43	37	6	8	3	4	3	0

FAPL Summary by Club

Chelsea	95-96 to 96-97	43	37	6	8	3	4	3	0
Total		*43*	*37*	*6*	*8*	*3*	*4*	*3*	*0*

GUPPY Steve — Leicester City

Full Name: Stephen Guppy DOB: 29-03-69 Winchester
Debut: Wimbledon v LEICESTER CITY 1/3/97
Debut Goal:

Previous Clubs Details			Apps				Goals		
Club	Signed	Fee	Tot	Start	Sub	FA	FL	Lge	FA FL
Wycombe W.	1989		41	41	0	8	4	8	2 0
Newcastle U.	Aug-94	£150,000	0	0	0	0	1	0	0 0
Port Vale *	Nov-94	£225,000	71	68	3	7	2	6	0 0
Leicester City	Feb-97	£850,000	13	12	1	0	0	0	0 0

FAPL Summary by Club

Leicester City	1996-97	13	12	1	0	0	0	0	0
Total		*13*	*12*	*1*	*0*	*0*	*0*	*0*	*0*

HAALAND Alf-Inge — Leeds United

Full Name: Alf-Inge Haaland DOB: 23-11-72 Stavanger, Norway
Debut: Southampton v NOTTINGHAM FOREST 17/9/94
Debut Goal: NOTTINGHAM FOREST v Ipswich Town 10/12/94

Previous Clubs Details			Apps					Goals	
Club	Signed	Fee	Tot	Start	Sub	FA	FL	Lge	FA FL
Young Boys									
N. Forest	Jan-94		74	66	6	6	7	7	0 0
Leeds Utd	Jun-97	Tribunal							

FAPL Summary by Club

N. Forest	94-95 to 96-97	74	66	6	6	7	7	0	0
Total		*74*	*66*	*6*	*6*	*7*	*7*	*0*	*0*

HALL Marcus — Coventry City

Full Name: Marcus Hall DOB: 24-03-76
Debut: COVENTRY CITY v Tottenham Hotspur 31/12/94 as sub
Debut Goal:

Previous Clubs Details			Apps					Goals	
Club	Signed	Fee	Tot	Start	Sub	FA	FL	Lge	FA FL
Coventry City			43	36	7	5	6	0	0 0

FAPL Summary by Club

Coventry City	94-95 to 96-97	43	36	7	5	6	0	0	0
Total		*43*	*36*	*7*	*5*	*6*	*0*	*0*	*0*

HALL Richard — West Ham United

Full Name: Richard Anthony Hall DOB: 14-03-72 Ipswich
Debut: SOUTHAMPTON v Tottenham Hotspur 15/8/92
Debut Goal: Oldham Athletic v SOUTHAMPTON 31/10/92

Previous Clubs Details				*Apps*				*Goals*		
Club	Signed	Fee	Tot	Start	Sub	FA	FL	Lge	FA	FL
Scunthorpe U.	Mar-90		22	22	0	3	2	3	0	0
Southampton	Feb-91	£200,000	126	119	7	15	12	12	3	1
West Ham U.	Jul-96		7	7	0	0	0	0	0	0
FAPL Summary by Club										
Southampton	92-93 to 95-96		99	98	1	10	7	9	1	1
West Ham U.	1996-97		7	7	0	0	0	0	0	0
Total			*106*	*105*	*1*	*10*	*7*	*9*	*1*	*1*

HALLE Gunnar   Leeds United

Full Name: Gunnar Halle   DOB: 11-08-65 Oslo, Norway
Debut: Chelsea v OLDHAM ATHLETIC 15/8/92
Debut Goal: OLDHAM ATH v Nottingham Forest 22/8/92

Previous Clubs Details				*Apps*				*Goals*		
Club	Signed	Fee	Tot	Start	Sub	FA	FL	Lge	FA	FL
Lillestrom										
Oldham Ath	Feb-91	£280,000	168	167	1	8	11	14	2	2
Leeds U.	Dec-96	£400,000	20	20	0	3	0	0	0	0
FAPL Summary by Club										
Oldham Ath	92-93 to 93-94		63	62	1	3	4	6	0	1
Leeds U.	1996-97		20	20	0	3	0	0	0	0
Total			*83*	*82*	*1*	*6*	*4*	*6*	*0*	*1*

HAMILTON Des   Newcastle United

Full Name: Derrick Vivian Hamilton   DOB: 15-08-76 Bradford
Debut: Debut Goal:

Previous Clubs Details				*Apps*				*Goals*		
Club	Signed	Fee	Tot	Start	Sub	FA	FL	Lge	FA	FL
Bradford C. *	Jun-94	Trainee	56	43	13	3	5	5	0	1
Newcastle U.	Mar-97	£1.6m +								

HARFORD Mick   Wimbledon

Full Name: Michael Gordon Harford   DOB: 12-02-59 Sunderland
Debut: CHELSEA v Oldham Athletic 15/8/92
Debut Goal: CHELSEA v Oldham Athletic 15/8/92

Previous Clubs Details				*Apps*				*Goals*		
Club	Signed	Fee	Tot	Start	Sub	FA	FL	Lge	FA	FL
Lincoln City	Jul-77		115	109	6	3	8	41	0	5
Newcastle U.	Dec-80	£180,000	19	18	1	0	0	4	0	0
Bristol City	Aug-81	£160,000	30	30	0	5	5	11	2	1
Birmingham C.	Mar-82	£100,000	92	92	0	7	10	25	2	6
Luton Town	Dec-84	£250,000	139	135	4	27	16	57	11	10
Derby County	Jan-90	£450,000	58	58	0	1	7	15	0	3
Luton Town	Sep-91	£325,000	29	29	0	0	1	12	0	0

Chelsea	Aug-92	£300,000	28	27	1	1	5	9	0	2
Sunderland	Mar-93	£250,000	11	10	1	0	0	2	0	0
Coventry City	Jul-93	£200,000	1	0	1	0	0	1	0	0
Wimbledon	Aug-94	£50,000	61	37	24	13	9	9	1	1
FAPL Summary by Club										
Chelsea		92-93 to 93-94	28	27	1	1	5	9	0	2
Coventry City		1993-94	1	0	1	0	0	1	0	0
Wimbledon		94-95 to 96-97	61	37	24	13	9	9	1	1
Total			*90*	*64*	*26*	*14*	*14*	*19*	*1*	*3*

HARKNESS Steve   Liverpool

Full Name: Steven Harkness   DOB: 27-08-71 Carlisle
Debut: Ipswich Town v LIVERPOOL 25/8/92
Debut Goal: LIVERPOOL v Tottenham Hotspur 8/5/93

Previous Clubs Details				*Apps*					*Goals*	
Club	Signed	Fee	Tot	Start	Sub	FA	FL	Lge	FA	FL
Carlisle U.	Mar-89		13	12	1	0	0	0	0	0
Liverpool	Jul-89	£75,000	71	62	9	4	10	3	0	1
Huddersfield T.	Sep-93	Loan	5	5	0	0	0	0	0	0
Southend U.	Feb-95	Loan	6	6	0	0	0	0	0	0
FAPL Summary by Club										
Liverpool		92-93 to 96-97	60	55	5	2	7	3	0	1
Total			*60*	*55*	*5*	*2*	*7*	*3*	*0*	*1*

HARRIS Jason   Crystal Palace

Full Name: Jason Harris   DOB: 24-11-76 Sutton
Debut: Debut Goal:

Previous Clubs Details				*Apps*					*Goals*	
Club	Signed	Fee	Tot	Start	Sub	FA	FL	Lge	FA	FL
C. Palace	Jul-95	Trainee	2	0	2	0	2	0	0	0

HARTE Ian   Leeds United

Full Name: Ian Harte   DOB: 31-08-77 Drogheda
Debut: LEEDS UTD v West Ham Utd 13/1/96
Debut Goal: Derby Co. v LEEDS UTD 17/8/96

Previous Clubs Details				*Apps*					*Goals*	
Club	Signed	Fee	Tot	Start	Sub	FA	FL	Lge	FA	FL
Leeds U.	Dec-95	Trainee	18	12	6	1	3	2	0	1
FAPL Summary by Club										
Leeds U.		95-96 to 96-97	18	12	6	1	4	2	0	1
Total			*18*	*12*	*6*	*1*	*4*	*2*	*0*	*1*

HARTSON John   West Ham United

Full Name: John Hartson   DOB: 05-04-75 Swansea
Debut: ARSENAL v Everton 14/1/95
Debut Goal: Coventry City v ARSENAL 21/1/95

Club	Signed	Fee	Tot	Start	Sub	FA	FL	Lge	FA	FL
					Apps				Goals	
Luton Town	Dec-92	Trainee	34	21	13	5	1	6	0	1
Arsenal	Jan-95	£2.5m	53	43	10	3	6	14	1	1
West Ham U.	Feb-97	£3.2m>£5m	11	11	0	0	0	5	0	0
FAPL Summary by Club										
Arsenal		94-95 to 96-97	53	43	10	3	6	14	1	1
West Ham U.		1996-97	11	11	0	0	0	5	0	0
Total			64	54	10	3	6	19	1	1

HASSELBAINK Jimmy Floyd Leeds United

Full Name: Jimmy Floyd Hasselbaink   DOB:
Debut: Debut Goal:

Previous Clubs Details

Club	Signed	Fee	Tot	Start	Sub	FA	FL	Lge	FA	FL
					Apps				Goals	
Boavista										
Leeds Utd	Jun-97	£2m								

HEALD Paul Wimbledon

Full Name: Paul Andrew Heald   DOB: 20-09-68 Wath-on-Dearne
Debut: SWINDON TOWN v Sheffield Wednesday 4/2/94 as sub
Debut Goal: (Goalkeeper)

Previous Clubs Details

Club	Signed	Fee	Tot	Start	Sub	FA	FL	Lge	FA	FL
					Apps				Goals	
Sheffield U.	Jun-87	Trainee	0	0	0	0	0	0	0	0
Leyton Orient	Dec-88	Unknown	176	176	0	9	13	0	0	0
Coventry City	Mar-92	Loan	2	2	0	0	0	0	0	0
Swindon Town	Mar-94	Loan	3	2	1	0	0	1	0	0
Wimbledon	Aug-95	£125,000	20	20	0	0	3	0	0	0
FAPL Summary by Club										
Swindon Town		93-94	3	2	1	0	0	1	0	0
Wimbledon		95-96 to 96-97	20	20	0	0	3	0	0	0
Total			23	22	1	0	3	1	0	0

HELDER Glenn Arsenal

Full Name: Glenn Helder   DOB: 28-10-68 Leiden, Holland
Debut: ARSENAL v Nottingham Forest 21/2/95
Debut Goal: Middlesbrough v ARSENAL 13/1/96

Previous Clubs Details

Club	Signed	Fee	Tot	Start	Sub	FA	FL	Lge	FA	FL
					Apps				Goals	
Sparta Rot.	1989		93					9		
Vitesse Arnhem	1993		52					12		
Arsenal	Feb-95	£2.3m	39	27	12	2	6	1	0	0
Benfica	Nov-96	Loan								

Arsenal	94-95 to 96-97	39	27	12	2	6	1	0	0
Total		*39*	*27*	*12*	*2*	*6*	*1*	*0*	*0*

HENDRIE Lee   Aston Villa
Full Name: Lee Hendrie   DOB: 18-05-77 Birmingham
Debut: QPR v ASTON VILLA 23/12/95 as sub
Debut Goal:

Previous Clubs Details

			Apps				Goals		
Club	Signed	Fee	Tot	Start	Sub	FA	FL	Lge	FA FL
Aston Villa		Trainee	7	2	5	3	0	0	0 0

FAPL Summary by Club

Aston Villa	95-96 to 96-97	7	2	5	3	0	0	0	0
Total		*7*	*02*	*5*	*3*	*0*	*0*	*0*	*0*

HENDRIE John   Barnsley
Full Name: John Hendrie   DOB: 24-10-63 Lennoxtown
Debut: Coventry City v MIDDLESBROUGH 15/8/92
Debut Goal: MIDDLESBROUGH v Leeds Utd 22/8/92

Previous Clubs Details

			Apps				Goals		
Club	Signed	Fee	Tot	Start	Sub	FA	FL	Lge	FA FL
Coventry City	May-81	Apprentice	21	15	6	0	2	2	0 0
Hereford U.	Jan-84	Loan	6	6	0	0	0	0	0 0
Bradford City	Jul-84	Free	173	173	0	11	17	46	6 4
Newcastle U.	Jun-88	£500,000	34	34	0	4	2	4	0 1
Leeds U.	Jun-89	£600,000	27	22	5	1	1	5	0 0
Middlesbrough	Jul-90	£550,000	192	181	11	10	23	45	2 6
Barnsley	Oct-96	£250,000	36	36	0	2	0	15	1 0

FAPL Summary by Club

Middlesbrough	92-93 to 95-96	45	38	7	0	3	10	0	0
Total		*45*	*38*	*7*	*0*	*3*	*10*	*0*	*0*

HENDRY Colin   Blackburn Rovers
Full Name: Edward Colin James Hendry   DOB: 07-12-65 Keith
Debut: Crystal Palace v BLACKBURN ROVERS 15/8/92
Debut Goal: BLACKBURN ROVERS v Coventry City 26/1/93

Previous Clubs Details

			Apps				Goals		
Club	Signed	Fee	Tot	Start	Sub	FA	FL	Lge	FA FL
Blackburn R.	Mar-87	£30,000	102	99	3	3	4	22	0 0
Man. City	Nov-89	£700,000	63	57	6	5	5	5	2 1
Blackburn R.	Nov-91	£700,000	200	195	5	14	22	11	0 0

FAPL Summary by Club

Blackburn R.	92-93 to 96-97	170	169	1	13	22	7	0	0
Total		*170*	*169*	*1*	*13*	*22*	*7*	*0*	*0*

HESKEY Emile   Leicester City

Full Name: Emile Heskey   DOB: 11-01-78 Leicester
Debut: QPR v LEICESTER CITY 8/3/95
Debut Goal: LEICESTER CITY v Southampton 21/8/97

Previous Clubs Details				*Apps*				*Goals*		
Club	Signed	Fee	Tot	Start	Sub	FA	FL	Lge	FA	FL
Leicester City	Oct-95	Trainee	66	56	10	3	11	17	0	2
FAPL Summary by Club										
Leicester City	94-95 to 96-97		36	36	0	3	9	10	0	2
Total			*36*	*36*	*0*	*3*	*9*	*10*	*0*	*2*

HILL Colin   Leicester City

Full Name: Colin Frederick Hill   DOB: 12-11-63 Uxbridge
Debut: LEICESTER CITY v Newcastle United 21/8/94
Debut Goal:

Previous Clubs Details				*Apps*				*Goals*		
Club	Signed	Fee	Tot	Start	Sub	FA	FL	Lge	FA	FL
Arsenal	Aug-81	Apprentice	46	46	0	1	4	1	0	0
Maritime (Por)		Free								
Colchester U.	Oct-87	Free	69	64	5	7	2	0	2	0
Sheffield U.	Aug-89	£85,000	82	77	5	12	5	1	0	0
Leicester City	Mar-92	Loan	10	10	0	0	0	0	0	0
Leicester City	Jul-92	£200,000	135	130	5	8	12	0	1	0
FAPL Summary by Club										
Leicester City	94-95 to 96-97		31	30	1	3	2	0	0	0
Total			*31*	*30*	*1*	*3*	*2*	*0*	*0*	*0*

HILLS John   Everton

Full Name: John Hills   DOB: 21-04-78 Blackpool
Debut: EVERTON v Wimbledon 28/12/96 as sub
Debut Goal:

Previous Clubs Details				*Apps*				*Goals*		
Club	Signed	Fee	Tot	Start	Sub	FA	FL	Lge	FA	FL
Blackpool										
Everton			3	1	2	0	0	0	0	0
FAPL Summary by Club										
Everton	1996-97		3	1	2	0	0	0	0	0
Total			*3*	*1*	*2*	*0*	*0*	*0*	*0*	*0*

HINCHCLIFFE Andy   Everton

Full Name: Andrew George Hinchcliffe   DOB: 05-02-69 Manchester
Debut: EVERTON v Sheffield Wednesday 15/8/92
Debut Goal: EVERTON v Nottingham Forest 13/3/93
Previous Clubs Details   *Apps*   *Goals*

Club	Signed	Fee	Tot	Start	Sub	FA	FL	Lge	FA	FL
Man. City	Feb-86		112	107	5	12	11	8	1	1
Everton	Jul-90	£800,000	165	155	10	14	20	6	1	1
FAPL Summary by Club										
Everton	92-93 to 96-97		126	119	7	9	15	6	1	1
Total			*126*	*119*	*7*	*9*	*15*	*6*	*1*	*1*

HIRST David   Sheffield Wednesday
Full Name: David Eric Hirst   DOB: 07-12-67 Cudworth
Debut: Everton v SHEFFIELD WEDNESDAY 15/8/92
Debut Goal: SHEFFIELD WED v Nottingham Forest 19/8/92

Previous Clubs Details				Apps				Goals		
Club	Signed	Fee	Tot	Start	Sub	FA	FL	Lge	FA	FL
Barnsley	Nov-85		28	26	2	0	1	9	0	0
Sheffield W.	Aug-86	£200,000	288	258	30	19	35	106	6	11
FAPL Summary by Club										
Sheffield W.	92-93 to 96-97		99	90	9	9	13	34	1	4
Total			*99*	*90*	*9*	*9*	*13*	*34*	*1*	*4*

HISLOP Shaka   Newcastle United
Full Name: Neil Hislop   DOB: 22-02-69 London
Debut: NEWCASTLE UNITED v Coventry City 19/8/95
Debut Goal: (Goalkeeper)

Previous Clubs Details				Apps				Goals		
Club	Signed	Fee	Tot	Start	Sub	FA	FL	Lge	FA	FL
Reading	Sep-92		104	104	0	3	10	0	0	0
Newcastle U.	Aug-95	£1.575m	40	40	0	3	5	0	0	0
FAPL Summary by Club										
Newcastle U.	95-96 to 96-97		40	40	0	3	5	0	0	0
Total			*40*	*40*	*0*	*3*	*5*	*0*	*0*	*0*

HITCHCOCK Kevin   Chelsea
Full Name: Kevin Joseph Hitchcock   DOB: 05-10-62 Canning Town
Debut: Manchester City v CHELSEA 20/9/92
Debut Goal: (Goalkeeper)

Previous Clubs Details				Apps				Goals		
Club	Signed	Fee	Tot	Start	Sub	FA	FL	Lge	FA	FL
N.Forest	Aug-83	£15,000	0	0	0	0	0	0	0	0
Mansfield T.	Feb-84	Loan	14	14	0	0	0	0	0	0
Mansfield T.	Jun-84	£140,000	168	168	0	10	12	0	0	0
Chelsea	Mar-88	£250,000	93	90	3	14	10	0	0	0
Northampton T.	Dec-90	Loan	17	17	0	0	0	0	0	0
FAPL Summary by Club										
Chelsea	92-93 to 96-97		58	55	3	10	8	0	0	0
Total			*58*	*55*	*3*	*10*	*8*	*0*	*0*	*0*

HOLDSWORTH Dean   Wimbledon

Full Name: Dean Christopher Holdsworth   DOB: 08-11-68 London
Debut: Leeds Utd v WIMBLEDON 15/8/92
Debut Goal: WIMBLEDON v Coventry City 22/8/92

Previous Clubs Details

Club	Signed	Fee		Apps					Goals		
			Tot	Start	Sub	FA	FL	Lge	FA	FL	
Watford	Nov-86	Apprentice	16	2	14	0	0	3	0	0	
Carlisle U.	Feb-88	Loan	4	4	0	0	0	1	0	0	
Port Vale	Mar-88	Loan	6	6	0	0	0	2	0	0	
Swansea City	Aug-88	Loan	5	4	1	0	0	1	0	0	
Brentford	Oct-88	Loan	7	2	5	0	0	1	0	0	
Brentford	Sep-89	£125,000	110	106	4	6	8	53	7	6	
Wimbledon	Jul-92	£720,000	164	144	20	20	18	58	7	11	

FAPL Summary by Club

Wimbledon	92-93 to 96-97		164	144	20	20	18	58	7	11	
Total			*164*	*144*	*20*	*20*	*18*	*58*	*7*	*11*	

HOLMES Matty   Blackburn Rovers

Full Name: Matthew Jason Holmes   DOB: 01-08-69 Luton
Debut: WEST HAM UNITED v Wimbledon 14/8/93
Debut Goal: WEST HAM UNITED v Manchester City 1/11/93

Previous Clubs Details

Club	Signed	Fee		Apps					Goals		
			Tot	Start	Sub	FA	FL	Lge	FA	FL	
Bournemouth	Aug-88	Trainee	114	105	9	10	7	8	0	0	
Cardiff City	Mar-89	Loan	1	0	1	0	0	0	0	0	
West Ham U.	Aug-92	£40,000	76	63	13	6	4	5	0	0	
Blackburn R.	Aug-95	£1.2m	9	8	1	0	0	1	0	0	

FAPL Summary by Club

West Ham U.	93-94 to 94-95		58	57	1	5	4	4	0	0	
Blackburn R.	1995-96		8	7	1	0	0	1	0	0	
Total			*66*	*64*	*2*	*5*	*4*	*5*	*0*	*0*	

HOPKIN David   Crystal Palace

Full Name: David Hopkin   DOB: 21-08-70 Greenock
Debut: Liverpool v CHELSEA 10/2/92
Debut Goal: Everton v CHELSEA 3/5/95

Previous Clubs Details

Club	Signed	Fee		Apps					Goals		
			Tot	Start	Sub	FA	FL	Lge	FA	FL	
Morton	1989	From NL	48	33	15	2	2	4	1	2	
Chelsea	Sep-92	£300,000	40	21	19	5	1	1	0	0	
C. Palace	Jul-95	£850,000	83	79	4	3	6	21	0	6	

FAPL Summary by Club

Chelsea	92-93 to 94-95		40	21	19	5	1	1	0	0	
Total			*40*	*21*	*19*	*5*	*1*	*1*	*0*	*0*	

HOTTIGER Marc   Everton

Full Name: Marc Hottiger   DOB: 07-11-67 Lausanne
Debut: Leicester City v NEWCASTLE UNITED 21/8/94
Debut Goal: Chelsea v NEWCASTLE UNITED 1/4/95

Previous Clubs Details					*Apps*				*Goals*	
Club	Signed	Fee	Tot	Start	Sub	FA	FL	Lge	FA	FL
Sion			0	0	0	0	0	0	0	0
Newcastle U.	Aug-94	£520,000	39	38	1	4	7	1	1	0
Everton	Mar-96	£700,000	17	13	4	0	1	1	0	0
FAPL Summary by Club										
Newcastle U.	94-95 to 95-96		39	38	1	4	7	1	1	0
Everton	95-96 to 96-97		17	13	4	0	1	1	0	0
Total			*56*	*51*	*5*	*4*	*8*	*2*	*1*	*0*

HOUGHTON Ray   Crystal Palace

Full Name: Raymond James Houghton   DOB: 09-01-62 Glasgow
Debut: Ipswich Town v ASTON VILLA 15/8/92
Debut Goal: ASTON VILLA v Norwich City 28/11/92

Previous Clubs Details					*Apps*				*Goals*	
Club	Signed	Fee	Tot	Start	Sub	FA	FL	Lge	FA	FL
West Ham U.	Jul-89		1	0	1	0	0	0	0	0
Fulham	Jul-82		129	129	0	4	12	16	3	2
Oxford U.	Sep-85	£147,000	83	83	0	3	13	10	0	3
Liverpool	Oct-87	£825,000	153	147	6	27	14	28	4	3
Aston Villa	Jul-92	£900,000	95	83	12	7	13	6	2	2
C. Palace	Mar-95	£300,000	72	69	3	4	6	7	0	0
FAPL Summary by Club										
Aston Villa	92-93 to 94-95		95	83	12	7	13	6	2	2
C. Palace	1994-95		10	10	0	2	0	2	0	0
Total			*105*	*93*	*12*	*9*	*13*	*8*	*2*	*2*

HOULT Russell   Derby County

Full Name: Russell Hoult   DOB: 28-03-91 Leicester
Debut: DERBY COUNTY v Leeds Utd 17/8/96
Debut Goal: (Goalkeeper)

Previous Clubs Details					*Apps*				*Goals*	
Club	Signed	Fee	Tot	Start	Sub	FA	FL	Lge	FA	FL
Leicester City	Mar-91		10	10	0	0	3	0	0	0
Lincoln City	Aug-91	Loan	2	2	0	0	1	0	0	0
Bolton W.	Nov-93	Loan	4	3	1	0	0	0	0	0
Lincoln City	Aug-94		15	15	0	0	0	0	0	0
Derby County	Feb-95	£300,000	88	86	2	1	2	0	0	0
FAPL Summary by Club										
Derby County	1996-97		32	31	1	0	0	0	0	0
Total			*32*	*31*	*1*	*0*	*0*	*0*	*0*	*0*

HOWELLS David   Tottenham Hotspur

Full Name: David Howells   DOB: 15-12-67 Guildford
Debut: Southampton v TOTTENHAM HOTSPUR 15/8/92
Debut Goal: Blackburn R. v TOTTENHAM HOTSPUR 7/11/92

Previous Clubs Details				Apps				Goals		
Club	Signed	Fee	Tot	Start	Sub	FA	FL	Lge	FA	FL
Tottenham H.	Jan-85	Apprentice	257	224	33	21	30	22	1	4
FAPL Summary by Club										
Tottenham H.	92-93 to 96-97		123	118	5	12	11	8	0	2
Total			*123*	*118*	*5*	*12*	*11*	*8*	*0*	*2*

HOWEY Steve   Newcastle United

Full Name: Stephen Norman Howey   DOB: 26-10-71 Sunderland
Debut: NEWCASTLE UNITED v Tottenham Hotspur 14/8/93
Debut Goal: NEWCASTLE UNITED v Leicester City 10/12/94

Previous Clubs Details				Apps				Goals		
Club	Signed	Fee	Tot	Start	Sub	FA	FL	Lge	FA	FL
Newcastle U.	Dec-89	Trainee	154	135	19	13	15	5	0	1
FAPL Summary by Club										
Newcastle U.	93-94 to 96-97		80	78	2	5	9	3	0	0
Total			*80*	*78*	*2*	*5*	*9*	*3*	*0*	*0*

HRISTOV Gjorgi   Barnsley

Full Name: Gjorgi Hiristov   DOB:
Debut: Debut Goal:

Previous Clubs Details				Apps				Goals		
Club	Signed	Fee	Tot	Start	Sub	FA	FL	Lge	FA	FL
Partizan Belgrade *			37	19	18			12		
Barnsley	Jun-97	£1.5m								

HUCKERBY Darren   Coventry City

Full Name: Darren Carl Huckerby   DOB: 27-04-76 Nottingham
Debut: NEWCASTLE UNITED v Bolton Wdrs 20/1/96 as sub
Debut Goal: COVENTRY CITY v Newcastle United 17/12/96

Previous Clubs Details				Apps				Goals		
Club	Signed	Fee	Tot	Start	Sub	FA	FL	Lge	FA	FL
Lincoln City	Jul-93	Trainee	30	20	10	0	2	3	0	0
Newcastle U.	Nov-95	£400,000	1	0	1	1	0	0	0	0
Millwall *	Sep-96	Loan								
Coventry City	Nov-96	£1m	25	21	4	4	0	5	2	0
FAPL Summary by Club										
Newcastle U.	95-96 to 96-97		1	0	1	1	0	0	0	0
Coventry City	1996-97		25	21	4	4	0	5	2	0
Total			*26*	*21*	*5*	*5*	*0*	*5*	*2*	*0*

HUGHES David   Aston Villa

Full Name: David Hughes   DOB:
Debut: ASTON VILLA v Liverpool 2/3/97 as sub
Debut Goal:
Previous Clubs Details

Club	Signed	Fee	Tot	Start	Sub	FA	FL	Lge	FA	FL
Aston Villa			7	4	3	0	0	0	0	0

FAPL Summary by Club

| Aston Villa | | 1996-97 | 7 | 4 | 3 | 0 | 0 | 0 | 0 | 0 |
| *Total* | | | *7* | *4* | *3* | *0* | *0* | *0* | *0* | *0* |

HUGHES Mark   Chelsea

Full Name: Leslie Mark Hughes   DOB: 01-11-63 Wrexham
Debut: Sheffield Utd v MANCHESTER UNITED 15/8/92
Debut Goal: Sheffield Utd v MANCHESTER UNITED 15/8/92
Previous Clubs Details

Club	Signed	Fee	Tot	Start	Sub	FA	FL	Lge	FA	FL
Manchester U.	Nov-80	Apprentice	89	85	4	10	6	37	4	4
Barcelona	Jul-86	£2.5m								
Bayern Munich	Oct-87	Loan								
Manchester U.	Jul-88	£1.5m	256	251	5	35	32	82	13	12
Chelsea	Jul-95	£1.5m	66	63	3	13	4	16	9	1

FAPL Summary by Club

Manchester U.		92-93 to 94-95	111	110	1	15	11	35	6	6
Chelsea		95-96 to 96-97	66	63	3	13	4	16	9	1
Total			*177*	*173*	*4*	*28*	*15*	*51*	*15*	*7*

HUGHES David   Southampton

Full Name: David Robert Hughes   DOB: 30-12-72 St Albans
Debut: Oldham Athletic v SOUTHAMPTON 5/12/94 as sub
Debut Goal: QPR v SOUTHAMPTON 28/12/94 as sub
Previous Clubs Details

Club	Signed	Fee	Tot	Start	Sub	FA	FL	Lge	FA	FL
Southampton	Jul-91	Juniors	31	9	22	5	4	3	1	0

FAPL Summary by Club

| Southampton | | 93-94 to 96-97 | 31 | 9 | 22 | 5 | 4 | 3 | 1 | 0 |
| *Total* | | | *31* | *9* | *22* | *5* | *4* | *3* | *1* | *0* |

HUGHES Steve — Arsenal

Full Name: Stephen John Hughes DOB: 18-09-76 Reading
Debut: ARSENAL v Aston Villa 26/12/94
Debut Goal: Southampton v ARSENAL 15/3/97

Previous Clubs Details

Club	Signed	Fee	Tot	Start	Sub	FA	FL	Lge	FA	FL
Arsenal		Trainee	16	10	6	2	1	1	1	0

FAPL Summary by Club

Arsenal	94-95 to 96-97	16	10	6	2	1	1	1	0
Total		*16*	*10*	*6*	*2*	*1*	*1*	*1*	*0*

HUGHES Michael — West Ham United

Full Name: Michael Eamonn Hughes DOB: 02-08-71 Larne
Debut: QPR v WEST HAM UNITED 4/12/94
Debut Goal: WEST HAM UNITED v Nottingham Forest 31/12/94

Previous Clubs Details

Club	Signed	Fee	Tot	Start	Sub	FA	FL	Lge	FA	FL
Man. City	Aug-88	Trainee	26	25	1	1	0	1	0	0
Strasbourg	Jul-92	£450,000	83	78	5	0	0	7	0	0
West Ham U.	Nov-94	Loan	78	74	4	7	6	5	1	0

FAPL Summary by Club

West Ham U.	94-95 to 96-97	78	74	4	7	6	5	1	0
Total		*78*	*74*	*4*	*7*	*6*	*5*	*1*	*0*

HUGHES Paul — Chelsea

Full Name: Paul Hughes DOB: 19-04-76 Hammersmith
Debut: CHELSEA v Derby Co. 18/1/97 as sub
Debut Goal: CHELSEA v Derby Co. 18/1/97 as sub

Previous Clubs Details

Club	Signed	Fee	Tot	Start	Sub	FA	FL	Lge	FA	FL
Chelsea		Trainee	12	8	4	1	0	2	0	0

FAPL Summary by Club

Chelsea	1996-97	12	8	4	1	0	2	0	0
Total		*12*	*8*	*4*	*1*	*0*	*2*	*0*	*0*

HUMPHREYS Richie — Sheffield Wednesday

Full Name: Richard John Humphreys DOB: 30-11-77 Sheffield
Debut: QPR v SHEFFIELD W. 9/9/95
Debut Goal: SHEFFIELD WEDNESDAY v Aston Villa 17/8/96

Previous Clubs Details

Club	Signed	Fee	Tot	Start	Sub	FA	FL	Lge	FA	FL
Sheffield W.	Feb-96	Trainee	34	15	19	4	1	3	2	0

FAPL Summary by Club

Sheffield W.	95-96 to 96-97	34	15	19	4	1	3	2	0
Total		*34*	*15*	*19*	*4*	*1*	*3*	*2*	*0*

HYDE Graham   Sheffield Wednesday

Full Name: Graham Hyde   DOB: 10-11-70 Doncaster
Debut: Everton v SHEFFIELD WEDNESDAY 15/8/92
Debut Goal: Nottingham Forest v SHEFFIELD WED 3/10/92

Previous Clubs Details				Apps			Goals		
Club	Signed	Fee	Tot	Start	Sub	FA	FL	Lge	FA	FL
Sheffield W.	May-88		130	97	33	13	19	8	1	2
FAPL Summary by Club										
Sheffield W.	92-93 to 95-96	117	88	29	11	18	8	1	2
Total			*117*	*88*	*29*	*11*	*18*	*8*	*1*	*2*

IMPEY Andy   West Ham United

Full Name: Andrew Rodney Impey   DOB: 30-09-71 Hammersmith
Debut: Manchester City v QPR 17/8/92
Debut Goal: Coventry City v QPR 26/8/92

Previous Clubs Details				Apps			Goals		
Club	Signed	Fee	Tot	Start	Sub	FA	FL	Lge	FA	FL
QPR *	Jun-90	£35,000	155	151	4	7	14	11	1	2
West Ham U.	Jun-97	£1.2m								
FAPL Summary by Club										
QPR	92-93 to 95-96	142	138	4	7	13	11	1	2
Total			*142*	*138*	*4*	*7*	*13*	*11*	*1*	*2*

IRWIN Dennis   Manchester United

Full Name: Joseph Dennis Irwin   DOB: 31-10-65 Cork
Debut: Sheffield Utd v MANCHESTER UNITED 15/8/92
Debut Goal: MANCHESTER UNITED v Ipswich Town 22/8/92

Previous Clubs Details				Apps			Goals		
Club	Signed	Fee	Tot	Start	Sub	FA	FL	Lge	FA	FL
Leeds U.	Nov-83	Apprentice	72	72	0	3	5	1	0	0
Oldham Ath	May-86		167	166	1	13	19	4	0	3
Manchester U.	Jun-90	£625,000	256	252	4	32	30	15	6	0
FAPL Summary by Club										
Manchester U.	92-93 to 96-97	184	182	2	26	15	11	6	0
Total			*184*	*182*	*2*	*26*	*15*	*11*	*6*	*0*

IVERSEN Steffen   Tottenham Hotspur

Full Name: Steffen Iversen   DOB:
Debut: TOTTENHAM HOTSPUR v Coventry City 07/12/96
Debut Goal: TOTTENHAM V Southampton 26/12/96

Previous Clubs Details				Apps			Goals		
Club	Signed	Fee	Tot	Start	Sub	FA	FL	Lge	FA	FL
Rosenborg	1995		25	8	17	0	0	8	0	0
Tottenham H.	Nov-96	£2.7m	16	16	0	0	0	6	0	0

Tottenham H.	1996-97	16	16	0	0	0	6	0	0
Total		*16*	*16*	*0*	*0*	*0*	*6*	*0*	*0*

IZZET Muzzy   Leicester City
Full Name: Mustafa Izzet   DOB: 31-10-74 Mile End, London
Debut: Sunderland v LEICESTER CITY 17/8/96
Debut Goal: Aston Villa v LEICESTER CITY 16/11/96

Previous Clubs Details				*Apps*				*Goals*	
Club	Signed	Fee	Tot	Start	Sub	FA	FL	Lge	FA FL
Chelsea	May-93	Trainee							
Leicester City	Feb-96	Loan	9	8	1	0	0	1	0 0
Leicester City	Jul-96	£800,000	35	34	1	3	8	3	0 1
FAPL Summary by Club									
Leicester City	1996-97	35	34	1	3	8	3	0	1
Total		*35*	*34*	*1*	*3*	*8*	*3*	*0*	*1*

JACKSON Mark   Leeds United
Full Name: Mark Graham Jackson   DOB: 30-09-77 Leeds
Debut: LEEDS UTD v Middlesbrough 30/3/96
Debut Goal:

Previous Clubs Details				*Apps*				*Goals*	
Club	Signed	Fee	Tot	Start	Sub	FA	FL	Lge	FA FL
Leeds U.	Jul-95	Trainee	18	11	7	4	0	0	0 0
FAPL Summary by Club									
Leeds U.	95-96 to 96-97	18	11	7	4	0	0	0	0
Total		*18*	*11*	*7*	*4*	*0*	*0*	*0*	*0*

JAMES David   Liverpool
Full Name: David Benjamin James   DOB: 01-08-70 Welwyn Garden City
Debut: Nottingham Forest v LIVERPOOL 16/8/92
Debut Goal: (Goalkeeper)

Previous Clubs Details				*Apps*				*Goals*	
Club	Signed	Fee	Tot	Start	Sub	FA	FL	Lge	FA FL
Watford	Jul-88	Trainee	89	89	0	2	6	0	0 0
Liverpool	Jul-92	£1m	161	160	1	17	17	0	0 0
FAPL Summary by Club									
Liverpool	92-93 to 96-97	161	160	1	17	17	0	0	0
Total		*161*	*160*	*1*	*17*	*16*	*0*	*0*	*0*

JOACHIM Julian   Aston Villa
Full Name: Julian Kevin Joachim   DOB: 12-09-74 Peterborough
Debut: LEICESTER CITY v Newcastle United 21/8/94
Debut Goal: LEICESTER CITY v Newcastle United 21/8/94

Previous Clubs Details				Apps				Goals		
Club	Signed	Fee	Tot	Start	Sub	FA	FL	Lge	FA	FL
Leicester City	Sep-92	Trainee	99	77	22	5	9	25	1	3
Aston Villa	Feb-96	£1.5m	26	7	19	1	1	4	0	0
FAPL Summary by Club										
Leicester City	94-95 to 96-97		15	11	4	0	2	3	0	0
Aston Villa	95-96 to 96-97		26	7	19	1	1	4	0	0
Total			*41*	*18*	*23*	*1*	*3*	*7*	*0*	*0*

JOBSON Richard — Leeds United

Full Name: Richard Ian Jobson   DOB: 09-05-63 Holderness
Debut: Chelsea v OLDHAM ATHLETIC 15/8/92
Debut Goal: Manchester City v OLDHAM ATHLETIC 29/8/92

Previous Clubs Details				Apps				Goals		
Club	Signed	Fee	Tot	Start	Sub	FA	FL	Lge	FA	FL
Watford	Nov-82	£22,000	28	26	2	1	2	4	0	0
Hull City	Feb-85	£40,000	221	219	2	13	12	17	1	0
Oldham Ath	Aug-90	£460,000	189	188	1	13	19	10	0	1
Leeds U.	Oct-95	£1m	22	22	0	1	3	1	0	0
FAPL Summary by Club										
Oldham Ath	92-93 to 93-94		77	77	0	9	7	7	0	0
Leeds U.	95-96 to 96-97		22	22	0	1	3	1	0	0
Total			*99*	*99*	*0*	*10*	*10*	*8*	*0*	*0*

JOHANSEN Michael — Bolton Wanderers

Full Name: Michael Johansen   DOB: 22-07-76, Glostrup
Debut: Debut Goal:

Previous Clubs Details				Apps				Goals		
Club	Signed	Fee	Tot	Start	Sub	FA	FL	Lge	FA	FL
Rosenhoj										
KB										
FC Copenhagen 1991										
Bolton W.	Aug-96	£1m	32	24	8	2	3	5	0	0

JOHNSEN Erland — Chelsea

Full Name: Erland Johnsen   DOB: 05-04-67 Fredrikstad, Norway
Debut: Nottingham Forest v CHELSEA 16/1/93
Debut Goal: CHELSEA v Blackburn R. 14/8/93

Previous Clubs Details				Apps				Goals		
Club	Signed	Fee	Tot	Start	Sub	FA	FL	Lge	FA	FL
Chelsea	Dec-89	£306,000	145	135	10	19	7	1	0	0
FAPL Summary by Club										
Chelsea	92-93 to 96-97		*114*	*105*	*9*	*15*	*7*	*1*	*0*	*0*
Total			*114*	*105*	*9*	*15*	*7*	*1*	*0*	*0*

JOHNSEN Ronnie   Manchester United

Full Name: Ronald Johnsen   DOB: 06-10-69
Debut: Wimbledon v MANCHESTER UTD 17/8/96 as sub
Debut Goal:

Previous Clubs Details					*Apps*			*Goals*		
Club	Signed	Fee	Tot	Start	Sub	FA	FL	Lge	FA	FL
Lillestrom	1995		23	23	0	0	0	4	0	0
Besiktas	1996		22	22	1	0	0	1	0	0
Manchester U.	Jul-96	£1.2m	31	26	5	2	0	0	0	0
FAPL Summary by Club										
Manchester U.		1996-97	31	26	5	2	0	0	0	0
Total			*31*	*26*	*5*	*2*	*0*	*0*	*0*	*0*

JOHNSON Tommy   Aston Villa

Full Name: Thomas Johnson   DOB: 15-01-71 Newcastle
Debut: ASTON VILLA v QPR 14/1/95
Debut Goal: ASTON VILLA v Wimbledon 11/2/95

Previous Clubs Details					*Apps*			*Goals*		
Club	Signed	Fee	Tot	Start	Sub	FA	FL	Lge	FA	FL
Notts County	Jan-89	Trainee	118	100	18	5	9	47	1	5
Derby County	Mar-92	£1.3m	88	81	7	5	6	30	2	1
Aston Villa	Jan-95	£2.9m +	59	40	19	7	5	13	1	2
FAPL Summary by Club										
Aston Villa		94-95 to 96-97	59	40	19	7	5	13	1	2
Total			*59*	*40*	*19*	*7*	*5*	*13*	*1*	*2*

JONES Scott   Barnsley

Full Name: Scott Jones   DOB: 01-05-75 Sheffield
Debut: Debut Goal:

Previous Clubs Details					*Apps*			*Goals*		
Club	Signed	Fee	Tot	Start	Sub	FA	FL	Lge	FA	FL
Barnsley	Feb-94	Trainee	21	16	5	2	0	0	0	0

JONES Lee   Liverpool

Full Name: Philip Lee Jones   DOB: 29-05-73 Wrexham
Debut: LIVERPOOL v Wimbledon 22/10/94 as sub
Debut Goal:

Previous Clubs Details					*Apps*			*Goals*		
Club	Signed	Fee	Tot	Start	Sub	FA	FL	Lge	FA	FL
Wrexham	Jul-91		39	24	15	5	3	9	1	0
Liverpool	Mar-92	£300,000	3	0	3	0	1	0	0	0
Crewe Alex.		Loan	8	4	4	0	0	0	0	0
Wrexham	Jan-97	Loan								

JONES Rob   Liverpool
Full Name: Robert Marc Jones   DOB: 05-11-71 Wrexham
Debut: LIVERPOOL v Sheffield Utd 19/8/92
Debut Goal:

Previous Clubs Details			Apps				Goals		
Club	Signed	Fee	Tot	Start	Sub	FA	FL	Lge	FA	FL
Crewe Alex.	Dec-88		75	59	16	3	9	2	0	0
Liverpool	Oct-91	£300,000	162	162	0	27	20	0	0	0

FAPL Summary by Club

Liverpool	92-93 to 96-97	134	134	0	18	20	0	0	0
Total		*134*	*134*	*0*	*18*	*20*	*0*	*0*	*0*

JONES Vinny   Wimbledon
Full Name: Vincent Peter Jones   DOB: 05-01-65 Watford
Debut: CHELSEA v Oldham Athletic 15/8/92
Debut Goal: Sheffield Wednesday v CHELSEA 22/8/92

Previous Clubs Details			Apps				Goals		
Club	Signed	Fee	Tot	Start	Sub	FA	FL	Lge	FA	FL
Wimbledon	Nov-86	£10,000NL	77	77	0	13	8	9	1	0
Leeds U.	Jun-89	£650,000	46	44	2	1	2	5	0	0
Sheffield U.	Sep-90	£700,000	35	35	0	1	4	2	0	0
Chelsea	Aug-91	£575,000	42	42	0	4	1	4	1	0
Wimbledon	Sep-92	£700,000	153	149	4	18	20	12	0	2

FAPL Summary by Club

Chelsea	1992-93	7	7	0	0	0	1	0	0
Wimbledon	92-93 to 96-97	153	149	4	18	20	12	0	2
Total		*160*	*156*	*4*	*18*	*20*	*13*	*0*	*2*

JUPP Duncan   Wimbledon
Full Name: Duncan Jupp   DOB: 25-01-75 Guildford
Debut: Everton v WIMBLEDON 28/12/96
Debut Goal:

Previous Clubs Details			Apps				Goals		
Club	Signed	Fee	Tot	Start	Sub	FA	FL	Lge	FA	FL
Fulham	Dec-93	Trainee	105	101	4	10	12	2	1	2
Wimbledon			6	6	0	2	1	0	0	0

FAPL Summary by Club

Wimbledon	1996-97	6	6	0	2	1	0	0	0
Total		*6*	*6*	*0*	*2*	*1*	*0*	*0*	*0*

KAAMARK Pontus   Leicester City
Full Name: Pontus Kaamark   DOB:
Debut: LEICESTER CITY v Blackburn R. 7/12/96 as sub
Debut Goal:

| *Previous Clubs Details* | | | | *Apps* | | | | *Goals* | | |
Club	Signed	Fee	Tot	Start	Sub	FA	FL	Lge	FA	FL
IFK	Nov-95	1990	126	114	12			1		
Leicester City	Nov-95	£840,000	11	10	1	2	3	0	0	0
FAPL Summary by Club										
Leicester City		1996-97	10	9	1	2	3	0	0	0
Total			*10*	*9*	*1*	*2*	*3*	*0*	*0*	*0*

KEANE Roy   Manchester United
Full Name: Roy Maurice Keane   DOB: 10-08-71 Cork
Debut: NOTTINGHAM FOREST v Liverpool 16/8/92
Debut Goal: Leeds Utd v NOTTINGHAM FOREST 5/12/92

| *Previous Clubs Details* | | | | *Apps* | | | | *Goals* | | |
Club	Signed	Fee	Tot	Start	Sub	FA	FL	Lge	FA	FL
Cobh Ramblers										
N. Forest	Jun-90	£10,000	114	114	0	18	17	22	3	6
Manchester U.	Jul-93	£3.75m	112	107	5	23	11	15	1	0
FAPL Summary by Club										
N. Forest		1992-93	40	40	0	4	5	6	1	1
Manchester U.		93-94 to 96-97	112	107	5	23	11	15	1	0
Total			*152*	*147*	*5*	*27*	*16*	*21*	*2*	*1*

KELLER Kasey   Leicester City
Full Name: Kasey Keller   DOB: 27-11-69 Washington USA
Debut: Sunderland v LEICESTER CITY 17/08/96
Debut Goal: (Goalkeeper)

| *Previous Clubs Details* | | | | *Apps* | | | | *Goals* | | |
Club	Signed	Fee	Tot	Start	Sub	FA	FL	Lge	FA	FL
Millwall	Feb-92	Free	176	176	0	8	14	0	0	0
Leicester City	Aug-96	£900,000	31	31	0	4	8	0	0	0
FAPL Summary by Club										
Leicester City		1996-97	31	31	0	4	8	0	0	0
Total			*31*	*31*	*0*	*4*	*8*	*0*	*0*	*0*

KELLY Gary   Leeds United
Full Name: Gary Kelly   DOB: 09-07-74 Drogheda
Debut: Manchester City v LEEDS UNITED 14/8/93
Debut Goal: Southampton v LEEDS UTD 23/11/96

| *Previous Clubs Details* | | | | *Apps* | | | | *Goals* | | |
Club	Signed	Fee	Tot	Start	Sub	FA	FL	Lge	FA	FL
Leeds U.	Sep-91		158	154	4	16	16	2	0	0

Leeds U.	93-94 to 96-97	154	152	2	16	15	2	0	0
Total		*154*	*152*	*2*	*16*	*15*	*2*	*0*	*0*

KENNA Jeff   Blackburn Rovers

Full Name: Jeffrey Jude Kenna   DOB: 27-08-70 Dublin
Debut: QPR v SOUTHAMPTON 19/8/92
Debut Goal: SOUTHAMPTON v Sheffield Utd 27/2/92

Previous Clubs Details				*Apps*				*Goals*	
Club	Signed	Fee	Tot	Start	Sub	FA	FL	Lge	FA FL
Southampton	Apr-89	Trainee	114	110	4	11	4	4	0 0
Blackburn R.	Mar-95	£1.5m	78	78	0	4	7	1	0 0
FAPL Summary by Club									
Southampton	92-93 to 94-95	98	95	3	7	4	4	0	0
Blackburn R.	94-95 to 96-97	78	78	0	4	7	1	0	0
Total		*176*	*173*	*3*	*11*	*11*	*5*	*0*	*0*

KENNEDY Mark   Liverpool

Full Name: Mark Kennedy   DOB: 15-05-76 Dublin
Debut: LIVERPOOL v Leeds Utd 9/4/95 as sub
Debut Goal:

Previous Clubs Details				*Apps*				*Goals*	
Club	Signed	Fee	Tot	Start	Sub	FA	FL	Lge	FA FL
Millwall	May-92	Trainee	43	37	6	4	7	9	1 2
Liverpool	Mar-95	£1.5m +	15	5	10	1	2	0	0 0
FAPL Summary by Club									
Liverpool	94-95 to 96-97	15	5	10	1	2	0	0	0
Total		*15*	*5*	*10*	*1*	*2*	*0*	*0*	*0*

KEOWN Martin   Arsenal

Full Name: Martin Raymond Keown   DOB: 24-07-66 Oxford
Debut: EVERTON v Coventry City 17/10/92
Debut Goal: Nottingham Forest v ARSENAL 3/12/94

Previous Clubs Details				*Apps*				*Goals*	
Club	Signed	Fee	Tot	Start	Sub	FA	FL	Lge	FA FL
Arsenal	Jan-84	Apprentice	22	22	0	5	0	0	0 0
Brighton & HA	Feb-85	Loan	23	21	2	0	2	1	0 1
Aston Villa	Jun-86	£200,000	112	109	3	6	13	3	0 0
Everton	Aug-89	£750,000	96	92	4	13	11	0	0 0
Arsenal	Feb-93	£2m	147	129	18	10	16	2	0 1
FAPL Summary by Club									
Everton		92-93	13	13	0	2	4	0	0 0
Arsenal	92-93 to 96-97	147	129	18	10	16	2	0	1
Total		*160*	*142*	*18*	*12*	*20*	*2*	*0*	*1*

KEWELL Harry
Leeds United

Full Name: Harold Kewell DOB: 22-09-78 Australia
Debut: LEEDS UTD v Middlesbrough 30/3/96
Debut Goal:

Previous Clubs Details				*Apps*				*Goals*		
Club	Signed	Fee	Tot	Start	Sub	FA	FL	Lge	FA	FL
Leeds U.			3	2	1	0	0	0	0	0
FAPL Summary by Club										
Leeds U.	95-96 to 96-97		3	2	1	0	0	0	0	0
Total			*3*	*2*	*1*	*0*	*0*	*0*	*0*	*0*

KHARINE Dimitri
Chelsea

Full Name: Dimitri Kharine DOB: 16-08-68 Moscow
Debut: QPR v CHELSEA 27/1/93
Debut Goal: (Goalkeeper)

Previous Clubs Details				*Apps*				*Goals*		
Club	Signed	Fee	Tot	Start	Sub	FA	FL	Lge	FA	FL
CSKA Moscow										
Chelsea	Dec-92	£200,000	107	107	0	12	8	0	0	0
FAPL Summary by Club										
Chelsea	92-93 to 95-96		107	107	0	12	8	0	0	0
Total			*107*	*107*	*0*	*12*	*8*	*0*	*0*	*0*

KIMBLE Alan
Wimbledon

Full Name: Alan Frank Kimble DOB: 06-08-66 Dagenham
Debut: West Ham Utd v WIMBLEDON 14/8/93
Debut Goal:

Previous Clubs Details				*Apps*				*Goals*		
Club	Signed	Fee	Tot	Start	Sub	FA	FL	Lge	FA	FL
Charlton Ath.	Aug-84		6	6	0	0	0	0	0	0
Exeter City	Aug-85	Loan	1	1	0	0	1	0	0	0
Cambridge U.	Aug-86	Free	299	295	4	29	24	24	1	0
Wimbledon	Jul-93	£175,000	102	99	3	17	14	0	0	0
FAPL Summary by Club										
Wimbledon	93-94 to 96-97		102	99	3	17	14	0	0	0
Total			*102*	*99*	*3*	*17*	*14*	*0*	*0*	*0*

KITSON Paul
West Ham United

Full Name: Paul Kitson DOB: 09-01-71 Peterlee
Debut: Aston Villa v NEWCASTLE UNITED 1/10/94
Debut Goal: NEWCASTLE UNITED v QPR 5/11/94

Previous Clubs Details				*Apps*				*Goals*		
Club	Signed	Fee	Tot	Start	Sub	FA	FL	Lge	FA	FL
Leicester City	Dec-88		50	39	11	2	5	6	1	3
Derby County	Mar-92	£1.3m	105	105	0	5	7	36	1	3

Club	Signed	Fee	Tot	Start	Sub	FA	FL	Lge	FA	FL
Newcastle U.	Sep-94	£2.25m	36	26	10	9	5	10	3	1
West Ham U.	Feb-97	£2.3m	14	14	0	0	0	8	0	0
FAPL Summary by Club										
Newcastle U.	94-95 to 96-97		36	26	10	9	5	10	3	1
West Ham U.	1996-97		14	14	0	0	0	8	0	0
Total			*50*	*40*	*10*	*9*	*5*	*18*	*3*	*1*

KVARME Bjorn Tore — Liverpool

Full Name: Bjorn Tore Kvarme — DOB: 17-07-72 Trondheim
Debut: LIVERPOOL v Aston Villa 18/1/97
Debut Goal:

Previous Clubs Details			*Apps*					*Goals*		
Club	Signed	Fee	Tot	Start	Sub	FA	FL	Lge	FA	FL
Rosenborg	1990		67	59	8			1		
Liverpool	Jan-97	Free	15	15	0	1	0	0	0	0
FAPL Summary by Club										
Liverpool	1996-97		15	15	0	1	0	0	0	0
Total			*15*	*15*	*0*	*1*	*0*	*0*	*0*	*0*

LAMBOURDE Bernard — Chelsea

Full Name: Bernard Lambourde — DOB:
Debut: — Debut Goal:

Previous Clubs Details			*Apps*					*Goals*		
Club	Signed	Fee	Tot	Start	Sub	FA	FL	Lge	FA	FL
Cannes			28	27	1			1		
Bordeaux *	1996									
Chelsea	Jun-97	£1.5m								

LAMPARD Frank — West Ham United

Full Name: Frank Lampard — DOB: 21-06-78 Romford
Debut: WEST HAM UTD v Coventry City 31/1/96 as sub
Debut Goal:

Previous Clubs Details			*Apps*					*Goals*		
Club	Signed	Fee	Tot	Start	Sub	FA	FL	Lge	FA	FL
West Ham U.		Trainee	15	3	12	1	2	0	0	0
Swansea City	Oct-95	Loan	9	8	1	0	0	1	0	0
FAPL Summary by Club										
West Ham U.	95-96 to 96-97		15	3	12	1	2	0	0	0
Total			*15*	*3*	*12*	*1*	*2*	*0*	*0*	*0*

LAURENT Pierre — Leeds United

Full Name: Pierre Laurent — DOB:
Debut: LEEDS UTD v Blackburn Rvrs 7/4/97
Debut Goal:

LAURSEN Jacob — Derby County

Full Name: Jacob Laursen   DOB:
Debut: DERBY COUNTY v Leeds Utd 17/8/96
Debut Goal: DERBY COUNTY v Manchester Utd 3/9/96

Previous Clubs Details

Club	Signed	Fee	Tot	Start	Sub	FA	FL	Lge	FA	FL
					Apps				Goals	
Silkeborg										
Derby County		£500,000	36	35	1	2	2	1	0	0

FAPL Summary by Club

| Derby County | 1996-97 | | 36 | 35 | 1 | 2 | 2 | 1 | 0 | 0 |
| *Total* | | | *36* | *35* | *1* | *2* | *2* | *1* | *0* | *0* |

LAWRENCE Jamie — Leicester City

Full Name: James Hubert Lawrence   DOB: 08-03-70 Balham
Debut: Crystal Palace v LEICESTER CITY 14/1/95
Debut Goal: LEICESTER CITY v Wimbledon 1/4/95 as sub

Previous Clubs Details

Club	Signed	Fee	Tot	Start	Sub	FA	FL	Lge	FA	FL
					Apps				Goals	
Sunderland	Oct-93	From NL	4	2	2	0	1	0	0	0
Doncaster R.	Mar-94	£20,000	25	16	9	1	2	3	0	0
Leicester City	Jan-95	£125,000	47	21	26	2	7	1	0	2

FAPL Summary by Club

| Leicester City | 94-95 to 96-97 | | 32 | 11 | 21 | 2 | 7 | 1 | 0 | 2 |
| *Total* | | | *32* | *11* | *21* | *2* | *7* | *1* | *0* | *2* |

LAZARIDIS Stan — West Ham United

Full Name: Stanley Lazaridis   DOB: 16-08-72 Perth, WA
Debut: Arsenal v WEST HAM UTD 16/9/95 as sub
Debut Goal: Wimbledon v WEST HAM UTD 17/3/97

Previous Clubs Details

Club	Signed	Fee	Tot	Start	Sub	FA	FL	Lge	FA	FL
					Apps				Goals	
West Adelaide (Aus)										
West Ham U.	Aug-95	£300,000	26	15	11	2	5	1	0	0

FAPL Summary by Club

| West Ham U. | 95-96 to 96-97 | | 26 | 15 | 11 | 2 | 5 | 1 | 0 | 0 |
| *Total* | | | *26* | *15* | *11* | *2* | *5* | *1* | *0* | *0* |

LEES Lars   Barnsley
Full Name: Lars Lees   DOB:
Debut: Debut Goal:
Previous Clubs Details   *Apps*   *Goals*
Club   Signed   Fee   Tot Start Sub FA FL   Lge FA FL
Bayer 04 Leverkusen
Barnsley   Jun-97   £250,000

LE SAUX Graeme   Blackburn Rovers
Full Name: Graeme Pierre Le Saux   DOB: 17-10-68 Jersey
Debut: CHELSEA v Ipswich Town 17/10/92
Debut Goal: Chelsea v BLACKBURN ROVERS 14/8/93
Previous Clubs Details   *Apps*   *Goals*
Club   Signed   Fee   Tot Start Sub FA FL   Lge FA FL
Chelsea   Dec-87   Free NL   90   77 13   8 13   8   0 1
Blackburn R.   Mar-93   Swap   130 128   2   8 10   7   0 0
FAPL Summary by Club
Chelsea   1992-93   14   10   4   1   4   0   0 0
Blackburn R.   92-93 to 96-97 130 128 2   8 10   7   0 0
Total   *144* *138* *6* *9* *14*   *7* *0* *0*

LE TISSIER Matthew   Southampton
Full Name: Matthew Paul Le Tissier   DOB: 14-10-68 Guernsey
Debut: SOUTHAMPTON v Tottenham Hotspur 15/8/92
Debut Goal: QPR v SOUTHAMPTON 18/8/92
Previous Clubs Details   *Apps*   *Goals*
Club   Signed   Fee   Tot Start Sub FA FL   Lge FA FL
Southampton   Oct-86   Apprentice 357 321 36 30 42 140 12 23
FAPL Summary by Club
Southampton   92-93 to 96-97 184 178 6 14 16   80   7 12
Total   *184* *178* *6* *14* *16*   *80* *7* *12*

LEBOEUF Frank   Chelsea
Full Name: Frank Leboeuf   DOB: 22-01-68 Marseille
Debut: Southampton v CHELSEA 18/8/96
Debut Goal: CHELSEA v Coventry City 24/8/96
Previous Clubs Details   *Apps*   *Goals*
Club   Signed   Fee   Tot Start Sub FA FL   Lge FA FL
Hyeres   1986   14   1
Meaux   1987   39   3
Laval   1988   69   10
Strasbourg   1991   189   49
Chelsea   Jul-96   £2.5m   26   26   0   7   2   6   1 0

LEE Dave   Bolton Wanderers

Full Name: David Mark Lee   DOB: 05-11-67 Blackburn
Debut: SOUTHAMPTON v Manchester United 24/8/92 as sub
Debut Goal: Middlesbrough v BOLTON WANDERERS 17/2/92

Previous Clubs Details				Apps				Goals	
Club	Signed	Fee	Tot	Start	Sub	FA	FL	Lge	FA FL
Bury	Aug-86		208	203	5	6	15	35	0 1
Southampton	Aug-91	£350,000	20	11	9	1	0	0	0 0
Bolton W.	Nov-92	£300,000	155	124	31	15	20	17	0 2

FAPL Summary by Club

Southampton	1992-93	1	0	1	0	0	0	0	0
Bolton W.	1995-96	18	9	9	1	4	1	0	0
Total		*19*	*9*	*10*	*1*	*4*	*1*	*0*	*0*

LEE David   Chelsea

Full Name: David John Lee   DOB: 26-11-69 Kingswood
Debut: Aston Villa v CHELSEA 2/9/92
Debut Goal: CHELSEA v Manchester United 19/12/92

Previous Clubs Details				Apps				Goals	
Club	Signed	Fee	Tot	Start	Sub	FA	FL	Lge	FA FL
Chelsea	Jul-88		150	118	32	14	18	10	0 1
Reading	Jan-92	Loan	5	5	0	0	0	5	0 0
Plymouth A.	Mar-92	Loan	9	9	0	0	0	1	0 0
Portsmouth	Aug-94	Loan	5	4	1	0	0	0	0 0

FAPL Summary by Club

Chelsea	92-93 to 96-97	78	65	13	9	11	4	0	0
Total		*78*	*65*	*13*	*9*	*11*	*4*	*0*	*0*

LEE Robert   Newcastle United

Full Name: Robert Martin Lee   DOB: 01-02-66 West Ham
Debut: NEWCASTLE UNITED v Tottenham Hotspur 14/8/93
Debut Goal: NEWCASTLE UNITED v Swindon Town 12/3/94

Previous Clubs Details				Apps				Goals	
Club	Signed	Fee	Tot	Start	Sub	FA	FL	Lge	FA FL
Charlton Ath	Jul-83		298	274	24	14	19	59	2 1
Newcastle U.	Sep-92	£700,000	181	180	1	14	13	39	4 3

FAPL Summary by Club

Newcastle U.	93-94 to 96-97	145	144	1	10	10	29	2	2
Total		*145*	*144*	*1*	*10*	*10*	*29*	*2*	*2*

LENNON Neil   Leicester City
Full Name: Neil Francis Lennon   DOB: 25-06-71 Lurgan
Debut: Sunderland v LEICESTER CITY 17/8/96
Debut Goal: Manchester United v LEICESTER CITY 30/11/96

Previous Clubs Details			*Apps*				*Goals*		
Club	Signed	Fee	Tot	Start	Sub	FA	FL	Lge	FA FL
Man. City	Aug-89	Trainee	1	1	0	0	0	0	0 0
Crewe Alex.	Sep-90	Free	147	142	5	12	9	15	1 0
Leicester City	Feb-96	£750,000	50	49	1	2	7	2	0 1
FAPL Summary by Club									
Leicester City	1996-97		35	35	0	2	7	1	0 1
Total			*35*	*35*	*0*	*2*	*7*	*1*	*0 1*

LEONHARDSEN Oyvind   Liverpool
Full Name: Oyvind Leonhardsen   DOB: 17-08-70 Norway
Debut: WIMBLEDON v Aston Villa 9/11/94
Debut Goal: WIMBLEDON v Aston Villa 9/11/94

Previous Clubs Details			*Apps*				*Goals*		
Club	Signed	Fee	Tot	Start	Sub	FA	FL	Lge	FA FL
Rosenborg	1992		63	63	0			20	
Wimbledon	Jan-95	£660,000	76	73	3	17	9	13	2 1
Liverpool	Jun-97	£3.5m							
FAPL Summary by Club									
Wimbledon	94-95 to 96-97		76	73	3	17	9	13	2 1
Total			*76*	*73*	*3*	*17*	*9*	*13*	*2 1*

LEWIS Neil   Leicester City
Full Name: Neil Anthony Lewis   DOB: 28-06-74 Wolverhampton
Debut: Wimbledon v LEICESTER CITY 10/9/94
Debut Goal:

Previous Clubs Details			*Apps*				*Goals*		
Club	Signed	Fee	Tot	Start	Sub	FA	FL	Lge	FA FL
Leicester City	Jul-92	Trainee	67	53	14	2	7	1	0 0
FAPL Summary by Club									
Leicester City	94-95 to 96-97		22	17	5	1	4	0	0 0
Total			*22*	*17*	*5*	*1*	*4*	*0*	*0 0*

LIDDELL Andy   Barnsley
Full Name: Andrew Mark Liddell   DOB: 28-06-73 Leeds
Debut: Debut Goal:

Previous Clubs Details			*Apps*				*Goals*		
Club	Signed	Fee	Tot	Start	Sub	FA	FL	Lge	FA FL
Barnsley	Jul-91	Trainee	154	126	28	7	9	32	0 1

LILLEY Derek   Leeds United

Full Name: Derek Lilley   DOB:
Debut: LEEDS UNITED v Blackburn Rovers 7/4/97
Debut Goal:

Previous Clubs Details				Apps				Goals		
Club	Signed	Fee	Tot	Start	Sub	FA	FL	Lge	FA	FL
Greenock Morton										
Leeds U.	Mar-97	£500,000 +	6	4	2	0	0	0	0	0
FAPL Summary by Club										
Leeds U.		1996-97	6	4	2	0	0	0	0	0
Total			*6*	*4*	*2*	*0*	*0*	*0*	*0*	*0*

LINIGHAN Andy   Crystal Palace

Full Name: Andrew Linighan   DOB: 18-06-62 Hartlepool
Debut: Sheffield United v ARSENAL 19/9/92
Debut Goal: Oldham Athletic v ARSENAL 20/2/93

Previous Clubs Details				Apps				Goals		
Club	Signed	Fee	Tot	Start	Sub	FA	FL	Lge	FA	FL
Hartlepool U.	Sep-80		110	110	0	8	8	4	0	1
Leeds U.	May-84	£200,000	66	66	0	2	6	3	0	1
Oldham Ath.	Jan-86	£65,000	87	87	0	3	8	6	0	2
Norwich City	Mar-88	£350,000	86	86	0	10	6	8	0	0
Arsenal	Jun-90	£1.25m	118	101	17	14	14	5	1	1
C. Palace	Jan-97	£110,000	19	19	0	0	0	2	0	0
FAPL Summary by Club										
Arsenal		92-93 to 96-97	91	79	12	10	12	5	1	1
Total			*91*	*79*	*12*	*10*	*12*	*5*	*1*	*1*

LOMAS Stephen   West Ham United

Full Name: Stephen Martin Lomas   DOB: 18-01-74 Hanover
Debut: Sheffield United v MANCHESTER CITY 25/9/93
Debut Goal: MANCHESTER CITY v Nottingham Forest 8/10/94

Previous Clubs Details				Apps				Goals		
Club	Signed	Fee	Tot	Start	Sub	FA	FL	Lge	FA	FL
Man. City *	Jan-91	Trainee	76	67	9	8	13	5	1	2
West Ham U.	Mar-97	£1.6m +	7	7	0	0	0	0	0	0
FAPL Summary by Club										
Manchester City		93-94 to 95-96	76	67	9	8	13	5	1	2
West Ham U.		96-97	7	7	0	0	0	0	0	0
Total			*83*	*74*	*9*	*8*	*13*	*5*	*1*	*2*

LUKIC John   Arsenal

Full Name: Jovan Lukic   DOB: 11-12-60 Chesterfield
Debut: LEEDS UNITED v Wimbledon 15/8/92
Debut Goal: Goalkeeper

Previous Clubs Details			Apps					Goals		
Club	Signed	Fee	Tot	Start	Sub	FA	FL	Lge	FA	FL
Leeds U.	Dec-78		146	146	0	9	7	0	0	0
Arsenal	Jul-83	£50,000	223	223	0	21	32	0	0	0
Leeds U.	Jun-90	£1m	209	209	0	19	23	0	0	0
Arsenal	Jul-96	Free	15	15	0	1	1	0	0	0
FAPL Summary by Club										
Leeds U.	92-93 to 95-96		129	129	0	12	12	0	0	0
Arsenal	96-97		15	15	0	1	1	0	0	0
Total			*144*	*144*	*0*	*13*	*13*	*0*	*0*	*0*

LUNDEKVAM Claus — Southampton

Full Name: Claus Lundekvam   DOB: 22-02-73 Norway
Debut: SOUTHAMPTON v Nottingham Forest 03/09/96
Debut Goal:

Previous Clubs Details			Apps					Goals		
Club	Signed	Fee	Tot	Start	Sub	FA	FL	Lge	FA	FL
SK Brann	1993		37	33	4			0		
Southampton	1996		29	28	1	1	8	0	0	0
Premiership Record										
Southampton	1996-97		29	28	1	1	8	0	0	0
Total			*29*	*28*	*1*	*1*	*8*	*0*	*0*	*0*

MABBUTT Gary — Tottenham Hotspur

Full Name: Gary Vincent Mabbutt   DOB: 23-08-61 Bristol
Debut: Wimbledon v TOTTENHAM HOTSPUR 25/10/92
Debut Goal: TOTTENHAM HOTSPUR v Nottingham Forest 18/12/92

Previous Clubs Details			Apps					Goals		
Club	Signed	Fee	Tot	Start	Sub	FA	FL	Lge	FA	FL
Bristol R.	Jan-79	Apprentice	131	122	9	6	10	10	1	1
Tottenham H.	Aug-82	£105,000	465	450	16	47	61	27	3	2
FAPL Summary by Club										
Tottenham H.	92-93 to 96-97		124	124	0	16	10	2	1	0
Total			*124*	*124*	*0*	*16*	*10*	*2*	*1*	*0*

MADDISON Neil — Southampton

Full Name: Neil Stanley Maddison   DOB: 02-10-69 Darlington
Debut: SOUTHAMPTON v Middlesbrough 28/9/92
Debut Goal: SOUTHAMPTON v Arsenal 5/12/92

Previous Clubs Details			Apps					Goals		
Club	Signed	Fee	Tot	Start	Sub	FA	FL	Lge	FA	FL
Southampton	Apr-88	Trainee	144	18	162	13	14	18	0	0
FAPL Summary by Club										
Southampton	92-93 to 96-97		142	133	9	10	12	16	0	0
Total			*142*	*133*	*9*	*10*	*12*	*16*	*0*	*0*

MAGILTON Jim   Southampton

Full Name: James Magilton   DOB: 06-05-69 Belfast
Debut: SOUTHAMPTON v Liverpool 14/2/94
Debut Goal: Arsenal v SOUTHAMPTON 19/11/94

Previous Clubs Details | | | | *Apps* | | | | *Goals* | |
|---|---|---|---|---|---|---|---|---|---|---|
| Club | Signed | Fee | Tot | Start | Sub | FA | FL | Lge | FA | FL |
| Liverpool | May-86 | Apprentice | 0 | 0 | 0 | 0 | 0 | 0 | 0 | 0 |
| Oxford U. | Oct-90 | £100,000 | 150 | 150 | 0 | 8 | 9 | 34 | 4 | 1 |
| Southampton | Feb-94 | £600,000 | 125 | 119 | 6 | 12 | 14 | 13 | 3 | 2 |
| *FAPL Summary by Club* | | | | | | | | | | |
| Southampton | 93-94 to 96-97 | | 125 | 119 | 6 | 12 | 14 | 13 | 3 | 2 |
| *Total* | | | *125* | *119* | *6* | *12* | *14* | *13* | *3* | *2* |

MANNINGER Alex   Arsenal

Full Name: Alex Manninger   DOB:
Debut: Debut Goal: (Goalkeeper)

Previous Clubs Details | | | | *Apps* | | | | *Goals* | |
|---|---|---|---|---|---|---|---|---|---|---|
| Club | Signed | Fee | Tot | Start | Sub | FA | FL | Lge | FA | FL |
| Casino Salzburg | | | | | | | | | | |
| Arsenal | Mar-97 | £500,000 | | | | | | | | |

MARCELLE Clint   Barnsley

Full Name: Clint Marcelle   DOB:
Debut: Debut Goal:

Previous Clubs Details | | | | *Apps* | | | | *Goals* | |
|---|---|---|---|---|---|---|---|---|---|---|
| Club | Signed | Fee | Tot | Start | Sub | FA | FL | Lge | FA | FL |
| Barnsley | | | 39 | 26 | 13 | 2 | 4 | 8 | 1 | 0 |

MARKER Nicky   Blackburn Rovers

Full Name: Nicholas Robert Marker   DOB: 03-06-65 Budleigh Salterton
Debut: BLACKBURN ROVERS v Oldham Athletic 26/9/92
Debut Goal:

Previous Clubs Details | | | | *Apps* | | | | *Goals* | |
|---|---|---|---|---|---|---|---|---|---|---|
| Club | Signed | Fee | Tot | Start | Sub | FA | FL | Lge | FA | FL |
| Exeter City | May-83 | | 202 | 196 | 6 | 8 | 11 | 3 | 0 | 1 |
| Plymouth A. | Oct-87 | £95,000 | 202 | 201 | 1 | 9 | 15 | 12 | 1 | 3 |
| Blackburn R. | Sep-92 | £250,000 + | 54 | 41 | 13 | 4 | 4 | 1 | 0 | 0 |
| *FAPL Summary by Club* | | | | | | | | | | |
| Blackburn R. | 92-93 to 96-97 | | 54 | 41 | 13 | 4 | 4 | 1 | 0 | 0 |
| *Total* | | | *54* | *41* | *13* | *4* | *4* | *1* | *0* | *0* |

MARSHALL Scott   Arsenal

Full Name: Scott Roderick Marshall   DOB: 01-05-73 Edinburgh
Debut: Sheffield Wednesday v ARSENAL 6/5/93
Debut Goal: ARSENAL v Newcastle United 23/3/96

Previous Clubs Details				Apps					Goals	
Club	Signed	Fee	Tot	Start	Sub	FA	FL	Lge	FA	FL
Arsenal	Mar-91	Trainee	21	18	3	1	0	1	0	0
Rotherham U.	Dec-93	Loan	10	10	0	1	0	0	0	0
Sheffield U.	Aug-94	Loan	17	17	0	0	0	0	0	0
FAPL Summary by Club										
Arsenal	92-93 to 96-97		21	18	3	0	0	1	0	0
Total			*21*	*18*	*3*	*0*	*0*	*1*	*0*	*0*

MARSHALL Ian   Leicester City

Full Name: Ian Paul Marshall   DOB: 20-03-66 Liverpool
Debut: Chelsea v OLDHAM ATHLETIC 15/8/92
Debut Goal: OLDHAM ATHLETIC v Ipswich Town 19/9/92

Previous Clubs Details				Apps					Goals	
Club	Signed	Fee	Tot	Start	Sub	FA	FL	Lge	FA	FL
Everton	Mar-84	Apprentice	15	9	6	0	2	1	0	1
Oldham Ath	Mar-88	£100,000	170	165	5	14	17	36	3	0
Ipswich Town	Aug-93	£750,000	82	77	5	9	3	32	3	2
Leicester City	Aug-96	£800,000	28	19	9	4	0	8	2	0
FAPL Summary by Club										
Oldham Ath	1992-93		27	26	1	1	3	2	0	0
Ipswich Town	93-94 to 94-95		47	42	5	5	3	13	3	2
Leicester City	1996-97		28	19	9	4	0	8	2	0
Total			*102*	*87*	*15*	*10*	*6*	*23*	*5*	*2*

MARTYN Nigel   Leeds United

Full Name: Nigel Anthony Martyn   DOB: 11-08-66 St Austell
Debut: CRYSTAL PALACE v Blackburn Rovers 15/8/92
Debut Goal: (Goalkeeper)

Previous Clubs Details				Apps					Goals	
Club	Signed	Fee	Tot	Start	Sub	FA	FL	Lge	FA	FL
Bristol R.	Aug-87	From NL	101	101	0	6	6	0	0	0
C. Palace	Nov-89	£1m	189	189	0	13	25	0	0	0
Leeds U.	1996		37	37	0	4	3	0	0	0
FAPL Summary by Club										
C. Palace	92-93 to 94-95		79	79	0	8	15	0	0	0
Leeds U.	1996-97		37	37	0	4	3	0	0	0
Total			*116*	*116*	*0*	*12*	*18*	*0*	*0*	*0*

MASKELL Craig   Southampton

Full Name: Craig Dell Maskell   DOB: 10-04-68 Aldershot
Debut: Sheffield United v SWINDON TOWN 14/8/93
Debut Goal: Southampton v SWINDON TOWN 25/8/93

MATTEO Dominic   Liverpool

Full Name: Dominic Matteo   DOB: 28-04-74 Dumfries
Debut: Manchester City v LIVERPOOL 23/10/93
Debut Goal:

Previous Clubs Details				*Apps*				*Goals*		
Club	Signed	Fee	Tot	Start	Sub	FA	FL	Lge	FA	FL
Liverpool	May-92	Trainee	49	29	20	3	5	0	0	0
Sunderland	Mar-95	Loan	1	1	0	0	0	0	0	0
FAPL Summary by Club										
Liverpool	93-94 to 96-97		49	29	20	3	5	0	0	0
Total			*49*	*29*	*20*	*3*	*5*	*0*	*0*	*0*

MAY David   Manchester United

Full Name: David May   DOB: 24-06-70 Oldham
Debut: Crystal Palace v BLACKBURN ROVERS 15/8/92
Debut Goal: Everton v BLACKBURN ROVERS 3/3/93

Previous Clubs Details				*Apps*				*Goals*		
Club	Signed	Fee	Tot	Start	Sub	FA	FL	Lge	FA	FL
Blackburn R.	Jun-88	Trainee	123	123	0	10	13	3	1	2
Manchester U.	Jul-94	£1.4m	64	54	10	4	4	6	0	1
FAPL Summary by Club										
Blackburn R.	92-93 to 93-94		74	74	0	7	10	2	1	2
Manchester U.	94-95 to 96-97		64	54	10	4	4	6	0	1
Total			*138*	*128*	*10*	*11*	*14*	*8*	*1*	*3*

MAYBURY Alan   Leeds United

Full Name: Alan Maybury   DOB: 08-08-78 Dublin
Debut: Aston Villa v LEEDS UNITED 3/2/96
Debut Goal:

Previous Clubs Details			Apps					Goals		
Club	Signed	Fee	Tot	Start	Sub	FA	FL	Lge	FA	FL
Leeds U.	Aug-95		1	1	0	0	0	0	0	0

FAPL Summary by Club

Leeds U.		1995-96	1	1	0	0	0	0	0	0
Total			*1*	*1*	*0*	*0*	*0*	*0*	*0*	*0*

McALLISTER Gary   Coventry City

Full Name: Gary McAllister   DOB: 25-12-64 Motherwell
Debut: LEEDS UNITED v Wimbledon 15/8/92
Debut Goal: LEEDS UNITED v Liverpool 29/8/92

Previous Clubs Details			Apps					Goals		
Club	Signed	Fee	Tot	Start	Sub	FA	FL	Lge	FA	FL
Leicester City	Aug-85	£125,000	201	199	2	5	15	46	2	3
Leeds U.	Jun-90	£1m	231	230	1	24	26	32	6	4
Coventry City	Aug-96	£3m	38	38	0	4	4	6	0	1

FAPL Summary by Club

Leeds U.		92-93 to 95-96	151	151	0	17	15	25	5	2
Coventry City		1996-97	38	38	0	4	4	6	0	1
Total			*189*	*189*	*0*	*21*	*19*	*31*	*5*	*3*

McALLISTER Brian   Wimbledon

Full Name: Brian McAllister   DOB: 30-11-70 Glasgow
Debut: Sheffield Utd v WIMBLEDON 25/8/92
Debut Goal:

Previous Clubs Details			Apps					Goals		
Club	Signed	Fee	Tot	Start	Sub	FA	FL	Lge	FA	FL
Wimbledon	Feb-89	Trainee	78	70	8	8	6	0	0	0
Plymouth A.	Dec-90	Loan	8	7	1	0	0	0	0	0
Crewe Alex.	Mar-96	Loan	13	13	0	0	0	1	0	0

FAPL Summary by Club

Wimbledon		92-93 to 96-97	65	60	5	8	6	0	0	0
Total			*65*	*60*	*5*	*8*	*6*	*0*	*0*	*0*

McANESPIE Steve   Bolton Wanderers

Full Name: Steve McAnespie   DOB: 01-02-72 Kilmarnock
Debut: BOLTON WANDERERS v QPR 30/9/95
Debut Goal:

Previous Clubs Details			Apps					Goals		
Club	Signed	Fee	Tot	Start	Sub	FA	FL	Lge	FA	FL
Aberdeen	May-88	Juniors	0	0	0	0	0	0	0	0
Vasterhaninge	Jun-93									
Raith R.	Jan-94		40	37	3	3	4	0	0	0
Bolton W.	Sep-95	£900,000	22	18	4	0	4	0	0	0

Bolton W.	1995-96	9	7	2	0	3	0	0	0
Total		*9*	*7*	*2*	*0*	*3*	*0*	*0*	*0*

McATEER Jason   Liverpool
Full Name: Jason McAteer   DOB: 18-06-71 Birkenhead
Debut: Wimbledon v BOLTON WANDERERS 19/8/95
Debut Goal: Arsenal v LIVERPOOL 24/3/97

Previous Clubs Details			Apps					Goals		
Club	Signed	Fee	Tot	Start	Sub	FA	FL	Lge	FA	FL
Bolton W.	Jan-92	NL	113	108	5	11	11	8	3	2
Liverpool	Sep-95	£4.5m	66	63	3	9	8	1	3	0

FAPL Summary by Club

Bolton W.		95-96	4	4	0	0	0	0	0	0
Liverpool		95-96 to 96-97	66	63	3	9	8	1	3	0
Total			*70*	*67*	*3*	*9*	*8*	*1*	*3*	*0*

McCLAIR Brian   Manchester United
Full Name: Brian John McClair   DOB: 08-12-63 Bellshill
Debut: Sheffield United v MANCHESTER UNITED 15/8/92
Debut Goal: Everton v MANCHESTER UNITED 12/9/92

Previous Clubs Details			Apps					Goals		
Club	Signed	Fee	Tot	Start	Sub	FA	FL	Lge	FA	FL
Celtic	Jul-83		0	0	0	0	0	0	0	0
Manchester U.	Jul-87	£850,000	339	294	45	42	44	88	14	19

FAPL Summary by Club

Manchester U.	92-93 to 96-97	149	104	45	18	16	18	3	5
Total		*149*	*104*	*45*	*18*	*16*	*18*	*3*	*5*

McGINLAY John   Bolton Wanderers
Full Name: John McGinlay   DOB: 08-04-64 Inverness
Debut: Aston Villa v BOLTON WANDERERS 30/8/95
Debut Goal: BOLTON WANDERERS v MIDDLESBROUGH 9/9/95

Previous Clubs Details			Apps					Goals		
Club	Signed	Fee	Tot	Start	Sub	FA	FL	Lge	FA	FL
Shrewsbury T.	Feb-89		60	58	2	1	4	27	2	0
Bury	Jul-90	£175,000	25	16	9	1	1	9	0	0
Millwall	Jan-91	£80,000	34	27	7	2	3	10	0	0
Bolton W.	Sep-92	£125,000	185	176	9	17	23	87	10	12

FAPL Summary by Club

Bolton W.	1995-96	32	29	3	2	6	6	1	2
Total		*32*	*29*	*3*	*2*	*6*	*6*	*1*	*2*

McGOWAN Gavin　　　　　　　　　　　　　　**Arsenal**
Full Name: Gavin Gregory McGowan　　　DOB: 16-01-76 Blackheath
Debut:　　Sheffield Wednesday v ARSENAL 6/5/93 as sub
Debut Goal:

Previous Clubs Details				Apps				Goals	
Club	Signed	Fee	Tot	Start	Sub	FA	FL	Lge	FA FL
Arsenal	Jul-94	Trainee	5	3	2	1	0	0	0 0
Luton	Mar-97	Loan							
FAPL Summary by Club									
Arsenal	94-95 to 96-97		5	3	2	1	0	0	0 0
Total			*5*	*3*	*2*	*1*	*0*	*0*	*0 0*

McGRATH Paul　　　　　　　　　　　　**Derby County**
Full Name: Paul McGrath　　　　　　　　DOB: 04-12-59 Ealing
Debut:　　ASTON VILLA v Ipswich Town 15/8/92
Debut Goal: ASTON VILLA v Nottingham Forest 12/12/92

Previous Clubs Details				Apps				Goals		
Club	Signed	Fee	Tot	Start	Sub	FA	FL	Lge	FA	FL
Manchester U.	Apr-82	£30,000	163	159	4	17	13	12	2	2
Aston Villa	Aug-89	£400,000	253	248	5	24	30	8	0	1
Derby County	Oct-96	£100,000	24	23	1	2	2	0	0	0
FAPL Summary by Club										
Aston Villa	92-93 to 95-96		142	137	5	12	21	6	0	1
Derby County	1996-97		24	23	1	2	2	0	0	0
Total			*166*	*160*	*6*	*14*	*23*	*6*	*0*	*1*

McKENZIE Leon　　　　　　　　　　　**Crystal Palace**
Full Name: Leon Mark McKenzie　　　　DOB: 17-05-78 Croydon
Debut:　　　　　　　　　　　　　　　Debut Goal:

Previous Clubs Details				Apps				Goals		
Club	Signed	Fee	Tot	Start	Sub	FA	FL	Lge	FA	FL
C.Palace	Oct-95	Trainee	33	8	25	4	4	2	0	1

McKINLAY Billy　　　　　　　　　　**Blackburn Rovers**
Full Name: William McKinlay　　　　　DOB: 22-04-69 Glasgow
Debut:　　West Ham Utd v BLACKBURN ROVERS 21/10/95 as sub
Debut Goal: Nottingham Forest v BLACKBURN ROVERS 13/4/96

Previous Clubs Details				Apps				Goals		
Club	Signed	Fee	Tot	Start	Sub	FA	FL	Lge	FA	FL
Dundee U.			222					23		
Blackburn R.	Oct-95	£1.75m	44	36	8	4	2	3	0	0
FAPL Summary by Club										
Blackburn R.	95-96 to 96-97		44	36	8	4	2	3	0	0
Total			*44*	*36*	*8*	*4*	*2*	*3*	*0*	*0*

McMANAMAN Steve   Liverpool

Full Name: Steven McManaman   DOB: 11-02-72 Bootle
Debut: Nottingham Forest v LIVERPOOL 16/8/92
Debut Goal: LIVERPOOL v Wimbledon 26/9/92

Previous Clubs Details | | | *Apps* | | | | *Goals* | |
|---|---|---|---|---|---|---|---|---|---|
| Club | Signed | Fee | Tot | Start | Sub | FA | FL | Lge | FA | FL |
| Liverpool | Feb-90 | Trainee | 208 | 197 | 11 | 28 | 28 | 31 | 5 | 10 |
| *FAPL Summary by Club* | | | | | | | | | | |
| Liverpool | 92-93 to 95-96 | | 176 | 171 | 5 | 19 | 23 | 26 | 2 | 7 |
| *Total* | | | *176* | *171* | *5* | *19* | *23* | *26* | *2* | *7* |

McVEIGH Paul   Tottenham Hotspur

Full Name: Paul McVeigh   DOB: 06-12-77 Belfast
Debut: Aston Villa v TOTTENHAM HOTSPUR 19,4,97
Debut Goal: TOTTENHAM HOTSPUR v Coventry City 11/5/97

Previous Clubs Details | | | *Apps* | | | | *Goals* | |
|---|---|---|---|---|---|---|---|---|---|
| Club | Signed | Fee | Tot | Start | Sub | FA | FL | Lge | FA | FL |
| Tottenham H. | | | 3 | 2 | 1 | 0 | 0 | 1 | 0 | 0 |
| *FAPL Summary by Club* | | | | | | | | | | |
| Tottenham H. | 1996-97 | | 3 | 2 | 1 | 0 | 0 | 1 | 0 | 0 |
| *Total* | | | *3* | *2* | *1* | *0* | *0* | *1* | *0* | *0* |

MIKLOSKO Ludek   West Ham United

Full Name: Ludek Miklosko   DOB: 09-12-61 Protesov, Czechoslovakia
Debut: WEST HAM UNITED v Wimbledon 14/8/93
Debut Goal: (Goalkeeper)

Previous Clubs Details | | | *Apps* | | | | *Goals* | |
|---|---|---|---|---|---|---|---|---|---|
| Club | Signed | Fee | Tot | Start | Sub | FA | FL | Lge | FA | FL |
| Banik Ostrava | | | | | | | | | | |
| West Ham U. | Feb-90 | £300,000 | 302 | 302 | 0 | 25 | 23 | 0 | 0 | 0 |
| *FAPL Summary by Club* | | | | | | | | | | |
| West Ham U. | 93-94 to 96-97 | | 156 | 156 | 0 | 13 | 13 | 0 | 0 | 0 |
| *Total* | | | *156* | *156* | *0* | *13* | *13* | *0* | *0* | *0* |

MILLER Kevin   Crystal Palace

Fullname: Kevin Miller   DOB: 15-03-69
Debut: Debut Goal: (Goalkeeper)

Previous Clubs Details | | | *Apps* | | | | *Goals* | |
|---|---|---|---|---|---|---|---|---|---|
| Club | Signed | Fee | Tot | Start | Sub | FA | FL | Lge | FA | FL |
| Exeter City | Mar-89 | NL | 163 | 163 | 0 | 12 | 7 | 0 | 0 | 0 |
| Birmingham C. | May-93 | £250,000 | 24 | 24 | 0 | 0 | 4 | 0 | 0 | 0 |
| Watford * | Aug-94 | £250,000 | 86 | 86 | 0 | 6 | 6 | 0 | 0 | 0 |
| C.Palace | Jun-97 | £1.55m | | | | | | | | |

MILOSEVIC Savo   Aston Villa

Full Name: Savo Milosevic   DOB: 02-09-73 Bijeljina, Yugoslavia
Debut: ASTON VILLA v Manchester United 19/8/95
Debut Goal: Blackburn Rovers v ASTON VILLA 9/9/95

Previous Clubs Details

Club	Signed	Fee	Tot	Start	Sub	FA	FL	Lge	FA	FL
				Apps					*Goals*	
Partizan Belgrade										
Aston Villa	Jul-95	£3.5m	67	65	2	8	8	22	1	1

FAPL Summary by Club

Aston Villa	95-96 to 96-97	67	65	2	8	8	22	1	1
Total		*67*	*65*	*2*	*8*	*8*	*22*	*1*	*1*

MOLENAAR Robert   Leeds United

Full Name: Robert Molenaar   DOB: 27-02-69 Zaandam, Holland
Debut: LEEDS UTD v Leicester City 11/1/97
Debut Goal: LEEDS UTD v Everton 8/3/97

Previous Clubs Details

Club	Signed	Fee	Tot	Start	Sub	FA	FL	Lge	FA	FL
				Apps					*Goals*	
FC Volendam	1992		107	107	0	0	0	3	0	0
Leeds U.	Jan-97	£1m	12	12	0	2	0	1	0	0

FAPL Summary by Club

Leeds U.	1996-97	12	12	0	2	0	1	0	0
Total		*12*	*12*	*0*	*2*	*0*	*1*	*0*	*0*

MONCUR John   West Ham United

Full Name: John Frederick Moncur   DOB: 22-09-66 Stepney
Debut: Sheffield United v SWINDON TOWN 14/8/93
Debut Goal: Sheffield United v SWINDON TOWN 14/8/93

Previous Clubs Details

Club	Signed	Fee	Tot	Start	Sub	FA	FL	Lge	FA	FL
				Apps					*Goals*	
Tottenham H.	Aug-84	Apprentice	21	10	11	0	3	1	0	0
Doncaster R.	Sep-86	Loan	4	4	0	0	0	0	0	0
Cambridge U.	Mar-87	Loan	4	3	1	0	0	0	0	0
Portsmouth	Mar-89	Loan	7	7	0	0	0	0	0	0
Brentford	Oct-89	Loan	5	5	0	0	0	1	0	0
Ipswich Town	Oct-91	Loan	6	5	1	0	0	0	0	0
N. Forest	Feb-92	Loan	0	0	0	0	0	0	0	0
Swindon Town	Mar-92	£80,000	58	53	5	1	4	5	0	0
West Ham U.	Jun-94	£900,000	77	75	2	4	10	4	1	2

FAPL Summary by Club

Swindon Town	1993-94	41	41	0	1	3	4	0	0
West Ham U.	94-95 to 96-97	77	75	2	4	10	4	1	2
Total		*118*	*116*	*2*	*5*	*13*	*8*	*1*	*2*

MONKOU Ken   Southampton
Full Name: Kenneth John Monkou   DOB: 29-11-64 Necare, Surinam
Debut: SOUTHAMPTON v Manchester United 24/8/92
Debut Goal: SOUTHAMPTON v Sheffield Wednesday 28/12/92

Previous Clubs Details				*Apps*				*Goals*		
Club	Signed	Fee	Tot	Start	Sub	FA	FL	Lge	FA	FL
Chelsea	Mar-89	£100,000	94	92	2	3	12	2	0	0
Southampton	Aug-92	£750,000	144	138	6	13	16	8	1	1
FAPL Summary by Club										
Southampton	92-93 to 96-97		144	138	6	13	16	8	1	1
Total			*144*	*138*	*6*	*13*	*16*	*8*	*0*	*1*

MORRIS Jody   Chelsea
Full Name: Jody Morris   DOB: 22-12-78 London
Debut: CHELSEA v Middlesbrough 4/2/96 as sub
Debut Goal:

Previous Clubs Details				*Apps*				*Goals*		
Club	Signed	Fee	Tot	Start	Sub	FA	FL	Lge	FA	FL
Chelsea	Jan-96	Trainee	13	6	7	0	2	0	0	1
FAPL Summary by Club										
Chelsea	95-96 to 96-97		13	6	7	0	2	0	0	1
Total			*13*	*6*	*7*	*0*	*2*	*0*	*0*	*1*

MOSES Adrian   Barnsley
Full Name: Adrian Paul Moses   DOB: 15-11-68 Doncaster
Debut: Debut Goal:

Previous Clubs Details				*Apps*				*Goals*		
Club	Signed	Fee	Tot	Start	Sub	FA	FL	Lge	FA	FL
Barnsley	Jul-93	Juniors	56	49	7	4	2	3	0	0

MOSS Neil   Southampton
Full Name: Neil Graham Moss   DOB: 10-05-75 New Milton
Debut: SOUTHAMPTON v Nottingham Forest 4/9/96
Debut Goal:

Previous Clubs Details				*Apps*				*Goals*		
Club	Signed	Fee	Tot	Start	Sub	FA	FL	Lge	FA	FL
Bournemouth	Jan-93	Trainee	22	21	1	4	1	0	0	0
Southampton	Dec-95	£250,000	3	3	0	0	2	0	0	0
FAPL Summary by Club										
Southampton	1996-97		3	3	0	0	2	3	0	0
Total			*3*	*3*	*0*	*0*	*2*	*3*	*0*	*0*

MURRAY Scott   Aston Villa
Full Name: Scott George Murray   DOB: 26-05-74 Aberdeen
Debut: ASTON VILLA v Middlesbrough 19/3/96
Debut Goal:

Previous Clubs Details			*Apps*				*Goals*		
Club	Signed	Fee	Tot	Start	Sub	FA	FL	Lge	FA	FL
Aston Villa	Mar 94	£35,000	4	4	0	0	0	0	0	0
FAPL Summary by Club										
Aston Villa	95-96 to 96-97		4	4	0	0	0	0	0	0
Total			*4*	*4*	*0*	*0*	*0*	*0*	*0*	*0*

MUSCAT Kevin   Crystal Palace
Full Name: Kevin Muscat   DOB: 07-08-73 Australia
Debut: Debut Goal:

Previous Clubs Details			*Apps*				*Goals*		
Club	Signed	Fee	Tot	Start	Sub	FA	FL	Lge	FA	FL
South Melbourne										
C. Palace	Jun-96		44	42	2	2	3	2	0	1

MYERS Andy   Chelsea
Full Name: Andrew John Myers   DOB: 03-11-73 Hounslow
Debut: Wimbledon v CHELSEA 28/12/92
Debut Goal: Sheffield Wednesday v CHELSEA 7/9/96

Previous Clubs Details			*Apps*				*Goals*		
Club	Signed	Fee	Tot	Start	Sub	FA	FL	Lge	FA	FL
Chelsea	Jun-91	Trainee	71	62	9	9	2	2	0	0
FAPL Summary by Club										
Chelsea	92-93 to 96-97		57	53	4	7	1	1	0	0
Total			*57*	*53*	*4*	*7*	*1*	*1*	*0*	*0*

NASH Carlo   Crystal Palace
Full Name: Carlo Nash   DOB: 13-09-73
Debut: Debut Goal:

Previous Clubs Details			*Apps*				*Goals*		
Club	Signed	Fee	Tot	Start	Sub	FA	FL	Lge	FA	FL
C.Palace	May-96	£35,000 NL	21	21	0	0	0	0	0	0

NDAH George   Crystal Palace
Full Name: George Ndah   DOB: 23-12-74 Dulwich
Debut: Liverpool v CRYSTAL PALACE 28/11/92 as sub
Debut Goal: CRYSTAL PALACE v Leicester City 14/1/95

Previous Clubs Details			*Apps*				*Goals*		
Club	Signed	Fee	Tot	Start	Sub	FA	FL	Lge	FA	FL
C. Palace	Aug-92	Trainee	74	31	43	4	12	8	1	1

NEILSON Alan   Southampton

Full Name: Alan Bruce Neilson   DOB: 26-09-72 Wegburg, Germany
Debut: Ipswich Town v NEWCASTLE UNITED 31/8/93 as sub
Debut Goal:

Previous Clubs Details				*Apps*				*Goals*	
Club	Signed	Fee	Tot	Start	Sub	FA	FL	Lge	FA	FL
Newcastle U.	Feb-91	Trainee	42	35	7	0	4	1	0	0
Southampton	Jun-95	£500,000	47	39	8	2	5	0	0	0

FAPL Summary by Club

		Tot	Start	Sub	FA	FL	Lge	FA	FL
Newcastle U.	93-94 to 94-95	20	15	5	0	1	0	0	0
Southampton	95-96 to 96-97	47	39	8	2	5	0	0	0
Total		*67*	*54*	*13*	*2*	*6*	*0*	*0*	*0*

NELSON Fernando   Aston Villa

Full Name: Fernando Nelson   DOB: 11-05-71
Debut: ASTON VILLA v Derby County 24/8/96 as sub
Debut Goal:

Previous Clubs Details				*Apps*				*Goals*	
Club	Signed	Fee	Tot	Start	Sub	FA	FL	Lge	FA	FL
Sporting Lisbon	1991		115	113	2			3		
Aston Villa	Jul-96	£1.75m	34	33	1	1	2	0	0	0

FAPL Summary by Club

		Tot	Start	Sub	FA	FL	Lge	FA	FL
Aston Villa	1996-97	34	33	1	1	2	0	0	0
Total		*34*	*33*	*1*	*1*	*2*	*0*	*0*	*0*

NETHERCOTT Stuart   Tottenham Hotspur

Full Name: Stuart David Nethercott   DOB: 21-03-73 Ilford
Debut: TOTTENHAM HOTSPUR v Norwich City 9/4/93 as sub
Debut Goal:

Previous Clubs Details				*Apps*				*Goals*	
Club	Signed	Fee	Tot	Start	Sub	FA	FL	Lge	FA	FL
Tottenham H.	Aug-91	Trainee	54	31	23	8	0	0	1	0
Maidstone U.	Sep-91	Loan	13	13	0	0	0	1	0	0
Barnet	Feb-92	Loan	3	3	0	0	0	0	0	0

FAPL Summary by Club

		Tot	Start	Sub	FA	FL	Lge	FA	FL
Tottenham H.	92-93 to 96-97	54	31	23	8	0	0	1	0
Total		*54*	*31*	*23*	*8*	*0*	*0*	*1*	*0*

NEVILLE Gary   Manchester United

Full Name: Gary Alexander Neville   DOB: 18-02-75 Bury
Debut: MANCHESTER UNITED v Crystal Palace 19/11/94

Debut Goal: MANCHESTER UNITED v Middlesbrough 5/5/97

Previous Clubs Details

Club	Signed	Fee	Tot	Start	Sub	FA	FL	Lge	FA	FL
Manchester U.	Jan-93	Trainee	80	76	4	13	5	1	0	0

FAPL Summary by Club

Club										
Manchester U.	94-95 to 96-97		80	76	4	13	5	1	0	0
Total			*80*	*76*	*4*	*13*	*5*	*1*	*0*	*0*

NEVILLE Phil · Manchester United

Full Name: Philip John Neville · DOB: 21-01-77 Bury
Debut: Manchester City v MANCHESTER UNITED 11/2/95
Debut Goal:

Previous Clubs Details

			Apps					*Goals*		
Club	Signed	Fee	Tot	Start	Sub	FA	FL	Lge	FA	FL
Manchester U.	Jun-94	Trainee	44	37	7	8	3	0	0	0

FAPL Summary by Club

Club										
Manchester U.	94-95 to 96-97		44	37	7	8	3	0	0	0
Total			*44*	*37*	*7*	*8*	*3*	*0*	*0*	*0*

NEWSOME Jon · Sheffield Wednesday

Full Name: Jonathan Newsome · DOB: 06-09-70 Sheffield
Debut: LEEDS UNITED v Wimbledon 15/8/92
Debut Goal: LEEDS UNITED v Blackburn Rovers 23/10/93

Previous Clubs Details

			Apps					*Goals*		
Club	Signed	Fee	Tot	Start	Sub	FA	FL	Lge	FA	FL
Sheffield Wed.	Jul-89	Trainee	7	6	1	0	3	0	0	0
Leeds U.	Jun-91	£150,000	76	62	14	4	3	3	0	0
Norwich City	Jun-94	£1m	62	61	1	5	9	7	1	0
Sheffield W.	Mar-96	£1.6m	18	18	0	3	1	2	0	0

FAPL Summary by Club

Club										
Leeds U.	92-93 to 93-94		66	55	11	4	3	1	0	0
Norwich City	1994-95		35	35	0	4	4	3	0	0
Sheffield W.	95-96 to 96-97		18	18	0	3	1	2	0	0
Total			*119*	*108*	*11*	*11*	*8*	*6*	*0*	*0*

NEWTON Eddie · Chelsea

Full Name: Edward John Ikem Newton · DOB: 13-12-71 Hammersmith
Debut: Norwich City v CHELSEA 19/8/92
Debut Goal: CHELSEA v Sheffield Wednesday 22/8/92

Previous Clubs Details

			Apps					*Goals*		
Club	Signed	Fee	Tot	Start	Sub	FA	FL	Lge	FA	FL
Chelsea	May-90	Trainee	140	121	19	18	13	8	1	1
Cardiff City	Jan-92	Loan	18	18	0	0	0	4	0	0

| Chelsea | 92-93 to 96-97 | 139 | 121 | 18 | 18 | 13 | 7 | 1 | 0 |
| *Total* | | *139* | *121* | *18* | *18* | *13* | *7* | *1* | *0* |

NICOL Steve   Sheffield Wednesday

Full Name: Stephen Nicol   DOB: 01-12-61 Irvine
Debut: Nottingham Forest v LIVERPOOL 16/8/92
Debut Goal: QPR v LIVERPOOL 18/8/93

Previous Clubs Details

				Apps				*Goals*	
Club	Signed	Fee	Tot	Start	Sub	FA	FL	Lge	FA FL
Liverpool	Oct-81	£300,000	343	328	15	50	42	36	3 4
Notts County	Jan-95	Free	32	32	0	1	1	2	0 0
Sheffield W.	Nov-95	Free	42	37	5	3	0	0	0 0

FAPL Summary by Club

Liverpool	92-93 to 94-95	67	63	4	3	7	1	0	0
Sheffield W.	95-96 to 96-97	42	37	5	3	0	0	0	0
Total		*109*	*100*	*9*	*6*	*7*	*1*	*0*	*0*

NIELSEN Allan   Tottenham Hotspur

Full Name: Allan Nielsen   DOB: 13-03-71
Debut: Wimbledon v TOTTENHAM HOTSPUR 3/9/96
Debut Goal: TOTTENHAM HOTSPUR v Aston Villa 12/10/96

Previous Clubs Details

				Apps				*Goals*	
Club	Signed	Fee	Tot	Start	Sub	FA	FL	Lge	FA FL
Bayern Munich			3					0	
Esbjerg									
OB Odense	1992		55	53	2			9	
FC Copenhagen	1995		26	25	1			3	
Brondby	1996	£100,000	38	38	0			9	
Tottenham H.			29	28	1	1	3	6	0 0

FAPL Summary by Club

| Tottenham H. | 1996-97 | 29 | 28 | 1 | 1 | 3 | 6 | 0 | 0 |
| *Total* | | *29* | *28* | *1* | *1* | *3* | *6* | *0* | *0* |

NOLAN Ian   Sheffield Wednesday

Full Name: Ian Robert Nolan   DOB: 09-07-70 Liverpool
Debut: SHEFFIELD WEDNESDAY v Tottenham Hotspur 20/8/94
Debut Goal: Liverpool v SHEFFIELD WEDNESDAY 1/10/94

Previous Clubs Details

				Apps				*Goals*	
Club	Signed	Fee	Tot	Start	Sub	FA	FL	Lge	FA FL
Preston (Non-League)		Trainee							
Tranmere R.	Aug-91	£10,000	88	87	1	7	10	1	1 0
Sheffield W.	Aug-94	£1.5m	109	109	0	8	10	4	0 0

FAPL Summary by Club

				Apps					Goals	
Sheffield W.	94-95 to 96-97	109	109	0	8	10		4	0	0
Total		*109*	*109*	*0*	*8*	*10*		*4*	*0*	*0*

O'CONNOR Jon   Everton

Full Name: Jonathon O'Connor   DOB: 29-10-76 Darlington
Debut: Manchester United v EVERTON 21/2/96
Debut Goal:

Previous Clubs Details				*Apps*				*Goals*	
Club	Signed	Fee	Tot	Start	Sub	FA	FL	Lge	FA FL
Everton	Oct-93	Trainee	4	3	1	0	0	0	0 0

FAPL Summary by Club

Everton	95-96 to 96-97	4	3	1	0	0	0	0	0
Total		*4*	*3*	*1*	*0*	*0*	*0*	*0*	*0*

O'KANE John   Manchester United

Full Name: John Andrew O'Kane   DOB: 15-11-74 Nottingham
Debut: Aston Villa v MANCHESTER UNITED 19/8/95 as sub
Debut Goal:

Previous Clubs Details				*Apps*				*Goals*	
Club	Signed	Fee	Tot	Start	Sub	FA	FL	Lge	FA FL
Manchester U.	Jan-93	Trainee	2	1	1	0	2	0	0 0
Bury	Oct-96	Loan							
Wrexham	Mar-97	Loan							

FAPL Summary by Club

Manchester U.	95-96 to 96-97	2	1	1	0	2	0	0	0
Total		*2*	*1*	*1*	*0*	*2*	*0*	*0*	*0*

O'NEILL Michael   Coventry City

Full Name: Michael O'Neill   DOB:
Debut: COVENTRY CITY v Nottingham Forest 17/8/96
Debut Goal:

Previous Clubs Details				*Apps*				*Goals*	
Club	Signed	Fee	Tot	Start	Sub	FA	FL	Lge	FA FL
Coventry City			1	1	0	0	0	0	0 0

FAPL Summary by Club

Coventry City	1996-97	1	1	0	0	0	0	0	0
Total		*1*	*1*	*0*	*0*	*0*	*0*	*0*	*0*

OAKES Michael   Aston Villa

Full Name: Michael Oakes   DOB: 30-10-73 Northwich
Debut: Sheffield Wednesday v ASTON VILLA 17/08/96
Debut Goal: (Goalkeeper)

Previous Clubs Details				Apps				Goals		
Club	Signed	Fee	Tot	Start	Sub	FA	FL	Lge	FA	FL
Aston Villa	Jul-91		20	18	2	0	1	0	0	0
Scarborough	Nov-93	Loan	1	1	0	0	0	0	0	0
FAPL Summary by Club										
Aston Villa		1996-97	20	18	2	0	1	0	0	0
Total			*20*	*18*	*2*	*0*	*1*	*0*	*0*	*0*

OAKES Scott   Sheffield Wednesday

Full Name: Scott John Oakes   DOB: 05-08-72 Leicester
Debut: SHEFFIELD WEDNESDAY v Aston Villa 17/08/96
Debut Goal: Sunderland v SHEFFIELD WEDNESDAY 25/11/96

Previous Clubs Details				Apps				Goals		
Club	Signed	Fee	Tot	Start	Sub	FA	FL	Lge	FA	FL
Leicester City	May-90	Trainee	3	1	2	0	0	0	0	0
Luton Town	Oct-91		173	136	37	14	6	27	5	1
Sheffield W.	Aug-96	£450,000	19	7	12	0	0	1	0	0
FAPL Summary by Club										
Sheffield W.		1996-97	19	7	12	0	0	1	0	0
Total			*19*	*7*	*12*	*0*	*0*	*1*	*0*	*0*

OAKLEY Matthew   Southampton

Full Name: Matthew Oakley   DOB: 17-08-77 Peterborough
Debut: Everton v TOTTENHAM HOTSPUR 6/5/95 as sub
Debut Goal: Wimbledon v SOUTHAMPTON 23/9/96

Previous Clubs Details				Apps				Goals		
Club	Signed	Fee	Tot	Start	Sub	FA	FL	Lge	FA	FL
Southampton			39	28	11	4	7	3	1	0
FAPL Summary by Club										
Southampton		94-95 to 96-97	39	28	11	4	7	3	1	0
Total			*39*	*28*	*11*	*4*	*7*	*3*	*1*	*0*

OGRIZOVIC Steve   Coventry City

Full Name: Steven Ogrizovic   DOB: 12-09-57 Mansfield
Debut: COVENTRY CITY v Middlesbrough 15/8/92
Debut Goal: (Goalkeeper)

Previous Clubs Details				Apps				Goals		
Club	Signed	Fee	Tot	Start	Sub	FA	FL	Lge	FA	FL
Chesterfield	Jul-77		16	16	0	0	2	0	0	0
Liverpool	Nov-77	£70,000	4	4	0	0	0	0	0	0
Shrewsbury Tn	Aug-82	£70,000	84	84	0	5	7	0	0	0
Coventry City	Jun-84	£72,000	478	478	0	32	45	1	0	0
FAPL Summary by Club										
Coventry City		92-93 to 96-97	162	162	0	13	13	0	0	0
Total			*162*	*162*	*0*	*13*	*13*	*0*	*0*	*0*

OMOYIMNI Emmanuel West Ham United

Full Name: Emmanuel Omoyimni DOB: 28-12-77 Nigeria
Debut: WEST HAM UNITED v Tottenham Hotspur 24/2/97 as sub
Debut Goal:

Previous Clubs Details			Apps					Goals		
Club	Signed	Fee	Tot	Start	Sub	FA	FL	Lge	FA	FL
West Ham U.			1	0	1	0	0	0	0	0
FAPL Summary by Club										
West Ham U.	1996-97		1	0	1	0	0	0	0	0
Total			*1*	*0*	*1*	*0*	*0*	*0*	*0*	*0*

OSTENSTAD Egil Southampton

Full Name: Egil Ostenstad DOB: 02-01-72 Haugesund
Debut: Coventry City v SOUTHAMPTON 13/10/96 as sub
Debut Goal: SOUTHAMPTON v Manchester United 26/10/96

Previous Clubs Details			Apps					Goals		
Club	Signed	Fee	Tot	Start	Sub	FA	FL	Lge	FA	FL
Viking FK	1990		104	81	23			31		
Southampton	1996		30	29	1	1	6	10	1	3
FAPL Summary by Club										
Southampton	1996-97		30	29	1	1	6	10	1	3
Total			*30*	*29*	*1*	*1*	*6*	*10*	*1*	*3*

OVERMARS Marc Arsenal

Full Name: Marc Overmars DOB: 29-03-73
Debut: Debut Goal:

Previous Clubs Details			Apps					Goals		
Club	Signed	Fee	Tot	Start	Sub	FA	FL	Lge	FA	FL
Go Ahead Eagles										
Willem II	1991		31	31	0			1		
Ajax *	1992		110	106	4			34		
Arsenal	Jun-97	£7m								

OWEN Michael Liverpool

Full Name: Michael Owen DOB:
Debut: Wimbledon v LIVERPOOL 6/5/97 as sub
Debut Goal: Wimbledon v LIVERPOOL 6/5/97 as sub

Previous Clubs Details			Apps					Goals		
Club	Signed	Fee	Tot	Start	Sub	FA	FL	Lge	FA	FL
Liverpool			2	1	1	0	0	1	0	0
FAPL Summary by Club										
Liverpool	1996-97		2	1	1	0	0	1	0	0
Total			*2*	*1*	*1*	*0*	*0*	*1*	*0*	*0*

PAATELAINEN Mixu — Bolton Wanderers

Full Name: Mixu Paatelainen DOB: 03-02-67 Helsinki
Debut: Wimbledon v BOLTON WANDERERS 19/8/95
Debut Goal: BOLTON WANDERERS v Everton 14/10/95

Previous Clubs Details

Club	Signed	Fee	Tot	Start	Sub	FA	FL	Lge	FA	FL
Valkeakosken										
Dundee U.	Oct-87		133	101	32	21	9	33	8	5
Aberdeen	Mar-92		59	55	4	2	9	12	0	2
Bolton W.	Aug-94	£300,000	69	58	11	2	9	14	0	2

FAPL Summary by Club

Bolton W.		1995-96	15	12	3	1	1	1	0	0
Total			*15*	*12*	*3*	*1*	*1*	*1*	*0*	*0*

PALLISTER Gary — Manchester United

Full Name: Gary Andrew Pallister DOB: 30-06-65 Ramsgate
Debut: Sheffield Utd v MANCHESTER UNITED 15/8/92
Debut Goal: MANCHESTER UNITED v Blackburn R. 3/5/93

Previous Clubs Details

Club	Signed	Fee	Tot	Start	Sub	FA	FL	Lge	FA	FL
Middlesbrough	Nov-84	Free NL	156	156	0	10	10	5	1	0
Darlington	Oct-85	Loan	7	7	0	0	0	0	0	0
Manchester U.	Aug-89	£2.3m	284	281	3	35	36	12	2	0

FAPL Summary by Club

Manchester U.		92-93 to 96-97	173	173	0	21	16	8	2	0
Total			*173*	*173*	*0*	*21*	*16*	*8*	*2*	*0*

PALMER Carlton — Leeds United

Full Name: Carlton Lloyd Palmer DOB: 05-12-65 Rowley Regis
Debut: Everton v SHEFFIELD WEDNESDAY 15/8/92
Debut Goal: SHEFFIELD WEDNESDAY v Oldham Athletic 17/10/92

Previous Clubs Details

Club	Signed	Fee	Tot	Start	Sub	FA	FL	Lge	FA	FL
WBA	Dec-84	Apprentice	121	114	7	4	8	4	0	1
Sheffield W.	Feb-89	£750,000	205	204	1	18	31	14	2	1
Leeds U.	Jun-94	£2.6m	102	100	2	12	12	5	1	0

FAPL Summary by Club

Sheffield W.		92-93 to 93-94	71	70	1	11	16	6	2	1
Leeds U.		94-95 to 96-97	102	100	2	12	12	5	1	0
Total			*173*	*170*	*3*	*23*	*28*	*11*	*3*	*1*

PARKER Paul — Derby County

Full Name: Paul Andrew Parker DOB: 04-04-64 West Ham
Debut: MANCHESTER UNITED v Liverpool 18/10/92

Debut Goal: MANCHESTER UNITED v Tottenham Hotspur 9/1/93

Previous Clubs Details				*Apps*				*Goals*	
Club	Signed	Fee	Tot	Start	Sub	FA	FL	Lge	FA FL
Fulham	Apr-82		153	140	13	11	16	2	0 1
QPR	Jun-87	£300,000	125	121	4	16	14	1	0 0
Manchester U.	Aug-91	£2m	105	100	5	15	15	1	0 0
Chelsea	Mar-97	Free	4	1	3	0	0	0	0 0
Derby County	Oct-97	Free	4	4	0	1	1	0	0 0
FAPL Summary by Club									
Manchester U.	92-93 to 95-96		79	76	3	12	9	1	0 0
Chelsea	1996-97		4	1	3	0	0	0	0 0
Derby County	1996-97		4	4	0	1	1	0	0 0
Total			*87*	*81*	*6*	*13*	*10*	*1*	*0 0*

PARKER Garry   Leicester City
Full Name: Garry Stuart Parker   DOB: 07-09-65 Oxford
Debut: Ipswich Town v ASTON VILLA 15/8/92
Debut Goal: Sheffield Utd v ASTON VILLA 29/8/92

Previous Clubs Details				*Apps*				*Goals*	
Club	Signed	Fee	Tot	Start	Sub	FA	FL	Lge	FA FL
Luton Town	May-83	Apprentice	42	31	11	8	4	3	0 1
Hull City	Feb-86	£72,000	84	82	2	4	5	8	0 0
N.Forest	Mar-88	£260,000	103	99	4	16	23	17	5 4
Aston Villa	Nov-91	£650,000	95	91	4	3	4	13	1 0
Leicester City	Feb-95	£300,000 +	85	72	13	7	13	7	1 1
FAPL Summary by Club									
Aston Villa	92-93 to 94-95		70	66	4	5	12	11	0 0
Leicester City	94-95 to 96-97		45	36	9	5	9	4	1 1
Total			*115*	*102*	*13*	*10*	*21*	*15*	*1 1*

PARKINSON Joe   Everton
Full Name: Joseph Simon Parkinson   DOB: 11-06-71 Eccles
Debut: EVERTON v Aston Villa 20/8/94 as sub
Debut Goal: Manchester City v EVERTON 30/8/95

Previous Clubs Details				*Apps*				*Goals*	
Club	Signed	Fee	Tot	Start	Sub	FA	FL	Lge	FA FL
Wigan Athletic	Apr-89	Trainee	119	115	4	9	11	6	0 1
Bournemouth	Jul-93	£35,000	30	30	0	4	4	1	0 1
Everton	Mar-94	£250,000	90	88	2	9	5	3	1 0
FAPL Summary by Club									
Everton	94-95 to 96-97		90	88	2	9	5	3	1 0
Total			*90*	*88*	*2*	*9*	*5*	*3*	*1 0*

PARLOUR Ray   Arsenal

Full Name: Raymond Parlour   DOB: 07-03-73 Romford
Debut: ARSENAL v Sheffield Wednesday 29/8/92
Debut Goal: ARSENAL v Sheffield Wednesday 29/8/92

Previous Clubs Details				*Apps*				*Goals*	
Club	Signed	Fee	Tot	Start	Sub	FA	FL	Lge	FA	FL
Arsenal	Mar-91	Trainee	136	101	35	12	16	6	1	0

FAPL Summary by Club

Arsenal	92-93 to 96-97		130	99	31	12	16	5	1	0
Total			*130*	*99*	*31*	*12*	*16*	*5*	*1*	*0*

PEACOCK Darren   Newcastle United

Full Name: Darren Peacock   DOB: 03-02-68 Bristol
Debut: Manchester City v QPR 17/8/92
Debut Goal: QPR v Coventry City 20/2/93

Previous Clubs Details				*Apps*				*Goals*	
Club	Signed	Fee	Tot	Start	Sub	FA	FL	Lge	FA	FL
Newport Co.	Feb-86	Apprentice	28	24	4	1	2	0	0	0
Hereford U.	Mar-89		59	56	3	6	6	4	1	0
QPR	Dec-90	£200,000	126	123	3	3	12	6	0	1
Newcastle U.	Mar-94	£2.7m	113	112	1	9	11	2	0	2

FAPL Summary by Club

QPR	92-93 to 93-94		68	65	3	2	8	5	0	1
Newcastle U.	93-94 to 96-97		113	112	1	9	11	2	0	2
Total			*181*	*177*	*4*	*11*	*19*	*7*	*0*	*3*

PEARCE Ian   Blackburn Rovers

Full Name: Ian Anthony Pearce   DOB: 07-05-74 Bury St Edmunds
Debut: CHELSEA v Liverpool 5/9/92 as sub
Debut Goal: West Ham Utd v BLACKBURN ROVERS 27/4/94

Previous Clubs Details				*Apps*				*Goals*	
Club	Signed	Fee	Tot	Start	Sub	FA	FL	Lge	FA	FL
Chelsea	Aug-91	Juniors	4	0	4	0	0	0	0	0
Blackburn R.	Oct-93	£300,000	57	42	15	3	8	2	0	1

FAPL Summary by Club

Chelsea	92-93 to 93-94		1	0	1	0	0	0	0	0
Blackburn R.	93-94 to 96-97		57	42	15	3	8	2	0	1
Total			*58*	*42*	*16*	*3*	*8*	*2*	*0*	*1*

PEDERSEN Per   Blackburn Rovers

Full Name: Per Pedersen   DOB: 30-03-69 Aalberg, Norway
Debut: Liverpool v BLACKBURN ROVERS 22/2/97 as sub
Debut Goal: Chelsea v BLACKBURN ROVERS 5/3/97

Previous Clubs Details			Apps					Goals		
Club	Signed	Fee	Tot	Start	Sub	FA	FL	Lge	FA	FL
OB (Denmark)	1990		22	20	2	0	0	8	0	0
Lyngby	1991		78	74	4	0	0	29	0	0
OB *	1996		32	31	1	0	0	16	0	0
Blackburn R.	Feb-97	£2.5m	11	6	5	0	0	1	0	0
FAPL Summary by Club										
Blackburn R.		1996-97	11	6	5	0	0	1	0	0
Total			*11*	*6*	*5*	*0*	*0*	*1*	*0*	*0*

PEMBRIDGE Mark   Sheffield Wednesday

Full Name: Mark Anthony Pembridge   DOB: 29-11-70 Merthyr Tydfil
Debut: Liverpool v SHEFFIELD WEDNESDAY 19/8/95
Debut Goal: SHEFFIELD WEDNESDAY v Blackburn Rovers 23/8/95

Previous Clubs Details			Apps					Goals		
Club	Signed	Fee	Tot	Start	Sub	FA	FL	Lge	FA	FL
Luton Town	Jul-89	Trainee	60	60	0	4	2	6	0	0
Derby County	Jun-92	£1.25m	110	108	2	6	9	28	3	1
Sheffield W.	Jul-95	£900,000	59	57	2	4	4	8	1	1
FAPL Summary by Club										
Sheffield W.		95-96 to 96-97	59	57	2	4	4	8	1	1
Total			*59*	*57*	*2*	*4*	*4*	*8*	*1*	*1*

PERRY Chris   Wimbledon

Full Name: Christopher John Perry   DOB: 26-04-73 Surrey
Debut: WIMBLEDON v Liverpool 4/4/94 as sub
Debut Goal: Manchester United v WIMBLEDON 29/1/97

Previous Clubs Details			Apps					Goals		
Club	Signed	Fee	Tot	Start	Sub	FA	FL	Lge	FA	FL
Wimbledon	Jul-91		98	90	8	17	11	1	0	1
FAPL Summary by Club										
Wimbledon		93-94 to 96-97	98	90	8	17	10	1	1	0
Total			*98*	*90*	*8*	*17*	*10*	*1*	*1*	*0*

PETRESCU Dan   Chelsea

Full Name: Dan Vasile Petrescu   DOB: 22-12-67 Bucharest
Debut: SHEFFIELD WEDNESDAY v Tottenham Hotspur 20/8/94
Debut Goal: SHEFFIELD WEDNESDAY v Tottenham Hotspur 20/8/94

Previous Clubs Details			Apps					Goals		
Club	Signed	Fee	Tot	Start	Sub	FA	FL	Lge	FA	FL
CSA Steaua	Jun-86		2	2	0	0	0	0	0	0
Olt Scornicesti	Jul-86		24	24	0	1	0	0	0	0
CSA Steaua	Jul-87		93	93	0	14	0	27	3	0
Foggia	Jul-91		55	55	0	6	0	7	0	0
Genoa	Jul-93		24	24	0	1	0	1	0	0
Sheffield W.	Aug-94	£1.25m	37	28	9	2	2	3	0	0

Chelsea	Nov-95 £2.3m	58	56	2	13	2	5	1	1

FAPL Summary by Club

Sheffield W.	94-95 to 95-96	37	28	9	2	2	3	0	0
Chelsea	95-96 to 96-97	58	56	2	13	2	5	1	1
Total		*95*	*84*	*11*	*15*	*4*	*8*	*1*	*1*

PETIT Emmanuel   Arsenal

Full Name: Emmanuel Petit   DOB: 22-09-70
Debut: Debut Goal:

Previous Clubs Details

			Apps				Goals		
Club	Signed	Fee	Tot	Start	Sub	FA	FL	Lge	FA FL
Monaco *	1985		155	154	1			4	
Arsenal	Jun-97 £3m								

PHELAN Terry   Everton

Full Name: Terence Michael Phelan   DOB: 16-03-67 Manchester
Debut: MANCHESTER CITY v Norwich City 26/8/92
Debut Goal: MANCHESTER CITY v Southampton 28/12/93

Previous Clubs Details

			Apps					Goals		
Club	Signed	Fee	Tot	Start	Sub	FA	FL	Lge	FA	FL
Leeds U.	Aug-84		14	12	2	0	3	0	0	0
Swansea City	Jul-86	Free	45	45	0	5	4	0	0	0
Wimbledon	Jul-87	£100,000	159	155	4	16	15	1	2	0
Man. City	Aug-92	£2.5m	103	102	1	8	11	1	1	0
Chelsea	Nov-95	£900,000	16	15	1	8	1	0	0	0
Everton	Dec-96	£850,00	15	15	0	1	0	0	0	0

FAPL Summary by Club

Man. City	92-93 to 95-96	103	102	1	8	11	1	1	0
Chelsea	95-96 to 96-97	16	15	1	8	1	0	0	0
Everton	96-97	15	15	0	1	0	0	0	0
Total		*134*	*132*	*2*	*17*	*12*	*1*	*1*	*0*

PHILLIPS Jimmy   Bolton Wanderers

Full Name: James Neil Phillips   DOB: 08-02-66 Bolton
Debut: Coventry City v MIDDLESBROUGH 15/8/92
Debut Goal: Liverpool v MIDDLESBROUGH 7/11/92

Previous Clubs Details

			Apps					Goals		
Club	Signed	Fee	Tot	Start	Sub	FA	FL	Lge	FA	FL
Bolton W.	Aug-83	Apprentice	108	103	5	7	8	2	0	0
Rangers	Mar-87	£95,000	25	19	6	4	0	0	0	0
Oxford U.	Aug-88	£110,000	79	79	0	4	3	6	0	0
Middlesbrough	Mar-90	£250,000	139	139	0	10	16	6	0	0
Bolton W.	Jul-93	£250,000	161	160	1	10	18	1	0	0

FAPL Summary by Club

Middlesbrough	92-93 to 95-96	40	40	0	0	0	2	0	0

Bolton W.		1995-96	37	37	0	2	6	0	0	0
Total			*77*	*77*	*0*	*2*	*6*	*2*	*0*	*0*

PITCHER Darren   Crystal Palace

Full Name: Darren Edward Pitcher   DOB: 12-10-69 Stepney
Debut: CRYSTAL PALACE v Liverpool 20/8/94
Debut Goal:

Previous Clubs Details				*Apps*				*Goals*		
Club	Signed	Fee	Tot	Start	Sub	FA	FL	Lge	FA	FL
Charlton Ath	Jan-88	Trainee	173	170	3	12	11	8	3	0
C.Palace	Aug-94	Swap	64	60	4	10	6	0	1	1
FAPL Summary by Club										
C.Palace		94-95 to 95-96	25	21	4	8	3	0	1	1
Total			*25*	*21*	*4*	*8*	*3*	*0*	*1*	*1*

PLATT David   Arsenal

Full Name: David Andrew Platt   DOB: 10-06-66 Oldham
Debut: ARSENAL v Middlesbrough 20/8/95
Debut Goal: Everton v ARSENAL 23/8/95

Previous Clubs Details				*Apps*				*Goals*		
Club	Signed	Fee	Tot	Start	Sub	FA	FL	Lge	FA	FL
Crewe Alex	Jan-85		134	134	0	3	0	55	1	0
Aston Villa	Feb-88	£200,000	121	121	0	4	14	50	2	10
Bari	Jul-91	£5.5m	29	29	0	0	0	11	0	0
Juventus			16	16	0	0	0	3	0	0
Sampdoria			29	29	0	0	0	9	0	0
Arsenal	Jul-95	£4.75m	57	54	3	2	6	10	0	1
FAPL Summary by Club										
Arsenal		95-96 to 96-97	57	54	3	2	6	10	0	1
Total			*57*	*54*	*3*	*2*	*6*	*10*	*0*	*1*

POBORSKY Karel   Manchester United

Full Name: Karel Poborsky   DOB: 30-03-72 Trebon, Czech R.
Debut: MANCHESTER UNITED v Everton 21/8/96
Debut Goal: Leeds United v MANCHESTER UNITED 7/9/96

Previous Clubs Details				*Apps*				*Goals*		
Club	Signed	Fee	Tot	Start	Sub	FA	FL	Lge	FA	FL
Dynamo Ceske	91-94		85	79	6			29		
Viktoria Zizkov	1994		28	28	0			7		
Slavia Prague	1995		26	26	0			11		
Manchester U.	Aug-96	£3.5m	22	15	7	2	2	3	0	0
FAPL Summary by Club										
Manchester U.		1996-97	22	15	7	2	2	3	0	0
Total			*22*	*15*	*7*	*2*	*2*	*3*	*0*	*0*

POLLOCK Jamie — Bolton Wanderers

Full Name: Jamie Pollock DOB: 16-02-74 Stockton
Debut: MIDDLESBROUGH v Leeds United 22/8/92 as sub
Debut Goal: Sheffield Wednesday v MIDDLESBROUGH 1/5/93

Previous Clubs Details			*Apps*					*Goals*		
Club	Signed	Fee	Tot	Start	Sub	FA	FL	Lge	FA	FL
Middlesbrough	Dec-91	Trainee	155	144	11	14	19	18	1	1
Osasuna	Sep-96	Free								
Middlesbrough	Nov-96	Free	51	46	5	3	6	2	1	0
Bolton W.	Nov-96	£1.5m	20	18	2	3	1	4	2	0
FAPL Summary by Club										
Middlesbrough	92-93 to 95-96		51	46	5	3	6	2	1	0
Total			*51*	*46*	*5*	*3*	*6*	*2*	*1*	*0*

POOLE Kevin — Leicester City

Full Name: Kevin Poole DOB: 21-07-63 Bromsgrove
Debut: Nottingham Forest v LEICESTER CITY 27/8/94
Debut Goal: (Goalkeeper)

Previous Clubs Details			*Apps*					*Goals*		
Club	Signed	Fee	Tot	Start	Sub	FA	FL	Lge	FA	FL
Aston Villa	Jun-81	Apprentice	28	28	0	1	2	0	0	0
Northampton T.	Nov-84	Loan	3	3	0	0	0	0	0	0
Middlesbrough	Aug-87		34	34	0	2	4	0	0	0
Hartlepool U.	Mar-91	Loan	12	12	0	0	0	0	0	0
Leicester City	Jul-91	£40,000	163	163	0	8	10	0	0	0
FAPL Summary by Club										
Leicester City	94-95 to 96-97		43	43	0	3	3	0	0	0
Total			*43*	*43*	*0*	*3*	*3*	*0*	*0*	*0*

POOM Mart — Derby County

Full Name: Mart Poom DOB: 03-02-72 Tallinn
Debut: Manchester United v DERBY COUNTY 5/4/97
Debut Goal: (Goalkeeper)

Previous Clubs Details			*Apps*					*Goals*		
Club	Signed	Fee	Tot	Start	Sub	FA	FL	Lge	FA	FL
FC Will										
Portsmouth	Aug-94	£200,000	4	4	0	0	4	0	0	0
FC Flora Tallinn			7	7	0	0	0	0	0	0
Derby County	Mar-97	£500,000	0	0	0	0	0	0	0	0
FAPL Summary by Club										
Derby County	1996-97		4	4	0	0	0	0	0	0
Total			*4*	*4*	*0*	*0*	*0*	*0*	*0*	*0*

PORFIRIO Hugo   **West Ham United**
Full Name: Hugo Cardoso Porfirio   DOB: 29-09-73
Debut: WEST HAM UNITED v Liverpool 29/9/96 as sub
Debut Goal: WEST HAM UNITED v Blackburn Rovers 26/10/96

Previous Clubs Details			*Apps*					*Goals*		
Club	Signed	Fee	Tot	Start	Sub	FA	FL	Lge	FA	FL
Uniao Leiria	1995		28	24	4			8		
Sporting Lisbon	Aug-96									
West Ham U.	Sep-96	Loan	23	15	8	2	2	2	1	1
FAPL Summary by Club										
West Ham U.		1996-97	23	15	8	2	2	2	1	1
Total			*23*	*15*	*8*	*2*	*2*	*2*	*1*	*1*

POTTS Steve   **West Ham United**
Full Name: Steven John Potts   DOB: 07-05-67 Hartford, USA
Debut: WEST HAM UNITED v Wimbledon 14/8/93
Debut Goal:

Previous Clubs Details			*Apps*					*Goals*		
Club	Signed	Fee	Tot	Start	Sub	FA	FL	Lge	FA	FL
West Ham U.	Jul-83		332	319	13	35	32	1	0	0
FAPL Summary by Club										
West Ham U.	93-94 to 96-97		137	134	3	12	11	0	0	0
Total			*137*	*134*	*3*	*12*	*11*	*0*	*0*	*0*

POWELL Chris   **Derby County**
Full Name: Christopher George Robin Powell   DOB: 08-09-69 Lambeth
Debut: DERBY COUNTY v Leeds United 17/8/96
Debut Goal:

Previous Clubs Details			*Apps*					*Goals*		
Club	Signed	Fee	Tot	Start	Sub	FA	FL	Lge	FA	FL
C.Palace	Dec-87	Trainee	3	2	1	0	1	0	0	0
Aldershot	Jan-90	Loan	11	11	0	0	0	0	0	0
Southend U.	Aug-90	Free	248	246	2	8	13	3	0	0
Derby County	Jan-96	£750,000	73	54	19	4	4	0	0	0
FAPL Summary by Club										
Derby County		1996-97	35	35	0	4	4	0	0	0
Total			*35*	*35*	*0*	*4*	*4*	*0*	*0*	*0*

POWELL Darryl   **Derby County**
Full Name: Darryl Anthony Powell   DOB: 15-11-71 Lambeth
Debut: DERBY COUNTY v Leeds United 17/8/96
Debut Goal: Arsenal v DERBY COUNTY 7/12/96

Previous Clubs Details			*Apps*					*Goals*		
Club	Signed	Fee	Tot	Start	Sub	FA	FL	Lge	FA	FL
Portsmouth	Dec-88	Trainee	132	83	49	10	14	16	0	3

| Derby County | Jul-95 | £750,000 | 70 | 64 | 6 | 7 | 9 | 6 | 0 | 0 |

FAPL Summary by Club

| Derby County | 1996-97 | 33 | 27 | 6 | 7 | 7 | 1 | 0 | 0 |
| *Total* | | *33* | *27* | *6* | *7* | *7* | *1* | *0* | *0* |

POYET Gustavo   Chelsea

Full Name: Gustavo Poyet   DOB: 15-11-67 Montevideo
Debut: Debut Goal:

Previous Clubs Details | | | | *Apps* | | | | *Goals* | |
Club	Signed	Fee	Tot	Start	Sub	FA	FL	Lge	FA	FL
River Plate										
Grenoble										
Bellavista										
Real Zaragoza			240					60		
Chelsea	May-97									

PRESSMAN Kevin   Sheffield Wednesday

Full Name: Kevin Paul Pressman   DOB: 06-11-67 Fareham
Debut: SHEFFIELD WEDNESDAY v Southampton 12/4/92
Debut Goal: (Goalkeeper)

Previous Clubs Details | | | | *Apps* | | | | *Goals* | |
Club	Signed	Fee	Tot	Start	Sub	FA	FL	Lge	FA	FL
Sheffield W.	Nov-85		196	196	0	12	27	0	0	0
Stoke City	Mar-92	Loan	4	4	0	0	0	0	0	0

FAPL Summary by Club

| Sheffield W. | 92-93 to 96-97 | 137 | 137 | 0 | 12 | 18 | 0 | 0 | 0 |
| *Total* | | *137* | *137* | *0* | *12* | *18* | *0* | *0* | *0* |

PRIOR Spencer   Leicester City

Full Name: Spencer Justin Prior   DOB: 22-04-71 Hockley
Debut: Sheffield Wednesday v NORWICH CITY 1/9/93
Debut Goal:

Previous Clubs Details | | | | *Apps* | | | | *Goals* | |
Club	Signed	Fee	Tot	Start	Sub	FA	FL	Lge	FA	FL
Southend U.	May-89		135	135	0	5	9	3	0	0
Norwich City	Jun-93	£200,000	73	67	6	2	11	1	0	1
Leicester City	Aug-96	£600,000	34	33	1	4	7	0	0	0

FAPL Summary by Club

Norwich City	93-94 to 94-95	30	25	5	1	4	0	0	0
Leicester City	1996-97	34	33	1	4	7	0	0	0
Total		*64*	*58*	*6*	*5*	*11*	*0*	*0*	*0*

QUINN Robert   Crystal Palace

Full Name: Robert John Quinn   DOB: 08-11-76 Sidcup

Debut:			Debut Goal:							
Previous Clubs Details				*Apps*				*Goals*		
Club	Signed	Fee	Tot	Start	Sub	FA	FL	Lge	FA	FL
C.Palace	Mar-95	Trainee	23	18	5	0	3	1	0	1

RADEBE Lucas   Leeds United

Full Name: Lucas Radebe   DOB: 12-04-69 Johannesburg
Debut: Sheffield Wednesday v LEEDS UNITED 26/9/94 as sub
Debut Goal:

Previous Clubs Details				*Apps*				*Goals*		
Club	Signed	Fee	Tot	Start	Sub	FA	FL	Lge	FA	FL
Kaiser Chiefs										
Leeds U.	Sep-94	£250,000	57	47	10	9	5	0	0	0
FAPL Summary by Club										
Leeds U.		94-95 to 96-97	57	47	10	9	5	0	0	0
Total			*57*	*47*	*10*	*9*	*5*	*0*	*0*	*0*

REDFEARN Neil   Barnsley

Full Name: Neil David Redfearn   DOB: 20-06-65 Dewsbury
Debut: Debut Goal:

Previous Clubs Details				*Apps*				*Goals*		
Club	Signed	Fee	Tot	Start	Sub	FA	FL	Lge	FA	FL
Bolton W.	Jun-82	N.For. Jnrs	35	35	0	4	2	1	0	0
Lincoln City	Mar-84	£8,250	100	96	4	3	3	13	1	0
Doncaster R.	Aug-86		46	46	0	3	2	14	1	0
C.Palace	Jul-87	£100,000	57	57	0	1	6	10	0	0
Watford	Nov-88	£150,000	24	22	2	6	1	3	3	0
Oldham Ath	Jan-90	£150,000	62	56	6	8	3	16	3	1
Barnsley	Sep-91	£150,000	255	252	3	14	18	61	4	4

REDKNAPP Jamie   Liverpool

Full Name: Jamie Frank Redknapp   DOB: 25-06-73 Barton on Sea
Debut: Leeds Utd v LIVERPOOL 29/8/92
Debut Goal: LIVERPOOL v Chelsea 5/9/92

Previous Clubs Details				*Apps*				*Goals*		
Club	Signed	Fee	Tot	Start	Sub	FA	FL	Lge	FA	FL
Bournemouth	Jun-90	Trainee	13	6	7	3	3	0	0	0
Liverpool	Jan-91	£350,000	157	134	23	15	22	16	1	5
FAPL Summary by Club										
Liverpool		92-93 to 96-97	150	129	21	12	22	15	0	5
Total			*150*	*129*	*21*	*12*	*22*	*15*	*0*	*5*

REEVES Alan   Wimbledon

Full Name: Alan Reeves   DOB: 19-11-67 Birkenhead
Debut: WIMBLEDON v Leicester City 10/9/94
Debut Goal: QPR v WIMBLEDON 24/9/94

Club	Signed	Fee	Tot	Start	Sub	FA	FL	Lge	FA	FL
						Apps			*Goals*	
Norwich City	Sep-88									
Chester City	Aug-89	£10,000	40	31	9	3	2	2	0	0
Rochdale	Jul-91	Free	121	119	2	6	12	9	0	1
Wimbledon	Sep-94	£300,000	58	53	5	8	1	4	0	0

FAPL Summary by Club

Wimbledon	94-95 to 96-97	58	53	5	8	1	4	0	0
Total		*58*	*53*	*5*	*8*	*1*	*4*	*0*	*0*

RIBERIO Bruno   Leeds United

Full Name: Bruno Riberio   DOB:
Debut: Debut Goal:

Previous Clubs Details

Club	Signed	Fee	Tot	Start	Sub	FA	FL	Lge	FA	FL
						Apps			*Goals*	
Vitoria Setubal										
Leeds Utd	Jun-97	£500,000								

RICHARDSON Kevin   Coventry City

Full Name: Kevin Richardson   DOB: 04-12-62 Newcastle
Debut: Ipswich Town v ASTON VILLA 15/8/92
Debut Goal: ASTON VILLA v Chelsea 2/9/92

Previous Clubs Details

Club	Signed	Fee	Tot	Start	Sub	FA	FL	Lge	FA	FL
						Apps			*Goals*	
Everton	Dec-80	Apprentice	109	95	14	13	13	16	1	3
Watford	Sep-86	£225,000	39	39	0	7	3	2	0	0
Arsenal	Aug-87	£200,000	96	88	8	9	16	5	1	2
Real Sociedad	Jun-90	£750,000	0	0	0	0	0	0	0	0
Aston Villa	Aug-91	£450,000	143	142	1	12	15	13	0	3
Coventry City	Feb-95	£300,000	75	72	3	7	8	0	0	1

FAPL Summary by Club

Aston Villa	92-93 to 94-95	101	100	1	7	13	8	0	3
Coventry City	94-95 to 96-97	75	72	3	7	8	0	0	1
Total		*176*	*172*	*4*	*14*	*21*	*8*	*0*	*4*

RIDEOUT Paul   Everton

Full Name: Paul David Rideout   DOB: 14-08-64 Bournemouth
Debut: EVERTON v Sheffield Wednesday 15/8/92
Debut Goal: Nottingham Forest v EVERTON 7/11/92

Previous Clubs Details

Club	Signed	Fee	Tot	Start	Sub	FA	FL	Lge	FA	FL
						Apps			*Goals*	
Swindon Town	Aug-81		95	90	5	7	3	38	1	2
Aston Villa	Jun-83	£200,000	54	50	4	2	6	19	0	3
Bari (Italy)	Jul-85	£400,000	0	0	0	0	0	0	0	0
Southampton	Jul-88	£430,000	75	68	7	7	13	19	0	2

Swindon Town	Mar-91	Loan	9	9	0	0	0	1	0	0
Notts County	Sep-91	£250,000	11	9	2	1	2	3	0	0
Rangers	Jan-92	£500,000								
Everton	Aug-92	£500,000	111	86	25	10	13	29	3	3
FAPL Summary by Club										
Everton		92-93 to 96-97	111	86	25	10	13	29	3	7
Total			*111*	*86*	*25*	*10*	*13*	*29*	*3*	*7*

RIEPER Marc   West Ham United

Full Name: Marc Rieper   DOB: 05-06-63 Rodoure, Denmark
Debut: Leeds United v WEST HAM UNITED 10/12/94
Debut Goal: WEST HAM UNITED v Blackburn Rovers 30/4/95

Previous Clubs Details					*Apps*				*Goals*	
Club	Signed	Fee	Tot	Start	Sub	FA	FL	Lge	FA	FL
Brondby			93	88	5			3		
West Ham U.	Dec-94	£500,000	85	78	7	4	7	4	0	0
FAPL Summary by Club										
West Ham U.		94-95 to 96-97	85	78	7	4	7	4	0	0
Total			*85*	*78*	*7*	*4*	*7*	*4*	*0*	*0*

RIPLEY Stuart   Blackburn Rovers

Full Name: Stuart Edward Ripley   DOB: 20-11-67 Middlesbrough
Debut: Crystal Palace v BLACKBURN ROVERS 15/8/92
Debut Goal: Crystal Palace v BLACKBURN ROVERS 15/8/92

Previous Clubs Details					*Apps*				*Goals*	
Club	Signed	Fee	Tot	Start	Sub	FA	FL	Lge	FA	FL
Middlesbrough	Nov-85	Apprentice	249	210	39	18	23	26	1	3
Bolton W.	Feb-86	Loan	5	5	0	0	0	0	1	0
Blackburn R.	Jul-92	£1.3m	158	147	11	11	18	11	2	0
FAPL Summary by Club										
Blackburn R.		92-93 to 96-97	158	147	11	11	18	11	2	0
Total			*158*	*147*	*11*	*11*	*18*	*11*	*2*	*0*

ROBERTS Andy   Crystal Palace

Full Name: Andrew James Roberts   DOB: 20-03-74 Dartford
Debut: Debut Goal:

Previous Clubs Details					*Apps*				*Goals*	
Club	Signed	Fee	Tot	Start	Sub	FA	FL	Lge	FA	FL
Millwall	Oct-91	Trainee	138	132	6	7	12	5	0	2
C.Palace	Jul-95	£2.52m	83	81	2	4	7	2	0	0

ROBERTSON David   Leeds United

Full Name: David Robertson   DOB: 17-10-68 Aberdeen
Debut: Debut Goal:

ROBINS Mark   Leicester City

Full Name: Mark Gordon Robins   DOB: 22-12-69 Ashton-under-Lyne
Debut: Arsenal v NORWICH CITY 15/8/92
Debut Goal: Arsenal v NORWICH CITY 15/8/92

Previous Clubs Details

Club	Signed	Fee		Apps					Goals	
			Tot	Start	Sub	FA	FL	Lge	FA	FL
Manchester U.	Dec-86	Apprentice	48	19	29	8	7	11	3	2
Norwich City	Aug-92	£800,000	67	57	10	0	9	20	0	1
Leicester City	Jan-95	£1m	56	40	16	6	9	12	0	5
FC Copenhagen	Oct-96	Loan								

FAPL Summary by Club

Norwich City	92-93 to 94-95		67	57	10	2	7	20	0	1
Leicester City	94-95 to 96-97		25	21	4	4	6	6	0	1
Total			*92*	*78*	*14*	*6*	*13*	*26*	*0*	*2*

ROBINSON Matt   Southampton

Full Name: Matthew Richard Robinson   DOB: 23-12-74 Exeter
Debut: TOTTENHAM HOTSPUR v Sheffield W. 29/4/95 as sub
Debut Goal:

Previous Clubs Details

Club	Signed	Fee		Apps					Goals	
			Tot	Start	Sub	FA	FL	Lge	FA	FL
Southampton	Jul-93	Trainee	7	3	4	3	0		0	0	0

FAPL Summary by Club

Southampton	94-95 to 96-97		14	3	11	3	0		0	0	0
Total			*14*	*3*	*11*	*3*	*0*		*0*	*0*	*0*

ROLLING Franck   Leicester City

Full Name: Franck Rolling   DOB:
Debut: Blackburn Rovers v LEICESTER CITY 11/5/97
Debut Goal:

Previous Clubs Details

Club	Signed	Fee		Apps					Goals	
			Tot	Start	Sub	FA	FL	Lge	FA	FL
Ayr Utd										
Leicester City	Sep-95	£100,000	18	18	0	1	5	0	0	0

FAPL Summary by Club

Leicester City	1996-97		1	1	0	0	2	0	0	0
Total			*1*	*1*	*0*	*0*	*2*	*0*	*0*	*0*

ROSENTHAL Ronny   Tottenham Hotspur

Full Name: Ronny Rosenthal   DOB: 11-10-63 Haifa, Israel
Debut: Nottingham Forest v LIVERPOOL 16/8/92 as sub
Debut Goal: LIVERPOOL v Aston Villa 19/9/92

Previous Clubs Details | | | | *Apps* | | | | *Goals* | |
|---|---|---|---|---|---|---|---|---|---|---|
| Club | Signed | Fee | Tot | Start | Sub | FA | FL | Lge | FA | FL |
| Liverpool | Mar-90 | £1m | 74 | 32 | 42 | 8 | 9 | 21 | 0 | 1 |
| Tottenham H. | Jan-94 | £250,000 | 88 | 55 | 33 | 9 | 3 | 4 | 6 | 1 |
| *FAPL Summary by Club* | | | | | | | | | | |
| Liverpool | 92-93 to 93-94 | | 30 | 16 | 14 | 1 | 3 | 6 | 0 | 1 |
| Tottenham H. | 93-94 to 96-97 | | 88 | 55 | 33 | 9 | 3 | 4 | 6 | 1 |
| *Total* | | | *118* | *71* | *47* | *10* | *6* | *10* | *6* | *2* |

ROWETT Gary   Derby County

Full Name: Gary Rowett   DOB: 06-03-74 Bromsgrove
Debut: Sheffield Wednesday v EVERTON 2/4/94 as sub
Debut Goal: DERBY COUNTY v Aston Villa 12/4/97

Previous Clubs Details | | | | *Apps* | | | | *Goals* | |
|---|---|---|---|---|---|---|---|---|---|---|
| Club | Signed | Fee | Tot | Start | Sub | FA | FL | Lge | FA | FL |
| Cambridge U. | Sep-91 | | 63 | 51 | 12 | 7 | 7 | 9 | 0 | 1 |
| Everton | May-94 | £200,000 | 4 | 2 | 2 | 0 | 0 | 0 | 0 | 0 |
| Blackpool | Jan-95 | Loan | 17 | 17 | 0 | 0 | 0 | 0 | 0 | 0 |
| Derby County | Jul-95 | £300,000 | 70 | 69 | 1 | 7 | 8 | 2 | 0 | 0 |
| *FAPL Summary by Club* | | | | | | | | | | |
| Everton | 93-94 to 94-95 | | 4 | 2 | 2 | 0 | 0 | 0 | 0 | 0 |
| Derby County | 1996-97 | | 35 | 35 | 0 | 6 | 6 | 2 | 0 | 0 |
| *Total* | | | *39* | *37* | *2* | *6* | *6* | *2* | *0* | *0* |

ROWLAND Keith   West Ham United

Full Name: Keith Rowland   DOB: 01-09-71 Portadown
Debut: Norwich City v COVENTRY CITY 16/1/93 as sub
Debut Goal: Newcastle United v WEST HAM UNITED 16/11/96

Previous Clubs Details | | | | *Apps* | | | | *Goals* | |
|---|---|---|---|---|---|---|---|---|---|---|
| Club | Signed | Fee | Tot | Start | Sub | FA | FL | Lge | FA | FL |
| Bournemouth | Oct-89 | Trainee | 72 | 65 | 7 | 8 | 5 | 2 | 0 | 0 |
| Coventry City | Jan-93 | Loan | 2 | 0 | 2 | 0 | 0 | 0 | 0 | 0 |
| West Ham U. | Aug-93 | £110,000 | 73 | 57 | 16 | 6 | 3 | 1 | 0 | 0 |
| *FAPL Summary by Club* | | | | | | | | | | |
| Coventry City | 1992-93 | | 2 | 0 | 2 | 0 | 0 | 0 | 0 | 0 |
| West Ham U. | 93-94 to 96-97 | | 73 | 57 | 16 | 6 | 3 | 1 | 0 | 0 |
| *Total* | | | *75* | *57* | *18* | *6* | *3* | *1* | *0* | *0* |

RUDDOCK Neil   Liverpool

Full Name: Neil Ruddock   DOB: 09-05-68 Wandsworth

Debut: Southampton v TOTTENHAM HOTSPUR 15/8/92
Debut Goal: TOTTENHAM HOTSPUR v Liverpool 31/10/92

Previous Clubs Details

Club	Signed	Fee	Tot	Start	Sub	FA	FL	Lge	FA	FL
								Goals		
Millwall	Mar-86	Apprentice	4	0	4	0	0	1	0	0
Tottenham H.	Apr-86	£50,000	9	7	2	2	0	0	1	0
Millwall	Jun-88	£300,000	2	0	2	0	2	1	0	3
Southampton	Feb-89	£250,000	107	100	7	10	15	9	3	1
Tottenham H.	Jul-92	£750,000	38	38	0	5	4	3	0	0
Liverpool	Jul-93	£2.5m	113	109	4	2	19	11	0	1

FAPL Summary by Club

Tottenham H.	1992-93		38	38	0	5	4	3	0	0
Liverpool	93-94 to 96-97		113	109	4	2	19	11	0	1
Total			*151*	*147*	*4*	*7*	*23*	*14*	*0*	*1*

RUSH Ian   Leeds United

Full Name: Ian James Rush   DOB: 20-10-61 St Asaph
Debut: Nottingham Forest v LIVERPOOL 16/8/92
Debut Goal: Manchester United v LIVERPOOL 18/10/92

Previous Clubs Details

Club	Signed	Fee	Tot	Start	Sub	FA	FL	Lge	FA	FL
								Goals		
Chester City	Sep-79	Apprentice	34	33	1	5	0	14	3	0
Liverpool	May-80	£300,000	224	224	0	25	47	139	20	25
Juventus (Italy)	Jun-87	£3.8m	0	0	0	0	0	0	0	0
Liverpool	Aug-88	£2.2m	245	223	22	36	30	90	19	23
Leeds U.	Jun-96	Free	36	34	2	4	2	3	0	0

FAPL Summary by Club

Liverpool	92-93 to 95-96		130	118	12	14	18	45	3	12
Leeds U.	1996-97		36	34	2	4	2	3	0	0
Total			*166*	*152*	*14*	*18*	*20*	*48*	*3*	*12*

SALAKO John   Coventry City

Full Name: John Akin Salako   DOB: 11-02-69 Nigeria
Debut: CRYSTAL PALACE v Blackburn Rovers 15/8/92
Debut Goal: Arsenal v CRYSTAL PALACE 1/10/94

Previous Clubs Details

Club	Signed	Fee	Tot	Start	Sub	FA	FL	Lge	FA	FL
								Goals		
C.Palace	Nov-86	Apprentice	215	172	43	20	24	22	4	5
Swansea City	Aug-89	Loan	13	13	0	0	0	3	0	0
Coventry City	Aug-95	£1.5m >£3m	61	57	4	4	7	4	1	1

FAPL Summary by Club

C.Palace	92-93 to 94-95		52	51	1	8	10	4	2	3
Coventry City	95-96 to 96-97		61	57	4	4	7	4	1	1
Total			*113*	*108*	*5*	*12*	*17*	*8*	*3*	*4*

SCALES John — Tottenham Hotspur

Full Name: John Robert Scales   DOB: 04-07-66 Harrogate
Debut: Leeds United v WIMBLEDON 15/8/92
Debut Goal: WIMBLEDON v Middlesbrough 9/3/93

Previous Clubs Details				*Apps*				*Goals*		
Club	Signed	Fee	Tot	Start	Sub	FA	FL	Lge	FA	FL
Bristol R.	Jul-85		72	68	4	6	3	2	0	0
Wimbledon	Jul-87	£70,000	240	235	5	21	19	11	1	0
Liverpool	Sep-94	£3.5m	65	65	0	14	10	2	0	2
Tottenham H.	Dec-96	£2.6m	12	10	2	0	0	0	0	0
FAPL Summary by Club										
Wimbledon	92-93 to 94-95		72	72	0	8	7	1	1	0
Liverpool	94-95 to 96-97		65	65	0	14	10	2	0	2
Tottenham H.	1996-97		12	10	2	0	0	0	0	0
Total			*149*	*147*	*2*	*22*	*17*	*3*	*1*	*2*

SCHMEICHEL Peter — Manchester United

Full Name: Peter Boleslaw Schmeichel   DOB: 18-11-68 Glodsone, Den.
Debut: Sheffield United v MANCHESTER UNITED 15/8/92
Debut Goal: (Goalkeeper)

Previous Clubs Details				*Apps*				*Goals*		
Club	Signed	Fee	Tot	Start	Sub	FA	FL	Lge	FA	FL
Manchester U.	Aug-91	£550,000	226	226	0	29	17	0	0	0
FAPL Summary by Club										
Manchester U.	92-93 to 96-97		186	186	0	26	11	0	0	0
Total			*186*	*186*	*0*	*26*	*11*	*0*	*0*	*0*

SCHOLES Paul — Manchester United

Full Name: Paul Scholes   DOB: 16-11-74 Salford
Debut: Ipswich Town v MANCHESTER UTD 24/9/94 as sub
Debut Goal: Ipswich Town v MANCHESTER UTD 24/9/94 as sub

Previous Clubs Details				*Apps*				*Goals*		
Club	Signed	Fee	Tot	Start	Sub	FA	FL	Lge	FA	FL
Manchester U.	Jan-93	Trainee	67	38	29	7	6	18	3	5
FAPL Summary by Club										
Manchester U.	94-95 to 96-97		67	38	29	7	6	18	3	5
Total			*67*	*38*	*29*	*7*	*6*	*18*	*3*	*5*

SCIMECA Ricky — Aston Villa

Full Name: Riccardo Scimeca   DOB: 13-08-75 Leamington
Debut: ASTON VILLA v Manchester United 19/8/95 as sub
Debut Goal:

Previous Clubs Details				*Apps*				*Goals*		
Club	Signed	Fee	Tot	Start	Sub	FA	FL	Lge	FA	FL

			Tot	Start	Sub	FA	FL	Lge	FA	FL
Aston Villa	Jul-93		34	18	16	5	5	0	0	0

FAPL Summary by Club

Aston Villa	95-96 to 96-97		34	18	16	5	5	0	0	0
Total			*34*	*18*	*16*	*5*	*5*	*0*	*0*	*0*

SEAMAN David   Arsenal

Full Name: David Andrew Seaman   DOB: 19-09-63 Rotherham
Debut: ARSENAL v Norwich City 15/8/92
Debut Goal: (Goalkeeper)

Previous Clubs Details

				Apps					Goals	
Club	Signed	Fee	Tot	Start	Sub	FA	FL	Lge	FA	FL
Leeds U.	Sep-81	Apprentice	0	0	0	0	0	0	0	0
Peterboro' U.	Aug-82	£4,000	91	91	0	5	10	0	0	0
Birmingham C.	Oct-84	£100,000	75	75	0	5	4	0	0	0
QPR	Aug-86	£225,000	141	141	0	17	13	0	0	0
Arsenal	May-90	£1.3m	249	249	0	32	30	0	0	0

FAPL Summary by Club

Arsenal	92-93 to 96-97		169	169	0	17	29	0	0	0
Total			*169*	*169*	*0*	*17*	*29*	*0*	*0*	*0*

SELLARS Scott   Bolton Wanderers

Full Name: Scott Sellars   DOB: 27-11-65 Sheffield
Debut: LEEDS UNITED v Aston Villa 13/9/92
Debut Goal: NEWCASTLE UNITED v Ipswich Town 23/3/94

Previous Clubs Details

				Apps					Goals	
Club	Signed	Fee	Tot	Start	Sub	FA	FL	Lge	FA	FL
Leeds U.	Jul-83		74	72	2	4	4	12	0	1
Blackburn R.	Jul-86	£20,000	202	194	8	11	12	35	1	3
Leeds U.	Jul-92	£800,000	7	6	1	0	2	0	0	0
Newcastle U.	Mar-93	£700,000	61	56	5	3	7	5	0	2
Bolton W.	Dec-95	£750,000	64	62	2	3	4	11	0	0

FAPL Summary by Club

Leeds U.		92-93	7	6	1	0	2	0	0	0
Newcastle U.		93-94 to 95-96	48	43	5	3	7	3	0	2
Bolton W.		1995-96	22	22	0	1	0	3	0	0
Total			*77*	*71*	*6*	*4*	*9*	*6*	*0*	*2*

SELLEY Ian   Arsenal

Full Name: Ian Selley   DOB: 14-06-74 Chertsey
Debut: ARSENAL v Blackburn Rovers 12/9/92
Debut Goal:

Previous Clubs Details

				Apps					Goals	
Club	Signed	Fee	Tot	Start	Sub	FA	FL	Lge	FA	FL
Arsenal	May-92		41	35	6	3	6	0	0	0
Southend	Dec-96	Loan								

Arsenal	92-93 to 96-97	41	35	6	3	6	0	0	0
Total		*41*	*35*	*6*	*3*	*6*	*0*	*0*	*0*

SHARPE Lee   Leeds United

Full Name: Lee Stuart Sharpe   DOB: 27-05-71 Halesowen
Debut: Aston Villa v MANCHESTER UNITED 7/11/92
Debut Goal: MANCHESTER UNITED v Coventry City 28/12/92

Previous Clubs Details

			Apps				Goals		
Club	Signed	Fee	Tot	Start	Sub	FA	FL	Lge	FA	FL
Torquay U.	May-88		14	9	5	0	0	3	0	0
Manchester U.	May-88	£185,000	193	160	33	29	23	21	3	9
Leeds U.	Jul-96	£4.5m	26	26	0	1	3	5	0	1

FAPL Summary by Club

Manchester U.	92-93 to 95-96	116	100	16	19	8	17	3	2
Leeds U.	1996-97	26	26	0	1	3	5	0	1
Total		*142*	*126*	*16*	*20*	*11*	*22*	*3*	*3*

SHAW Paul   Arsenal

Full Name: Paul Shaw   DOB: 04-09-73 Burnham
Debut: Nottingham Forest v ARSENAL 3/12/94 as sub
Debut Goal: ARSENAL v Southampton 4/12/96

Previous Clubs Details

			Apps				Goals		
Club	Signed	Fee	Tot	Start	Sub	FA	FL	Lge	FA	FL
Arsenal	Sep-91	Trainee	12	1	11	1	0	2	0	0
Burnley	Mar-95	Loan	9	8	1	0	0	4	0	0
Cardiff	Aug-95	Loan	6	6	0	0	0	0	0	0
Peterborough	Oct-95		12	12	0	0	0	5	0	0

FAPL Summary by Club

Arsenal	94-95 to 96-97	12	1	11	1	0	2	0	0
Total		*12*	*1*	*11*	*1*	*0*	*2*	*0*	*0*

SHAW Richard   Coventry City

Full Name: Richard Edward Shaw   DOB: 11-09-68 Brentford
Debut: CRYSTAL PALACE v Blackburn Rovers 15/8/92
Debut Goal:

Previous Clubs Details

			Apps				Goals		
Club	Signed	Fee	Tot	Start	Sub	FA	FL	Lge	FA	FL
C.Palace	Sep-86	Apprentice	207	193	14	18	30	3	0	0
Hull City	Dec-89	Loan	4	4	0	0	0	0	0	0
Coventry City	Nov-95	£1m	56	56	0	7	3	0	0	0

FAPL Summary by Club

C.Palace	92-93 to 94-95	74	73	1	9	11	0	0	0
Coventry City	95-96 to 96-97	56	56	0	7	3	0	0	0
Total		*130*	*129*	*1*	*16*	*14*	*0*	*0*	*0*

SHEARER Alan — Newcastle United

Full Name: Alan Shearer
DOB: 13-08-70 Newcastle
Debut: Crystal Palace v BLACKBURN ROVERS 15/8/92
Debut Goal: Crystal Palace v BLACKBURN ROVERS 15/8/92

Previous Clubs Details				*Apps*				*Goals*		
Club	Signed	Fee	Tot	Start	Sub	FA	FL	Lge	FA	FL
Southampton	Apr-88		118	105	13	14	18	23	4	11
Blackburn R.	Jul-92	£3.6m	138	132	6	8	16	112	2	12
Newcastle U.	Jul-96	£15m	31	31	0	3	1	25	1	1
FAPL Summary by Club										
Blackburn R.	92-93 to 95-96		138	132	6	8	16	112	2	12
Newcastle U.	1996-97		31	31	0	3	1	25	1	1
Total			*169*	*163*	*6*	*11*	*17*	*137*	*3*	*13*

SHEPHERD Paul — Leeds United

Full Name: Paul Shepherd
DOB: 17-11-77 Leeds
Debut: Arsenal v LEEDS UNITED 26/10/96
Debut Goal:

Previous Clubs Details				*Apps*				*Goals*		
Club	Signed	Fee	Tot	Start	Sub	FA	FL	Lge	FA	FL
Leeds U.			1	1	0	0	0	0	0	0
FAPL Summary by Club										
Leeds U.	1996-97		1	1	0	0	0	0	0	0
Total			*1*	*1*	*0*	*0*	*0*	*0*	*0*	*0*

SHERIDAN Darren — Barnsley

Full Name: Darren Stephen Sheridan
DOB: 01-10-64 Stretford
Debut:
Debut Goal:

Previous Clubs Details				*Apps*				*Goals*		
Club	Signed	Fee	Tot	Start	Sub	FA	FL	Lge	FA	FL
Barnsley	Aug-93	£10,000	NL120	114	6	5	5	4	0	0

SHERIDAN John — Bolton Wanderers

Full Name: John Joseph Sheridan
DOB: 01-10-64 Manchester
Debut: SHEFFIELD WEDNESDAY v Blackburn Rovers 31/10/92
Debut Goal: SHEFFIELD WEDNESDAY v Manchester United 26/12/92

Previous Clubs Details				*Apps*				*Goals*		
Club	Signed	Fee	Tot	Start	Sub	FA	FL	Lge	FA	FL
Leeds U.	Mar-82		230	225	5	12	14	47	1	3
N.Forest	Jul-89	£650,000	0	0	0	0	1	0	0	0
Sheffield W.	Nov-89	£500,000	197	187	10	18	24	25	3	3
Birmingham C.	Feb-96	Loan	2	1	1	0	2	0	0	0
Bolton W.	Dec-96	£180,000	19	12	7	2	2	2	0	0

SHERINGHAM Teddy   Manchester United

Full Name: Edward Paul Sheringham   DOB: 02-04-66 Walthamstow
Debut: NOTTINGHAM FOREST v Liverpool 16/8/92
Debut Goal: NOTTINGHAM FOREST v Liverpool 16/8/92

Previous Clubs Details				Apps					Goals		
Club	Signed	Fee	Tot	Start	Sub	FA	FL		Lge	FA	FL
Millwall	Jan-84	Apprentice	220	205	15	12	17		93	5	8
Aldershot	Feb-85	Loan	5	4	1	0	0		0	0	0
N.Forest	Jul-91	£2m	42	42	0	4	10		14	2	5
Tottenham H.	Aug-92	£2.1m	166	163	3	17	14		76	13	7
Man. Utd	Jun-97	£3.5m									

FAPL Summary by Club

Club				Apps					Goals		
N.Forest	1992-93		3	3	0	0	0		1	0	0
Tottenham H.	92-93 to 96-97		166	163	3	17	14		76	13	7
Total			*169*	*166*	*3*	*17*	*14*		*77*	*13*	*7*

SHERWOOD Tim   Blackburn Rovers

Full Name: Timothy Alan Sherwood   DOB: 06-02-69 St Albans
Debut: Crystal Palace v BLACKBURN ROVERS 15/8/92
Debut Goal: BLACKBURN ROVERS v Norwich City 3/10/92

Previous Clubs Details				Apps					Goals		
Club	Signed	Fee	Tot	Start	Sub	FA	FL		Lge	FA	FL
Watford	Feb-87	Trainee	32	23	9	9	5		2	0	0
Norwich City	Jul-89	£175,000	71	66	5	4	7		10	0	1
Blackburn R.	Feb-92	£500,000	196	191	5	13	22		17	2	1

FAPL Summary by Club

Club				Apps					Goals		
Blackburn R.	92-93 to 96-97		186	185	1	13	21		17	2	1
Total			*186*	*185*	*1*	*13*	*21*		*17*	*2*	*1*

SHIPPERLEY Neil   Crystal Palace

Full Name: Neil Shipperley   DOB: 30-10-74 Chatham
Debut: Southampton v CHELSEA 10/4/93 as sub
Debut Goal: CHELSEA v Wimbledon 12/4/93

Previous Clubs Details				Apps					Goals		
Club	Signed	Fee	Tot	Start	Sub	FA	FL		Lge	FA	FL
Chelsea	Sep-92	Trainee	37	26	11	3	6		7	1	1
Watford	Dec-94	Loan	6	5	1	0	0		1	0	0
Southampton	Jan-95	£1.25m	66	65	1	10	6		13	5	4
C.Palace	Oct-96	£1m	32	29	3	2	0		12	0	0

		Tot	Start	Sub	FA	FL	Lge	FA	FL
Chelsea	92-93 to 94-95	37	26	11	3	6	7	1	1
Southampton	94-95 to 96-97	66	65	1	10	6	13	5	4
Total		*103*	*91*	*12*	*13*	*12*	*20*	*6*	*5*

SHIRTLIFF Peter — Barnsley

Full Name: Peter Andrew Shirtliff   DOB: 06-02-61 Hoyland
Debut: Crystal Palace v SHEFFIELD WEDNESDAY 25/8/92
Debut Goal:

Previous Clubs Details					*Apps*			*Goals*		
Club	Signed	Fee	Tot	Start	Sub	FA	FL	Lge	FA	FL
Sheffield W.	Oct-78		188	188	0	18	18	4	1	0
Charlton Ath	Jul-86	£125,000	103	102	1	5	10	7	0	0
Sheffield W.	Jul-89	£500,000	84	84	0	6	13	4	2	1
Barnsley			13	12	1	0	0	0	0	0
FAPL Summary by Club										
Sheffield W.	92-93 to 94-95		20	20	0	3	5	0	0	0
Total			*20*	*20*	*0*	*3*	*5*	*0*	*0*	*0*

SHORT Craig — Everton

Full Name: Craig Short   DOB: 25-06-68
Debut: Nottingham Forest v EVERTON 17/9/95
Debut Goal: EVERTON v Middlesbrough 26/12/95

Previous Clubs Details					*Apps*			*Goals*		
Club	Signed	Fee	Tot	Start	Sub	FA	FL	Lge	FA	FL
Scarborough	Oct-87	free NL	63	63	0	0	0	7	0	0
Notts Co	Jul-89	£100,000	128	128	0	8	6	6	1	1
Derby County	Sep-92	£2.5m	118	118	0	7	11	9	4	0
Everton	Jul-95	£2.7m	46	41	5	4	3	4	0	0
FAPL Summary by Club										
Everton	95-96 to 96-97		46	41	5	4	3	4	0	0
Total			*46*	*41*	*5*	*4*	*3*	*4*	*0*	*0*

SIMPSON Paul — Derby County

Full Name: Paul David Simpson   DOB: 26-07-66 Carlisle
Debut: DERBY COUNTY v Leeds United 17/8/96 as sub
Debut Goal: DERBY COUNTY v Leeds United 17/8/96

Previous Clubs Details					*Apps*			*Goals*		
Club	Signed	Fee	Tot	Start	Sub	FA	FL	Lge	FA	FL
Man. City	Aug-83	Apprentice	121	99	22	12	11	18	4	2
Oxford U.	Oct-88	£200,000	144	138	6	9	10	43	2	3
Derby County	Feb-92	£500,000	185	133	52	5	11	48	1	6
Sheffield U.	Dec-96	Loan								
FAPL Summary by Club										
Derby County	1996-97		19	0	19	0	0	2	0	1
Total			*19*	*0*	*19*	*0*	*0*	*2*	*0*	*1*

SINCLAIR Frank   Chelsea

Full Name: Frank Mohammed Sinclair   DOB: 03-12-71 Lambeth
Debut: Manchester City v CHELSEA 20/9/92
Debut Goal: Wimbledon v CHELSEA 10/4/95

Previous Clubs Details

Club	Signed	Fee	Tot	Start	Sub	FA	FL	Lge	FA	FL
Chelsea	May-90	Trainee	147	143	4	18	13	6	1	1
WBA	Dec-91	Loan	6	6	0	0	0	1	0	0

FAPL Summary by Club

Chelsea	92-93 to 96-97		135	131	4	17	13	5	1	1
Total			*135*	*131*	*4*	*17*	*13*	*5*	*1*	*1*

SINTON Andy   Tottenham Hotspur

Full Name: Andrew Sinton   DOB: 19-03-66 Newcastle
Debut: Manchester City v QPR 17/8/92
Debut Goal: Manchester City v QPR 17/8/92

Previous Clubs Details

Club	Signed	Fee	Tot	Start	Sub	FA	FL	Lge	FA	FL
Cambridge U.	Apr-83	Apprentice	93	90	3	3	6	13	0	1
Brentford	Dec-85	£25,000	149	149	0	11	8	28	1	3
QPR	Mar-89	£350,000	160	160	0	13	14	22	2	0
Sheffield W.	Aug-93	£2.75m	60	54	6	13	5	3	0	0
Tottenham H.	Jan-96	£1.5m	42	40	2	1	2	6	0	0

FAPL Summary by Club

QPR	92-93 to 95-96		36	36	0	2	4	7	0	0
Sheffield W.	93-94 to 95-96		60	54	6	13	5	3	0	0
Tottenham H.	95-96 to 96-97		42	40	2	1	2	6	0	0
Total			*138*	*130*	*8*	*16*	*11*	*16*	*0*	*0*

SLATER Robbie   Southampton

Full Name: Robert David Slater   DOB: 22-11-64 Skelmersdale
Debut: Southampton v BLACKBURN ROVERS 20/8/94
Debut Goal: Blackburn Rovers v WEST HAM UNITED 2/12/95

Previous Clubs Details

Club	Signed	Fee	Tot	Start	Sub	FA	FL	Lge	FA	FL
Lens										
Blackburn R.	Aug-94	£300,000	18	12	6	1	1	0	0	0
West Ham U.	Aug-95	£600,000	25	18	7	1	3	2	0	0
Southampton	Aug-96	£250,000	30	22	8	1	7	2	0	0

FAPL Summary by Club

Blackburn R.	94-95 to 95-96		18	12	6	1	1	0	0	0
West Ham U.	95-96 to 96-97		25	18	7	1	3	2	0	0
Southampton	1996-97		30	22	8	1	7	2	0	0
Total			*73*	*52*	*21*	*3*	*11*	*4*	*0*	*0*

SMALL Bryan
Bolton Wanderers

Full Name: Bryan Small   DOB: 15-11-71 Birmingham
Debut: ASTON VILLA v Blackburn Rovers 19/10/92
Debut Goal:

Previous Clubs Details

Club	Signed	Fee	Tot	Start	Sub	FA	FL	Lge	FA	FL
Aston Villa	Jul-90		35	31	4	3	2	0	0	0
Birmingham C.	Sep-94	Loan	3	3	0	0	0	0	0	0
Bolton W.	Mar-96	Free	12	11	1	3	1	0	0	0

FAPL Summary by Club

Aston Villa	92-93 to 94-95		28	23	5	0	2	0	0	0
Bolton W.	1995-96		1	1	0	0	0	0	0	0
Total			29	24	5	0	2	0	0	0

SOLIS Mauricio
Derby County

Full Name: Mauricio Solis   DOB:
Debut: Aston Villa v DERBY COUNTY 12/4/97
Debut Goal:

Previous Clubs Details

Club	Signed	Fee	Tot	Start	Sub	FA	FL	Lge	FA	FL
CS Heridiano										
Derby County	Mar-97	£600,000	2	0	2	0	0	0	0	0

FAPL Summary by Club

Derby County	1996-97		2	0	2	0	0	0	0	0
Total			2	0	2	0	0	0	0	0

SOLSKJAER Ole Gunnar
Manchester United

Full Name: Ole Gunnar Solskjaer   DOB: 26-02-73 Kristiansund
Debut: MANCHESTER UNITED v Blackburn Rovers 25/8/96 as sub
Debut Goal: MANCHESTER UNITED v Nottingham Forest 14/9/96

Previous Clubs Details

Club	Signed	Fee	Tot	Start	Sub	FA	FL	Lge	FA	FL
Molde	1995		26	26	0	0	0	20	0	0
Manchester U.	Jul-96	£1.5m	33	25	8	3	0	18	0	0

FAPL Summary by Club

Manchester U.	1996-97		33	25	8	3	0	18	0	0
Total			33	25	8	3	0	18	0	0

SOUTHALL Neville
Everton

Full Name: Neville Southall   DOB: 16-09-58 Llandudno
Debut: EVERTON v Sheffield Wednesday 15/8/92
Debut Goal: (Goalkeeper)

Previous Clubs Details

Club	Signed	Fee	Tot	Start	Sub	FA	FL	Lge	FA	FL
Bury	Jun-80	£6,000	39	39	0	5	0	0	0	0

Everton	Jul-81	£150,000	566	566	0	70	64	0	0	0
Port Vale	Jan-83	Loan	9	9	0	0	0	0	0	0
FAPL Summary by Club										
Everton	92-93 to 96-97		195	195	0	15	17	0	0	0
Total			*195*	*195*	*0*	*15*	*17*	*0*	*0*	*0*

SOUTHGATE Gareth   Aston Villa

Full Name: Gareth Southgate   DOB: 03-09-70 Watford
Debut: CRYSTAL PALACE v Blackburn Rovers 15/8/92
Debut Goal: CRYSTAL PALACE v Blackburn Rovers 15/8/92

Previous Clubs Details				*Apps*					*Goals*	
Club	Signed	Fee	Tot	Start	Sub	FA	FL	Lge	FA	FL
C.Palace	Jan-89	Trainee	152	148	4	9	24	15	0	7
Aston Villa	Jul-95	£2.5m	59	59	0	7	9	2	0	1
FAPL Summary by Club										
C.Palace	92-93 to 94-95		75	75	0	8	13	4	0	4
Aston Villa	95-96 to 96-97		59	59	0	7	9	2	0	1
Total			*134*	*134*	*0*	*15*	*22*	*6*	*0*	*5*

SPEED Gary   Everton

Full Name: Gary Andrew Speed   DOB: 08-09-69 Hawarden
Debut: LEEDS UNITED v Wimbledon 15/8/92
Debut Goal: Aston Villa v LEEDS UNITED 19/8/92

Previous Clubs Details				*Apps*					*Goals*	
Club	Signed	Fee	Tot	Start	Sub	FA	FL	Lge	FA	FL
Leeds U.	Jun-88	Trainee	248	231	17	21	26	39	5	11
Everton	Jul-96	£3.5m	37	37	0	2	2	9	1	1
FAPL Summary by Club										
Leeds U.	92-93 to 95-96		143	142	1	11	14	22	5	5
Everton	1996-97		37	37	0	2	2	9	1	1
Total			*180*	*179*	*1*	*13*	*16*	*31*	*6*	*6*

SRNICEK Pavel   Newcastle United

Full Name: Pavel Srnicek   DOB: 10-03-68 Ostrava, Czechoslovakia
Debut: NEWCASTLE UNITED v Tottenham Hotspur 14/8/93
Debut Goal: (Goalkeeper)

Previous Clubs Details				*Apps*					*Goals*	
Club	Signed	Fee	Tot	Start	Sub	FA	FL	Lge	FA	FL
Banik Ostrava										
Newcastle U.	Feb-91	£350,000	148	147	1	11	11	0	0	0
FAPL Summary by Club										
Newcastle U.	93-94 to 96-97		96	95	1	7	9	0	0	0
Total			*96*	*95*	*1*	*7*	*9*	*0*	*0*	*0*

STAUNTON Steve Aston Villa

Full Name: Stephen Staunton DOB: 19-01-69 Drogheda
Debut: Ipswich Town v ASTON VILLA 15/8/92
Debut Goal: ASTON VILLA v Crystal Palace 5/9/92

Previous Clubs Details			Tot	Start	Sub	*Apps* FA	FL	Lge	*Goals* FA	FL
Club	Signed	Fee								
Liverpool	Sep-86	£20,000	65	55	10	16	8	0	1	4
Bradford City	Nov-87	Loan	8	7	1	0	2	0	0	0
Aston Villa	Aug-91	£1.1m	181	178	3	16	19	15	0	1
FAPL Summary by Club										
Aston Villa	92-93 to 96-97		144	141	3	12	17	12	0	1
Total			*144*	*141*	*3*	*12*	*17*	*12*	*0*	*1*

STEFANOVIC Dejan Sheffield Wednesday

Full Name: Dejan Stefanovic DOB:
Debut: Nottingham Forest v SHEFFIELD WEDNESDAY 26/12/95
Debut Goal: Chelsea v SHEFFIELD WEDNESDAY 28/2/97

Previous Clubs Details			Tot	Start	Sub	*Apps* FA	FL	Lge	*Goals* FA	FL
Club	Signed	Fee								
Red Star Belgrade										
Sheffield W.	Dec-95	£2m	35	32	3	2	1	2	0	0
FAPL Summary by Club										
Sheffield W.	95-96 to 96-97		35	32	3	2	1	2	0	0
Total			*35*	*32*	*3*	*2*	*1*	*2*	*0*	*0*

STIMAC Igor Derby County

Full Name: Igor Stimac DOB: 09-06-67
Debut: Tottenham Hotspur v DERBY COUNTY 21/8/96
Debut Goal: DERBY COUNTY v Sheffield Wednesday 19/2/97

Previous Clubs Details			Tot	Start	Sub	*Apps* FA	FL	Lge	*Goals* FA	FL
Club	Signed	Fee								
Hadjuk Split										
Cadiz										
Hadjuk Split										
Derby County	Oct-95	£1.5m	48	48	0	10	9	2	0	0
FAPL Summary by Club										
Derby County	1996-97		21	21	0	9	9	1	0	0
Total			*21*	*21*	*0*	*9*	*9*	*1*	*0*	*0*

STRACHAN Gordon Coventry City

Full Name: Gordon David Strachan DOB: 09-02-57 Edinburgh
Debut: LEEDS UNITED v Wimbledon 15/8/92
Debut Goal: QPR v LEEDS UNITED 24/10/92

Club	Signed	Fee	Tot	Start	Sub	FA	FL	Lge	FA	FL
Manchester U.	Aug-84	£500,000	160	155	5	22	13	33	2	1
Leeds U.	Mar-89	£300,000	197	188	9	14	19	37	2	3
Coventry City	Mar-95	Free	26	13	13	3	4	0	0	0

FAPL Summary by Club

Club			Tot	Start	Sub	FA	FL	Lge	FA	FL
Leeds U.	92-93 to 94-95		70	62	8	7	6	7	1	1
Coventry City	94-95 to 96-97		26	13	13	3	4	0	0	0
Total			*96*	*75*	*21*	*10*	*10*	*7*	*1*	*1*

STUART Graham   Everton

Full Name: Graham Charles Stuart   DOB: 24-10-70 Tooting
Debut: CHELSEA v Oldham Athletic 15/8/92
Debut Goal: Norwich City v CHELSEA 19/8/92

Previous Clubs Details

				Apps					*Goals*	
Club	Signed	Fee	Tot	Start	Sub	FA	FL	Lge	FA	FL
Chelsea	Jun-89	Trainee	87	70	17	7	11	14	1	2
Everton	Aug-93	£850,000	122	102	20	13	6	20	5	2

FAPL Summary by Club

Chelsea	92-93 to 94-95		39	31	8	1	6	9	0	1
Everton	93-94 to 96-97		122	102	20	13	6	20	5	2
Total			*161*	*133*	*28*	*14*	*12*	*29*	*5*	*3*

STURRIDGE Dean   Derby County

Full Name: Dean Constantine Sturridge   DOB: 27-07-73 Birmingham
Debut: DERBY COUNTY v Leeds Utd 17/8/96
Debut Goal: DERBY COUNTY v Leeds Utd 17/8/96

Previous Clubs Details

				Apps					*Goals*	
Club	Signed	Fee	Tot	Start	Sub	FA	FL	Lge	FA	FL
Derby County	Jul-91	Trainee	92	78	14	9	9	32	2	1
Torquay U.	Dec-94	Loan	10	10	0	0	0	5	0	0

FAPL Summary by Club

Derby County	1996-97		30	29	1	9	9	11	2	1
Total			*30*	*29*	*1*	*9*	*9*	*11*	*2*	*1*

SULLIVAN Neil   Wimbledon

Full Name: Neil Sullivan   DOB: 24-02-70 Sutton
Debut: Southampton v WIMBLEDON 17/10/92
Debut Goal: (Goalkeeper)

Previous Clubs Details

				Apps					*Goals*	
Club	Signed	Fee	Tot	Start	Sub	FA	FL	Lge	FA	FL
Wimbledon	Jul-88	Trainee	68	67	1	15	7	0	0	0
C.Palace	May-92	Loan	1	1	0	0	0	0	0	0

FAPL Summary by Club

Wimbledon	92-93 to 96-97		66	65	1	15	7	0	0	0
Total			*66*	*65*	*1*	*15*	*7*	*0*	*0*	*0*

SUTTON Chris
Blackburn Rovers

Full Name: Christopher Roy Sutton   DOB: 10-03-73 Nottingham
Debut: Arsenal v NORWICH CITY 15/8/92
Debut Goal: NORWICH CITY v QPR 17/10/92

Previous Clubs Details

Club	Signed	Fee	Tot	Start	Sub	FA	FL	Lge	FA	FL
Norwich City	Jul-91	Trainee	102	89	13	10	9	35	5	3
Blackburn R.	Jul-94	£5m	78	73	5	4	9	26	2	4

FAPL Summary by Club

Norwich City	92-93 to 93-94		79	73	6	4	7	33	2	3
Blackburn R.	94-95 to 96-97		78	73	5	4	9	26	2	2
Total			157	146	11	8	16	59	4	5

TAGGART Gerry
Bolton Wanderers

Full Name: Gerald Paul Taggart   DOB: 18-10-70 Belfast
Debut: BOLTON WANDERERS v Middlesbrough 9/9/95
Debut Goal: Sheffield Wednesday v BOLTON WANDERERS 1/1/96

Previous Clubs Details

Club	Signed	Fee	Tot	Start	Sub	FA	FL	Lge	FA	FL
Man. City	Jul-89	Trainee	12	10	2	0	0	1	0	0
Barnsley	Jan-90	£75,000	212	209	3	14	15	16	2	1
Bolton W.	Aug-95	£1.5m	54	54	0	2	5	3	0	1

FAPL Summary by Club

Bolton W.	1995-96		11	11	0	2	2	1	0	0
Total			11	11	0	2	2	1	0	0

TAYLOR Scott
Bolton Wanderers

Full Name: Scott James Taylor   DOB: 05-05-76 Chertsey
Debut: BOLTON WANDERERS v Chelsea 8/4/96 as sub
Debut Goal:

Previous Clubs Details

Club	Signed	Fee	Tot	Start	Sub	FA	FL	Lge	FA	FL
Millwall	Feb-95	£15,000 NL	28	13	15	1	2	0	1	2
Bolton W.	Mar-96	£150,000	12	2	10	1	3	1	1	1

FAPL Summary by Club

Bolton W.	1995-96		1	0	1	0	0	0	0	0
Total			1	0	1	0	0	0	0	0

TAYLOR Maik
Southampton

Full Name: Maik Stefan Taylor   DOB: 04-09-71 Germany
Debut: Middlesbrough v SOUTHAMPTON 11/1/97
Debut Goal: (Goalkeeper)

Previous Clubs Details

Club	Signed	Fee	Tot	Start	Sub	FA	FL	Lge	FA	FL
Barnet	Jun-95	From NL	45	45	0	2	2	0	0	0

| Southampton | Dec-96 | £500,000 | 18 | 18 | 0 | 0 | 0 | 0 | 0 | 0 |

FAPL Summary by Club

| Southampton | | 1996-97 | 18 | 18 | 0 | 0 | 0 | 0 | 0 | 0 |
| *Total* | | | *18* | *18* | *0* | *0* | *0* | *0* | *0* | *0* |

TAYLOR Ian   Aston Villa

Full Name: Ian Kenneth Taylor   DOB: 04-06-68 Birmingham
Debut: SHEFFIELD WEDNESDAY v Tottenham Hotspur 20/8/94
Debut Goal: SHEFFIELD WEDNESDAY v Newcastle United 22/10/94

Previous Clubs Details

				Apps				Goals		
Club	Signed	Fee	Tot	Start	Sub	FA	FL	Lge	FA	FL
Port Vale	Jul-92	£15,000 NL	83	83	0	6	4	28	1	2
Sheffield W.	Jul-94	£1m	14	9	5	0	4	1	0	1
Aston Villa	Dec-94	£1m	81	75	6	5	8	6	1	2

FAPL Summary by Club

Sheffield W.		1994-95	14	9	5	0	4	1	0	1
Aston Villa		94-95 to 96-97	81	75	6	5	8	6	1	2
Total			*95*	*84*	*11*	*5*	*12*	*7*	*1*	*3*

TELFER Paul   Coventry City

Full Name: Paul Norman Telfer   DOB: 12-10-91 Edinburgh
Debut: Newcastle United v COVENTRY CITY 19/8/95
Debut Goal: COVENTRY CITY v Manchester City 23/8/95

Previous Clubs Details

				Apps				Goals		
Club	Signed	Fee	Tot	Start	Sub	FA	FL	Lge	FA	FL
Luton Town	Nov-88	Trainee	144	136	8	14	5	19	2	0
Coventry City	Jul-95	£1.5m	65	62	3	7	8	1	1	2

FAPL Summary by Club

| Coventry City | | 95-96 to 96-97 | 65 | 62 | 3 | 7 | 8 | 1 | 1 | 2 |
| *Total* | | | *65* | *62* | *3* | *7* | *8* | *1* | *1* | *2* |

THATCHER Ben   Wimbledon

Full Name: Benjamin David Thatcher   DOB: 30-11-75 Swindon
Debut: WIMBLEDON v Manchester United 17/8/96
Debut Goal:

Previous Clubs Details

				Apps				Goals		
Club	Signed	Fee	Tot	Start	Sub	FA	FL	Lge	FA	FL
Millwall	Jun-96	Trainee	90	87	3	7	6	1	0	0
Wimbledon	Jul-96	£1.8m	9	9	0	0	0	0	0	0

FAPL Summary by Club

| Wimbledon | | 1996-97 | 9 | 9 | 0 | 0 | 0 | 0 | 0 | 0 |
| *Total* | | | *9* | *9* | *0* | *0* | *0* | *0* | *0* | *0* |

THOMAS Michael   Liverpool

Full Name: Michael Lauriston Thomas   DOB: 24-08-67 Lambeth

Debut: LIVERPOOL v Southampton 1/9/92
Debut Goal: LIVERPOOL v Norwich City 25/10/92

Previous Clubs Details

Club	Signed	Fee	Tot	Start	Sub	FA	FL	Lge	FA	FL
					Apps				*Goals*	
Arsenal	Dec-84	Apprentice	163	149	14	17	23	24	1	5
Portsmouth	Dec-86	Loan	3	3	0	0	0	0	0	0
Liverpool	Dec-91	£1.5m	112	85	27	17	9	9	2	1
FAPL Summary by Club										
Liverpool		92-93 to 96-97	95	69	26	13	9	5	0	1
Total			*95*	*69*	*26*	*13*	*9*	*5*	*0*	*1*

THOMPSON David   Liverpool
Full Name: David Thompson   DOB: 12-09-77 Birkenhead
Debut: LIVERPOOL v Arsenal 19/8/96 as sub
Debut Goal:

Previous Clubs Details

Club	Signed	Fee	Tot	Start	Sub	FA	FL	Lge	FA	FL
					Apps				*Goals*	
Liverpool		Trainee	3	1	2	0	0	0	0	0
FAPL Summary by Club										
Liverpool		1996-97	3	1	2	0	0	0	0	0
Total			*3*	*1*	*2*	*0*	*0*	*0*	*0*	*0*

THOMPSON Alan   Bolton Wanderers
Full Name: Alan Thompson   DOB: 22-12-73 Newcastle
Debut: Wimbledon v BOLTON WANDERERS 19/8/95
Debut Goal: Wimbledon v BOLTON WANDERERS 19/8/95

Previous Clubs Details

Club	Signed	Fee	Tot	Start	Sub	FA	FL	Lge	FA	FL
					Apps				*Goals*	
Newcastle U.	Mar-91	Trainee	16	13	3	1	0	0	0	0
Bolton W.	Jul-93	£250,000	124	110	14	7	21	25	2	4
FAPL Summary by Club										
Bolton W.		1995-96	26	23	3	1	5	1	0	1
Total			*26*	*23*	*3*	*1*	*5*	*1*	*0*	*1*

THOMPSON Neil   Barnsley
Full Name: Neil Thompson   DOB: 02-10-63 Beverley
Debut: IPSWICH TOWN v Aston Villa 15/8/92
Debut Goal: Oldham Athletic v IPSWICH TOWN 19/9/92

Previous Clubs Details

Club	Signed	Fee	Tot	Start	Sub	FA	FL	Lge	FA	FL
					Apps				*Goals*	
N. Forest Jnrs										
Hull City	Nov-81	Free	31	29	2	0	0	0	0	0
Scarborough	Aug-83	Free	87	87	0	4	8	15	0	1

| Ipswich Town | Jun-89 | £100,000 | 206 | 199 | 7 | 17 | 15 | 19 | 1 | 1 |
| Barnsley | Jun-96 | | 24 | 24 | 0 | 1 | 3 | 5 | 0 | 0 |

THOMSEN Claus   Everton

Full Name: Claus Thomsen   DOB: 31-05-70 Aarhus, Denmark
Debut: IPSWICH TOWN v Manchester United 24/9/94
Debut Goal: IPSWICH TOWN v Blackburn Rovers 19/11/94

Previous Clubs Details				*Apps*					*Goals*	
Club	Signed	Fee	Tot	Start	Sub	FA	FL	Lge	FA	FL
AGF Aarhus	1990		96	95	1	0	0	13	0	0
Ipswich Town	Jun-94	£250,000	70	67	3	4	4	7	0	1
Everton	Jan-97	£900,000	16	15	1	0	0	0	0	0
FAPL Summary by Club										
Ipswich Town		1994-95	33	31	2	1	2	5	0	0
Everton		1996-97	16	15	1	0	0	0	0	0
Total			*49*	*46*	*3*	*1*	*2*	*5*	*0*	*0*

THORN Andy   Wimbledon

Full Name: Andrew Charles Thorn   DOB: 12-11-66 Carshalton
Debut: CRYSTAL PALACE v Blackburn Rovers 15/8/92
Debut Goal: CRYSTAL PALACE v Leeds United 20/12/92

Previous Clubs Details				*Apps*					*Goals*	
Club	Signed	Fee	Tot	Start	Sub	FA	FL	Lge	FA	FL
Wimbledon	Nov-84	Apprentice	107	106	1	9	7	2	0	0
Newcastle U.	Aug-88	£850,000	36	36	0	0	4	2	0	1
C.Palace	Dec-89	£650,000	128	128	0	10	19	3	0	4
Wimbledon	Oct-94	Free	37	33	4	3	2	1	0	0
FAPL Summary by Club										
C.Palace		1992-93	34	34	0	0	5	1	0	1
Wimbledon		94-95 to 95-96	37	33	4	3	3	1	0	0
Total			*71*	*67*	*4*	*3*	*8*	*2*	*0*	*1*

THORNLEY Ben   Manchester United

Full Name: Benjamin Lindsay Thornley   DOB: 21-04-75 Bury
Debut: West Ham United v MANCHESTER UNITED 26/2/94 as sub
Debut Goal:

Previous Clubs Details				*Apps*					*Goals*	
Club	Signed	Fee	Tot	Start	Sub	FA	FL	Lge	FA	FL
Manchester U.	Jan-93	Trainee	4	1	3	0	2	0	0	0
Stockport Co.	Nov-95	Loan	10	8	2	0	0	1	0	0
Huddersfield T.	Feb-96	Loan	12	12	0	0	0	2	0	0
FAPL Summary by Club										
Manchester U.		93-94 to 96-97	4	1	3	0	2	0	0	0
Total			*4*	*1*	*3*	*0*	*2*	*0*	*0*	*0*

TISDALE Paul   Southampton

Full Name: Paul Tisdale   DOB: 14-01-73 Malta
Debut: Sheffield W. v TOTTENHAM HOTSPUR 2/1/95 as sub
Debut Goal: Manchester City v SOUTHAMPTON 16/3/96

Previous Clubs Details			*Apps*					*Goals*		
Club	Signed	Fee	Tot	Start	Sub	FA	FL	Lge	FA	FL
Southampton	Jun-91	Junior	16	5	11	1	1	1	0	0
Northampton T.	Mar-92	Loan	5	5	0	0	0	0	0	0
Huddersfield T.	Nov-96	Loan								
Ipswich Town	Jan-97	Loan								
FAPL Summary by Club										
Southampton	94-95 to 95-96		15	5	10	1	1	1	0	0
Total			*15*	*5*	*10*	*1*	*1*	*1*	*0*	*0*

TODD Andy   Bolton Wanderers

Full Name: Andrew John James Todd   DOB: 21-09-74 Derby
Debut: Liverpool v BOLTON WANDERERS 23/9/95 as sub
Debut Goal: Liverpool v BOLTON WANDERERS 23/9/95 as sub

Previous Clubs Details			*Apps*					*Goals*		
Club	Signed	Fee	Tot	Start	Sub	FA	FL	Lge	FA	FL
Middlesbrough	Jun-92	Trainee	8	7	1	0	2	0	0	0
Swindon Town	Feb-95	Loan	13	13	0	0	0	0	0	0
Bolton W.	Aug-95	£250,000	27	15	12	0	8	3	0	0
FAPL Summary by Club										
Bolton W.	1995-96		12	9	3	0	4	2	0	0
Total			*12*	*9*	*3*	*0*	*4*	*2*	*0*	*0*

TOWNSEND Andy   Aston Villa

Full Name: Andrew David Townsend   DOB: 23-07-63 Maidstone
Debut: CHELSEA v Oldham Athletic 15/8/92
Debut Goal: CHELSEA v Norwich City 12/9/92

Previous Clubs Details			*Apps*					*Goals*		
Club	Signed	Fee	Tot	Start	Sub	FA	FL	Lge	FA	FL
Southampton	Jan-85	£35,000	83	77	6	5	8	5	0	0
Norwich City	Aug-88	£300,000	71	66	5	10	4	8	2	0
Chelsea	Jul-90	£1.2m	110	110	0	7	17	12	0	7
Aston Villa	Jul-93	£2.1m	129	128	1	12	20	8	0	2
FAPL Summary by Club										
Chelsea	1992-93		41	41	0	1	6	4	0	3
Aston Villa	93-94 to 96-97		129	128	1	12	20	8	0	2
Total			*170*	*169*	*1*	*13*	*26*	*12*	*0*	*5*

TROLLOPE Paul   Derby County

Full Name: Paul Jonathan Trollope   DOB: 03-06-72 Swindon

Debut: Leeds United v DERBY COUNTY 29/1/97
Debut Goal: DERBY COUNTY v Tottenham Hotspur 22/3/97

Previous Clubs Details

Club	Signed	Fee	Apps					Goals		
			Tot	Start	Sub	FA	FL	Lge	FA	FL
Swindon Town	Dec-89	Trainee	0	0	0	0	0	0	0	0
Torquay U.	Mar-92	Free	106	103	3	7	10	16	0	1
Derby County	Dec-94	Loan	5	4	1	0	0	1	0	0
Derby County	Jan-95	£100,000	50	39	11	4	5	4	0	0
C.Palace	Oct-96	Loan	9	0	9	0	0	0	0	0
FAPL Summary by Club										
Derby County		1996-97	14	13	1	3	3	1	0	0
Total			*14*	*13*	*1*	*3*	*3*	*1*	*0*	*0*

TRUSTFULL Orlando   Sheffield Wednesday
Full Name: Orlando Trustfull   DOB:
Debut: Newcastle United v SHEFFIELD WEDNESDAY 24/08/96
Debut Goal: SHEFFIELD WEDNESDAY v Nottingham Forest 18/11/96

Previous Clubs Details

Club	Signed	Fee	Apps					Goals		
			Tot	Start	Sub	FA	FL	Lge	FA	FL
Dordrecht 90	1991		22	22	0			0		
Feyenoord	1992		78	63	15			13		
Sheffield W.	Aug-96	£750,000	19	9	10	1	2	3	0	0
FAPL Summary by Club										
Sheffield W.		1996-97	19	9	10	1	2	3	0	0
Total			*19*	*9*	*10*	*1*	*2*	*3*	*0*	*0*

TUTTLE David   Crystal Palace
Full Name: David Philip Tuttle   DOB: 06-02-72 Reading
Debut: TOTTENHAM HOTSPUR v Crystal Palace 22/8/92
Debut Goal:

Previous Clubs Details

Club	Signed	Fee	Apps					Goals		
			Tot	Start	Sub	FA	FL	Lge	FA	FL
Tottenham H.	Feb-90		13	10	3	0	4	0	0	0
Peterboro' U.	Jan-93	Loan	7	7	0	0	0	0	0	0
Sheffield U.	Aug-93	£350,000	63	63	0	3	2	1	0	0
C.Palace	Mar-96		49	48	1	1	3	3	0	0
FAPL Summary by Club										
Tottenham H.		1992-93	5	4	1	0	2	0	0	0
Sheffield U.		1993-94	31	31	0	1	1	0	0	0
Total			*36*	*35*	*1*	*1*	*3*	*0*	*0*	*0*

ULLATHORNE Robert   Leicester City
Full Name: Robert Ullathorne   DOB: 11-10-71 Wakefield
Debut: Sheffield United v NORWICH CITY 6/11/93
Debut Goal: Manchester United v NORWICH CITY 16/4/94

Previous Clubs Details			*Apps*					*Goals*		
Club	Signed	Fee	Tot	Start	Sub	FA	FL	Lge	FA	FL
Norwich City	Jul-90	Trainee	94	86	8	8	12	7	0	1
Osasuna										
Leicester City	Feb-97	£600,000	0	0	0	0	1	0	0	0
FAPL Summary by Club										
Norwich City	1993-94 to 1994-95		43	38	5	5	2	4	0	0
Leicester City	1996-97		0	0	0	0	1	0	0	0
Total			*43*	*38*	*5*	*5*	*3*	*4*	*0*	*0*

UNSWORTH David Everton

Full Name: David Gerald Unsworth   DOB: 16-10-73 Chorley
Debut: EVERTON v Liverpool 7/12/92
Debut Goal: EVERTON v Arsenal 29/10/94

Previous Clubs Details			*Apps*					*Goals*		
Club	Signed	Fee	Tot	Start	Sub	FA	FL	Lge	FA	FL
Everton	May-92	Trainee	116	108	8	7	7	11	0	0
FAPL Summary by Club										
Everton	92-93 to 96-97		114	107	7	7	7	10	0	0
Total			*114*	*107*	*7*	*7*	*7*	*10*	*0*	*0*

UPSON Matthew Arsenal

Full Name: Matthew James Upson   DOB: 18-04-79 Hartismere
Debut: Debut Goal:

Previous Clubs Details			*Apps*					*Goals*		
Club	Signed	Fee	Tot	Start	Sub	FA	FL	Lge	FA	FL
Luton Town	Apr-96	Trainee								
Arsenal	May-97	£1m								

VAN DER GOUW Raimond Manchester United

Full Name: Raimond Van der Gouw   DOB: 24-03-63 Oldenzaal
Debut: Aston Villa v MANCHESTER UNITED 21/9/96
Debut Goal: (Goalkeeper)

Previous Clubs Details			*Apps*					*Goals*		
Club	Signed	Fee	Tot	Start	Sub	FA	FL	Lge	FA	FL
Vitesse Arnhem	1990		188	188	0	0	0	0	0	0
Manchester U.	Jul-96	undisclosed	2	2	0	0	2	0	0	0
FAPL Summary by Club										
Manchester U.	1996-97		2	2	0	0	2	0	0	0
Total			*2*	*2*	*0*	*0*	*2*	*0*	*0*	*0*

Van Der LAAN Robin Derby County

Full Name: Robertus Petrus Van Der Laan   DOB: 05-09-68
Schiedam, Holland
Debut: Aston Villa v DERBY COUNTY 24/8/96 as sub

Debut Goal: DERBY COUNTY v Tottenham Hotspur 22/3/97

Previous Clubs Details				Apps				Goals		
Club	Signed	Fee	Tot	Start	Sub	FA	FL	Lge	FA	FL
Wageningen										
Port Vale	Feb-91	£80,000	176	154	22	10	12	24	1	1
Derby County	Aug-95	£475,000	55	54	1	2	4	8	3	0
W'hampton W.	Oct-96	Loan								
FAPL Summary by Club										
Derby County		1996-97	16	15	1	1	1	2	3	0
Total			*16*	*15*	*1*	*1*	*1*	*2*	*3*	*0*

VAN GOBBEL Ulrich   Southampton
Full Name: Ulrich Van Gobbel   DOB: 16-01-71 Surinam
Debut: SOUTHAMPTON v Sunderland 19/10/96
Debut Goal: SOUTHAMPTON v Leicester City 22/3/97

Previous Clubs Details				Apps				Goals		
Club	Signed	Fee	Tot	Start	Sub	FA	FL	Lge	FA	FL
Feyenoord	-1990		110	96	14			2		
Galatasaray	Dec-95		16	16	0			2		
Southampton	Oct-96	£1.3m	25	24	1	1	6	1	0	1
FAPL Summary by Club										
Southampton		1996-97	25	24	1	1	6	1	0	1
Total			*25*	*24*	*1*	*1*	*6*	*1*	*0*	*1*

VEART Carl   Crystal Palace
Full Name: Carl Thomas Veart   DOB: 21-05-70 Whyalla, Australia
Debut: Debut Goal:

Previous Clubs Details				Apps				Goals		
Club	Signed	Fee	Tot	Start	Sub	FA	FL	Lge	FA	FL
Adelaide City										
Sheffield U.	Jul-94	£250,000	66	47	19	3	3	15	1	1
C.Palace	Mar-96		51	40	11	2	3	6	0	2

VEGA Ramon   Tottenham Hotspur
Full Name: Ramon Vega   DOB: 14-06-71
Debut: TOTTENHAM HOTSPUR v Manchester United 12/1/97
Debut Goal: Aston Villa v TOTTENHAM HOTSPUR 19/4/97

Previous Clubs Details				Apps				Goals		
Club	Signed	Fee	Tot	Start	Sub	FA	FL	Lge	FA	FL
Grasshopper	1990		156	154	2	0	0	13	0	0
Cagliari	Aug-96									
Tottenham H.	Jan-97	£3.75m	8	8	0	0	0	1	0	0
FAPL Summary by Club										
Tottenham H.		1996-97	8	8	0	0	0	1	0	0
Total			*8*	*8*	*0*	*0*	*0*	*1*	*0*	*0*

VENISON Barry   Southampton

Full Name: Barry Venison   DOB: 16-08-64 Consett
Debut: NEWCASTLE UNITED v Tottenham Hotspur 14/8/93
Debut Goal: NEWCASTLE UNITED v Aston Villa 25/2/95

Previous Clubs Details   *Apps*   *Goals*

Club	Signed	Fee	Tot	Start	Sub	FA	FL	Lge	FA	FL
Sunderland	Jan-82	Apprentice	173	169	4	8	21	2	0	0
Liverpool	Jul-86	£200,000	110	103	7	21	17	1	0	0
Newcastle U.	Jul-92	£250,000	109	108	1	11	9	1	0	0
Galatasaray	Jun-95	£750,000								
Southampton	Oct-95	£850,000	24	23	1	3	2	0	0	0

FAPL Summary by Club

Newcastle U.	93-94 to 94-95		65	64	1	7	5	1	0	0
Southampton	95-96 to 96-97		24	23	1	3	2	0	0	0
Total			*89*	*87*	*2*	*10*	*7*	*1*	*0*	*0*

VIALLI Gianluca   Chelsea

Full Name: Gianluca Vialli   DOB: 09-07-64 Cremona
Debut: Southampton v CHELSEA 18/8/96
Debut Goal: CHELSEA v Coventry City 24/8/96

Previous Clubs Details   *Apps*   *Goals*

Club	Signed	Fee	Tot	Start	Sub	FA	FL	Lge	FA	FL
Cremonese	1980		105					23		
Sampdoria	1984		223					82		
Juventus	1992		102					38		
Chelsea	Jun-96	Free	28	23	5	5	1	9	2	0

FAPL Summary by Club

Chelsea	1996-97		28	23	5	5	1	9	2	0
Total			*28*	*23*	*5*	*5*	*1*	*9*	*2*	*0*

VIERRA Patrick   Arsenal

Full Name: Patrick Vierra   DOB: 23-06-76 Dakar, Senegal
Debut: ARSENAL v Sheffield Wednesday 16/9/96
Debut Goal: ARSENAL v Derby County 7/12/96

Previous Clubs Details   *Apps*   *Goals*

Club	Signed	Fee	Tot	Start	Sub	FA	FL	Lge	FA	FL
AS Cannes	1993		36	32	4			2		
Milan	1995		2	1	1			0		
Arsenal	Aug-96	£3.5m	31	30	1	3	3	2	0	0

FAPL Summary by Club

Arsenal	1996-97		31	30	1	3	3	2	0	0
Total			*31*	*30*	*1*	*3*	*3*	*2*	*0*	*0*

WALKER Des   Sheffield Wednesday

Full Name: Desmond Sinclair Walker   DOB: 26-11-65 Hackney
Debut: SHEFFIELD WEDNESDAY v Aston Villa 18/8/93
Debut Goal:

Previous Clubs Details

Club	Signed	Fee	Tot	Start	Sub	FA	FL	Lge	FA	FL
N.Forest	Nov-83	Apprentice	264	259	5	27	40	1	0	0
Sampdoria	Aug-92	£1.5m	0	0	0	0	0	0	0	0
Sheffield W.	Jul-93	£2.7m	152	152	0	12	15	0	0	0

FAPL Summary by Club

Sheffield W.	93-94 to 96-97		152	152	0	12	15	0	0	0
Total			*152*	*152*	*0*	*12*	*15*	*0*	*0*	*0*

WALKER Ian   Tottenham Hotspur

Full Name: Ian Michael Walker   DOB: 31-10-71 Watford
Debut: Southampton v TOTTENHAM HOTSPUR 15/8/92
Debut Goal: (Goalkeeper)

Previous Clubs Details

Club	Signed	Fee	Tot	Start	Sub	FA	FL	Lge	FA	FL
Tottenham H.	Dec-89	Trainee	163	162	1	15	13	0	0	0
Oxford U.	Aug-90	Loan	2	2	0	0	1	0	0	0

FAPL Summary by Club

Tottenham H.	92-93 to 95-96		107	106	1	14	8	0	0	0
Tottenham H.	1996-97		37	37	0	1	4	0	0	0
Total			*144*	*143*	*1*	*15*	*12*	*0*	*0*	*0*

WALLACE Rod   Leeds United

Full Name: Rodney Seymour Wallace   DOB: 02-10-69 Greenwich
Debut: LEEDS UNITED v Wimbledon 15/8/92
Debut Goal: LEEDS UNITED v Tottenham Hotspur 25/8/92

Previous Clubs Details

Club	Signed	Fee	Tot	Start	Sub	FA	FL	Lge	FA	FL
Southampton	Apr-88	Trainee	128	111	17	10	19	45	3	6
Leeds U.	Jun-91	£1.6m	181	158	23	17	15	43	3	6

FAPL Summary by Club

Leeds U.	92-93 to 95-96		147	124	23	16	12	32	3	4
Total			*147*	*124*	*23*	*16*	*12*	*32*	*3*	*4*

WALSH Steve   Leicester City

Full Name: Steven Walsh   DOB: 03-11-64 Preston
Debut: LEICESTER CITY v Newcastle United 21/8/94
Debut Goal: LEICESTER CITY v Everton 23/11/96

Previous Clubs Details				Apps				Goals		
Club	Signed	Fee	Tot	Start	Sub	FA	FL	Lge	FA	FL
Wigan Athletic	Sep-82	Juniors	125	123	2	6	7	4	0	0
Leicester City	Jun-86	£100,000	309	307	2	11	31	47	1	3
FAPL Summary by Club										
Leicester City		96-97	27	27	0	2	8	2	1	0
Total			*27*	*27*	*0*	*2*	*8*	*2*	*1*	*0*

WANCHOPE Paulo　　　　　　　　　　　　Derby County

Full Name: Paulo Wanchope　　　　　　　DOB:
Debut: Manchester United v DERBY COUNTY 5/4/97
Debut Goal: Manchester United v DERBY COUNTY 5/4/97

Previous Clubs Details				Apps				Goals		
Club	Signed	Fee	Tot	Start	Sub	FA	FL	Lge	FA	FL
CS Heridiano										
Derby County	Mar-97	£600,000	5	2	3	0	0	1	0	0
FAPL Summary by Club										
Derby County		1996-97	5	2	3	0	0	1	0	0
Total			*5*	*2*	*3*	*0*	*0*	*1*	*0*	*0*

WARD Ashley　　　　　　　　　　　　　Derby County

Full Name: Ashley Stuart Ward　　　　　　DOB: 24-11-70 Manchester
Debut: NORWICH CITY v Chelsea 10/12/94
Debut Goal: NORWICH CITY v Chelsea 10/12/94

Previous Clubs Details				Apps				Goals		
Club	Signed	Fee	Tot	Start	Sub	FA	FL	Lge	FA	FL
Man. City	Aug-89	Trainee	1	0	1	2	0	0	0	0
Wrexham	Jan-91	Loan	4	4	0	0	0	2	0	0
Leicester City	Jul-91	£80,000	10	2	8	1	3	0	0	0
Blackpool	Nov-92	Loan	2	2	0	0	0	1	0	0
Crewe Alex	Dec-92	£80,000	61	58	3	2	4	25	4	2
Norwich City	Dec-94	£500,000	53	53	0	1	6	18	0	3
Derby County	Mar-96	£1m	37	30	7	2	2	11	1	0
FAPL Summary by Club										
Norwich City		94-95 to 96-97	25	25	0	0	0	8	0	0
Derby County		1996-97	30	25	5	2	2	10	1	0
Total			*55*	*50*	*5*	*2*	*2*	*18*	*1*	*0*

WARHURST Paul　　　　　　　　　　Blackburn Rovers

Full Name: Paul Warhurst　　　　　　　DOB: 26-09-69 Stockport
Debut: Everton v SHEFFIELD WEDNESDAY 15/8/92
Debut Goal: Nottingham Forest v SHEFFIELD WEDNESDAY 12/9/92

Previous Clubs Details				Apps				Goals		
Club	Signed	Fee	Tot	Start	Sub	FA	FL	Lge	FA	FL
Man. City	Jun-88	Trainee	0	0	0	0	0	0	0	0

Oldham Ath	Oct-88	£10,000	67	60	7	9	8	2	0	0
Sheffield W.	Jul-91	£750,000	66	60	6	8	9	6	5	4
Blackburn R.	Aug-93	£2.7m	57	30	27	9	16	4	5	3
FAPL Summary by Club										
Sheffield W.		1992-93	33	29	4	7	7	6	5	3
Blackburn R.	93-94 to 96-97		57	30	27	9	16	4	5	3
Total			*90*	*59*	*31*	*16*	*23*	*10*	*10*	*6*

WARNER Tony   Liverpool
Full Name: Anthony Warner   DOB: 11-05-74 Liverpool
Debut: Debut Goal: (Goalkeeper)

Previous Clubs Details				*Apps*					*Goals*	
Club	Signed	Fee	Tot	Start	Sub	FA	FL	Lge	FA	FL
Liverpool	Trainee									

WARREN Christer   Southampton
Full Name: Christer Warren   DOB: 10-10-74 Bournemouth
Debut: Arsenal v SOUTHAMPTON 23/9/95 as sub
Debut Goal:

Previous Clubs Details				*Apps*					*Goals*	
Club	Signed	Fee	Tot	Start	Sub	FA	FL	Lge	FA	FL
Southampton	Mar-95	£40,000 NL	8	1	7	0	1	0	0	0
Fulham	Mar-97	Loan								
FAPL Summary by Club										
Southampton	95-96 to 96-97		8	1	7	0	1	0	0	0
Total			*8*	*1*	*7*	*0*	*1*	*0*	*0*	*0*

WATKINSON Russ   Southampton
Full Name: Russ Watkinson   DOB: 03-12-77 Epsom
Debut: SOUTHAMPTON v Tottenham Hotspur 14/9/96
Debut Goal:

Previous Clubs Details				*Apps*					*Goals*	
Club	Signed	Fee	Tot	Start	Sub	FA	FL	Lge	FA	FL
Southampton	From NL		2	0	2	1	1	0	0	0
FAPL Summary by Club										
Southampton	1996-97		2	0	2	1	1	0	0	0
Total			*2*	*0*	*2*	*1*	*1*	*0*	*0*	*0*

WATSON Dave   Everton
Full Name: David Watson   DOB: 20-11-61 Liverpool
Debut: EVERTON v Sheffield Wednesday 15/8/92
Debut Goal: Middlesbrough v EVERTON 10/4/93

Previous Clubs Details				*Apps*					*Goals*	
Club	Signed	Fee	Tot	Start	Sub	FA	FL	Lge	FA	FL
Liverpool	May 79	Juniors	0	0	0	0	0	0	0	0

Norwich City	Nov-80	£100,000	212	212	0	18	21	11	1	3
Everton	Aug-86	£900,000	369	367	2	2	0	23	5	6
FAPL Summary by Club										
Everton	92-93 to 96-97		169	168	1	14	12	6	2	1
Total			*169*	*168*	*1*	*14*	*12*	*6*	*2*	*1*

WATSON David   Barnsley

Full Name: David Neil Watson   DOB: 10-11-73 Barnsley
Debut: Debut Goal:

Previous Clubs Details				*Apps*					*Goals*	
Club	Signed	Fee	Tot	Start	Sub	FA	FL	Lge	FA	FL
Barnsley	Jul-92	Trainee	142	142	0	5	13	0	0	0

WATSON Steve   Newcastle United

Full Name: Stephen Craig Watson   DOB: 01-04-74 North Shields
Debut: NEWCASTLE UNITED v Tottenham Hotspur 14/8/93
Debut Goal: NEWCASTLE UNITED v Swindon Town 12/3/94

Previous Clubs Details				*Apps*					*Goals*	
Club	Signed	Fee	Tot	Start	Sub	FA	FL	Lge	FA	FL
Newcastle U.	Apr-91	Trainee	172	145	27	13	13	11	0	1
FAPL Summary by Club										
Newcastle U.	93-94 to 96-97		118	99	19	6	13	10	0	1
Total			*118*	*99*	*19*	*6*	*13*	*10*	*0*	*1*

WATTS Julian   Leicester City

Full Name: Julian Watts   DOB: 17-03-71 Sheffield
Debut: Liverpool v SHEFFIELD WEDNESDAY 3/3/93
Debut Goal: SHEFFIELD WEDNESDAY v Wimbledon 10/2/96 as sub

Previous Clubs Details				*Apps*					*Goals*	
Club	Signed	Fee	Tot	Start	Sub	FA	FL	Lge	FA	FL
Rotherham U.	Jul-90	Trainee	20	17	3	4	1	1	0	0
Sheffield W.	Mar-92	£80,000	16	11	5	0	1	1	0	0
Shrewsbury T.	Dec-92	Loan	9	9	0	0	0	0	0	0
Leicester City	Mar-96	£210,000	35	31	4	3	6	1	0	0
FAPL Summary by Club										
Sheffield W.	92-93 to 95-96		15	12	3	0	1	1	0	0
Leicester City	1996-97		26	22	4	3	6	1	0	0
Total			*41*	*34*	*7*	*3*	*7*	*2*	*0*	*0*

WETHERALL David   Leeds United

Full Name: David Wetherall   DOB: 14-03-71 Sheffield
Debut: Southampton v LEEDS UNITED 19/9/92
Debut Goal: LEEDS UNITED v Chelsea 24/3/93

Previous Clubs Details				*Apps*					*Goals*	
Club	Signed	Fee	Tot	Start	Sub	FA	FL	Lge	FA	FL
Sheffield W.	Jul-89	Trainee	0	0	0	0	0	0	0	0

| Leeds U. | Jul-91 | £125,000 | 147 | 141 | 6 | 17 | 16 | 9 | 3 | 0 |

FAPL Summary by Club

| Leeds U. | 92-93 to 96-97 | 146 | 141 | 5 | 17 | 16 | 9 | 3 | 0 |
| *Total* | | *146* | *141* | *5* | *17* | *16* | *9* | *3* | *0* |

WHELAN Noel   Coventry City

Full Name: Noel Whelan   DOB: 30-12-74 Leeds
Debut: Sheffield Wednesday v LEEDS UNITED 4/5/93
Debut Goal: LEEDS UNITED v Arsenal 23/8/94 as sub

Previous Clubs Details				*Apps*				*Goals*		
Club	Signed	Fee	Tot	Start	Sub	FA	FL	Lge	FA	FL
Leeds U.	Mar-93	Trainee	48	28	20	2	5	7	0	1
Coventry City	Dec-95	£2m	56	55	1	7	4	14	3	0

FAPL Summary by Club

Leeds U.	92-93 to 95-96	48	28	20	2	5	7	0	1
Coventry City	95-96 to 96-97	56	55	1	7	4	14	3	0
Total		*104*	*83*	*21*	*9*	*9*	*21*	*3*	*1*

WHITLOW Mike   Leicester City

Full Name: Michael William Whitlow   DOB: 13-01-68 Liverpool
Debut: LEICESTER CITY v Newcastle United 21/8/94
Debut Goal: Manchester United v LEICESTER CITY 28/12/94

Previous Clubs Details				*Apps*				*Goals*		
Club	Signed	Fee	Tot	Start	Sub	FA	FL	Lge	FA	FL
Leeds U.	Nov-88	£10,000 NL	77	62	15	5	5	4	0	0
Leicester City	Mar-92	£250,000	147	141	6	6	12	6	0	1

FAPL Summary by Club

| Leicester City | 94-95 to 96-97 | 45 | 42 | 3 | 3 | 5 | 2 | 0 | 0 |
| *Total* | | *45* | *42* | *3* | *3* | *5* | *2* | *0* | *0* |

WHITTINGHAM Guy   Sheffield Wednesday

Full Name: Guy Whittingham   DOB: 10-11-64 Evesham
Debut: ASTON VILLA v Manchester United 23/8/93 as sub
Debut Goal: Everton v ASTON VILLA 31/8/93

Previous Clubs Details				*Apps*				*Goals*		
Club	Signed	Fee	Tot	Start	Sub	FA	FL	Lge	FA	FL
Portsmouth	Jun-89	Free NL	160	149	11	10	9	88	10	3
Aston Villa	Jul-93	£1.2m	25	17	8	0	5	5	0	1
W'hampton W.	Feb-94	Loan	13	13	0	1	0	8	0	0
Sheffield W.	Dec-94	£700,000	83	72	11	7	6	18	1	2

FAPL Summary by Club

Aston Villa	93-94 to 94-95	25	17	8	0	5	5	0	1
Sheffield W.	94-95 to 96-97	83	72	11	7	6	18	1	2
Total		*108*	*89*	*19*	*7*	*11*	*23*	*1*	*3*

WILCOX Jason   **Blackburn Rovers**

Full Name: Jason Malcolm Wilcox   DOB: 15-03-71 Farnworth
Debut: BLACKBURN ROVERS v Arsenal 18/8/92
Debut Goal: Middlesbrough v BLACKBURN ROVERS 5/12/92

Previous Clubs Details				*Apps*				*Goals*		
Club	Signed	Fee	Tot	Start	Sub	FA	FL	Lge	FA	FL
Blackburn R.	Jun-89		188	174	14	13	16	24	1	0
FAPL Summary by Club										
Blackburn R.	92-93 to 96-97		131	125	6	13	14	20	1	0
Total			*131*	*125*	*6*	*13*	*14*	*20*	*1*	*0*

WILKINSON Paul   **Middlesbrough**

Full Name: Paul Wilkinson   DOB: 30-10-64 Louth
Debut: Coventry City v MIDDLESBROUGH 15/8/92
Debut Goal: MIDDLESBROUGH v Leeds United 22/8/92

Previous Clubs Details				*Apps*				*Goals*		
Club	Signed	Fee	Tot	Start	Sub	FA	FL	Lge	FA	FL
Grimsby Town	Nov-82	Amateur	71	69	2	6	10	27	1	5
Everton	Mar-85	£250,000	31	19	12	3	4	6	1	7
N.Forest	Mar-87	£200,000	34	32	2	5	3	5	2	1
Watford	Aug-88	£300,000	134	133	1	7	4	52	0	1
Middlesbrough	Aug-91	£550,000	164	160	4	14	16	50	5	8
Oldham	Oct-95	Loan								
Watford	Dec-95	Loan								
Luton Town	Mar-96	Loan								
Barnsley			45	45	0	2	4	9	0	2
FAPL Summary by Club										
Middlesbrough	1992-93		43	42	1	3	0	15	0	0
Total			*43*	*42*	*1*	*3*	*0*	*15*	*0*	*0*

WILLEMS Ron   **Derby County**

Full Name: Ron Willems   DOB:
Debut: DERBY COUNTY v Leeds United 17/8/96
Debut Goal: Blackburn Rovers v DERBY COUNTY 9/9/96

Previous Clubs Details				*Apps*				*Goals*		
Club	Signed	Fee	Tot	Start	Sub	FA	FL	Lge	FA	FL
Grasshopper Club										
Derby County	Jul-95	£300,000	49	38	11	1	2	13	2	1
FAPL Summary by Club										
Derby County	1996-97		16	7	9	0	0	2	2	0
Total			*16*	*7*	*9*	*0*	*0*	*2*	*2*	*0*

WILLIAMS Paul   **Coventry City**

Full Name: Paul Darren Williams   DOB: 26-03-71 Burton
Debut: Newcastle United v COVENTRY CITY, 19/8/95

Debut Goal: COVENTRY CITY v Tottenham Hotspur 4/11/95

Previous Clubs Details

Club	Signed	Fee	Tot	Start	Sub	FA	FL	Lge	FA	FL
								Apps		Goals
Derby County	Jul-89	Trainee	160	153	7	8	12	25	3	2
Lincoln City	Nov-89	Loan	3	3	0	2	0	0	0	0
Coventry City	Aug-95	£750,000+	64	59	5	5	6	4	1	1
FAPL Summary by Club										
Coventry City	95-96 to 96-97		64	59	5	5	6	4	0	1
Total			*64*	*59*	*5*	*5*	*6*	*4*	*0*	*1*

WILLIAMS Mike   Sheffield Wednesday

Full Name: Michael Antony Williams   DOB: 21-11-69 Bradford
Debut: SHEFFIELD WEDNESDAY v Southampton 12/4/93
Debut Goal: SHEFFIELD WEDNESDAY v Ipswich Town 14/5/95

Previous Clubs Details

Club	Signed	Fee	Tot	Start	Sub	FA	FL	Lge	FA	FL
								Apps		Goals
Sheffield W.	Feb-91	Free NL	23	16	7	0	5	1	0	0
Halifax Town	Dec-92	Loan	9	9	0	0	0	1	0	0
Huddersfield T.	Oct-96	Loan								
FAPL Summary by Club										
Sheffield W.	92-93 to 96-97		23	16	7	0	5	1	0	0
Total			*23*	*16*	*7*	*0*	*5*	*1*	*0*	*0*

WILLIAMSON Danny   West Ham United

Full Name: Daniel Alan Williamson   DOB: 05-12-73 Newham
Debut: Arsenal v WEST HAM UNITED 30/4/94 as sub
Debut Goal: WEST HAM UNITED v Southampton 7/5/94

Previous Clubs Details

Club	Signed	Fee	Tot	Start	Sub	FA	FL	Lge	FA	FL
								Apps		Goals
West Ham U.	Jul-92	Trainee	51	47	4	5	3	5	0	0
FAPL Summary by Club										
West Ham U.	93-94 to 96-97		51	47	4	5	3	5	0	0
Total			*51*	*47*	*4*	*5*	*3*	*5*	*0*	*0*

WILSON Stuart   Leicester City

Full Name: Stuart Wilson   DOB:
Debut: LEICESTER CITY v Derby County 22/2/97
Debut Goal: Blackburn Rovers v LEICESTER CITY 11/5/97

Previous Clubs Details

Club	Signed	Fee	Tot	Start	Sub	FA	FL	Lge	FA	FL
								Apps		Goals
Leicester City			2	0	2	1	0	1	0	0
FAPL Summary by Club										
Leicester City	1996-97		2	0	2	1	0	1	0	0
Total			*2*	*0*	*2*	*1*	*0*	*1*	*0*	*0*

WILSON Clive   Tottenham Hotspur

Full Name: Clive Euclid Aklana Wilson   DOB: 13-11-61 Manchester
Debut: Manchester City v QPR 17/8/92
Debut Goal: QPR v Manchester City 6/2/93

Previous Clubs Details | | | | *Apps* | | | | *Goals* | |
|---|---|---|---|---|---|---|---|---|---|---|
| Club | Signed | Fee | Tot | Start | Sub | FA | FL | Lge | FA | FL |
| Man. City | Dec-79 | Juniors | 109 | 107 | 2 | 2 | 10 | 9 | 0 | 2 |
| Chester City | Sep-82 | Loan | 21 | 21 | 0 | 0 | 0 | 2 | 0 | 0 |
| Chelsea | Mar-87 | £250,000 | 81 | 68 | 13 | 4 | 6 | 5 | 0 | 0 |
| QPR | Jul-90 | £450,000 | 172 | 170 | 2 | 8 | 16 | 12 | 1 | 1 |
| Tottenham H. | Jun-95 | Free | 54 | 51 | 3 | 5 | 6 | 1 | 1 | 0 |
| *FAPL Summary by Club* | | | | | | | | | | |
| QPR | 92-93 to 94-95 | | 119 | 119 | 0 | 6 | 10 | 6 | 1 | 1 |
| Tottenham H. | 95-96 to 96-97 | | 54 | 51 | 3 | 5 | 6 | 1 | 1 | 0 |
| *Total* | | | *173* | *170* | *3* | *11* | *16* | *7* | *2* | *1* |

WINTERBURN Nigel   Arsenal

Full Name: Nigel Winterburn   DOB: 11-12-63 Nuneaton
Debut: ARSENAL v Norwich City 15/8/92
Debut Goal: ARSENAL v Oldham Athletic 26/8/92

Previous Clubs Details | | | | *Apps* | | | | *Goals* | |
|---|---|---|---|---|---|---|---|---|---|---|
| Club | Signed | Fee | Tot | Start | Sub | FA | FL | Lge | FA | FL |
| Wimbledon | Sep-83 | Free | 165 | 164 | 1 | 12 | 13 | 8 | 0 | 0 |
| Arsenal | May-87 | £407,000 | 346 | 345 | 1 | 33 | 45 | 7 | 0 | 3 |
| *FAPL Summary by Club* | | | | | | | | | | |
| Arsenal | 92-93 to 96-97 | | 176 | 176 | 0 | 16 | 26 | 3 | 0 | 1 |
| *Total* | | | *176* | *176* | *0* | *16* | *26* | *3* | *0* | *1* |

WISE Dennis   Chelsea

Full Name: Dennis Frank Wise   DOB: 15-12-66 Kensington
Debut: CHELSEA v Blackburn Rovers 26/8/92
Debut Goal: Aston Villa v CHELSEA 2/9/92

Previous Clubs Details | | | | *Apps* | | | | *Goals* | |
|---|---|---|---|---|---|---|---|---|---|---|
| Club | Signed | Fee | Tot | Start | Sub | FA | FL | Lge | FA | FL |
| Wimbledon | Mar-85 | | 135 | 127 | 8 | 11 | 14 | 27 | 3 | 0 |
| Chelsea | Jul-90 | £1.6m | 218 | 211 | 7 | 25 | 23 | 44 | 6 | 6 |
| *FAPL Summary by Club* | | | | | | | | | | |
| Chelsea | 92-93 to 96-97 | | 147 | 141 | 6 | 20 | 14 | 24 | 4 | 3 |
| *Total* | | | *147* | *141* | *6* | *20* | *14* | *24* | *4* | *3* |

WOODS Chris   Southampton

Full Name: Christopher Charles Eric Woods   DOB: 14-11-59 Boston
Debut: Everton v SHEFFIELD WEDNESDAY 15/8/92
Debut Goal: (Goalkeeper)

Club	Signed	Fee	Tot	Start	Sub	FA	FL	Lge	FA	FL
									Apps → *Goals*		
N.Forest	Dec-76	Apprentice	0	0	0	0	7	0	0	0
QPR	Jul-79	£250,000	63	63	0	1	8	0	0	0
Norwich City	Mar-81	£225,000	216	216	0	19	26	0	0	0
Rangers	Jul-86	£600,000								
Sheffield W.	Aug-91	£1.2m	107	106	1	10	13	0	0	0
Reading	Oct-95	Loan	5	5	0	0	0	0	0	0
Colorado Rapids										
Southampton	Oct-96	Loan	4	4	0	0	1	0	0	0

FAPL Summary by Club

Club			Tot	Start	Sub	FA	FL	Lge	FA	FL
Sheffield W.	92-93 to 95-96		66	65	1	8	9	0	0	0
Southampton	1996-97		4	4	0	0	1	0	0	0
Total			*70*	*69*	*1*	*8*	*10*	*0*	*0*	*0*

WRIGHT Mark — Liverpool

Full Name: Mark Wright   DOB: 01-08-63 Dorchester on Thames
Debut: Nottingham Forest v LIVERPOOL 16/8/92
Debut Goal: LIVERPOOL v Southampton 1/9/92

Previous Clubs Details

Club	Signed	Fee	Tot	Start	Sub	FA	FL	Lge	FA	FL
Oxford U.	Aug-80		10	8	2	1	0	0	0	0
Southampton	Mar-82	£80,000	170	170	0	17	25	7	1	2
Derby County	Aug-87	£760,000	144	144	0	5	15	10	0	0
Liverpool	Jul-91	£2.2m	152	150	2	18	16	5	0	1

FAPL Summary by Club

Club			Tot	Start	Sub	FA	FL	Lge	FA	FL
Liverpool	92-93 to 96-97		131	129	2	9	15	5	0	2
Total			*131*	*129*	*2*	*9*	*15*	*5*	*0*	*2*

WRIGHT Ian — Arsenal

Full Name: Ian Edward Wright   DOB: 03-11-63 Woolwich
Debut: ARSENAL v Norwich City 15/8/92
Debut Goal: Liverpool v ARSENAL 23/8/92

Previous Clubs Details

Club	Signed	Fee	Tot	Start	Sub	FA	FL	Lge	FA	FL
C.Palace	Aug-85	Free	225	206	19	11	19	89	3	9
Arsenal	Sep-91	£2.5m	197	190	7	15	28	118	12	28

FAPL Summary by Club

Club			Tot	Start	Sub	FA	FL	Lge	FA	FL
Arsenal	92-93 to 96-97		167	160	7	15	25	94	12	26
Total			*167*	*160*	*7*	*15*	*25*	*94*	*12*	*26*

WRIGHT Alan — Aston Villa

Full Name: Alan Geoffrey Wright   DOB: 28-09-71 Ashton-under-Lyme
Debut: Crystal Palace v BLACKBURN ROVERS 15/8/92
Debut Goal: Middlesbrough v ASTON VILLA 1/1/96

Previous Clubs Details			Apps					Goals		
Club	Signed	Fee	Tot	Start	Sub	FA	FL	Lge	FA	FL
Blackpool	Apr-89	Juniors	98	91	7	8	12	0	0	0
Blackburn R.	Oct-91	£400,000	74	67	7	5	8	1	0	0
Aston Villa	Mar-95	£1m	84	84	0	8	10	3	0	0
FAPL Summary by Club										
Blackburn R.	92-93 to 94-95	41	35	6	4	8	0	0	0	
Aston Villa	94-95 to 96-97	84	84	0	8	10	3	0	0	
Total			*125*	*119*	*6*	*12*	*18*	*3*	*0*	*0*

YATES Dean — Derby County

Full Name: Dean Richard Yates DOB: 26-10-67 Leicester
Debut: DERBY COUNTY v Leeds United 17/8/96
Debut Goal:

Previous Clubs Details			Apps					Goals		
Club	Signed	Fee	Tot	Start	Sub	FA	FL	Lge	FA	FL
Notts County	Jun-85	Apprentice	314	312	2	20	24	33	0	0
Derby County	Jan-95	£350,000	59	57	2	1	3	3	0	0
FAPL Summary by Club										
Derby County	1996-97	10	8	2	0	0	0	0	0	
Total			*10*	*8*	*2*	*0*	*0*	*0*	*0*	*0*

YEBOAH Anthony — Leeds United

Full Name: Anthony Yeboah DOB: 06-06-66 Kumasi, Ghana
Debut: LEEDS UNITED v QPR 24/1/95 as sub
Debut Goal: LEEDS UNITED v Everton 22/2/95

Previous Clubs Details			Apps					Goals		
Club	Signed	Fee	Tot	Start	Sub	FA	FL	Lge	FA	FL
Eintracht Frankfurt										
Leeds U.	Jan-95	£3.4m	48	45	3	8	7	24	2	3
FAPL Summary by Club										
Leeds U.	94-95 to 96-97	48	45	3	8	7	24	2	3	
Total			*48*	*45*	*3*	*8*	*7*	*24*	*2*	*3*

YORKE Dwight — Aston Villa

Full Name: Dwight Yorke DOB: 03-11-71 Tobago
Debut: ASTON VILLA v Leeds United 19/8/92
Debut Goal: ASTON VILLA v Crystal Palace 5/9/92

Previous Clubs Details			Apps					Goals		
Club	Signed	Fee	Tot	Start	Sub	FA	FL	Lge	FA	FL
Aston Villa	Dec-89	£120,000	200	164	36	22	21	61	11	8
FAPL Summary by Club										
Aston Villa	92-93 to 96-97	148	129	19	15	18	48	7	8	
Total			*148*	*129*	*19*	*15*	*18*	*48*	*7*	*8*

ZOLA Gianfranco   Chelsea

Full Name: Gianfranco Zola   DOB: 05-07-66 Oliena (Sardinia)
Debut: Blackburn Rovers v CHELSEA 16/11/96
Debut Goal: CHELSEA v Everton 07/12/96

| Previous Clubs Details | | | | Apps | | | | Goals | | |
Club	Signed	Fee	Tot	Start	Sub	FA	FL	Lge	FA	FL
Nuorse (C2/Int)	1984		31					10		
Torres (C1)	1986		88					21		
Napoli	1989		105	102	3			32		
Parma	1993		94	93	1			47		
Chelsea	Nov-96	£4.5m	23	22	1	7	0	8	4	0
FAPL Summary by Club										
Chelsea		1996-97	23	22	1	7	0	8	4	0
Total			*23*	*22*	*1*	*7*	*0*	*8*	*4*	*0*

A-Z PREMIER LEAGUE MANAGERS

	Start	Finish	P	W	D	L	F	A	Pts	PG
ARDILES, Ossie										
Tottenham Hot.	19-Jun-93	30-Oct-94	54	16	14	24	75	83	62	1.15
ATKINSON, Ron										
Aston Villa	Jun-91	10-Nov-94	98	38	27	33	118	114	141	1.44
Coventry City	15-Feb-95	21-Oct-96	62	17	17	28	56	81	68	1.10
		Total	160	55	44	61	174	195	209	1.31
BALL, Alan										
Southampton	20-Jan-94	Jul-95	60	19	22	19	87	93	79	1.32
Manchester City	Jul-95	1996	38	9	11	18	33	58	38	1.00
		Total	98	28	33	37	120	151	117	1.19
BASSETT, Dave										
Sheffield United	21-Jan-88	12-Dec-95	84	22	28	34	96	113	94	1.12
BONDS, Billy										
West Ham United	23-Apr-90	10-Aug-94	42	13	13	16	47	58	52	1.24
BRANFOOT, Ian										
Southampton	Jun-91	11-Jan-94	66	18	14	34	77	97	68	1.03
BURLEY, George										
Ipswich Town	28-Dec-94		22	4	2	16	16	53	14	0.64
CLARK, Frank										
N. Forest	12-May-93	19-Dec-96	97	38	31	28	136	126	145	1.49
CLOUGH, Brian										
N. Forest	6-Jan-75	1-May-93	42	10	10	22	41	62	40	0.95
COPPELL, Steve										
Crystal Palace	1984	20-May-93	42	11	16	15	48	61	49	1.17
DALGLISH, Kenny										
Blackburn Rovers	Oct-91	May-95	126	72	28	26	211	121	244	1.94
Newcastle United	14-Jan-97		16	8	6	2	33	16	30	1.88
		Total	142	80	34	28	244	137	274	1.93

	Start	Finish	P	W	D	L	F	A	Pts	PG
DEEHAN, John										
Norwich City	7-Jan-94	1995	61	12	23	26	66	89	59	0.97
EVANS, Roy										
Liverpool	28-Jan-94		134	65	35	34	212	131	230	1.72
FERGUSON, Alex										
Manchester United	6-Nov-86		202	123	52	27	373	176	421	2.08
FRANCIS, Gerry										
QPR	Jun-91	11-Nov-94	56	24	14	18	88	76	86	1.54
Tottenham Hot.	15-Nov-94		105	40	32	33	139	121	152	1.45
		Total	161	64	46	51	227	197	238	1.48
FRANCIS, Trevor										
Sheffield Wed.	17-Jun-91	20-May-95	126	44	42	40	180	162	174	1.38
GORMAN, John										
Swindon Town	4-Jun-93	21-Nov-94	42	5	15	22	47	100	30	0.71
GOULD, Bobby										
Coventry City	24-Jun-92	23-Oct-93	54	16	19	19	66	73	67	1.24
GRAHAM, George										
Arsenal	14-May-86	21-Feb-95	112	41	38	33	132	98	161	1.44
Leeds United	10-Sep-96		33	9	12	12	23	29	39	1.18
		Total	145	50	50	45	155	127	200	1.38
GULLITT, Ruud										
Chelsea	1-Jun-96		38	16	11	11	58	55	59	1.55
HARFORD, Ray										
Blackburn Rovers	May-95	25-Oct-96	58	18	19	21	79	89	69	1.19
HODDLE, Glenn										
Chelsea	4-Jun-93	31-May-96	122	38	41	43	145	152	155	1.27
HODGSON, Roy										
Blackburn Rovers	Jun-97									
HORTON, Brian										
Manchester City	27-Aug-93	16-May-95	80	21	30	29	90	108	93	1.16
KEEGAN, Kevin										
Newcastle United	5-Feb-92	8-Jan-97	143	78	30	35	253	147	264	1.85

	Start	Finish	P	W	D	L	F	A	Pts	PG
KENDALL, Howard										
Everton	Nov-90	4-Dec-93	60	22	11	27	73	78	77	1.28
Everton	Jun-97									
KINNEAR, Joe										
Wimbledon	19-Jan-92		202	72	56	74	264	289	272	1.35
LAWRENCE, Lennie										
Middlesbrough	10-Jul-91	2-May-94	42	11	11	20	54	75	44	1.05
LITTLE, Brian										
Leicester City	May-91	22-Nov-94	14	2	3	9	14	26	9	0.64
Aston Villa	25-Nov-94		103	43	30	30	131	98	159	1.54
		Total	117	45	33	39	145	124	168	1.44
LIVERMORE/CLEMENCE, Doug/Ray										
Tottenham Hot.	27-May-92	Jun-93	42	16	11	15	60	66	59	1.40
LYALL, John										
Ipswich Town	11-May-90	5-Dec-94	101	24	34	43	101	146	106	1.05
McFARLAND, Roy										
Bolton Wanderers	Jun-95	Jan-96	22	2	4	16	21	44	10	0.45
McGHEE, Mark										
Leicester City	14-Dec-94	Dec-95	24	3	7	14	26	47	16	0.67
MERRINGTON, Dave										
Southampton	Jul-95	Jul-96	38	9	11	18	34	52	38	1.00
NEAL, Phil										
Coventry City	23-Oct-93	14-Feb-95	58	18	18	22	54	69	72	1.24
O'NEILL, Martin										
Leicester City	Dec-95		38	12	11	15	46	54	47	1.24
PEARCE, Stuart										
N. Forest	20-Dec-96	Jun-97	21	5	9	7	17	30	24	1.14
PLEAT, David										
Sheffield Wednesday	Jun-95		76	24	25	27	98	112	97	1.28
PORTERFIELD, Ian										
Chelsea	1991	15-Feb-93	29	9	10	10	32	36	37	1.28
REDKNAPP, Harry										
West Ham United	10-Aug-94		118	37	32	49	126	148	143	1.21

	Start	Finish	P	W	D	L	F	A	Pts	PG
REID, Peter										
Manchester City	1990	26-Aug-93	46	15	13	18	57	56	58	1.26
Sunderland	Mar-93		38	10	10	18	35	53	40	1.05
		Total	84	25	23	36	92	109	98	1.17
RIOCH, Bruce										
Arsenal	8-Jun-95	12-Aug-96	38	17	12	9	49	32	63	1.66
ROBSON, Bryan										
Middlesbrough	May-94		76	21	22	33	86	110	82	1.08
ROYLE, Joe										
Oldham Athletic	14-Jul-82	10-Nov-94	84	22	23	39	105	142	89	1.06
Everton	10-Nov-94	23-Mar-97	97	36	31	30	136	116	139	1.43
		Total	181	58	54	69	241	258	228	1.26
SMITH, Alan										
Crystal Palace	3-Jun-93	15-May-95	42	11	12	19	34	49	45	1.07
SMITH, Jim										
Derby County	Jun-93		38	11	13	14	45	58	46	1.21
SOUNESS, Graeme										
Liverpool	1991	28-Jan-94	68	28	18	22	106	87	102	1.50
Southampton	Jul-96	Jul-97	38	10	11	17	50	56	41	1.08
		Total	106	38	29	39	156	143	143	1.35
STRACHAN, Gordon										
Coventry City	22-Oct-96		28	8	11	9	34	40	35	1.25
TODD, Colin										
Bolton Wanderers	2-Jan-96		16	6	1	9	18	27	19	1.19
WALKER, Mike										
Norwich City	1-Jun-92	7-Jan-94	65	31	16	18	97	91	109	1.68
Everton	7-Jan-94	8-Nov-94	31	6	9	16	29	52	27	0.87
		Total	96	37	25	34	126	143	136	1.42
WEBB, David										
Chelsea	15-Feb-93	11-May-93	13	5	4	4	19	18	19	1.46
WENGER, Arsène										
Arsenal	1-Oct-96		30	14	9	7	45	24	51	1.70
WILKINS, Ray										
QPR	15-Nov-94		108	35	25	48	136	156	130	1.20

	Start	Finish	P	W	D	L	F	A	Pts	PG

WILKINSON, Howard
Leeds United   10-Oct-88   8-Sep-96   174   66   53   55   231   214   250   1.44

WILSON, Danny
Barnsley

CARETAKER MANAGERS

BARRON, Jim
Aston Villa   10-Nov-94   25-Nov-94   1   1   0   0   4   3   3   3.00

EVANS, Allan
Leicester City   22-Nov-94   13-Dec-94   4   1   1   2   5   7   4   1.00

GODDARD, Paul
Ipswich Town   5-Dec-94   28-Dec-94   3   0   2   1   4   7   2   0.67

HARVEY, Colin
Everton   4-Dec-93   6-Jan-94   7   0   1   6   2   12   1   0.14

HOUSTON, Stuart
Arsenal   21-Feb-95   8-Jun-95   14   5   2   7   13   17   17   1.21
Arsenal   12-Aug-96   13-Sep-96   5   2   2   1   9   7   8   1.60
                 Total   19   7   4   8   22   24   25   1.32

McDERMOTT, Terry
Newcastle United   11-Jan-97   13-Jan-97   1   0   1   0   2   2   1   1.00

MORTIMORE, John
Southampton   11-Jan-94   20-Jan-94   1   1   0   0   1   0   3   3.00

PARKES, Tony
Blackburn Rovers   26-Oct-96   11-May-97   28   9   11   8   36   29   38   1.36

PERRYMAN, Steve
Tottenham Hot.   1-Nov-94   14-Nov-94   1   0   0   1   0   2   0   0.00

RICE, Pat
Arsenal   13-Sep-96   30-Sep-96   3   3   0   0   8   1   9   3.00

WATSON, Dave
Everton   5-Apr-97   Jun-97   7   1   3   3   7   12   6   0.86

FA Premier League
Stadium Guide

Notes: The following pages contain brief directions to each of the Premiership grounds for the forthcoming season. These are supplemented by maps which provide a generalised picture of the area and roads surrounding the stadium. They do not provide a complete picture of all roads and are not to scale. However, used in conjunction with the directions and other details in the book they should allow you to find your way to and locate the stadium in question. Stadiums are represented by the football on each map. Local train stations are also shown. Clubs' telephone numbers and those relating to ticket purchase are also provided – note some of these numbers are charged at premium rate. Contact the clubs for further details.

Club	Number	Ticket Details
Arsenal	0171 704 4000	0171 704 4242
Aston Villa	0121 327 2299	0891 121848
Barnsley	01226 295353	
Blackburn Rovers	01254 698888	0891 121179
Bolton Wanderers	01204 698800	01204 389200
Chelsea	0171 385 5545	0891 121011
Coventry City	01203 234000	01203 23020
Crystal Palace	0181 768 6000	0181 771 8841
Derby County	01332 340105	01332 672226
Everton	0151 521 2020	0891 121599
Leeds United	0113 271 6037	0891 121180
Leicester City	0115 255 5000	0116 291 5232
Liverpool	0151 263 2361	0151 260 9999
Manchester United	0161 872 1661	0161 872 0199
Newcastle United	0191 232 8361	0891 121190
Sheffield Wednesday	0114 243 3122	0114 233 7233
Southampton	01703 220505	01703 228575
Tottenham Hotspur	0181 365 5000	0181 365 5050
West Ham United	0181 548 2748	0181 548 2700
Wimbledon	0181 771 2233	0181 771 8841

ARSENAL

Arsenal Stadium, Highbury, London, N5 1BU

Highbury is a mixture of old and new. The East and West Stands reek tradition and invite images of the famous marble halls. In truth though they are antiquated and the views from the back of the lower section of these stands is awful. They can also be very stuffy and hot. In contrast, the two-tier North (Bank) Stand is immaculate inside and offers modern facilities – it is however designated for home supporters. The South (Clock End) Stand entertains away supporters and also executive boxes – there is talk of rebuilding this to increase the ground's capacity.

Directions

From North: M1, J2 follow sign for the City. After Holloway Road station (c 6 miles) take third left into Drayton Park. Then right into Aubert Park after ¾ mile and 2nd left into Avenell Road. *From South:* Signs for Bank of England then Angel from London Bridge. Right at traffic lights towards Highbury roundabout. Follow Holloway Road then third right into Drayton Park, thereafter as above. *From West:* A40 (M) to A501 ring road. Left at Angel to Highbury roundabout, then as above. *Parking:* It's worth considering parking away from the ground and then taking the Tube. Otherwise get there early and leave late.
Rail: Finsbury Park or Drayton Park.   *Tube:* Arsenal – Piccadilly Line.

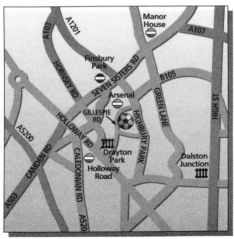

ASTON VILLA

Villa Park, Trinity Road, Birmingham, B6 6HE

Villa Park is easy to find but often difficult to get to due to snarl-ups on the motorway. Always allow plenty of time and think about spending the morning in Brum. Villa Park's stature as a home for many an FA Cup semi-final speaks volumes for the ground which is well placed and has an enjoyable atmosphere. The Trinity Road Stand is one of the most distinctive in the country with its towers and red brick frontage. The North Stand and Doug Ellis Stand are fairly typical of the new stands in England with away seating for both in adjacent corners. Facilities do leave a little to be desired. The Hoult Stand was built on what was one of the biggest kop areas in England and offers an excellent view.

Directions

M6 J6, follow signs for Birmingham NE. Third exit at roundabout then right into Ashton Hall Rd after ½ mile

Parking: Another ground where if you are coming by car you need to arrive early to find somewhere to park within an acceptable walking distance of the ground. It's not easy but possible – just make a note of where you parked!

Rail. Witton.

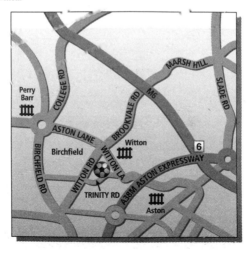

BARNSLEY

Oakwell Ground, Grove Street, Barnsley, S71 1ET

Oakwell has been pretty much rebuilt during the past few years and, with a capacity of some 19,000, is one of the smallest stadiums in the Premiership. Dominating the four sides is the 7,000 seater, two-tier East Stand. Opposite is the older West Stand which is where the visitors' seating is located and this may flow into the Spion Kop area where red bucket seats have been bolted on to the terraces and are at the mercy of the elements. The South Stand at the Pontefract Road end is the newest development, a single-tiered stand with distinctive cantilevered roof.

Directions

From North and West: M1 J37, take A628 towards Barnsley and continue towards the town centre. After about half a mile, take the fourth exit from the Town End roundabout on to the Barnsley Western Relief Road (dual carriageway) heading towards Pontefract. At next roundabout take second exit (Pontefract A628) and continue down Harborough Hill. At the roundabout at the bottom of hill, turn back on yourself up Harborough Hill. Turn left at sign for Pontefract (half mile), and ground is about half a mile along Pontefract Road on left.
From South: M1, J37 onto A61 (Barnsley South). Take first exit at Birdwell roundabout towards town centre. Follow town centre signs which eventually leads on to Harborough Hill – then as above.
Parking: Plenty at ground but, as always, arrive early.

BLACKBURN ROVERS

Ewood Park, Blackburn, BB2 4JF

Ewood Park could be described as the House that Jack built – but that would be rather unkind, not least because the visiting supporters' facilities are amongst the best in the Premiership. Jack Walker's steely millions helped rebuild a decaying ground and it is ironic that the three new stands make the stand first rebuilt in 1987 – the Walkersteel Stand – look rather dated. On the opposite side the Jack Walker Stand contains the executive boxes whilst home support is located mainly in the Blackburn Stand itself. The Darwen End is where visiting supporters are housed. The Darwen River runs alongside the ground and this is a good landmark to use.

Directions

From North, South & West: M6 J31, follow signs for Blackburn then Bolton Road. Turn left after 1½ miles into Kidder Street.

From East: A677 or A679 following signs for Bolton Road, then as above.

Parking: Reasonable all around and it's a case of what you can get when you arrive, either in the streets, the local industrial estates or the schools.

Rail: Blackburn Central.

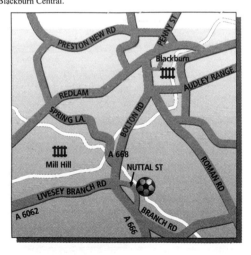

BOLTON WANDERERS

The Reebok Stadium, Mansell Way, Horwich

Judgement will have to be passed during 1997-98 on Bolton's new ground but one thing is for sure – it will be amongst the most futuristic-looking in the country. Four looping-roofed stands dominate each side and these have been coded into Blue, Green, Red and Yellow for ticketing purposes with the Red and Yellow ends being behind the goals. Each stand will encompass two levels. It is probably that these stands will be allocated names in due course but at the time of writing Bolton were referring to the stands by their designated colour. Signs at the ground also direct fans to their seats using designated colours. Visiting supporters have been allocated red tickets.

Directions

From all directions: M6, J6, head towards Horwich A6027 (at which point the ground will be visible). The Reebok Stadium is located approximately 0.25 miles on the left.
Parking: At ground and in local industrial parks (further along A6027).
Rail: Horwich.

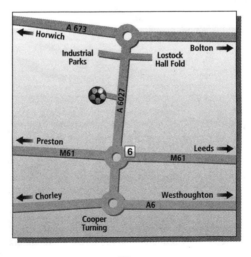

CHELSEA

Stamford Bridge, London, SW6 1HS

Stamford Bridge had a complete overhaul during the close season with West Stand and old Shed End (South Stand) undergoing a rebuild to completely enclose the stadium and bring it in line with the main East Stand and Matthew Harding Stand. All-in-all this should make it one of the most atmospheric grounds in the Premiership. The South Stand forms part of the Chelsea Village complex and also houses a line of executive boxes. It, like the Matthew Harding Stand, includes a large video screen. In recent seasons the lower parts of the East Stand have been used to house visiting supporters.

Directions

From North & East: A1 or M1 to central London and Hyde Park corner. Follow signs for Guildford (A3) and then Knightsbridge (A4). After a mile, turn left into Fulham Road. *From South:* A219 Putney Bridge then follow signs for West End joining A308 and then into Fulham Road. *From West:* M4 then A4 to central London. Follow A3220 to Westminster; after ¾ mile right at crossroads into Fulham Road. *Parking:* Forget it. If travelling from the north leave your car at Stanmore and travel in on the tube.
Rail/Tube: Fulham Broadway (District line).

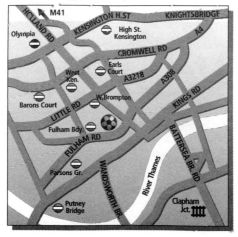

COVENTRY CITY

Highfield Road, King Richard St, Coventry, CV2 4FW

Highfield Road was famous as being the first all-seater stadium in England, years before the 'concept' was ever mooted. The ground though is rather nondescript but does provide a good atmosphere to make for an enjoyable event. Visiting supporters are normally located at the west end of the Sky Blue Stand and the view in general is excellent. Not all Sky Blue fans can say the same though; in recent years the corners of the ground have been closed in and the view from seats here is wanting to say the least.

Directions
From North & West: M6 J3, after 3¹⁄₂ miles turn left into Eagle Street and straight on to Swan Lane. *From South & East:* M1 to M45 then A45 to Ryton-on-Dunsmore where third exit at roundabout is A423. After one mile turn right into B4110. Left at T-junction then right into Swan Lane.
Parking: There is plenty of street parking. In fact, you can get within a few minutes walk of the ground even close to kick-off times, but you need to know your way around the side streets to achieve this.
Rail: Coventry.

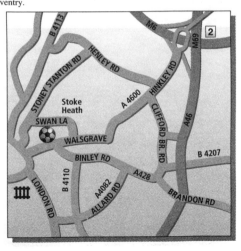

CRYSTAL PALACE

Selhurst Park, South Norwood, London, SE25 6PU

Selhurst Park is located in the suburbs of south-east London and is one of those places where you always under-estimate the amount of time you need to get there. Always allow extra time and then some, no matter how you plan to get there. The home supporters have seen some big developments in recent years with new stands behind each goal giving impressive views of the playing area. The same cannot be said of the accommodation for visiting supporters in the Arthur Waite Stand. This is quite awful, with obstructed views and a shallow slope to the steps making most occupants stand to get a view of the game. The facilities match the stand and the narrow gangways and lack of toilets make it an accident waiting to happen.

Directions
From North: M1/A1 to North Circular A406 and Chiswick. Follow South Circular A205 to Wandsworth then the A3 and A214 towards Streatham and A23. Then left on to B273 for one mile and turn left at end into High Street and Whitehorse Lane.
From South. On A23 follow signs for Crystal Palace along B266 going through Thornton Heath into Whitehorse Lane. *From East:* A232 Croydon Road to Shirley joining A215, Norwood Road. Turn left after 2¹/₂ miles into Whitehorse Lane.
From West: M4 to Chiswick then as above.
Parking: If early you can use Sainsbury's at the Whitehorse Lane End or in local streets. *Rail:* Selhurst, Norwood Junction or Thornton Heath.

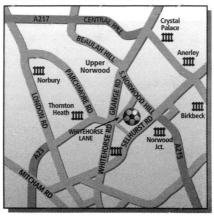

DERBY COUNTY

Pride Park Stadium, Derby

Pride Park Stadium is the brand new home for the Rams, after its official opening by the Queen in July 1997. The 30,000 capacity stadium is one of the modern 'horseshoe' designs with upper and lower decks. There are positions for disabled people in the north-east corner. The South Stand has been allocated to away supporters and the accommodation in this stand will be adjusted to suit the number of visitors. The concourse behind the horseshoe contains good facilities, including food outlets and adequate toilets for men and women. There are also TV screens so that you don't miss any action. The 'Baseball Ground' pub is sited in the north-east corner by the ticket office, club shop and administration . The main West Stand contains executive boxes, players' facilities and a restaurant. There are additional boxes and a business club in the north-west corner stand.

Directions

From North & West: Follow signs for A52 and Nottingham, left off A52 after Derby city centre. *From South & East:* M1 J25, onto A52. Follow yellow signs for football stadium. First slip road off dual carriageway into Pride Park. You can see the stadium and car parks ahead, beyond retail park.
Parking: 2200 capacity next to the stadium. There are buses from Derby city centre.
Rail: Derby Station, 10 minutes walk.

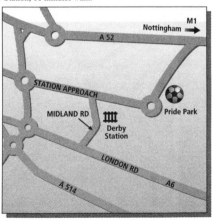

EVERTON

Goodison Park, Liverpool, L4 4EL

Goodison Park was always at the forefront of development – it was the first ground to have a two-tier stand and then the first to go one better with a three-tier stand. Visiting supporters occupy the open end of the Bullens Road Stand which itself swings around into the Gwladys Street Stand sandwiched in between here and the Main Stand is, uniquely, a church – St Luke the Evangelist has probably seen a lot of Evertonians praying for wins down the years! The Park End Stand is the most recent development, being completed in 1994, and this now tends to house the main Evertonian support.

Directions

From North: M6 J8, take A58 to A580 and follow into Walton Hall Avenue.
From South & East: M6 J21A to M62, turn right into Queen's Drive then, after 4 miles, left into Walton Hall Avenue.
From West: M53 through Wallasey Tunnel, follow signs for Preston on A580. Walton Hall Avenue is signposted.
Parking: The Stanley Park car park has 100 spaces for a couple of quid. This is actually located at the Anfield end of the park.
Rail: Liverpool Lime Street.

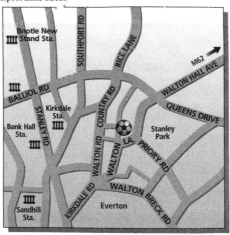

LEEDS UNITED

Elland Road, Leeds, LS11 0ES

Elland Road towers out of the southern end of Leeds and is actually best viewed from a northbound train, out to the right were the massive East Stand dominates the ground. With a capacity of 17,000, this makes the rest of the ground look rather small in contrast. Facilities here are very good with its open plan nature. Visiting supporters are allocated the corner between the East and South Stands and the facilities here leave a little to be desired. That said, the view is good if you don't mind watching the game from this point.

Directions

From North & East: A58, A61, A63 or A64 into city centre and then on to M621. Leave motorway after 1½ miles on to A643 and Elland Road.
From West: take M62 to M621 then as above.
From South: M1 then M621 then as above.
Parking: Plenty of space, car parks near the ground fill up early.
Rail: Leeds City – about 30 minute walk (1.5 miles).

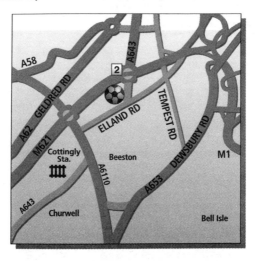

LEICESTER CITY

City Stadium, Filbert Street, Leicester, LE2 7FL

Filbert Street is one of my favourite grounds, with a mixture of old and new. The new Carling Stand dominates the stadium and sitting in the upper tier of this you can easily look over the tops of the other stands. Opposite, the low East Stand is used to house visiting supporters and its compact nature helps to add to the atmosphere for those inside it. The Filbert Street end contains the famous executive boxes which extend over seated areas.

Directions

From South: M1 J21. Follow A5460 towards Leicester (avoid Ring Road). Continue for close on two miles until dual carriageway ends and you go under a railway bridge. At next set of lights turn right into Upperton Road. Go over bridge and Leicester City ground is located in the street running parallel to Upperton Road. This is a one-way system and access is only available to official cars for the LCFC club car park. *From North:* Leave M1 J22, or take A46, A607 to town centre. Towards Rugby via Almond Road, Aylestone Road, and then left into Walnut Street and Filbert Street for the ground

From West: M69 and A50 to Aylestone Road, and then as North.

Parking: Try one of the roads running off to the left at the point around the railway bridge mentioned in the directions above. There is a maze of roads here. Avoid going further down Upperton Road.

Rail: Leicester.

LIVERPOOL

Anfield Road, Liverpool, L4 OTH

Anfield minus the standing Kop really isn't the same. The Kop Stand is an excellent facility and blends in perfectly with the rest of the ground, but... At the opposite end of the ground the Anfield Road Stand is where the visitors' accommodation is located. The Main Stand includes a paddock at the front with a two-tier Centenary Stand completing the ground.

Directions
From North: M6 J8, follow A58 to Walton Hall Avenue and pass Stanley Park, turning left into Anfield Road. *From South/East:* To end of M62 and right into Queens Drive (A5058). After three miles turn left into Utting Avenue and right after one mile into Anfield Road. *From West:* M53 through Wallasey Tunnel, follow signs for Preston then turn into Walton Hall Avenue and right into Anfield Road before Stanley Park.
Parking: Very, very difficult. The Stanley Park Car Park is utilised mainly by the club on match days and unless you arrive very early there is little chance of getting a space. *Rail:* Liverpool Lime Street (main). Sandhills (local).

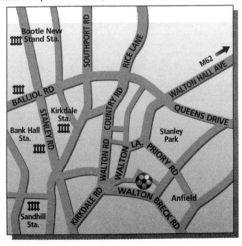

MANCHESTER UNITED

Old Trafford, Manchester, M16 0RA

Old Trafford has the biggest capacity of any football ground in England except Wembley. The North Stand had a third tier added prior to Euro '96 to bring the total accommodation possibility to over 55,000. The view from the top of here though leaves a bit to be desired, especially when the ball is on the far touchline. That apart, Old Trafford is arguably the best football stadium in England and is one that has been able to retain its own atmosphere despite going all-seater. Facilities are excellent and visiting supporters are generally located at the East Stand end.

Directions
From North: From the M63 Junction 4 follow the signs for Manchester (A5081). Turn right after 2¹/₂ miles into Warwick Road. *From South:* From the M6 Junction 19 follow the A556 then the A56 (Altrincham). From Altrincham follow the signs for Manchester, turning left into Warwick Road after six miles. *From East:* From the M62 Junction 17 take the A56 to Manchester. Follow the signs South and then to Chester. Turn right into Warwick Road after two miles.

Parking: Pretty good – a case of finding a location you like in one of the many 'Match-day' car parks. Getting away is murder. *Rail:* Old Trafford (Metrolink).

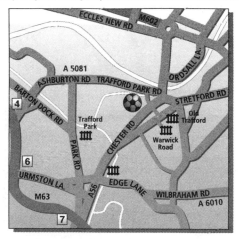

NEWCASTLE UNITED

St James's Park, Newcastle-Upon-Tyne, NE1 4ST

St James's Park remains one of the noisiest grounds in England but there has still been a loss of atmosphere here since it was redeveloped by Sir John Hall, who has the Leazes End stand named in his honour. Visiting fans are located in the corner here. The Gallowgate End is the first stand you come to when walking up from the town centre. The main Milburn Stand includes an exclusive seated area which will set you back £3000 a seat for the season. No wonder it's called the Platinum Club. I'll take three…

Directions
From South: Follow A1, A68 then A6127 to cross the Tyne. At roundabout, first exit into Moseley Street. Left into Neville Street, right at end for Clayton Street and then Newgate Street. Left for Leaze Park Road. *From West:* A69 towards city centre. Left into Clayton Street for Newgate Street, left again for Leaze Park Road. *From North:* A1 then follow signs for Hexham until Percy Street. Right into Leaze Park Road.
Parking: There are some designated areas but it is so close to the town centre that using one of the city centre multi-storeys and taking the short walk is easy.
Rail: Newcastle Central (¹/₂ mile).

SHEFFIELD WEDNESDAY

Hillsborough, Sheffield, S6 1SW

Hillsborough has always had a reputation as being one of the best grounds in the country. From a visiting supporters' point of view this will probably be true as the away fans have generally been accommodated in the upper tier of the West Stand behind the goal. In general the ground is rather plain although the introduction of the Sheffield Wednesday Bank last season was an inspiration and certainly adds to the entertainment value.

Directions

From North: M1 J34 then A6109 to Sheffield. At roundabout after 1½ miles take third exit then turn left after three miles into Harries Road. *From South & East:* M1 J31 or 33 to A57. At roundabout take Prince of Wales Road exit. A further six miles then turn left into Herries Road South.

From West: A57 to A6101 then turn left after four miles at T junction into Penistone Road.

Parking: The streets off the A61 are good hunting grounds for a car parking space. Try and get close to the ground – this area is hilly!

Rail: Sheffield Midland.

415

SOUTHAMPTON

The Dell, Milton Road, Southampton, SO9 4XX

After 31 applications, Southampton have finally got permission to build a new ground. It can't come soon enough. **The Dell** is very distinctive but also very cramped and even the addition of new stands behind each of the goals has done little to help matters. Visiting supporters are normally directed to the Archers Road end of the East Stand.

Directions

From North: A33 into The Avenue then right into Northlands Road. Right at the end into Archer's Road. *From East:* M27 then A334 and signs for Southampton along A3024. Follow signs for the West into Commercial Road, right into Hill Lane then first right into Milton Road.

From West: Take A35 then A3024 towards city centre. Left into Hill Lane and first right into Milton Road.

Parking: The Dell is probably the worst place in the Premiership for parking. The best bet is to arrive early and find a school selling spaces in its playground, otherwise the city centre and a short walk.

Rail: Southampton Central.

TOTTENHAM HOTSPUR

White Hart Lane, High Road, London, N17 0AP

White Hart Lane is now pretty much complete and the majority of seats offer a good view of the pitch. For those unsighted moments you can glance at one of the two JumboTrons as games are normally fed live straight to them (no contentious replays though). The screens are located high at each end of the ground as is the octagonal-shaped ground control room which hangs from the South Stand. This stand also has a rather peculiar (I think) translucent roof. The redevelopment has virtually enclosed the ground into what some describe as a Sugar Bowl!

Directions:

A406 North Circular to Edmonton. At traffic lights follow signs for Tottenham along A1010 then Fore Street for ground.

Parking: Traffic along the High Street on match days (and shopping Saturdays) is a nightmare. Parking is equally as fraught. Arrive early, park, walk and expect to leave late.

Rail: White Hart Lane (adjacent). *Tube:* Seven Sisters and Tottenham Hale (Victoria Line) or Manor House (Piccadilly Line).

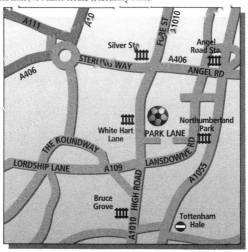

WEST HAM UNITED

Boleyn Ground, Green St, Upton Park, London, E13

Upton Park has its own unique atmosphere and an excellent range of facilities which includes Chinese and Mexican take-aways! The Bobby Moore Stand at the Castle Street end of the ground is the main focal point – two-tiers and the executive suites. Visiting supporters generally find themselves at the other end in the North Stand where the facilities are not quite as good.

Directions:

From North & West: North Circular to East Ham then Barking Rd for 1½ miles until traffic lights. Turn right into Green Street.

From South: Blackwall Tunnel then A13 to Canning Town. Then A124 to East Ham, Green Street on left after two miles.

From East: A13 then A117 and A124. Green Street on right after ¾ miles.

Parking: Plenty of off-street parking available but beware that the traffic can become quite congested.

Tube: Upton Park (¼ mile).

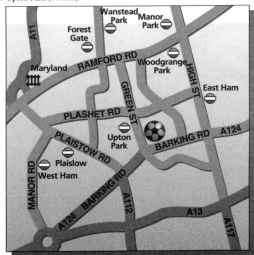

WIMBLEDON

Selhurst Park, South Norwood, London, SE25

Selhurst Park is the home from home for the Dons who share the ground with Crystal Palace. It is located in the suburbs of south-east London and is one of those places where you always under estimate the amount of time you need to get there. Always allow extra time and then some, no matter how you plan to get there. See the Palace entry for more details.

Directions

From North: M1/A1 to North Circular A406 and Chiswick. Follow South Circular A205 to Wandsworth then A3 and A214 towards Streatham and A23. Then left on to B273 for one mile and turn left at end into High Street and Whitehorse Lane.
From South: On A23 follow signs for Crystal Palace along B266 going through Thornton Heath into Whitehorse Lane. *From East:* A232 Croydon Road to Shirley joining A215, Norwood Road. Turn left after 2½ miles into Whitehorse Lane.
From West: M4 to Chiswick then as above.
Parking: If early you can use Sainsbury's at the Whitehorse Lane End or in local streets. *Rail:* Selhurst, Norwood Junction or Thornton Heath.

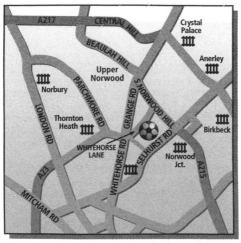

Form 'n' Encounter Guide

Our unique *Form 'n' Encounter Guide* will allow you to plan your season's FA Carling Premiership schedule by providing you with a form guide which helps you to predict what are likely to be the most exciting games to attend on a day-by-day basis. Listed are the results from the previous Premiership encounters for the matches. Please do check that the game you are looking to attend is on before you set out. Match dates and kick-off times are all subject to change to cope with TV schedules and the like.

Cup matches and World Cup qualifiers for the home countries are shown in italic type.

Dates given for the European club competitions are based on the Wednesday of the week – however, this date is normally reserved exclusively for UEFA Champions' League fixtures. UEFA Cup matches are generally played on the Tuesday and Cup-Winners' Cup ties on the Thursday. Clubs involved in the latter may move subsequent league matches to the Sunday.

Matches listed in **bold** type have been selected for live transmission on Sky Sports at the time of going to press.

Date	Match /Event	93-94	94-95	95-96	96-97
03-Aug	*FA Charity Shield:* Chelsea v Manchester Utd				
09-Aug	Barnsley v West Ham Utd ....-	-	-	-
09-Aug	Blackburn Rvrs v Derby County ......-	-	-	1-2
09-Aug	Coventry City v Chelsea..............1-1	2-2	1-0	3-1
09-Aug	Everton v Crystal Palace	3-1	-	-
09-Aug	Leeds Utd v Arsenal 2-1	1-0	0-3	0-0
09-Aug	Leicester City v Aston Villa ....-	1-1	-	1-0
09-Aug	Newcastle Utd v Sheffield W. 4-2	2-1	2-0	1-2
09-Aug	Southampton v Bolton Wdrs ....-	-	1-0	-
09-Aug	Wimbledon v Liverpool 1-1	0-0	1-0	2-1
10-Aug	**Tottenham H. v Manchester Utd** 0-1	0-1	4-1	1-2
11-Aug	**Arsenal v Coventry City** 0-3	2-1	1-1	0-0
12-Aug	Crystal Palace v Barnsley	-	-	-
13-Aug	Aston Villa v Blackburn Rvrs 0-1	0-1	2-0	1-0
13-Aug	Derby County v Wimbledon ....-	-	-	0-2
13-Aug	Liverpool v Leicester City ....-	2-0	-	1-1
13-Aug	Manchester Utd v Southampton 2-0	2-1	4-1	2-1

420

Date	Match/Event	93-94	94-95	95-96	96-97
13-Aug	Sheffield W. v Leeds Utd	3-3	1-1	6-2	2-2
13-Aug	West Ham Utd v Tottenham H.	1-3	1-2	1-1	4-3
23-Aug	Blackburn Rvrs v Liverpool	2-0	3-2	2-3	3-0
23-Aug	Coventry City v Bolton Wdrs	-	-	0-2	-
23-Aug	Everton v West Ham Utd	0-1	1-0	3-0	2-1
23-Aug	Leeds Utd v Crystal Palace	-	3-1	-	-
23-Aug	Leicester City v Manchester Utd	-	0-4	-	2-2
23-Aug	Newcastle Utd v Aston Villa	5-1	3-1	1-0	4-3
23-Aug	Southampton v Arsenal	0-4	1-0	0-0	0-2
23-Aug	Tottenham H. v Derby	-	-	-	1-1
23-Aug	Wimbledon v Sheffield W.	2-1	0-1	2-2	4-2
24-Aug	**Barnsley v Chelsea**	-	-	-	-
25-Aug	**Blackburn Rvrs v Sheffield W.**	1-1	3-1	3-0	4-1
26-Aug	Barnsley v Bolton Wanderers	-	-	-	-
26-Aug	Leeds Utd v Liverpool	2-0	0-2	1-0	0-2
26-Aug	Wimbledon v Chelsea	1-1	1-1	1-1	0-1
27-Aug	Coventry City v West Ham Utd	1-1	2-0	2-2	1-3
27-Aug	Everton v Manchester Utd	0-1	1-0	2-3	0-2
27-Aug	Leicester City v Arsenal	-	2-1	-	0-2
27-Aug	Southampton v Crystal Palace	-	3-1	-	-
27-Aug	Tottenham H. v Aston Villa	1-1	3-4	0-1	1-0
30-Aug	Arsenal v Tottenham H.	1-1	1-1	0-0	3-1
30-Aug	Aston Villa v Leeds Utd	1-0	0-0	3-0	2-0
30-Aug	Chelsea v Southampton	2-0	0-2	3-0	1-0
30-Aug	Crystal Palace v Blackburn Rvrs	-	0-1	-	-
30-Aug	Derby County v Barnsley	-	-	-	-
30-Aug	Manchester Utd v Coventry City	0-0	2-0	1-0	3-1
30-Aug	Sheffield W. v Leicester City	-	1-0	-	2-1
30-Aug	West Ham Utd v Wimbledon	0-2	3-0	1-1	0-2
31-Aug	**Liverpool v Newcastle Utd**	0-2	2-0	4-3	4-3
01-Sep	**Bolton Wdrs v Everton**	-	-	1-1	-
10-Sep	*World Cup Qualifier:* England v Moldova				
13-Sep	Arsenal v Bolton Wdrs	-	-	2-1	-
13-Sep	Barnsley v Aston Villa	-	-	-	-
13-Sep	Coventry City v Southampton	1-1	1-3	1-1	1-1
13-Sep	Crystal Palace v Chelsea	-	0-1	-	-

Date	Match/Event	93-94	94-95	95-96	96-97
13-Sep	Derby County v Everton	-		-	0-1
13-Sep	Leicester City v Tottenham H.		3-1		1-1
13-Sep	Liverpool v Sheffield W.		4-1	1-0	0-1
13-Sep	Manchester Utd v West Ham Utd	3-0	1-0	2-1	2-0
13-Sep	Newcastle Utd v Wimbledon	4-0	2-1	6-1	2-0
14-Sep	**Blackburn Rvrs v Leeds Utd**	2-1	1-1	1-0	0-1
17-Sep	*Coca-Cola League Cup 2nd Round, 1st Leg*				
20-Sep	Aston Villa v Derby	-	-	-	2-0
20-Sep	Bolton Wdrs v Manchester Utd	-		0-6	-
20-Sep	Everton v Barnsley	-			
20-Sep	Leeds Utd v Leicester City		2-1	-	3-0
20-Sep	Sheffield W. v Coventry City	0-0	5-1	4-3	0-0
20-Sep	Southampton v Liverpool	4-2	0-2	1-3	0-1
20-Sep	Tottenham H. v Blackburn Rvrs.	0-2	3-1	2-3	2-1
20-Sep	West Ham Utd v Newcastle Utd	2-4	1-3	2-0	0-0
20-Sep	Wimbledon v Crystal Palace	-	2-0	-	-
21-Sep	**Chelsea v Arsenal**	0-2	2-1	1-0	0-3
22-Sep	**Liverpool v Aston Villa**	2-1	3-2	3-0	3-0
23-Sep	Arsenal v West Ham Utd	0-2	0-1	1-0	2-0
23-Sep	Bolton Wdrs v Tottenham H.	-	-	2-3	-
23-Sep	Wimbledon v Barnsley	-	-	-	-
24-Sep	*Coca-Cola Cup 2nd Round, 2nd Leg*				
24-Sep	Coventry City v Crystal Palace	-	1-4	-	-
24-Sep	Leicester City v Blackburn Rvrs	-	0-0	-	1-1
24-Sep	Manchester Utd v Chelsea	0-1	0-0	1-1	1-2
24-Sep	Newcastle Utd v Everton	1-0	2-0	1-0	4-1
24-Sep	Sheffield W. v Derby	-	-	-	0-0
24-Sep	Southampton v Leeds Utd	0-2	1-3	1-1	0-2
27-Sep	Aston Villa v Sheffield W.	2-2	1-1	3-2	0-1
27-Sep	Barnsley v Leicester City				
27-Sep	Chelsea v Newcastle Utd	1-0	1-1	1-0	1-1
27-Sep	Crystal Palace v Bolton Wdrs	-	-	-	-
27-Sep	Derby County v Southampton	-	-	-	1-1
27-Sep	Everton v Arsenal	1-1	1-1	0-2	0-2
27-Sep	Leeds Utd v Manchester Utd	0-2	2-1	3-1	0-4
27-Sep	Tottenham H. v Wimbledon	1-1	1-2	3-1	1-0
27-Sep	West Ham Utd v Liverpool	1-2	3-0	0-0	1-2

Date	Match/Event	93-94	94-95	95-96	96-97
28-Sep	**Blackburn Rvrs v Coventry City** 2-1	4-0	5-1	4-0
30-Sep	*UEFA Cup*			
01-Oct	*Champions' League*			
02-Oct	*Cup-Winners' Cup*			
04-Oct	Arsenal v Barnsley ....-	-	-	-
04-Oct	Bolton Wdrs v Aston Villa...............-		0-2	
04-Oct	Coventry City v Leeds Utd 0-2	2-1	0-0	2-1
04-Oct	Manchester Utd v Crystal Palace ......-	3-0		
04-Oct	Newcastle Utd v Tottenham H. 0-1	3-3	1-1	7-1
04-Oct	Sheffield W. v Everton 5-1	0-0	2-5	2-1
04-Oct	Southampton v West Ham Utd 0-2	1-1	0-0	3-0
04-Oct	Wimbledon v Blackburn Rvrs 4-1	0-3	1-1	1-0
05-Oct	**Liverpool v Chelsea** 2-1	3-1	2-0	5-1
06-Oct	**Leicester City v Derby County** ......-		-	4-2
11-Oct	*World Cup Qualifier:* Italy v England			
15-Oct	*Coca-Cola Cup 3rd Round*			
18-Oct	Aston Villa v Wimbledon 0-1	7-1	2-0	5-0
18-Oct	Blackburn Rvrs v Southampton 2-0	3-2	2-1	2-1
18-Oct	Chelsea v Leicester City...................-	4-0	-	2-1
18-Oct	Crystal Palace v Arsenal ...., ...-	0-3	-	-
18-Oct	Derby County v Manchester Utd .....-	-	-	1-1
18-Oct	Everton v Liverpool 2-0	2-0	1-1	1-1
18-Oct	Leeds Utd v Newcastle Utd 1-1	0-0	0-1	0-1
18-Oct	West Ham Utd v Bolton Wdrs ....-	-	1-0	-
19-Oct	**Tottenham H. v Sheffield W.** 1-3	3-1	1-0	1-1
20-Oct	**Barnsley v Coventry City**................-	-	-	-
21-Oct	*UEFA Cup*			
22-Oct	*Champions' League*			
23-Oct	*Cup-Winners' Cup*			
25-Oct	Bolton Wdrs v Chelsea ....-	-	2-1	-
25-Oct	Coventry City v Everton...............2-1	0-0	2-1	0-0
25-Oct	Liverpool v Derby County ....-	-	-	2-1
25-Oct	Manchester Utd v Barnsley ....-			
25-Oct	Newcastle Utd v Blackburn Rvrs ...1-1	1-1	1-0	2-1
25-Oct	Sheffield W. v Crystal Palace...........-	1-0	-	
25-Oct	Southampton v Tottenham H. 1-0	4-3	0-0	0-1

Date	Match/Event	93-94	94-95	95-96	96-97
25-Oct	Wimbledon v Leeds Utd..............1-0		0-0	2-4	2-0
26-Oct	**Arsenal v Aston Villa** 1-2		0-0	2-0	2-2
27-Oct	**Leicester City v West Ham Utd** ......-		1-2	-	0-1
01-Nov	Aston Villa v Chelsea...................1-0		3-0	0-1	0-2
01-Nov	Barnsley v Blackburn Rovers............-		-	-	-
01-Nov	Bolton Wdrs v Liverpool ....-		-	0-1	-
01-Nov	Derby County v Arsenal...................-		-	-	1-3
01-Nov	Manchester Utd v Sheffield W. 5-0		1-0	2-2	2-0
01-Nov	Newcastle Utd v Leicester City ....-		3-1	-	4-3
01-Nov	Tottenham H. v Leeds Utd 1-1		1-1	2-1	1-0
01-Nov	Wimbledon v Coventry City 1-2		2-0	0-2	2-2
02-Nov	**Everton v Southampton** 1-0		0-0	2-0	7-1
03-Nov	**West Ham Utd v Crystal Palace** ......-		1-0	-	-
04-Nov	*UEFA Cup*				
05-Nov	*Champions' League*				
06-Nov	*Cup-Winners' Cup*				
08-Nov	Blackburn Rvrs v Everton 2-0		3-0	0-3	1-1
08-Nov	Chelsea v West Ham Utd 2-0		1-2	1-2	3-1
08-Nov	Coventry City v Newcastle Utd 2-1		0-0	0-1	2-1
08-Nov	Crystal Palace v Aston Villa ....-		0-0	-	-
08-Nov	Leeds Utd v Derby County................-		-	-	0-0
08-Nov	Liverpool v Tottenham H. 1-2		1-1	0-0	2-1
08-Nov	Sheffield W. v Bolton Wdrs ....-		-	4-2	-
08-Nov	Southampton v Barnsley ....-		-	-	-
09-Nov	**Arsenal v Manchester Utd** 2-2		0-0	1-0	1-2
10-Nov	**Leicester City v Wimbledon** ....-		3-4	-	1-0
22-Nov	Aston Villa v Everton...................0-0		0-0	1-0	3-1
22-Nov	Blackburn Rvrs v Chelsea 2-0		2-1	3-0	1-1
22-Nov	Derby County v Coventry City ....-		-	-	2-1
22-Nov	Leicester City v Bolton Wdrs............-		-	-	-
22-Nov	Liverpool v Barnsley ....-		-	-	-
22-Nov	Newcastle Utd v Southampton 1-2		5-1	1-0	0-1
22-Nov	Sheffield W. v Arsenal 0-1		3-1	1-0	0-0
22-Nov	Wimbledon v Manchester Utd 1-0		0-1	2-4	0-3
23-Nov	**Leeds Utd v West Ham Utd**.........1-0		2-2	2-0	1-0

Date	Match/Event	93-94	94-95	95-96	96-97
24-Nov	**Tottenham H. v Crystal Palace** ......-	0-0		-	-
25-Nov	*UEFA Cup*				
26-Nov	*Champions' League*				
27-Nov	*Cup-Winners' Cup**				
26-Nov	Chelsea v Everton 4-2	0-1	0-0	2-2
29-Nov	Barnsley v Leeds Utd ....-	-	-	--
29-Nov	Bolton Wdrs v Wimbledon...............-	-	1-0	-
29-Nov	Chelsea v Derby County...................-	-	-	3-1
29-Nov	Coventry City v Leicester City ....-	4-2	-	0-0
29-Nov	Crystal Palace v Newcastle Utd ....-	0-1	-	-
29-Nov	Everton v Tottenham H. 0-1	0-0	1-1	1-0
29-Nov	Manchester Utd v Blackburn Rvrs ...1-1	1-0	1-0	2-2
29-Nov	Southampton v Sheffield W. 1-1	0-0	0-1	2-3
29-Nov	West Ham Utd v Aston Villa 0-0	1-0	1-4	0-2
30-Nov	**Arsenal v Liverpool** 1-0	0-1	0-0	1-2
01-Dec	**Bolton Wdrs v Newcastle Utd** ....-	-	1-0	
04-Dec	*World Cup Finals Draw*				
06-Dec	Aston Villa v Coventry City 0-0	0-0	4-1	2-1
06-Dec	Blackburn Rvrs v Bolton Wdrs ....-	-	3-1	-
06-Dec	Derby County v West Ham Utd ....-	-	-	1-0
06-Dec	Leeds Utd v Everton 3-0	1-0	2-2	1-0
06-Dec	Leicester City v Crystal Palace ....-	0-1	-	-
06-Dec	**Liverpool v Manchester Utd** 3-3	2-0	2-0	1-3
06-Dec	Newcastle Utd v Arsenal 2-0	1-0	2-0	1-2
06-Dec	Tottenham H. v Chelsea 1-1	0-0	1-1	1-2
07-Dec	**Wimbledon v Southampton**.........1-0	0-2	1-2	3-1
08-Dec	**Sheffield W. v Barnsley** ....-	-	-	-
09-Dec	*UEFA Cup*				
10-Dec	*Champions' League*				
11-Dec	*Cup-Winners' Cup*				
13-Dec	Arsenal v Blackburn Rvrs 1-0	0-0	0-0	1-1
13-Dec	Barnsley v Newcastle Utd ....-	-	-	-
13-Dec	Chelsea v Leeds Utd 1-1	0-3	4-1	0-0
13-Dec	Coventry City v Tottenham H. 1-0	0-4	2-3	1-2
13-Dec	Crystal Palace v Liverpool ....-	1-6	-	-
13-Dec	Everton v Wimbledon 3-2	0-0	2-4	1-3

Date	Match/Event	93-94	94-95	95-96	96-97
13-Dec	Southampton v Leicester City ....-		2-2	-	2-2
13-Dec	West Ham Utd v Sheffield W. 2-0		0-2	1-1	5-1
14-Dec	**Bolton Wdrs v Derby County** ....-		-	-	-
15-Dec	**Manchester Utd v Aston Villa** 3-1		1-0	0-0	0-0
17-Dec	Newcastle Utd v Derby County ....-		-	-	3-1
20-Dec	Aston Villa v Southampton 0-2		1-1	3-0	1-0
20-Dec	Blackburn Rvrs v West Ham Utd ...0-2		4-2	4-2	2-1
20-Dec	Derby County v Crystal Palace ....-		-	-	
20-Dec	Leeds Utd v Bolton Wdrs ....-			0-1	
20-Dec	Leicester City v Everton....................-		2-2	-	1-2
20-Dec	Liverpool v Coventry City 1-0		2-3	0-0	1-2
20-Dec	Sheffield W. v Chelsea 3-1		1-1	0-0	0-2
20-Dec	Tottenham H. v Barnsley ....-				
21-Dec	**Newcastle Utd v Manchester Utd** 1-1		1-1	0-1	5-0
22-Dec	**Wimbledon v Arsenal** 0-3		1-3	0-3	2-2
26-Dec	Arsenal v Leicester City...................-		1-1	-	2-0
26-Dec	**Aston Villa v Tottenham H.**..........1-0		1-0	2-1	1-1
26-Dec	Bolton Wdrs v Barnsley ....-		-	-	-
26-Dec	Chelsea v Wimbledon 2-0		1-1	1-2	2-4
26-Dec	Crystal Palace v Southampton ....-		0-0		
26-Dec	Derby County v Newcastle Utd ....-		-	-	0-1
26-Dec	Liverpool v Leeds Utd 2-0		0-1	5-0	4-0
26-Dec	Manchester Utd v Everton 1-0		2-0	2-0	2-2
26-Dec	Sheffield W. v Blackburn Rvrs 1-2		0-1	2-1	1-1
26-Dec	West Ham Utd v Coventry City 3-2		0-1	3-2	1-1
28-Dec	Barnsley v Derby County ....-		-	-	-
28-Dec	Blackburn Rvrs v Crystal Palace .....-		2-1	-	
28-Dec	Coventry City v Manchester Utd ...0-1		2-3	0-4	0-2
28-Dec	Everton v Bolton Wdrs ....-		-	3-0	
28-Dec	Leeds Utd v Aston Villa 2-0		1-0	2-0	0-0
28-Dec	Leicester City v Sheffield W............-		0-1	-	1-0
28-Dec	**Newcastle Utd v Liverpool** 3-0		1-1	2-1	1-1
28-Dec	Tottenham H. v Arsenal 0-1		1-0	2-1	0-0
28-Dec	Wimbledon v West Ham Utd 1-2		1-0	0-1	1-1
29-Dec	**Southampton v Chelsea** 3-1		0-1	2-3	0-0
03-Jan	*FA Cup 3rd Round*				

Date	Match/Event 93-94	94-95	95-96	96-97
07-Jan	*Coca-Cola League Cup 5th Round*			
10-Jan	Arsenal v Leeds Utd 2-1	1-3	2-1	3-0
10-Jan	Aston Villa v Leicester City ....-	4-4	-	1-3
10-Jan	Bolton Wdrs v Southampton ....-		0-1	-
10-Jan	Chelsea v Coventry City...............1-2	2-2	2-2	2-0
10-Jan	Crystal Palace v Everton ....-	1-0		
10-Jan	Derby County v Blackburn Rvrs ......-	-	-	0-0
10-Jan	Liverpool v Wimbledon 1-1	3-0	2-2	1-1
10-Jan	Manchester Utd v Tottenham H. ...2-1	0-0	1-0	2-0
10-Jan	Sheffield W. v Newcastle Utd 0-1	0-0	0-2	1-1
10-Jan	West Ham Utd v Barnsley ....-			
17-Jan	Barnsley v Crystal Palace ...., ...-	-	-	-
17-Jan	Blackburn Rvrs v Aston Villa 1-0	3-1	1-1	0-2
17-Jan	Coventry City v Arsenal...............1-0	0-1	0-0	1-1
17-Jan	Everton v Chelsea 4-2	3-3	1-1	1-2
17-Jan	Leeds Utd v Sheffield W. ...., ...2-2	0-1	2-0	0-2
17-Jan	Leicester City v Liverpool ....-	1-2		0-3
17-Jan	Newcastle Utd v Bolton Wdrs ....-	-	2-1	-
17-Jan	Southampton v Manchester Utd ...1-3	2-2	0-1	6-3
17-Jan	Tottenham H. v West Ham Utd ..., 1-4	3-1	0-1	1-0
17-Jan	Wimbledon v Derby County ....-	-	-	1-1
24-Jan	*FA Cup 4th Round*			
31-Jan	Arsenal v Southampton ...., ...1-0	1-1	4-2	3-1
31-Jan	Aston Villa v Newcastle Utd 0-2	0-2	1-1	2-2
31-Jan	Bolton Wdrs v Coventry City............-		1-2	-
31-Jan	Chelsea v Barnsley ....-	-	-	-
31-Jan	Crystal Palace v Leeds Utd ....-	1-2	-	-
31-Jan	Derby County v Tottenham H. ....-	-	-	4-2
31-Jan	Liverpool v Blackburn Rvrs 0-1	2-1	3-0	0-0
31-Jan	Manchester Utd v Leicester City ....-	1-1	-	3-1
31-Jan	Sheffield W. v Wimbledon.............2-2	0-1	2-1	3-1
31-Jan	West Ham Utd v Everton 0-1	2-2	2-1	2-2
07-Feb	Arsenal v Chelsea 1-0	3-1	1-1	3-3
07-Feb	Barnsley v Everton ....-	-	-	-
07-Feb	Blackburn Rvrs v Tottenham H......1-0	2-0	2-1	0-2
07-Feb	Coventry City v Sheffield W........1-1	2-0	0-1	0-0
07-Feb	Crystal Palace v Wimbledon ....-	0-0	-	-
07-Feb	Derby County v Aston Villa ....-	-	-	2-1

Date	Match/Event	93-94	94-95	95-96	96-97
07-Feb	Leicester City v Leeds ....-		1-3	-	1-0
07-Feb	Liverpool v Southampton 4-2		3-1	1-1	2-1
07-Feb	Manchester Utd v Bolton Wdrs ....-		-	3-0	-
07-Feb	Newcastle Utd v West Ham Utd ...2-0		2-0	3-0	1-1
14-Feb	*FA Cup 5th Round*				
14-Feb	Aston Villa v Barnsley ....-		-	-	-
14-Feb	Bolton Wdrs v Arsenal ....-		-	1-0	-
14-Feb	Chelsea v Crystal Palace ....-		0-0	-	-
14-Feb	Everton v Derby County..................-		-	-	1-0
14-Feb	Leeds Utd v Blackburn Rvrs 3-3		1-1	0-0	0-0
14-Feb	Sheffield W. v Liverpool 3-1		1-2	1-1	1-1
14-Feb	Southampton v Coventry City 1-0		0-0	1-0	2-2
14-Feb	Tottenham H. v Leicester City ....-		1-0	-	1-2
14-Feb	West Ham Utd v Manchester Utd ...2-2		1-1	0-1	2-2
14-Feb	Wimbledon v Newcastle Utd 4-2		3-2	3-3	1-1
18-Feb	*Coca-Cola League Cup Semi-Final 1st Leg*				
21-Feb	Arsenal v Crystal Palace..................-		1-2	-	-
21-Feb	Bolton Wdrs v West Ham Utd ....-		-	0-3	-
21-Feb	Coventry City v Barnsley ....-		-	-	-
21-Feb	Leicester City v Chelsea..................-		1-1	-	1-3
21-Feb	Liverpool v Everton 2-1		0-0	1-2	1-1
21-Feb	Manchester Utd v Derby County ......-		-	-	2-3
21-Feb	Newcastle Utd v Leeds Utd 1-1		1-2	2-1	3-0
21-Feb	Sheffield W. v Tottenham H. 1-0		3-4	1-3	2-1
21-Feb	Southampton v Blackburn Rvrs 3-1		1-1	1-0	2-0
21-Feb	Wimbledon v Aston Villa 2-2		4-3	3-3	0-2
22-Feb	*Coca-Cola League Cup Semi-Final 2nd Leg*				
28-Feb	Aston Villa v Liverpool 2-1		2-0	0-2	1-0
28-Feb	Barnsley v Wimbledon ....-		-	-	-
28-Feb	Blackburn Rvrs v Leicester City ......-		3-0	-	2-4
28-Feb	Chelsea v Manchester Utd 1-0		2-3	1-4	1-1
28-Feb	Crystal Palace v Coventry City ....-		0-2	-	-
28-Feb	Derby County v Sheffield W.............-		-	-	2-2
28-Feb	Everton v Newcastle Utd 0-2		2-0	1-3	2-0
28-Feb	Leeds Utd v Southampton 0-0		0-0	1-0	0-0
28-Feb	Tottenham H. v Bolton Wdrs............-		-	2-2	-
28-Feb	West Ham Utd v Arsenal 0-0		0-2	0-1	1-2

Date	Match/Event	93-94	94-95	95-96	96-97
03-Mar	*UEFA Cup Quarter-Finals 1st Leg*				
04-Mar	*Champions' League Quarter-Final 1st Leg*				
05-Mar	*Cup-Winners' Cup Quarter-Final 1st Leg*				
07-Mar	*FA Cup 6th Round*				
07-Mar	Arsenal v Derby County	-		-	2-2
07-Mar	Blackburn Rvrs v Barnsley	-		-	-
07-Mar	Chelsea v Aston Villa	1-1	1-0	1-2	1-1
07-Mar	Coventry City v Wimbledon	1-2	1-1	3-3	1-1
07-Mar	Crystal Palace v West Ham Utd	-	1-0	-	-
07-Mar	Leeds Utd v Tottenham H.	2-0	1-1	1-3	0-0
07-Mar	Leicester City v Newcastle Utd	-	1-3	-	2-0
07-Mar	Liverpool v Bolton Wdrs	-	-	5-2	-
07-Mar	Sheffield W. v Manchester Utd	2-3	1-0	0-0	1-1
07-Mar	Southampton v Everton	0-2	2-0	2-2	2-2
14-Mar	Aston Villa v Crystal Palace	-	1-1	-	-
14-Mar	Barnsley v Southampton	-	-	-	-
14-Mar	Bolton Wdrs v Sheffield W.	-	-	2-1	-
14-Mar	Derby County v Leeds Utd	-	-	-	3-3
14-Mar	Everton v Blackburn Rvrs	0-3	1-2	1-0	0-2
14-Mar	Manchester Utd v Arsenal	1-0	3-0	1-0	1-0
14-Mar	Newcastle Utd v Coventry City	4-0	4-0	3-0	4-0
14-Mar	Tottenham H. v Liverpool	3-3	0-0	1-3	0-2
14-Mar	West Ham Utd v Chelsea	1-0	1-2	1-3	3-2
14-Mar	Wimbledon v Leicester City	-	2-1	-	1-3
17-Mar	*UEFA Cup Quarter-Finals 2nd Leg*				
18-Mar	*Champions' League Quarter-Final 2nd Leg*				
19-Mar	*Cup-Winners' Cup Quarter-Final 2nd Leg*				
28-Mar	Arsenal v Sheffield W.	1-0	0-0	4-2	4-1
28-Mar	Barnsley v Liverpool	-	-	-	-
28-Mar	Bolton Wdrs v Leicester City	-	-	-	-
28-Mar	Chelsea v Blackburn Rvrs	1-2	1-2	2-3	1-1
28-Mar	Coventry City v Derby County	-	-	-	1-2
28-Mar	Crystal Palace v Tottenham H.	-	1-1	-	-
28-Mar	Everton v Aston Villa	0-1	2-2	1-0	0-1
28-Mar	Manchester Utd v Wimbledon	3-1	3-0	3-1	2-1
28-Mar	Southampton v Newcastle Utd	2-1	3-1	1-0	2-2
28-Mar	West Ham Utd v Leeds Utd	0-1	0-0	1-2	0-2
29-Mar	*Coca-Cola League Cup Final*				

Date	Match/Event	93-94	94-95	95-96	96-97
31-Mar	*UEFA Cup Semi-Finals 1st Leg*				
01-Apr	*Champions' League Semi-Final 1st Leg*				
02-Apr	*Cup-Winners' Cup Semi- Final 1st Leg*				
04-Apr	Aston Villa v West Ham Utd 3-1	0-2	1-1	0-0	
04-Apr	Blackburn Rvrs v Manchester Utd ...2-0	2-4	1-2	2-3	
04-Apr	Derby County v Chelsea.................-		-	3-2	
04-Apr	Leeds Utd v Barnsley ....-	-	-		
04-Apr	Leicester City v Coventry City ....-	2-2	-	0-2	
04-Apr	Liverpool v Arsenal 0-0	3-0	3-1	2-0	
04-Apr	Newcastle Utd v Crystal Palace ....-	3-2	-		
04-Apr	Sheffield W. v Southampton 2-0	1-1	2-2	1-1	
04-Apr	Tottenham H. v Everton 3-2	2-1	0-0	0-0	
04-Apr	Wimbledon v Bolton Wdrs...............-	-	3-2		
05-Apr	*FA Cup Semi-Final*				
11-Apr	Arsenal v Newcastle Utd 2-1	2-3	2-0	0-1	
11-Apr	Barnsley v Sheffield W. ....-	-	-	-	
11-Apr	Bolton Wdrs v Blackburn Rvrs ....-	-	2-1	-	
11-Apr	Chelsea v Tottenham H. 4-3	1-1	0-0	3-1	
11-Apr	Coventry City v Aston Villa 0-1	0-1	0-3	1-2	
11-Apr	Crystal Palace v Leicester City ....-	2-0	-	-	
11-Apr	Everton v Leeds Utd 1-1	3-0	2-0	0-0	
11-Apr	Manchester Utd v Liverpool 1-0	2-0	2-2	1-0	
11-Apr	Southampton v Wimbledon 1-0	2-3	0-0	0-0	
11-Apr	West Ham Utd v Derby County ....-	-	-	1-1	
13-Apr	Aston Villa v Manchester Utd 1-2	1-2	3-1	0-0	
13-Apr	Blackburn Rvrs v Arsenal 1-1	3-1	1-1	0-2	
13-Apr	Derby County v Barnsley ....-	-	-	-	
13-Apr	Leeds Utd v Chelsea 4-1	2-3	1-0	2-0	
13-Apr	Leicester City v Southampton ....-	4-3	-	2-1	
13-Apr	Liverpool v Crystal Palace ....-	0-0	-	-	
13-Apr	Newcastle Utd v Barnsley ....-	-	-	-	
13-Apr	Sheffield W. v West Ham Utd 5-0	1-0	0-1	0-0	
13-Apr	Tottenham H. v Coventry City 1-2	1-3	3-1	1-2	
13-Apr	Wimbledon v Everton 1-1	2-1	2-3	4-0	
14-Apr	*UEFA Cup Semi-Finals 2nd Leg*				
15-Apr	*Champions' League Semi-Final 2nd Leg*				
16-Apr	*Cup-Winners' Cup Semi- Final 2nd Leg*				

Date	Match/Event 93-94	94-95	95-96	96-97
18-Apr	Arsenal v Wimbledon.................1-1	0-0	1-3	0-1
18-Apr	Barnsley v Tottenham H. ....-	-	-	-
18-Apr	Bolton Wdrs v Leeds Utd ....-	-	0-2	-
18-Apr	Chelsea v Sheffield W. 1-1	1-1	0-0	2-2
18-Apr	Coventry City v Liverpool 1-0	1-1	1-0	0-1
18-Apr	Crystal Palace v Derby County ....-	-	-	-
18-Apr	Everton v Leicester City................-	1-1	-	1-1
18-Apr	Manchester Utd v Newcastle Utd ...1-1	2-0	2-0	0-0
18-Apr	Southampton v Aston Villa 4-1	2-1	0-1	0-1
18-Apr	West Ham Utd v Blackburn Rvrs ...1-2	2-0	1-1	2-1
25-Apr	Aston Villa v Bolton Wdrs......., ...-	-	1-0	-
25-Apr	Barnsley v Arsenal ..., ...-	-	-	-
25-Apr	Blackburn Rvrs v Wimbledon 3-0	2-1	3-2	3-1
25-Apr	Chelsea v Liverpool 1-0	0-0	2-2	1-0
25-Apr	Crystal Palace v Manchester Utd ......-	1-1	-	-
25-Apr	Derby County v Leicester City ....-	-	-	2-0
25-Apr	Everton v Sheffield W. 0-2	1-4	2-2	2-0
25-Apr	Leeds Utd v Coventry City...........1-0	3-0	3-1	1-3
25-Apr	Tottenham H. v Newcastle Utd 1-2	4-2	1-1	1-2
25-Apr	West Ham Utd v Southampton 3-3	2-0	2-1	2-1
29-Apr	*UEFA Cup Final 1st Leg*			
02-May	Arsenal v Everton 2-0	1-1	1-2	3-1
02-May	Bolton Wdrs v Crystal Palace ....-	-	-	-
02-May	Coventry City v Blackburn Rvrs ...2-1	1-1	5-0	0-0
02-May	Leicester City v Barnsley ....-	-	-	-
02-May	Liverpool v West Ham Utd 2-0	0-0	2-0	0-0
02-May	Manchester Utd v Leeds Utd 0-0	0-0	1-0	1-0
02-May	Newcastle Utd v Chelsea 0-0	4-2	2-0	3-1
02-May	Sheffield W. v Aston Villa............0-0	1-2	2-0	2-1
02-May	Southampton v Derby County ....-	-	-	3-1
02-May	Wimbledon v Tottenham H. 2-1	1-2	0-1	1-0
06-May	*Cup-Winners' Cup Final*			
10-May	Aston Villa v Arsenal 1-2	0-4	1-1	2-2
10-May	Barnsley v Manchester Utd ....-	-	-	-
10-May	Blackburn Rvrs v Newcastle Utd ...1-0	1-0	2-1	1-0
10-May	Chelsea v Bolton Wdrs ....-	-	3-2	-
10-May	Crystal Palace v Sheffield W............-	2-1	-	-
10-May	Derby County v Liverpool ....-	-	-	0-1

Date	Match/Event	93-94	94-95	95-96	96-97
10-May	Everton v Coventry City...............0-0		0-2	2-2	1-1
10-May	Leeds Utd v Wimbledon...............4-0		3-1	1-1	1-0
10-May	Tottenham H. v Southampton 3-0		1-2	1-0	3-1
10-May	West Ham Utd v Leicester City ....-		1-0	-	1-0
13-May	*UEFA Cup Final 2nd Leg*				
10-May	*Football League Play-off Semi Finals 1st Leg*				
13-May	*Football League Play-off Semi Finals 2nd Leg*				
16-May	*FA Cup Final*				
20-May	*Champions' Cup Final*				
25-May	*Football League Division 1 Play-off Final*				
10-Jun	*France '98 World Cup finals start*				
12-Jul	*World Cup Final*				

FA Carling
PREMIERSHIP
98-99

Pocket Annual

The 6th edition of the
Premiership *bible* will be
available in August 1998.
Reserve your copy now.